ENGLAND
& WALES

Edited by John Julius Norwich

Published in Association with
English Heritage & the National Trust

KNOPF GUIDES

PREFACE

As this book so eloquently illustrates, the heritage of England and Wales is nothing short of inspiring.

The National Trust and English Heritage are fortunate in being able to care for hundreds of outstanding heritage properties that demonstrate this diversity and richness and it is part of our duty to ensure that these properties are properly looked after for current and future generations to enjoy.

Our responsibilities are mirrored by scores of other devoted organisations, agencies and private owners who are as committed as we are to enabling today's society to enjoy and learn from all that heritage has to offer. Collectively, our task can be daunting, but its scale reflects the very positive fact that millions of people care deeply about its outcome.

As this book shows, heritage is literally all around us – from fine houses to fantastic coastline; from Victorian street signs to neolithic burial mounds; from old mills to Norman castles. Heritage is part of our everyday experience and it enriches our daily lives. That is why we are delighted to have sponsored this book.

Fiona Reynolds. Simon Thurley.

Fiona Reynolds
Director General
The National Trust

Simon Thurley
Chief Executive
English Heritage

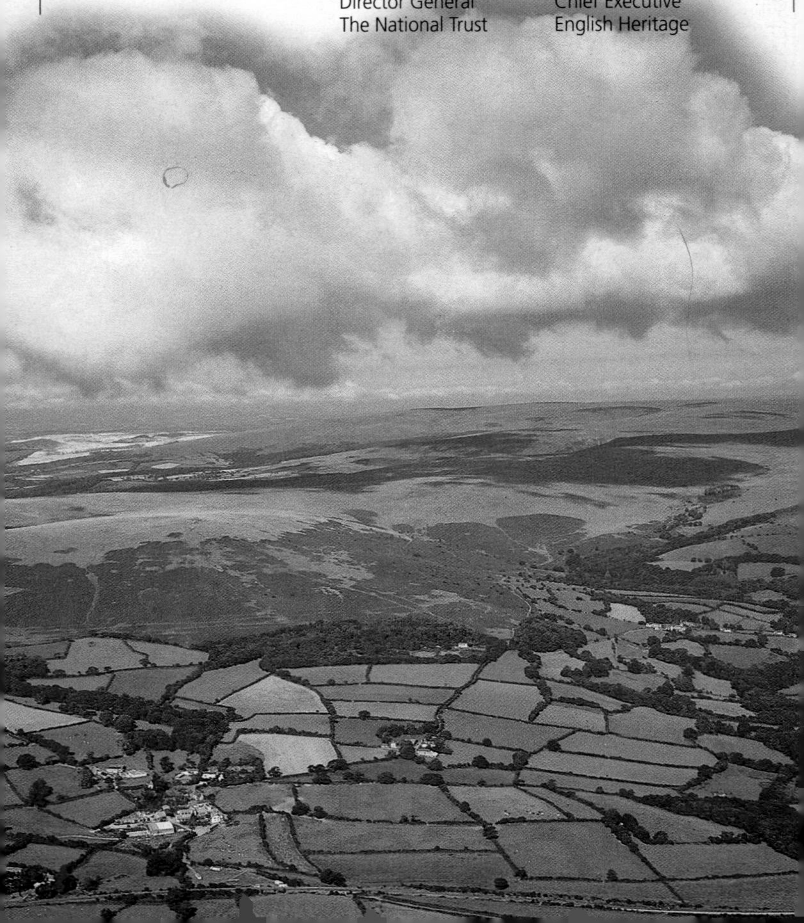

Nowhere in the world – not in France, not in Germany or Spain, not even in Italy – will you find less than 60,000 square miles containing such a profusion of medieval cathedrals and churches, of historic houses and castles spanning well over a thousand years, of dazzling museums and galleries, of glorious gardens and superb scenery. To describe it all between the covers of a single book is an impossible task. All we can hope to do is to give you some idea of the wonders awaiting you, to help you make your selection and to guide you on your way.

But there is an admission to be made: the sad fact is that a century ago our architectural heritage was considerably richer than it is today. Many of the losses – particularly in the City of London, in industrial areas like Coventry and in ports like Portsmouth – were the result of enemy action in World War II; but far, far more were due to the so-called planners of the decades immediately following. It was they who – in the name of progress – gutted one historic town after another, replacing the twisted street patterns with shopping malls and piazzas and "recreational spaces"; and substituting, in the place of the old variety and character, a grim concrete uniformity that deadens the spirit. In several magnificent old cities – Gloucester and Worcester in particular spring to mind – they destroyed so much that one is mildly surprised to see the Cathedral still standing. Nor were they alone among the guilty. National governments, by refusing to give owners of historic houses any significant exemption from their crippling taxation, made the continuing maintenance of these buildings impossible. Between 1945 and 1974, over 250 historic houses were demolished. Here was official vandalism on a scale unparalleled since Henry VIII's Dissolution of the Monasteries over four centuries before.

Today, fortunately, things are a good deal better. Organizations such as English Heritage, the Historic Houses Association and the National Trust are doing a magnificent job; meanwhile the fact that almost everyone in the country owns or has access to a car has led to a huge increase in interest on the part of the general public, together with a new respect for architecture. All this means that if the present climate of opinion continues, it is difficult to imagine any further barbarities of the kind which were all too frequent half a century ago.

Where the countryside is concerned, on the other hand, the future looks a good deal less secure. Hedgerows, for example, are vital for many species of flowering plants, birds and insects, serving too as important corridors for animals to move from one place to another; yet the increase in the size of fields and the relentless spread of urban development has caused the disappearance of well over half of our hedgerows in the past 50 years, some 70,000 miles between 1984 and 1993. A degree of legal protection was secured in 1997, but this still protects only one in five of the hedges in England alone. Much the same is true of our flower-rich meadows and pastures, traditionally used for hay-making and the grazing of livestock; since 1945, 95 percent of those meadows have gone and in the past decade alone, we have lost an area of permanent grassland the size of Bedfordshire, while what remains is still at risk.

What is to be done? One real contribution is to join the Council for the Protection of Rural England, English Heritage and the National Trust (see pages 495-7). But the purpose of this introduction is not to hold out a begging bowl. The important thing is that you should make the most of your time in England and Wales, planning your itinerary in such a way as to see as many as possible of the things that interest you most. If this book helps you to do that, and if it succeeds in giving you some idea of the richness and variety of what our country has to offer, it will not have been written in vain.

John Julius Norwich
John Julius Norwich

● Encyclopedia section

NATURE The natural heritage: species and habitats characteristic to the area covered by the guide, annotated and illustrated by a naturalist author and artists.

HISTORY The impact of international historical events on British history, from the arrival of the first inhabitants, with key dates appearing in a timeline beside the text.

ARTS AND TRADITIONS Customs and traditions and their continuing role in contemporary life.

ARCHITECTURE The architectural heritage, focusing on style and topology, a look at rural and urban buildings, major civil, religious and military monuments.

PAINTERS A selection of paintings by different artists and schools, arranged chronologically or thematically.

AS SEEN BY WRITERS An anthology of texts focusing on the city or country, taken from works of all periods and countries, arranged thematically.

▲ Itineraries

Each itinerary begins with a map of the area to be explored.

★ EDITOR'S CHOICE Sites singled out by the editor for special attention.

INSETS On richly illustrated double pages, these insets turn the spotlight on subjects deserving more in-depth treatment.

◆ Practical information

All the travel information you will need before you go and when you get there.

MUSEUMS AND MONUMENTS A handy list of contact numbers.

HOTELS AND RESTAURANTS A selection of the best hotels and restaurants compiled by an expert.

APPENDICES Bibliography, list of illustrations and general index.

MAP SECTION Maps of all the areas covered by the guide.

● ▲ ◆
The above symbols within the text provide cross references to a place or a theme discussed elsewhere in the guide.

Left and right: objects c. 1800 by William Libery, from the Usher Art Gallery, Lincoln

USHER ART GALLERY Built in 1927 with money left by James Ward Usher, whose collection of watches, portrait miniatures, blue and white china and antique silver were the foundation of the present collection. There is a good collection of paintings by the watercolorist Peter de Wint, who was associated with the town (above right, *Lincoln from the South West*). For the poetic visitor, Tennyson's cloak and large-brimmed hat are also on display.

Chancel and crossing, St Mary's Church, Stow

In the large village of STOW is ST MARY'S CHURCH ★, o the best early parish churches in England. The nave a crossing with its narrow transepts are a mixture of late and early Norman work, all from the 11th century; the complicated history of building and rebuilding can be the stonework of the walls. The chancel is a very gran example of Norman church architecture, accurately re to its original glory in the 1850s.

GAINSBOROUGH OLD HALL ★ rises up grandly out of v ordinary urban surroundings, proclaiming itself a late medieval house of the first importance. Sir Thomas B entertained King Richard III here in 1484, and Sir Th enormous Great Hall with its elaborate timber roof st along with the great kitchen and other catering rooms kitchen is possibly the most complete medieval kitche England. Other parts of the mansion were rebuilt in the

NEWARK

Newark is a handsome town on the River Trent which became rich from the wool and coal shipped up the ri was defended by a strong castle, but during the Civil V was besieged by Parliamentary forces, who damaged t castle walls. The town was important as a staging place Great North Road and as a center of agriculture. Som great sheds built for malting still survive at its edge. A heart is the broad and active market square with the s medieval CHURCH OF ST MARY MAGDALEN ★ – one of grandest parish churches in England. T building has the tall proportions a large windows typical of the late century. Also square is the Palladian Mar of 1774 by Joh All around are of Georgian h A couple of m north of Newa across the Tre remote church HOLME BY LAN is worth a visit rebuilt in 1491

St Mary's Church, Stow

The mini-map pinpoints the itinerary within the wider area covered <u>by the guide.</u>

The itinerary map shows the main sites, towns and cities covered in the <u>chapter.</u>

John Barton out of profits from the wool trade, and is a perfect and moving example of a Tudor church.
LAXTON A few miles north of Newark (south of Worksop) is the village of Laxton, remarkable as the only place left in the country that still uses the medieval open field system of cultivation, with all the land surrounding the village divided into long strips.
SOUTHWELL is a quiet little town,

ORD TO GAINSBOROUGH

1. SHREWSBURY 2. CHESTER 3. STOKE IN TRENT 4. BURTON UPON TRENT 5. DERBY 6. CHESTERFIELD 7. LEICESTER

8. NOTTINGHAM 9. GAINSBOROUGH 10. MELTON MOWBRAY 11. GRANTHAM 12. LINCOLN 13. STAMFORD 14. BOSTON

Below left: Burghley House exterior and (bottom) the Great Hall
Below right: Lady Adelaide Talbot by Lord Leighton, Belton House

SIR ISAAC NEWTON (1642-1727) was a mathematician whose discoveries laid the foundations for much of the progress in science since his time. Besides inventing calculus, he solved some of the mysteries of light and, most importantly of all, evolved the theory of

STAMFORD TO GAINSBOROUGH

STAMFORD ★ A perfect small Georgian town that has been used for countless film locations, although the church steeples that punctuate the skyline serve as a reminder that Stamford has an older past, still visible in many places. **ALL SAINTS CHURCH** is the hub of the town and much more conspicuous than the 18th-century town hall in St Mary's Street. Most of the buildings are the excellent local building stone, and a large proportion are still owned by the Cecil family from nearby Burghley House. Many of the 18th-century houses which line the streets have ornamental door and window surrounds copied directly out of the pattern books of the time.
BURGHLEY HOUSE ★ Just beyond the boundary of the town, this is one of four great houses built by William Cecil, Secretary of State to Elizabeth I. Begun in the 1550s and finished by 1587, Burghley was meant for showing off, and the enormous stone palace with its fantastic silhouette of towers and chimneys is an unforgettable sight. The rooms inside were redecorated in the 1680s by the 5th Earl of Exeter and the ceilings of the state rooms covered with paintings by Antonio Verrio – most spectacularly in the Heaven Room. The Cecil family's huge collection of paintings covers the walls.
GRIMSTHORPE HALL is a magnificent muddle. The great north entrance front and the cavernous stone great hall behind it are the work of Sir John Vanbrugh, architect of Blenheim Palace and Castle Howard. Vanbrugh was employed to rebuild the whole house, but he died in 1715 and the Tudor house round its courtyard, with

parts of the medieval castle still embedded in it, was left more or less untouched. The gardens are still partly formal, in a way that complements Vanbrugh's work.
GRANTHAM Grantham was clearly a highway town and takes much of its character from the fact that the Great North Road passed through the center of it. There are countless inns, notably THE ANGEL AND ROYAL HOTEL, with its 15th-century carved stone front where King Richard III signed the Duke of Buckingham's death warrant; the inn is still serving its original function 500 years later. The other conspicuous building and a monument to the medieval wealth accumulated from the wool trade is the CHURCH OF ST WULFRAM ★ with its staggeringly tall spire.
WOOLSTHORPE MANOR Seven miles south of the town is a limestone house of about 1620, where Isaac Newton was born in 1642 and where, in 1665, he discovered the principles of differential calculus.
HARLAXTON MANOR Westward of Grantham lies the wildest and most fanciful 1830s mansion in England. The architects – first Anthony Salvin then William Burn – copied parts of all the major Jacobean houses they could think of and combined them with an eye to theatrical effect. The interior is just as wild as the outside.
BELTON HOUSE ★ Built for Sir John Brownlow between 1685 and 1688, it still gives an excellent impression of a great late 17th-century mansion. The inside has some splendid plaster ceilings, wood carvings and much furniture and silver of the period, as well as Soho tapestries, a fine cross-section of 17th-century English portraiture, and remnants of a major collection of Old Masters. One room is entirely decorated with large bird paintings by Hondecoeter.

gravity. Newton was born at Woolsthorpe Manor and educated at Grantham Grammar School and Trinity College, Cambridge. During the 1680s he formulated his three laws of motion and from them derived the theory of universal gravitation that was published in his book *Philosophiae Naturalis Principia Mathematica* (1687). Newton helped to resist the efforts of King James II to make Cambridge University Roman Catholic and was rewarded by being made Master of the Royal Mint in 1693 and later President of the Royal Society.

Belton House

359

★ The star symbol signifies sites singled out by the editor for special attention.

1. Anglesey, North Wales
2. Arnside and Silverdale: Cumbria/Lancashire
3. Blackdown Hills: Devon/Somerset
4. Cannock Chase: Staffordshire
5. Chichester Harbour: Hampshire/West Sussex
6. Chilterns: Bedfordshire/Hertfordshire/ Buckinghamshire/Oxfordshire
7. Clwydian Range: Denbighshire/Flintshire, North Wales
8. Cornwall
9. Cotswolds: Gloucestershire/Wiltshire/ Warwickshire/Worcestershire/ Somerset
10. Cranborne Chase and West Wiltshire Downs: Dorset/Hampshire/Somerset/ Wiltshire
11. Dedham Vale: Essex/Suffolk
12. Dorset
13. East Devon
14. East Hampshire
15. Forest of Bowland: Lancashire/North Yorkshire
16. Gower: Swansea, South Wales
17. High Weald: Kent/Surrey/East Sussex/West Sussex
18. Howardian Hills: North Yorkshire
19. Isle of Wight
20. Isles of Scilly
21. Kent Downs
22. Lincolnshire Wolds
23. Lleyn: Gwynedd, North Wales
24. Malvern Hills: Herefordshire/Worcestershire/ Gloucestershire
25. Mendip Hills: Somerset
26. Nidderdale: North Yorkshire
27. Norfolk Coast
28. North Devon
29. North Pennines: Cumbria/Durham/ Northumberland
30. Northumberland Coast
31. Quantock Hills: Somerset
32. Shropshire Hills
33. Solway Coast: Cumbria
34. South Devon
35. South Hampshire Coast
36. Suffolk Coast and Heaths
37. Surrey Hills
38. Sussex Downs
39. Tamar Valley: Cornwall/Devon
40. North Wessex Downs: Berkshire/Hampshire/ Oxfordshire/Wiltshire
41. Wye Valley: Monmouthshire/ Gloucestershire/Herefordshire

Lake District

Snowdonia

Shropshire Hills

Wye Valley

North Cornwall

Northumberland coast

North York Moors

Chilterns

Dorset coast

● Encyclopedia section

▲ Itineraries in England and Wales

CONTENTS

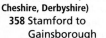

◆ Practical information

Numerous specialists and academics have contributed to this guide, under the general editorship of John Julius Norwich and with the advice of Alastair Laing, Colin Amery, Giles Waterfield, Neil Burton, Simon Jenkins and Penelope Hobhouse.

Advisors

Alastair Laing
Advisor on pictures and sculpture to The National Trust
Colin Amery
Special Advisor to the World Monuments Fund; Architectural Correspondent of the Financial Times for 20 years; recent publications include Art and Architecture – The Story of the Sainsbury Wing at the National Gallery
Giles Waterfield
Formerly director of Dulwich Picture Gallery; recent publications include Art Treasures of England *(1998)*
Neil Burton
Secretary of the Georgian Group, author of Life in the Georgian City
Simon Jenkins
Times columnist and author of England's Thousand Best Churches
Penelope Hobhouse
Writer, designer and lecturer: author of Garden Design *(1996)*

●

Encyclopedia section

■ **NATURE**
John Woodward
Author of several books and CD-ROMS on wildlife and the landscape over the last 20 years
■ **HISTORY**
David Boyle
Journalist specializing in history and economics; recent publications include Funny Money
■ **ARTS AND TRADITIONS**
Anna Gilbert
(Theater and Cheeses)
Michael Rose
(Music and Opera)
Hugh Matheson
(Sports)
Catherine Blake
(Customs and Ceremonies)
■ **ARCHITECTURE**
Colin Amery
■ **PAINTING IN ENGLAND AND WALES**
Giles Waterfield
■ **ENGLAND AND WALES AS SEEN BY WRITERS**
Lucinda Gane
Co-director of the publishing company Ondt & Gracehopper and the theater company Mama Quillo

▲

Itineraries in England & Wales

■ **LONDON**
Colin Amery and **Ian Collins**

■ **SOUTH EAST**
Ian Sutton
Author of Western Architecture *(2000)*
David Lloyd
Contributor to Buildings of England
■ **SOUTH WEST**
Geoffrey Beard
Author of 15 books, including The National Trust Book of English House Interiors *(1989) and* The Work of Grinling Gibbons *(1990)*
■ **WEST COUNTRY**
Jeremy Pearson
Historian for the National Trust; previously worked in several museums
■ **SOUTH MIDLANDS**
Lucy Worsley
Inspector of Historic Buildings for English Heritage, specializing in great houses in the Midlands
■ **HOME COUNTIES**
Emily Cole
Historian for English Heritage; researcher and writer on Architecture of England and Ireland
■ **EAST ANGLIA**
Ian Collins
London correspondent of the Eastern Daily Press newspaper; books include A Broad Canvas: Art in East Anglia since 1880
■ **NORTH MIDLANDS**
Neil Burton

■ **NORTH EAST**
Jane Hatcher
Local and architectural historian and lecturer at the University of Leeds; author of several books including Richmondshire Architecture *(1990)*
■ **NORTH WEST**
Frank Kelsall
Architectural historian, previously inspector of historic buildings for English Heritage in the North West; now works as a consultant to the Ancient Monuments Society
■ **NORTH AND SOUTH WALES**
Lindsay Evans
Trustee of the National Heritage Memorial Fund until 1999; author of several books including Castles of Wales *(1998)*

Practical information

Matthew Fort
(hotels and restaurants)
Tom Fort
(fishing)
Robert Lloyd Parry
(walking)
John Woodward
(birdwatching)
Sandra Pisano
(general research)

KNOPF GUIDES

This is a Borzoi Book
published by Alfred A. Knopf

Completely revised
and updated in 2007

Copyright © 2000 Alfred A. Knopf, New York.
All rights reserved under International
and Pan-American Copyright Conventions.
Published in the United States by Alfred
A Knopf, a division of Random House, Inc.,
New York, and simultaneously in Canada by
Random House of Canada Limited, Toronto.
Distributed by Random House, Inc., New York

Knopf, Borzoi Books and the colophon are
registered trademarks of Random House, Inc

www.aaknopf.com

ISBN 10: 0-375-71107-4
ISBN 13: 978-0-375-71106-0

Originally published in the UK by
Everyman Publishing Plc in association
with English Heritage and the National
Trust and Editions Nouveaux-Loisirs, a
subsidiary of Gallimard, Paris. © 2000
Everyman Publishing Plc

SERIES EDITORS
Shelley Wanger and Clémence Jacquinet

PRINTED AND BOUND IN ITALY BY
Editoriale Lloyd

ENGLAND AND WALES

GENERAL EDITOR
John Julius Norwich

ADVISORS
Colin Amery, Neil Burton, Penelope
Hobhouse, Simon Jenkins, Alastair Laing,
Giles Waterfield

PROJECT EDITOR
Grapevine Publishing Services

EDITORIAL
Catherine Blake, Gill Paul, Yvonne Worth

DESIGN
Anikst Design, Thanh Tung Uong

PICTURE RESEARCH
Elaine Willis, Josine Meier, Sarah Yates,
Sandra Pisano

MAPS
Landscape maps on opening pages of
itinerary chapters: Frederique Lieval and
(Atelier Duplantier, Bordeaux)

The Editor's Choice Maps on the
endpapers, the maps in the Practical
Information, and pages 561-574 © Oxford
Cartographers.

Locator maps on opening pages of
itinerary chapters and on pages 20-21:
Sylvie Rabbe

Map of the areas of outstanding natural
beauty: supplied by courtesy of the
Countryside Agency and reproduced
by kind permission of Ordnance Survey
© Crown Copyright NC/00/788

NATURE AND ARCHITECTURE ILLUSTRATIONS
International Artworks

RESTAURANTS AND HOTELS
The section on restaurants and hotels on
pages 514–33 was originally written by
Matthew Fort. It was updated for the
subsequent editions by Everyman.

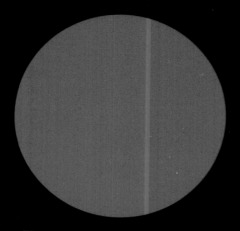

ENCYCLOPEDIA SECTION

Coal miners in the pits at Bargoed, near Cardiff, stand waiting to go up to the surface after working a shift, December 1910.

Queens Docks, Liverpool, 1880s.

King George V and Prince Henry being pursued by a gypsy at the Epsom Derby, 1920.

A news vendor in April 1910, with a headline protesting about a proposed tax.

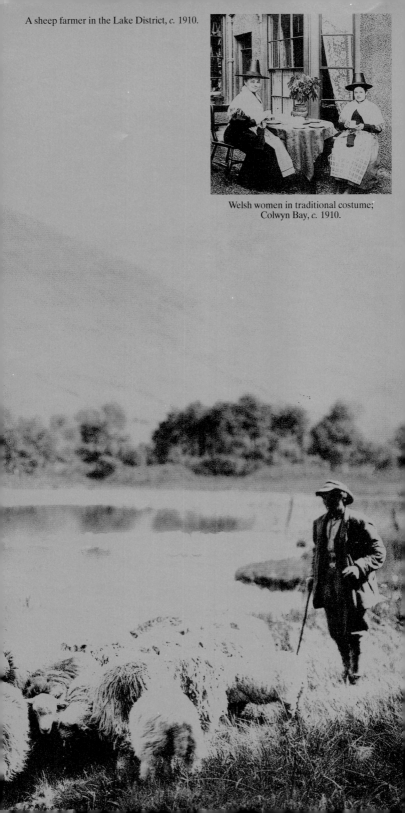

A sheep farmer in the Lake District, *c.* 1910.

Welsh women in traditional costume;
Colwyn Bay, *c.* 1910.

NATURE
John Woodward

The nature of England and Wales has been shaped by their geology and climate. In the west and north – in Cornwall, Devon, Wales and the Lake District – ancient rocks have been buckled, cooked and hardened by titanic earth movements to create rugged mountain landscapes. As part of this process huge masses of molten rock welled up and solidified deep underground as granite. The biggest of these granite intrusions occurred in the southwest, where it is now exposed at the surface as Dartmoor, Bodmin Moor, Land's End and the Scilly Isles. These uplands have a high annual rainfall, swept in from the Atlantic on the prevailing south-westerly winds. The combination of hard, unyielding rock and heavy rain creates acid, infertile soils and bleak moorlands. To the southeast, the old rocks are covered with layer upon layer of younger, softer rocks, tilted gently to the southeast. The tilted layers of rock and clay have been eroded into a series of gentle ridges separated by clay vales, such as the Cotswold Hills, the Chiltern Hills and the chalk Downs of the southeast. The softer rocks and milder climate have created gentle landscapes, fertile soils and a rich farming tradition.

Gulf Stream

ANNUAL RAINFALL
- ■ 20–30 in
- ■ 30–40 in
- ■ 40–60 in
- ■ 60–96 in

SNOWDONIA
The slates and volcanic rocks of north Wales survived the ice ages as splintered crags, divided by deep valleys gouged out by glaciers.

CHILTERN HILLS
Thick layers of chalk, laid down in warm seas during the age of dinosaurs, now form many of the hills and cliffs of southeast England.

YORKSHIRE DALES
The Carboniferous limestone of the Yorkshire Dales is eroded into spectacular cliffs and gorges, honeycombed with caves.

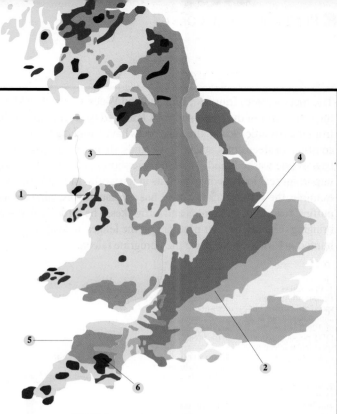

GEOLOGY

- Tertiary clay and sand: up to 65 million years old (myo)
- Cretaceous chalk: 65–140 myo
- Jurassic limestone and clay: 140–195 myo
- Triassic sandstone: 195–230 myo
- Permian limestone: 230–280 myo
- Carboniferous limestone, sand and coal: 280–345 myo
- Older sandstones, shales and slate: 345–1000 myo
- Granite intrusions
- Volcanic rocks

EAST ANGLIAN FENLAND
In eastern England the hard rocks are buried beneath layers of clay laid down by ice sheets, creating broad, flat farmlands.

NORTH DEVON COAST
In southwest England the layered rocks were buckled and squeezed by continental collisions over 250 million years ago.

DARTMOOR
The acid moorlands of Dartmoor have developed on part of a vast mass of hard, crystalline granite that lies beneath southwest England.

The rocky western fringes of England and Wales are much wilder than the soft shores of the south and east. Pounded by storm waves rolling in from the Atlantic Ocean, the hard rocks have formed a fractured coastline of steep cliffs, stacks and islands, sheltering narrow coves and bays of tide-washed sand. These remote shores are among the most important seabird breeding habitats in the world. In South Wales, for example, the Pembrokeshire coast has spectacular breeding colonies of puffins, razorbills, guillemots and kittiwakes. The birds hunt at sea, bringing fish back to their nestlings on the ledges and clifftops, and are hunted in turn by raptors like the peregrine falcon.

1. PEREGRINE
Famous for its high-speed attack dive, but almost wiped out in the mid 20th century by DDT poisoning, this spectacular falcon is now a frequent sight on remote rocky coasts.

2. GUILLEMOT
During the breeding season the sheer cliffs are packed with guillemots jostling for space on the narrow ledges.

3. CHOUGH
Named for its sneezing call, the chough is a rare treat for birdwatchers visiting western Wales.

4. FULMAR
It may look like a gull, but this stiff-winged glider is really a miniature albatross.

5. PUFFIN
Resplendent in their clown-like breeding colors, puffins whirr through the air like clockwork toys, their bills full of sand-eels for their young.

6. RAZORBILL
A large proportion of the world razorbill population breeds on British coasts, often on cliff ledges alongside guillemots.

7. CORMORANT
The diving cormorant does not have water-proof plumage, so after hunting it dries its wings in the breeze.

8. GREY SEAL
Grey seals breed on secluded beaches and islands.

9. KITTIWAKE
This small gull breeds in great colonies on the cliffs, wheeling and calling with their "kitti way-ake" chorus.

10. OYSTERCATCHER
With its bright orange bill, white wing-bars and piping call the oystercatcher is quite unmistakable. It uses its powerful bill as a hammer to crack shellfish.

11. GANNET
The plunge-dive of the gannet is a breathtaking sight, but is usually seen only out at sea. There are vast breeding colonies of these magnificent ocean birds just off the Welsh coast.

12. RABBIT
Rabbits often share their burrows with puffins.

13. BASKING SHARK
Huge plankton-feeding basking sharks regularly trawl the waters off the Welsh coast, their fins just visible above the surface.

14. SHORE CRAB
The shore crab can survive long periods out of the water.

■ THE LAKE DISTRICT

1. RED DEER
Originally woodland
animals, red deer have
adapted to life on open
moorlands.

The Lake District of northwest England is a great dome of hard rock, etched by deep, radiating valleys. Like those of nearby Snowdonia, the valleys were gouged out by glaciers during the ice age that ended some 15,000 years ago. They now contain deep lakes flanked by farmland, while the rainswept hillsides support moorland vegetation such as heather, bracken and coarse grasses, with bog plants in patches of waterlogged peat. These crags and moorlands are among the last

2. GOLDEN-RINGED DRAGONFLY
This spectacular insect lays its eggs in mountain streams.

3. COMMON LIZARD
A warm stone makes a good basking site for this little lizard.

4. DIPPER
A plump little bird that hunts underwater in fast-flowing streams.

5. SHORT-EARED OWL
This large owl nests on moorland and often hunts by day.

wildernesses in England. Golden eagles nest here, along with buzzards and bird-hunting peregrines and merlins. Ravens scavenge the remains of dead sheep and rabbits, their harsh croaks punctuating the liquid, bubbling calls of the curlews that breed on the moorlands, and during the autumn rut the valleys echo to the roars of red deer stags.

6. SUNDEW
The poor bog soils are colonized by the insect-eating sundew plant.

7. BUZZARD
Soaring buzzards wheel on rising air currents as they search for prey.

8. CURLEW
Although it winters on estuaries this big wader breeds on open moors.

9. STOAT
This slender, fierce rabbit-killer is widespread but elusive.

10. RAVEN
The heavy-billed raven finds plenty to eat on the wild uplands.

11. MERLIN
This miniature moorland falcon catches small birds out of the air.

25

■ THE FOREST OF DEAN

WREN (RIGHT)
Astonishingly noisy for such a tiny creature, the wren is one of the most common and widespread woodland birds in Britain.

1. TAWNY OWL
Although hard to see by day, the tawny owl's hooting call is a familiar sound at night.

2. GREAT SPOTTED WOODPECKER
The rapid drumming of this colorful woodpecker is a territorial call, made by hammering at a dead branch carefully selected for its musical tone.

3. BADGER
The badger builds vast burrow systems called setts in woodlands and hedgerows.

4. ROE DEER
The smallest native deer in England and Wales is becoming more common every year. It normally forages in small groups at dawn and dusk.

5. DORMOUSE
The dormouse is rarely seen in England and Wales now, and may be declining.

6. TREECREEPER
Braced by its stiff tail, the little treecreeper spirals up tree trunks and searches the bark for insects with its curved tweezer bill.

BLUEBELL
Glorious drifts of
bluebells transform the
broadleaved woodlands
of England and Wales in
spring: a spectacle that is
unique to Britain.

Dense forests of oak, ash, beech and other broadleaved
deciduous trees once covered England and Wales, but
most of the forest was cleared over two thousand years ago.
Patches remained, though, and during the Middle Ages large areas of
native woodland were set aside as royal hunting forests. Later these
became valuable sources of oak used for building the wooden warships of
Nelson's navy. The Forest of Dean, on the borders of England and Wales,
was originally a royal forest. In spring the great oaks preside over carpets
of bluebells, wood anemones and other spring flowers. The rich flora
supports a wealth of insects and other small animals, which attract birds
such as the woodcock, woodpecker and treecreeper. Roe deer graze
among the trees, and at dusk badgers emerge to root through the leaf
litter for worms and other morsels.

7. GREY SQUIRREL
Introduced from the
eastern USA in the
1870s, the grey
squirrel is now found
in every oak
woodland in England
and Wales, and most
of the native red
squirrels have
retreated to the pine
forests of the west
and north.

8. SPARROWHAWK
The sparrowhawk's
short wings and long
tail give it tremendous
agility in the air.

9. POLECAT
Centuries of
persecution made the
polecat almost extinct
in England, but it
survived in Wales and
is slowly spreading
across the border.

10. BLUE TIT
Common birds with
distinctive coloring.

11. PURPLE EMPEROR
This rare butterfly
lives in treetops.

12. OTTER
Although the otter
has vanished from the
more populated parts
of England it can still
be seen playing in the
clear streams of the
west.

13. JAY
Jays help regenerate
the oak forest by
burying acorns for
winter food.

14. WOODCOCK
The woodcock is most
likely to be seen in
flight at dawn or
dusk, spending the
rest of its day hidden
in the undergrowth.

THE NORFOLK BROADS

SWALLOW (RIGHT)
Migrating swallows may roost in their thousands in reedbeds before making their way inland to breed.

1. LAPWING
The tumbling display flight of the lapwing is becoming a less common sight in England, possibly because modern farming methods destroy its nests on the ground.

3. GRASS SNAKE
The grass snake is a good swimmer, using its skills to hunt amphibians like the common frog.

2. KINGFISHER
A flash of electric blue is often all you see of the kingfisher as it plunges into the water to seize a fish.

4. BITTERN
The bittern has suffered from marsh drainage and is now reduced to about 20 breeding pairs in Britain, although its booming call can still be heard on the Norfolk Broads.

5. MALLARD
Commonest of all Britain's wild ducks, the mallard will live anywhere there is fresh water – from remote marshes to urban boating lakes.

6. GREAT CRESTED GREBE
Once rare in Britain, this diving bird nests on a floating platform of reeds after an elaborate courtship display.

7. PIKE AND 8. PERCH
Voracious predators lurk beneath the surface, ready to snap up any small fish, frogs, and even fledgeling birds.

MUTE SWAN (RIGHT)
Common and widespread, the swan can be dangerously aggressive during the spring breeding season.

The rivers and freshwater wetlands of England and Wales are havens for a wide variety of wildlife. The nature of the water determines how rich the habitat is, so while the clear, often acidic waters of an upland stream support relatively few animals and plants, the fertile waters of lowland rivers and lakes teem with life. The Norfolk Broads in eastern England are among of the richest of these lowland wetlands. Created by peat digging in the Middle Ages, and linked by a network of rivers, these lakes and marshes are gradually becoming overgrown to create peat fens and pockets of swampy woodland. In places where there is little boat traffic this process has created tangled thickets of reeds, marsh flowers, willows and alder alongside the open water, harboring marsh birds like the grey heron, bittern and reed bunting, and mammals such as the water vole and mink.

9. WATER VOLE
Now rare in Britain, the water vole is a casualty of modern farming, which has destroyed most of the wild marshlands where it once hid from predators.

10. AMERICAN MINK
Introduced for its valuable fur, the predatory mink now breeds in the wild and is blamed for the disappearance of native animals like the water vole.

11. GREY HERON
The grey heron stands sentinel in the shallows, watching for fish and frogs to spear with its dagger bill.

12. REED BUNTING
The black head of the male reed bunting in breeding plumage is a common sight among the reedbeds.

13. MOORHEN
The long toes of the moorhen help spread its weight as it pads over floating vegetation at the water's edge.

■ DEVON FARMLAND

MAGPIE This raucous crow is often blamed for eating the eggs and nestlings of smaller birds, but domestic cats are far more destructive.

BARN OWL (left) The ghostly white form of the barn owl can sometimes be seen floating over the fields at dusk.

SKYLARK The warbling song of the skylark is becoming less common in Britain, but it is still one of the classic sounds of open grassland.

DUNNOCK The dunnock is notorious for its complex sex life, with both male and female having up to three mates each.

The traditional English farming landscape of fields, hedgerows and small woods evolved over centuries as a way of marking boundaries, confining cattle and sheep and providing useful timber. But it also offered wildlife a habitat that made a good substitute for the primeval forests. In regions such as Devon, where the hedgerows are still maintained, wild mammals such as weasels, foxes, and hedgehogs use them as corridors between the woodlands. The insects that live on the wide variety of plants in old hedgerows attract songbirds such as blackbirds and robins, and the undergrowth harbors mice, voles and reptiles like the slow worm. Brown hares and partridges feed on grasses and seeds out in the fields, while moles burrow through the rich earth in search of worms and grubs.

1. KESTREL Britain's most widespread raptor, the kestrel is celebrated for its ability to hover in one spot as it searches for prey on the ground below.

2. ROOK Groups of big, white-billed rooks probing for grubs in the damp soil are a frequent sight on farmland.

3. GREY PARTRIDGE Bustling coveys of grey partridges feed in the long grass, bursting up on whirring wings if they are disturbed.

4. HEDGEHOG This nocturnal animal lives on insects and worms found in the undergrowth.

WEASEL Slim enough to chase voles through their runs and tunnels, the weasel is a ferocious hunter that can kill a rabbit many times its own size.

MOLE Although it rarely comes to the surface, evidence of the mole's presence can be seen everywhere on old pastures.

GOLDFINCH
In late summer goldfinches feast on the seeds of thistles and teasels growing at the field margins.

Red Admiral

BUTTERFLIES The flowering and fruiting shrubs in the hedgerows attract bright-winged butterflies such as the yellow brimstone, the comma and the red admiral.

ROBIN For some reason the English robin is much bolder than its continental cousins, and its bright red breast is one of the most familiar sights of the countryside.

Brimstone

Comma

HEDGES Most of the hedges on English farms were planted in the 19th century. Little more than fences of live hawthorn, many of these have been ripped out to make bigger fields suitable for modern farm machinery. Unfortunately some of the old, dense hedges have been destroyed too, but this is now being discouraged by financial incentives to conserve farm wildlife.

5. BROWN HARE Although superbly adapted for life on open grassland, the long-legged hare is becoming scarce thanks to modern farming methods.

6. DOR BEETLE The dung scattered on Devon fields by cattle and sheep is gathered and buried by dor beetles, who use it as a food store for their young.

RED FOX Despite hunting, shooting and trapping the red fox remains Britain's most successful wild predator. It is common everywhere, from the fields and woods of Devon to the streets of London.

7. LITTLE OWL Often seen perched on fence posts in daylight, the little owl may sit stock-still for hours.

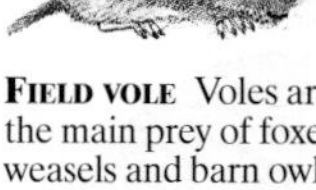

FIELD VOLE Voles are the main prey of foxes, weasels and barn owls.

■ THE NEW FOREST

One of the most interesting yet threatened wildlife habitats in Europe, heathland develops on poor, dry, often sandy or stony soil that has been stripped of its natural forest cover. The vegetation is dominated by heather and gorse, which often catches fire in the heat of summer. The parts that stay unburned are colonized by birch and then pine, and may eventually revert to forest. Large areas of the New Forest in southern England are actually open heath, grazed by rabbits and half-wild ponies. In summer lizards and snakes such as the adder and the rare smooth snake bask in the sun, and the teeming insect life is preyed upon by heathland birds like the hobby, nightjar and Dartford warbler.

Hobby

Emperor moth

Green Hairstreak

Adder

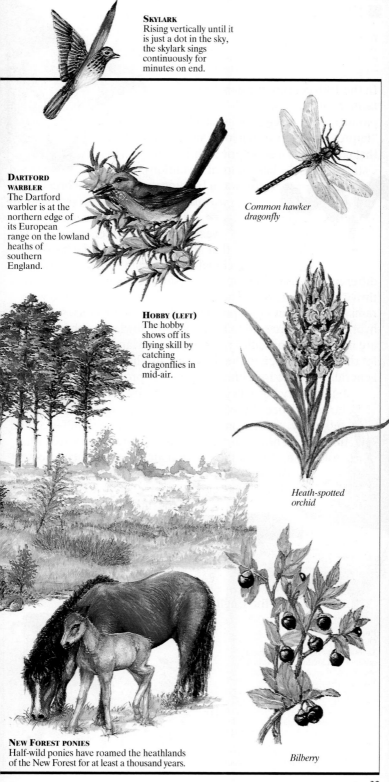

SKYLARK
Rising vertically until it is just a dot in the sky, the skylark sings continuously for minutes on end.

DARTFORD WARBLER
The Dartford warbler is at the northern edge of its European range on the lowland heaths of southern England.

Common hawker dragonfly

HOBBY (LEFT)
The hobby shows off its flying skill by catching dragonflies in mid-air.

Heath-spotted orchid

NEW FOREST PONIES
Half-wild ponies have roamed the heathlands of the New Forest for at least a thousand years.

Bilberry

■ FARM ANIMALS

Hereford bull

DAIRY COWS
While the black and white Friesian produces most of the milk in the UK, specialist breeds like the Jersey are kept for cream and dairy produce.

In the 18th century the gentleman farmers of England and Wales pioneered the science of livestock breeding, "improving" their rough local stock into animals that could fetch a good price while still making the best of local conditions. The result was a baffling variety of local breeds, many of which still survive, mainly in the uplands of the north and west where the farmers need animals that are well adapted to the harsh climate and terrain. There are many different breeds of hill sheep, for example: tough animals that thrive on poor grazing. The hill ewes (females) are mated with rams of softer, yet more productive breeds to produce strong hybrids. These are sold to farmers in the lowlands, where they are mated with muscular rams to produce lambs for market. A lot of the cattle seen in the fields are also hybrids. Cattle are generally suitable for either milk or beef production, but not both. Dairy farmers get around this by mating their dairy cows with beef-breed bulls to produce calves that they can sell easily, so it is common to see a burly beef bull in a field full of lean, bony dairy cows. Their hybrid calves are either sold for beef or, if they are female, used as "suckler cows" to rear beef calves on hill farms. Most of the old pig breeds have been superseded by long, lean breeds that are kept in big sheds. But free-range pigs are becoming more common, and again these are usually strong hybrids that can put up with the English or Welsh weather.

PIGS
Old breeds like the ginger Tamworth are now rare, and most outdoor pigs are hybrids between breeds like the Large White and British Saddleback.

SHEEP
The horned Swaledale is a typical British hill breed. Longwool sheep like the Romney are scarce, but the meat quality of the black-faced Suffolk ram makes it popular with lamb producers.

HISTORY

David Boyle

*The circle of stones
at Stonehenge ▲ 212*

THE STONE AGE TO THE VIKINGS

*Above: Celtic human
sacrifice in a giant
wicker man*

55 BC
*Julius Caesar arrives in
Britain for the first
time.*

AD 43
*Roman general Aulus
Plautius arrives under
orders from the
Emperor Claudius.*

410
*Emperor Honorius
abandons Britain to
marauding Saxon
raiders.*

825
*Egbert, the King of
Wessex, defeats the
Mercians in battle and
becomes king of all
England.*

*Right: Bronze Age
bracelet found in Kent
Below: Mercury bronze
from Colchester,
Roman
period*

BEGINNINGS Legends say that this rocky outcrop of Europe was once the mythical Isle of Albion, populated by a race of giants, although in fact the British Isles were connected to the European mainland until only about 7,000 years ago. Evidence of human habitation has been uncovered, near Swanscombe to the east of London, that stretches back to 250,000 BC; and a human tooth found in a cave near Denbigh in Wales is thought to belong to nomadic settlers who lived there before the Ice Age forced them south. We know they wandered across the dry land that is now the English Channel in search of animals to hunt, probably in small bands of 25 people or so, settling in camps for the summer. The thawing of the most recent Ice Age created the island, but did not stop the wave of Neolithic settlers, who first started arriving around 3500 BC, bringing their new farming techniques, clearing the forests and building their strange turf-covered mounds known as long barrows. By 2250 BC, they seem to have been capable of moving the 123 enormous bluestones which made up the double circle at Stonehenge (each of them weighing up to 4 tons) all the way from the Prescelly Mountains in Dyfed to their present site.

BRONZE AND IRON AGES Bronze Age settlers developed fortifications, either because of population pressures or because the new arrivals were more aggressive: Bronze Age artefacts tend to be for killing and subjugation, compared to Stone Age implements, fashioned for handling stone and wood. The years around 600 BC saw the emergence of the Celts – probably arriving from central Europe with their culture, ironwork skills and language, which is the basis for modern Welsh and Cornish. Their religion was complex, embracing many deities, but included faith in the sacred value of oak trees, wells and mistletoe, and they had a sophisticated social structure led by poets, warriors and ritual priests known as druids. Celtic warriors had a fierce reputation: they made their hair stick out before battle, wore striped cloaks and bright tunics, and kept the heads of enemies in wall niches as souvenirs.

THE ROMANS Julius Caesar made a half-hearted invasion in 55 BC and came back a year later with 800 ships, taking the first British captives to parade through the streets of Rome. In AD 43 the Emperor Claudius needed a military triumph to prop up his tentative hold over the army, and took advantage of the death of the British King Cunobelin (the model for Shakespeare's Cymbeline) to achieve his ends. Flanked by a large force that included camels and elephants, Roman troops reached South Wales in four years, despite constant harassment from the British tribes along the way. Their resistance culminated in the Roman destruction of the Druid stronghold of Anglesey and the surrender of the

Stonehenge: a place of ritual
Below: Coin with the head of Emperor Claudius

British guerrilla chief Caractacus (Cunobelin's son) in Wales in the year 50. Even then, the invaders faced a serious challenge from the queen of the Iceni tribe in East Anglia. Boudicca (known later as Boadicea) burned the Roman towns of Camolodunum (Colchester) and Verulamium (St Albans) in 61 before wreaking devastation upon the new Roman city of Londinium, but her forces were finally defeated. By 79, the Romans had subdued Wales and the north of England, and in 130 had completed Hadrian's Wall, which ran from the Solway to the Tyne to mark the northern limit of the Empire.

886
King Alfred formally recognizes the Danelaw, the area of eastern England occupied by Danes.

1066
Death of Edward the Confessor and the Norman Conquest.

THE SAXONS By the 4th century AD, Saxon raiders from Germany were already making their presence felt along the southern and eastern coasts. The Romans were forced to cut their British colony adrift, and within half a century the Saxons, Angles and Jutes were settling on the British Isles and beginning a slow conquest. They were resisted by a range of mysterious Romano-British leaders (one of whom was known later as King Arthur) but the British resistance was pushed back far into Wales, the southwest and Cumbria, where the flame of Celtic Christianity was kept alive through the Dark Ages. By the end of the 6th century the rest of England had been divided into the pagan Anglo-Saxon kingdoms of Wessex, Kent, East Anglia, Mercia and Northumbria. Christianity returned in 597 when St Augustine arrived in Kent, accompanied by 40 monks. The local king Ethelbert allowed him to found a monastery on the site of the present Canterbury Cathedral, where he was baptized, along with some 10,000 others, at an enormous Christmas ceremony. His missionaries proceeded to spread the new religion widely.

Below: Anglo-Saxon warriors
Bottom: King Arthur's legendary Round Table

THE VIKINGS After the death of the powerful Mercian king Offa, Wessex became the dominant English kingdom, and by 825 Egbert, its king, had won the allegiance of all the others. Wales was also being united through the efforts of Rhodri the Great and his descendants Hywel Dda and Gruffydd ap Llewellyn. But it was English kings such as Alfred the Great (871-99) who bore the brunt of the increasingly frequent raids by Vikings from Scandinavia, which began with destructive incursions and ended with a permanent invasion. The northern part of England under Viking control was known as the Danelaw. A short Viking dynasty of kings, notably Canute (1016-35), ruled over England after Ethelred the Unready (978-1016) had fled to Normandy. But Saxons were restored briefly to the throne under Edward the Confessor, who built the first Westminster Abbey and died childless, paving the way for the Norman Conquest.

William the Conqueror (right) and setting out from Normandy, as portrayed by contemporaries in the Bayeux Tapestry (opposite page, top)

THE 11TH TO 13TH CENTURIES: MEDIEVAL TIMES

Battle of Hastings

INVASION The last Saxon king of England, Harold II, was crowned in Westminster Abbey in 1066, but was killed months later fighting William, Duke of Normandy at the Battle of Hastings. William (1066-87) was crowned king on Christmas Day of the same year, earning himself the nickname "the Conqueror". He was a tireless administrator and imposed a new military aristocracy on the country, guarded over by strongholds including the new Tower of London, and compiled a detailed inventory of his new lands known as the Domesday Book. This provided the basis for a set of feudal obligations throughout society, in which everyone owed allegiance to him as king and |to a complex system of overlords. It puts England's population at that time at between 1 and 3 million, sparsely spread in the north but dense in the east. The Welsh kings were forced to pay homage, but William and his immediate descendants left it to newly appointed "Marcher Lords" to rule the lawless border area between England and Wales.

KING AND BARONS The new system ushered in an era of tension between the king and his increasingly powerful barons, which overwhelmed the reigns of his two sons William Rufus (1087-1100) and Henry I (1100-35), and contributed to the 19-year civil war (1135-54). Henry II (1154-89) reasserted royal authority, founding the Norman dynasty of Plantagenet kings, which ruled over territory stretching from Hadrian's Wall to the Pyrenees in France. It was Henry who introduced trial by jury, but his battle with the church authorities turned sour in 1170, when four knights took him |at his word and murdered the Archbishop of Canterbury, Thomas Becket, in his own cathedral. Becket was canonized just three years later and became the center of a cult extending across Europe. Two of Henry's sons reigned in quick succession. Richard I (1189-99), known as "the Lionheart", spent most of his reign on crusade and once had to be ransomed after being imprisoned in central Europe on his journey home. King John (1199-1216) was forced by the barons to agree to a charter that guaranteed their rights and privileges. The Magna Carta was signed at Runnymede in 1215. He repudiated it shortly afterward, but its principles remain in English law, and can be found echoed in the US Declaration of Independence and the UN Declaration of Human Rights: "No freeman shall be arrested or imprisoned or deprived of his freehold or outlawed or exiled or in any way brought to destruction ... except by the lawful judgement of his peers and by the law of the land."

Center: Richard I ("the Lionheart") Above: St Thomas Becket, the turbulent priest

MEDIEVAL LIFE

MEDIEVAL LIFE A series of miracles reinforced the cult of Thomas Becket and brought pilgrims flocking from all over Europe to the shrines or great fairs, such as Stourbridge, St Giles or Bartholomew Fair in London. It was a period that saw much brutality, but also learning, understanding of herbal medicine and a rapidly developing legal system, within a world where complex feudal hierarchies on earth were seen as a mirror of the great hierarchies of heaven, with every peasant owing allegiance to his lord, and via his lord and king to God. The increasingly wealthy monasteries provided hospital and teaching services across the country: by 1300 there were over 17,000 monks and nuns in England alone.

Medieval kings of England

CONTROL OF WALES John also led campaigns into Wales, aiming to re-impose his control over the shrewd king Llewelyn ap Iowerth (1196-1240), who was progressively uniting the remaining Welsh kingdoms of Powys and Gwynedd. His grandson Llywelyn ap Gruffydd (1246-82) expelled the English from most of Wales, forcing Henry III (1216-72) to recognize him as "Prince of Wales". But after an assault by Edward I, the Treaty of Aberconwy in 1277 stripped him of almost all his land, leaving him with the title alone, and a string of spectacular new castles such as Caernarfon (Carnarvon) and Harlech were left to impose English royal authority. After a series of uprisings, Wales was left at the mercy of the English lords for a century.

King John

THE BARONS AND THE SCOTS Henry III was plunged into a renewed struggle with the barons, even falling captive to their leader Simon de Montfort in 1265. His son Edward escaped, killed de Montfort at the Battle of Evesham, and as Edward I (1272-1307) presided over a revolution in parliamentary development, extending the boundaries of his rule by annexing Wales and imposing his authority on a divided Scotland. But in 1314 Edward's achievements began to unravel when his son Edward II (1307-27) faced a crushing defeat at the hands of the Scottish leader Robert Bruce at the Battle of Bannockburn. This was the final straw for an unpopular homosexual king, who was overthrown by his French wife Isabella and her lover Roger Mortimer, and eventually murdered in Berkeley Castle ▲ 257 with a red hot poker. It was said that his screams could be heard across three counties.

1086
The Domesday Book is compiled.

1215
King John signs the Magna Carta.

1265
Simon de Montfort's parliament and his defeat at the Battle of Evesham.

1282
Rebellion in Wales and the death of King Llewelyn.

The coronation of Edward I

THE 14TH AND 15TH CENTURIES: THE HIGH MIDDLE AGES

CHIVALRY At the age of 15, Edward's heir Edward III (1327-77) seized Mortimer and his mother – executing one and imprisoning the other – and assumed full power himself to become one of England's best known kings. His reign marked the height of the age of chivalry, and he created his own version of the Arthurian ideal of a Round Table dedicated to chivalry and courtly love, the Order of the Garter. Edward used his mother's claim to the throne of France as the pretext for launching the Hundred Years War in 1337, with early English victories at the battles of Crecy and Poitiers, and the capture of Calais in 1347. English kings continued to style themselves "King of France" for the next 400 years.

Above: the Hundred Years War
Right: a Knight of the Garter
Below right: the Black Death

1337
The start of the Hundred Years War.

1348
The Black Death strikes England.

1400
Owen Glendower's revolt against English rule in Wales.

1485
The Wars of the Roses end with the Battle of Bosworth.

PLAGUE The so-called "Little Ice Age" and floods between 1315 and 1317 ushered in a period of serious inflation and food shortages. By the time the Black Death struck England in 1348, the poor in London had already been weakened by a diet comprising dogs, cats and pigeons. The plague killed about a third of the population of England. In the aftermath of the devastation, a smaller, richer and more literate population emerged, able to extract more pay from landowners and employers and to break the feudal ties once and for all. A new mercantile period was beginning, when the old arable fields were converted to sheep pasture, and cloth merchants joined the great barons as some of the wealthiest men in the land.

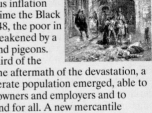

Chaucer at the court of Edward III, by Ford Madox Brown

FERMENT AND REVOLT Economic upheavals and rising wages led to the Peasants' Revolt against a poll tax in 1381. The rebels burst into London and their leader Wat Tyler met the boy king Richard II (1377-99) at Smithfield. A scuffle with the Mayor of London led to Tyler's death; the revolt petered out, but brought terrible retribution. There was intellectual ferment, too, as Geoffrey Chaucer (c. 1340-1400) wrote one of the most important books in the English language, *The Canterbury Tales*.

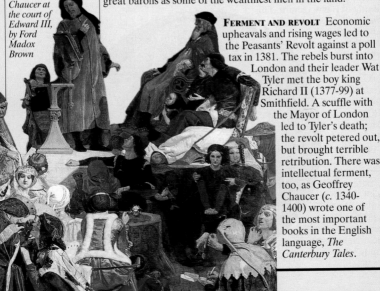

At the same time the Oxford scholar John Wyclif (*c.* 1330-84) defied convention by translating the Bible into English. Meanwhile the booming English cloth industry improved the dress of all sections of the population: people began to wear stockings and the close-fitting lined tunic known as doublet and hose, while women experimented with gigantic head-dresses.

GLYNDWR AND HENRY V The confused reign of Richard II, with his favorites and his extravagance, was too much for the aristocracy: he was overthrown in 1399 by his cousin Henry Bolingbroke, who founded the House of Lancaster, thus dividing the English ruling classes for almost a hundred years. Henry's coup was the signal for the charismatic Owain Glyndwr (Owen Glendower) to rebel against the King in 1400. Henry's response was to restrict Welsh land ownership, but this only swelled the revolt, and by 1404 Glyndwr controlled most of Wales. He summoned a parliament at Machynlleth and had himself crowned in front of diplomatic envoys from Scotland and France. But a series of defeats followed, and by 1416 Glyndwr had disappeared from history. Henry's son Henry V (1413-22) revived the war with France to bolster his legitimacy, winning a superb victory at Agincourt in 1415 and forcing the mad French king Charles VI to sign the Treaty of Troyes in 1420, naming him as his successor. After only two years, however, Henry had died, and the French had rallied under Joan of Arc. By 1454, only Calais was left in English hands.

THE WARS OF THE ROSES Henry VI (1422-61 and 1470-71) suffered from bouts of insanity as his long reign progressed, and the Wars of the Roses broke out between the supporters of the Lancastrian dynasty and those of Richard, Duke of York, another direct descendant of Edward III. Richard was killed in 1460 at the Battle of Wakefield; but a year later Richard's son had taken his revenge and crowned himself Edward IV (1461-70 and 1471-83), the first king from the House of York. Edward returned from a brief exile in 1471, soundly defeating his rivals at the battles of Barnet and Tewkesbury, and sending Henry to the Tower of London. He reigned until 1483, when he was succeeded by his 12-year-old son, Edward V. Only two months later, young Edward and his brother Richard, Duke of York, were murdered in the Tower of London, almost certainly on the orders of their uncle Richard III (1483-5), who was killed by his Welsh cousin Henry Tudor at the decisive Battle of Bosworth in 1485. The Wars of the Roses – and the House of Plantagenet – were at an end.

Henry VI: saintly, but a weak king

*Below: Henry VIII
in full regalia*

THE 16TH AND 17TH CENTURIES: THE TUDORS AND STUARTS

THE TUDOR DYNASTY Henry VII (1485-1509) ended the rivalry between the houses of Lancaster and York by marrying Edward IV's daughter Elizabeth, whose portrait is still the traditional image for queens on packs of playing cards. He was a ruthless administrator and, as the wool and cloth trades grew, he presided over a period of unprecedented growth in English wealth and influence.

THE REFORMATION The divorce between Henry VIII (1509-47) and Catherine of Aragon, who had failed to give birth to a male heir, changed England's position in Europe and played a major role in the reformation of the church. Although the Pope had awarded him the title "Defender of the Faith" for a book criticizing the Protestant reformer Martin Luther, he refused to annul Henry's marriage. A furious Henry cut the English church off from Rome and forced it to accept him as its head. From 1536, he also began dissolving the ancient monasteries, taking over their land and enormous wealth and changing the social structure of the English countryside. The Dissolution of the Monasteries was efficiently executed by his advisor Thomas Cromwell (*c.* 1485-1540) and there was little opposition, except in the north where the Pilgrimage of Grace, organized in protest in 1536-7, was savagely put down. All the monastic cathedrals except Coventry were refounded as secular colleges.

PROTESTANT AND CATHOLIC Henry was married another five times, beheading two of his wives (Anne Boleyn and Catherine Howard) on grounds of adultery. His heir, Edward VI, was only nine when he came to the throne in 1547, but his brief reign firmly established Protestantism in the English church. The pendulum swung back again when he was succeeded

ACTS OF UNION
The Acts of Union of 1536 and 1543 gave the English and Welsh equality under the law. But Welsh gentry were getting increasingly English; the Welsh language was banned and their courts used English, which Welsh peasants did not understand.

Queen Elizabeth I

by the fervently Catholic Mary (1553-8). She forced an alliance with Catholic Spain – marrying their king Philip II – which led to war with France and the loss of Calais, whose name she claimed she would always find "graven on her heart". Mary burned the leaders of the English Reformation at the stake at Oxford, including the Archbishop of Canterbury and author of the first English prayer book, Thomas Cranmer.

THE VIRGIN QUEEN When Mary's half-sister Elizabeth (1558-1603) succeeded to the throne, the country was threatened from outside by Spain and from inside by bitter religious factions. The Spanish threat was averted with the spectacular defeat of the Armada in 1588, and Elizabeth's 45-year reign became known as the "English Renaissance", opening the world to English commerce with the skills of piratical seafarers such as Francis Drake (*c.* 1542-96), and with an outpouring of literature and drama from playwrights, among them William Shakespeare.

Mr. WILLIAM
SHAKESPEARES
COMEDIES,
HISTORIES, &
TRAGEDIES.
Published according to the True Originall Copies.

LONDON
Printed by Isaac Iaggard, and Ed. Blount. 1623.

Above: William Shakespeare and admiring contemporaries, and a collection of his plays. Left: the Spanish Armada, with Sir Francis Drake (inset) Below: The Globe Theatre

SHAKESPEARE The area of London known as Bankside, which until 1546 had been a neighborhood of prostitutes licensed by the Bishop of Winchester, became in the late 16th century the site of London's new theaters. One of the first English playhouses, the Globe, was the home of the King's Men, among them William Shakespeare (1564-1616). Shakespeare was the son of a tradesman in Stratford-upon-Avon ▲ 271, who had attracted the patronage of the Earl of Southampton, to whom he dedicated two poems. The Globe ● 57, constructed in timber in 1599 near Southwark Cathedral, saw the first performances of many of Shakespeare's great plays.

Oliver Cromwell (right) and (below) the execution of Charles I in 1649, with the signatures on his death warrant shown underneath.

During one of these, the roof caught fire and the theater burned down. It was rebuilt, but was finally to be demolished under Cromwell in 1644.

THE STUART DYNASTY

Elizabeth named the Scottish king James VI (1603-25) as her heir. He became James I of England, uniting the two kingdoms under his rule. Two years later he narrowly avoided a coup by Catholic conspirators, known as the "Gunpowder Plot". But the absolute rule of James and his son Charles I (1625-49) was increasingly challenged by a newly articulate Parliament, dominated by the landed gentry who refused to accept the "divine right" of kings. In Wales, Walter Cradock and William Wroth had already set up the first Welsh non-conformist church at Llanfaches in Monmouthshire in 1639, starting a powerful dissenting tradition in the country. Charles was forced to recall Parliament in 1640 after he antagonized the Scots with his Anglican prayer book, but found them increasingly hostile. He therefore withdrew to Nottingham and raised his standard against them, launching the Civil War against Parliament which would end in revolution, defeat and his execution on the scaffold.

1605
The Gunpowder Plot.

1642
The start of the English Civil War.

1649
The execution of Charles I.

1660
The restoration of the monarchy.

1665
The Great Plague.

1688
The Glorious Revolution deposes James II.

1707
The Act of Union with Scotland.

London in flames: the Great Fire, 1666

THE COMMONWEALTH

For 11 years the country came under the increasingly arbitrary rule of the parliamentary leader and creator of the victorious New Model Army Oliver Cromwell (1599-1658), who gave his military commissioners the power to interfere in a range of country pleasures

(including horse-racing, bear-baiting and cock-fighting), and launched a brutal repression in Ireland. After his death, and two more years under his incompetent son Richard, Parliament voted to restore the monarchy with Charles's son Charles II (1660-85). To symbolize the end of Cromwellian rule, a 130-foot maypole was erected in the Strand.

Above: London Bridge before the Great Fire
Below: A quack sells remedies for the Great Plague in London

RESTORATION

Charles II's return to England was swiftly followed by the Great Plague of 1665, and the Great Fire, which all but destroyed medieval London, the following year. But the torrent of political excitement and debate after the Civil War was transformed into new exuberance of architecture, literature and drama, after the years of parliamentary rule when theatres had been closed. Coffee houses were now increasingly widespread: the first opened in Oxford in 1650, and there were almost 2,000 in London by the end of the century.

Left: A London coffee house
Below: William and Mary sharing the throne
Bottom: Queen Anne

THE GLORIOUS REVOLUTION Charles II was succeeded by his Catholic brother James II (reigned 1685-8), but civil war threatened when one of Charles's illegitimate sons, the Duke of Monmouth, landed at Lyme Regis in opposition. His forces were defeated at the Battle of Sedgemoor, Monmouth was beheaded and hundreds of rebels were executed or deported. When James's son was born, destined to be brought up a Catholic, messengers were sent to his son-in-law – the Dutch Protestant William of Orange – who was acclaimed king in the Glorious Revolution of 1688. William ruled jointly with James's daughter Mary, having first signed the Bill of Rights of 1689, which limited the power of the monarch, and then the Act of Settlement of 1701, which banned Catholics from the throne. Mary's sister Anne (1702-14) won a series of spectacular victories on the continent and established a Mediterranean base at Gibraltar. Her reign also saw the 1707 Act of Union, which united England and Scotland, turning the English parliament at Westminster into a British one.

Below (from top): Walpole, the first Prime Minister; Dr Johnson's great Dictionary; a pamphlet satirizing the South Sea Bubble; Sir Isaac Newton (right)

THE 18TH CENTURY: THE GEORGIAN AGE

GEORGE I Queen Anne had 17 children, none of whom survived her. Under the terms of the Act of Settlement, the throne passed to her nearest Protestant relative – the Elector of Hanover, who arrived in London to rule as George I (1714-27). He spoke no English, so the relationship between the monarchy and government changed, with the king no longer coming to cabinet meetings, and his place taken by England's first Prime Minister, Sir Robert Walpole (1676-1745).

THE ENLIGHTENMENT The early 18th century was a period of peace and cultural renaissance known as the Enlightenment, when the discoveries of Sir Isaac Newton (1642-1727) and the dictionary of Samuel Johnson (1709-84) ushered in the modern world. There was the occasional financial disaster, like the South Sea Bubble in 1720 – one of the most famous share collapses in British history – but life was becoming steadily more civilized. The laws against witchcraft were repealed in 1736; the wild boar, which had once infested the medieval forests, finally became extinct. The first turnpike tolls had been levied in 1683, and new roads were ploughing deep into the countryside. But it was a tough period as well, when amputations were carried out without anaesthetic, when highwaymen and press gangs roamed, when fashionable people rushed to replace their teeth with ivory imitations – and when 14,000 black slaves were employed in the country houses of the gentry.

George III

WAR AND THE JACOBITES The period of peace ended in the reign of George II (1727-60). England declared war on Spain in 1739 at the start of the War of the Austrian Succession. Six years later, the country faced the most serious attempt to replace the Hanoverian monarchy with the Catholic Stuarts. The grandson of James II, Charles Edward Stuart (1720-88) – known as Bonnie Prince Charlie – landed in Scotland and advanced as far south as Derby, just 130 miles from London, before he retreated north to a brutal defeat at Culloden.

THE EMERGING EMPIRE English armies were successful around the world, taking control of Canada from the French and building an empire in India. And when Captain James Cook (1728-89) set sail from Plymouth in 1768, his maps of Australia and New Zealand added to the scope of what would soon become the British Empire. But the 60-year reign of George III (1760-1820) – the first English-born Hanoverian – was soon overshadowed by the loss of the American colonies in the American War of Independence (1775-83).

Wellington at Waterloo in 1815

METHODISM The emergence of Methodism, led by the charismatic preacher John Wesley (1703-91), brought a concern for education and social justice. In Wales, the Society for Promoting Christian Knowledge had been setting up schools since 1699, and soon half the population of Wales was able to read. The Methodist revival produced hymns, organized schools and revived the Welsh literary tradition, so that the chapel became the center of social life.

NAPOLEONIC WARS As the 18th century reached its end, England and Wales faced a threatening adversary in the shape of Napoleon Bonaparte; only the navy stood in the way of invasion. "I do not say that he cannot come," reassured the English admiral Lord St Vincent (1735-1823). "I only say that he cannot come by sea." Napoleon's ambitions were stopped short by a British victory over the combined French and Spanish fleets at the Battle of Trafalgar in 1805, where Horatio Nelson (1758-1805) laid the foundations for the supremacy of British sea power – to continue for well over a century. Napoleon's final defeat took place ten years later at Waterloo, at the hands of the Duke of Wellington (1769-1852).

The Duke of Wellington (1769-1852) gave his name to the Wellington boot.

Power loom weaving in one of the new factories

THE INDUSTRIAL REVOLUTION When the Scottish engineer James Watt (1736-1819) patented his steam engine in 1781, the advent of steam power turned the coalfields of the Midlands and north of England into the "workshop of the world", with the rural population flooding into the new factories and mechanized cotton mills. Between the beginning of George III's reign in 1760 and its end in 1820 the country's population had doubled, and returning soldiers and widespread unemployment had led to mounting political discontent. The romantic movement was by now in full swing, with poets such as Lord Byron (1788-1824) and William Wordsworth (1770-1850), thrilled by the political upheaval and reminding readers of a lost rural innocence.

1745
The Jacobite uprising and the Battle of Culloden.

1770
James Cook starts his exploration of the coast of New South Wales.

1781
James Watt invents the steam engine.

1815
The Battle of Waterloo marks the end of the Napoleonic Wars.

THE REGENCY AND REFORM When George III died, after years of insanity, his place was taken by his son, the Prince Regent, who succeeded him as George IV (1820-30). The Prince – fun-loving, corpulent and spendthrift – was also a great patron of architecture. His reign saw the beginnings of reform, from the new police force to the Factory Acts to control of child labor. More such legislation came during the reign of his brother William IV (1830-7), when the Reform Act of 1832 modernized Parliament and acknowledged the principle of popular representation.

John Nash, architect, (1752-1835), and (left) his buildings around Regent's Park ▲ 159.

The first Victoria Cross, made from captured guns from the Crimean War.

Prince Albert

THE 19TH CENTURY: THE VICTORIAN ERA

QUEEN VICTORIA Victoria (1837-1901) gave her name to an age that saw the British Empire reach its apotheosis, with thousands of young men from England and Wales leaving their native land to explore it or administer it. At the age of only 18, she was woken and given the news that she was Queen. After a little thought, Victoria replied that she would "be good". Her marriage to Albert, Prince of Saxe-Coburg-Gotha, brought a relentless reformer to the palace, whose energy lay behind some of the enormous scientific and technological achievements of her reign.

TECHNOLOGICAL CHANGE The Industrial Revolution was culminating in the age of railways, with the opening of the Liverpool to Manchester line by George Stephenson (1781-1848) in 1830. The railways changed the shape of the cities and the lives of all classes: the Duke of

Queen Victoria as a young woman

Wellington famously disapproved on the grounds that they encouraged the working classes to move about. By the mid 1840s there were over 8,000 miles of track and people like the "Railway King" George Hudson (1800-71) were making a fortune in railway shares. Excursion trains brought millions to see Prince Albert's brainchild, the Great Exhibition of 1851, which demonstrated British engineering prowess to the world. In the year Victoria came to the throne the first message was sent by electric telegraph between Camden Town station and Euston in London. Within 30 years, messages could be sent in Morse code across the Atlantic. The penny post, introduced in 1840, was just as successful. Within the same period, nearly 700 million letters and packages were being sent around the country every year.

Posters urging a penny post: it began in 1840; early stamps (above right)
Right: Stephenson's North Star, 1837

INTELLECTUAL CHANGE Probably the greatest scientific impact of the age, with all its cultural and theological ramifications, was the publication in 1859 of the book that introduced evolution, *The Origin of Species* by Charles Darwin (1809-82). This was also the period when novelist and journalist Charles Dickens (1812-70) was roaming the capital reporting the appalling social conditions – notably in his 1837 novel *Oliver Twist*. It was also the era of the Crimean War (1853-6) against the Russians, which first brought the nursing reformer Florence Nightingale (1820-1910) to prominence as the "Lady with the Lamp".

CHARTISM

The Chartists' campaign for democratic reform culminated in a petition signed by over a million people, which was taken to London in an enormous demonstration in 1848, but was rejected by Parliament. Chartism had particularly brutal consequences in Wales, where marchers in Newport walked straight into a trap set by troops, who killed over 20 demonstrators and captured their leader John Frost (d. 1877). The so-called Rebecca Riots continued the tradition of Welsh political dissent from 1843, when demonstrators disguised themselves as women to tear down the hated tollgates on the roads. Welsh political aspirations for the rest of the century were focused on the rights of non-conformists against the privileges of the Anglican Church of Wales, and for land to be reformed. The extension of the voting franchise to farm labourers led to increasing success, culminating in the 1881 Welsh Sunday Closing Act, which forced Welsh pubs to shut on the sabbath.

WELSH LANGUAGE

Although the Church of Wales did not lose its prime position until 1920, there were notable successes extending education to Wales, including the opening of the first Welsh university college in Aberystwyth in 1872. But the Welsh language had been falling into disuse, especially after the 1846 inspectors' report, known as the Treason of the Blue Books, dismissed it as "the language of slavery". The Welsh Language Society was formed in 1885 to redress the balance, and *eisteddfodau* were reintroduced into rural life to encourage an understanding of Welsh culture. At the same time, the minefields of South Wales became the centre of trade unionism in the battle over pay with the mine-owners.

GLADSTONE AND DISRAELI

William Ewart Gladstone (1809-98), the Liberal Prime Minister, passed most of his important reforms in the first of his four ministries between 1868 and 1874, including the legalisation of trade unions and compulsory education. Even so, it was his arch-rival, the Conservative leader Benjamin Disraeli (1804-81), who extended the franchise further with the Second Reform Act of 1867. Gladstone's attempt to give home rule to Ireland divided his party; he left office for the last time in 1894.

EMPIRE AND TRADE

From the Indian Mutiny in 1857 to the Boer War in South Africa in 1899, British soldiers and sailors were kept increasingly busy policing an empire which – despite the reluctance of Gladstone – continued to grow until it covered nearly a quarter of the globe. The Empire spread British goods across the world, and brought an increasing range of products back to England, filling the new department stores which began appearing in English cities. The first was Whiteley's in London, founded in 1863 by William Whiteley, the "Universal Provider", whose hard-pressed staff worked from 7am to 11pm, providing "anything from a pin to an elephant at short notice"

Top: the Liverpool to Manchester railway
Above: Sherlock Holmes, the fictional detective, and Benjamin Disraeli, Prime Minister and novelist.

1837
Queen Victoria comes to the throne

1851
The Great Exhibition in Hyde Park

1853
The Crimean War begins

1857
The Indian Mutiny

JACK THE RIPPER

The series of horrific murders of prostitutes in Whitechapel in 1888 has never been solved, but popular newspaper coverage at the time dubbed the murderer "Jack the Ripper", and brought the plight of inner city poverty to the public's attention. It also led to a new interest in detective stories – the first Sherlock Holmes story had been published the year before.

*Queen Elizabeth II
and Prince Philip*

Pageantry around Britain includes the dignity of the medieval processions of the City of London, the Edinburgh Tattoo and the Welsh tradition of *eisteddfodau*, the literary and musical events held in Wales since the 12th century. Most royal ceremonies are newer than that, but they have their origins in older traditions, such as the annual State Opening of Parliament and the Trooping of the Colour. Kings and queens have lived in London since Edward the Confessor set up his court in Westminster 900 years ago. The Tower of London became a palace to his successors, but the biggest royal household in London for more than 300 years was Whitehall Palace – in its heyday stretching across 20 acres between Whitehall and the river. The palace was burned down in 1698, but its Banqueting House still survives in Whitehall, as does St James's Palace, where new kings and queens are proclaimed. It was built by Henry VIII on the site of an old leper hospital. Henry was also responsible for the magnificent palace at Hampton Court.

ROYAL PALACES

Above, from the far left: the original Whitehall Palace, long since burned down; the Queen opens the Parliamentary year at the Palace of Westminster, better known as the Houses of Parliament; the Garter Ceremony outside Windsor Castle; and the Tower of London, London's oldest palace and, in different periods, also its prison, mint, zoo and place of execution.

CROWN JEWELS

The crown jewels include all the priceless items of ritual from the coronation, many of them not used since 1953. The ritual itself dates back to the time of Edward the Confessor, almost a millennium ago. Most of the jewels were actually made for the coronation of Charles II in 1660, though the extraordinary Imperial State Crown dates from 1838, and includes 2,800 diamonds and the Black Prince's ruby, worn by Henry V at the Battle of Agincourt in 1415. The State Crown of Queen Elizabeth the Queen Mother includes the infamous Koh-I-Noor diamond. These and other royal jewels are on show at the Jewel Tower of the Tower of London. They are the most precious of all the paraphernalia of pageantry.

TRADITION

Royal processions, like the coronation, are creations of the last two centuries. Other pageants and rituals are passed from generation to generation. Many of the peculiar uniforms – like those of the Pikemen and Musketeers who protect the Lord Mayor of London – are reconstructions of this century.

PROCESSIONS

Royal ceremonials are some of the newer events, but they have their origins in older traditions. At the State Opening of Parliament, which takes place every year, the Queen, plus 109 troopers and seven officers, the Australian State Coach and the Imperial State Crown – made for Queen Victoria's coronation in 1838 – process from Buckingham Palace to the Houses of Parliament. At the back of the procession are two farriers, whose traditional role is to kill lame horses and chop off their hooves to prove they had not simply sold the horse along the way. Trooping the Colour, the celebration of the Queen's official birthday, takes place in June on London's Horse Guards Parade. The Lord Mayor's Show in November features the new Lord Mayor of the City of London in procession in a golden state coach.

Left: Lily Langtry, mistress of Edward VII
Below right: going "over the top" on the Western Front

THE 20TH CENTURY: MODERN TIMES

THE EDWARDIAN ERA Queen Victoria was succeeded by her son Edward VII (r. 1901-10) who, until then, had spent his adult life as a leisurely playboy prince; one of his mistresses, Lily Langtry (1853-1929), became a celebrity in her own right. His short reign was a period of unprecedented opulence, but also of political turmoil, with fierce battles over wages, votes for women and the so-called People's Budget that introduced old age pensions and was vetoed by the House of Lords.

1914
The outbreak of World War I.

1926
The General Strike.

1936
The abdication of Edward VIII.

1945
The end of World War II.

WORLD WAR I The period ended unexpectedly with the outbreak of war on August 4, 1914, when Britain honored its 80-year-old promise to defend Belgium. By the end of the war in November 1918, nearly a million had been killed, and a new camaraderie between the classes

meant that the country could never be the same again. The shortage of men led to women taking on roles that would have been unthinkable a few years before. They became bus conductors from 1916, and housemaids left their jobs to work in factories; as many as 900,000 women were working in the munitions factories by the end of the war. By 1922, 900,000 war pensions were being paid out; six years later, 65,000 shell-shock victims were still in mental hospitals. A revulsion against jingoism spread through the country as the true horrors became apparent, and the politicians struggled to fulfil the promise made by Prime Minister David Lloyd George (1863-1945) to build a "land fit for heroes to live in".

Wartime ration books; and an image of civil unrest during the General Strike

DEPRESSION AND UNREST A new socialist party had been emerging as a separate political force, with Keir Hardie (1856-1915) becoming the first Labour MP in 1900. The party formed a brief minority government under Ramsay MacDonald (1877-1937) in 1924. Social unrest erupted into the General Strike in 1926, lasting for nine days and involving half a million workers. Wales, the heartland of trade unionism, was gripped by massive unemployment, running at 27 percent. Welsh nationalism had also begun to emerge in 1925 with the launch of the political party Plaid Cymru under the literary critic Saunders Lewis (1893-1985), who was imprisoned in 1936 for a token act of arson at an RAF base.

Neville Chamberlain after the Munich Agreement of 1938

SOCIAL CHANGE Women were finally given the vote in November 1918, although they still had to be over 30: men and women were not given equality in the polling booths until 1929. At the forefront of the women's revolution was Marie Stopes (1880-1958), whose books, *Married Love* and *Wise Parenthood,* published in 1918, openly discussed contraception and sold 700,000 copies. She opened the first birth control clinic in 1921. In 1936, the royal family was shaken by domestic crisis when the new king Edward VIII decided to

"We are seven" say the Minor Range

Cars become widely affordable

abdicate his throne because he wanted to marry the twice-divorced American Wallis Simpson. It was a period of other changes as well. Driving tests were introduced in 1934 and the first Motor Show was held at Olympia in 1937. With its "ribbon development" and new commuter suburbs such as Hendon, Morden and Wembley, London grew to a peak population of 8 million.

WORLD WAR II Prime Minister Neville Chamberlain (1869-1940) met Adolf Hitler at Munich in 1938 and caved in to his territorial demands for Czechoslovakia. Chamberlain returned to a hero's welcome, waving the signed agreement and declared that it meant "peace in our time". It did not, and when the war broke out in September 1939, Britain was still seriously unprepared. Expecting an immediate assault from the air, the government evacuated millions of children to rural areas, many of them ending up in Wales. When Chamberlain stepped down in favor of the charismatic Winston Churchill (1874-1965), invasion was expected on the English coast at any moment. Thanks largely to a heroic air defence (the Battle of Britain), this invasion never occurred, but nevertheless elaborate precautions were put in place. The Blitz, which began in 1940, caused enormous damage to cities, especially London, Liverpool, Manchester, Sheffield and Coventry; 58,000 civilians were killed, and 200,000 houses destroyed. The war put civilians in the front line for the first time, with women playing a central role. By 1944, there were 500,000 women in the forces. The end of the war in 1945 left Britain victorious but exhausted and all but bankrupt.

Top: Winston Churchill and his famous victory sign
Above: the Blitz strikes Coventry in 1940

1958
The Campaign for Nuclear Disarmament is founded.

THE WELFARE STATE Peace brought a hunger for political reform, and after VE Day in 1945 the Labour Party under Clement Attlee (1883-1967) was returned to power by a huge majority, with a program to nationalize the coal, gas, iron, steel and electricity industries. It also backed a plan by Sir William Beveridge (1879-1963) that included a National Health Service and National Insurance system and laid the foundations for the modern welfare state. Green belts around London and other big cities and a string of new towns like Stevenage and Harlow changed the look of England. There was continuing confusion about the UK's post-colonial role: Anglo-French forces invaded Egypt to protect the Suez Canal in 1956, but were withdrawn after international condemnation. It was also a period of growing prosperity: most people, said Prime Minister Harold Macmillan (1894-1986) in 1957, "had never had it so good".

Parents hand over wartime evacuees

● HISTORY OF ENGLAND AND WALES

Below left: Clement Attlee (1883-1967), the post-war Prime Minister.
Below right: The Beatles.
Middle page: The miners on strike and (bottom) Margaret Thatcher.

FROM THE BEATLES TO BLAIR

1959
The development of the Morris Mini.

1969
Divorce Act ushers in no-fault divorces, and Britain's first motorway is opened.

1975
Britain enters the European Economic Community, now the European Union.

1982
The Falklands War.

1994
The opening of the Channel Tunnel.

1999
The first elections to a devolved assembly governing Wales.

2001, 2005
Tony Blair re-elected prime minister.

2005
July 6: London wins the 2012 Olympic bid.

2005
July 7: In Britain's first suicide bombing, four terrorists blow up the London Underground, killing 56.

SOCIAL UPHEAVAL The post-war economy had recovered by the 1960s, and under Prime Minister Harold Wilson (1916-95) – thanks to the emergence of The Beatles and other English bands – London suddenly became the trendiest city in the world, at the very heart of the cultural revolution. The Mini car (1959) and the mini skirt (1965) put British design on the map, and a string of legal changes altered the moral atmosphere of England and Wales. Homosexuality was legalized, the birth control pill appeared, the death penalty was abolished and the voting age cut to 18, but the most influential was probably the 1969 Divorce Act, which allowed fault-free divorce after the "irretrievable breakdown" of the marriage. The divorce rate has risen steadily ever since.

POLITICAL UPHEAVAL The discovery of oil in the North Sea helped contribute to the collapse of manufacturing because it drove up the value of the pound. In Wales, the slow closure of the mines – from 212 in 1945 to just 11 in 1989 – meant growing unemployment, just as stricter limits on public spending began reducing traditional services. The 1963 Beeching Report had closed many of the railway branch lines that connected smaller communities across the country. The motor car was taking over, and in 1969, the first motorway – the M1 – was opened between London and Yorkshire. There were political changes too, when Prime Minister Edward Heath (b. 1916) took Britain into the EEC, and the oil crisis and rising inflation led to a decade of industrial unrest and recession.

THATCHER AND BLAIR In 1979 Margaret Thatcher (b. 1925) became Britain's first woman prime minister, ushering in a period of polarization, civil unrest and economic boom, when the Conservative Party dominated politics by winning three successive election victories. It was a decade that saw a major clampdown on trade union power and widespread inner city rioting (1981 and 1985), an epic miners' strike (1984-5) and the successful outcome of the Falklands War (1982). In 1990 Mrs Thatcher was overthrown by colleagues, critical of her increasing arrogance, but the Conservatives scraped back in under John Major (b. 1943) in 1992, pushing ahead with the privatization of the railways and parts of the health service. In this period the Conservatives became increasingly divided over Britain's relations with the European Union. The year 1994 also brought important changes, with the opening of the Channel Tunnel and the start of Britain's national lottery – the biggest in the world. Tony Blair's (b. 1953) Labour Party was swept to office in 1997, and has succeeded in devolving power to a Scottish parliament in Edinburgh, and a Welsh assembly in Cardiff. The relations between the different parts of the UK look set for an exciting period of change.

ARTS AND TRADITIONS

*Below: London's Shaftesbury Avenue
Inset: Dame Judy Dench (top) and
(bottom) Harold Pinter in conversation
with Tom Stoppard*

PANTOMIME DAMES
The cross-dressing comic hero in a Christmas pantomime is a very English tradition. These seasonal shows combine sentimental fairy tales with broad comedy, farce and gentle satire.

London, regarded internationally as the capital of world theater, is the crowning glory in a dramatic tradition that stretches back to Roman times and beyond. The Royal National Theatre, the reconstruction of Shakespeare's Globe, the glamorous West End and the radical fringe all make the city a mecca for theater-goers worldwide. Throughout the country, from the Royal Shakespeare Company's home in Stratford-on-Avon to Theatre Clwyd in Wales, English and Welsh towns and cities have a wealth of distinguished repertory theaters. Touring companies like Shared Experience and Théâtre de Complicité take groundbreaking work to audiences all over Britain, as well as touring internationally to enormous critical acclaim.

ROYAL SHAKESPEARE COMPANY
Founded in 1961, the RSC uses three different theaters in Stratford-on-Avon, Shakespeare's birthplace. They also tour and have a diverse London season, producing classical and contemporary drama as well as Shakespeare.
Left: a production of Webster's *The White Devil* in the Swan Theatre, Stratford-on-Avon, which combines the intimacy of Elizabethan stage with the comfort and technology of a modern auditorium.

Punch and Judy shows (right), based on early Commedia dell' Arte masks, combine slapstick violence with traditional characters.

THE GREATS

Sir Henry Irving, perhaps the greatest 19th-century actor, was most famous for his melodramatic performance in *The Bells* and was the first actor to be knighted for his services to the profession.

Dame Ellen Terry was one of a large theatrical dynasty, including her parents, siblings, and her son Edward Gordon Craig, who became one of the great designers of the age.

SHAKESPEARE'S GLOBE (below)

The Globe opened on London's South Bank in 1997, on a site very close to the original Globe of Shakespeare's day. Modern audiences can stand in the pit, which is open to the elements, or book a seat under cover, for an authentic Elizabethan experience.

In his day one of the most controversial figures in society, Oscar Wilde was also one of theater's great comic geniuses. His plays remain popular for their wit and style.

ROYAL NATIONAL THEATRE

Founded in 1961 by Laurence Olivier, the National Theatre on London's South Bank boasts three auditoria and has an international reputation for excellence. Past artistic directors have included Olivier himself, Sir Peter Hall and Sir Richard Eyre; the current incumbent is Trevor Nunn. The company also tours, provides workshop facilities for new writing, and maintains an extensive education program.

Below: Fiona Shaw stars in *The Prime of Miss Jean Brodie*.

Noel Coward's plays, musicals, popular songs, comic revues and his own cabaret act kept him at the forefront of popular entertainment for over 50 years, both in Britain and the United States.

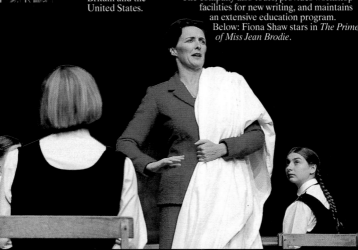

MUSIC

e human voice has been at the heart of British music since the ddle Ages. John Dunstable (d. 1453), the first English composer European reputation, headed a school of polyphonic composition t blossomed a century later in the rich choral legacy of Thomas lis and his pupil William Byrd, and in the great flood of madrigals d lute songs that characterized the reign of Elizabeth I. The brief eer of Henry Purcell seemed to herald a v era, but its promise faded in the ly 18th century with the arrival of ndel, whose oratorios kept choral cieties busy for the next 200 years c whose influence on native mposers was suffocating. It was not the late 19th century that British sic recovered its individuality and ntured into modern orchestral ritory in the powerfully mantic scores of Edward gar, the quintessentially glish music of Ralph ughan Williams, and works of a prolific st-war generation ging from Benjamin tten and Michael ppett to the tougher modern oms of Peter Maxwell Davies d Harrison Birtwistle.

SIR SIMON RATTLE
Appointed conductor to the City of Birmingham Symphony Orchestra at the age of 24, he transformed it over 18 years into a world-class ensemble.

THE PROMS
An annual 8-week festival of music at the Royal Albert Hall that is probably the most comprehensive to be found anywhere in the world, attracting artists and orchestras at the highest international level. The Last Night, complete with audience participation, has become a regular British institution. Here Malcolm Sargent (left), chief conductor from 1948 to 1967, officiates at the celebrations.

BRITTEN
Composer, conductor, pianist, Britten (below) was a practical musician whose genius touched most aspects of British musical life in the years after World War II.

HUDDERSFIELD
The choral tradition at the heart of British music still thrives, from the male voice choirs of Wales to the amateur choruses of Northern England; this is the home of the Huddersfield Choral Society (above), one of the oldest and most famous of all.

HANDEL
A German trained in Italy, Handel (below) lived in London for nearly half a century and became a naturalized Englishman. As well as operas and oratorios, he provided a series of magnificent choral and orchestral works for royal and public occasions.

BRASS BANDS
Amateur brass bands have been popular, especially in the north, since the early 19th century. By 1900, there were said to be over 20,000 in Great Britain. The tradition continues in famous ensembles like the Black Dyke Mills Band (above).

● OPERA AND BALLET

The restoration of the Stuarts in the late 17th century brought
new influences from the continent, among them opera. Purcell
was the first English composer to tackle the new form with any
persistence, and his little masterpiece *Dido and Aeneas* is the
earliest English opera to be regularly performed today. But
within a few years the invasion of Handel and his Italian rivals
was to create a lasting taste for foreign importations; in English
only satire and humor survived – from the *Beggar's Opera* in 1728
to the operettas of Gilbert and Sullivan 150 years later – until
the 20th century, when Benjamin Britten emerged on the world
stage with *Peter Grimes* and a succession of stage works that
opened a new era in British music theater. Meanwhile ballet,
encouraged by the visits of Diaghilev's *Ballets Russes*, took root
in England, first as the Vic-Wells Ballet in 1931, then as the
Sadlers Wells Ballet, whose outstanding success brought it the
title of Royal Ballet in 1956.

"GAWAIN"
John Tomlinson as
the Green Knight in
the spectacular
production of
Harrison Birtwistle's
opera at Covent
Garden, 1991.

**THE ROYAL OPERA
HOUSE** (right),
the third theater on
the site, dates from
1858 after the Royal
Italian Opera had
been destroyed by
fire. Its recent
renovation has put it
on a level with any
opera house in the
world.

FONTEYN
Margot Fonteyn, legendary prima ballerina of the Sadler's Wells Ballet the Royal Ballet from 1956) in Stravinsky's *Firebird*. Her partnership with Rudolf Nureyev provided some of Covent Garden's most memorable evenings in the 1960s.

JOHN BULL
Thomas Rowlandson's picture of *John Bull at the Italian Opera* (*c.* 1811).

GLYNDEBOURNE
Glyndebourne Festival Opera was launched by John Christie at his family home in Sussex in 1934, with the intention of presenting opera in ideal conditions. The quality of performance in the purpose-built theater is equalled by the beauty of the surrounding gardens, in which members of the audience are encouraged to picnic.

PURCELL
Henry Purcell, who died at 36, took the first significant steps in English opera. His *Dido and Aeneas*, written for a girls' school in Chelsea, has outlived his more ambitious works for the musical theater.

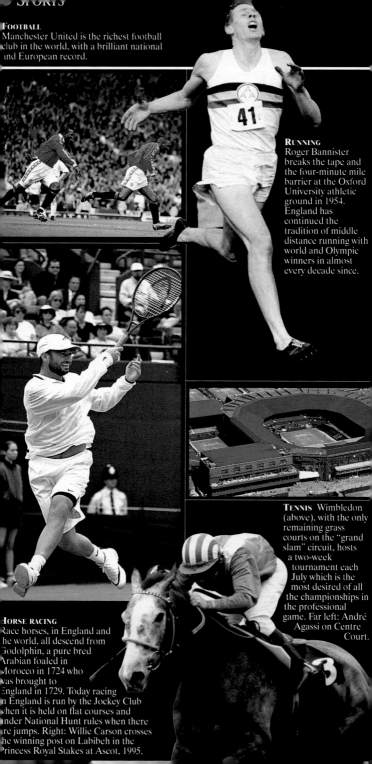

SPORTS

FOOTBALL
Manchester United is the richest football club in the world, with a brilliant national and European record.

RUNNING
Roger Bannister breaks the tape and the four-minute mile barrier at the Oxford University athletic ground in 1954. England has continued the tradition of middle distance running with world and Olympic winners in almost every decade since.

TENNIS Wimbledon (above), with the only remaining grass courts on the "grand slam" circuit, hosts a two-week tournament each July which is the most desired of all the championships in the professional game. Far left: André Agassi on Centre Court.

HORSE RACING
Race horses, in England and the world, all descend from Godolphin, a pure bred Arabian foaled in Morocco in 1724 who was brought to England in 1729. Today racing in England is run by the Jockey Club when it is held on flat courses and under National Hunt rules when there are jumps. Right: Willie Carson crosses the winning post on Labibeh in the Princess Royal Stakes at Ascot, 1995.

e new Millennium
dium in Cardiff (far
ht) hosts rugby
ernationals and was
venue for the 1999
gby World Cup.

England likes to claim the invention of many of the world's most popular sports during the 19th century and to lament its inability to win any of them in the 20th century. Games – mostly crude versions of football played with an inflated pig's bladder – were fought between villages throughout the pre-industrial world. They took on rules only when the railways spread through England and Wales. The work disciplines of new factories and mines were applied to playtime and the new codes were pushed out round the world and especially to the Empire. So the cabbage patch at Twickenham became the headquarters of Rugby Union, which remains there today. Lords moved from an overcrowded square in the Marylebone district of London to St John's Wood, and the retired heroes of the game continue to rule from the Long Room in the pavilion. The English are more baffled than resentful of the change in their fortunes and still love to debate what sport should be and how high it might aspire.

ROWING
Matthew Pinsent (left) training at Henley-on-Thames with the world's most successful rower and five times Olympic gold medallist, Steve Redgrave (now retired).

CRICKET
avid Gower, captain of Leicester
d England is bowled out by
ran Khan, who captained
ford University
d
kistan,
d was
e of the
rld's great
t bowlers in
e 1970s.

njit Singh (above),
Indian prince who
yed as an amateur
England in the
mative years of the
ernational game.

LORDS CRICKET GROUND
Lords, crowned by its 21st-century media center, is still at the heart of the game, 100 years after the first world-renowned player W.G. Grace (right) last played there.

GUY FAWKES NIGHT

On November 5, 1605, the government was saved by the last-minute discovery of Guy Fawkes's plot to blow up the Houses of Parliament, an event that is remembered every anniversary with fireworks displays and bonfires on which a "guy" is destroyed in the flames.

STATE OPENING OF PARLIAMENT

After the summer recess, the monarch reopens Parliament in October/early November. "Black Rod", the royal emissary, is sent to summon the members of the Commons, where no monarch has entered since Charles I's ill-fated attempt to arrest five members in 1641. He knocks three times with his black rod then is permitted to deliver his message.

MAY DAY - MAY 1

The Celtic festival of Beltane, invoking the protection of the gods for the herds in their summer pastures, was celebrated with bonfires and the ritual gathering of wood. At sunrise May flowers and a straight-growing trunk (maypole) were brought in as a focus for dancing and games (below). Of the old luck-bringing May beasts, only a few – such as the Padstow Hobby Horse (right) – now survive.

MUMMERS

Mumming plays, most commonly performed around Christmas, date back to the Middle Ages when they were supposed to bring good luck and fertility. The mummers (right) wear strips of cloth; their speeches are topical.

The often bizarre ceremonies and customs of England and Wales show little sign of dying out. In fact those that have survived into the 21st century are being revived with vigor, not only as merchandizing opportunities but also, in a world dominated by new technology, global trading and rapid change, as an expression of people's increasing need to reinforce a sense of time and place within the community. Most of these rituals and celebrations originate in a rural and agrarian past, in a cyclical existence governed by sowing, harvesting and stock-rearing. Some have their roots in ancient folklore and pagan rites, such as many May Day celebrations. Others have survived because they became inextricably bound up with the festivals of the Christian calendar. Through television, the official rites of crown and state are now accessible to all, thus widening the shared heritage of ritual that has over the centuries played such an integral part in binding and uplifting the community spirit.

The cheese-making tradition goes back over a thousand years in England and Wales, and today there is a revival in the craft of local independent cheese-makers. Tangy, nutty Cheddars, crumbly Caerphilly and salty, creamy, blue-veined Stilton are all world-class cheeses, delicious when eaten with crusty bread and equally wonderful in traditional dishes such as Welsh Rarebit (melted cheese and seasonings on buttered toast).

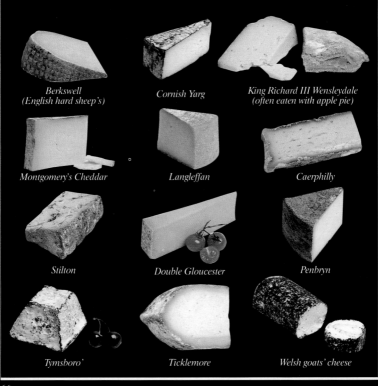

Berkswell
(English hard sheep's)

Cornish Yarg

King Richard III Wensleydale
(often eaten with apple pie)

Montgomery's Cheddar

Langleffan

Caerphilly

Stilton

Double Gloucester

Penbryn

Tymsboro'

Ticklemore

Welsh goats' cheese

ARCHITECTURE

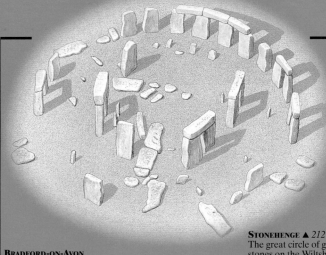

STONEHENGE ▲ 212
The great circle of giant upright stones on the Wiltshire plain dates from prehistory, probably 2nd or 3rd millennium BC. It is the annual focus of Druidic solstice rituals.

BRADFORD-ON-AVON CHURCH ▲ 216
This church, founded by St Aldhelm, is dedicated to St Lawrence and was built in AD 700. For a long time it was in secular use but is now recognized as the most important Saxon church in England.

MAIDEN CASTLE ▲ 205
An Iron Age hill fort near Dorchester in Dorset, which was fought over by the Romans in a famous battle in AD 44 under Vespasian. Excavations in the 1930s uncovered Iron Age and Roman artifacts.

AVEBURY ▲ 213
Huge ceremonial and memorial stones arranged to some arcane and mystical plan. Covering 28 acres, the stones are now mixed up inside the boundaries of the present-day Wiltshire village.

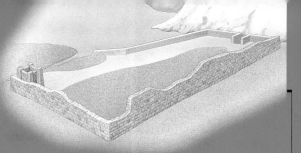

TINTAGEL ▲ 249
More bleak coastal
scenery than
architecture,
"Black cliffs and
caves and storm
and wind", wrote
Tennyson, although
he was moved, as
visitors are today,
by the ruined castle
and its associations
with King Arthur.

It could be misleading to call some of the earliest man-made
artifacts that litter the soil of England and Wales "architecture"
– but they do embody techniques of construction that subsequently
develop and refine. Stonehenge today seems very isolated and
remote from any known building type but its great stones
supporting lintels use a way of building that was well known in
Mycenean Greece. Earthworks, tombs and rough stone walls
evoke a distant way of life that is defensive and yet vulnerable to
the activities of unknown pre-Christian gods. The Anglo-Saxons
who arrived in England in the 5th and 6th centuries did not
achieve anything like the standards of the Roman colonizers.
In fact, they were indifferent to the built inheritance of Rome –
they were unable to comprehend the values of Roman life and
either ignored the architecture of the Empire or pillaged it for
building materials.

DOVER CASTLE ▲ 186
Built to defend the "front
door of England", what we
admire today is mainly King
Henry's 12th-century keep
and curtain walls. The
Constable's tower and the
chapel are
spectacular remains
of ancient English
power.

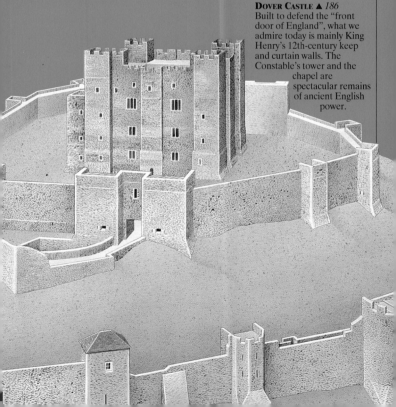

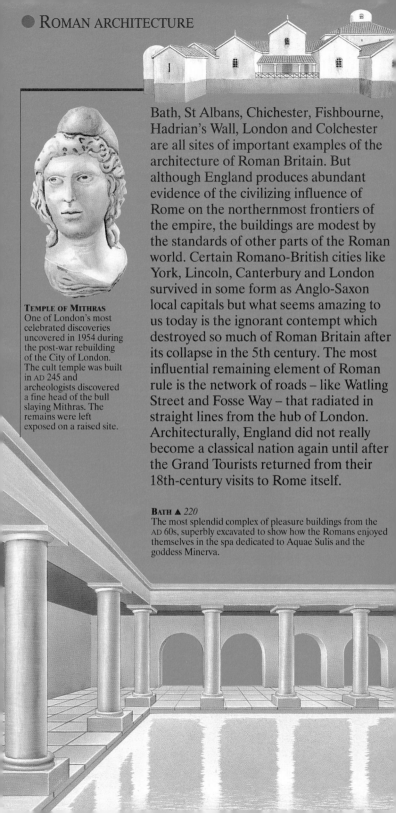

TEMPLE OF MITHRAS
One of London's most celebrated discoveries uncovered in 1954 during the post-war rebuilding of the City of London. The cult temple was built in AD 245 and archeologists discovered a fine head of the bull slaying Mithras. The remains were left exposed on a raised site.

Bath, St Albans, Chichester, Fishbourne, Hadrian's Wall, London and Colchester are all sites of important examples of the architecture of Roman Britain. But although England produces abundant evidence of the civilizing influence of Rome on the northernmost frontiers of the empire, the buildings are modest by the standards of other parts of the Roman world. Certain Romano-British cities like York, Lincoln, Canterbury and London survived in some form as Anglo-Saxon local capitals but what seems amazing to us today is the ignorant contempt which destroyed so much of Roman Britain after its collapse in the 5th century. The most influential remaining element of Roman rule is the network of roads – like Watling Street and Fosse Way – that radiated in straight lines from the hub of London. Architecturally, England did not really become a classical nation again until after the Grand Tourists returned from their 18th-century visits to Rome itself.

BATH ▲ *220*
The most splendid complex of pleasure buildings from the AD 60s, superbly excavated to show how the Romans enjoyed themselves in the spa dedicated to Aquae Sulis and the goddess Minerva.

LULLINGSTONE, KENT (LEFT) ▲ 172
A Roman middle-class villa, typical of many of the smaller Roman villas built in southern England. This reconstruction shows how it was built around its sheltered atrium garden.

VERULAMIUM – ST ALBANS ▲ 282
Clearly a very important Roman city; some of the brick and flint walls from AD 125 still stand. There is evidence of the Forum, theater, temples and good examples of the hypocaust system that warmed the chilly Roman occupiers.

FISHBOURNE, SUSSEX
The best villa in Britain – more of a palace, which suggests that it might have been one of the residences of a ruler. Grand mosaics and decoration evoke a sunnier world than damp Sussex.

LULLINGSTONE, KENT ▲ 172
The wall paintings and mosaics – including Europa the Bull being abducted by Jupiter – date from the 4th century. Lullingstone is remarkable because it shows that both pagan and later Christian rituals were practised here.

HADRIAN'S WALL
Long fragments of Roman walls and gates remain along the Northumberland borders, designed to keep out Picts and Scots. The most complete remaining Roman fortification in Europe.

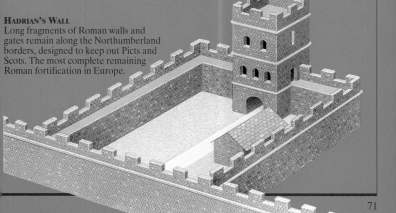

● NORMAN CASTLES AND CATHEDRALS

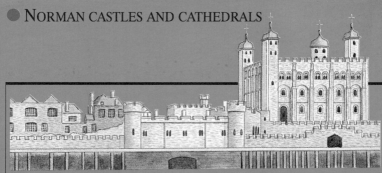

After the Norman Conquest of 1066, England gained its own version of the Romanesque architecture that was weighing heavily on the soil of continental Europe. The round arch and the solidity of the great cathedral walls are its distinctive features. The abbots from Normandy rebuilt the churches, cathedrals and monasteries of England and the style reflects both the strength of the faith and the power of the Conquest. Today the great naves of Durham, Rochester, Ely, Winchester and St Albans continue to impress. The carvings of Norman moldings are both geometric in their chevron patterns and reminiscent of the Norse past with their strange pagan figures. The secular defensive architecture in the castles survives well and there are some small Norman manors and their parallel smaller churches.

TOWER OF LONDON (ABOVE) ▲ *142*
The Norman White Tower at the heart of the Tower of London, begun by William the Conqueror after the Battle of Hastings in 1066, once dominated London and is now the most important Norman fortified building in Britain. Successors each added their own features, Edward I building the outer curtain wall and moat in the late 13th century.

BODIAM, SUSSEX ▲ *176*
Bodiam is a late example of a French type of castle – it feels Norman but was not built until 1385. It is a perfect square sitting in the moat, preceded by a gatehouse. It was saved and restored by Lord Curzon in 1919.

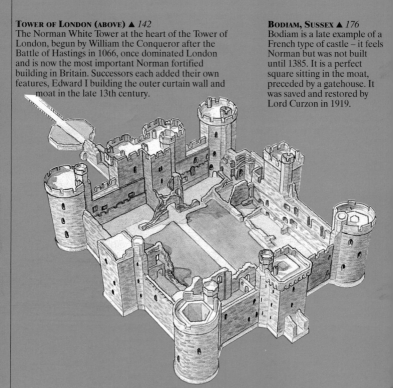

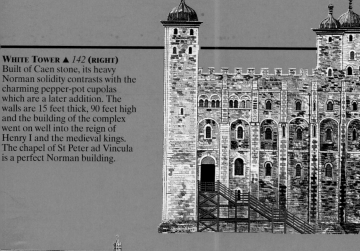

WHITE TOWER ▲ *142* **(RIGHT)**
Built of Caen stone, its heavy
Norman solidity contrasts with the
charming pepper-pot cupolas
which are a later addition. The
walls are 15 feet thick, 90 feet high
and the building of the complex
went on well into the reign of
Henry I and the medieval kings.
The chapel of St Peter ad Vincula
is a perfect Norman building.

ST BARTHOLOMEW THE GREAT ▲ *145* **(LEFT)**
St Bartholomew's was part of an Augustinian Priory
founded in 1123. It is the most impressive
Romanesque survival in London.

**ROMSEY ABBEY, HAMPSHIRE
▲** *197* **(ABOVE)**
The rebuilding began in 1120 and
went on until 1230. It is the nave that
impresses in its uniformity and the
detail of the scalloped capitals.

**DURHAM CATHEDRAL
▲** *408-9* **(ABOVE)**
The great Norman nave was
finished in 1133. The gigantic
arcade of massive cylindrical
columns with their incised
patterns is one of the wonders
of the Norman world.

After the Romanesque, the Medieval period in England produced the finest masterpieces of ecclesiastical architecture – some of the cathedrals and parish churches are the most impressive in Europe. The three phases of medieval architecture are known as Early English (roughly 1150 to 1275), Decorated (1275 to 1375) and Perpendicular (1375 to 1530). The style is entirely Gothic – i.e. the arches are pointed. There was a transitional period when round arches and pointed arches occur in one building. Early English is seen at its purest in Salisbury Cathedral and the retro-choir of Southwark Cathedral. York Minster, Exeter Cathedral and St Mary Redcliffe in Bristol are all fine examples of the Decorated style and King's College Chapel in Cambridge is the high point of Perpendicular.

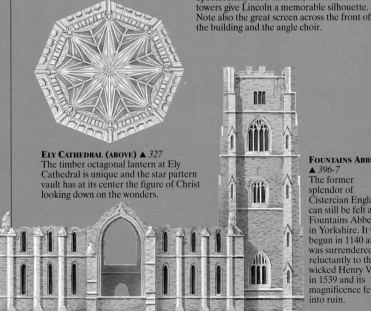

LINCOLN CATHEDRAL (ABOVE) ▲ *362*
Spectacularly sited on a hill, the three slender towers give Lincoln a memorable silhouette. Note also the great screen across the front of the building and the angle choir.

ELY CATHEDRAL (ABOVE) ▲ *327*
The timber octagonal lantern at Ely Cathedral is unique and the star pattern vault has at its center the figure of Christ looking down on the wonders.

FOUNTAINS ABBEY
▲ *396-7*
The former splendor of Cistercian England can still be felt at Fountains Abbey in Yorkshire. It was begun in 1140 and was surrendered reluctantly to the wicked Henry VIII in 1539 and its magnificence fell into ruin.

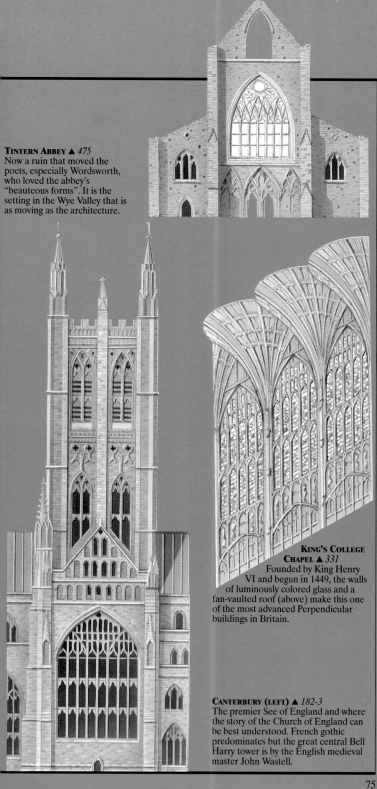

TINTERN ABBEY ▲ 475
Now a ruin that moved the
poets, especially Wordsworth,
who loved the abbey's
"beauteous forms". It is the
setting in the Wye Valley that is
as moving as the architecture.

**KING'S COLLEGE
CHAPEL ▲ 331**
Founded by King Henry
VI and begun in 1449, the walls
of luminously colored glass and a
fan-vaulted roof (above) make this one
of the most advanced Perpendicular
buildings in Britain.

CANTERBURY (LEFT) ▲ 182-3
The premier See of England and where
the story of the Church of England can
be best understood. French gothic
predominates but the great central Bell
Harry tower is by the English medieval
master John Wastell.

Tudor monarchs ruled from the accession of Henry VII to the death of Queen Elizabeth in 1603. Gothic architecture was flattening out at the beginning of this period and there was a gradual understanding and spread of Renaissance ideas. The Tudor style shows the infusion of classical styles onto medieval plans. After the Dissolution of the Monasteries, the newly enriched gentry built grand houses, often known as prodigy houses because of their extravagance. The Stuart period falls into two parts – James I and Charles I (1603-49), and Charles II and James II (1660-88) – separated by the Commonwealth republican period. Out of simple Palladian buildings comes the age of Wren and the rise of the English Baroque. The Fire of London gave Wren the opportunity of all time to rebuild the City of London and he left us St Paul's and all the City churches.

HAMPTON COURT ▲ 170 (GATEHOUSE ABOVE)
Here is some of the finest Tudor architecture in England. Built for Cardinal Wolsey and seized by Henry VIII, the palace and its gardens rapidly became England's Versailles – especially after Wren expanded it for William and Mary.

BOLSOVER CASTLE (RIGHT) ▲ 384
The interior of Bolsover is probably the work of John Smythson, who took over from his father Robert Smythson. The Pillar Chamber of 1616 is a mixture of Gothic vaulting, Renaissance columns and a typically Jacobean fireplace.

ST PAUL'S AND LONDON
After the Great Fire of 1666, Christopher Wren planned the new formal City – his triumph was St Paul's Cathedral ▲ 142, surrounded by the spires of his city churches as recorded by Hollar in this engraving.

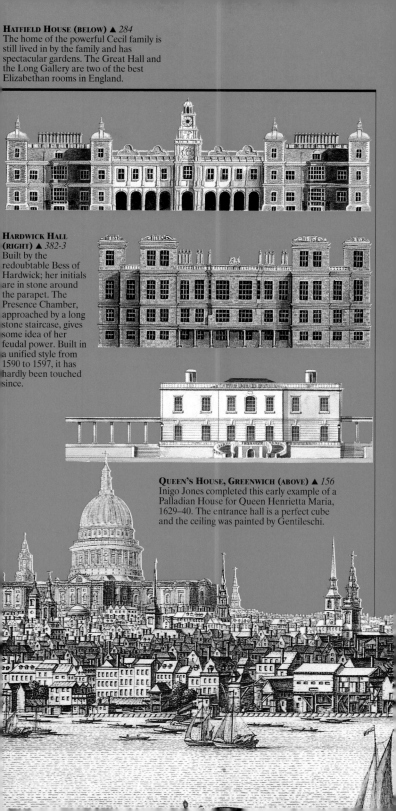

HATFIELD HOUSE (BELOW) ▲ *284*
The home of the powerful Cecil family is still lived in by the family and has spectacular gardens. The Great Hall and the Long Gallery are two of the best Elizabethan rooms in England.

HARDWICK HALL (RIGHT) ▲ *382-3*
Built by the redoubtable Bess of Hardwick; her initials are in stone around the parapet. The Presence Chamber, approached by a long stone staircase, gives some idea of her feudal power. Built in a unified style from 1590 to 1597, it has hardly been touched since.

QUEEN'S HOUSE, GREENWICH (ABOVE) ▲ *156*
Inigo Jones completed this early example of a Palladian House for Queen Henrietta Maria, 1629–40. The entrance hall is a perfect cube and the ceiling was painted by Gentileschi.

MAUSOLEUM AT CASTLE HOWARD, YORKSHIRE ▲ 403
One of the most sublime classical temples in England designed for Lord Carlisle by Nicholas Hawksmoor. The tight circle of columns seems determined to keep the dead inside.

The reign of Queen Anne (1702–14) was not really a complete architectural period but her name became synonymous with a domestic classicism that characterizes some of the best small houses of the period. Her years also coincided with the rise of Baroque architecture in England. The four King Georges reigned from 1714 to 1830 and the period is one of pure Classicism when order, restraint, dignity and elegance are the key elements of the style. The period had some experiments like Gothick and Rococo and even Chinoiserie but homogeneity is the trademark. The certainty of the universal rules rediscovered from Greece and Rome underlie this confident period.

BELTON HOUSE, LINCOLNSHIRE (BELOW) ▲ 359
A really good late 17th-century house given a facelift in 1777 by James Wyatt. Inside there is a great marble hall and beautiful chimneypieces.

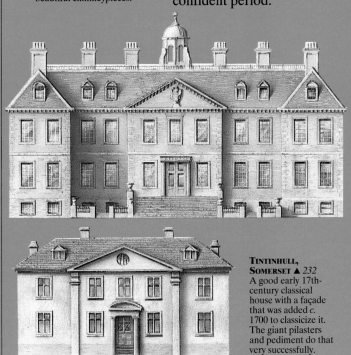

TINTINHULL, SOMERSET ▲ 232
A good early 17th-century classical house with a façade that was added c. 1700 to classicize it. The giant pilasters and pediment do that very successfully.

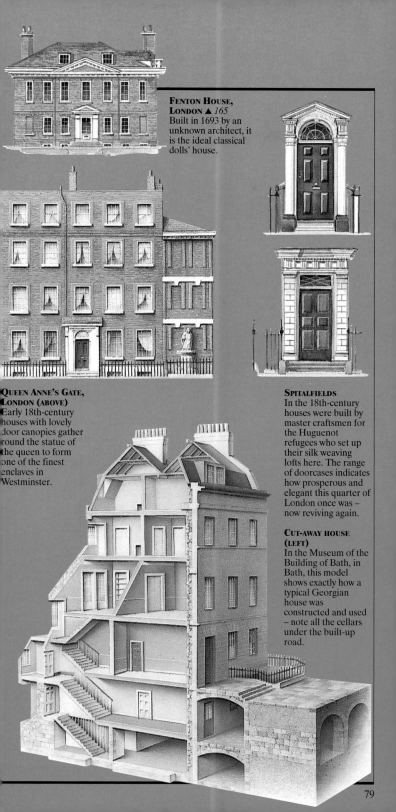

FENTON HOUSE, LONDON ▲ *165*
Built in 1693 by an unknown architect, it is the ideal classical dolls' house.

QUEEN ANNE'S GATE, LONDON (ABOVE)
Early 18th-century houses with lovely door canopies gather round the statue of the queen to form one of the finest enclaves in Westminster.

SPITALFIELDS
In the 18th-century houses were built by master craftsmen for the Huguenot refugees who set up their silk weaving lofts here. The range of doorcases indicates how prosperous and elegant this quarter of London once was – now reviving again.

CUT-AWAY HOUSE (LEFT)
In the Museum of the Building of Bath, in Bath, this model shows exactly how a typical Georgian house was constructed and used – note all the cellars under the built-up road.

● ARCHITECTS

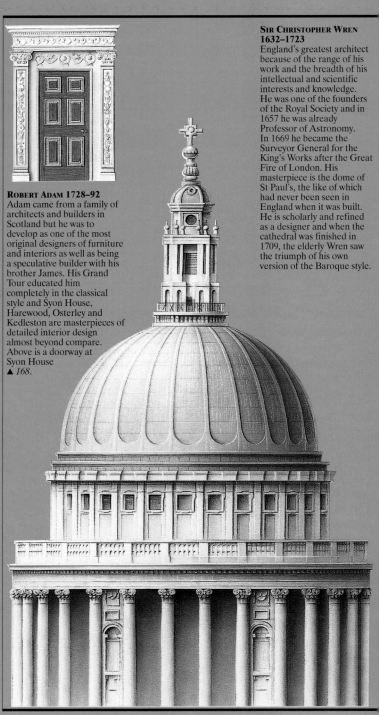

ROBERT ADAM 1728–92
Adam came from a family of
architects and builders in
Scotland but he was to
develop as one of the most
original designers of furniture
and interiors as well as being
a speculative builder with his
brother James. His Grand
Tour educated him
completely in the classical
style and Syon House,
Harewood, Osterley and
Kedleston are masterpieces of
detailed interior design
almost beyond compare.
Above is a doorway at
Syon House
▲ *168*.

**SIR CHRISTOPHER WREN
1632–1723**
England's greatest architect
because of the range of his
work and the breadth of his
intellectual and scientific
interests and knowledge.
He was one of the founders
of the Royal Society and in
1657 he was already
Professor of Astronomy.
In 1669 he became the
Surveyor General for the
King's Works after the Great
Fire of London. His
masterpiece is the dome of
St Paul's, the like of which
had never been seen in
England when it was built.
He is scholarly and refined
as a designer and when the
cathedral was finished in
1709, the elderly Wren saw
the triumph of his own
version of the Baroque style.

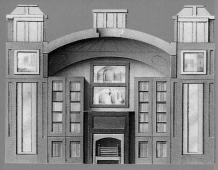

SIR JOHN SOANE 1753–1837

One of the world's most original neoclassical architects, Soane has left us his own house as a museum which says more about the architectural creativity of his mind than any of his surviving buildings. He trained under George Dance and Henry Holland. Much of his work has perished but his house and the Dulwich Art Gallery give you the essence. A section of his Breakfast Room is shown above ▲ *140*.

SIR JOHN VANBRUGH 1664–1726

Not just an architect but a soldier, playwright, adventurer, possibly a spy and also a herald. He worked alongside Wren as Comptroller at the Office of Works as a result of the patronage of Lord Carlisle, for whom he was building Castle Howard. Blenheim Palace, built for the Duke of Marlborough, is his triumph, where the interior and exterior demonstrate his theatrical as well as his architectural skills. Above is the bridge over the lake at Blenheim and below left is a section of the Great Hall ▲ *312*.

NICHOLAS HAWKSMOOR 1661–1736

From the age of 18, he was Wren's assistant and he worked especially closely with him at Greenwich. He designed Easton Neston on his own in 1702 and went on to design six major London churches as well as parts of All Souls at Oxford and the Gothic west towers of Westminster Abbey. On the right is his spire for Christ Church, Spitalfields, in London ▲ *148*. Soaring above the arched pediment of the portico, it dominates the whole design of the church. Inside is a flat ceiling with barrel-vaulted side aisles.

England's most original and valuable esthetic contribution to the world is the designed Arcadian landscape. This is seen to its best advantage in relation to country houses where the park and gardens are harmoniously designed together. The skills of landscape designers like Capability Brown and Humphry Repton are unique and England is the home of the Picturesque landscape. They banished for ever the formality of French gardening, killing off the knot garden and pushing the parterre out of sight. The *jardin anglais* spread all over the civilized world and is perhaps seen at its very best in Russia where it was adopted by Catherine the Great and her architect Charles Cameron.

CHINESE PAGODA AT KEW ▲ *169*
Designed by Sir William Chambers in 1762, it is 163 feet high and was, on completion, very elaborately decorated. It is one of a series of ornamental buildings that Chambers scattered around the royal park at Kew.

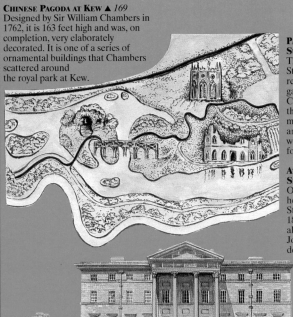

PAINSHILL PARK SURREY ▲ *314*
The predecessor of Stourhead, this recently restored garden was laid out by Charles Hamilton in the 1740s. It has a magnificent grotto and a Turkish Tent as well as lakes and follies.

ATTINGHAM PARK, SHROPSHIRE ▲ *375*
One of the grandest houses by George Steuart of the early 18th century and altered later on by John Nash. Repton designed the Park.

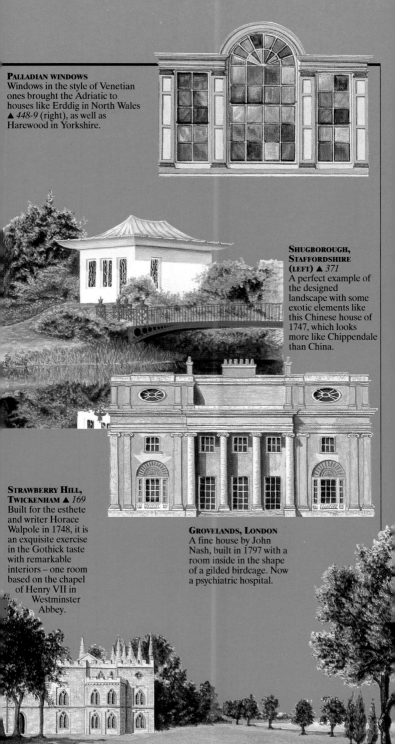

PALLADIAN WINDOWS
Windows in the style of Venetian ones brought the Adriatic to houses like Erddig in North Wales ▲ *448-9* (right), as well as Harewood in Yorkshire.

SHUGBOROUGH, STAFFORDSHIRE (LEFT) ▲ *371*
A perfect example of the designed landscape with some exotic elements like this Chinese house of 1747, which looks more like Chippendale than China.

STRAWBERRY HILL, TWICKENHAM ▲ *169*
Built for the esthete and writer Horace Walpole in 1748, it is an exquisite exercise in the Gothick taste with remarkable interiors – one room based on the chapel of Henry VII in Westminster Abbey.

GROVELANDS, LONDON
A fine house by John Nash, built in 1797 with a room inside in the shape of a gilded birdcage. Now a psychiatric hospital.

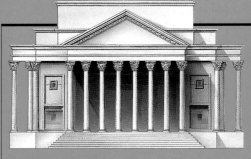

ST GEORGE'S HALL, LIVERPOOL ▲ 423
Unusually pure for the time, the new civic hall with a concert hall and law courts was completed in 1856. The classical design by Harvey Lonsdale Elmes won the competition in 1839 – he was only 25. C.R. Cockerell took over after Elmes's early death in 1847.

The Victorian era is architecturally eclectic to a degree. All styles flourished to the point when there was a "Battle of the Styles" which came to a head over the design of the Foreign Office when Gothic and Classical designs fought it out. In the end Classicism won the day. Earlier in the reign of Queen Victoria (1837-1901) the Houses of Parliament were erected in a rich Gothic style but on a classical plan, and the collaboration of Charles Barry and Augustus Welby Pugin seemed to predict the richness of the architecture of the reign. The Gothic Revival was probably the most distinctive feature of the period and it was a very serious undertaking by a whole range of architects. Historicism seems to march alongside technological improvements and radical uses of newer materials like cast iron and glass. The Victorian clients were rich, the Empire flourished and so architects were encouraged to create wonderful fantasy worlds in the most unlikely places. The reaction to Georgian reticence was extreme but the seeds had been planted in the Regency.

ST BARTHOLOMEW'S, BRIGHTON (LEFT) ▲ 189
Taller than Westminster Abbey, this church is so Victorian in its aspiring piety. Built in 1872–4, it has a silver altar and is overpowering in its hugeness.

ST PANCRAS, LONDON (RIGHT) ▲ 135
George Gilbert Scott's masterpiece – engineering extravagance meets the Gothic hotel.

ALBERT DOCK, LIVERPOOL
▲ *422* Jesse Hartley's massive granite buildings for the Liverpool docks are still remarkable – now shops and museums occupy them.

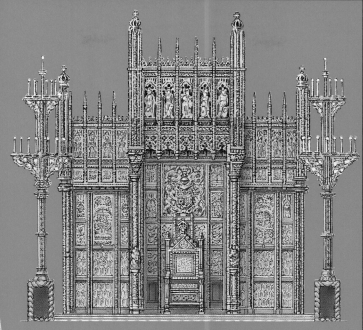

HOUSES OF PARLIAMENT ▲ *128*
Pugin's design for a throne in the House of Lords (above) made the British sovereign appear like a medieval monarch. The interiors were all designed by Augustus Welby Pugin while Charles Barry did the outsides from winning the competition in 1832. The whole interior is a riot of manic medieval decoration.

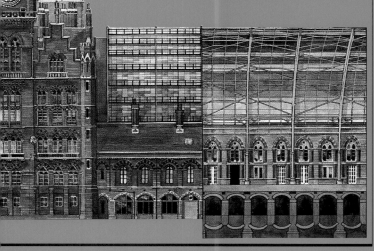

ROYAL COURTS OF JUSTICE ▲ 141
Architect George Edmund Street was worn out by this huge project and died in 1881, before the completion of his masterly Gothic design (1874-82). Its style is pure 13th-century and it was the only major government-funded building erected in the Gothic style.

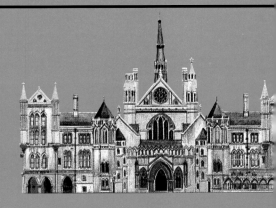

THE RED HOUSE ▲ 177
Built for William Morris by Philip Webb in 1859, it is now regarded as a pioneer of Victorian domestic comfort and style. It is medieval and romantic, in Bexleyheath, Kent.

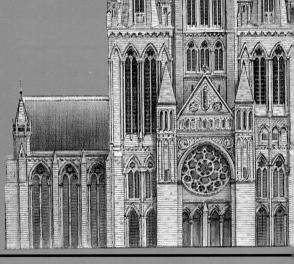

TRURO CATHEDRAL ▲ 243
John Loughborough Pearson's masterpiece was built in 1880 and finished by his son in the Normandy Gothic style.

ALBERT MEMORIAL ▲ *160* **(RIGHT)**
Completed in 1876 and restored in 1999, the
gilded statue of the Prince Consort sits under
the high Gothic canopy designed by George
Gilbert Scott; the prince is holding the
catalogue of the Great Exhibition of 1851.

KENNINGTON HOUSES
Prince Albert designed these model
homes for the Great Exhibition and
they survive in Kennington, London,
to show how he was in the forefront
of workers' care.

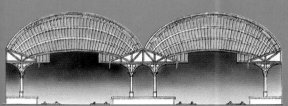

YORK STATION
Celebrated for its
curved shed, which
is 800 feet long and
was a pioneer of
railway architecture
of the 1840s.

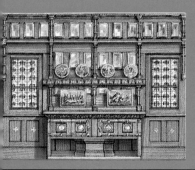

CARDIFF CASTLE
▲ *470*
William Burges's
dream home for the
Marquess of Bute
has some of the
finest Victorian
fantasy interiors
in the country.

The era that followed the long reign of Queen Victoria was a kind of Imperial sunset before World War I. It was a time when large prosperous houses were built and public buildings were grand and pompous. The "Battle of the Styles" was declared a truce and Gothic was the style for churches while secular buildings were in the Classical manner. It was a period when the apprenticeship system ensured that the standard of craftsmanship remained high and Edwardian buildings are almost the last traditional constructions before the age of movement, war and machines. One architect dominates the period – Sir Edwin Lutyens (1869-1944). He was as good as Wren, with greater opportunities, including the design of New Delhi, the Imperial capital of British India.

ROYAL GEOGRAPHICAL SOCIETY ▲ *161*
The London home of the society of geographers and explorers was built by Norman Shaw as a house for the Hon. William Lowther. Although it dates from 1874, it embodies the characteristics of many Edwardian houses.

CASTLE DROGO ▲ *239*
The last castle built in Devon by Lutyens for a family who had made a fortune from "Home and Colonial" grocery shops. Building was tragically interrupted by World War I. The granite pile is a poignant place on the edge of Dartmoor.

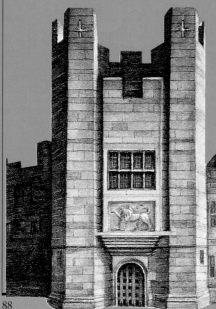

TIGBOURNE COURT
On the road to Brighton stands this beautifully built house by Lutyens, with his trademark giant chimneys.

VICTORIA MEMORIAL, LONDON
The great queen sits forever on Sir Aston Webb's pompous pile in front of Buckingham Palace, under the shadow of an enormous winged Victory.

BROADLEYS, CARTMEL FELL, LAKE WINDERMERE
▲ *439* C. F. Voysey was the Edwardian domestic architect who built magical houses of great simplicity; this one in the Lake District typifies the whole idea of "home".

LADY LEVER ART GALLERY ▲ *426*
The gallery is at the heart of Port Sunlight near Liverpool – a well-designed company town for the makers of soap. It is a classical centerpiece to the vernacular garden suburb.

THE LADY LEVER ART GALLERY

● MODERN ARCHITECTURE

MILLENNIUM BRIDGE ▲ *151*
A new bridge over the River
Thames by Sir Norman Foster
and sculptor Anthony Caro.

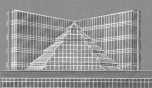

England had to rebuild itself after the devastation of World War II and the development of modern architecture both benefitted and suffered from the scale of rebuilding. Before the war things looked promising, with garden cities, new underground railways for London and an occasional flourish of Art Deco. The war changed everything and rehousing became a priority; the dire influence of theorists like Le Corbusier damaged many lives in tower blocks and concrete town centers.

HOOVER BUILDING, PERIVALE ▲ *168* **(ABOVE)**
Built in 1933 as a factory, it was designed by
Wallis Gilbert and Partners on the Great West
Road north of London as a potent Art Deco
advertisement for the streamlined product. It
now houses offices and a supermarket.

LLOYD'S OF LONDON ▲ *144* **(BELOW)**
The dynamic home of the insurance market in
Leadenhall Street, EC3, was designed in the
early 1980s by Richard Rogers and houses the
underwriting rooms and the old Lutine Bell in
a spectacular modern atrium building with
glass lifts.

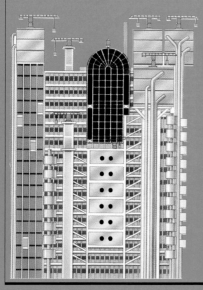

HISTORY FACULTY, CAMBRIDGE
James Stirling designed this striking
library in 1964 and it remains a
controversial greenhouse building to
this day.

ARNOS GROVE UNDERGROUND STATION
Charles Holden designed the extension
of the Piccadilly Line into the northern
suburbs in the 1930s. His brick and
concrete stations have lasted well and
are now listed historic buildings.

**LIVERPOOL ROMAN CATHOLIC
CATHEDRAL OF CHRIST THE KING** ▲ *422*
Built on top of the crypt of Lutyens'
cathedral,
"paddy's
wigwam" was
designed by
Sir Frederick
Gibberd in the
early 1960s.

PAINTING IN ENGLAND AND WALES

Giles Waterfield

FROM THE MIDDLE AGES TO THE EARLY 1600S

The flourishing art of medieval England survives primarily in churches. In the 16th century numerous continental artists, notably Hans Holbein, settled in England, while miniature painting developed through such native masters as Nicholas Hilliard.

HANS HOLBEIN, "THE AMBASSADORS" (1533)
Hans Holbein brought international sophistication to England during his London stays in the 1520s and 1530s. His portrait of the French ambassador and a bishop is executed with meticulous realism and filled with symbolic detail, such as the lute with broken string and the anamorphic skull (shown in distorted perspective) in the foreground. Such works raised courtly portraiture to a new level of sophistication.

NICHOLAS HILLIARD, "UNKNOWN YOUTH" (1500s)

Trained as a jeweler, Hilliard became famous as a miniaturist and received the patronage of Queen Elizabeth I. Influenced by Holbein, he and his younger contemporary Isaac Oliver developed the art of the miniature, a private form of art generally intended to be enjoyed only by those close to the sitter, into a powerful independent medium. In this study of a contemplative *Unknown Youth*, he combines the clear outlines of the engraver with the fresh strong colors of the jeweler in a stylized and poetic image.

SLEEPING JESSE (1400s)

Many of the great works of medieval British art have been lost, but notable pieces survive such as this fragment of a 15th-century carving of the sleeping Jesse, once highly colored and part of a larger sculpture. It comes from St Mary's Priory, Abergavenny.

THOMAS GAINSBOROUGH, COUNTESS HOWE (c. 1763-4) Gainsborough was one of the most gifted of British artists, forced by financial need to paint portraits although it was landscapes he most enjoyed. Around 1753 he painted this dazzling portrait of Lady Mary, wife of a naval hero. The artist performs the difficult feat of suggesting that his sitter is moving through the landscape. The shimmering silks and lace of her costume, while extremely lavish, suggest clothing suitable for a country walk. She eyes the viewer confidently, at ease in the appealing English countryside which Gainsborough studies with such affection.

THOMAS LAWRENCE, "POPE PIUS VII" (c.1816) At the end of the Napoleonic Wars in 1815, the allied victors met to discuss the future of Europe. King George IV commissioned the celebrated portrait painter Lawrence to paint all the sovereigns for the new Waterloo Chamber at Windsor Castle, named after the Battle of Waterloo. Pius VII had been forced by Napoleon to live as a near-prisoner in Paris. This sensitive and clever man is shown in a strangely tense pose, coiled on the throne whose arms he grips. Beneath the glittering surface of his paint, Lawrence applied great psychological penetration: here he depicts the conflicts of a man who has suffered international humiliation.

WILLIAM HOGARTH, "CAPTAIN CORAM" (1740)
Portraiture by British rather than foreign artists became a crucial aspect of British art in the 18th century, and found an increasing market in a generally prosperous society. Captain Coram was not a fashionable sitter: he was a naval captain, famous for his acts of charity. Moved by the plight of children abandoned by their mothers, he founded the Foundling Hospital in London, where they would be looked after. Hogarth, a supporter of the charity and champion of British art, paints Coram in the manner of a grand portrait, giving him a strong unpolished individuality.

ALLAN RAMSAY, 'THE ARTIST'S WIFE" (1754-5)
The most remarkable Scottish portraitist of the 18th century, Ramsay was influenced by French pastel painting in his creation of beautifully executed and psychologically acute portraits. In this portrait of Margaret Lindsay, his second wife, she is shown as though at home arranging flowers, which suggest the freshness and happiness of their love. She turns toward the artist as though interrupted in her task. This work reflects the growing interest in intimate expressions of affection in the mid-18th century, compared to the formality of earlier painting.

JOHN CONSTABLE, "GOLDING CONSTABLE'S FLOWER GARDEN" (1816) (ABOVE)
THOMAS GAINSBOROUGH, "HARVEST WAGON" (1767) (RIGHT)
Landscape painting has long been one of the major preoccupations of British artists, important to the definition of a national identity. Constable paints the garden from an upstairs window in his parents' house at East Bergholt, Suffolk. Apparently a small and unambitious painting, this is a highly innovative landscape, with hedges and shrubs arranged in a bold diagonal across the center of the canvas, and foreground shadows creating distance. Gainsborough, too, was passionately fond of painting landscapes. These were inspired by Dutch 17th-century painting but developed in works like *The Harvest Wagon* a soft melting style in which vegetation and figures are suffused with light.

CANALETTO, "OLD WALTON BRIDGE" (1754) (LEFT)
JOHN SELL COTMAN, "BRIGNALL BANKS ON THE GRETA" (1805)
(ABOVE) During his extended stays in England, the Venetian artist
Canaletto reacted enthusiastically to the soft changing light, painting
with a freshness which in Venice he sometimes forgot. Here he paints
an elaborate view of the bridge at Walton-on-Thames for his patron
Thomas Hollis. Hollis, with a friend and his dog, stand in the
foreground. By contrast, fifty years later, the watercolor painter
Cotman chooses a picturesque East Anglian landscape to create a
highly individual view of the countryside. He seems emotionally
engaged in his subject, expressing the character of this deep gorge and
its surrounding trees with a sympathy for nature quite unlike the
cheerful topographical approach of the Italian artist.

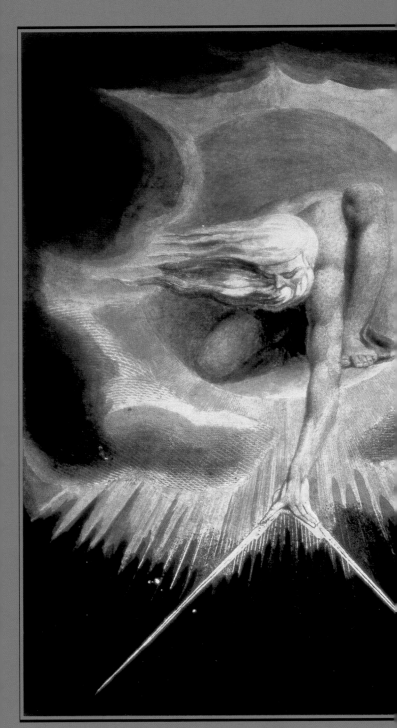

WILLIAM BLAKE, "ANCIENT OF DAYS" (1824) (LEFT)
One of the most inspired of mystical artists and writers, Blake created several illustrated poetic books. The watercolor/print of *The Ancient of Days* was intended as the frontispiece to *Europe*, in which he prophesied the defeat of inhuman and cruel reason by what he regarded as the truer power of imagination. Urizen, creator of the universe and enforcer of reason, is shown imposing the compass on "the face of the depth" as he creates the world. Inspired by Michelangelo, this is a powerful work of imagination and bold design, executed in a combination of etching and watercolor peculiar to Blake.

GEORGE STUBBS, "CHEETAH AND STAG WITH TWO INDIANS" (*c.* 1765)
The greatest of British animal painters, Stubbs painted this work around 1765. The year before, the Governor-General of Madras had given a cheetah to King George III of England, and it is shown here with its two Indian keepers on the point of being released to chase the stag. Stubbs was fascinated by the power of raw nature and by the challenge of depicting the strength and the anatomy of animals. Here he contrasts the graceful energy of the cheetah with the perturbed uncertainty of its likely victim. The picture, set against a brooding sky, creates a sense of uncanny aggression.

HENRY FUSELI, "LADY MACBETH SEIZING THE DAGGERS" (1812?)
A Swiss artist living in London for most of his life, Fuseli painted bold, sexually charged images in which traditional literary stories provided the motif for an exploration of human desire, cruelty and repression.

WILLIAM POWELL FRITH, "RAILWAY STATION" (1860-2)
One of the most successful Victorian painters, Frith was admired for his detailed studies of everyday life. At the Royal Academy, his works had to be protected by a barrier. In this study of Paddington Station he shows a crowd hurrying to catch a train. The figures include two boys saying goodbye to their mother before departing for school, a bride and groom leaving for their honeymoon, and (on the right) two detectives arresting an escaping criminal.

FORD MADOX BROWN, "WORK" (*c*.1863)

The Pre-Raphaelite Brotherhood, founded in 1848, had a powerful influence on 19th-century British painting. One of its members, Ford Madox Brown, executed this realistic and closely detailed study of a London street. The laborers symbolize the dignity of manual labor in contrast to the ragged children and the unemployed who have never been taught to work. On the right stand two intellectuals (Thomas Carlyle on the left), advocates of education for all, epitomizing the importance of labor for the health of society.

WILLIAM HOLMAN HUNT, "ISABELLA AND THE POT OF BASIL" (1866-8)

The story, from a poem by Keats, tells how Isabella, whose lover has been murdered by her brothers, places his head in a pot planted with basil. She is shown adoring this grisly memento in a painting loaded with sinister eroticism. The careful, almost oppressive, detail is typical of Pre-Raphaelitism.

FREDERIC LEIGHTON, "MOTHER AND CHILD" (C.1865) Leighton was an academic late Victorian painter and President of the Royal Academy. His luxurious house survives in London ▲ *161*. He was famous for his richly executed and sensuous studies of classical subjects. In this painting, exhibited in 1865, he shows a modern subject, maternal love, but gives it a strange inward-looking quality and a highly ornate pictorial surface.

**WALTER RICHARD SICKERT,
"THE JUVENILE LEAD" (1908)**
Sickert was one of the most prominent early
20th-century British artists who reacted
against the conservatism of much Victorian
painting and formed societies such as the
Camden Town Group. They were inspired by
modern French art (Sickert worked with
Degas) as well as by everyday urban subjects.
This picture is one of Sickert's numerous self
portraits, reflecting his fascination with the
stage. He paints in deliberately low tones as
was his custom, but the paint is thickly
applied while the construction of the painting
is carefully organized.

FRANCIS BACON, "FIGURE STUDY II" (1945-6)
Still one of the most disturbing of artists, Bacon became prominent in the
1940s. His savage works are inspired by his feeling for traditional art, in
particular Italian Renaissance painting (as here) and the work of
Velázquez. In *The Magdalene*, he shows an ambiguous and disturbing
figure, its mouth open in a scream of grief – a comment on the plight of
humanity.

HENRY MOORE, "KING AND QUEEN" (1952-3)
Moore was one of Britain's most internationally influential 20th-century sculptors and draughtsmen. Abandoning the classical ideal of beauty which had dominated the British tradition, he used his knowledge of ancient Mexican and African work, as well as classical art, to create a semi-abstract, highly energized style, reflecting his feeling for his materials. As he wrote, "The human figure is what interests me most deeply." In this sculpture, intended for a wild open-air site, he develops the theme of the linked king and queen (or family) which he had been exploring for years.

STANLEY SPENCER, "RESURRECTION OF SOLDIERS" (1928-9) (below) Spencer represented a highly personal mystical/sexual tradition. This painting is set near an abandoned village at Kalinora in Macedonia, where Spencer served during the World War I. He was inspired by a sermon by John Donne which discussed the soul journeying from one life to the next. Here, among the debris of war, the dead are resurrected in an atmosphere of tranquility.

GWEN JOHN, "MÈRE POUSSEPIN"
A private and highly serious artist, Gwen John (sister of Augustus) spent much of her life in France. This is one of six studies of the founder of an order of nuns, painted for the sisters. It is notable for its serenity, sense of design and restrained palette.

DAVID HOCKNEY, "MR AND MRS CLARK AND PERCY" (1970-
This is one of the most famous paintings by an artist who in his early wo
epitomized the Swinging Sixties. He shows his friends Ozzie and Celia Clark
their London living room. In this cool sunlit space, painted in a hyper-real
style, they are spare and elegant, yet curiously self-conscious and detache

LUCIAN FREUD, "MAN'S HEAD" (1963) Born in Berlin of a celebrated German family, Freud
moved to England at an early age. He is now recognized as one of the leading British painters
of his generation. Highly aware of the art of the past, he brings to his work a powerful direct
technique, confronting the fragility and sexuality of the human body while responding to men
and women as social beings. His accomplished yet agonized portraits reflect the conflict
between the social and the private human being, and a fascination with the peculiarities of
human nature and the human body.

ENGLAND AND WALES
AS SEEN BY WRITERS
Lucinda Gane

HISTORICAL PERSPECTIVES

EARLY BRITONS

The Greek navigator and geographer Pytheas (fl. 325–285 BC) described Britain as triangular in shape, with a perimeter of 4,670 miles (about twice what it actually is) and pictured the island's peoples as follows:

❝The inhabitants of Britain are said to be sprung from the soil and to serve a primitive style of life. They make use of chariots in wars, such as the ancient Greek heroes are reputed to have employed in the Trojan War; and their habitations are rough-and-ready, being for the most part constructed of wattles or logs. They harvest their grain crops by cutting off the ears without the haulms and stowing them in covered granges; from these they pull out the oldest and prepare them for food. They are simple in their habits, and far removed from the cunning and knavishness of modern man. Their diet is inexpensive and quite different from the luxury that is born of wealth. The island is thickly populated, and has an extremely chilly climate, as one would expect in a sub-Arctic region. It has many kings and potentates, who live for the most part in a state of mutual peace.❞

PYTHEAS, QUOTED IN M. CARY AND E.H. WARMINGTON,
THE ANCIENT EXPLORERS, 1929

Hecateus of Abdera found evidence of strange religions in Britain, c. 350 BC:

❝This [island] is in the far North, and is inhabited by people called the Hyperboreans from their location beyond the Boreas, the North Wind... There are men who serve as priests of Apollo because this god is worshipped every day with continuous singing and is held in exceptional honour. There is also in the island a precinct sacred to Apollo and suitably imposing, and a notable spherical temple decorated with many offerings. There is also a community sacred to this god, where most of the inhabitants are trained to play the lyre and do so continuously in the temple, worshipping the god with singing.❞

THE ROMANS

In the Eclogues (42-37 BC), Virgil describes Britons as being "wholly sundered from the world" and Pope Gregory I famously commented on English captives for sale in Rome that they were "Not Angles but Angels". According to Bede, this defenceless nation invited the Romans to come and prevent invasions by other tribes.

❝From the time [the Romans ceased to rule], the south part of Britain, destitute of armed soldiers, or martial stores, and of all its active youth, which had been led away by the harshness of the tyrants, never to return, was wholly exposed to rapine, as being totally ignorant of the use of weapons. Whereupon they suffered many years under two very savage foreign nations, the Scots from the west, and the Picts the north. We call these foreign nations, not on account of their being seated out of Britain, but because they were remote from that part of it which was possessed by the Britons. . .On account of the irruption of these nations, the Britons sent messengers to Rome with letters in mournful manner, praying for succour, and promising perpetual subjection, provided that the impending enemy should be driven away. An armed legion was immediately sent, which, arriving in the island, and engaging the enemy, slew a great multitude of them, drove the rest out of the territories of their allies, and having delivered them from their cruel oppressors, advised them to build a wall between the two seas across the island, that it might secure them, and keep off the enemy; and thus they returned home with great triumph. The islanders raising the wall, as they had been directed, not of stone, as having no artist capable of such a work, but of sods, made it of no use. . . .Then the Romans declared to the Britons, that they could not for the future undertake such troublesome expeditions for their sake, advising them rather to handle their weapons like men, and undertake themselves the charge of engaging their enemies, who would not prove too powerful for them, unless they were deterred by cowardice; and, thinking that it might be some help to the allies, whom they were forced to abandon, they built a strong stone wall from sea to sea, in a straight line between the towns that had been there built for fear of the enemy, and not far from the trench of Severus. This famous wall, which is still to be seen, was built at the public and private expense, the Britons also lending their assistance. It is eight feet in breadth, and twelve in height, in a straight line from west to east, and is still visible to beholders.**"**

THE VENERABLE BEDE, *THE ECCLESIASTICAL HISTORY OF THE ENGLISH NATION*, 731

SNOWDONIA

In 1188, Giraldus Cambrensis (Gerald of Wales, c.1145–1223) accompanied the Archbishop of Canterbury on a preaching tour to Wales, trying to raise support for the Third Crusade.

"I must not fail to tell you about the mountains which are called Eryri by the Welsh and by the English Snowdon, that is the Snow Mountains . . . At the very top of these mountains two lakes are to be found, each of them remarkable in its own way. One has a floating island, which moves about and is often driven to the opposite side by the force of the winds. Shepherds are amazed to see the flocks which are feeding there carried off to distant parts of the lake . . . The second lake has a remarkable and almost unique property. It abounds in three different kinds of fish, eels, trout and perch, and all of them have only one eye, the right one being there but not the left. If the careful reader asks me the cause of such a remarkable phenomenon, I can only answer that I do not know. It is worth noticing that in Scotland, too, in two different places, one to the east and one to the west, the fish called mullet are found in the sea with only one eye. They lack the left eye but have the right one.**"**

GIRALDUS CAMBRENSIS, *THE JOURNEY THROUGH WALES*, TRANS. L. THORPE, 1978

A JEWELLED ISLE . . .

William Shakespeare (1564–1616) described a proud, regal nation, one that would never be conquered by foreign powers but could be rotted internally by laws and corrupt government.

"This royal throne of kings, this scept'red isle,
This earth of majesty, this seat of Mars,
This other Eden, demi-paradise,
This fortress built by Nature for herself
Against infection and the hand of war,
This happy breed of men, this little world,
This precious stone set in the silver sea
Which serves it in the office of a wall,
Or as a moat defensive to a house,
Against the envy of less happier lands,
This blessed plot, this earth, this realm, this England,
This nurse, this teeming womb of royal kings, . . .
This land of such dear souls, this dear dear Land.**"**

SHAKESPEARE,
RICHARD THE SECOND,
c. 1595–6

HISTORY LESSONS

In her vivid account of the Mitford family, Jessica Mitford (b. 1917) describes the way in which they learned history.

"Muv taught English history from a large illustrated book called *Our Island Story*, with a beautiful picture of Queen Victoria as its frontispiece. 'See, England and all our Empire possessions are a lovely pink on the map,' she explained. 'Germany is a hideous, mud-coloured brown.' The illustrations, the text, and Muv's interpretative comments created a series of vivid scenes: Queen Boadicea, fearlessly riding at the head of her army . . . the poor little Princes in the Tower . . . Charlemagne, claimed by Grandfather as our ancestor . . .hateful, drab Cromwell . . . Charles I, Martyred King . . . the heroic Empire-builders, bravely quelling the black hordes of Africa for the glory of England . . . the wicked Indians of the Black Hole of Calcutta . . . the Americans, who had been expelled from the Empire for causing trouble, and who no longer had the right to be a pretty pink on the map . . .the Filthy Huns, who shot Uncle Clem in the war . . . the Russian Bolshies, who shot down the Czar's dogs in cold blood (and, as a matter of fact, the little Czarevitch and Czarevnas, only their fate didn't seem quite so sad as that of the poor, innocent dogs) . . . the good so good, and the bad so bad, history as taught by Muv was on the whole very clear to me."
JESSICA MITFORD, *HONS AND REBELS*, 1960

CITY VIEWS

DEFOE'S YORK

Daniel Defoe (1660-1731) produced a guide book to the British Isles in three volumes, based on his own observations of the state of the country.

"The antiquity of York, though it was not the particular enquiry I proposed to make, yet showed itself so visibly at a distance, that we could not but observe it before we came quite up to the city, I mean the mount and high hills, where the ancient castle stood, which, when you come to the city, you scarcely see, at least not so as to judge of its antiquity. . . . It boasts of being the seat of some of the Roman emperors, and the station of their forces for the north of Britain, being itself a Roman colony . . .But now things infinitely modern, compared to those, are become marks of antiquity; for even the castle of York, built by William the Conqueror, anno 1069, is not only become ancient and decayed, but even sunk into time, and almost lost and forgotten; fires, sieges, plunderings and devastations, have often been the fate of York; so that one should wonder there could be any thing of a city left. But 'tis risen again, and we see now is modern; the bridge is vastly strong, and has one arch which, they tell me, was near 70 foot in diameter; it is, without exception, the greatest in England, some say it is as large as the Rialto at Venice, though I think not."
DANIEL DEFOE, *A TOUR THROUGH THE WHOLE ISLAND OF GREAT BRITAIN*, 1724–6

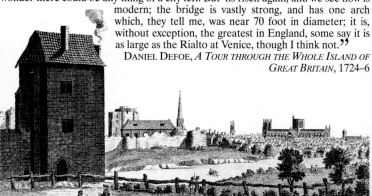

BOSWELL'S LONDON

Dr Johnson's volatile biographer James Boswell (1740–95) enjoyed all the facilities that 18th-century London had to offer.

"When we came upon Highgate Hill and had a view of London, I was all life and joy. I repeated Cato's soliliquy on the immortality of the soul, and my soul bounded forth to a certain prospect of happy futurity. I sung all manner of songs, and began to make one about an amorous meeting with a pretty girl, the burthen of which was as follow:

She gave me *this*, I gave her *that*;
And tell me, had she not tit for tat?

I gave three huzzas and we went briskly in.

I got from Digges' a list of the best houses on the road, and also a direction to a good inn at London. I therefore made the boy drive me to Mr. Hayward's, at the Black Lion, Water Lane, Fleet Street. The noise, the crowd, the glare of shops and signs agreeably confused me. I was rather more wildly struck than when I first came to London. My companion could not understand my feelings. He considered London just as a place where he was to receive orders from the East India Company.**"**

LONDON JOURNAL, NOVEMBER 19, 1762

"After dinner I sauntered in a pleasing humour to London Bridge, viewed the Thames's silver expanse and the springy bosom of the surrounding fields. I then went up to the top of the Monument. This is a most amazing building. It is a pillar two hundred feet high. In the inside, a turnpike stair runs up all the way. When I was about half way up, I grew frightened. I would have come down again, but thought I would despise myself for my timidity. Thus does the spirit of pride get the better of fear. I mounted to the top and got upon the balcony. It was horrid to find myself so monstrous a way up in the air, so far above London and all its spires. I durst not look round me. There is no real danger as there is a strong rail both on the stair and balcony. But I shuddered, and as every heavy waggon passed down Gracechurch Street, dreaded that the shaking of the earth would make the tremendous pile tumble to the foundation.**"**

LONDON JOURNAL, APRIL 2, 1763

SMOLLETT'S BATH

"The Expedition of Humphry Clinker", by Tobias Smollett (1721–71), is written as a series of letters sent during a round trip from Wales to London to Scotland and back again. Here the curmudgeonly character Matthew Bramble describes Bath.

"The same artist who planned the Circus, has likewise projected a Crescent; when that is finished, we shall probably have a Star; and those who are living thirty years hence, may, perhaps, see all the signs of the Zodiac exhibited in architecture at Bath . . . but the rage of building has laid hold on such a number of adventurers, that one sees new houses starting up in every out-let and every corner of Bath; contrived without judgement, executed without solidity, and stuck together with so little regard to plan and propriety, that the different lines of the new rows and buildings interfere with, and intersect one another in every different angle of conjunction. They look like th wreck of streets and squares disjointed by an earthquake, which hath broken th ground into a variety of holes and hillocks; or, as if some Gothic devil had stuffe them altogether in a bag, and left them to stand higgledy piggledy, just as chanc directed. What sort of a monster Bath will become in a few years, with those growin excrescences, may be easily conceived: but the want of beauty and proportion is no the worst effect of these new mansions; they are built so slight, with the so crumbling stone found in this neighbourhood, that I shall never sleep quietly in on of them, when it blowed (as the sailors say) a cap-full of wind. **"**

TOBIAS SMOLLETT, *THE EXPEDITION OF HUMPHRY CLINKER*, 177

THE GROWTH OF LONDON

Thomas Macaulay (1800–59) wrote a 4-volume History England that was widely read in its day and admired for i meticulous research.

"Whoever examines the maps of London which wer published towards the close of the reign of Charles th Second will see that only the nucleus of the presen capital then existed. The town did not, as now, fade b imperceptible degrees into the country. No long avenue of villas, embowered in lilacs and laburnums, extende from the great centre of wealth and civilisation almost t the boundaries of Middlesex and far into the heart of Kent and Surrey. In the eas no part of the immense line of warehouses and artificial lakes which now stretche from the Tower to Blackwall had even been projected. On the west, scarcely one those stately piles of building which are inhabited by the noble and wealthy was i existence; and Chelsea, which is now peopled by more than forty thousand huma beings, was a quiet country village with about a thousand inhabitants. On the north cattle fed, and sportsmen wandered with dogs and guns, over the site of the boroug of Marylebone, and far the greater part of the space now covered by the boroughs Finsbury and of the Tower Hamlets. Islington was almost a solitude; and poets love to contrast its silence and repose with the din and turmoil of monster London. O the south the capital is now connected with its suburb by several bridges, not inferio in magnificence and solidity to the noblest works of the Caesars. In 1685, a singl line of irregular arches, overhung by piles of mean and crazy houses, and garnished, after a fashion worthy of the naked barbarians of Dahomey, with scores of mouldering heads, impeded the navigation of the river. **"**

T.B. MACAULAY, *HISTORY OF ENGLAND*, 1849–61

JAMES'S CHESTER

Henry James (1843–1916) surveys the town of Chester from an American point of view.

"It is full of that delightful element of the crooked, the accidental, the unforeseen, which, to American eyes, accustomed to our eternal straight lines and right angles, is the striking feature of European street scenery. An American strolling in the Chester streets finds a perfect feast of crookedness – of those random corners, projections and recesses, odd domestic interspaces charmingly saved or lost, those innumerable architectural surprises and caprices and fantasies which lead to such refreshing exercise a vision benumbed by brownstone fronts. . . . Next after its wall – possibly even before it – Chester values its Rows, an architectural idiosyncrasy which ust be seen to be appreciated. They are a sort of Gothic edition of the blessed rcades and porticoes of Italy, and consist, roughly speaking, of a running public assage tunnelled through the second storey of the houses. The low basement is thus irectly on the drive-way, to which a flight of steps descends, at frequent intervals, rom this superincumbent verandah. . . .If the picturesque be measured by its hostility to our modern notions of convenience, Chester is probably the most romantic city in the world. This arrangement is endlessly rich in opportunities for amusing effect, but the

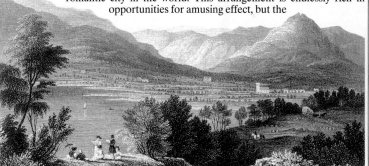

ull charm of the architecture of which it is so essential a part must be observed from he street below. Chester is still an antique town, and medieval England sits bravely nder her gables. Every third house is a 'specimen' – gabled and latticed, timbered nd carved, and wearing its years more or less lightly.**"**

HENRY JAMES, *ENGLISH HOURS*, 1981

LANDSCAPES

THE LAKES

The prodigious output of William Wordsworth (1770–1850) comprised many essays and number of prose works as well as the poetry for which he is best known.

"I do not indeed know any tract of country in which, within so arrow a compass, may be found an equal variety in the nfluences of light and shadow upon the sublime or beautiful eatures of landscape; and it is owing to the combined ircumstances to which the reader's attention has been irected. From a point between Great Gavel and Scawfell, a hepherd would not require more than an hour to descend into ny one of eight of the principal vales by which he would be urrounded; and all the others lie (with the exception of Iawswater) at but a small distance. Yet, though clustered ogether, every valley has its distinct and separate character: in some instances, as if hey had been formed in studied contrast to each other, and in others with the nited pleasing differences and resemblances of a sisterly rivalship. This oncentration of interest gives to the country a decided superiority over the most ttractive districts of Scotland and Wales, especially for the pedestrian traveller. In cotland and Wales are found, undoubtedly, individual scenes, which, in their everal kinds, cannot be excelled. But, in Scotland, particularly, what long tracts of esolate country intervene! so that the traveller, when he reaches a spot deservedly f great celebrity, would find it difficult to determine how much of his pleasure is wing to excellence inherent in the landscape itself; and how much to an nstantaneous recovery from an oppression left upon his spirits by the barrenness nd desolation through which he has passed.**"**

THE PROSE WORKS OF WILLIAM WORDSWORTH, VOL. II,
ED. W.J.B. OWEN AND JANE WORTHINGTON SMYSER, 1974

KESWICK

Beatrix Potter (1866–1943) bought a farm at Sawrey in the Lake District in 1905. The following journal entries date from 1885.

"Sunday, August 16th. Being Sunday, five Keswick men and one from Penrith went to the Lodore Hotel to drink, and coming back at 8 o'clock, dusk, began fighting, upset the boat, and they were drowned. The Hotel has a very bad name. Keswick roughs have a regular habit of getting drunk there every Sunday, and Saturday too. . . .

There have been many drownings on this lake, but invariably caused by drink. The landlord of the Derwentwater Hotel at Portinscale went out with another man, both drunk, and both drowned. Twenty-two years later to the very day, his son and one of the others went out in a similar condition, and the son fell out of the boat near Fawe Park where the butler heard a scuffle, but thought little of it at the time. The other returned, sat down in a chair remarking casually, 'oh me, someone was drowned'. He was too bad to say more, but people at the Inn hurried out and found the body standing where the butler heard the noise, with hardly an inch of water over the head. Bodies are always upright, on their head or feet. . . .

The lake is very rough sometimes, great white waves, but one never hears of misfortunes then. Sensible people keep off it. When this happened it was a most lovely evening, warm and sultry, not a breeze of wind. The sunset was still fiery in the west and south, the moon was rising, the reflections of the great blue mountains lay broad and motionless in the water, undisturbed save now and then by the ripple of a passing boat. East, south and north, the blue mountains with their crimson crests towered up against a clear blue heaven, flecked with little white fleecy clouds. Westwards the thunder clouds came rolling across the fire; yet under such a sky, and amidst such peace and calm, one hears shouting and drunken voices singing 'hold the fort' in a variety of discords."

THE JOURNAL OF BEATRIX POTTER FROM 1881–1897

ALDEBURGH

A small town on the coast of Suffolk, pounded by the North Sea, Aldeburgh has an annual music festival. E.M. Forster (1879–1970) gave this talk in 1948.

"The situation of [Aldeburgh] is curious. A slight rise of the ground – I'll call it a hill, though the word is too emphatic – projects from the fenlands of Suffolk towards the North Sea. On this hill stands the church, a spacious Gothic building with very broad aisles, so that it has inside rather the effect of a hall. At the foot of the hill lies the town – a couple of long streets against which the sea is making an implacable advance. There used to be as many as five streets – three of them have disappeared beneath the shallow but violent waters . . . the Elizabethan moot hall, which used to be in the centre of the place, now stands on a desolate beach. During the past twelve months the attack has been frightening. I can remember a little shelter erected for visitors on the shingle. Last autumn it was at the edge of a cliff, so that fishermen at the high tide actually sat in it to fish. This spring it has vanished, and the waters actually broke into the High Street – huge glassy waves coming in regularly and quietly, and each exploding when it hit the shore with the sound of a gun. This sort of attack went on a hundred and fifty years ago, . . . but the zone of operation lay further out. To-day only the hill is safe. Only at the church . . . is there security and peace."

E.M. FORSTER, TWO CHEERS FOR
DEMOCRACY, 1951

GAD'S HILL

Charles Dickens (1812–70) bought Gad's Hill Place ▲ 178, 2 miles from Rochester, in 1856. After spending a considerable sum on improvements, he moved there permanently in 1860. This letter to a French friend was written in July 1858.

"At this present moment I am on my little Kentish freehold looking on as pretty a view out of my study window as you will find in a long day's English ride. My little place is a grave red brick house (time of George the First, I suppose) which I have added to and stuck bits upon in all manner of ways, so that it is pleasantly irregular, and as violently opposed to all architectural ideas, as the most hopeful man could possibly desire. It is on the summit of Gad's Hill. The robbery was committed before the door, on the man with the treasure, and Falstaff ran away from the identical spot of ground now covered by the room in which I write. A little rustic alehouse, called the Sir John Falstaff, is over the way – has been over the way ever since, in honour of the event. Cobham Woods and park are behind the house; the distant Thames in front; the Medway, with Rochester, and its old castle and cathedral on one side. The whole stupendous property is on the old Dover Road, so when you come, come by the North Kent Railway (not the South Eastern) to Strood or Higham, and I'll drive over to fetch you."

THE LETTERS OF CHARLES DICKENS,
ED. MADELEINE HOUSE AND GRAHAM STOREY, 1995

DERBYSHIRE

Son of a miner, D.H. Lawrence (1885–1930) grew up in Nottinghamshire. "Sons and Lovers" is often claimed to be the first English novel with a truly working-class background.

"She went over the sheep-bridge and across a corner of the meadow to the cricket-ground. The meadows seemed one space of ripe, evening light, whispering with the distant mill-race. She sat on a seat under the alders in the cricket-ground, and fronted the evening. Before her, level and solid, spread the big green cricket-field, like the bed of a sea of light. Children played in the bluish shadow of the pavilion. Many rooks, high up, came cawing home across the softly-woven sky. They stooped in a long curve down into the golden glow, concentrating, cawing, wheeling, like black flakes on a slow vortex, over a tree-clump that made a dark boss among the pasture.

A few gentlemen were practising, and Mrs. Morel could hear the chock of the ball, and the voices of men suddenly roused; could see the white forms of men shifting silently over the green, upon which already the under shadows were smouldering. Away at the grange, one side of the hay-stacks was lit up, the other sides blue-grey. A waggon of sheaves rocked small across the melting yellow light.

The sun was going down. Every open evening, the hills of Derbyshire were blazed over with red sunset. Mrs. Morel watched the sun sink from the glistening sky, leaving a soft flower-blue overhead, while the western space went red, as if all the fire had swum down there, leaving the bell cast flawless blue. The mountain-ash berries across the field stood fierily out from the dark leaves, for a moment. A few shocks of corn in the corner of the fallow stood up as if alive; she imagined them bowing; perhaps her son would be a Joseph. In the east, a mirrored sunset floated pink opposite the west's scarlet. The big haystacks on the hillside, that butted into the glare, went cold."

D.H. LAWRENCE, *SONS AND LOVERS*, 1913

113

In the Harbour, St. Ives, Cornwall.

St Ives

"I remember looking at St Ives – from the height of the bus stop at Malakoff and further up from Tregenna Steps – it was the perfect picture-postcard. A piece of land flung out like a small bent finger into the Atlantic; the C of the harbour; the waves coming in like horizons in reverse; a few fishing boats; gulls; the lighthouse in the bay; the island criss-crossed like a hot cross bun; and the pretty little sand beaches. But in the back streets, in condemned cottages with the water tap outside and soapy water stagnant in the gutter, they were living on national assistance. Damp funeral cards. 'Bed and Breakfast' signs. The retired middle class on the terraces who came here with their savings and bought their graves. And the careless people who come to places like St Ives anxious for the new holiday encounter because they need for their existence – to feed their pretence of being 'a painter', 'a writer', – a lot of strangers passing through. Then shot through the poverty, the squalor, the boredom (like those fantastic balloon shapes that the wind makes blowing through the spokes of a wheel which has passed through fish slime) were the lyrical absurdities of the summer. When the stenographers and the typists and the art students came down. . . . swimming at night in the nude in the harbour . . . the all-night parties in cottages on the moors; the homosexuals down from London; the rats squeezing a night down the drains; the tiny rooms with the walls damp, the light from the gas bracket . . .
But from a height how could one see this or guess it?"

NORMAN LEVINE, *Canada Made Me*, 1958

Dartmoor

Karel Capek (1890–1938) found Dartmoor uncannily beautiful.

"The journey is along prettily winding roads across curved hills through that shaggiest of green regions, which contains the densest of quickset hedges, the biggest of sheep, the greatest quantities of ivy, coppices and hawthorn, as well as the bushiest trees and cottages covered with the thickest thatches that I have ever seen. An old tree in Devonshire is as compact as a rock and as perfect as a statue. Then come straggling, bare, forlorn hills without a single tree; this is Dartmoor. Here and there projects on the solitude of furze a granite boulder upraised like the altar of giants or primeval lizards; these are tors, I may tell you. Sometimes among the furze there flows a black streamlet, a sunken pool darkens, an overgrown swamp glistens; they say that a rider on horseback will vanish there without a trace, but this I could

not try, because I had no horse. The low ridges become overcast; I do not know whether it is the droop of the straggling clouds, or the fumes from the ceaselessly oozing earth. A misty veil of rain obscures the region of granite and marsh, the clouds ponderously roll together and for a while a baleful twilight reveals the forlorn stretches of furze, juniper and bracken, which just now were an impenetrable wood. **"**

KAREL CAPEK, *LETTERS FROM ENGLAND*, TRANS. P. SELVER, 1925

GOWER

In 1949, Dylan Thomas (1914–53) moved to Laugharne with his wife Caitlin.

"Gower is a very beautiful peninsula, some miles from this blowsy town, and so far the Tea-Shop philistines have not spoilt the more beautiful of its bays. Gower, as a matter of fact, is one of the loveliest sea-coast stretches in the whole of Britain, and some of its tiny villages are as obscure, as little inhabited, and as lovely as they were a hundred years ago*. [In the margin: *This sounds like a passage from a Tourists' Guide.] I often go down in the mornings to the furthest point of the Gower – the village of Rhosilli – and stay there until evening. The bay is the wildest, bleakest, and barrennest I know – four or five miles of yellow coldness going away into the distance of the sea. And the Worm, a seaworm of rock pointing into the channel, is the very promontory of depression. Nothing lives on it but gulls and rats, the millionth generation of the winged and tailed families that screamed in the air and ran through the grass when the first sea thudded on the Rhossilli beach.

There is one table of rock on the

Worm's back that is covered with long yellow grass, and, walking on it, one [feels] like something out of the Tales of Mystery & Imagination treading, for a terrible eternity, on the long hairs of rats. Going over that grass is one of the strangest experiences; it gives under one's feet; it makes little sucking noises, & smells – and this to me is the most grisly smell in the world – like the fur of rabbits after rain. **"**

THE COLLECTED LETTERS OF DYLAN THOMAS,
ED. PAUL FERRIS, 1985

DINING OUT

In her autobiography Edith Sitwell (1887–1964) describes a visit to the home of Sir Edmund and Lady Gosse.

"The house was ruled in part by Parker the parlour-maid, a very famous character, and, still more, by Buchanan, a large black and white cat. Buchanan had apparently entered the house from some unknown place, and had taken over the charge of it. He would not come down to meals until the whole family was assembled in the dining-room, and this being done, he insisted upon Sir Edmund mounting the stairs and ringing the dinner-bell. Buchanan would then walk downstairs, in a dignified way, and eat his dinner with the rest of the family. When tea-time came, Buchanan refused, firmly, and without showing any signs of yielding, to drink his cream unless Lady Gosse, kneeling, held the saucer for him. If, as occasionally happened, he was indignant for some reason or another, he would leave the room, and an awed silence would fall. I remember one occasion when I was dining at the house and Buchanan left the room after dinner in a marked manner, Sir Edmund and Lady Gosse discussing, in a frightened whisper, all possible causes which could have given Buchanan offence. He had his own writing paper and envelopes specially made for him, not too large, and when Sir Edmund went away on a visit, Buchanan would dictate letters to him every day (Lady Gosse told me in a whisper that she was afraid Buchanan was a sad gossip) and Sir Edmund would reply."

EDITH SITWELL, *TAKEN CARE OF*, 1965

TRAMS

Quintessential Yorkshireman Alan Bennett (b. 1934) bemoans the passing of the tram.

"It is not just the passage of time that makes me invest the trams of those days with such pleasure. To be on a tram sailing down Headingley Lane on a fine evening lifted the heart at the time just as it does in memory. . . .Odd details about trams come back to me now, like the slatted platforms, brown with dust, that were slung underneath either end, like some urban cowcatcher; or the little niche in the glass of the window on the seat facing the top of the stairs so that you could slide it open and hang out; and how convivial trams were, the seats reversible so that if you chose you could make up a four whenever you wanted. . . . Buses have never inspired the same affection – too cushioned and comfortable to have a moral dimension. Trams were bare and bony, transport reduced to its basic elements, and they had a song to sing, which buses never did. I was away at university when they started to phase them out, Leeds as always in too much of a hurry to get to the future, and so doing the wrong thing. I knew at the time that it was a mistake . . . . and that life was starting to get nastier. If trams ever come back, though, they should come back not as curiosities, nor, God help us, as part of the heritage, but as a cheap and sensible way of getting from point A to point B, and with a bit of poetry thrown in."

ALAN BENNETT,
WRITING HOME, 1994

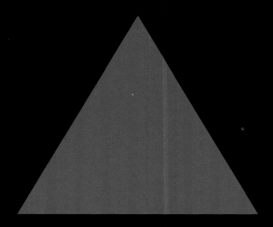

ITINERARIES

PREVIOUS PAGES: DERWENTWATER ▲ *438*

▲ NYMANS GARDEN, WEST SUSSEX ▲ *190*

▲ WEST WYCOMBE PARK, BUCKINGHAMSHIRE ▲ *289*

▼ COTTESBROOKE HALL GARDEN, NORTHAMPTON ▲ *279*

▲ PATCHWORK OF FIELDS, DARTMOOR, DEVON *238*

▲ WINKWORTH ARBORETUM, SURREY *318*

▼ STONEHENGE, WILSTHIRE, *212*

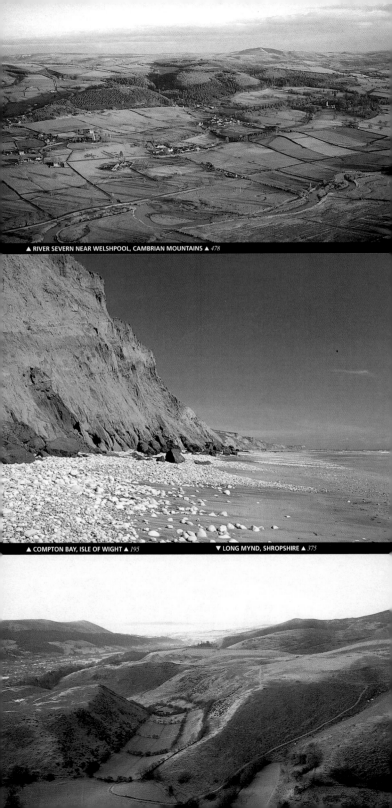

▲ RIVER SEVERN NEAR WELSHPOOL, CAMBRIAN MOUNTAINS ▲ *478*

▲ COMPTON BAY, ISLE OF WIGHT ▲ *195*

▼ LONG MYND, SHROPSHIRE ▲ *375*

LONDON

Colin Amery and Ian Collins

▲ THE WEST END

1. HOLLAND PARK
2. ALBERT HALL
3. BATTERSEA PARK
4. HARRODS
5. REGENT'S PARK
6. BATTERSEA POWER STN
7. BUCKINGHAM PALACE
8. BRITISH MUSEUM
9. TRAFALGAR SQ
10. TATE BRITAIN

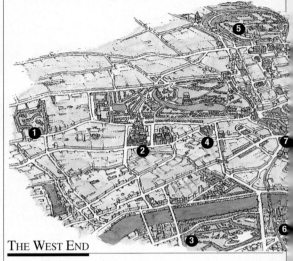

TRAFALGAR SQUARE
Conceived by John
Nash and constructed
mostly in the 1830s,
Trafalgar Square
recalls the 1805 battle
and its hero and
casualty Admiral
Lord Nelson. He
gazes with his one
good eye from a 165-
foot column, guarded
by four 1860s lions by
Sir Edwin Landseer.
The square is popular
with protesters, New
Year's Eve revelers
and pigeons.

*Above: Nelson's
Column, Trafalgar
Square
Right: St Martin-in-
the-Fields*

*George Stubbs's study
of a half-rearing, half-
wild racehorse named
"Whistlejacket" has
been recently acquired
by the National
Gallery.*

THE WEST END

NATIONAL GALLERY ★ Begun in 1824 when Lord Liverpool
helped to secure the public purchase of 38 paintings, including
works by Titian, Raphael, Rembrandt and Rubens, the
stupendous national collection now fills an 1830s neoclassical
building by William Wilkins facing Trafalgar Square – with
Early Renaissance art and temporary exhibitions in the recent
Sainsbury Wing. This international building shows European
painting from 1260 to 1920 (Giotto to
Picasso). Over 2,200 pictures, all on
permanent display, include Leonardo da
Vinci's cartoon of the Virgin and *Child
with St Anne and John the Baptist, The
Ambassadors* by Holbein, the *Rokeby
Venus* by Velázquez and Seurat's *Bathers
at Asnières*. There are major works by
British artists such as Gainsborough,
Constable and Stubbs.

NATIONAL PORTRAIT GALLERY Behind
the National Gallery, British history is portrayed through more
than 9,000 famous faces and figures from Tudor times to the
present day. There are portraits of monarchs, courtiers, writers
(including the only known likeness of
Shakespeare taken from life), artists,
scientists, statesmen, heroes and villains.
The 20th-century galleries are crowded
with paintings and photos of household
names, from politicians and princes to
pop musicians, film stars and sports
personalities.

ST MARTIN-IN-THE-FIELDS This church
by James Gibbs, now noted for
concerts and social work, upset
many a zealous Protestant in the
1720s with its catholic use of
ornament. Famous people buried
here include Charles II's mistress

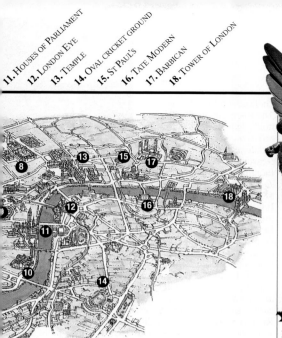

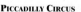

PICCADILLY CIRCUS
Now a blaze of gaudy neon signs, Piccadilly Circus was once part of John Nash's grand plan for Regent Street. The "Eros" statue (above), unveiled in 1893, is by Alfred Gilbert. It was originally named the Angel of Christian Charity and dedicated to the philanthropic 7th Earl of Shaftesbury. London's first statue cast in aluminum has lately been revived after metal fatigue.

Plaque to the poet laureate John Dryden, in Gerrard Street, Soho

Nell Gwynne, artist Sir Joshua Reynolds, cabinet-maker Thomas Chippendale and highwayman Jack Sheppard.

LONDON COLISEUM Frank Matcham's exuberant 1904 building, topped with a floodlit globe, boasts an unaltered Edwardian interior. It is the largest theater in London and now the home of English National Opera.

MAYFAIR was laid out in the area between Hyde Park, Oxford Street, Regent Street and Piccadilly by the earls of Grosvenor. Grosvenor Square (1720-5), with the US embassy on its west side, has been "Little America" since Ambassador John Adams moved to No. 9 in 1785; No. 44 Berkeley Square (1737-47) is by William Kent. Besides grand residences (Queen Elizabeth II was born at 17 Bruton Street) this expensive enclave embraces embassies, Bond Street shops and art galleries, Savile Row tailors and Claridge's hotel.

Wren thought **ST JAMES'S PICCADILLY**, finished in 1684, one of his finest churches, and even bomb damage and alterations have not ruined the effect. Note the tall windows and slim spire (a cunning fibreglass replica of 1966). The altar screen and marble font are by 17th-century master carver Grinling Gibbons.

On the columned Albemarle Street site of the **ROYAL INSTITUTION** – a scientific body founded in 1799 for the "improvement of life through demonstration" – Michael Faraday conducted pioneering work into electricity and magnetism. His laboratory has been recreated in a basement museum.

ROYAL ACADEMY OF ARTS The Academy was founded in 1768 by 34 painters, sculptors and architects, with George III as its patron and Sir Joshua Reynolds its president, to promote art and design, and to train artists. A century later the RA moved into Burlington House in Piccadilly – England's first Palladian town house – building galleries over the gardens. Displays staged throughout the year include the Summer Exhibition, held annually since 1769 and where all artists can submit work for possible inclusion. Sir Norman Foster's 1991 Sackler

London Coliseum

Chinatown

ST PAUL'S, COVENT GARDEN
All that remains of an Inigo Jones plan for a residential square based on the piazza at Livorno in northern Italy, this actors' church has been dubbed "the handsomest barn in England". The walls are lined with memorials to stage and screen stars; leading artists and writers lie in the crypt and adjoining graveyard. The closed east portico is now a stage for street entertainers.

"Taddei Tondo" by Michelangelo Buonarroti (1475-1564) at the Royal Academy

THE THEATRE MUSEUM, COVENT GARDEN
(Tavistock Street)
This focuses on the history of all the performing arts – drama, opera, ballet, music hall, rock, pop, pantomime and circus – through playbills, programmes, props, costumes and fragments of lost venues. Productions are staged in a small theater.

Galleries host smaller shows. The RA permanent collection holds diploma works given by artists on election as Royal Academicians. But its greatest treasure, given by Sir George Beaumont, is Michelangelo's *Taddei Tondo* – one of only four sculptures by the artist outside Italy, depicting the Virgin and Christ with the Infant St John the Baptist.

LEICESTER SQUARE Scores of West End theaters extend to all points of the central London compass, but are most concentrated in and around Victorian SHAFTESBURY AVENUE. LEICESTER SQUARE, with its 1874 Shakespeare fountain, 1981 Charlie Chaplin statue and half-price ticket booth, is animated with street entertainers, souvenir shops, amusement arcades and cinemas. The square began sedately in 1670, its early residents including Sir Isaac Newton.

REGENT STREET was originally built 1813-23 to designs by John Nash as a majestic route of stucco-fronted houses and shops linking the Prince Regent's Carlton House home in St James's Park to Regent's Park. Rebuilt from 1898, the street now houses luxury shops, most notably LIBERTY's department store, founded in 1875, behind a mock-Tudor façade on Great Marlborough Street. Crossing Regent Street at Oxford Circus, OXFORD STREET is London's longest shopping street, running 1½ miles from Marble Arch to Tottenham Court Road.

SOHO This cosmopolitan district between Regent Street and Charing Cross Road, with its smart restaurants and cafés, strip clubs, pornographic bookshops and bars of all kinds, has long mixed sleaze and glamor. Wardour Street hosts the British film industry. Old Compton Street is London's latest gay mecca. Specialty food stores and Berwick Street market lure gourmets. Pubs proliferate: General de Gaulle drank at the French House in Dean Street and bohemians have been trying to drain the Coach and Horses in Romilly Street since the 1940s. Carnaby Street, favorite haunt of dedicated followers of fashion in the days of Mary Quant and the Swinging Sixties, is now a precinct of tourist shops and unexciting boutiques. Three Chinese arches straddle GERRARD STREET, where the Chinese New Year is marked in late January/early February with a vibrant festival. The surrounding area is crammed with restaurants and shops selling oriental produce. Once based around the East End's Limehouse docks in the 19th century, London's thriving Chinese community has now moved west.

COVENT GARDEN PIAZZA Although most buildings are Victorian, Inigo Jones's original plans can be glimpsed in colonnaded Bedford Chambers, rebuilt in 1879. Charles Fowler's 1833 glass-and-iron-roofed design for a central market has held chic small shops and crafts stalls since the fruit and vegetable wholesalers moved south of the Thames in the 1970s.

LONDON TRANSPORT MUSEUM The old Victorian Flower Market has been converted into a giant tram, train, bus and

THE RITZ, PICCADILLY
Edwardian opulence oozes from the colonnaded château-style Ritz Hotel, with period charm still preserved in its institution of afternoon tea.

Regent Street (below)

carriage shed tracking past and present public transport. Children may sit in the drivers' seats.

THEATRE ROYAL Nell Gwynne, mistress of Charles II, acted in the first theater on this Drury Lane site when it was one of only two London venues where drama could legally be staged. Three successive buildings burned down, including one designed by Sir Christopher Wren. The present theater, by Benjamin Wyatt, opened in 1812.

ROYAL OPERA HOUSE Much of the song and dance associated with this celebrated site since 1732 has centred on the building rather than the stage. Fires raged in 1808 and 1856. E.M. Barry's design of 1858 – incorporating John Flaxman's earlier portico frieze of tragedy and comedy – has been lately enlarged and redesigned to create a better home for the Royal Opera and Royal Ballet companies ● *60-1*.

WESTMINSTER

WHITEHALL is principally occupied by ministries and other government offices – such as the 1844 Treasury building by Sir Charles Barry, which retains the columns and frieze of its predecessor by Sir John Soane. The Banqueting House ▲ *132*, by Inigo Jones is all that survives of the old Whitehall Palace.

CENOTAPH This austere 1920 memorial by Sir Edwin Lutyens to the dead of World War I, its name meaning "empty tomb", is devoid of decoration save for the flags of the three services and Merchant Navy. A service to honor the dead from both world wars, attended by the Royal Family and leading politicians, is held at the eleventh hour on the Sunday nearest to the eleventh day of the eleventh month.

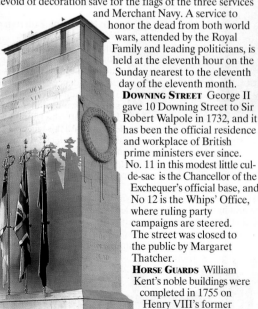

DOWNING STREET George II gave 10 Downing Street to Sir Robert Walpole in 1732, and it has been the official residence and workplace of British prime ministers ever since. No. 11 in this modest little cul-de-sac is the Chancellor of the Exchequer's official base, and No 12 is the Whips' Office, where ruling party campaigns are steered. The street was closed to the public by Margaret Thatcher.

HORSE GUARDS William Kent's noble buildings were completed in 1755 on Henry VIII's former tournament ground. Mounted sentries stand guard outside.

BURLINGTON ARCADE
One of three 19th-century arcades off Piccadilly selling traditional British luxury goods, Burlington Arcade was built by Lord Cavendish in 1819 to stop passers-by throwing garbage into his garden. Beadles still patrol to ensure that suitable standards prevail. As splendid and less crowded is John Nash's Royal Opera Arcade off the Haymarket, completed in 1818.

GREEN PARK
The peace of Green Park, planned by Charles II, was often broken by the sound of pistol shots in the 18th century, when it was a favorite site for duels.

10 Downing Street

HORSE GUARDS PARADE
Changing of the Guard still occurs here at 11am daily. Trooping the Colour, marking the Queen's official birthday, is performed on the second Saturday in June.

Left: Cenotaph

▲ WESTMINSTER

Stone carving outside Westminster Abbey

BOADICEA

In a sculpture by Thomas Thornycroft, Boadicea appears to be aiming her chariot at the Palace of Westminster. After her rebellion against the Romans was finally smashed, the English queen killed herself. Legend puts her burial place beneath Platform 10, King's Cross Station, although others claim it to be on Parliament Hill on Hampstead Heath.

GUNPOWDER PLOT

The Houses of Parliament have seen many explosive confrontations. The worst would have been in 1605 had not plotters led by Guy Fawkes been arrested just in time (and then horribly tortured and executed). The Gunpowder Plot is remembered with fireworks each November 5.

Right: Joseph Nash, "Interior of the House of Commons," 1858, oil on canvas.
Below: The Palace of Westminster

CABINET WAR ROOMS

Below Government Offices north of Horse Guards Parade is a warren of bomb-proofed rooms where Britain's World War II campaign was plotted.

WESTMINSTER ABBEY ★ is the very heart of England. The abbey church begun by Edward the Confessor has hosted every coronation since 1066. Every monarch save two (Edwards V and VIII) has been crowned and most have been buried here, from Harold Harefoot (1040) to George II (1760), many beneath splendid tombs. Amid masses of monuments, Shakespeare and Dickens have memorials in Poets' Corner. The present building mixes most beautifully the architectural styles from the 13th century onward – with noble French Gothic in the nave and exquisite Tudor decoration in Henry VII's Chapel. The two great West Front towers were built in 1734-45 to the design of Nicholas Hawksmoor. English Heritage runs the Abbey's octagonal 13th-century Chapter-House, with original sculpture and floor-tiles still intact, and the Pyx Chamber museum, with amazing wood and wax effigies of notable figures from medieval monarchs to Nelson. An arch near the Abbey's west

door leads into the peaceful square of Dean's Yard (buildings not open) and the entrance to Westminster School. Old boys include Ben Jonson and Christopher Wren.

THE HOUSES OF PARLIAMENT

Work began on the first Palace of Westminster for Edward the Confessor in 1042, and the building was a royal residence until a fire in 1512. It then developed as the seat of a two-chamber Parliament – the House of Lords, with a large hereditary element (until the recent reforms enacted under Tony Blair), and the elected House of Commons. After an all-consuming fire in 1834 it was rebuilt by Sir Charles Barry, with decoration and detail by A.W. Pugin. The House of Commons was again rebuilt after destruction during the Blitz.

WESTMINSTER HALL, dating from 1199, and with Europe's biggest hammerbeam roof added under Richard II in the late 14th century, has been a debating chamber, law court, banqueting hall and shopping arcade.

Westminster Abbey

The **Jewel Tower** was built around 1365 as a moated three-storey safe for Edward III, and used for royal treasures until the reign of Henry VIII. This outpost of the Palace of Westminster later held parliamentary records.

Parliament Square was laid out in the 1840s to show off the new Houses of Parliament. Today it is a traffic island containing statues of soldiers and statesmen – including the best bulldog image of Sir Winston Churchill, by Ivor Roberts-Jones. The mock-Gothic Middlesex Guildhall of 1913 stands behind a seated Abraham Lincoln.

St Margaret's Church Founded in the 12th century, Parliament's parish church has a window marking Prince Arthur's engagement to Catherine of Aragon (he died before the wedding; his younger brother Henry VIII succeeded to the bride and later the throne). Pepys, Milton and Churchill were all wed here; Sir Walter Raleigh was buried here after his 1618 execution.

The Guards Museum, in the Wellington Barracks on Birdcage Walk, tells the story of five regiments of Foot Guards over 350 years to the Gulf War.

Westminster Cathedral

St John's Smith Square Thomas Archer's 1728 feat of English Baroque, known as Queen Anne's footstool, has been struck by fire, lightning and aerial bombing. It has now been restored as a concert venue, holding regular lunchtime and evening chamber concerts.

Central Hall Westminster is a flamboyant example of the Beaux-Arts style, belying its 1911 origins as a Methodist meeting hall. The first General Assembly of the United Nations was held here in 1946.

Queen Anne's Gate Terraced houses in this elegant enclave date from 1704, the earliest with ornate front door canopies.

Blewcoat School Built in 1709 by a local brewer to teach poor children to "read, write, cast accounts and the catechism", and in use as a school until 1939, this pleasing red-brick building is now a National Trust shop.

Westminster Cathedral John Francis Bentley's neo-Byzantine building for the Catholic diocese of Westminster was completed on this former prison site in 1903. A striking red-brick tower with horizontal stripes of white stone rises 261 feet high. An interior rich in colored marble and mosaics also includes Eric Gill's *Stations of the Cross*, completed by the controversial sculptor during World War I.

Augustus Pugin (1812-1852) championed the Gothic Revival through his writings and buildings. He created more than 60 churches and many country houses; and, working under Barry, designed much of the elaborate ornament and fittings of the Palace of Westminster. When in his prime he suffered a complete breakdown, said to have been brought on by overwork, and died insane.

Big Ben Broadcast daily, the deep chimes of Big Ben (above) have become a symbol of Britain. A resonant 14-ton bell has been sounding for the famous four-faced clock in the 320-foot tower since 1858. The light above the clock is switched on when Parliament is sitting.

DAVID DES GRANGES
"THE SALTONSTALL FAMILY" (C. 1637)
(below) Every picture tells a story and "The Saltonstall Family", painted by David Des Granges around 1637, reveals Sir Richard Saltonstall at the death-bed of his first wife, who is gesturing toward their two surviving children. He, however, gazes on his new wife and baby.

Sugar magnate Sir Henry Tate funded the neo-baroque building by Sydney Smith that opened as a gallery of British art in 1897. Extended down the decades, the Millbank base has established a global reputation for daring modernism – hosting shows of conceptual art and giving the annual Turner Prize for young avant-garde (often controversial) artists. With the opening of the new Tate Gallery of Modern Art on Bankside ▲ *154-5*, Millbank will focus more coherently and comprehensively on British painting and sculpture since 1500. Annual rehangings – and regular dispersals of work to St Ives, Liverpool, Norwich and elsewhere – are putting many more of the nation's treasures on public view. Here are masterpieces by Gainsborough, Constable, Stubbs, Hogarth, William Blake and Joseph Wright of Derby. Sir John Everett Millais's portrait of the drowned Ophelia, pride of a strong Pre-Raphaelite section, was among 67 works given by Sir Henry Tate. Joseph Mallord William Turner, Britain's greatest Romantic painter, left 300 oils and 20,000 watercolors and drawings to the nation in 1851, with the stipulation that they should be stored and shown in a home of their own. That wish was fully granted only with the opening of the Tate's Clore Gallery, in a postmodern building lit by natural light designed by James Stirling, in 1987 (entered to the right of the main gallery).

JAMES WHISTLER, "MISS CICELY ALEXANDER" (c. 1872-4)
American-born artist James Abbot McNeill Whistler (1834-1903) lived mostly in London from the 1860s, creating esthetic color harmonies from moonlit scenes of the Thames near his Chelsea home. His portraits, like the one shown here, were also studies in tonal values.

JOSEPH MALLORD WILLIAM TURNER,
"PEACE – BURIAL AT SEA" (1842) (BOTTOM)
One of the magnificent seascapes Turner left
to the nation, now displayed in the Clore
Gallery.

JOHN WILLIAM WATERHOUSE,
"THE LADY OF SHALOTT" (1888) (BELOW)
This painting represents the zenith of Pre-
Raphaelite romanticism. Inspired by Rossetti
and Burne-Jones, the Victorian artist depicts
the beautiful weaver in Tennyson's poem
drifting in a boat to her death.

Banqueting House

INIGO JONES
(1573-1652),
England's first
professional architect,
studied in Italy and
introduced the
classical style of
Palladio. Besides
designing halls and
palaces he planned
squares such as
Lincoln's Inn Fields
and was surveyor-
general of works
under James I and
Charles I. He created
court masques for
both kings, and his
theatrical innovations
are said to have
included the
proscenium arch and
movable scenery.

St James's Palace

ST JAMES'S PARK
Enclosed by Henry
VIII as part of a
string of hunting
grounds (along with
Green Park and Hyde
Park), St James's Park
was originally a
marsh. Charles II
landscaped it with
avenues and a canal,
and added an aviary
along what is now
Birdcage Walk. The
Mall was converted
into a processional
route from Trafalgar
Square to
Buckingham Palace in
the late 19th century.

*Right: The Victoria
Memorial by Sir
Thomas Brock, facing
Buckingham Palace*

BANQUETING HOUSE ★ Whitehall Palace was once the biggest
royal residence in Europe – shrinking dramatically in 1698,
after a maid left drying linen too near a fire. All was lost save
for the 1622 Banqueting House, one of London's first purely
Renaissance buildings, designed by Inigo Jones for state
occasions, plays and masques. Its majestic Rubens ceiling was
commissioned by Charles I to celebrate the life of his father,
James I. From here Charles stepped on to the scaffold on
January 30, 1649 ● *44*.

SPENCER HOUSE Said by some to be London's most
beautiful building, Spencer House is the former
home of the family of Diana, Princess of Wales.
It is a Palladian palace, completed in 1766 –
chiefly to designs by John Vardy – for the 1st Earl
Spencer. With interiors now restored, the house
is open by appointment and available for formal
entertaining.

ST JAMES'S SQUARE was laid out and lined with
exclusive houses as early as the 1670s, intended
for members of the nobility who wanted to
live close to St James's Palace, then the
monarch's official residence. The London
Library (No. 14) was founded here in
1841 by Thomas Carlyle.

ST JAMES'S PALACE (not open). Built by
Henry VIII in the 1530s on the site of
a former leper colony, it always been
primarily a royal residence. Foreign
ambassadors are officially accredited
to the Court of St James but
received at Buckingham Palace.
The gatehouse is a distinctive
Tudor landmark.

Now separated from St James's
Palace by Marlborough Gate,
THE QUEEN'S CHAPEL was built
by Inigo Jones for Charles I's
wife, Henrietta Maria,
in 1627. England's first

*pencer House Great Room (below)
nd exterior (below right)*

Cleopatra's Needle

lassical church has a Carracci altarpiece. George III married Charlotte of Mecklenburg-Strelitz here in 1761. The exquisite nterior is open only for regular Sunday worshippers.

BUCKINGHAM PALACE Built in 1703 by the Duke of Buckingham and bought by George III as a private town dwelling for Queen Charlotte in 1762, this house-turned-palace has been the London home of British monarchs since he accession of Queen Victoria in 1837. When the sovereign s in residence the Royal Standard flies above it. The present 00-room palace was built from 1821 to designs by John Nash, ut has a later façade by Sir Aston Webb. The 18 State Rooms re open to the public in August and September. Chambers in rimson and gold contain vast chandeliers, Sèvres porcelain, Gobelins tapestries, mirrors, inlaid furniture and portraits of ings and queens. The Picture Gallery has works by Van Dyck, oussin, Rubens and Rembrandt.

ROYAL MEWS A quadrangle of stables and coach houses built o John Nash's design in 1825 holds the stateliest examples of orse-drawn transport. Here are landaus, barouches and haetons, as well as the Irish State Coach bought by Queen Victoria in 1852 and used for the State Opening of Parliament nd the Glass Coach used at royal weddings. The Gold State Coach, which conveyed George III to the 1762 State Opening f Parliament, has panels painted by Cipriani.

CLEOPATRA'S NEEDLE This granite monument, whose nscriptions praise the pharaohs, was raised in Heliopolis round 1500 BC and presented to Britain by Mohammed Ali, Viceroy of Egypt, in 1819. Erected on the newly completed Embankment along with Victorian bronze sphinxes in 1878, it as a time capsule (including photos of 12 fleshy beauties and train timetable) placed in its base. A twin stands in New York's Central Park.

PALL MALL Named after the croquet-cum-golf game played ere in the 17th century, elegant Pall Mall has been the heart f London clubland for almost 200 years – from Nash's 1827 United Services Club (No 116; now the Institute of Directors) nd at No 107 Decimus Burton's Athenaeum (1830), to Barry's Travellers' (No 106; 1832) and Reform (No 104; 1837). But he pride of Pall Mall is Wren's **MARLBOROUGH HOUSE**, ommissioned by Queen Anne for the Duke of Marlborough nd completed in 1711. Enlarged for use by 19th-century oyalty – and the social center of London when home to the uture Edward VII – it now houses the Commonwealth ecretariat.

ir Aston Webb's **ADMIRALTY ARCH** (not open), at the end of he Mall, was completed in 1911. The Latin inscription above he Corinthian columns is Edward VII's tribute to his mother and an echo of the Victoria Monument outside Buckingham alace – but he did not live to see its unveiling.

INSTITUTE OF CONTEMPORARY ARTS
The eastern end of John Nash's classical Carlton House Terrace (1833), built on the site of George IV's residence, is now given over to contemporary art, with a cinema, gallery, auditorium, bookshop, bar and restaurant. Entrance is on the Mall. It hosts exhibitions, films, concerts, talks and plays.

Changing the Guard

British Museum exhibits: an Easter Island statue and the Portland Vase

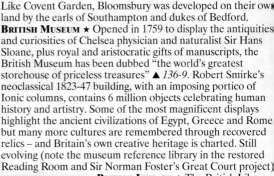

BLOOMSBURY

Like Covent Garden, Bloomsbury was developed on their own land by the earls of Southampton and dukes of Bedford.

BRITISH MUSEUM ★ Opened in 1759 to display the antiquities and curiosities of Chelsea physician and naturalist Sir Hans Sloane, plus royal and aristocratic gifts of manuscripts, the British Museum has been dubbed "the world's greatest storehouse of priceless treasures" ▲ *136-9*. Robert Smirke's neoclassical 1823-47 building, with an imposing portico of Ionic columns, contains 6 million objects celebrating human history and artistry. Some of the most magnificent displays highlight the ancient civilizations of Egypt, Greece and Rome but many more cultures are remembered through recovered relics – and Britain's own creative heritage is charted. Still evolving (note the museum reference library in the restored Reading Room and Sir Norman Foster's Great Court project)

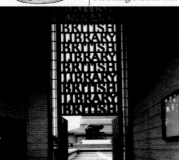

The British Library

BRITISH LIBRARY ★ The British Library at St Pancras is the UK's largest 20th-century public building. Fully opened in 1999, it cost £511 million, provides seats for 1,200 readers and stores 12 million books in deep basements. Architect Sir Colin St John Wilson has housed a state-of-the-art storage, retrieval and display system in a building that some think is a great work of art in itself. A celebration of human knowledge begins in the piazza, with Sir Eduardo Paolozzi's statue of Sir Isaac Newton plotting with a pair of dividers the immensity of the universe. Different reading rooms allow researchers to study manuscripts, maps, rare books and musical scores, the Humanities, the Sciences and the Oriental and India Office collections. The 65,000-volume King's Library, collected by George III and given to the nation by George IV, is held in a six-storey glass tower. Public exhibitions focus on the scope of the library, on postage stamps, and on the history of communication. Best of all are the treasures in the John Ritblat Gallery: the Codex Sinaiticus (*c.* 350), the Lindisfarne Gospels (*c.* 700), the Magna Carta (1215), the Gutenberg Bible (1455) and Shakespeare's First Folio (1623). The gallery also displays samples of the handwriting of Leonardo da Vinci, Lewis Carroll and many others.

CORAM FOUNDATION Retired sea-captain Thomas Coram established the Foundling Hospital in 1739 and a legacy of care for abandoned children continues in a 1937 building in Brunswick Square. Displayed gifts from artistic benefactors include paintings by Hogarth and Gainsborough and Handel's copy of the *Messiah*. Adults are barred from Coram's Fields playground (Guilford Street) unless accompanied by children

WELLCOME LIBRARY Sir Henry Wellcome's collections charting medical and scientific history – now with a 500,000-volume library and 100,000 prints, drawings, photos, films and paintings – are held in the Wellcome Building in Euston Road

DICKENS'S HOUSE Charles Dickens lived at 48 Doughty Street for only two years (1837-9) but made his literary name here by working on *The Pickwick Papers*, *Oliver Twist* and *Nicholas Nickleby*. Saved from demolition in 1923, the house

FITZROVIA
The name Fitzrovia was coined between World Wars I and II for the Fitzroy Square and Charlotte Street area – whose pubs (such as the Fitzroy Tavern) were favored by poets and painters including Dylan Thomas and Augustus John. Its skyline is now dominated by the 580-ft Telecom Tower of 1964.

THE BLOOMSBURY GROUP

The Bloomsbury Group was an early 20th-century coterie of friends, relations and kindred creative spirits bent on personal and artistic freedom. The area's Georgian squares have held the homes of novelist Virginia Woolf, biographer Lytton Strachey and painters Duncan Grant and Vanessa Bell. Roger Fry set up the Post-Impressionist art and crafts Omega Workshop at 33 Fitzroy Square in 1913.

*Dickens's House:
a portrait of the writer
as a young man, by
Laurence, and the
Drawing Room
(bottom)*

contains a museum filled with memorabilia. The Dickens Library is in the basement.

PERCIVAL DAVID FOUNDATION

Exceptional Chinese ceramics, dating from the 10th century and left to London University by scholar and collector Sir Percival David, are now displayed in a Georgian town house in Gordon Square. Some exquisite wares have come from

the imperial collection. There is a gallery for special exhibitions of East Asian art and a reference library.

PETRIE MUSEUM OF EGYPTIAN ARCHAEOLOGY University College in Gower Street exhibits antiquities assembled by its first professor of Egyptology, Sir Flinders Petrie. His discoveries in Egypt included King Akhnaton's palace, the Greek city of Naucratis and pieces of a huge statue of Ramesses II.

ST PANCRAS STATION Sir George Gilbert Scott's 250-bedroom Grand Midland Hotel opened in 1874 as the last word in comfort and modernity. The gingerbread Gothic fantasy, best

of the three rail termini along Euston Road, was used for offices from 1935, until restored as a hotel in recent years. The train shed behind is a miracle of Victorian engineering: its roof stretches for 700 feet and soars 100 feet high.

ST PANCRAS PARISH CHURCH (1822) was designed by William Inwood and his son Henry in uncompromising Greek Revival style. The caryatids on the side are in terracotta over cast iron; they are casts of those on the Erechtheum in Athens – and are now a good deal better preserved.

SELENE'S HORSE
This horse's head, one of four drawing the goddess Selene's chariot, comes from the Parthenon's east pediment. It was completed in 447-432 BC.

In the British Museum millions of objects span the millennia as archeology merges into anthropology. History and geography contract. The neoclassical exterior and entrance hall reflect the fact that the core collections are those of Classical Antiquity – including the Elgin and Townsley Marbles and the Nereid Temple of Xanthus. Children make a bee-line for the mummies in the Egyptian galleries – where cats as well as courtiers are embalmed for eternity. There is also the Lindow Man, a 2000-year-old corpse found in a Cheshire bog. But adult interest may lead to the Greek Antiquities section, in which the fabulous 5th-century BC Elgin Marbles have been a controversial centerpiece since 1816. They were taken from the Parthenon in Athens by a British diplomat; Greece still presses for their return. There are major displays of later Asiatic, Islamic and European art and artifacts, hordes of coins and medals, jewels and a huge department of prints and drawings. There is also a program of fee-charging temporary exhibitions in this otherwise free museum.

MILDENHALL TREASURE
Thirty-four pieces of 4th-century AD silver tableware, including the Great Disk (above), were ploughed up from a Suffolk field in the 1940s.

THE SNETTISHAM GREAT TORQUE
This masterpiece of Celtic artistry using twisted gold wire, is the best of many such finds in Norfolk. It was buried around the time Boadicea's revolt against Roman rule was being crushed (60-70 AD).

THE WARREN CUP
The recently acquired Warren Cup shows a Roman homosexual orgy. Rather more controversy has surrounded the tiny vessel's origins, authenticity and purchase price than its risqué subject matter.

RAMESSES II
Part of a gigantic 13th-century BC granite statue of Ramesses II, one of ancient Egypt's most powerful pharaohs, displayed in the Egyptian Sculpture Gallery.

EGYPTIAN COFFINS
Beautifully carved and painted coffins show the serene faces of ancient Egyptians who were sure their mummified bodies were destined for the afterlife. On the left is the inner coffin of the Libyan Pasentor, *c*. 700 BC.

SUTTON HOO
The richly worked buckle shown far right was found on the Sutton Hoo burial ship for an early 7th-century king of East Anglia ▲ *345*.

LIONESS BAS RELIEF (BELOW)
This bas-relief image of a hunted lioness was found in the Assyrian palace at Nineveh *c*. 645 BC. It is among several carvings depicting the feats of King Assurbanipal (ruled 669 to 627 BC) and his warriors who subjugated Babylon and conquered Egypt.

HOXNE HOARD
The Hoxne coins, jewels and domestic objects were buried in Suffolk by a wealthy family when the Roman legions were leaving Britain early in the 5th century AD. The Roman coins shown right were part of the treasure. Coins minted all over the Roman empire were circulated around Britain by traders and soldiers. The British Museum's ancient and modern coin collection is now one of the greatest in the world.

"Study of Adam" by Michelangelo

*Sutton Hoo buckle,
7th century AD*

ROSETTA STONE
Carved in 196 BC,
the Rosetta Stone
was found in the
Nile Delta in 1799.
A royal decree
written in Egyptian
hieroglyphics (the
language of priests),
in demotic (the
common language)
and in Greek, it
provided the key
to the texts of
ancient Egypt.

*Human-headed bull and
attendant genie, Khorsabad,
Assyria, c. 710 BC*

*Bronze head of
Hadrian from the
Thames at London
Bridge*

Sir John Soane's Museum

HOLBORN AND EMBANKMENT

SIR JOHN SOANE'S MUSEUM ★ An Aladdin's cave of treasures and architectural tricks left to the nation by maverick Sir John Soane in 1837. The Lincoln's Inn Fields home of the architect (son of a bricklayer who wed a wealthy builder's daughter) is adorned with domes, mirrors and lantern lights. Soane's taste in rooms ran to Catacombs, a Monk's Parlour and a Sepuchral Chamber containing the sarcophagus of Pharaoh Seti I. The house is crammed with ancient artifacts, paintings (Hogarth, Canaletto, Turner, Watteau), books, fine furnishings and architectural drawings. A joy.

Scholar and lexicographer **SAMUEL JOHNSON** lived at many addresses in his beloved London, but only **17 GOUGH SQUARE** has survived. The fine 1700 house alone was saved when alleys off Fleet Street were blitzed and bulldozed for offices. Living here from 1746 until 1759, Dr Johnson wrote his *Dictionary of the English Language* in an austere garret which can now be seen in a poignant museum to his memory.

FLEET STREET The 1980s flight of newspapers from Fleet Street has seen the "street of shame" redeveloped for City offices. Even the Wig and Pen Club, which survived the Great Fire, has closed – although the 1610 Prince Henry's Room, with a richly decorated plaster ceiling and display about diarist Samuel Pepys, remains open. Elderly journalists still totter into El Vino's Wine Bar after memorial services at St Bride's Church, but Ye Olde Cheshire Cheese (where scribes like Pepys, Johnson, Dickens and Mark Twain once slaked their thirst) is for tourists.

INNS OF COURT Lawyers have been based around Temple Bar since the Middle Ages – at first coming to London for sessions of the Royal Courts of Justice and lodging in taverns, the ancestors of the Inns of Court. Law schools also arose here. Compared with

SAVOY HOTEL
Opening on the site of the medieval Savoy Palace in 1889, the Savoy Hotel is so grand that its forecourt is the only street in Britain where traffic keeps to the right. The Savoy Theatre, built for D'Oyly Carte opera, is a restored Art Deco delight.

Fleet Street

TWININGS TEAS
Twinings have been selling tea at 216 The Strand since 1706 – the doorway with two Chinese figures and a golden lion dates from 1787. A museum at the back of the shop outlines the company's history.

Left: Somerset House
Below left: Middle Temple Hall
Below right: Temple Gateway

HATTON GARDEN
Close to the London Silver Vaults in Chancery Lane is Hatton Garden – the capital's diamond and jewelry center. A pawnbroker still trades here.

GRAY'S INN HALL
Shakespeare's *A Comedy of Errors* was first performed in Gray's Inn Hall in 1594. Middle Temple Hall, its Elizabethan interior still marvelously intact, hosted the 1601 premiere of *Twelfth Night* – with the Queen herself attending.

0 Inns in the 14th century, there are now only Lincoln's Inn, Middle Temple, Inner Temple and Gray's Inn. Each has its own all, church, library, cloister and gardens – a tranquil and imeless world (although much rebuilt after Hitler's bombs).

ROYAL COURTS OF JUSTICE With 1,000 rooms, 3½ miles of orridors and 35 million bricks faced with Portland stone, his warren houses the nation's main civil courts. Completed 1 1882, G.E. Street's neo-Gothic building deals with such natters as divorce, libel, civil liability and appeals. Designed y Christopher Wren, **ST CLEMENT DANES** is now the church of he Royal Air Force and isolated on a traffic island. Its bells till ring to the tune of the English nursery rhyme "Oranges nd Lemons".

STAPLE INN, in High Holborn, is the last remnant of Elizabethan half-timbering left in central London. It was nce the wool staple – where wool was weighed and taxed.

SOMERSET HOUSE Home to the Courtauld Galleries, this is classical 1770s quadrangle by Sir William Chambers. Built n the site of a Renaissance palace, it was Britain's first urpose-built government office block. The Gilbert Collection f European gold, English silver and mosaics can now be seen ere. Fabulous art galleries occupy the former Fine Rooms f the Royal Academy of Arts. Impressionist and Post-mpressionist masterpieces amassed by textile magnate Samuel Courtauld have been augmented by other superb gifts, particu-

The Royal Courts of Justice exterior (above) and interior (left)

larly of Italian and Flemish Old Master paintings. The Hermitage Rooms hold exhibitions of some of the magnificent treasures of The State Hermitage Museum in St Petersburg. A fine collection of 20th-century British art is not entirely eclipsed.

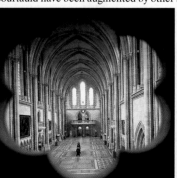

ROMAN BATH
Beside a large window in Surrey Street, a light switch illuminates an antique bathing pool. Popular for cold plunges in the 19th century, the bath probably began as part of Arundel House – one of several Strand palaces in Tudor times.

CEREMONY OF THE KEYS After each of the Tower's gates has been locked for the night, the last post sounds and the Ceremony of the Keys proceeds to Queen's House. As the Crown Jewels were stolen by Colonel Blood in 1671, this security drill is rather more than a ritual.

Right: Royal crowns, orbs and scepters

THE CITY

RAVENS
Legend claims that if the ravens ever desert the Tower the kingdom will fall – so a small colony of wing-clipped birds is pampered by one of 40 resident Yeoman Warders (dressed in distinctive uniforms and dubbed "Beef-eaters"). Perhaps the birds first settled here when the cliff-like White Tower of 1097 was London's tallest building.

ROYAL ARMOURIES
A tourist attraction at the Tower since 1660, the Royal Armouries now contain 40,000 pieces of arms and armor on show in London and Leeds. The White Tower selection covers sporting and tournament equipment, suits of armor, cannons, swords, pistols and early machine guns.

THE TOWER OF LONDON For many visitors to the Tower over the last 900 years, the experience has been more chilling than thrilling. As a fortress, jail, torture chamber and place of execution, the stark gray compound beside the Thames issued one-way tickets, especially to those who entered by boat through Traitors' Gate.

Although a medieval palace was founded by Henry III in 1220, and high-ranking prisoners enjoyed comfortable confinement in Beauchamp Tower, most inmates suffered terribly. Even royal status was no guarantee of protection – the Bloody Tower is linked to two boy princes, Edward V and his brother, who vanished in 1483 (skeletons were found nearby in 1674).

CROWN JEWELS The jewels in the Tower's crown are priceless regalia used at royal coronations and other state occasions since 1661 (earlier relics were sold or melted down by Cromwell). A moving walkway takes visitors around cases of swords, rings, orbs, sceptres and 12 crowns. St Edward's Crown is the oldest, and the Imperial State Crown made for Queen Victoria the most opulent (with 2,800 diamonds, the Black Prince's Ruby given to Edward III's eldest son in 1367, the Stuart Sapphire taken into exile by James III in 1688 and pearls worn by Elizabeth I). The legendary Koh-i-Noor or Mountain of Light diamond, set in the Queen Mother's crown, is said to bring bad luck to men.

ST PAUL'S CATHEDRAL ★ On the site of a Roman temple to Diana, the first St Paul's was built in 604 and rebuilt between the 11th and 13th centuries as the largest medieval church in Europe. Wren's restoration plans for St Paul's won approval one week before the structure was razed in the Great Fire; amid many rows, his subsequent designs for a new cathedral were much altered and 35 years in the building. The compromise gave a Latin cross-shape to the interior, but the outline is dominated by the great dome, which some still think less suited to London than Rome. The view over London from its Golden Gallery is superb, the Whispering Gallery acoustics astounding. Grinling Gibbons carved the

St Paul's Cathedral painted by Canaletto in 1745

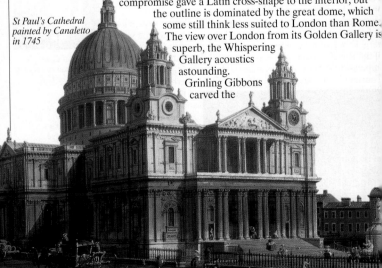

MUSEUM OF LONDON

A showcase on the edge of the Barbican for life in London since Roman times, with recreated interiors and street scenes, exhibits from excavated everyday items and treasures to the Lord Mayor's State Coach and Selfridges' Art Deco lifts. An animated model of the 1666 Great Fire is accompanied by Samuel Pepys's eyewitness report.

Above left: the Lord Mayor's coach in the Museum of London
Left: Egyptian Hall, Mansion House

SIR CHRISTOPHER WREN (1632-1723)

won early note as a scientist – teaching mathematics at Gresham's College in London, co-founding the Royal Society and becoming a professor of astronomy at Oxford. But he found lasting fame as the genius of English Baroque architecture. Although many of his plans remained as drawings or models, numerous ecclesiastical and secular masterpieces were executed in stone. His tomb is in St Paul's Cathedral, whose much-delayed completion he lived to see. The epitaph translates as: "If you seek his memorial look around."

choir stalls, bishop's throne and organ case; Sir James Thornhill almost fell to his death while adorning the cupola with paintings showing the life of St Paul. A pantheon since 1790, the cathedral contains the tombs of Wellington and Nelson (the latter in a black marble sarcophagus once earmarked for Henry VIII's Cardinal Wolsey). During the Blitz, the continued survival of the great cathedral seemed to Londoners like a miracle as the City burned around it.

MANSION HOUSE A Palladian façade with six Corinthian columns gives a suitably grand appearance to the Lord Mayor's official residence. The building, completed to George Dance the Elder's design in 1753, boasts splendid state rooms – including the spectacular Egyptian Hall and the Samuel collection of excellent Dutch 17th-century paintings. It also includes 11 holding cells, for the Mayor is the City's chief magistrate and his residence doubles as a court.

OLD BAILEY Its dome topped by a bronze statue of a blindfolded Justice brandishing her sword and scales, the new Central Criminal Courts have tried major cases since 1907. But a Sessions House operated from 1539, and Judge Jeffreys dispensed injustice here in the 1670s. Part of the site was also occupied by the notorious Newgate prison.

CHARTERHOUSE A 14th-century gateway in Charterhouse Square leads to the remains of a Carthusian monastery closed by Henry VIII. In 1611 the buildings were converted to a hospital for needy pensioners and the Charterhouse charity school, whose pupils included writer William Makepeace Thackeray and Boy Scout movement founder Robert Baden-Powell. The school moved to Surrey in 1872, but apartments for the genteel old remain.

BARBICAN CENTRE A large residential, commercial and arts complex dating from 1962, with ornamental lake, fountains, lawns and conservatory. Marooned in this modernity is the church of **ST GILES CRIPPLEGATE** where Oliver Cromwell was married and the poet John Milton is buried.

Gateway in Charterhouse Square

POSTMAN'S PARK
Postman's Park was converted in 1880 from St Botolph, Aldersgate churchyard. The green was much used by staff from the nearby General Post Office (where a National Postal Museum can now be visited). Victorian artist G.F. Watts dedicated one of the park's walls to plaques hailing the bravery of ordinary people.

CLOTH FAIR
The quiet backwater of Cloth Fair is named after boisterous Bartholomew Fair – the main cloth fair in medieval and Tudor England, held annually until 1855. The late poet laureate Sir John Betjeman lived at No 43.

Below: the Stock Exchange
Below right: the Royal Exchange
Bottom: the Bank of England

COLLEGE OF ARMS The home of the royal heralds, rebuilt after the Great Fire by Maurice Emmett – although records dating from medieval times were rescued. Still recording pedigrees and examining armorial bearings, the college was presented with wrought-iron gates and railings from Goodrich Court in Hertfordshire by an American benefactor in 1956.

LLOYD'S OF LONDON was founded in the late 17th century and named after the coffee house where ships and marine insurance were traded. It soon became the world's main stock exchange for insurance contracts, with the Lutine bell tolling for good or bad news. Since 1986 Lloyd's has been based in a brilliant glass and steel building by Richard Rogers ● *90*, co-designer of the Pompidou Centre in Paris. With an arch-roofed central atrium, satellite towers and external lifts and piping, the assembly looks most effective when floodlit in blue at night.

LEADENHALL MARKET A food market has existed on the site of the Roman forum since medieval times. The present ornate covered shopping precinct of 1881 was designed by Sir Horace Jones, who also built Smithfield and Billingsgate (the Thames side fish market that moved to the Isle of Dogs in 1982).

STOCK EXCHANGE From coffee houses to a base in Threadneedle Street and finally to its present home in Old Broad Street, the Stock Exchange has seen frenzied dealing. But computerization has calmed the trading floor in this 1969 building.

The **GUILDHALL** has been the seat of municipal power since 1192, with the present structure begun in 1411 and ravaged by the Great Fire and Blitz. Surviving 15th-century fabric comprises the porch, crypts and great-hall walls – the roof of the latter rebuilt by Sir Giles Gilbert Scott. Each November, soon after the Lord Mayor's parade, the Prime Minister addresses a banquet here. A magnificent library, founded with a bequest by Richard ("Dick") Whittington, Lord Mayor in the 14th and 15th centuries, was seized by the Duke of Somerset in 1549 and restored in 1828.

ROYAL EXCHANGE The City's oldest mercantile institution was founded by Sir Thomas Gresham in 1567. William Tite's lofty neoclassical building, dating from 1844, is the third on this site. Outside stands Sir Francis Chantrey's equestrian statue of the Duke of Wellington – cast in bronze from French cannons captured at Waterloo.

BANK OF ENGLAND MUSEUM Founded in 1694 when William III needed a public loan to fund his war against France, the mighty Bank (left) has been satirized by Sheridan as The Old Lady of Threadneedle Street and devalued – architecturally – by rebuilding schemes reducing Sir John Soane's late 18th-century masterpiece to an outer wall. But a fragment of the finest neoclassical interiors in Europe has been recreated for a display of bank notes and gold bars in a museum of money.

ST JOHN'S GATE was once an entrance to the Priory of the Knights of St John of Jerusalem in Clerkenwell. It is now a

MONUMENT (below) Wren's memorial to the Great Fire of 1666
is the tallest free-standing stone column in the world (205 ft high).
Reliefs show Charles II restoring the ruined capital. A viewing
platform is reached by 311 steps.

museum telling the
story of the Order of
St John (Malta), a
body founded during
the Crusades.

**SADLER'S WELLS
THEATRE** Built as a
"musick house" by
Thomas Sadler in
1683, and rebuilt in
1927 by the
redoubtable Lilian
Baylis (also a
benefactor of the
Old Vic in Waterloo),
this dance center on
Rosebery Avenue
reopened in 1999.

ST BARTHOLOMEW'S
Inside the gates of
Bart's Hospital,
ST BARTHOLOMEW
THE LESS has served
patients and their
families, doctors and nurses for five centuries. Architect Inigo
Jones was baptized here; the post-Wren octagonal dome was
constructed in 1789 and has twice been rebuilt. Inside the
hospital itself is a stunning series of murals by Hogarth. Also
once part of the ancient priory is ST BARTHOLOMEW THE GREAT
(1123), the oldest parish church in the City.

WESLEY'S CHAPEL The "Methodists' Cathedral"
– with ship-mast columns and a beautiful
austerity – was consecrated by founder John
Wesley in 1778. He lived next door for his last
11 years, where many of his personal effects
are now on display, and is buried behind
the chapel. A crypt museum outlines the
history of Methodism (note the
electric-shock machine which Wesley
used to treat cases of depression).

BUNHILL FIELDS Designated a
cemetery after the Great Plague of
1665, Bunhill Fields was soon allocated
to Nonconformists (who were banned
from churchyard burial). John Bunyan,
Daniel Defoe and William Blake lie
here. John Milton wrote the epic poem
Paradise Lost while living in Bunhill Row
in the years before his death in 1674.

BEVIS MARKS, the Spanish and
Portuguese Synagogue. Jews were
expelled from England in 1290 and
allowed back by Cromwell. The oldest
surviving English synagogue was built for
Sephardic worship in 1699-1701 by
Quaker carpenter Joseph Avis. It is a
handsome red-brick box with galleried
interior, Tuscan columns and carved
woodwork.

LIVERY COMPANIES
have played a key role
in the City's
commerce and
government since
medieval times.
A hundred of these
trade guilds survive
today – Mercers,
Goldsmiths, Salters
and Vintners among
them – and a third
have halls where plate
and other treasures
are held and some-
times displayed.
Timepieces owned by
the Clockmakers'
Company (and Mary
Queen of Scots'
skull-shaped watch)
can be seen in the
Guildhall Library.

**ST BARTHOLOMEW
AND THE JESTER**
Rahere, Henry I's
court jester, had a
dream in which St
Bartholomew saved
him from a winged
monster. He became
a monk and in 1123
founded the church of
St Bartholomew the
Great where he is
buried.

*Left: Statue of
St Bartholomew,
Bank of England*

TEMPLE CHURCH (above), a religious castle built in the 12th and 13th centuries for the Knights Templar, is one of the few circular churches to survive in England. A military order protecting pilgrims to the Holy Land, the Templars were based here from 1185 until suppressed by the Crown in 1312.

ST VEDAST (above) St Vedast Foster Lane, a humble medieval church remodeled along loftier lines by Wren, boasts a unique baroque spire. This intricate beacon in the manner of Borromini was added from 1709, probably by Hawksmoor.

ST STEPHEN WALBROOK ★ St Stephen Walbrook (right) is one of Wren's most elaborate and most classical designs. The church itself has a centralized interior and dome, a practice piece for St Paul's. It now has an austere altarpiece by Henry Moore. Prebendary Chad Varah founded the Samaritans in the crypt.

ST BRIDE'S FLEET STREET (right) Wren's tallest and most celebrated spire (226 feet), topping the journalists' church, is composed of successively diminishing octagonal tiers. A City baker of the time copied the design for a wedding cake, and created a tradition. A crypt museum looks at the eight churches to have occupied this site, as well as at the history of printing.

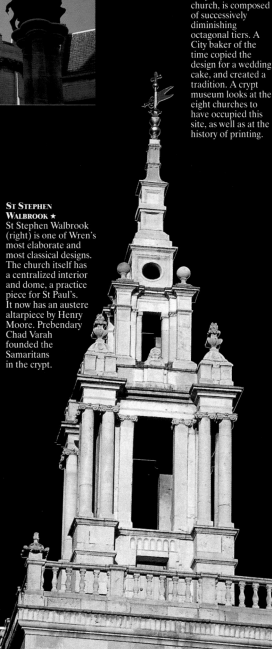

ST MARY WOOLNOTH ★ (below)
Nicholas Hawksmoor's small baroque church (1716-27) contains groups of Corinthian columns supporting a clerestory with large lunettes. The jewel-like interior seems oddly larger than the outside walls.

Medieval London had over 100 churches, but 87 were destroyed or damaged when the Great Fire of 1666 cleared 400 City acres. The calamity gave Sir Christopher Wren scope to design a new capital. Grand plans for thoroughfares radiating from St Paul's and the Royal Exchange were rejected as too expensive – to be picked up over a century later for Washington, DC. But the great cathedral and 51 churches were rebuilt.

ALL HALLOWS BY THE TOWER OF LONDON took the bodies of those executed in the nearby fortress, and gave Samuel Pepys a safe vantage point during the Great Fire. Rebuilt after the Blitz, it has an Undercroft Museum with relics from Roman times. Church registers record the baptism of William Penn, founder of Pennsylvania, and the marriage of John Quincy Adams, 6th US president.

Whitechapel Art Gallery

Geffrye Museum exterior (far right) and its Regency Period Room (right)

GEFFRYE MUSEUM
Recreated domestic interiors between the reigns of Elizabeths I and II are shown in the Geffrye Museum, with a special exhibition every Christmas contrasting festive celebrations down the centuries.

William Morris Gallery

WHITECHAPEL ART GALLERY enjoys an international reputation for contemporary art shows staged in the airy space behind C. Harrison Townsend's Art Nouveau façade.

Right: Christ Church, Spitalfields

BETHNAL GREEN MUSEUM OF CHILDHOOD is an outpost of the Victoria and Albert Museum – and actually occupied part of the present V&A site until dismantled and re-erected in the deprived East End in 1872. Baby equipment, nursery furniture, children's clothes and teenage fashions all feature. But the strongest focus is on toys, with charming displays of puppets, automata, dolls and dolls' houses. A Nuremberg house dates from 1673 and a model of Queen Victoria in coronation robes from the 1840s.

GEFFRYE MUSEUM Founded in 1901 for the people of the East End, the Geffrye Museum is set in almshouses built in 1715 on land bequeathed by trader and Lord Mayor of London Sir Robert Geffrye. A central chapel survives with box pews and inscriptions of the Creed, Commandments and Lord's Prayer. Outside lies a new walled herb garden.

SPITALFIELDS Just north of the City walls, this area has given refuge to waves of migrants – Huguenot weavers from the 17th century, then Jews, now Bangladeshis. Workshops, small factories, ethnic restaurants and places of worship have succeeded one another. Petticoat Lane, a clothing market since the 16th-century, is packed on Sunday mornings as crowds flow to the Bengali food shops in Brick Lane. Around Fournier Street, where 18th-century houses have light attics for silk-weaving, beautiful buildings have only lately been saved from demolition. The Spitalfields Historic Buildings Trust headquarters has a Victorian synagogue in its garden.

CHRIST CHURCH, SPITALFIELDS ★ is the most impressive of Nicholas Hawksmoor's six London churches. Built between 1714 and 1729, and disfigured by Victorian alterations and 20th-century vandalism, it was restored and reopened in 1987. The soaring spire and arched portico on four pedimented Tuscan columns dominate the surrounding streets as they were always intended to do, the church being designed to combat the spread of Nonconformism in a Huguenot stronghold.

SUTTON HOUSE With original brickwork, large fireplaces and linenfold paneling still intact, this Tudor merchant's house is a unique East End survival (though when it was built, in 1535, Hackney was a village).

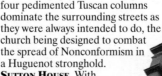

Right: St Katharine's Dock
Below: Great Chamber,
Sutton House

An exhibition traces the history of the house and its occupants.

QUEEN ELIZABETH'S HUNTING LODGE, CHINGFORD was actually built for her father, Henry VIII, in 1543 as a grandstand for blood sports in the forest below. But Gloriana did shoot her crossbow from the first-floor room in which a hunt breakfast has now been recreated.

WILLIAM MORRIS MUSEUM, WALTHAMSTOW In its garden setting, 18th-century Water House was the elegant early home of artist, writer, designer, craftsman and social reformer William Morris (1834-96). The fields in which he found inspiration have been engulfed by Walthamstow (whose old church is well worth visiting for its monuments), but the house cherishes his achievements and those of the Arts and Crafts movement. Exhibits include the Kelmscott Chaucer and the Woodpecker Tapestry, plus Mackmurdo furniture, tiles by de Morgan, Burne-Jones stained glass and pottery by the Martin brothers. The Sir Frank Brangwyn Collection adds 19th and early 20th-century paintings.

SUTTON HOUSE
Built for Henry VIII's courtier Sir Ralph Sadleir, it successively became home to traders, Huguenot silk-weavers, Victorian teachers, Edwardian clergy and a trade union.

CANARY WHARF Pinnacle of the Docklands development – on docks left derelict when trade shifted down river to Tilbury's modern container port – Canary Wharf is planned as a mini-city of 21 office blocks, plus shops, flats and leisure facilities. Cesar Pelli's 50-storey One Canada Square, like a great white pencil, is the tallest office building in Europe. Best viewed from the overhead Docklands Light Railway.

ST KATHARINE'S DOCK, whose 1820s building had razed a medieval district and displaced 11,000 people, was the first of London's docks to close, in 1969. It has been revived as a leisure and residential center, with the 1854 Ivory House now flats and a three-storey warehouse the Dickens Inn. One basin is a marina and another holds the Historic Ship Collection, with tugs, traders, lightship and Captain Scott's HMS *Discovery* recalling the ages of sail and steam.

Canary Wharf

COLUMBIA ROAD
A street of small Victorian shops erupts with crowds and color each Sunday as the Columbia Road Flower Market opens for business. Britain's passion for gardening has rarely seemed more exciting or less peaceful!

149

▲ LONDON BRIDGES

Before 19th-century engineering created bridges that barely impeded river flow, the Thames often froze over – allowing mass revels known as "frost fairs". In the winter of 1683-4 an ox was roasted on the ice and booths stretched from Temple to Southwark.

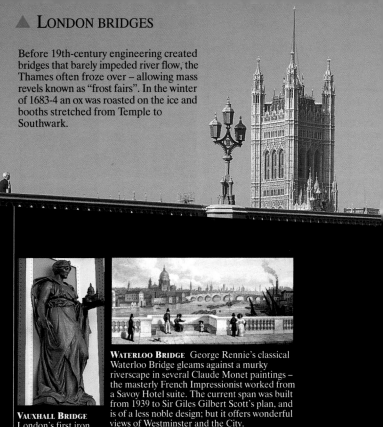

WATERLOO BRIDGE George Rennie's classical Waterloo Bridge gleams against a murky riverscape in several Claude Monet paintings – the masterly French Impressionist worked from a Savoy Hotel suite. The current span was built from 1939 to Sir Giles Gilbert Scott's plan, and is of a less noble design; but it offers wonderful views of Westminster and the City.

VAUXHALL BRIDGE London's first iron bridge, originally known as Regent's Bridge, was built from 1811 and replaced by a granite and steel model of Edwardian design. Its piers, with their statues of the Arts and Sciences, look like a Tate Gallery overspill.

TOWER BRIDGE The first bridge to be built downstream from London Bridge opened in 1894. Now its Gothic profile, looking like two Scottish castles, is more famous than the Tower it echoes and overshadows. Described by architect Sir Horace Jones as "steel skeletons clothed in stone", the turrets house equipment to lift two 1200-ton bascules (French for "seesaw") and let ships into the Pool of London. The high-level footbridge, now glassed-in as part of the Tower Bridge Experience museum, gives superb views across London and beyond.

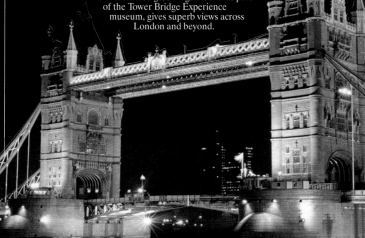

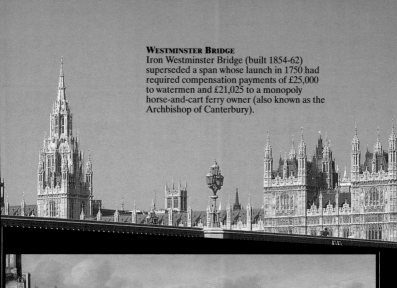

WESTMINSTER BRIDGE
Iron Westminster Bridge (built 1854-62)
superseded a span whose launch in 1750 had
required compensation payments of £25,000
to watermen and £21,025 to a monopoly
horse-and-cart ferry owner (also known as the
Archbishop of Canterbury).

LONDON BRIDGE (above, "Old
London Bridge" by Claude de
Jongh, 1630, at Kenwood House
▲ *166*) London Bridge has been
rebuilt many times over two
millennia, and until 1729 was the
city's only span across the
Thames. From 1209 the first stone
bridge had 19 arches and a narrow
street of overhanging shops and
houses, but the buildings were lost
with a widening scheme started in
1758. George Rennie's 1820s
bridge now crosses Lake Havasu
in Arizona. The present (1972)
bridge is the dullest to date.

ALBERT BRIDGE Opened in 1873, Rowland Ordish's
beautiful web-like structure links Chelsea and Battersea
and was the first river crossing to incorporate suspended
central and side spans. At night it is one of London's most
brilliant pieces of illumination.

HUNGERFORD BRIDGE (not
illustrated) was one of the last
Millennium projects to be
completed. Two beautiful new
footbridges, slung either side of
the existing Hungerford rail and
pedestrian bridge, linking
Charing Cross and the Royal
Festival Hall, were opened
in 2002.

MILLENNIUM BRIDGE The first new span across the
Thames in central London for 100 years is a walkway
linking St Paul's and the City to the new Tate Modern
gallery at Bankside. This low-dip suspension bridge, by
architect Sir Norman Foster and sculptor Sir Anthony
Caro, represents the cutting edge of technology. Today
London has 34 bridges (including railway bridges); some
of the most elegant constructions are in Victorian
ironwork. Blackfriars Bridge, opened amid great fanfare
by Queen Victoria in 1869, replaced a lovely Portland
stone structure by Piranesi-influenced Robert Mylne
of a century earlier.

Southwark Cathedral

DESIGN MUSEUM
Once a banana warehouse, the Design Museum is the first center in the world to celebrate the history, theory and practice of design in mass-produced consumer goods. The imprint of style guru Sir Terence Conran now spills across the trendy restaurants of Butler's Wharf.

HMS *BELFAST*, a Royal Navy last light cruiser, was launched just before World War II. It has been moored opposite the Tower of London as a floating museum since 1971.

GLOBE THEATRE In the late Elizabethan period the Bankside area of Southwark saw London's first fixed theaters – the Swan, the Hope, the Rose and, most famously, the Globe. The great Wooden O, in which Shakespeare acted and invested, was gutted in 1613 when a cannon fired during a performance of Henry VIII set the thatched roof ablaze. Puritanism felled the replacement. Now, thanks to the late American actor and director Sam Wanamaker, a replica of the original building runs summer seasons. There is also a Shakespeare museum.

SOUTHWARK CATHEDRAL A church dating from the 12th century and a cathedral since 1905, Southwark is rich in medieval features and memorials – including the 1408 tomb of poet John Gower, friend of Geoffrey Chaucer. But Shakespeare is the poet who seems most in residence: his south aisle memorial was carved by Henry McCarthy in 1912, and an annual birthday service is held in his honor.

Below: British Airways London Eye
Bottom: The Globe Theatre

In the chilling OLD OPERATING THEATRE, in the loft of St Thomas's parish church, between 1821 and 1862 surgeons carved into gagged and bound women in front of student audiences. The gory spectacle predated antiseptic surgery and anaesthetics.

FLORENCE NIGHTINGALE MUSEUM The hospital reformer became the legendary Lady of the Lamp after working among Crimean War casualties. Lately reassessed, her life is recalled in a museum within St Thomas's Hospital, where she set up the first school of nursing after returning to England in 1856.

SOUTH BANK The site of the 1951 Festival of Britain, celebrating the Great Exhibition's centenary, now hosts London's main center for the visual and performing arts in concrete buildings: Royal National Theatre, Hayward Gallery, Queen Elizabeth Hall, Royal Festival Hall, Purcell Room, and National Film Theatre. The BRITISH AIRWAYS LONDON EYE – the Millennium Wheel – is a gigantic ferris wheel, offering panoramic views over London.

THE IMPERIAL WAR MUSEUM is housed in the old Bedlam lunatic asylum, which was built in 1815, the same year as the Battle of Waterloo. Its exhibits relate to conflicts involving British or Commonwealth troops since 1914. A huge central hall holds military hardware from planes (Sopwith Camel, Spitfire, Mustang) and tanks (Churchill,

Poussin's "The Triumph of David", c. 1631-33, at the Dulwich Picture Gallery

Sherman, Grant) to submarines and Polaris missiles. Elsewhere medals, firearms, artworks, photos, ephemera, books, films and recordings recall land, sea and air warfare and life on the home front. Recreated "experiences" simulate trauma in a Flanders trench and in the London Blitz.

LAMBETH PALACE The Thames-side Palace has been the London base of the Archbishop of Canterbury, senior cleric of the Church of England, for 800 years. Although the building is much restored, the chapel and undercroft date from the 13th century and a fine Tudor gatehouse from 1486. The large library (entry by prior request) began with Archbishop Bancroft's 1610 bequest: treasures include the 1150 Lambeth Bible and Sir Thomas More's *Utopia* (More was interrogated in the Guard Room for refusing to endorse Henry VIII's break with Rome ● *42*).

Horniman Museum

MUSEUM OF GARDEN HISTORY. Housed in and around the 14th-century tower of St Mary-at-Lambeth church, the Museum and Garden honor the Tradescant pioneer plantsmen of the 17th century (father and son who lie in the charming churchyard beside Captain Bligh of the Bounty).

DULWICH PICTURE GALLERY ★ Britain's first public art gallery stands in a village setting 4 miles south of Trafalgar Square. Designed by Sir John Soane and opened in 1814, the building contains 12 galleries and a mausoleum (with sarcophagi of donors). A stupendous collection of Old Masters includes works by Rembrandt, Rubens, Van Dyck, Canaletto, Claude, Poussin and Watteau. Here you can see Gainsborough's sublime double portrait of the Linley Sisters, Elizabeth evidently all set to elope to France with the playwright Sheridan.

HORNIMAN MUSEUM The Art Nouveau building surrounded by elegant gardens (with a Victorian conservatory) was given by tea merchant Frederick J. Horniman to Londoners in 1901. A mosaic panel on the façade shows an allegory of life's journey, and the exhibits include natural history specimens, musical instruments and ethnographic art from the donor's travels.

CLINK PRISON MUSEUM
Close to the faked historical horrors of the London Dungeon, this museum in Clink Street recreates the real thing. This jail for prostitutes, drunkards, religious dissenters and debtors – long run by the Bishops of Winchester, whose ruined palace is now reduced to a west gable end with an unusual round window – was burned down by rioters in 1780.

St Thomas's Hospital

CARL ANDRÉ "EQUIVALENT VIII FIREBRICKS" (1966)

This sculpture caused a media sensation along the lines of "Tate Buys Heap of Bricks Shock". André made a series of sculptures by arranging 120 fire bricks in two layers in different combinations – creating visual diversity within the same volume.

GILBERT AND GEORGE "DEATH HOPE LIFE FEAR" (1984) (ABOVE RIGHT)

Gilbert and George met in 1967 while studying sculpture at St Martins School of Art. They turned themselves into "living sculptures" before producing photopieces from their base in Spitalfields.

ANISH KAPOOR "AS IF TO CELEBRATE, I DISCOVERED A MOUNTAIN BLOOMING WITH RED FLOWERS" (1981)

The Indian-born sculptor moved to London in 1971.

Monuments and monoliths, rather than hot air, are now rising in the old Bankside Power Station designed by Sir Giles Gilbert Scott and adapted by Herzog and Meuron. The Tate Gallery of Modern Art, with seven levels and dazzling Thames views, promises to be one of the world's most dynamic display spaces for international art created since 1900. Its heart lies in the old Turbine Hall, which resembles a vast version of an artist's loft.

**PABLO PICASSO
"THE THREE DANCERS" (1925)**
Picasso, the towering genius of 20th-century painting, created this image in 1925 at a crucial moment in his development.

The Three Dancers marks the start of a new period of emotional violence and Expressionist distortion. It seems both a passionate tango and a dance of death.

ERNST KIRCHNER "BATHERS AT MORTIZBURG" 1909/26)
Kirchner is among the leading Expressionist painters on display.

**PAUL NASH "TOTES MEER
(DEAD SEA)" (1940-1)**
Nash was an official war artist in both world conflicts.

Millennium Dome

CRYSTAL PALACE
Moved from Hyde
Park to Sydenham
after the 1851 Great
Exhibition, a huge
glass conservatory
was at the center of
an amusement park
until it burned down
in 1936. Crystal
Palace Park retains
two Victorian
curiosities: a circular
Tea Maze and a
menagerie of 29
painted bronze
prehistoric monsters.

*The Royal
Observatory*

THAMES BARRIER
Londoners lived with
a fear of flooding
until the 1,700-foot-
long Thames Barrier
was completed in
1984. Before perilous
tides 10 gates,
pivoting from their
normal position flat
on the river bed,
swing up to 6 feet
above the level
reached by the surge
of 1953. Best seen by
boat.

*Greenwich
Hospital*

GREENWICH is best reached by the new Jubilee line tube or by
river bus from Tower Bridge, a journey that reveals how many
derelict wharves and warehouses have been converted into
chic Docklands. There is also a foot tunnel under the Thames
from Island Gardens, opened for dock workers in 1902.
Now known for the Zero Meridian – the courtyard of the Old
Royal Observatory marking the spot from which Greenwich
Mean Time is measured – the "green village" existed in 1427
when the Duke of Gloucester, Henry V's brother, built a
palace here and enclosed 200 acres to form Greenwich Park.
Henry VIII, Mary and Elizabeth I were all born here – the

King loving to hunt in the park (the deer were penned rather
recently, after a stag gored an unwary visitor) and to look
down on his fleet and dockyards. The view over London
remains stunning.
In 1615 James I commissioned Inigo Jones to build the
H-shaped Palladian-style QUEEN'S HOUSE for his wife, Anne
of Denmark. And in 1694 William and Mary hired Sir
Christopher Wren and assistants Nicholas Hawksmoor
and John Webb to transform the ruined palace into a
hospital for seamen. Their sublime symmetry became
the Royal Naval College in 1873 and is now occupied
by Greenwich University. The Painted Hall, with walls
and ceilings decorated in baroque style by Sir James
Thornhill, Wren's neoclassical Chapel (remodeled by
"Athenian" Stuart after a fire in 1799) and the grounds
are open to the public.
The NATIONAL MARITIME MUSEUM, long based around
the Queen's House, has been enlarged for the
Millennium. New galleries tell the saga of mankind's

Above left: the entrance hall at Eltham Palace Ranger's House: exterior (top) and a portrait of Lady Diana Cecil by William Larkin, c. 1615 (above)

relationship with the sea. But, with the 200th anniversary of the Battle of Trafalgar looming on October 21, 2005, Horatio Nelson retains pride of place. The most poignant exhibit is the naval hero's bloodstained uniform, the fatal bullet-hole visible in the left shoulder.

MILLENNIUM DOME A controversial big tent costing £758 million; described by its ministerial champion as "the largest concentration of inspiration, education and entertainment under one roof anywhere in the world", and by its opponents as an over-priced theme park. Fourteen interactive exhibition zones include Home Planet, with a simulated ride through space, and the Body Zone, in the shape of an embracing couple. The building was emptied in January 2001 and is still waiting to be put to new use.

Beside Greenwich Park stands **RANGER'S HOUSE**, a handsome 18th-century red-brick villa housing the splendid Suffolk Collection – including nine full-length Stuart portraits displaying Jacobean power, costume and style.

One 18th-century house in Greenwich's lovely Croom's Hill holds the **FAN MUSEUM**. Around 3,000 fans, some dating back to Tudor times, come from all over the world.

ST ALFEGE'S CHURCH Dedicated to an archbishop of Canterbury murdered by Danes in Greenwich in 1012, the church saw Henry VIII's baptism and composer Thomas Tallis's burial (1585). The church was remodeled by Nicholas Hawksmoor in 1712-18 and beautifully restored after bomb damage – a Thornhill altarpiece was repainted by Glyn Jones.

ELTHAM PALACE This moated medieval palace, extended by Edward IV, was a childhood home of Henry VIII. The building crumbled over centuries, and the Great Hall was used as a barn before it was renovated as a grand music room in the 1930s for an adjoining Art Deco fantasy house. The home of socialites Stephen and Virginia Courtauld – now restored and with reproduction furnishings – crosses Hollywood film set with Cunard liner.

The Queen's House

CUTTY SARK (above and left) Dwarfing the nearby Gipsy Moth IV, in which Francis Chichester sailed single-handedly around the world in 1966-7, this 1869 tea clipper is now rigged up as a nautical museum. Exhibits include the Long John Silver Collection of carved figureheads.

157

LONDON CENTRAL MOSQUE
A copper dome gleams among the white and cream classicist sweeps of Nash terraces partly ringing Regent's Park. It is the London Central Mosque, designed by Sir Frederick Gibberd and completed in 1978.

REGENT'S PARK Designed as a garden suburb by John Nash and enclosed in 1812, the park never received most of its intended villas, nor the pleasure palace conceived for the Prince Regent. But delights include the summer Open-Air Theatre, Queen Mary's Rose Gardens, a boating lake teeming with native and ornamental waterfowl and, in the north-west corner, the LONDON ZOO. Opened in 1828, the menagerie ranges from midges to mammals and is both tourist attraction and conservation center. Three features are of architectural interest – Berthold Lubetkin's Penguin Pool of 1936, Sir Hugh Casson's Elephant House and Lord Snowdon's 1964 aviary.

WALLACE COLLECTION ★ This sublime collection was amassed by four generations of the Hertford family and given to the nation in 1897. Sèvres porcelain, clocks, furniture, armor, sculpture and paintings spill through 25 galleries. Old Master highlights include Frans Hals's *The Laughing Cavalier*, Rembrandt's poignant portrait of his son Titus and Nicolas Poussin's *A Dance to the Music of Time*. The range of 18th-century French pictures (by Watteau, Boucher, Fragonard) rivals that in the Louvre.

Frans Hals "The Laughing Cavalier", Wallace Collection, Manchester Square

Wax-modeler **MADAME TUSSAUD** made death masks of famous figures beheaded in the French Revolution, and displayed her macabre work in Baker Street from 1835. The frequently updated cast of characters now spans celebrities in Garden Party and Grand Hall settings, and Chamber of Horrors villains. A Spirit of London finale takes visitors in stylized taxis on a historical journey from the 1666 Great Fire to the Swinging 1960s. Part of the same complex is the LONDON PLANETARIUM, with its spectacular star show and interactive Space Trail exhibition.

LORD'S CRICKET GROUND has been the home of the MCC (Marylebone Cricket Club) and the headquarters of Britain's chief summer sport since 1787. A museum display outlines the history of the site and explains a sport which both baffles and beguiles. Exhibits include an urn containing burned wood, known as the Ashes, which is the object of fierce competition between the English and Australian national teams.

The Duke of Wellington, by Sir Thomas Lawrence, c. 1815, and Apsley House (above and left)

HYDE PARK, the largest of the royal parks, has been a prized public space since James I opened it in the early 17th century. Henry VIII had seized the ancient manor from Westminster Abbey at the Dissolution of the Monasteries in 1536, retaining it as a private hunting ground. The Serpentine, an artificial boating and bathing lake, was created when Caroline, wife of George II, ordered the damming of the River Westbourne in 1730; here Harriet, pregnant and abandoned wife of poet Percy Bysshe Shelley, drowned herself in 1816. Down the centuries the park has hidden highwaymen and duellists and hosted fairs, firework displays, balloon ascents, concerts and the 1851 Great Exhibition. Since 1872 Speakers' Corner has attracted Sunday orators and ranters who compete with hecklers and each other. John Nash's Marble Arch, moved from Buckingham Palace in 1851 because it was too narrow for stately coaches, stands close to the site of Tyburn gallows, where public hangings took place until 1783.

Now a museum on a traffic island, **APSLEY HOUSE** once had a parkland setting and the splendid address of Number One London – when it was a suitably grand residence for the Duke of Wellington. The Iron Duke had the Adam house remodeled by Benjamin and Philip Wyatt in 1829 and filled it with a victor's spoils, including a huge and almost nude Canova statue of the vanquished Napoleon. The Waterloo Gallery holds fine paintings by the likes of Rubens, Goya, Murillo and Velázquez. The gates behind Apsley House (left) were erected to celebrate the long life of Queen Elizabeth the Queen Mother with painted panels by the sculptor David Wynn.

The **REGENT'S CANAL**, linking the Grand Junction Canal at Paddington with the London docks at Limehouse since 1820, is now a leisure amenity. The paved towpath is a popular walkway and boat trips meander between London Zoo, Little Venice and the crafts market at Camden Lock.

SHERLOCK HOLMES
Sir Arthur Conan Doyle's fictional detective lived at 221b Baker Street. Now the Sherlock Holmes Museum honors that imaginary address, though it actually sits between Nos 237 and 239.

The Royal Albert Hall

Lately restored by English Heritage, Sir George Gilbert Scott's **Albert Memorial** now glitters as it did when completed in 1876, 15 years after Queen Victoria was cast into a desolate widowhood. Near the site of the Great Exhibition, which the capable and progressive prince helped to plan, the monumental hero sits beneath a gilded spire and colored marble canopy, amid mosaics, enamels, polished stone, wrought iron and nearly 200 sculpted figures. The Gothic memorial faces the 1871 Francis Fowke building echoing a Roman amphitheater, which was to have been called the Hall of Arts and Science until Victoria demanded another tribute to her lost love. The Royal Albert Hall now hosts concerts (notably the annual "Proms" series), with very occasional sporting contests and conferences.

Kensington Gardens were the grounds of Kensington Palace until turned into a public park in 1841. In contrast to prairie-like Hyde Park, with which they merge to the east, the gardens are packed with charming features. A Sunken Garden was laid out in 1909. A 1912 bronze by Sir George Frampton of Peter Pan, the boy who never grew up and who forever plays his pipe to the animals and fairies in a column below his feet, is among London's best-loved statues. Also popular is the Elfin Oak, a treetrunk carved with woodland figures, by Ivor Innes. Childen pay their respects to both sculptures then sail model

Kensington Palace

Rotten Row
(from the French *route de roi*) links Kensington Palace to St James's. It was the first road in England to have street lighting when William III ordered hundreds of lanterns to be hung from the trees as a defence against highwaymen. Today, riders on this route are more peaceful – ranging from children on ponies to Horse Guards.

The Albert Memorial

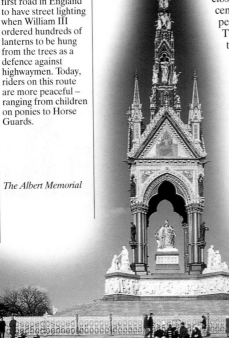

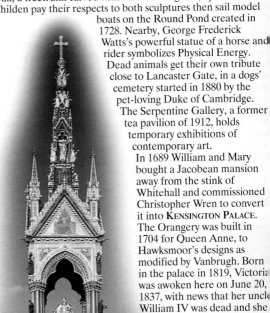

boats on the Round Pond created in 1728. Nearby, George Frederick Watts's powerful statue of a horse and rider symbolizes Physical Energy. Dead animals get their own tribute close to Lancaster Gate, in a dogs' cemetery started in 1880 by the pet-loving Duke of Cambridge.

The Serpentine Gallery, a former tea pavilion of 1912, holds temporary exhibitions of contemporary art.

In 1689 William and Mary bought a Jacobean mansion away from the stink of Whitehall and commissioned Christopher Wren to convert it into **Kensington Palace**. The Orangery was built in 1704 for Queen Anne, to Hawksmoor's designs as modified by Vanbrugh. Born in the palace in 1819, Victoria was awoken here on June 20, 1837, with news that her uncle William IV was dead and she

Kensington Palace Cupola Room (left) and Bedchamber (above)

THE ROYAL GEOGRAPHICAL SOCIETY ● 89
The Society, based in Kensington Gore, has supported intrepid explorers since it was founded in 1830. The Map Room – with more than 900,000 maps and charts, plus atlases, globes and gazetteers – is now open for inspection.

was now queen. Visitors can tour a series of ornate state rooms and a display of court dress since 1760. The rest of the palace is a warren of royal apartments. Diana Princess of Wales lived here from 1981 until her death in 1997 and some of her clothes are on show. The Diana, Princess of Wales children's playground in Kensington Gardens is based on a Peter Pan theme, with pirate ship, seaside path, wigwam village, tree house encampment and "movement and musical" garden, complete with wooden xylophone and water piano. The regal female figure carved in stone outside the palace is the young Victoria by her daughter, Princess Louise.

KENSINGTON HIGH STREET Until the onset of the Victorian era this was a village lane amid market gardens and mansions – most notably the rambling Jacobean HOLLAND HOUSE, largely demolished in the 1950s after war-time bombing. A remnant survives in lovely Holland Park, with a 1630s Orangery now a gallery and the old Garden Ballroom a restaurant.

In this neighborhood of smart shops, villas, mansion flats and terraces stands LINLEY SAMBOURNE HOUSE (18 Stafford Terrace), where a perfectly preserved late Victorian domestic interior recalls a Punch magazine illustrator's work and family life.

Nearby LEIGHTON HOUSE (12 Holland Park Road) is a startling Moorish palace with marble columns, glazed tiles, mosaics and fountain; it was built for the celebrated painter Frederic, Lord Leighton, by George Aitchinson, 1865.

Arab Hall, Leighton House

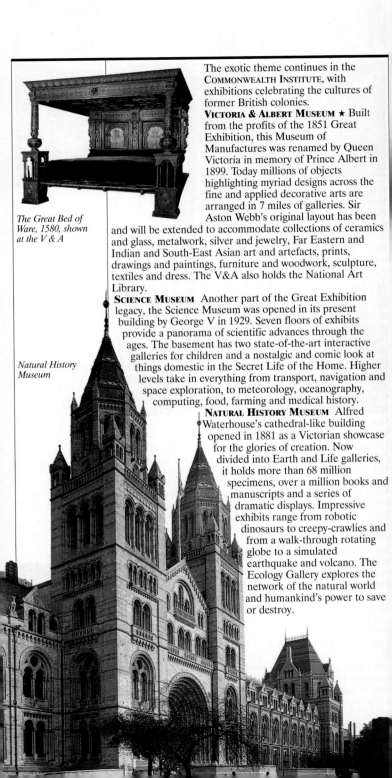

The Great Bed of Ware, 1580, shown at the V & A

Natural History Museum

The exotic theme continues in the COMMONWEALTH INSTITUTE, with exhibitions celebrating the cultures of former British colonies.

VICTORIA & ALBERT MUSEUM ★ Built from the profits of the 1851 Great Exhibition, this Museum of Manufactures was renamed by Queen Victoria in memory of Prince Albert in 1899. Today millions of objects highlighting myriad designs across the fine and applied decorative arts are arranged in 7 miles of galleries. Sir Aston Webb's original layout has been and will be extended to accommodate collections of ceramics and glass, metalwork, silver and jewelry, Far Eastern and Indian and South-East Asian art and artefacts, prints, drawings and paintings, furniture and woodwork, sculpture, textiles and dress. The V&A also holds the National Art Library.

SCIENCE MUSEUM Another part of the Great Exhibition legacy, the Science Museum was opened in its present building by George V in 1929. Seven floors of exhibits provide a panorama of scientific advances through the ages. The basement has two state-of-the-art interactive galleries for children and a nostalgic and comic look at things domestic in the Secret Life of the Home. Higher levels take in everything from transport, navigation and space exploration, to meteorology, oceanography, computing, food, farming and medical history.

NATURAL HISTORY MUSEUM Alfred Waterhouse's cathedral-like building opened in 1881 as a Victorian showcase for the glories of creation. Now divided into Earth and Life galleries, it holds more than 68 million specimens, over a million books and manuscripts and a series of dramatic displays. Impressive exhibits range from robotic dinosaurs to creepy-crawlies and from a walk-through rotating globe to a simulated earthquake and volcano. The Ecology Gallery explores the network of the natural world and humankind's power to save or destroy.

Left: Brompton Oratory
Below: Royal Hospital

BELGRAVIA

In 1849 Henry Charles Harrod, formerly a tea-dealer in Eastcheap, took over a small grocer's shop in Brompton Road and diversified into stationery, perfumes and patent medicines. The increasing splendor of **HARRODS** – with 100 assistants by 1880 – matched that of the surrounding Knightsbridge district. Completed in 1939, the vast department store is ablaze in light bulbs at night, like a seaside pavilion.

The Italianate **BROMPTON ORATORY** is a monument to the late 19th-century English Catholic revival. Established by John Henry Newman – later Cardinal Newman – and designed by the young Herbert Gribble, the church is enriched by earlier treasures. Marble figures of the Apostles were carved by Giuseppe Mazzuoli for Siena Cathedral in the late 17th century. Belgravia was a marshy haunt of robbers until Thomas Cubitt (1777-1855) used earth from the St Katharine's Dock excavation as a foundation for elegant squares and terraces. The best is Belgrave Square, by George Basevi.

CHELSEA Once a riverside village, Chelsea has been fashionable since Henry VIII's day – fine Tudor monuments (including one to Sir Thomas More) line Chelsea Old Church, rebuilt after war-time bombing. A Bohemian reputation established by the Chelsea Set of writers and artists in the 19th century – when Turner, Whistler and Rossetti were drawn to the Thames views from Cheyne Walk – survives in Carlyle's House and the Chelsea Arts Club. A raffish tradition continued in the King's Road from the hippy 1960s to the punk 1980s, but this shopping street is now sedately chic. Antique shops and galleries proliferate, though high rents have forced artists and writers to move out. Sloane Square, laid out in the late 18th century, holds the well-designed 1936 Peter Jones department store by William Crabtree. **CROSBY HALL** (not open) is the remnant of a mansion built for wealthy grocer Sir John Crosby on the Embankment from 1466 and later owned by Sir Thomas More.

ROYAL HOSPITAL
Some 400 veterans live in the noble Royal Hospital which Charles II commissioned from Christopher Wren as a retirement home for old and wounded soldiers. Wearing scarlet coats and black tricorn hats, residents have been known as Chelsea Pensioners since the late 17th century. Wren's chapel remains; his paneled Great Hall is still in use as a dining room.

CHELSEA PHYSIC GARDEN
Founded by the Society of Apothecaries in 1673 for the study of medicinal plants, Chelsea Physic Garden was saved from closure in 1722 by the wealthy physician and collector Sir Hans Sloane. The benefactor's statue survives, as does one of London's most fascinating cultivated spaces – complete with a rock garden dating from 1772.

Above left: Peter Jones, Sloane Square
Below: Crosby Hall

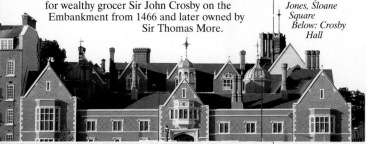

Carlyle's House

Thomas Carlyle, carbon photograph by Elliot and Fry, 1865

CARLYLE'S HOUSE This plain Queen Anne house in Cheyne Row was the home of writer and historian Thomas Carlyle from 1834 until his death. Furniture, portraits and books recall his residency, as does the Victorian walled garden. Dickens, Chopin, Tennyson and George Eliot and many other luminaries called here.

The history of British land forces over almost six centuries since Agincourt is charted in the NATIONAL ARMY MUSEUM, with relics, paintings, dioramas and archive film clips illustrating major battles.

NOTTING HILL

NOTTING HILL was best known as the scene of Europe's biggest street carnival, with costumed parades flooding the streets and gyrating to a Caribbean beat every August holiday weekend since 1966.

"Chelsea Interior" by Robert Tait, 1858, at Carlyle's House

HAMPSTEAD
Writers and artists have long lived hereabouts. A blue plaque on the wall of 16 Phillimore Place recalls Kenneth Grahame, author of the children's classic *The Wind in the Willows*, who resided at this address from 1901 until 1908 dreaming of wild woods and riverbanks.

Then the area gave its name to a film starring Hugh Grant and Julia Roberts and became one of the trendiest and costliest parts of London, rife with specialist small shops and cafés. But the locality's greatest abiding glory is Portobello Road, where a market has been held since 1837. Antiques, bric-a-brac and junk are traded from 2,000 stalls each Saturday (a must for collectors and souvenir hunters who might also venture to Camden Passage on Wednesday, Bermondsey on Friday and Greenwich on Sunday – but only the earliest birds catch the bargains).

HAMPSTEAD AND HIGHGATE

HAMPSTEAD is one of London's best villages. Dotted with blue plaques recording once-resident writers and artists, its leafy streets of Georgian houses ascend to the 800 acres of Hampstead Heath, Parliament Hill Fields and Kenwood. Woods, meadows and bathing ponds (male, female and mixed) abound with wildlife and strolling celebrities.

Fenton House

Three Meissen porcelain figures, c. 1740, Fenton House

FENTON HOUSE (Windmill Hill) is a splendid house of 1693 named after Baltic merchant Philip Fenton, who bought it a century later. Outside is a walled garden with roses, vegetables and orchard, but the main delights lie inside: 18th-century furniture and porcelain, a dozen William Nicholson paintings and, best of all, the Benton Fletcher Collection of Keyboard Instruments. The Queen has lent a 1612 harpsichord probably used by Handel.

KEATS'S HOUSE originated as a pair of attached cottages built from 1815 in a shared garden, but combined in Victorian times and now a museum. John Keats (1795-1821) lodged in one

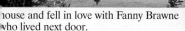

house and fell in love with Fanny Brawne who lived next door.

2 WILLOW ROAD was the former home of Modernist architect and high-rise enthusiast Ernö Goldfinger – the central house in a terrace of three he designed and built in 1939. Contents include furniture also by Goldfinger, and art works by Henry Moore and Max Ernst.

BURGH HOUSE Dubbed "the finest Queen Anne house in London," Burgh House was built in 1703 in New End Square and became the home of spa physician Dr William Gibbons. It now hosts the Hampstead Museum and music-room recitals and lectures. There is a café in the basement.

FREUD MUSEUM Old and ill, Sigmund Freud fled Nazi Austria for London in 1938. He moved his furniture (including the celebrated desk and couch), books and antiquities, and recreated Vienna in Hampstead at 20 Maresfield Road. He died the following year. His house, bequeathed by his analyst daughter Anna, is now a museum with a research archive, educational resource and cultural center.

HISTORIC PUBS

On top of the heath is Jack Straw's Castle, a historic wooden pub visited by Charles Dickens. The novelist also frequented the Spaniard's Inn, the Spanish ambassador's residence during the reign of James II. In 1780 the landlord got the Gordon Rioters drunk to stop them burning Kenwood House.

Keats's House and a portrait of the poet by Joseph Severn, c.1818

KEATS'S HOUSE ★

Much of the poet's best work was written here – including "Ode to a Nightingale", penned under a plum tree. Keats died in Rome before his planned marriage. A heart-rending display includes the poet's love letters and the engagement ring Fanny wore until her death. The house at 10 Keats Grove is now a museum dedicated to the poet and open to the public.

2 Willow Road

Robert Adam

Jan Vermeer's "The Guitar Player" (detail)

Above center: The Library, Kenwood Far right: a Robert Adam design for Kenwood

Kenwood House

KENWOOD HOUSE ★ Its lake-centered parkland merging into Hampstead Heath, Kenwood encloses outstanding neoclassical interiors, containing an even more impressive art collection – with works by Vermeer, Turner, Gainsborough and Reynolds, and the Rembrandt self-portrait lately voted the most prized painting in Britain. An opulent Robert Adam library, modeled with Corinthian columns and a curved ceiling dating to 1764, remains intact. The house of the earls of Mansfield was bought by brewing magnate the 1st Earl of Iveagh, who bequeathed both the house and his picture collection to London in 1927. There is a lovely café in the old stables and a walled garden, and summer concerts are held beside the lake.

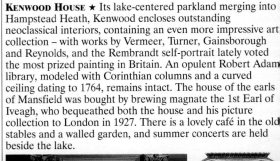

HIGHGATE is a mainly Georgian village with a few modernist flourishes, notably the 1930s apartment blocks Highpoint 1 and 2 by Lubetkin and Tecton, which Le Corbusier hailed as "a vertical garden city". On Highgate Hill, Lauderdale House (Tudor remains behind a late Georgian façade) is said to have been the residence of Nell Gwynne and her baby son by Charles II; now it is a museum and cultural center. Nearby **CROMWELL HOUSE** (not open) is a rare, Inigo Jones-influenced survival from 1637.

HIGHGATE CEMETERY Bisected by Swains Lane, the overgrown and wildly romantic burial ground was designed from 1838 by Stephen Geary and now holds almost 170,000 bodies in 51,000 graves. The Victorian fascination with death is reflected in startling architecture, ranging from Gothic follies to an Egyptian Avenue and the Cedar of Lebanon Catacombs. No wonder Hammer House of Horror filmed here. Eminent Victorian residents include Christina and Dante Gabriel Rossetti, Michael Faraday, George Eliot and John Galsworthy. Atheists make pilgrimages to the monumental tomb of Karl Marx; Herbert Spencer lies appropriately opposite.

TURN AGAIN WHITTINGTON
At the bottom of Highgate Hill the statue of a black cat marks the legendary spot where a penniless apprentice with his pet heard the bells of St Mary-le-Bow urging him to return and become Lord Mayor of London. Richard Whittington, thrice mayor, bequeathed a fortune in 1423 to endow the Guildhall and inspired a perennial pantomime.

Strand on the Green

WEST LONDON

PITSHANGER MANOR MUSEUM (Mattock Lane) Magpie architect Sir John Soane's country villa from 1800, long ago engulfed in the suburb of Ealing, has been restored and partly filled with bizarre Martinware pottery.

GUNNERSBURY PARK The neoclassical mansion, altered for the Rothschilds by Sidney Smirke in the 1830s, is now a local museum. The bath-house of George II's daughter Princess Amelia, who used the then-Palladian house as a summer residence 1763-86, survives in the grounds.
Between the Thames and the A4, a stretch of fine houses runs from Upper Mall to Chiswick Mall via Hammersmith Terrace. Façades date from the 17th century; interiors may be older. Artists, writers and actors have lived here. Built around 1780, **KELMSCOTT HOUSE** helped Sir Francis Ronalds to invent the electric telegraph in 1816 (he planted 8 miles of cable in the garden). William Morris based his printing and design works here after 1877 and died here in 1896. The house retains Morris wallpaper and the fireplace designed by Philip Webb as a wedding gift.

STRAND ON THE GREEN, Chiswick, is a riverside pocket of handsome 18th-century houses. Painter John Zoffany resided at No 65 between 1790 and 1810. Novelist Nancy Mitford lived at Rose Cottage and poet Dylan Thomas at Ship House Cottage.

Portrait of Henrietta of Lorraine by Sir Anthony Van Dyck, Kenwood House

Gravestone at Highgate cemetery (left)

167

*Ham House,
"The Duke and
Duchess of
Lauderdale" by
Sir Peter Lely*

HOGARTH'S HOUSE In 1749 William Hogarth chose this "little country box by the Thames" for its tranquil location; now traffic flows alongside. The artist spent much time here, leaving the night before he died for his Leicester Square town house. A museum since 1909, the restored retreat celebrates Hogarth's life and work. A mulberry tree in the garden dates from his day.

CHISWICK HOUSE is a Palladian villa built by the 3rd Earl of Burlington in the 1720s and based on Palladio's Villa Capra near Vicenza; its gardens are scattered with statues and follies. Sumptuous William Kent interiors include the gilded Blue Velvet Room and the recently redecorated octagonal Domed Saloon, which housed the Earl's art collection. Handel, Pope and Swift were early guests in a building designed for entertaining.

Gilbert and Partners
with green windows
and red-and-blue
striped faience as a
"palace of work, now
a supermarket"; and
the Coty Factory on
the Great West Road,
complete with
majestic doorway.

OSTERLEY PARK ★ The house is the adaptation of a four-turreted house completed for Sir Thomas Gresham, founder of the Royal Exchange, in 1575 – the stable block remains unchanged. In the 1760s, working for the Child family,

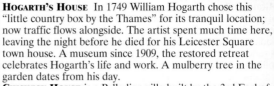

Robert Adam created a wonderful colonnaded screen, filled the house with decorations and furniture of his own design, and erected a greenhouse. The garden and Doric Temple of Pan are by Sir William Chambers.

*Top: Hoover Building
Above right: Osterley
Park
Below: fountain at
Syon House
Bottom: Strawberry Hill
Below right: Chiswick
House*

SYON HOUSE ★ The only large mansion in London still in its hereditary ownership, Syon has been home to the earls and dukes of Northumberland for 400 years. A 15th-century convent was remodeled by Robert Adam ● 80 from 1761 and his lavish neoclassical interiors survive. Amid many fine paintings, some walls have Spitalfields silk hangings. Gardens laid out by Capability Brown now include the London Butterfly House, an aquarium and 400 varieties of rose.

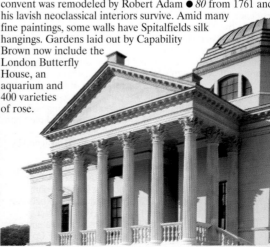

Marble Hill House exterior (far left) and its Great Room (left), richly gilded, with inset paintings by Panini.

Ham House interiors (left)

ORLEANS HOUSE Only the Octagon, with its fine interior plasterwork, survives of this 1720 James Gibbs building. It was named after the Duke of Orleans, who lived in exile here 1800-17, before becoming King Louis-Philippe of France in 1830. Exhibitions are held in the adjacent gallery.

MARBLE HILL HOUSE This ravishing Thames-side Palladian villa, set in a 66-acre park, was built in the 1720s for Henrietta Howard, Countess of Suffolk and mistress of George II. The house also contains important early Georgian furniture and pictures, and the Lazenby Bequest of Chinoiserie.

STRAWBERRY HILL As an antidote to prevailing Palladian fashion, Horace Walpole's eclectic miniature castle of 1749-76 was the most influential Gothic Revival building in England. A fireplace is modeled on Edward the Confessor's tomb; the staircase balustrade is copied from Rouen Cathedral. The house ● *80* is now a college (open by arrangement).

HAM HOUSE ★ A fine Stuart house of 1610, enlarged in the 1670s when it was home to the Duke and Duchess of Lauderdale and at the center of Restoration court life and intrigue. Ham has outstanding interior decorations and original furnishings. Formal 17th-century gardens, admired by diarist John Evelyn, were recently restored. A foot-passenger ferry runs on some days in summer to Marble Hill House.

KEW BRIDGE STEAM MUSEUM A 19th-century pumping station, which used to supply Londoners with water, is now a museum of steam power. The earliest of five giant engines dates from 1820 and once pumped out Cornish tin and copper mines.

ROYAL BOTANIC GARDENS, KEW ★ Princess Augusta, George II's mother, established a small garden here in 1759, with Sir William Chambers adding the Orangery and Chinese pagoda. Subsequently combining his Richmond and Kew estates, George III employed Capability Brown and encouraged naturalist Sir Joseph Banks to oversee a botanic garden to which specimens could be sent from all over the globe. He and his wife summered at Kew, latterly at Kew Palace – dubbed the "Dutch House" because of its 1631 gabling. Queen Charlotte's 1771 Cottage echoes Marie Antoinette's Petit Trianon at Versailles. Acquired by the state in 1840, the Royal Botanic Gardens grew apace under first director Sir William Hooker and

Right: Richmond Park
Far right: White Lodge,
Richmond Park
Below: Royal Botanic
Gardens, Kew

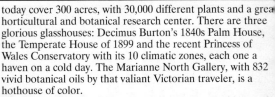

today cover 300 acres, with 30,000 different plants and a great horticultural and botanical research center. There are three glorious glasshouses: Decimus Burton's 1840s Palm House, the Temperate House of 1899 and the recent Princess of Wales Conservatory with its 10 climatic zones, each one a haven on a cold day. The Marianne North Gallery, with 832 vivid botanical oils by that valiant Victorian traveler, is a hothouse of color.

RICHMOND Lovely Richmond was the summer residence of the Plantagenet kings. Elizabeth I and her grandfather Henry VII died here: his coat of arms adorns the gatehouse of the otherwise vanished palace, just off what some think England's finest green. There are many historic houses and elegant shops. Riverside walks take in James Paine's five-arched Richmond Bridge of 1777. The view from the top of Richmond Hill, of the Thames meandering in the valley below, has inspired artists such as Richard Wilson, Turner and Constable. Sir Joshua Reynolds (1723-92) lived here, at Wick House, for his last two decades.

A royal hunting ground enclosed by Charles I, 2,470-acre **RICHMOND PARK** is the largest in Greater London. There are lakes, deer-grazed grassland and trees that include several splendid medieval oaks. Capability Brown designed Richmond Gate, in the northwest corner, in 1798. At Henry

Hampton Court
(above and right)

HAMPTON COURT
Decorators ranged from carvers Caius Cibber and Grinling Gibbons, to painters Sir James Thornhill, Louis Laguerre and Antonio Verrio, and ironsmith Jean Tijou. Treasures include Nicholas Oursian's Astronomical Clock and Andrea Mantegna's nine-canvas *Triumph of Julius Caesar* painted in 1492 and bought by Charles I.

VIII's Mound, with views from Windsor Castle to the Tower of London, the king awaited the signal that Anne Boleyn had been executed. Palladian White Lodge, built for George II, and birthplace of the future Edward VIII (later Duke of Windsor) in 1894, is home to the Royal Ballet School.

HAMPTON COURT ★ is essentially an English Renaissance palace, constructed around two courtyards; but, much amended and extended in the 16th and 17th centuries, it is in fact three palaces in one. Built to reflect Cardinal Wolsey's mighty status, the red-brick riverside residence so impressed Henry VIII that he confiscated it. The King rebuilt the hall, finished the chapel and added a kitchen court and royal apartments now lost save for the Great Watching Chamber. Wren's baroque overhaul for William and Mary, begun in 1689, brought the East Front, Versailles-influenced Fountain Court, Cartoon Gallery and Queen's Wing. Hampton Court, open since 1838 (Queen Victoria chose to live at Windsor), is also noted for its gardens – with canal, lime avenues and maze. The **GREAT VINE** grew from a root planted in 1768.

SOUTH EAST
Ian Sutton and David W. Lloyd

▲ SEVENOAKS TO HASTINGS

1. ROMSEY 2. ISLE OF WIGHT 3. BEAULIEU 4. SOUTHAMPTON 5. WINCHESTER 6. PORTSMOUTH 7. CHICHESTER 8. ARUNDEL 9. SHOREHAM-BY-SEA 10. BRIGHTON 11. LEWES 12. SEVENOAKS 13. TONBRIDGE 14. EASTBOURNE 15. MAIDST

CHARLES DARWIN
(below) lived at Down
House (right) in
Downe for most of his
life and died there in
1882. Knowing that
his theory of natural
selection would
scandalize
conventional
Christians, he waited
many years before
publishing.

*Below right: Lady
Frances Cranfield, of
Knole, by Van Dyck. A
rich heiress, she
married Richard
Sackville, 5th Earl of
Dorset.*

*Few of the excavated
Roman villas in
England give such a
vivid idea of the
sophistication and
luxury of contemporary
life as that of
Lullingstone. The
mosaic shows the
figure of Summer.*

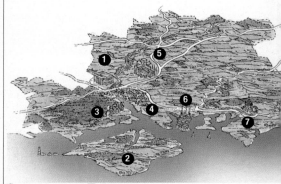

SEVENOAKS TO TONBRIDGE

The road from London to Sevenoaks passes close to Down
House, the home of Charles Darwin, where he wrote *The Origin
of Species* and *The Descent of Man*, works that put forward the
theory of natural selection – one of the cornerstones of
modern thought. The house, restored by English Heritage, is
now maintained as it was in his time, vividly conveying the
great scientist's personality.

EYNSFORD Further east, near the pretty village of Eynsford,
which still has a ford across the river for cars and horses, is
Lullingstone Castle, Tudor in origin but largely rebuilt under
Queen Anne, with its charming little parish church in the
grounds. The Roman villa of Lullingstone, excavated in the
1950s, dates from the 1st to the 4th centuries AD and is chiefly
notable for its mosaic floor depicting the Rape of Europa. It
also includes a Christian chapel, virtually the only evidence for
Christianity in Britain during the Roman
period.

KNOLE ★ Outside Sevenoaks, in a
spacious park, stands Knole, seat of the
Sackville family. Knole is one of the most
atmospheric late medieval houses in
England, and also one of the largest,
with 365 rooms, 4 long galleries and 7
courtyards. Entry is via a gatehouse into
the Green Court, added in the 16th
century to an earlier house begun in

172

THE BALLROOM AT KNOLE When the Sackvilles acquired Knole in 1563, they initiated a program of new work, of which the most outstanding was the ballroom (below left). Paneling and ceiling are particularly lavish, but the most sumptuous feature is the chimneypiece in a variety of marbles; and in the upper part carved flowers and musical instruments.

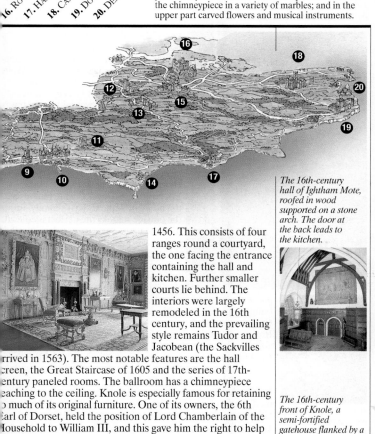

The 16th-century hall of Ightham Mote, roofed in wood supported on a stone arch. The door at the back leads to the kitchen.

1456. This consists of four ranges round a courtyard, the one facing the entrance containing the hall and kitchen. Further smaller courts lie behind. The interiors were largely remodeled in the 16th century, and the prevailing style remains Tudor and Jacobean (the Sackvilles arrived in 1563). The most notable features are the hall screen, the Great Staircase of 1605 and the series of 17th-century paneled rooms. The ballroom has a chimneypiece reaching to the ceiling. Knole is especially famous for retaining so much of its original furniture. One of its owners, the 6th Earl of Dorset, held the position of Lord Chamberlain of the Household to William III, and this gave him the right to help himself to any of the royal furnishings that were deemed to be in need of replacement. Thus he brought to Knole a whole set of chairs of state covered in purple velvet and walnut chairs upholstered in blue silk damask made for Charles II (marked "WP" for Whitehall Palace). There are also some splendid four-poster beds with their original hangings, superb tapestries and some important pictures. Knole "slept" during the late 17th and 18th centuries, leaving its contents miraculously undisturbed.

The 16th-century front of Knole, a semi-fortified gatehouse flanked by a gabled range.

IGHTHAM MOTE Nearby, to the east, is another medieval house, more modest than Knole but older and exceptionally picturesque: Ightham Mote. It consists of four wings round a courtyard, surrounded by a moat. The oldest part is a 13th-century crypt; the hall dates from the 14th century.

SQUERRIES COURT AND QUEBEC HOUSE West of Sevenoaks, near Westerham, are two

Below: Squerryes Court, Westerham, a typical gentleman's seat of the 18th century

fine 17th- and 18th-century gentry houses, Squerries Court and Quebec House, both of brick with stone dressings. The latter was the home of General Wolfe, conqueror of Quebec, whose statue stands on Westerham Green. Emmet's Garden, at Ide Hill, was laid out in the 19th century and contains many rare exotic trees and shrubs. Finally, 2 miles to the south, is Winston Churchill's house, Chartwell, mostly rebuilt in 1923. Here Churchill lived, wrote and painted for more than 40 years.

HEVER CASTLE Further south, near Edenbridge, is Hever Castle, famous as the home of Anne Boleyn's family. From the outside it looks the perfect medieval fortified manor – ivy-covered walls, moat and drawbridge. The interior is a disappointment. By the 19th century it was a ruin and was bought in 1903 by Lord Astor, who restored it with some fine Edwardian woodwork. For extra guest accommodation, rather than compromise the old building, he built a convincing "Tudor" village next door.

CHIDDINGSTONE CASTLE, a mile to the east, is an exercise in Romantic "Gothick", a 17th-century house with battlements added between 1808 and 1830. The next village, Chiddingstone Causeway, has a notable church by J.F. Bentley (the architect of the Catholic Westminster Cathedral), with attractive Arts and Crafts fittings.

PENSHURST PLACE Also close by is the second of the great medieval houses of Kent, Penshurst Place. The oldest part (1341) was built by Sir John de Pulteney, Lord Mayor of London. Of this house the great hall survives virtually intact with its timber roof and paneled screen, and the central hearth and (restored) louvre. By this date it had become customary for the lord to take his meals not with the retainers in the great hall but in a private room (the "solar") reached by a staircase at one end. The one at Penshurst is among the earliest of such rooms. The rest of Penshurst Place, ranges of buildings forming three courtyards, dates from the 15th and 16th centuries. The Sidney family acquired it in 1552, and it was the home of the poet Sir Philip Sidney. The long gallery was built by his brother, Sir Robert, *c.* 1600. During the 19th century, the gardens were restored to their 17th-century appearance and the village of Penshurst was rebuilt in a Tudor style that can easily deceive the visitor.

Winston Churchill as a young man by Sir John Lavery, displayed at Chartwell

The south front of Penshurst Place: the oldest part (1338-49) is in the center – the great hall, octagonal stair turret and "solar" to the left

ONBRIDGE, a busy town on the Medway, is dominated by its Norman castle, with a shell keep standing on a mound and well-preserved gatehouse of about 1300. The Victorian school also repays a visit, with its fine chapel of 1900.

TONBRIDGE TO RYE

On the way to Tunbridge Wells it is worth stopping at the church of Speldhurst to see the stained glass by Morris and Co. There are ten windows by the firm, made in the 1870s and designed by Morris and Burne-Jones.

GROOMBRIDGE PLACE, south of Speldhurst, is a well-preserved brick house of about 1600, surrounded by a moat, with classical features such as Ionic columns and gate-piers surmounted by pineapples. Inside are some Wren-period plaster ceilings.

TUNBRIDGE WELLS is an attractive town developed as a spa in the late 17th century. Of that date is the church of King Charles the Martyr (a rare dedication) which has splendid plasterwork by craftsmen who probably worked on Wren's churches in the City of London ▲ *146*. Of the 18th and 19th centuries are the Pantiles (rows of shops behind raised arcades next to the medicinal spring) and Calverley Park, a semi-circle of nineteen Regency villas by Decimus Burton.

OLD BAYHAM ABBEY Continuing east one soon reaches Old Bayham Abbey, founded about 1210 by the Premonstratensian Order. There are substantial remains of the church and monastic buildings – cloister, chapterhouse and undercroft of the dormitory. The grounds were landscaped in the picturesque style by Humphry Repton to harmonize with a later (but now Victorian) house. A similar combination of medieval ruin and Victorian mansion is to be seen at nearby Scotney Castle. Here the remains of the old castle, lying low beside a lake, were made into a romantic landscape in the 1870s to accompany a neo-Gothic house by Anthony Salvin.

Above left: Chartwell, the home of Winston Churchill from 1922 to 1964
Above center: Chiddingstone Castle
Above right: Bayham Abbey

OLD BAYHAM ABBEY (left): Bayham Abbey is just across the border in Sussex. Like Scotney, it was preserved as a romantic ruin. Originally it belonged to the Premonstratensian Order and was founded in 1210. The monastic layout is still partly preserved, the south wall of the church (left) standing to a considerable height.

Scotney Castle, the ruins of a 14th-century fortified house modernized in the 17th century. It is now simply a feature in a picturesque park.

175

Sissinghurst

FINCHCOCKS A mile to the east is Finchcocks, a fine baroque house of 1725 in the style of Vanbrugh, chiefly notable today for its collection of over ninety historic keyboard instruments, which are often played when the house is open.

SISSINGHURST ★ A little further east is Sissinghurst, the remains of a big Elizabethan courtyard house which Harold Nicolson and Vita Sackville-West transformed with a garden in the 1930s. Divided into sections by hedges and walls, this garden forms a combination of sophisticated planting and charming informality that has no equal in the country.

BODIAM CASTLE Due south of Sissinghurst is Bodiam Castle, the perfect picture of the medieval castle, with towers and battlements reflected in the dark waters of a moat. It was built in 1383 as a secure place against French invaders. Inside the walls not much remains, but one can trace the hall, living quarters, kitchen and chapel.

BURWASH A short diversion to the west takes us to Burwash, and Rudyard Kipling's home, Bateman's, part of a house of 1634 built by a Sussex ironmaster. Most of the rooms, including his book-lined study, are much as Kipling left them, and his Rolls Royce is also on display. At Northiam to the east stands Great Dixter, a splendid example of a 15th-century half-timbered cottage. It owes much to its restoration in 1910 by Sir Edwin Lutyens, who used his own imagination when evidence was lacking. By Lutyens too is the garden, which displays an ingenious use of architectural features.

RYE We reach the coast at Rye, once a busy port, now abandoned by the sea: a small picturesque hill town, its cobbled streets sloping down from the medieval church. Henry James chose to live here (Lamb House). On the beach outside the town stands Camber Castle, built under Henry VIII

Rudyard Kipling, poet and novelist, lived at Batemans (above left), a sturdy 17th-century house in the village of Burwash.

on the model of Walmer and Deal castles, with six lobes surrounding a circular tower. Close by is Winchelsea, a planned town founded by Edward I in 1283 on a grid pattern. The plan can still be recognized. The very ambitious church, of which only the chancel remains, contains five amazing 14th-century tombs with ogee canopies.

ROMNEY MARSH East of Rye is the flat landscape of Romney Marsh, to some strangely attractive, to others strangely sinister. Brookland church is most remarkable for its free-standing, octagonal wooden belfry with three diminishing stages of roof; the interior, with four vast vertical posts, is worth inspecting. Inside the church are 13th-century wall paintings and a Norman lead font with reliefs illustrating the labors of the months and the signs of the zodiac. Further east, the church of St Mary-in-the-Marsh has an unrestored interior of around 1300. Old and New Romney both have interesting churches, the first with 18th-century furnishings, the second with a sturdy Norman arcade and three spectacular east windows of reticulated tracery. Nearby LYDD is equally grand in scale, reflecting the importance of the area when Romney was one of the Cinque Ports (along with Hastings, Hythe, Dover and Sandwich).

DUNGENESS At the tip of the peninsula is Dungeness, with its stylish new lighthouse of 1959 and its nuclear power station of 1960. More appealing to the visitor, however, is the garden that the writer and film-maker Derek Jarman created round his tiny cottage on the bleak, stony east-facing beach. Here, where it seemed that nothing would grow, he lovingly assembled flowering plants and bushes that could live among pebbles and sand, interspersed with pieces of old timber and iron rescued from the sea – a unique and poetic landscape.

THE RED HOUSE William Morris lived at the Red House (above) for only five years. To him it was "in the style of the 13th century". To us, it seems eminently of its time, 1860.

BEXLEYHEATH TO RAMSGATE VIA ROCHESTER

Hall Place, parts of which go back to the 16th century

BEXLEYHEATH, now practically part of London, was in William Morris's time the beginning of rural Kent. Here in 1859 he decided to build a home for himself and his bride, designed by his friend Philip Webb. It was to be a milestone in domestic architecture, a rejection of the prevailing classical style and, for Morris, "very medieval in spirit". In the event, the RED HOUSE is a free adaptation of many periods, and full of individual details expressive of the characters of both men.

Close to it, at Bexley, is HALL PLACE, a 16th-century house of which the hall and one range survive, with a 17th-century addition at the back. It has been much altered over the years and is now run as a museum by the local council. In front are some splendid 18th-century iron gates. Off the road to the south is Sutton-

Upnor Castle

Upnor Castle, on the north bank of the Medway, was built by Elizabeth I between 1559 and 1567 to defend the dockyard at Chatham. Unlike Henry VIII's forts at Deal and Walmer ▲ *185* and the new Italian type of fortification introduced at Berwick ▲ *416*, it consists of a two-storeyed block in the center flanked by towers at either side.

ROCHESTER CASTLE
Rochester Castle is a typical Norman keep with massive walls and four corner towers. There are remains of an inner and outer bailey. The castle has played its part in English history – occupied by the barons fighting King John, captured by him in 1215 and by the French in 1216, but holding out against Simon de Montfort in 1264.

at-Hone, which has a rare survival, a "commandery" of the Knights Hospitallers of St John of Jerusalem, going back to the 13th century. It was adapted as a Georgian house in the 18th century. Back north, on the other side of the main road to Rochester, is the particularly fine 13th-century church of Stone, so sophisticated in its details (rib-vaulted chancel, arcading with lush foliage carving) that it seems likely to have been built by the same masons as Westminster Abbey.

COBHAM South of the road again is Cobham, a small village with three buildings of outstanding interest: the church (which contains the best collection of monumental brasses in England), the college (a 14th-century foundation, originally two courtyards surrounded by brick ranges) and Cobham Hall. This is one of England's major Elizabethan houses – very large, very ornate and at the time very modern. It consists of three wings, the middle one later than the other two (1660s). It is now a school, stripped of its contents, but many original features remain, notably a series of extravagant chimneypieces. In the grounds is a mausoleum by James Wyatt (1783), a severely classical design of Doric columns surmounted by a pyramid. It has had to be walled up because of vandalism.

GADSHILL Before Rochester, literary pilgrims will want to make a small detour to see Gadshill, the last home of Charles Dickens, in which he died. Dickens lived as a boy in Rochester (*Great Expectations* is set there and in the marshes nearby), and buying this house was the fulfilment of a childhood dream. It is now a school, and the only room with any atmosphere is Dickens' study, the door of which is lined with fake book-spines with titles such as *The Life of the Cat, in Nine Volumes*, among others in a similar vein.

ROCHESTER The historic center of Rochester is still unspoilt for the most part, although isolated by the main road and railway. The high street is lined with pleasant Georgian and Regency shops (many cashing in on the Dickens connections), a 17th-century town hall and Eastgate House, of the 16th century, now a Dickens museum; at the west end is a second-hand bookshop that claims to be the largest in England.

The CASTLE and CATHEDRAL bear witness to Rochester's importance in Norman times. The castle keep, guarding the crossing of the Medway, is the tallest in England. Begun in 1123, it is square, with corner turrets. Inside it is a ruin, but one can still identify the great hall, occupying the third and fourth storeys and divided by an arcade.

The CATHEDRAL was begun even earlier, but of the original building only the stump of a tower (Gandulf's Tower, next to the north transept)

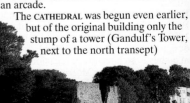

survives. The rest belongs to
the 12th and early 13th
centuries. The exterior has
been so restored that much
of what one sees is Victorian;
an exception is the main west
door, a rare example of
Norman sculpture (but
compare Barfreston and
Patrixbourne, ▲ 184). The
tympanum shows Christ in
Majesty and the door is
flanked by column-figures of
Solomon and the Queen of
Sheba. The interior has its
nave arcade of round arches,
its choir (unusually between
solid walls, not arcades) and
its Early English east end,
the most architecturally
sophisticated part of the
building, with sexpartite vaults and graceful Purbeck marble
shafts.

UPNOR CASTLE At the mouth of the Medway stands the
Elizabethan Upnor Castle, built to guard the new Dockyard
at Chatham. The Dockyard itself, on the east bank, was
founded by Henry VIII but most of the existing buildings
date from the 18th century. Until recently firmly closed to the
public, these are now accessible. The main gate, of 1720, has
a huge royal coat-of-arms over the entrance. Inside, the most
interesting buildings are the storehouse (1780s and 1790s)
with original tackle; the Ropery (1785), nearly a third of a
mile long (last used in the Falklands War); the Admiral's
House and Officer's Terrace, and the so-called slips,
Victorian boat-sheds roofed with iron.

NORTH KENT COAST The north Kent coast beyond Chatham
has a distinctive character. On the Isle of Sheppey, a flat
isolated area, rarely visited, is the remarkable church of
Minster, a Saxon foundation which partly survives. Further
east is Faversham, a small town of great atmosphere, well
worth exploring. The streets are lined with 16th, 17th and
18th-century houses, including that of Arden of Faversham,
murdered by his wife's lover and the subject of a famous
Elizabethan play. Close to Faversham to the north is the very
attractive, unspoiled church of Graveney, mostly of the 14th
century: it contains notable brasses (1381 and 1436). South of
Faversham is Belmont, a charming late 18th-century villa by
Samuel Wyatt, complete with original decor and furniture.
Whitstable, Herne Bay, Westgate-on-Sea, Margate and
Broadstairs have lost most of the charm that made them
popular holiday resorts in the first half of the 20th century.

QUEX PARK, near Birchington, is a curiosity. It was the home
of Major Percy Powell-Cotton, who between 1887 and 1938
spent much of his time in Africa killing wild animals. The
whole house is full of these animals, stuffed, and arranged in
vivid dioramas imitating the jungle. One show-case exhibits
the bloodstained shirt in which the Major was mauled by a
lion, as well as the lion itself. In the garden stands an
extraordinary bell-tower, built in 1819 to commemorate the

CHATHAM DOCKYARD,
(above) founded in
the 16th century, was
developed as one of
the main bases of the
English fleet in the
1720s, and continued
to be enlarged into
the early 20th century.
It closed in 1984 but
the buildings remain
remarkably intact.
They include an
entrance gate, a
chapel, sheds for
repairing and fitting
ships, offices and
residential quarters.
The Admiral's offices,
designed by Edward
Holl, were completed
in 1809, but the
doorway (above) is
flanked by two
fantastic sculptures
like figure-heads
ending in fishtails,
which came from an
18th-century yacht.

*A Swiss chalet from
Gadshill, now in
Rochester Museum*

GODINTON HOUSE The east front of Godinton House (1628), with its series of shaped gables. The brick exterior conceals an earlier half-timbered house built round a small internal courtyard.

Augustus Welby Northmore Pugin, pioneer of the Gothic Revival ● 84, settled at Ramsgate and built his own church and house, now taken over by the Landmark Trust.

KIT'S COTY HOUSE The megalithic burial chamber known as Kit's Coty was originally covered with an earth mound.

ALLINGTON CASTLE Dating originally from 1281, it was remodeled in the early 16th century, when it was the home of the poet Sir Thomas Wyatt. In 1929 it had become a ruin and was carefully restored by the architect D.W. Caröe.

Battle of Waterloo. It is crowned by an openwork spire made of cast iron, a bit like a miniature Eiffel Tower.

RAMSGATE Finally, at the end of the so-called Isle of Thanet (not an island) is Ramsgate. Here the architect A.W.N. Pugin built himself a house, the Grange, and next to it his own Catholic church, St Augustine's, where he is buried. It is small but spatially satisfying, serious and personal.

MAIDSTONE TO ASHFORD

MAIDSTONE, the county town of Kent, has suffered from over-development, but the group of buildings by the river is still worth inspecting – the large parish church, the college and the archbishop's palace and stables (which contain a museum of carriages). Maidstone Museum and Art Gallery, in the 16th-century Chillington Manor, has Dutch and Italian paintings and items of local history. The area to the north-west of Maidstone has several places of interest. **TROTTISCLIFFE CHURCH** contains an amazing pulpit with the sounding board resting on a palm-tree. It was made for Westminster Abbey in 1775 by Henry Keene and moved here in 1826. Near West Malling is Great Comp Garden, seven acres of trees, shrubs and woodland walks laid out round a 17th-century manor house. Nearer Maidstone, **AYLESFORD** was a house of Carmelite friars, which fell into ruin after the Dissolution and was turned into a large house, severely damaged by fire in 1930. In 1949 the Carmelites returned. A new church was built and became a center of modern Catholicism: it is interesting on that account, whatever one's religious affiliation. A mile or so away is **KIT'S COTY HOUSE**, a megalithic burial chamber consisting of four big stones. Finally, near the river, is **ALLINGTON CASTLE**, from the outside a well-preserved 13th-century castle, modernized inside and now owned by the Carmelites of Aylesford.

MEREWORTH CASTLE Southwest of Maidstone stands the very notable Palladian mansion of Mereworth Castle (1723), inspired by the Villa Rotonda outside Vicenza and designed by Lord Burlington's protégé Colen Campbell. The house is not open to the public but can be seen from the road. The **CHURCH** next to it of 1744, by an unknown architect, is a fine example of neoclassicism in Britain. In the nave two rows of Tuscan columns support a flat entablature and a barrel vault.

To the west, **OLD SOAR** forms part of a Wealden house of about 1290. The hall range has gone, replaced by a Georgian brick house, but the solar, opening off the hall, remains.

BOUGHTON MONCHELSEA is south of Maidstone. An Elizabethan house, built in 1567 and altered in the 19th century, it incorporates a charming mixture of styles, with decoration and furniture of all periods. There are two walled gardens.
LEEDS CASTLE The main road to Ashford passes Leeds Castle, a enchanting sight from a distance, several stone buildings on an island in a lake. Parts of it indeed go back to the 13th century, but mostly it is Victorian pastiche, the interiors containing little of interest. On the outskirts of Ashford lies **GODINTON PARK**, a sumptuous 17th-century house concealing a 14th-century core. It has an ambitious staircase and an impressive Great Chamber with a vast Jacobean chimneypiece. Godinton Park also houses an impressive collection of pictures, Chinese, Chippendale and other furniture, and English and continental porcelain.

LEEDS CASTLE
claims to be "the most beautiful castle in England", and its romantic silhouette and setting in a lake give it some justification for the title. It owes its appearance very largely to the restorations of the then owner Fiennes Wykeham-Martin in 1821.

ASHFORD TO SANDWICH VIA CANTERBURY

CHILHAM, about half way between Ashford and Canterbury, is a small village powerfully evocative of the past. The church (over-restored) contains three outstanding 17th-century monuments, of which one is by Nicholas Stone, and several of the 19th century. Across the village square stand the remains of a 12th-century castle and an ambitious Jacobean house. The castle's unusual plan is laid out as five sides of a hexagon, one side left open. Within the house, finished in 1616, not a great deal survives apart from the staircase and a few chimneypieces. The next village, Chartham, has a splendid church of about 1300, the windows displaying typical "Kentish" tracery (that is, with split cusps).
CANTERBURY was badly damaged in World War II, but besides the CATHEDRAL ★ there are still several medieval churches which repay a visit, one city gate, the remains of a castle, Eastbridge Hospital (with a chapel and hall) and St John's Hospital, founded soon after the Conquest. A bizarre surprise is the former SYNAGOGUE in King Street, now a church hall, a replica of an ancient Egyptian temple in cement. The Canterbury Museum and Art Gallery, High Street, exhibits work by local artists and military memorabilia.

CHARTHAM CHURCH
The chancel of Chartham church, with its amazing east window of about 1296. This is the epitome of the Decorated style ● 74 in a particular local form. The top of the lights consists of cusped quatrefoils with each cusp split, the so-called "Kentish" tracery.

Above: a winged beast on one of the capitals in the Norman crypt
Below: the crypt, with columns from 1176

The Cathedral of Christ Church, Canterbury, is the most important medieval building in Britain, both architecturally and historically, but it is not one that reveals all its secrets at first glance. The first cathedral, a large early Norman building of which nothing survives, was built by William the Conqueror's archbishop Lanfranc. Between 1096 and 1130 the eastern part was lavishly rebuilt on a much larger scale under Archbishop Anselm but four years later it was gutted by fire, leaving only a smoking shell. The French master-mason William of Sens was appointed to rebuild the cathedral between 1175 and 1179 and his work introduced the new Gothic style to England with pointed arches, sexpartite vaulting and a system of buttressing concealed under the aisle roofs.

Above: stained glass portrait of St Thomas, the murdered archbishop, Trinity Chapel. (The face is a restoration.)

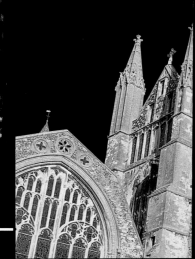

THE LATER MIDDLE AGES

Only in 1378 was it decided to demolish the old nave and rebuild it in the new Perpendicular style (left). The architect was Henry Yevele; his work is higher, lighter, more rational than the old nave, making an immediate impact as one first enters the cathedral. A new west front was also begun, but only one tower was built. The other (on the north) did not replace the Norman one until 1832. The cathedral's crowning glory, the tower over the crossing, known as Bell Harry, was designed by John Wastell and built between 1496 and 1503.

TRINITY CHAPEL

When William was seriously injured by a fall, the work was taken over by another William, 'the Englishman', who built the Trinity Chapel which contained the shrine of Thomas Becket, a marvel of mosaic and rich decoration. The stained-glass windows, still largely intact, form the greatest collection of 13th-century glass in Britain. Besides Biblical subjects, they tell stories of the miraculous cures at Becket's tomb.

THE CATHEDRAL FROM THE NORTH

From the cloister one sees the big window of the chapterhouse on the left, the crossing tower, "Bell Harry" in the center and the 14th-century nave on the right.

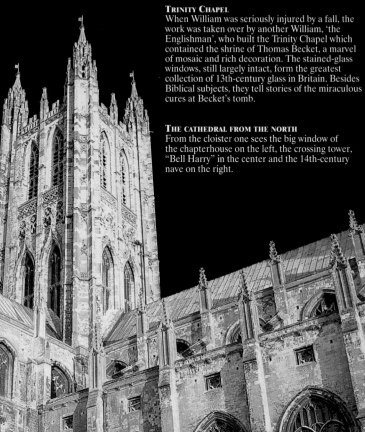

Bronze figurine of reclining river god, Roman period, Richborough Castle

Right: exterior and interior of the Norman parish church of St Nicholas, Barfreston, 12th century. The taller half is the nave, with its sculptured doorway, the smaller the chancel with its rose window and gable. Inside, the chancel arch is flanked by two blank arches.

Steelyard weight in the form of a satyr, Richborough Castle

After **Christ Church Cathedral**, the other great ecclesiastical foundation of Canterbury was **St Augustine's Abbey**. This has now disappeared, apart from a lavish gateway, and only foundations are visible. These are not easy to interpret because several buildings are superimposed and have to be separated in the mind. There were originally two Saxon churches, linked to the middle by an 11th-century rotunda unique in England. This curious arrangement was swept away for a big new church built at the same time as the cathedral and equally impressive. It lasted until the Reformation, when it was completely demolished.

BARFRESTON Beyond Canterbury to the southeast is Barfreston, famous for one of the most sumptuous and best preserved Norman parish churches in England. On the tympanum of the south doorway is a relief of about 1160 showing Christ blessing, flanked by foliage scrolls containing a king and queen. The arch framing it is carved into three orders with many tiny figures in foliated circles and ovals: humans, animals, fabulous beasts and scenes of daily life. In the south wall of the chancel is a relief of St Michael slaying the Dragon and there is further sculptural enrichment to the east wall. Patrixbourne, closer to Canterbury, belongs to the same school, with a similarly carved south doorway.

SANDWICH, now a mile from the sea, was in the Middle Ages one of the Cinque Ports. Its commercial decline has had the advantage of preserving much of its medieval fabric and many houses of the 16th and

ROMAN WALL
Part of the Roman wall of Richborough Castle (right), built about AD 285 when Britain was threatened by the Saxons. It is eleven feet thick and consists mostly of concrete and rubble; the stone facing has disappeared.

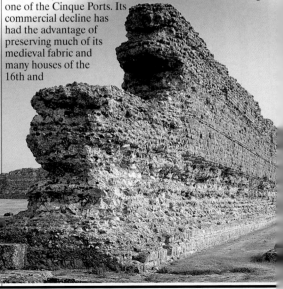

WALMER CASTLE, originally built by Henry VIII, has been drastically remodeled to make it the official residence of the Lord Warden of the Cinque Ports. The only clue to its original form is the circular shape of the rooms (below center).

Left: The Duke of Wellington's bedroom painted by Thomas Shotter Boys, displayed at Walmer Castle Above: part of the nave arcade of St Margaret at Cliffe. The arches are decorated with zig-zag and some of the capitals have faces staring out of the corners.

17th centuries. A mile to the north is Richborough, the site of the Emperor Claudius's landing in AD 43, which marks the beginning of the Roman occupation. Not much is to be seen except ruined walls and ditches, and the foundation of a huge monument in the form of a two-way triumphal arch (two arches crossing at right angles). Difficult to visualize, it is luckily represented by a fine model in the museum on the site.

SANDWICH TO HYTHE VIA DOVER

Between Sandwich and Dover are two forts built by Henry VIII around 1534-40: DEAL and WALMER CASTLES. Both consist of a circular center surrounded by semi-circular bastions (Deal has six, Walmer four) giving them a distinctively geometrical appearance (perhaps symbolic of the Tudor rose). Deal is the larger and is well preserved, though some of its battlements were rebuilt during World War II. Inside, visitors can see the living quarters of the garrison, the rooms nearly all segments of circles. Walmer Castle was once very similar, but the interior was remodeled to make it a comfortable residence for the Lord Wardens of the Cinque Ports. The Duke of Wellington died here in 1852. The gardens were laid out about 1800 and extended by the present warden, Queen Elizabeth the Queen Mother.

DEAL CASTLE, the largest and best preserved of Henry VIII's three castles on the Kentish coast, *c.* 1539. The circular keep rises slightly above the six bastions, and has six smaller bastions of its own.

ST MARGARET'S-AT-CLIFFE At St Margaret's-at-Cliffe, on the way to Dover, there is a very large and impressive NORMAN CHURCH. Its west doorway, arcade, wide chancel arch and four-bay chancel are typical of about 1150 and not too drastically restored, although the aisle windows are Victorian.

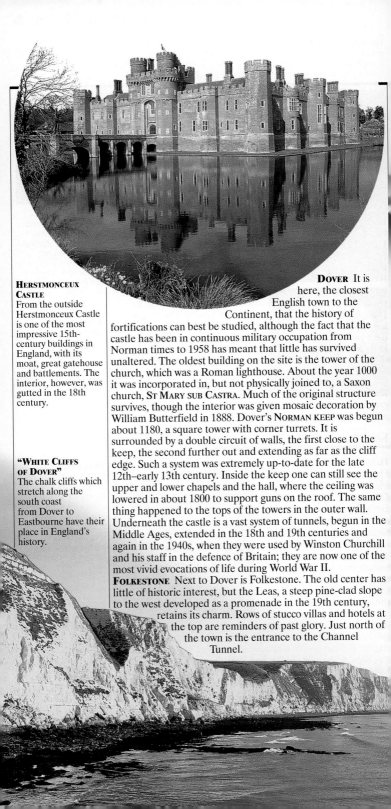

HERSTMONCEUX CASTLE
From the outside Herstmonceux Castle is one of the most impressive 15th-century buildings in England, with its moat, great gatehouse and battlements. The interior, however, was gutted in the 18th century.

"WHITE CLIFFS OF DOVER"
The chalk cliffs which stretch along the south coast from Dover to Eastbourne have their place in England's history.

DOVER It is here, the closest English town to the Continent, that the history of fortifications can best be studied, although the fact that the castle has been in continuous military occupation from Norman times to 1958 has meant that little has survived unaltered. The oldest building on the site is the tower of the church, which was a Roman lighthouse. About the year 1000 it was incorporated in, but not physically joined to, a Saxon church, ST MARY SUB CASTRA. Much of the original structure survives, though the interior was given mosaic decoration by William Butterfield in 1888. Dover's NORMAN KEEP was begun about 1180, a square tower with corner turrets. It is surrounded by a double circuit of walls, the first close to the keep, the second further out and extending as far as the cliff edge. Such a system was extremely up-to-date for the late 12th–early 13th century. Inside the keep one can still see the upper and lower chapels and the hall, where the ceiling was lowered in about 1800 to support guns on the roof. The same thing happened to the tops of the towers in the outer wall. Underneath the castle is a vast system of tunnels, begun in the Middle Ages, extended in the 18th and 19th centuries and again in the 1940s, when they were used by Winston Churchill and his staff in the defence of Britain; they are now one of the most vivid evocations of life during World War II.

FOLKESTONE Next to Dover is Folkestone. The old center has little of historic interest, but the Leas, a steep pine-clad slope to the west developed as a promenade in the 19th century, retains its charm. Rows of stucco villas and hotels at the top are reminders of past glory. Just north of the town is the entrance to the Channel Tunnel.

DOVER CASTLE
The keep of Dover Castle ● 72, built by the Normans, is surrounded by fortifications dating from almost every century up to the 20th. Crowning the hill above the town, it is the main bastion of defence against any invader from the Continent.

HYTHE Further along the coast is Hythe, once a major port but now, like the other Cinque Ports, a picturesque backwater. Underneath the chancel of the MEDIEVAL CHURCH, accessible from the outside, is a rare "bone house" containing, for those with a taste for the macabre, rows of skulls on shelves. Nearby is SALTWOOD CASTLE, the grounds of which are often open; it was the seat of Sir Kenneth (later Lord) Clark, who achieved public recognition with his television series *Civilization*.

LYMPNE Beyond Hythe is Lympne (pronounced "Lim"). LYMPNE CASTLE is a 15th-century manor house, restored from a ruin and made habitable around 1910. Near it is a private zoo owned by John Aspinall, well worth a visit to see a variety of wild animals in something like their natural surroundings. The property included Port Lympne, a house built before World War I by Sir Herbert Baker and decorated after it by Phillip Tilden. Its Art Deco interior features a garden room painted by Rex Whistler in 1933. (The coast between Hythe and Hastings is described on pages *176-7*.)

HASTINGS TO BRIGHTON

Hastings is a town of dual character: on the one hand, it is a brash modern holiday resort full of amusement arcades, and on the other a picturesque old port of narrow streets and a sea front specially notable for its strange collection of net-stores, all black timber structures like towers, used to haul in the fishermen's nets. In Pelham Crescent is the strange church of St-Mary-in-the-Castle, a rotunda dug into the cliff behind; it is now a concert hall.

THE BATTLE OF HASTINGS (1066) was fought not at Hastings but inland at a site now appropriately called Battle. William the Conqueror built a monastery here as an offering of thanks. The church has gone but the gatehouse (1338) and the 13th-century dormitory survive.

ST LEONARDS Further west along the coast is ST LEONARDS, a stylish planned suburb of Hastings designed by Decimus Burton (1828). Then comes BEXHILL, whose claim to fame is the DE LA WARR PAVILION by Erich Mendelssohn and Serge Chermayeff (1933), one of the first examples of International Modern architecture in Britain. The best view is from the beach; go inside to see the graceful glazed spiral staircase.

HERSTMONCEUX Inland again is Herstmonceux, a fairy-tale castle surrounded by a moat. Built in 1440, it was a ruin in the 18th century and was only restored in 1933, complete with its fine garden. In 1948 it was taken over by the Royal Observatory when it moved from smog-polluted Greenwich. Michelham Priory, to the west, was an Augustinian monastery, then a private house. There are some medieval remains.

Moorish kiosk opposite the De la Warr Pavilion in Bexhill

The De la Warr Pavilion

SHEFFIELD PARK ★
The gardens of
Sheffield Park
(above), laid out by
Repton before 1794
but continuously
added to during the
19th century, are
particularly luxuriant.
They surround four
lakes linked by
cascades and
waterfalls. The
rhododendrons and
azaleas are specially
notable, and there are
vivid patches of
daffodils and
bluebells in the
spring.

*Detail from statue of
Sir John Gage, Firle
church, 1557*

Head back to the coast for Pevensey, where William actually
landed, and where the ruins of the big Norman castle repay
examination. From here one soon reaches Eastbourne and the
high white cliffs of Beachy Head, parts of which occasionally
fall into the sea. The pretty village of Alfriston is tucked away
inland, along with the ruined medieval priory of Wilmington.
Between here and Lewes are Firle Place, basically an 18th-
century house with attractive period rooms; Glynde Place, an
Elizabethan mansion, much altered; Glyndebourne ▲ *61*,
famous for its opera house founded in the 1930s by a music-
loving millionaire and rebuilt in 1995 by his son on a much
larger scale; and Charleston Farmhouse, the home of Vanessa
Bell and Duncan Grant, an "outpost of Bloomsbury" from
1916 to 1958. It is full of paintings and ceramics by them and
their friends. A few miles further north is Sheffield Park. The
house is closed but the magnificent garden (120 acres) is
among the most exotic in the southeast.

LEWES is the county town of Sussex, with a castle, a prison and
a richly rewarding High Street, lined with harmoniously
blending houses of all periods. An Elizabethan house, wrongly
called "Anne of Cleves's House", is now a museum and has an
interesting furniture collection.

It is worth making an expedition to the north, perhaps more
easily visited from Surrey, to East Grinstead to see two
notable houses – STANDEN and HAMMERWOOD. Standen, of
1891, is Philip Webb's best house, an informal Arts and Crafts
composition reflecting a mixture of periods and preserved
complete with all its furniture and Morris wallpaper. The
eccentric Hammerwood House is virtually the only English
work of Benjamin Latrobe, who emigrated to America in 1795
and is famous as the architect of Baltimore Catholic
Cathedral and part of the Capitol in Washington.

BRIGHTON Brighthelmstone was a small fishing village until
the mid-18th century, when it began to be developed as a
seaside spa. In 1786 the Prince of Wales (later George IV)
chose it as a holiday home where he could be with Mrs
Fitzherbert, whom he had secretly married, and began
converting an old farmhouse into what is now the ROYAL
PAVILION ★. His first architect was Henry Holland, who gave it
two wings with bow windows linked by a central rotunda. In
1815 John Nash began transforming it into the wonderful

Brighton Pavilion (left) (from the Old Steine) The domed room on the right of the picture is the Saloon, and on the left the Banqueting Room and its gallery.

Hindu-Chinese fantasy that we see today. It is equally amazing inside and out; the climax is the Banqueting Room, with a huge chandelier hanging from a silver dragon. Next to the Pavilion are the very large domed stables (1804) by William Porden, already Indian in style, which have been converted into a theater. The very enterprising Brighton Museum can be found next door.

The old fishing village of BRIGHTHELMSTONE still exists – an area of tiny houses and alleys known as The Lanes, now mostly boutiques and antique shops. Outside this and along the sea front there are still attractive Regency terraces, although insensitive modern development is compromising Brighton's old character. There are two piers, of which the older, the West Pier, is now closed but due to be restored at enormous cost.

Brighton is rich in interesting 19th-century churches. ST PETER'S, of 1824, is by Sir Charles Barry, architect of the Houses of Parliament. ST BARTHOLOMEW'S, of 1872, is by a local architect, Edmund Scott – a vast brick church, higher than Westminster Abbey, with outstanding metalwork by the Arts and Crafts designer Henry Wilson. ST MICHAEL'S is two churches, a small one by G.F. Bodley (1858-61), which became the south chapel of a much larger one by William Burges (see Cardiff Castle and Castell Coch in South Wales ▲ 470).

HOVE, the westward extension of Brighton, is marked by much grander terraces and squares, some of them opening toward the sea on their fourth side. It has one of J.L. Pearson's best churches, All Saints (1890) and the British Engineerium, a museum of engineering.

One of the dragons on the ceiling of the Music Room, Brighton Pavilion

SHOREHAM TO ARUNDEL

SHOREHAM TO ARUNDEL

NYMANS GARDENS
(below right)
Nymans, the creation of the Messel family and the home of Lady Rosse, founder of the Victorian Society. Its collection of plants, shrubs and trees is hardly surpassed in England.

STEYNING CHURCH
The nave arcade of Steyning church, 11th century, has typical circular piers, round arches and zig-zag ornament. The church was founded by St Cuthman in the 8th century, the subject of Christopher Fry's play *Boy with a Cart*.

WAKEHURST PLACE,
an Elizabethan mansion at Ardingly dating from 1590. The present south front is only one wing, containing the hall, of an original courtyard house of four wings.

Old Shoreham has a fine Norman church, much restored in 1839, while New Shoreham can boast the still grander church of ST MARY DE HAUSA. It was originally much larger (the nave disappeared in the 17th century) but what remains is the transitional choir and crossing of about 1180, with a three-storey elevation (arcade, gallery, clerestory), all lavishly decorated, and a quadripartite stone vault. Curiously, the piers of the north and south arcades do not match. One can reach ARUNDEL along the coast road or by a detour further inland. If one progresses along the coast one soon sees the giant chapel of Lancing College, standing proudly on the slope of the Downs. Designed by R.C. Carpenter, who died in

1855, only a year after building had begun, it is of cathedral proportions but was never properly completed. The west front is a modern compromise. Nearby is SOMPTING, a notable Anglo-Saxon church with a tower ending in a gabled pyramid, the so-called "Rhenish helm" unique in England. On the other side of Worthing, at Goring, the Catholic church looks extremely unprepossessing, but those who go inside are in for a surprise. It is covered by a complete replica (naturally on a reduced scale) of Michelangelo's ceiling of the Sistine Chapel in Rome.

The inland route takes us as far as Horsham. BRAMBER is a village with a small Norman church, and one of the best timber-framed houses in Sussex, ST MARY'S, which contains interesting old furniture and a display of costume dolls. STEYNING CHURCH is also Norman and much more impressive, and has a nave with an arcade ornamented with deeply cut zig-zag. Within the parish of Steyning is CHANCTONBURY RING, a circular prehistoric earthwork planted with beeches, around which many legends have accumulated: if you run round it seven times the Devil will appear and offer you a bowl of soup (don't accept it), or the ghost of Julius Caesar can be raised by counting the trees. Further north is another

Henry Frederick, Prince of Wales, attributed to Robert Peake, c. 1611, in the collection at Parham

ood Norman
hurch, Shipley,
uilt about 1125
y the Knights
emplar. North
gain is Christ's
ospital, a large
ictorian public
chool designed by
ir Aston Webb (architect of the Victoria and Albert
luseum) and finished in 1902.

PARHAM PARK was begun in 1577, altered in the 18th century and restored to its original appearance in the 20th. The house is entered from the north, but the main show façade faces the garden on the south.

RUNDEL AND PETWORTH

rom the south Arundel presents what seems to be a perfect
iedieval silhouette – a hill town dominated by a castle on one
de and a cathedral on the other. In fact, both are creations
f the 19th century. Of the old castle, one of the seats of the
uke of Norfolk, the shell keep on a mound, the gatehouse
nd a few fragments remain. The rest was built by C.A. Buckler
etween 1890 and 1903, though including an interesting
arlier room, the Library, in Regency Gothick of 1801.

T NICHOLAS' CHURCH Genuinely medieval is the church of
t Nicholas (1380), actually two churches in one; the nave
elongs to the parish, the Fitzalan Chapel to the Norfolk
mily. It has a spectacularly elaborate Gothic pulpit and a
lendid series of 15th- and 16th-century tombs, including one
ade famous by Philip Larkin.

he cathedral-like church that we saw from a distance is the
ATHOLIC CHURCH OF ST PHILIP NERI, a successful pastiche of
3th-century French Gothic by J.A. Hansom (1870) – very
ompetent, very expensive, with plenty of carved capitals and
stone vault.

here is another remarkable Norman church at CLIMPING, just
outh of Arundel. The tower has a flat buttress on each side,
nd in the buttress a narrow window with deeply carved zig-zag
rnamentation all round, not just top and sides, an extraordinary
ffect. At West Chiltington, to the north, the special feature is
ie wall paintings, dating from the 12th to the 14th centuries,
ot all in very good condition.

ARUNDEL CASTLE (from the air) The ancient round keep is in the center. The building in the foreground is a 19th-century reconstruction of what the castle was once like.

A 17th-century needlework and walnut armchair in the great parlor at Parham

ARHAM, to the south, is an Elizabethan house
f understated charm, although now it is a
ood deal restored. It has a nearly symmetrical
rey stone front begun in 1577; inside is a typical Tudor long
allery and hall. Not far away, the large Roman villa of
ignor once consisted of a series of lavish rooms round a
ourtyard, some of them with mosaic pavements: Venus
ith a peacock and gladiator-cupids.

IDHURST Between Petworth and Chichester one
asses Midhurst, another rewarding town, just
utside which are the ruins of Cowdray Park,
nce one of the grandest Elizabethan houses in
ngland, but largely destroyed by fire in 1793.
nough remains of the gatehouse, hall and
napel to show that it combined elegant
erpendicular Gothic with the latest Italian
enaissance ornament. Trotton, north-west of
lidhurst, has a 13th-century church with a fine
ollection of brasses.

▲ Petworth House ★

Below (from top): Doric Temple; "Mrs Robinson" by William Owen; exterior of Petworth; "Thomas Wentworth, 1st Earl of Strafford" and "Lady Anne Carr, Countess of Bedford", both by Anthony van Dyck. Right: Page from 15th-century version of "Canterbury Tales"

Petworth, further north, is Sussex's major country house. Apart from a few earlier fragments in the chapel, what we see today dates from 1688-90. It is very large – the front of 21 bays – but very plain, although it did originally have a central dome. The architect is unknown. Ostentation is reserved for the interiors: the Marble Hall, solemn but austere; the Grand Staircase, with painted decoration by Laguerre, the staircase itself, rebuilt in the 19th century; and the Grinling Gibbons room, with the wood-carver at his most brilliant. The chapel is basically 13th century

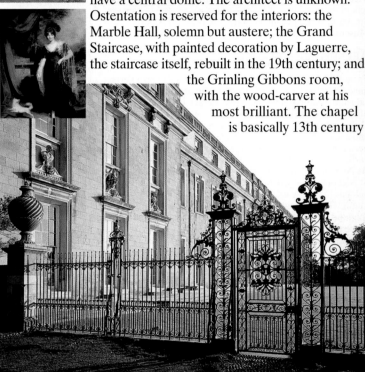

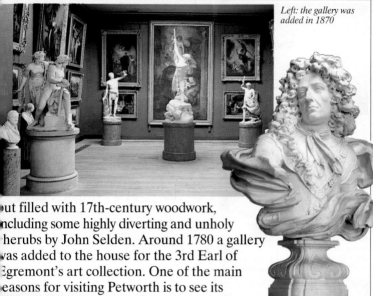

Left: the gallery was added in 1870

ut filled with 17th-century woodwork, ncluding some highly diverting and unholy herubs by John Selden. Around 1780 a gallery vas added to the house for the 3rd Earl of Egremont's art collection. One of the main easons for visiting Petworth is to see its

etail of the oodwork by rinling Gibbons

outstanding paintings and sculpture, including works by Turner (whose most generous patron was the Earl), Van Dyck and numerous others, as well as Greek, Roman and Renaissance pieces. The park of Petworth, with its herd of deer, was laid out by Capability Brown, and the little town outside the gates is one of the most attractive in Sussex.

The bust has long been called William III but there are reasons for thinking it may be a – broken-nosed – James II.

Dewy Morning at etworth" by M.W. Turner

▲ CHICHESTER

UPPARK, by William Talman, built 1685-90, but rebuilt in the 1990s (see below), is a typically English "brick box" with a pediment over its central three bays. The saloon (below-right) is in the style made popular by Robert Adam ● *80-1*, with an elegant stucco ceiling and classical fireplace.

"Seapiece, Morning" by Joseph Vernet, Uppark

CHICHESTER CATHEDRAL, the nave looking east, the walls of 1090, the vault 1187. At the end of this view stands the Arundel Screen, a beautiful stone screen made about 1460. In the 19th century it was taken out to

"improve the vista", but in 1960 it was re-erected in its original position.

GOODWOOD ESTATE
Goodwood, exterior (right) and interior (Yellow Drawing Room, far right). The corners of this strange three-sided composition are marked by domed pavilions. The Goodwood estate was bought in 1720 by the first Duke of Richmond, the bastard son of Charles II and Louise de Kéroualle, Duchess of Portsmouth. Their portraits by Lely are among the treasures of the house.

CHICHESTER

Chichester has Sussex's only cathedral, small in scale but high in quality. It was begun about 1090 and is still structurally a Norman building with thick walls, round arches and a minimum of ornament. In 1187 a great fire destroyed the wooden roof. This was replaced by an Early English stone vault, and the way in which the vaulting shafts were added to the old piers can easily be seen. In 1861 the central tower and spire collapsed and were rebuilt in replica by Sir Gilbert Scott. Inside are two sculptured reliefs showing the Raising of Lazarus and Christ in the House of Mary and Martha. Once thought to be Saxon, they are now dated about 1125.
There are several places worth visiting all round Chichester, including two major country houses.

GOODWOOD was designed by James Wyatt in about 1790. It was intended to be much bigger, on an octagonal plan, but only three of the eight wings were built. Inside are some impressive neoclassical rooms, including the Tapestry Room and the Library. Goodwood is best known for its race-course.
UPPARK Near Midhurst, UPPARK is square, plain, brick-built, and has the quiet dignity of the age of William and Mary. The interior was mostly 18th century in style, the Saloon its grandest room. The house was gutted by fire in 1989, but the contents were saved and it has since been restored. It is now more popular than before it was burnt.

*Lord Nelson by
Sir William Beechey*

PORTSMOUTH

Portsmouth Dockyard has been a base for the British navy for 500 years. The centrepiece is HMS *Victory*, one of the finest surviving wooden ships anywhere, restored as she was when commanded by Lord Nelson at the Battle of Trafalgar in 1805 and set in a stone-sided dry dock which itself dates from 1802. In a nearby dock are the reassembled remains of the *Mary Rose*, one of Henry VIII's ships, which sank off Portsmouth during a skirmish with the French in 1545 and was dramatically recovered from the sea bed in 1982.

*Freshwater,
Isle of Wight*

OLD PORTSMOUTH The original town, still an entity, grew beside the harbor entrance. It was badly bombed in 1940-1 but there are several fine Georgian or earlier houses fronting the long High Street and streets leading off, such as Lombard Street. The old parish church became the CATHEDRAL in 1927; the remarkable east end of *c.* 1200 survives.

THE VICTORIAN FORTS In the mid-19th century fears of a serious French invasion had taken hold, and a series of forts (called "Palmerston's Folly" after the then Prime Minister) was constructed along Portsdown Hill, a chalk ridge to the north of the city, and across the Gosport peninsula to the west. They are huge constructions of brick and earth, strong enough to withstand shells and surrounded by moats, which on Portsdown Hill had to be dry. They were made as inconspicuous as possible from the landward sides, but on the sides facing the sea they are prominent, with massive brick walls and stone- (or granite-) lined entrances and gun openings. One, FORT NELSON on Portsdown Hill, is now a branch of the Royal Armouries, with armaments on display; another, FORT BROCKHURST, north of Gosport, is regularly open to the public.

PORTCHESTER CASTLE is the oldest military monument in the area. A fort was built by the Romans in *c.* 280 on the north shore of the harbor – the most westerly of several built to resist raids by Anglo-Saxons and others. Most of the external walls survive (among the most substantial Roman structural remains north of the Alps). They were adapted for a Norman castle, of which the shell of the impressive keep is intact. Within the castle enclosure is the mid-12th-century St Mary's, originally part of a priory and now the parish church; its west front is particularly impressive.

PORTSMOUTH CATHEDRAL
The present choir of the cathedral dates from 1692-3. Extension westward began in 1935 under the architect Sir Charles Nicholson but was stopped by the war; the new west end was completed in 1991 under Michael Drury.

ISLE OF WIGHT

Diamond-shaped, 23 miles from east to west and 13 north to south, the island is full of variety. A chalk range marks the east–west axis, ending in the Needles peninsula, the dramatic series of detached rocks at the western extremity, with Alum Bay, famous for its many-colored sands.

RYDE developed from the 1820s, and has a late-Georgian to mid-Victorian character; its best building is the ROYAL VICTORIA ARCADE (1836) with a splendid classical interior by William Westmacott. To the west is QUARR ABBEY; the remains of the medieval abbey are fragmentary but the present abbey, built from 1908 for Benedictine monks originally from France, to the design of Dom Paul Bellot, has a magnificent church.

Quarr Abbey

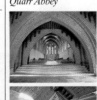

Interior of St Nicholas Chapel (restored from ruin in the 1920s), Carisbrooke Castle

Top: Yarmouth Castle (left), Appuldurcombe House (right)

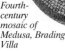

Fourth-century mosaic of Medusa, Brading Villa

OSBORNE HOUSE
Osborne (below) is an Italianate, classical palace of many parts, dominated by two towers of different heights. The formal gardens have been restored, and the grounds have, among other attractions, the Swiss Cottage built for the royal children, with a toy fort nearby.

APPULDURCOMBE HOUSE, north of Ventnor, is the preserved shell of a great house of 1701-13, by John James (with alterations *c.* 1805-10) in a beautiful setting; the main façade has been completely restored.

CARISBROOKE CASTLE On the outskirts of Newport, Carisbrooke Castle is one of the most interesting in southern England. It has a keep on a Norman motte; a former Great Hall altered in the 19th century and now a museum; Norman and later curtain walls, and a 14th-century Great Gateway; outer defences added in the Elizabethan period; and a treadwheel over a well regularly operated by a donkey. Charles I was imprisoned here, tried unsuccessfully to escape and was brought hence to his execution in London in 1649.

OSBORNE HOUSE was built from 1845 on an estate bought by Queen Victoria in that year; it was designed essentially by Prince Albert in partnership with Thomas Cubitt, the successful builder of much of Belgravia, in London. The main domestic section is open to the public, furnished as in the Queen's time. It was Victoria's favorite home; she spent most of her time there after Prince Albert's death in 1861, and died there in 1901.

SOUTHAMPTON

Southampton has been a major port intermittently for 1200 years. With its open quays and almost perpetual deep water (owing to double tides), Southampton proved more practicable than Liverpool for the great transatlantic liners; the *Titanic* was one of the first to sail from there in 1912. The Bargate, the northern gate of the walled town, is late 12th-century at its core; the impressive north face is largely 13th–14th; the south side is more restored. The wall survives intermittently east of the Bargate toll; at ruined Arundel Tower it meets the original shoreline. The wall continues past the Westgate – the old town gate, quite small, which opened onto the quay – and now ends near a monument, erected in 1913, to commemorate the sailing of the Pilgrim Fathers in 1620. THE WOOL HOUSE, a 14th-century warehouse, is now the excellent Maritime Museum. Beside it, Bugle Street, the best historic street in Southampton, leads to the heart of the Old Town. Tudor House Museum is a basically 15th-century house with a striking, much altered, timber-framed front. At the back is a modern replica of a typical Tudor garden and the entrance to the so-called KING JOHN'S HOUSE – a stone-built shell with its original fireplace and window openings, and a rare

Mottisfont Abbey

xample of a medieval chimney, re-erected here from a
ombed site elsewhere. Opposite is St Michael's, a survivor of
everal medieval churches, with a needle-like spire on its
entral tower (which is supported internally on simple,
mpressive 11th-century arches). GOD'S HOUSE TOWER AND
GATE, 14th-15th century, now an archeological museum, are at
he southeastern corner of the walled town. The Art Gallery
as an Art Deco interior and fine collections, including
urne-Jones's *Perseus* cycle and the Arthur Jeffries Bequest of
0th-century, mainly British, art.

NETLEY ABBEY, on the southeastern city outskirts, is the
nagnificent ruin of a 13th-14th century Cistercian monastery.
n the fast-developing area between Southampton and
ortsmouth are several old villages which retain their historic
enters, such as Hamble, Botley, Bishop's Waltham and

*Medieval Merchant's
House, Southampton*

*Left: Titchfield Abbey
Below: "Perseus and
the Sea Nymphs", Sir
Edward Burne-Jones*

TITCHFIELD; the last is
amazingly well preserved with
Tudor timber-framed houses,
and others fronted in 17th-
or 18th-century brick. The
lower part of the church
tower dates from around
800; inside is fine 15th-
century work

nd a sumptuous monument to the 1st Earl and
Countess, and 2nd Earl, of Southampton; the 3rd
Earl was Shakespeare's patron.

*Left: "In the Park" by
Malcolm Drummond*

ROMSEY, an interesting market town, is dominated by the
athedral-like 12th-century ABBEY CHURCH which the
ownspeople bought for the value of its building materials
£100) to be their outsize parish church when the nunnery was
losed at the Reformation. It is, internally, the most complete
najor Norman church in England, although the western part
early Gothic. Earl Mountbatten of Burma is buried under a
tone slab in the Abbey; his family home is BROADLANDS, just
outh of the town, open to the public in the summer; it was
esigned c. 1768 by Capability Brown (who also remodeled
he landscape) and enlarged in 1788 by Henry Holland; there
an exhibition of the life of Earl Mountbatten. In Victorian
mes this was the home of Lord Palmerston, Prime Minister.
o the northeast are Sir Harold Hillier Gardens with a
onderful collection of trees and garden plants.

MOTTISFONT ABBEY is a mainly Georgian house with remains
f a medieval abbey (and a room with *trompe-l'oeil* murals of
939 by Rex Whistler), set in a garden with a famous
ollection of old varieties of roses.

TITCHFIELD ABBEY
The 1st Earl of
Southampton
converted Titchfield
Abbey (north of the
village) into his
mansion at the
Reformation; he built
the magnificent
gatehouse, now a
shell, across the
former nave.
Fragments remain of
the 13th-century
abbey, and nearby is a
fine monastic barn,
now a farm shop.

▲ WINCHESTER

Below and right: Winchester School; the stained-glass window shows Bishop William of Wykeham

WINCHESTER CATHEDRAL
The cathedral is austere externally, but inside is full of fine details, including medieval wall-paintings of outstanding quality, and delicate 14th-century choir stalls (although the screen in the same style is of 1875 by Sir George Gilbert Scott). The nave was remodeled under Bishop William of Wykeham before 1400 in the newly established Perpendicular style, with William Wynford as master mason.

CHAWTON (above)
Jane Austen lived here from 1809 to 1817; her house is open to the public. She is buried under a stone slab in the north aisle of Winchester Cathedral.

Right: Stratfield Saye House

WINCHESTER was the capital of Wessex, which became the dominant Anglo-Saxon kingdom under King Alfred (871-901), and was later considered the capital of England until, by the 12th century, London assumed that status.

The CATHEDRAL ★ was built from 1079 on a site slightly overlapping its Saxon predecessor (whose outlines are indicated in the ground). The north transept remains as built in strong, basic Norman style with little ornament; the tower was rebuilt after a fall in 1107. The delicately formed retrochoir was added after 1200 in contrasting Gothic style, and is filled with a series of richly detailed tomb-chapels, or chantries, of later medieval bishops.

WINCHESTER COLLEGE was founded in 1382 by Bishop William of Wykeham for boys whom he intended to go on to New College, Oxford, already founded by him. Little comparable education was then available outside monasteries so this was a pioneer institution in secular schooling. Most of the original buildings survive, little altered outwardly, with two gateways, a complete courtyard, and chapel – together with numerous later accretions to serve what has always been one of the most prestigious boarding schools in Britain.

The HIGH STREET follows the line of the main thoroughfare of the Roman town of Venta Belgarum – which declined after the Romans left Britain and was re-established as a town under King Alfred. (A statue of him dating from 1901 stands in the middle of the street.) Past the ornate Guildhall (1873), the street narrows between shops, often under old upper storeys – especially in The Pentice, where the top storeys project over the pavement and are supported by pillars. Nos 33-4 have 16th-century decorative wooden bargeboards on their gables. The BUTTER CROSS is a rare survival of a civic "cross"; the top is restored but the lower part is 15th-century with later statues. Of the great medieval CASTLE not much remains except for the Great Hall, internally one of the

*...e Vyne (below) and casket in the
...teroom at the Vyne (right)*

...nest secular medieval buildings of its kind surviving – with
...cades of *c.* 1230, partly in Purbeck marble. Its great feature
... the top of the so-called "King Arthur's Round Table"
...anging on a wall and dating from the late 13th century,
...hen stories of the legendary figure were fashionable; the
...ainting, including representations of the knights' seating,
...as added later.

...t Cross Hospital, on the southern outskirts of
...inchester, is a medieval charity – a retirement
...ome founded by Bishop Henry of Blois in 1136
...d augmented by another bishop in 1445. The
...agnificent chapel is largely 12th-century and
...ustrates the transition from Norman to
...othic. The 15th-century Hospital buildings
...clude residents' lodgings and hall. The
...sidents still wear distinctive robes or gowns.

...ELBORNE, a village not far from Winchester, was
...ome to Gilbert White (d. 1793), one of the best early
...riters on natural history. At his house, **THE WAKES**, the
...arden is being restored as he knew it.

...INTON AMPNER is a good example of neo-Regency taste; the
...arden is superb – a mixture of formal and informal. Crondall
...as a particularly fine 12th- to 13th-century church (especially
... side), with a 17th-century tower.

...LDERSHOT has been the chief base of the British army since
...e 1850s; of interest to visitors are several museums,
...cluding the Aldershot Military Museum and the Airborne
...orces Museum. At Farnborough is St Michael's Abbey,
...stablished in 1886 by the exiled Empress Eugénie, together
...ith an elaborate mausoleum for her husband, Napoleon III,
...d their son, killed fighting in 1879 in the Zulu Wars.

...TRATFIELD SAYE HOUSE (17th to 19th centuries) was bought
... the government and presented to the Duke of Wellington
...ter the battle of Waterloo; it contains works of art and relics
... the Iron Duke.

...ASING HOUSE, which began as a Norman castle, became a
...alatial Tudor mansion and was destroyed during and after a
...emorable siege (with Oliver Cromwell personally in
...mmand) in 1645. A Tudor garden has recently been re-
...eated and there is a fine, undamaged, Tudor barn, but the
...mains are otherwise limited to extensive earthworks.
...urther north is **THE VYNE**, a magnificent brick house built by
... courtier of Henry VIII, with one of the earliest classical

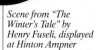

*Scene from "The
Winter's Tale" by
Henry Fuseli, displayed
at Hinton Ampner*

BREAMORE, to the northwest of the New Forest, is a combination of a country house open to the public, museums, church and picturesque village. The house is partly Elizabethan, but the center section was rebuilt after a fire in 1856; it is full of fine furnishings.

The Georgian stables house a collection of carriages; the Countryside Museum illustrates farming and farm-workers' lives through the ages. The church is exceptional – substantially of about AD 1000 with later alterations. (View of Breamore by J. Sigrist, above)

*"The Boy with the Bat"
c. 1760, Breamore*

porticos in England (added 1655), and much superb internal detail and furnishings of the 16th to 18th centuries, in a landscaped park with a lake.

SILCHESTER, now a scattered village, contains the site of Calleva Atrebatum, abandoned following the Roman withdrawal after AD 400 and, unlike many Roman cities in England (such as Winchester), not re-established later. Most of the town wall, in flint with rough stone, survives.

HIGHCLERE CASTLE, home of successive Earls of Carnarvon, 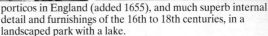 a sumptuous mansion designed by Sir Charles Barry. Among its treasures are relics from the Tomb of Tutankhamun which the 5th Earl, with Howard Carter, discovered in 1922. The park was landscaped by Capability Brown.

SANDHAM MEMORIAL CHAPEL, in the village of Burghclere, has a plain exterior which contains some remarkable wall paintings by Stanley Spencer depicting scenes of army life in World War I (*Ablutions and Moving Kit Bags*, right),  culminating in a battlefield, with soldiers rising with white crosses toward a figure of Christ ▲ *103*. It commemorates Henry Sandham, who died after war service.

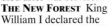

THE NEW FOREST King William I declared the area a royal forest in 1079. Then as now, more than half was probably heathland, grassland or bog, the rest woodland. Local people were permitted to graze animals there but the requirements of royal hunting were paramount. Later, its timber came to be valued as a reserve for the Royal Navy. In the last 150 years many conifers have been planted, but now the emphasis is on maintaining the Forest for wildlife and recreation. The New Forest Museum at Lyndhust provides a good introduction.

ST MICHAEL AND ALL ANGELS at Lyndhurst is one of the fines Victorian churches, built by William White in brick and varie stones, with outstanding glass by William Morris and Burne-Jones; Mrs Alice Hargraves, who as a girl inspired *Alice in Wonderland*, is buried in the churchyard.

BEAULIEU was a Cistercian abbey founded in 1204 at the head of a tidal estuary. The abbey lands passed after the Reformation to an ancestor of the present Lord Montagu of Beaulieu, and Palace House was built in the 19th century. There are picturesque ruins of claustral buildings and an intact range including a museum; the present parish church was the monks' refectory. The National Motor Museum grew from a private collection of earl cars and now displays a remarkable series of vehicles

THE SOUTH WEST

Geoffrey Beard

JOHN TRADESCANT
(1570–1638),
responsible for
planting the gardens
at Cranborne Manor,
was also the official
gardener to Charles I.
He traveled widely,
visiting Russia in 1618
and northern Africa
in 1620, and
introduced many
plants from overseas
to the British Isles.

*Wimborne Minster:
southeast view
(below); St Cuthberga
window (bottom left);
the nave, looking east
(bottom right)*

BOURNEMOUTH TO LYME REGIS

CHRISTCHURCH This attractive old town, with its
wide, shallow harbor and narrow outlet to the sea, is
small and bustling. It takes its name from its impressive
church ★ (once part of an Augustinian priory), the longest
parish church in the country. The towering stone reredos of
c. 1350 is awe-inspiring, with its crowded figures, tiers and
niches, rising to the height of the chancel. The carved wood
misericords afford a fascinating glimpse into medieval life:
here are animals, jesters, even a fox wearing a cowl.
Christchurch also has the remains of a Norman house and
castle, built originally of wood on an artificial mound to
dominate the surrounding countryside. By the late 13th
century the castle had acquired walls 30 feet high and 10 feet
thick, only to be reduced to ruins in the Civil War.
BOURNEMOUTH In a valley surrounded by 100-foot cliffs,
where pine trees line the chines that lead through the chalk
hills down to the long stretches of beach, shelters the sedate
seaside town of Bournemouth. It underwent its greatest
period of expansion with the coming of the railways in the
19th century, when, with its superb sands and generally mild
climate, it became a popular holiday destination. The erection
of its grand stuccoed villas was soon underway, along with
even more impressive Italianate structures such as the Royal
Bath Hotel. The private house (1894) of the hotel's original
owner, Sir Merton Russell-Cotes, is now a museum and art
gallery bearing his name. The Museum houses a splendidly
eclectic range of exhibits that include oil-paintings, shells,
accoutrements of the actor Sir Henry
Irving, and local and exotic butterflies
and moths, arranged within an Italian-
style interior.
WIMBORNE ★ The twin-towered
Wimborne Minster, girdled by busy
streets, dominates this market town.
Within the largely Norman building (11th
century) is a fine nave that has later (13th
century) Purbeck shafts at the transept
entrances. There are good stained-glass
windows (1838) by Thomas Willement.
KINGSTON LACY Not far from Wimborne
and the great Iron Age hill fort of
Badbury Rings is Kingston Lacy, a
precise 17th-century house. It was built
for Sir Ralph Bankes in 1663-5 to replace
the ruined Corfe Castle, 12 miles to the
south, which had been defended in the
Civil War by Sir Ralph's mother, Dame
Mary. The original design for Kingston
Lacy was the work of architect Sir Roger

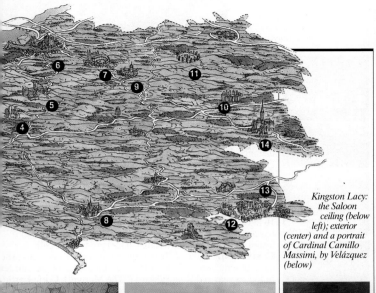

Kingston Lacy: the Saloon ceiling (below left); exterior (center) and a portrait of Cardinal Camillo Massimi, by Velázquez (below)

Pratt, but the house was remodeled in 1835-41 by Sir Charles Barry, changing it from brick to Chilmark stone without and marble within. There is an important collection of some 150 oil paintings, including fine Spanish works by Velázquez, Murillo and Zurbaran, displayed on the gilded leather-lined walls of the Spanish Room. The room also has a Venetian ceiling from one of the Contarini palaces, acquired by William Bankes in 1838.

CHETTLE and **CRANBORNE MANOR** are country houses about 10 miles northeast of Blandford. Chettle, dating to about 1710-20, has a most unusual plan to commend it. It is shaped with curved corners, and bears a curved projection with flat pilasters on its west front; these tricks were inspired by the Italian travels of the architect, Thomas Archer. Within, there is a fine double staircase which continues through an archway at the upper level, a spacial conceit beloved by artists versed, like Archer, in Roman Baroque. At Cranborne, there is a fine Jacobean manor house created for Robert Cecil. The house is closed, but Cranborne's splendid gardens are open to visitors.

BLANDFORD FORUM The elegant Georgian town of Blandford Forum is now mercifully bypassed by the constant flow of traffic to and from the coast. A fire in 1731 destroyed most of the town, but enabled the two surveyors in charge of the rebuilding, William and John Bastard, to exercise their talents. The Parish Church (with the Bastard family tomb in its churchyard) and the town hall (1734) are two examples. Within the church the paneled galleries are slung between giant Portland stone columns with Ionic capitals, and the box pews, font cover and mayor's chair (1748) are all finely crafted.

MILTON ABBEY ★
There is exquisite architectural detail in Milton Abbas abbey, which was founded in 933, destroyed in a storm in 1309 and rebuilt in the 14th, 15th and 18th centuries. Next to it is a huge 18th-century country house, by William Chambers.

FIDDLEFORD MANOR has been called "the most spectacular medieval manor house interior in Dorset". Its late 14th-century roof structures are shaped into great ogee curves, trefoils and quatrefoils.

203

▲ DORSET COAST

Right: Brownsea Island; Far right: Durdle Door

Top: Brownsea Island; Above and center: Lulworth Castle

Corfe Castle

DORSET COAST

From Poole to Weymouth, and from there to Lyme Regis, Dorset's dramatic coastline is ever dominant.

POOLE, with its great harbor, enjoyed a long history of prosperity until the early 19th century, when the attractions of Bournemouth came into the ascendant. Down at the Quay one can still appreciate the scale of the harbor, while in the distance lies Brownsea Island, with its Henrician castle, a garrison in the Civil War. The island, acquired by the National Trust in 1962, is now a haven for a rich variety of wildlife, including the threatened red squirrel. There are boat trips to the island from Poole, Swanage and Bournemouth. Be sure to see St Osmund's Church in Bournemouth Road, built in 1913-16 in the Byzantine style by E.S. Prior and Arthur Grove; it has a great rose window and intricate façades. The altar inscriptions in the Incarnation Chapel are by Eric Gill.

CORFE CASTLE One of Britain's most majestic ruins, the castle has a bloody history. It was the scene, in AD 978, of the murder of the 18-year-old King Edward ("The Martyr"). Corfe Castle once controlled the gateway to the Isle of Purbeck, and had been an important fortification until it was besieged by Cromwell in 1646. Lady Bankes defended it against an army of more than 500 Parliamentarians for six weeks, until it eventually fell through an act of betrayal. It was finally rent asunder, its stone then used in local buildings. Although it is now little more than an assorted jumble of walls, ramparts and steep ditches, it is still impressive on its hilltop site.

SMEDMORE HOUSE, a short distance southwest of Corfe, is a mainly 18th-century building that contains fine marquetry furniture, paintings and a collection of antique dolls. There is also a beautiful walled garden.

LULWORTH Close to the coast stands Lulworth Castle. After a long history of in-fighting among the Howard family, Thomas Howard, the 3rd Viscount Bindon, acquired the estate of Lulworth in 1600. Lord Salisbury at Cranborne gave him the idea to build a house there, and by 1610 it was habitable. But Bindon's death and subsequent problems led to its sale in 1641 to Humphrey Weld. This amazing house, with its compact plan and four corner towers, a little like "the centre of the Jacobean stage", still remains in the family's possession. Much was destroyed in a fire in 1929 but it has been recently restored by English Heritage.

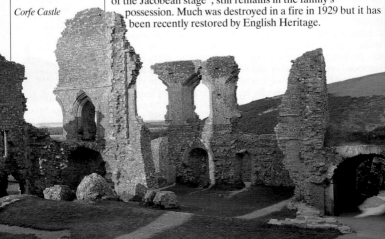

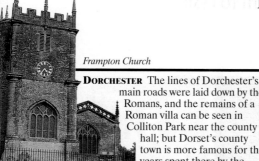

Frampton Church

DORCHESTER The lines of Dorchester's main roads were laid down by the Romans, and the remains of a Roman villa can be seen in Colliton Park near the county hall; but Dorset's county town is more famous for the years spent there by the Victorian writer, Thomas Hardy. The character of the town may be absorbed merely by walking the length of the high street, which has changed very little since Hardy's day. In High Street West is the excellent County Museum, whose collections cover all aspects of Dorset's history, geology and natural history. It has an interior exhibition hall supported on cast-iron columns and, as one would expect, there is a Thomas Hardy Memorial Room. Close by is ST PETER'S CHURCH ★, a stunning example of Perpendicular architecture, the mid-19th century town hall by Benjamin Ferrey, and his church of Holy Trinity of 20 years later (1875).

MAIDEN CASTLE A few miles southwest of Dorchester is Maiden Castle, one of the most impressive earthwork fortifications in Europe. The site was first occupied some 4,000 years ago by a thriving community. The great oval ramparts, enclosing an area about half a mile long and half as wide, were erected several centuries before Christ, and when the Romans arrived in AD 44 under Vespasian they constructed a temple within its confines. In places the ramparts (60 to 90 feet high) were faced with stone and timber, but only the lower courses remain, and these are buried beneath the turf-covered slopes of the earthen mounds they once strengthened (right).

ATHELHAMPTON HOUSE Built for Sir William Martyn in 1493, this is one of the finest examples of a manor house of the period. It has the usual (Tudor) Great Hall, with a four-sided oriel window rising through its substantial height (terminating on the outside in battlements), a splendid timber roof, and a great deal of armorial stained-glass. The east wing was restored after a fire in 1992. The house is surrounded by 20 acres of GROUNDS ★, laid out in 1891, including a Great Court, with 12 giant pyramids of yew. There is also a 16th-century dovecote and three formal enclosed gardens, one with a crest of obelisks. Take the time to look at the church of ST JOHN AT TOLPUDDLE with its 14th-century roof, where a headstone (1934) by Eric Gill is dedicated to the memory of one of the Tolpuddle Martyrs. Six farm laborers from his village attempted in 1834 to form a union. They were sentenced to seven years' transportation, but after public protest in 1836 their sentences were remitted. The church at FRAMPTON also has some interesting monuments.

CERNE ABBAS
The Cerne Abbas Giant is a simple figure cut in the turf through to chalk, with long outstretched arms, erect phallus and club. The Giant, thought to be associated with ancient fertility rites, was probably cut in the 2nd century AD.

*Below: Maiden Castle
Bottom: Tudor Great
Hall at Athelhampton
House*

HARDY'S COTTAGE
This cob and thatch cottage in Higher Brockhampton was built by Hardy's great-grandfather, and has been altered little since then. Thomas Hardy was born there in 1840, and it was from here that he would make the daily trek to school in Dorchester. In 1885, Hardy designed his own house, Max Gate, in Alington Avenue in Dorchester, where he wrote *Tess of the D'Urbervilles* and *Jude the Obscure*. Both houses are open to the public.

*Above: Mapperton
Above right: Parnham
House*

PARNHAM HOUSE
The Drawing Room
at Parnham House
has a memorable
overmantel, with an
inset portrait group of
the early 17th-century
– crude, but with a
fascinating relief of
Joseph with
Potiphar's wife. She
accused him, falsely,
of an attempt on
her virtue.

BRIDPORT In this, the best of Dorset's small towns, three broad streets form a junction at which the late 18th-century town hall stands. The town is famous for its long history of rope-making (a "Bridport dagger" is a hangman's halter). Its wide pavements were originally "rope-walks" where the cord was laid out for twisting and drying. The wonderful views of the surrounding hills complement the architecture of Bridport's elegant Georgian and Victorian façades. The road northeast leads to nearby **POWERSTOCK**, with its church of St Mary high on a knoll amid Victorian houses.

PARNHAM HOUSE This large Tudor manor house, close to Beaminster, and set among acres or formal and informal gardens, was built in 1540. It was enlarged by John Nash in 1840 and beautifully restored by John and Jennie Makepeace, with grant-aid by English Heritage. The house and gardens are open by appointment only.

WOLFETON HOUSE Toward Yeovil is Wolfeton House, both medieval and Elizabethan, which lies in the water meadows near the confluence of the rivers Cerne and Frome. The house has a splendid stone chimneypiece in the Long Gallery (*c.* 1600), reminiscent of much West Country work in houses such as Montacute ▲ *231* and Winterbourne Herringston.

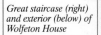

MAPPERTON ★ This is a Jacobean and Carolean manor house with Tudor features and a classical north front. The seat of the Earl and Countess of Sandwich, Mapperton has fine Italianate gardens with an orangery, and topiary and formal borders which descend to fish ponds and shrub gardens. The undulating Dorset hills and dark woodlands that surround the house provide a dramatic setting, and it has been much featured in film and television adaptations of classics such as Henry Fielding's *Tom Jones* and Jane Austen's *Emma*.

*Great staircase (right)
and exterior (below) of
Wolfeton House*

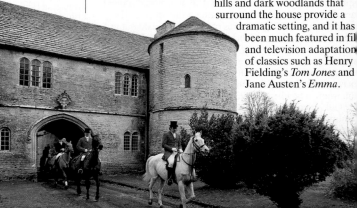

Interior of Forde Abbey (left), and view of the front elevation and long pond border (above)

FORDE ABBEY Just into Somerset is Forde Abbey, a house that developed from the beautiful remains of a Cistercian abbey founded in 1138, but today largely dates from the middle of the 17th century. It has wonderful plaster ceilings, Mortlake tapestries from Raphael's cartoons, and splendid woodwork. There are also award-winning gardens, stretching over some 30 acres, with five lakes.

LYME REGIS At the western end of Dorset sits the ancient town of Lyme Regis, its steep and narrow streets leading down to Lyme Bay. Jane Austen had a cottage on the sea front and set parts of *Persuasion* here. Lyme is a quiet haven, with five small beaches beloved of fossil collectors clustering around the 14th-century breakwater, The Cobb. The little Philpot Museum contains prints, documents, lace, and the fossilized remains of an ichthyosaurus, a 30-foot-long aquatic reptile that lived around 140 million years ago.

"Elizabeth I in Procession", British School, one of the paintings in Sherborne Castle's historic collection

SHERBORNE has an imposing ABBEY ★, with the historic boys' public school in its shadow. Seek out the monument to John Digby, Earl of Bristol, in the Abbey, cut in 1698 by John Nost. In the complex of surrounding buildings there is much that is medieval, mixed in with good 19th-century work in the same style.

SHERBORNE CASTLE, a little further south, was built by Sir Walter Raleigh in 1594 and has been home to the Digbys since 1617. The parkland surrounding the castle rolls away to a 50-acre serpentine lake at the north of Capability Brown's landscaped park. The 12th-century Old Castle, ruined by the Parliamentarians in 1645, still stands 400 yards away from the later castle, across the water.

Sherborne Castle, detail

SANDFORD ORCAS The Tudor manor house of Sandford Orcas has lovely terraced gardens, while nearby PURSE CAUNDLE MANOR is a 15th- and 16th-century manor house with a Great Hall and Minstrels' Gallery. The upper Great Chamber has a barrel ceiling and an oriel window.

Mompesson House

WILTSHIRE

SALISBURY The cathedral city has its origins at Old Sarum, a prehistoric hill fort built around 500 BC that was occupied in succession by the Romans, the Saxons and finally the Normans. Today it is a fine earthwork with a deep ditch and steep ramparts, spreading over 50 acres. It is a favorite spot for picnickers, who enjoy wonderful views - not least of the 404-foot cathedral spire immortalized in John Constable's oil painting (1823). The cathedral lies at the center of one of the loveliest walled closes in England: the gates are still locked at night. Covering at least 1000 square feet, green lawns stretch away to its perimeter. There are trees to give summer shade and cars are banished to the distant fringes.

Above: chapter house roof vaulting, Salisbury Cathedral

Above right: Malmesbury House, main staircase and sundial (below right)

SALISBURY CATHEDRAL was built in one phase (1220-58) with Chilmark stone (quarried 12 miles from the site). The octagonal chapter house, begun in the 1260s and completed about 1300, contains an interesting medieval frieze depicting scenes from Genesis and the finest surviving copy of the Magna Carta. The spire, on a heightened tower, was added about 1334. Note the wide use of Purbeck marble in the shafting, and the enormous brass honoring Bishop Wyville (d.1375) in the northeast transept. On the north side of the Close lie two engaging town houses. At the east end is **MALMESBURY HOUSE**, originally a 13th-century canonry, but leased to the Harris family, whose descendant became the first Earl of Malmesbury, in 1660. There is wonderful Rococo plasterwork within. At the west end is **MOMPESSON HOUSE** (Queen Anne), now furnished as the town house of a Georgian gentleman. It is enclosed by a small walled garden. On the west side, in The King's House (No. 65), a Grade One listed building, are the internationally renowned collections of the Salisbury and South Wiltshire Museum.

Salisbury Cathedral spire

Outside is the alluring oblong space of the Market, with the porticoed Guildhall (1788) in the southeast corner, and other varied and interesting buildings all around, dating mainly from the early years of the 18th century.

SHAFTESBURY The Saxon hilltop town of Shaftesbury, close to the Dorset–Wiltshire border, once had the richest Benedictine nunnery in the county. The church survives in excavated form with its floor tiles still visible – more are on display in the adjacent museum in Park Walk. Down the very steep cobbled slopes of Gold Hill, there is a local history museum, and beyond lie the vast green reaches of Dorset.

TISBURY Tisbury's large church of St John Baptist has a delightful wide interior and splendid timber roofs – the nave has a wagon roof dating to about 1470, where horizontal angels adorn the hammer beams. The ceiled aisle roofs are later, but have molded and decorated beams, as well as St Andrew's crosses in the panels.

OLD WARDOUR CASTLE ★ A mile south of Tisbury is the old Castle at Wardour, set on a wooded bank above an 18th-century lake. Unusually, its courtyard is enclosed on six sides, and its battlements date back to 1393, when it was licensed to crenellate. There are interesting Elizabethan features added in the 1570s for Sir Matthew Arundell, the new owner; the main staircase to the hall dates from this period.

A mile across the park is the new house of Wardour Castle, designed in 1769-74 by James Paine for the 8th Lord Arundell. A wing of this great classical house contains a splendid chapel. When the castle became a school (it is now private apartments) the chapel continued its function as the most impressive of the small but fascinating group of 18th-century Roman Catholic chapels. Paine conceived it and Sir John Soane enlarged it in about 1790. Their work had the support of Father John Thorpe, a Jesuit settled in Rome. He coped with Lord Arundell's perfectionist ways for over 20 years, arranging for an altar for the chapel to be made in Rome by Giacomo Quarenghi.

PYT HOUSE This country house at Newtown was designed in 1805 by its owner, John Benett. Don't miss the imposing Italian chimneypieces, one dated 1553, in two of the principal rooms; they are an example of the curious and unexpected treasures that made fashionable additions to country houses.

Place farm gatehouse, Tisbury

Above: Salisbury Cathedral
Top: Fonthill Abbey

FONTHILL ABBEY
The abbey stands on the spot where the rich Englishman William Beckford ▲ 221 used to live in a dramatic building by James Wyatt, which collapsed soon after it was built. Lord Nelson had Christmas dinner there in 1800.

Below: Old Wardour Castle

▲ WILTON HOUSE ★

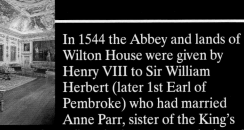

In 1544 the Abbey and lands of Wilton House were given by Henry VIII to Sir William Herbert (later 1st Earl of Pembroke) who had married Anne Parr, sister of the King's sixth wife. After a fire, the house was redesigned by Inigo Jones, who was responsible for the Single and Double Cube Rooms. It has superb historic architecture, beautiful gardens and fine art collections.

THE HOUSE AND GARDENS
The 17th-century diarist, John Aubrey, wrote that "King Charles the First did love Wilton above all places; and came thither every Sommer". Seen from the southwest, the Tudor tower dominates, and the glorious rest, in Chilmark stone, is dated between 1630 and 1655. The gardens contain a splendid "Palladian" bridge (1737) (shown far right).

Amongst the paintings on display is Van Dyck's conversation-piece painting of the 4th Earl of Pembroke and his family (bottom). The Earl was Lord Chamberlain to Charles I.

DOUBLE CUBE ROOM
What Inigo Jones created in the State Rooms of Wilton House was a Double Cube Room (60 x 30 x 30 ft, shown top), and a Single Cube Room (30 x 30 x 30 ft, shown right), each with painted ceilings and redolent of the precise geometrical relations which Jones had observed in the work of Andrea Palladio (1508-80).

*The circle at
Stonehenge*

A ROYAL VISIT
Charles II and his
Queen, Catherine of
Braganza, came to
Longleat while they
were staying in Bath.
The Queen was
taking the waters in
the hope they might
help her to produce
the needed heir to the
throne. They started
out late on their
journey because the
Queen had kept the
King waiting while
she attended Mass.
On the way there
were fears of the
coach overturning in
the narrow lanes and
the Queen vowed she
would never again
venture out in "such
a mountainous
country".

LONGLEAT In the west of the county, as it borders Somerset,
you will find both the great Elizabethan house of Longleat,
seat of the Marquess of Bath, and the landscaped park created
at Stourhead ▲ *214-15* for Henry Hoare. Longleat – the first
stately home to be opened, in 1949, on a commercial basis –
is set in a park of 900 acres landscaped by Capability Brown.
The house was built for Sir John Thynne and was more or less
complete by 1580. Enjoy the great canvases of hunting scenes
by John Wootton in the Entrance Hall; the rest of the house
is largely Victorianized, the work of J.D. Crace and Co. in
the 1860s.
If you motor through the surrounding Safari Park, you will see
hundreds of animals (among them lions, tigers, wolves and
elephants) kept in a natural parkland setting.

THE STONE AGE TRAIL

Many visitors to Wiltshire come with the intention of seeking
out its awesome vestiges of Stone Age civilization: the
mystical, daunting stone circles at STONEHENGE ★
(a World Heritage Site), and at Avebury.
Stonehenge, north of Salisbury, is perhaps the
best-known prehistoric monument in
western Europe, and was probably part
of some great astronomical calendar
erected some 5,000 years ago. Its
unique circle of stones is oriented on
the rising and
setting

Longleat

un, but the origin and placing of the stones themselves has always excited attention, for they seem to match outcrops in north Pembrokeshire in Wales ▲ *463*. Answers are not conclusive. The stones need to be seen (most dramatically at sunset) as part of a remote landscape and plans are afoot to relandscape the site. The busy A303 road will be diverted, with stretches hidden in a tunnel, and visitor resources more discreetly sited.

AVEBURY ★ The site at Avebury, near Marlborough, is less well known than Stonehenge. It is scattered over a site of some 28 acres, its stone circles enclosed by a ditch and external bank also encompassing an avenue of about 100 pairs of standing stones. The most thorough investigation of the Avebury stone circles was undertaken by Alexander Keiller in the 1930s. The collections can be seen in the museum at Avebury bearing his name. A mile away on the Bath-Marlborough road is **SILBURY HILL,** a giant man-made

Top: Windmill Hill
Above left: West Kennett Long Barrow
Above: Silbury Hill

earthern mound, 130 feet high, presumed to be of pre-Roman date. Its purpose is uncertain. Almost opposite, and across the fields from the Bath-Marlborough road, is the splendid **WEST KENNETT LONG BARROW**, over 100 yards long, with the burial chamber at its east end. Here are prehistoric works on a grand scale indeed.

The army has used Salisbury Plain for over 100 years as a training ground and many areas are closed to the public. There are nevertheless many interesting views, walks, churches and houses. Ten miles northwest of Salisbury is the Tudor house of **LITTLE CLARENDON** at Dinton, as well as the neo-Grecian **PHILIPPS HOUSE** built in 1820 by Sir Jeffry Wyatville for William Wyndham. The surrounding landscaped park, recently restored, offers many attractive walks, starting from the car park.

BURIAL SITES
A number of the burials in the barrows on Salisbury Plain and elsewhere, are remarkable for the richness of the objects buried with the dead. They betoken kings or chiefs. Women of rank were also given magnificent burials – armlets and other gold ornaments and a necklace of amber beads have been excavated.

Avebury Circle (left and above left)

▲ STOURHEAD ★

ART COLLECTIO
The fine collection of pictur
and furniture – some by Thom
Chippendale the Younger,
mostly due to the collecti
acumen of Sir Richard Co
Hoare (1758-1838

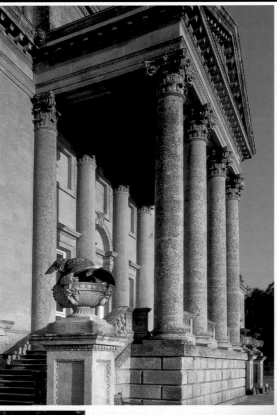

STOURHEAD HOUSE
The east front of
Stourhead House
(left) comprises the
villa which the
Scottish architect,
Colen Campbell,
designed for Henry
Hoare between 1721
and 1725. The most
striking feature is the
pedimented front,
with its four
Corinthian columns,
giving a sense of the
calm observation of
proportion which
pertains throughout.
It is as if a Greek or
Roman temple had
been added to the
house. Indeed the
source is Italian – the
Palladian Villa Emo
near Vicenza
(c. 1560).
The length of the
front was extended i
1792 when Colt
Hoare added
pavilions for a librar
and a picture gallery

THE PANTHEON
The Cheere statue
of Neptune (1751)
(above) is eclipsed
somewhat by the
elegant proportions
of the domed
Pantheon (right),
commanding
attention from every
vantage point around
the lake.

Stourhead, arguably one of the greatest English landscape gardens, was laid out from 1741 by Henry I. Hoare, a member of the London banking family. At the head of the park is the Palladian house designed by Colen Campbell in 1721-4, containing a notable collection of pictures. Walk a mile around the lake from the five-arched bridge, passing the Temple of Flora and coming eventually to the dark Grotto and John Cheere's statue of Neptune (1751). From here there is a splendid view back through the stone-framed opening across the lake to the bridge and church. At its most distant point from the house is the Pantheon (1753), with statues in niches in the rotunda, the principal of which is Rysbrack's *Flora* (1762).

TEMPLE OF APOLLO
The Temple of Apollo (above) was designed in 1765 by the London architect, Henry Flitcroft, to supplement Stourhead's classical offerings. It looks high across the lake and the canopy of circling beech trees – a painterly landscape of form and mass.

Above: Great Chalfield Manor
Right: The Courts, Holt

IFORD MANOR ★
This Tudor house is surrounded by spectacular gardens laid out by Sir Harold Peto in the early 20th century, with pools, statuary, fountains, and a loggias and a colonnade.

WESTWOOD MANOR
One of the rich 16th-century clothiers who worked in Bradford-on-Avon, Thomas Horton, owned Westwood Manor. In a little bedroom is stained glass of his time, with his rebus therein – a barrel ("TUN"), surmounted by the letters ("HOR").

BRADFORD-ON-AVON The picturesque town, surrounded by steep hills, has many interesting features. In the center of its nine-arched bridge is the 17th-century chapel, replacing a medieval one. By the early 19th century Bradford had 32 cloth factories. Climbing the hillsides all around it are the larger houses of the merchants and the crowded 18th- and 19th-century shops which served them. The Church of Holy Trinity with its nave of *c.* 1300, has two good monuments: Charles Steward (d. 1701) by John Nost and Anthony Methuen (d. 1737) by J. M. Rysbrack. The tiny **CHURCH OF ST LAWRENCE ★** is one of the most important late Anglo-Saxon churches in Great Britain: the nave is only 23 feet long by 13 feet wide, yet it is over 25 feet high.

There are some fascinating country houses in the vicinity: Westwood Manor a mile or so southwest of Bradford-on-Avon, Great Chalfield Manor close by Melksham, Bowood ▲ *218* near Calne, and Corsham Court ▲ *218* on the way from Bath to Chippenham.

WESTWOOD MANOR is a 15th-century stone manor house, altered in the 16th century, with late Gothic and Jacobean windows and rich plaster ceilings. Close by is the late 14th-century castle at **FARLEIGH HUNGERFORD**, which contains the tomb of its builder; the little church of 1443 has his portrait in stained glass.

GREAT CHALFIELD MANOR Between Bradford-on-Avon and Melksham is Great Chalfield Manor, a superb late 15th-century manor house enclosed by a moat and a defensive wall. The Great Hall has a daïs for the high table; on the first floor in the east wing, is the Great Chamber. There are good oriel windows: the window of the Great Chamber has a lierne-vaulted ceiling with three pendants. The adjacent church of All Saints, with its

Westwood Manor

agon-roofed Tropnell Chapel completed about 1480, is also
orth a visit. In the area east and southeast of Bradford-on-
von are important churches, those of St Mary, St Katherine
d All Saints at Edington, and to the east the long church of
Michael at Urchfont. The church of the rare Bonshommes
anons, Edington, was completed by 1361. It is a remarkable
:ample of how the Perpendicular linear style replaced the
nate Decorated style, and looks like a small fortified citadel.
y contrast a Decorated chancel can be seen at Urchfont,
o-vaulted and perhaps of 1320 or 1325.

:attered across the chalk uplands of Wiltshire are the 18th-
entury WHITE HORSES cut into the turf. Westbury is the best
own, but there are others at Cherhill (1780), Pewsey (1785)
d Preshute (1864). The horse at Cherhill can be easily seen
om the main road to Marlborough from Calne. Alongside it,
d visible for many miles, is the Lansdowne Obelisk, erected in

THE COURTS
At The Courts in Holt
there are charming
gardens set within an
arboretum. It
contains water
features, topiary and
fine specimen trees
and there is an
interesting use of
color in the flower
and herbaceous
borders.

"The White Horse
at Westbury is 166
feet long and 163 feet
high. It was
apparently made in
the early 18th
century, but in 1873 it
was alas 'rectified',
and now it looks a
moderately correct,
dispirited animal."
Sir Nikolaus Pevsner,
*Buildings of England,
Wiltshire* (1963)

*Above right: the White
Horse at Westbury
Left, and above left:
Farleigh Hungerford
Castle*

e 1840s by the 3rd Marquess of Lansdowne to commemorate
s ancestor, the 17th-century economist, Sir William Petty.

RATTON Around 30 miles from Salisbury stands Bratton
astle, a fine Iron Age fort, commanding breathtaking views.
is protected by a double row of earthworks rising in parts
feet high. The great White Horse cut into the turf is much
der than those at Westbury or Pewsey; in fact it is believed
at it was carved out of the ground to celebrate Alfred's
ctory over the Danes. The horse measures 180 feet long,
7 feet high, and its eye has a circumference of 25 feet. As
ell as its castle and its white horse, Bratton has one other
ique feature: a 13th-century church, standing alone on a
llside and reached by 180 steps. It is one of the most
arming small churches in the country. Its 15th-century
wer has a stair turret and is embattled like the aisles, and all
ve big gargoyles. Its chancel is severely true to 13th-century
adition, and the north transept has delightful corbel angels,
ther playing musical instruments or carrying shields.

Corsham Court

Bowood House terraces (right), and gallery (below right)

TROWBRIDGE The county town of Trowbridge was center of the weaving trade from the 14th century, and is now an excellent base from which to tour the Wiltshire Downs. Fore Street and Roundstone Street have fine houses built by prosperous merchants, and the church of St James, restored in 1847, is a copy of an earlier church endowed by the clothier John Terumber, who died in 1483.

DEVIZES The busy market town of Devizes is pervaded by the wonderful hops and malt smell from Wadsworth's Brewery. Its CHURCH OF ST JOHN ★ has a splendid Norman chancel (*c.* 1125) with elaborate and interlocking zig-zag arches. There is also the ornate Beauchamp Chapel with its riot of heraldry. Thomas Baldwin's Town Hall of 1806 is a five bay building by the Bath architect, with restrained Adamesqu plasterwork within. In Long Street is the Wiltshire Heritage Museum, housing a large collection of prehistoric, Roman, Saxon and medieval effects. On a hillside near the town is an astonishing flight of 29 locks, the longest in Britain, which carry the Kennet and Avon Canal over the 230-foot Caen Hil

MARLBOROUGH The town is known for its celebrated boys' public school, founded in 1845. This stands at the southern end of a very long and wide high street, the result, it is said, of a great fire in 1653. All postdates this, and everything worth seeing is ranged either side of the High Street.

CHIPPENHAM Chippenham, with its high viaduct on the Brunel railway line from Paddington, is a good point from which to drive to Lacock, and, nearby, to the idyllic village of CASTLE COMBE. The church, the adjoining Manor House and the Market Cross are what England does best.

BOWOOD was begun about 1720, and became the family hom of the Earl and Countess of Shelburne in about 1754, when the house was purchased by the second Earl. The Henry Keene and Adam house at its core was demolished in 1955, leaving a perfectly proportioned Georgian home. The Diocletian wing, designed by Robert Adam, contains a splendid Library, and the laboratory where Joseph Priestley discovered oxygen in 1774. The Sculpture Gallery exhibits some of the famous Lansdowne marbles.

CORSHAM COURT ★ An Elizabethan house of 1582, bought by Paul Methuen (1723-95) in the mid 18th century to house an outstanding collection of paintings, and much altered in the 18th and 19th centuries. Note in particular Capability Brown's Picture Gallery (he also worked, more characteristically, in the surrounding park) in which paintings are se

Photograph of W.H. Fox Talbot from a daguerreotype made in 1840 at Lacock Abbey

Lacock Abbey

over the 1760s crimson damask that also covers the large suite of Chippendale-style settees and chairs, below a coved plaster ceiling by Thomas Stocking of Bristol.

Above: the Capability Brown Picture Gallery at Corsham Court

LACOCK The whole village of Lacock is owned by the National Trust. The Abbey was founded in 1232 but converted finally into a Tudor country house, with later 18th-century Gothick façades. The medieval cloisters and chapter-house survive. Nearby is the FOX TALBOT MUSEUM commemorating the pioneering photography of the family member, William Henry Fox Talbot (d. 1877). Thanks to his calotype process of about 1839, he is generally credited with the invention of photography.

Left and below: Malmesbury Abbey

CASTLE COMBE This Cotswold village, set in a river valley, is of renowned beauty. It has a 15th-century stone-canopied market cross, mellowed stone houses and cottages, and a church that is mostly Perpendicular; it was restored in 1851 but the original tower still stands. Inside lies the 13th-century effigy of Walter de Dunstanville, who built the original castle (of which only a few traces remain). The little river Bybrook flows under a triple-arched bridge.

MALMESBURY ABBEY
In the 11th century a monk called Oliver broke both legs when attempting to fly from the abbey roof, using home-made wings. The event is portrayed in a stained-glass window in the church.

MALMESBURY Within the ancient town – its charter of 924 supports its claim to be the oldest borough in England – pride of place goes to the magnificent nave – now sadly truncated – of a 12th-century Benedictine ABBEY CHURCH ★ and the excellent south porch, its eight orders of relief sculptures as fine as any in England.

SWINDON The great locomotive workshops of the old railway town of Swindon are now silent, but it is still possible to see historic locomotives made there, with other railway memorabilia, in the Great Western Railway Museum in Faringdon Road. The town's Art Gallery contains paintings by Graham Sutherland, Ben Nicholson and others.

LYDIARD TREGOZE This ancestral home of the Bolingbrokes, built in the late 1740s, has interior decoration that is partly in the style of William Kent and partly 1750s Rococo. The church of St Mary of *c.* 1653 is rich with imposing monuments, a wonderful Chancel ceiling, and a wrought-iron communion rail. On the 1633 monument of Sir Giles and Lady Mompesson, the stone figures sit facing one another, and she has a skull in her lap. There is also a tomb by Rysbrack of the builder of the house, Viscount St John, who died in 1749.

BATH

BATH SPA – the only city in England to be classified as a World Heritage Site – rises from the hillsides as a froth of honey-colored stone buildings. The Georgian terraces climb high as if set around a giant bowl, with the River Avon flowing over a weir below. Bath is a city to walk in – to arrive by train from Bristol or London is ideal, or if you drive here, abandon your car in a "Park and Ride" facility for the day. The car is unwelcome in this maze of one-way systems and narrow streets, and parking is restricted and expensive.

It is said that the hot mineral spa that made Bath famous was discovered by Bladud, a Briton prince, who noted the waters' healing effects on his leprous swine wallowing joyously in the mud. Roman soldiers proved forerunners of those who felt th waters could cure; Charles II came in 1677 ▲ *212*, James II ten years later, and the wealthy and fashionable throughout the succeeding 150 years. They bathed, wrapped themselves in cold sheets, and perhaps felt better for the effort. Their wealt increased or decreased in proportion to their success in the "New" **ASSEMBLY ROOMS**, at cards and games of chance.

Two architects, father and son, both named John Wood, profited from this affluence, and soon began to transform the medieval city, clustered around its ancient walls and church. John Wood the elder (1704-54) proposed buildings and spaces based on Roman architecture – a Royal Forum, a grand Circus, an Imperial Gymnasium.

Above and top: the Assembly Rooms Right and below: the Roman Baths with the Abbey Church in the background

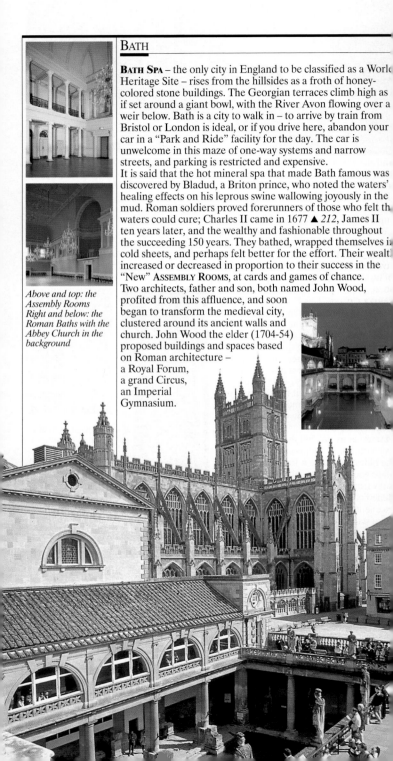

Royal Crescent, Bath

ome
f this he
arried out,
tarting in 1728 with
Queen Square. He lived there himself,
nd as the buildings rose they proved to be a twofold success,
oth through their proportioned appearance and their
ndoubted commercial value. His CIRCUS, approached by
nree streets, is a great circle of 30 houses, 318 foot in
iameter. Their façades bear three tiers of columns,
uperimposed one above the other – Roman Doric, Ionic and
Corinthian. John Wood the younger (1727-81) became as well
nown as his father through his modification of the plans for
ne ROYAL CRESCENT (1767-75), the first and most famous
uch crescent in the world. At its head is No. 1, headquarters
f the Bath Preservation Trust, restored with windows of
orrect height and glazing bars, and furnished as a
entleman's town house.

he younger Wood was also the architect of the ASSEMBLY
ROOMS, a mere stone's throw away along Bennett Street (to
ne northeast of the Circus, toward Lansdown Road), and
nother significant part of Bath's Georgian life of rout, dances
nd assemblies. Further over the hill (on a Wednesday walk
own steep Guinea Lane, with its antique market) is the
ountess of Huntingdon's Chapel, now administered as a
Building of Bath Museum" by the Bath Preservation Trust –
an essential stop for all those interested in how
the Georgian city was built. Selina, Countess
of Huntingdon (1707-91), having been
converted to evangelical Methodism, built the
Bath Chapel in 1765. A beautiful but lesser-
known crescent (but arguably more
successful and elegant than the Royal
Crescent) is the high-looming Lansdown
Crescent, designed and built by John
Palmer in 1789-93. Sheep graze to the
railings, as if in some Claudian landscape,
and it still has its overthrow lamps
astride the porches leading to its fan-
headed doors. No. 19, at its west end, was
the home of the writer William Beckford
from 1822. With some of his West
Indian fortune still intact,
he slung a bridge to
incorporate the next
house, and from the
back of his
property he could
ride up across the
hills to his folly,
"Beckford's
Tower", built for
him in 1823-27 by
H.E. Goodridge.

"Me think it cannot
be clean to go so
many bodies together
in the same water."
Samuel Pepys, 1668

"You disliked the
killibeate taste,
perhaps?"
"I don't know much
about that 'ere," said
Sam. "I thought
they'd a wery strong
flavour o' warm flat-
irons."
Samuel Weller, in
Charles Dickens, The
Pickwick Papers
(1837)

The Circus is a
"... pretty bauble,
contrived for shew
and looks like
Vespasian's
amphitheatre turned
inside out."
Matthew Bramble, in
Tobias Smollett, The
Expedition of
Humphry Clinker
(1771) ● *109-10*

*Landsdown Tower,
Bath*

*Above right: Prior Park
Top: Henrietta Laura
Pulteney by Angelica
Kauffman at the
Holburne Museum
Above: the façade of
the Museum, painting
by Ray Williams, 1994*

**THE HOLBURNE
MUSEUM**
Set in a fine 18th-
century building, this
museum houses
collections of
porcelain and
antiques, as well as
paintings by
Gainsborough and
Stubbs.

Dyrham Park

THE ABBEY CHURCH ★ has heavy carved doors of 1617, and stone angels climbing their ladders to heaven. Oliver King, who had been appointed as Bishop in 1495, had a dream in which he heard a voice telling him "Let an Olive establish a Crown and let a King restore the Church"; and the ladders, olive tree and crown were put there by him in his rebuilding program. They are now much restored. Within the church (entered by a door at the northwestern corner) are fine fan-vaulted ceilings dating to 1499, comparatively early in the Perpendicular style. The nave ceiling, which looks medieval, was in fact erected in 1869 under the architectural direction of Sir Gilbert Scott, and the Jacobean timber roof was demolished. The Abbey had ceased to exist by the time of the Dissolution, but became, in its rebuilt state, the grandest parish church in England. While the bishop of this Somerset diocese is called the Bishop of Bath and Wells – a double title confirmed by Pope Innocent IV in 1245 – it is at Wells ▲ *228-9* that he has his cathedral, palace, dean and chapter.

There are more surprises in Bath city center. The OCTAGON CHAPEL in Milsom Street (Bath's principal shopping street) now, in converted form, houses the Royal Photographic Society's exhibitions. But its glory, designed by Thomas Lightoler in 1765, is its eight-sided continuous gallery. Nearby is the GUILDHALL, designed by Thomas Baldwin in 1776 and containing, on its first floor, a grand ballroom. It is the most magnificent room in Bath, Adamesque in decoration, and an outstanding achievement for a young architect, then but 26 years old. Its lesser-known east side also has a fine façade, where there is the entrance to the covered 19th-century market. Pass by the bacon, biscuits, ground coffee and vegetables and emerge at the east side across from Robert Adam's Pulteney Bridge: there are tiny shops on either side of the bridge, which spans the Avon. It was designed in 1769 and put there to connect Lord Pulteney's Bathwick estates to the city. At the end of Pulteney Street is the lovely HOLBURNE MUSEUM with its glorious collection of art and decorative arts.

CLAVERTON MANOR On the bowl high above Bath, near the University, is the American Museum, housed in a fine classical Bath stone building of 1819-20 designed by Sir Jeffry Wyattville. There are historic American interiors constructed to fit their new spaces, with quilts, Pennsylvania German and Shaker artifacts. Nearby are the beautiful landscaped gardens of **PRIOR PARK**, now a property of the National Trust. The great house, now a school, was begun by the elder Wood for Ralph Allen in 1735. Allen, whose lovely town house is tucked away behind buildings on the south side of the Abbey Church, was an energetic tycoon, not only quarrying Bath stone but profiting from a countrywide system of cross-posts which he introduced when postmaster in Bath. In the park below the house is the wonderfully sited Palladian Bridge, a 1750 copy of the famous one at Wilton House ▲ *210*.

Dyrham Park: Diogenes Room, (above left); State Bed in Queen Anne Room (top); and "Peasant woman and boy", Bartolomé Esteban Murillo (1618-82)

DYRHAM PARK Designed by William Talman, this country mansion, crowned with a balustrade affording fine views of the surrounding parkland, was built in 1698 for William Blathwayt, politician and secretary of state for William III. Its rooms, paneled with oak, walnut and cedar, have changed little since then. The house has a fine collection of portraits and tapestries, and blue-and-white delftware, reflecting the contemporary taste for Dutch fashion.

The American Museum, Claverton Manor

BADMINTON HOUSE ★ The classical mansion of the dukes of Beaufort since the 17th century, Badminton underwent alterations in 1740, possibly by William Kent, who also laid out the grounds (later extended by Capability Brown). Badminton contains a collection of Italian, Dutch and English paintings and some fine carving by Grinling Gibbons. The annual Badminton Horse Trials are held within the 15,000-acre estate each April, and the stables are open for viewing.

LITTLE SODBURY MANOR is a 15th-century gabled mansion with a magnificent Great Hall built for Sir John Walsh, the king's Champion; Henry VIII stayed here with Anne Boleyn. William Tyndale resided here as chaplain and tutor to Walsh's children, and it was here that he resolved to make an English translation of the Bible. He started his labor in the attic, which remains much as he knew it then. The northwest wing, however, burnt down in 1702.

HORTON COURT This Cotswold house is probably the oldest rectory in England. It was much altered in the 19th century, but the magnificent 12th-century Great Hall survives, and elsewhere in the house there remain early Renaissance features, including stucco caricatures of classical figures. There is an exceptionally fine detached loggia and an unusual late Perpendicular ambulatory in the garden.

223

▲ BRISTOL

Lord Mayor's Chapel of St Mark on College Green

Bristol Cathedral, choir

Clifton Suspension Bridge over the Avon Gorge

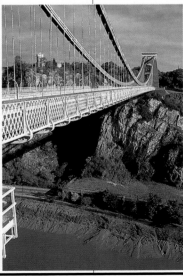

BRISTOL The Anglo-Saxon settlement at Bristol grew up around the bridge and harbor on the River Avon. With access to the sea, it increased in importance. Wool from the flocks of sheep grazing on the local pastureland, most of it originally monastic, was sent out in the 14th century to the Baltic countries and Ireland. In 1497 John Cabot sailed from here to find the Americas, landing in Newfoundland (a replica ship accomplished the journey again in 1997), and in 1552 the Society of Merchant Venturers was founded here. The port did a flourishing trade, importing wines, tobacco, chocolate, and slaves bought in West Africa to be sold in the Indies. The emancipation of slaves in the 1820s, and the growing competition from Liverpool, led to Bristol's decline. Further opportunities to develop came with the launching of Isambard Kingdom Brunel's steamships *Great Western* and *Great Britain*, however, in 1837 and 1843. The *Great Britain*, the first screw-propeled passenger ship, returned to Bristol in 1970 (for its restoration and an honored place in the dock) after it had been abandoned in the Falkland Islands in 1886. Brunel, whose London–Bristol railway line (1841) terminated in his Gothic-style station of Temple Meads, had long been involved with Bristol. He had remodeled the docks in 1830 and six years later designed the **CLIFTON SUSPENSION BRIDGE** over the 250-foot-deep Avon Gorge. This, however, was delayed through inadequate funding, and not built until 1864 (five years after Brunel's death) by the Institute of Civil Engineers. Clifton, residential suburb of Bristol, spreads from the Downs above the city with its Georgian and Regency terraces – Royal York Terrace, which looks out across the gorge, is the largest crescent in England. During the bombing raids of World War II many churches and historic houses were lost. Fortunately, the finest parish church in England, **ST MARY REDCLIFFE ★** with its 292-foot spire, survived, although traffic now swirls all around it. The decorated doorway of the north porch (*c.* 1325), with its triple-tiered display of naturalistic foliage, leads into a Perpendicular-style interior.

BRISTOL CATHEDRAL ★ was founded as an Augustinian abbey in the 1140s and became a cathedral in 1542. The Norman chapter-house is particularly fine. The chancel was begun in 1298 and completed 30 years later. The city boasts many other superb churches. The Norman CHURCH OF ST NICHOLAS acts as an ecclesiastical museum, containing the great altarpiece painted by William Hogarth taken from St Mary Redcliffe. The outstanding Christ Church of 1786 by William Paty has wooden figures striking bells to chart each quarter-hour. St Stephen's has a fine Perpendicular tower, and the LORD MAYOR'S CHAPEL OF ST MARK on College Green is noted for its remarkable German, French and English stained glass (some bought by the Corporation at the 1823 sale of William Beckford's Fonthill ▲ *209*). There are also some minor treasures – the wrought-iron sword rest of 1702 by William Edney, and the Poyntz chantry chapel of the 1530s with its Spanish floor tiles. Bristol has some interesting Georgian churches, too, including Redland Chapel (1741-3) built by William Halfpenny for the London grocer John Cossins (his bust by Rysbrack is kept here). Regular concerts are given in ST GEORGE'S (on Brandon Hill, off steep Park Street), a church by Sir Robert Smirke of 1823, now transformed into a concert hall and used by the BBC as a recording studio.

At the top of Park Street, in Queen's Road, is the imposing **WILLS TOWER** (1925) of the University, one of the landmarks of Bristol. Here also is the MUSEUM AND ART GALLERY, with its collections of maritime effects, its "Bristol blue" glass, Cookworthy porcelain, and paintings by the "Bristol School" – Francis Danby and others – of the Avon Gorge and elsewhere. There is also an excellent collection of French and Italian paintings from the 17th to 19th centuries, including Bellini's *Descent of Christ into Limbo*, Le Brun's *Worship of the Brazen Serpent* and Antonio da Solario's *Withypool Triptych*. Don't miss the houses maintained by Bristol's Museums Service, especially the 16th-century RED LODGE and the GEORGIAN HOUSE, which contains 18th-century furniture and fittings. There is almost too much to see in Bristol: other gems include John Wood's CORN EXCHANGE of 1743, the COOPERS' HALL by William Halfpenny, of the same year, the 1739 GROTTO at Goldney House in Clifton, the long south façade (1635) of ASHTON COURT, and the 1669 CHRISTMAS STEPS (off the beginning of Park Road). At the top is the tiny Perpendicular chapel of the THREE KINGS OF COLOGNE (1504), with Foster's Almshouses of 1861 now around it.

BLAISE HAMLET To the west of the church in Henbury, one of Bristol's villages, you will find the picturesque layout of tiny cottages at Blaise Hamlet (1811) designed by John Nash to accommodate Blaise Estate pensioners. With the fairytale village green, complete with water pump, and the quaint assortment of cottages, there is a subtly maintained degree of artificiality throughout. There is a city-administered folk museum in the nearby BLAISE CASTLE HOUSE, built originally by William Paty in 1796 for a Quaker banker, and set in delightful grounds adjacent to Blaise Woods.

Wills Tower

KING'S WESTON
At the end of the road from Silchester, on the Avon estuary, stood the small port of Abone, where lie the remains of a Roman villa. The site has been extensively excavated, and the findings are on display. The skeleton of a man killed by a sword was among the discoveries made by archeologists.

Nash cottages, Blaise Hamlet

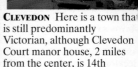

Congresbury church (far right) and stonework detail (right)

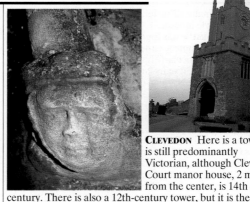

CLEVEDON Here is a town tha is still predominantly Victorian, although Clevedon Court manor house, 2 miles from the center, is 14th century. There is also a 12th-century tower, but it is the splendid collection of Nailsea glass and pottery by the English art potter, Sir Edmund Elton (1846-1920), that attracts most visitors. Clevedon Court was the Elton family home.

WRAXALL Eight miles due east of Clevedon is the impressive Perpendicular church of All Saints, Wraxall, atmospherically lit through its preponderance of Victorian stained-glass by C.E. Kempe. The windows afford almost too little light to permit a proper examination of the 15th-century tomb, with recumbent effigies of Sir Edmund and Lady Gorges.

YATTON At Yatton, the early 14th-century church of St Mary has the finest decorated (south) porch in Somerset. Thin Perpendicular stone lines rise up over the ogee curved doorway to the crocketed and pierced balustrade. Continue southeast through **CONGRESBURY**, a village of beautiful doorways, not least the church doorway. The church is 13th century, and has one of the most gracefu of Somerset's few spires. Inside is a font with a bucket-shaped Norman bowl on a 13th-century pedestal, and with a Jacobean cover. Between the clerestory windows i a collection of little people in red and green, many of whom are obviously suffering from toothache. Their swollen faces are believed to be here in memory of Bishop Button, whose wonderful cures are

GORGES TOMB
On the Gorges tomb at Wraxall find some light to take note of the splendid kneeling winged angels holding the coats-of-arms of the family, all flanking the grandly positioned central family arms, with its many quarterings betokening family liaisons.

Above and right: All Saints Church, Wraxall

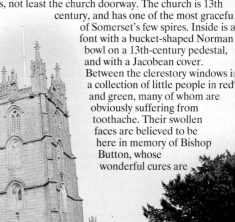

*Roadside cottage near
Stanton Drew*

STANTON DREW
At one time it is
obvious that stone
avenues stood at
Stanton Drew, very
similar to those
surviving at Avebury
and Stonehenge. In
fact, the Stanton
Drew site is a small
version of that at the
more imposing
Stonehenge
▲ 212-13.

remembered in his cathedral at Wells ▲ 228-9. Five miles
southwest is the church of St Andrew at **BANWELL**. It has a
very high tower (101 feet) with buttresses, pinnacles and a
parapet. Here you will find the best of carved rood screens,
dated to 1522.

CHEDDAR GORGE consists of steep limestone rocks and caves
that are rich in the remains left by prehistoric man. Follow the
A371 toward the cathedral city of Wells, making a detour up
the Cheddar Gorge road
(B3135) to Charterhouse and
the Bronze Age sanctuary at
GORSEY BIGBURY. Visitors can
see the earthwork, a circular
enclosure 160 feet across. From
here you can travel to the
important stone circles at
STANTON DREW, the most
important prehistoric
monument in Somerset, with
some 44 stones comprising
three circles, the largest 120
yards across.

Clevedon Court

CHEWTON MENDIP The church of St Mary Magdalene, at
Chewton Mendip, is Norman but has an imposing 16th-
century tower, and contains fragments of medieval glass and
14th-century effigies.

PRIDDY CIRCLES Four miles north of Wells is Priddy, with its
long barrows and the four large earthen rings, each some 550
feet in diameter, placed side by side in the Bronze Age.
Before continuing on to the city, pause to explore **WOOKEY
HOLE,** a mile north of Wells, where evidence of human
occupation has been found dating back to 35,000 BC. The
caves are now owned by Madame Tussaud's, who have added,
among other things, a museum.

Wells is England's smallest city but it has the most magnificent of cathedrals, which dominates its narrow streets. The west front makes a vast and amazing backdrop for some 400 figures of saints, prophets and angels. Many were defaced in the Civil War, but they have all benefited from the recent extensive restoration. Within, the great strainer arches of interlocked ogee curves, erected about 1340, straddle each side of the crossing and help to bear the crossing tower's great weight. The two west towers were built *c.* 1386. There is a famous astronomical clock in the north transept, dating from about 1390.

CONSTRUCTION OF THE CATHEDRAL

Wells Cathedral is the work of two main periods, *c.* 1180 to 1240 and *c.* 1290 to 1340. The first date gave the building a Gothic style. The later and original treatment of space gave us the remarkable Chapter House, Lady Chapels and the wondrous arches at the crossing. Moreover, on the West front is the richest display of 13th-century sculpture in England, dating to about 1235. The central Tower (left), like those at Hereford, Salisbury and Pershore, has a clarity of design in its soaring Perpendicular lines. Such buildings as Wells Cathedral are the work of talented craftsmen aided by the religious community raising funds. At Wells the work was under the supervision of the master-mason, William Wynford (fl. 1360-1404).

Left: Vicar's Close
Far left: The astronomic clock

The 36 ribs of the Chapter House rise from a fluted pier to support the center vault of its roof – one of the finest examples in England of the tierceron rib vaulting style. You reach it by a memorable flight of bifurcating steps of about 1270. Outside, on the northwest side of the cathedral, is a similarly astounding view – of the Vicar's Close, a street nearly 500 feet long, lined on both sides with precise early houses and their walled gardens, and ending in a small chapel of about 1470.

Glastonbury Abbey

The ruined 15th-century tower at Glastonbury

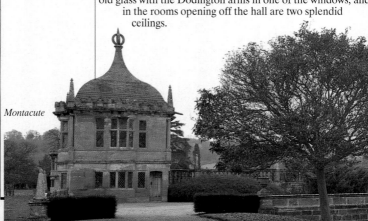

CROSCOMBE The church of St Mary at Croscombe has a high Jacobean rood screen with obelisks of about 1620; the pulpit is dated 1616 and has a large tester with similar obelisks on top.

GLASTONBURY There are two great legends linked to this bustling town, with its Victorian market cross at the center. Joseph of Arimathea is said to have journeyed to Glastonbury from the Holy Land, intent on converting the British, and to have buried the Holy Grail (the cup used by Christ at the Last Supper) beneath a spring at Tor Hill, to the east of the present town. He is also supposed to have built a chapel on which site the abbey was erected. A few remains are left, some merely foundations in the grass. The transept side of the Abbey Church (1184) rears up symmetrically, the masonry remains of doors and arches cut off against the sky. Tor Hill is also claimed as the legendary Avalon, the burial-place of King Arthur.

WESTON ZOYLAND In the church of St Mary, the initials of Richard Bere, abbot of Glastonbury (1493-1524), are carved on one of the buttresses. Of particular interest is the timber ceiling, with its pierced horizontal tie-beams and the large angels holding the central king posts that rise to the ridge of the roof.

BRIDGWATER Once Bridgwater was a busy port but was soon eclipsed by Bristol to the northeast. Cromwell's troops savaged it, but its low-slung Church of St Mary survived, a mixture of Decorated and Perpendicular styles, with a fine Jacobean screen in the south transept. Castle Street was begun in 1723 for the first Duke of Chandos; "The Lions" on West Quay is a fine mansion of about 1730. There is plenty of other good early Georgian architecture, some by the London builder-architects Thomas Fort and Edward Shepherd (both of whom worked on Cannons, demolished in 1747, the Duke's great Middlesex house).

DODINGTON HALL The hall of this Elizabethan manor house has a magnificent dark roof of solid oak, formed of richly carved panels, and supported on angel corbels. There is also a minstrel's gallery. The date 1581 is over the fireplace, which has an elaborate mantelpiece supported on one side by a man's head and on the other by a woman's. There is a little old glass with the Dodington arms in one of the windows, and in the rooms opening off the hall are two splendid ceilings.

COLERIDGE COTTAGE
In Lime Street, Nether Stowey, is Coleridge Cottage, where Samuel Taylor Coleridge lived from 1797 to 1800. He wrote part of "Christabel" there, as well as the "Rime of the Ancient Mariner", and there are mementos of the poet on display.

Montacute

Lytes Cary Manor, near Charlton Mackrell

Barrington Court

HESTERCOMBE ★
The 50-acre gardens of Hestercombe House were designed by Lutyens in 1906 and planted by Gertrude Jekyll.

From the collection at Montacute:
Below left: Elizabeth Knollys, Lady Layton (attributed to George Gower, 1577)
Below: Col. Edward Phelips (attributed to Jacob Huysmans, 1633)

TAUNTON Taunton has Georgian architecture in abundance, but one of the most interesting buildings, in Fore Street in the center of town, is the Elizabethan town-house of the Portman family (1578). Nearby is the Market House (1770-2), which has a pediment over a five-bay front. The church of St Mary Magdalene is a remodeling of the 15th-century church by Benjamin Ferrey and Sir George Gilbert Scott (1862). It has an imposing Perpendicular tower of red Quantock sandstone. The local museum at Taunton Castle in North Street has collections relevant to the whole county.

BARRINGTON COURT Gertrude Jekyll-inspired plantings surround the Tudor manor house restored in the 1920s by the Lyle family, just outside Ilminster.

LYTES CARY MANOR The south wing contains the Great Parlour, dated 1533, and above this lies the Great Chamber with an early plaster ceiling decorated with stars and diamonds. The arms of Henry VIII appear in the plasterwork.

MONTACUTE ★ Another great country house in this part of Somerset is Montacute, not far from the formal gardens of Tintinhull ▲ *232*. Built in Ham Hill stone, a warm biscuit tan in color, Montacute rears up on either side of its impressive entrance, with three tiers of windows, surmounted by statues of heroes. It was built about 1590 for Col. Edward Phelips, Speaker of the House of Commons – the date 1599 appears on one of the interior chimneypieces. Visitors glide round this fascinating house in felt over-slippers to protect the floors, although the imposing

Long Gallery (189 feet) was covered in apple-matting in 1998 when it was repainted. These improvements admirably set off the rearranged and wonderful display of Tudor and Jacobean portraits, on loan from the National Portrait Gallery in London.

Cleeve Abbey

Tintinhull House and garden

Exmoor National Park

Dunster Castle (below) and the Outer Hall (bottom)

YEOVILTON The Fleet Air Museum was opened at the Royal Naval Air Station in Yeovilton in 1964, to celebrate 50 years of naval flying. As well as displays charting its history and development, there are over 50 aeroplanes on show, including the Sea Vampire, the craft that made the first jet deck-landing in 1945, and Concorde 002.

TINTINHULL GARDEN A formal garden near Montacute House, Tintinhull is a 20th-century creation surrounding a perfect 17th-century manor house with a façade of *c*. 1720. The garden, enclosed within walls and clipped hedges, is quite small; but the uneven paths, cobbles, roses, honeysuckle and other scented plants make it seem far larger.

EXMOOR NATIONAL PARK Extending to the northern coastline from Minehead and Ilfracombe in Somerset to Combe Martin in Devon, Exmoor covers about 170,000 acres, a plateau of moorland and upland farms with deep wooded combes along the main rivers – the Exe, the Barle and the Lyn. Most of the land is owned by the National Trust. The coastline, stretching about 30 miles, is beautiful and dramatic, with key tourist centers at Minehead, Porlock and Lynmouth. Exmoor has a proliferation of ling, bellheather and gorse. The climate is often wet, with sea breezes. The moor is a haven for an enormous variety of flora and fauna.

DUNSTER CASTLE The little town of Dunster, at the west side of the county, is dominated by the Luttrell Arms (the Dunster residence of the abbots of Cleeve), by the octagonal market cross and by the castle. This is set dramatically on a wooded hilltop, above the River Tor. Though there has been a castle on the site since Norman times, the present building was largely rebuilt in 1868-72, under the direction of the architect Anthony Salvin. Salvin was working for George Luttrell, whose family had lived at Dunster for over 600 years. Within the house there are fine plaster-work ceilings, such as that in the Dining Room, dated to 1681, attributed to the leading London master, Edward Goudge. There is also a splendid staircase with an oak handrail and panels of hunting and military trophies, even coins, carved flowers and foliage, all in elm, dating to about 1683 (as do some of the Charles II shillings on display).

CLEEVE ABBEY Five miles southeast of Dunster are the extensive remains of Cleeve Abbey, founded as a Cistercian house in 1198. Best preserved is the complete grouping of cloister buildings. The refectory was rebuilt in the 16th century and has a fine timber wagon roof.

WEST COUNTRY
Jeremy Pearson

Scilly Isles

SHUTE, near Axminster, is the former home of the Pole family, who built a magnificent gatehouse flanked by two pavilions in 1560. Behind lies the Barton, a confusing mixture of medieval, Elizabethan and much later buildings.

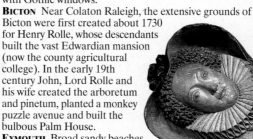

HONITON Renowned for the hand-made lace industry based here from the 16th century, Honiton flourished through the patronage of Queen Victoria, whose wedding dress was decorated with the local lace. The small **ALLHALLOWS MUSEUM** contains some very fine examples of local lace and has demonstrations of lacemaking.

OTTERY ST MARY ★ The important church of **ST MARY** was founded by John de Grandison, Bishop of Exeter in 1337, and was based on the design of Exeter Cathedral. Elaborate vaults, exceptional roof bosses, fine bench ends and corbels embellish the interior – among the most charming figures are elephants and a "green man".

SIDMOUTH The largely Regency town became a fashionable resort in the early years of the 19th century and still retains a genteel air. Throughout the town there are thatched Regency cottages, mostly with elaborate, dripping bargeboards and good ironwork, often with Gothic windows.

BICTON Near Colaton Raleigh, the extensive grounds of Bicton were first created about 1730 for Henry Rolle, whose descendants built the vast Edwardian mansion (now the county agricultural college). In the early 19th century John, Lord Rolle and his wife created the arboretum and pinetum, planted a monkey puzzle avenue and built the bulbous Palm House.

EXMOUTH Broad sandy beaches encouraged the development of this still-charming resort in the 19th century. Houses of note include (at Foxholes)

Ottery St Mary

COLERIDGE
Samuel Taylor Coleridge's father was the vicar and schoolmaster in Ottery St Mary; the poet lived here from 1772–81. He never lost his affection for the town, about which he wrote several poems.

Exeter Cathedral monument (right)

Exeter Cathedral

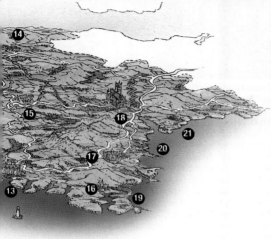

14th-century corbel from Exeter Cathedral showing a Virgin and Child

The Barn, a splendid Arts and Crafts house by E.S. Prior, and on another hill at the other end of the town, À LA RONDE. This sixteen-sided *cottage orné* was built by Miss Jane Parminter and her cousin Mary in 1798. All the wedge-shaped rooms open out of the central hall (fancifully said to be based on the Church of San Vitale in Ravenna), with an extraordinary shellwork grotto on the top floor.

EXETER Roman legions established a fortress here in AD 55-60. The remains of the Roman Bath House, with its mosaic floor, now lie buried under the Green, near the west front of the cathedral. By the 13th century there were over 20 churches within the walls, together with St Nicholas Priory (now a museum) and the CATHEDRAL ★, dedicated to St Peter. The twin towers crown the transepts, while the Purbeck columns of the nave support the longest unbroken Gothic vault in the world. There is a 60-foot high Bishop's Throne constructed in 1316 entirely without nails.

EXETER CASTLE, with its imposing gateway at Rougemont, protected and dominated a city that was already prosperous through its cloth trade. This developing wealth is evident in the late medieval clergy houses overlooking the cathedral, in the several half-timbered merchants' houses that survive in the High Street and in the GUILDHALL. The front of the present building, with its four massive granite Tuscan columns, was added to the earlier hall in about 1592-5. On the Quay, the CUSTOMS HOUSE of 1681, with its first-floor rooms decorated with extravagant plasterwork ceilings in high relief, is also a symbol of the thriving wool trade. The ROYAL ALBERT MEMORIAL MUSEUM AND ART GALLERY comprises a college, art school, library and museum, built with several varieties of local stone and completed in 1866. Many of the exhibits are by locally born artists such as Reynolds, Hudson, White Abbot, Payne and Prout.

A La Ronde

Above: Powderham Castle staircase (left) and libraries (right)

Below: Killerton House, and a display in the Museum of Costume (bottom)

CREDITON was birthplace of St Boniface and the seat of the western bishopric from 909 until 1050. The church of the Holy Cross ★ has a Perpendicular air and a range of monuments.

KILLERTON The grounds that surround the plain house of 1778-9 are full of rare and tender shrubs and command views across the valley of the Culm to the valley of the Exe. The Aclands, who have lived here since the early 17th century, planned a large and elaborate house by James Wyatt; but it was never built, and their "temporary" home now accommodates the National Trust collection of costume, charmingly displayed in period settings.

POWDERHAM CASTLE ★ This ancient home of the Courtenays, earls of Devon, was reordered by Charles Fowler in the mid-1840s. The silhouette was embellished and made more romantic and the interior was reorganized. The apsidal-ended Music Room by James Wyatt of 1794-6, with portraits by Richard Cosway, is a masterpiece of light and delicate neoclassical work. Commissioned by the 3rd Viscount Courtenay (later 9th Earl of Devon), he decorated some roundels in the room with the help of his 13 daughters. The Great Staircase has notable plasterwork by John Jenkins dating from the 1750s, including exuberant trophies and great garlands of fruit and flowers. The deer park stretches in front of the castle down to the River Exe, while behind the house is the mid-18th-century triangular Belvedere, mirrored by the **HALDON BELVEDERE** near Dunchideock. This triangular tower, with corner turrets and Gothic windows, was built in 1788 by Sir Robert Palk, a local landowner, in memory of his friend from his days in India, General Stringer Lawrence. An over-lifesize statue of the General in classical garb, in Coade stone, stands on the ground floor. The upstairs rooms command magnificent views.

UGBROOKE HOUSE Set within a Capability Brown park, the plain but castellated house of the Cliffords was built by Robert Adam for the 4th Lord Clifford (d. 1783). His ancestor was Charles II's Lord Chancellor, and this office had done much to improve the family's fortunes. A magnificent silver-gilt bowl and ewer connected with this Lord Clifford (the first member of the CABAL) is still on show in the house. Other treasures include magnificent 18th-century embroideries executed by the Cliffords or their kinswomen, the Howards, for they were Catholics and rigidly stuck to the old ways. The chapel wing has a plain Adam exterior which does not prepare the visitor for the mid-19th-century marble exuberance within.

Dartmouth Castle

TORQUAY The English Riviera has long been a popular holiday resort for those in need of recuperation – Elizabeth Barrett and John Keats both came here for their health, and Charles Kingsley brought his wife. On the seafront are the remains of Torre Abbey, which together with the Art Gallery and the Spanish Barn form the cultural heart of the town. Another popular stop is the pretty hamlet of COCKINGTON, with its 16th-century Court, its forge, and a fine inn designed in the 1930s by Sir Edwin Lutyens. In PAIGNTON is Oldway Manison (pictured on page 233), the remarkable home of Isaac Singer (of the sewing-machine company). Finished by his third son, Paris, in 1907, it is modeled on Versailles. Up the grand imperial staircase with its marble walls, visitors can see the first-floor rooms where Isadora Duncan once danced.

Below: Berry pomeroy Castle
Bottom left: Totnes Castle
Bottom right: Compton Castle Courtyard

BERRY POMEROY CASTLE The castle was much drawn in the 18th century by artists seeking the romantic. The oldest walls date from the second half of the 15th century, and beyond lie the ruins of the ambitious house built for Edward, Duke of Somerset, the Protector. As the castle was begun in 1547, not much can have been completed at the time of Edward's execution in 1552, but later descriptions tell of great chimneypieces of marble and statues of alabaster.

BRIXHAM Brixham is still a bustling fishing port, as it was in 1688 when William of Orange landed here with 15,000 men and 6,000 horses to claim the English throne. His statue (right) stands near the excellent National Fisheries Museum. Between Brixham and Kingswear lies COLETON FISHACRE, first acquired by the National Trust for its magnificent coastline, but now both the house and garden, created 1923-26 by Oswald Milne for Rupert D'Oyly Carte (of the family of the Gilbert and Sullivan operas and the Savoy Hotel) are open to the public.

Statue of William of Orange in Brixham

DARTMOUTH A richly decorated church and the timbered Butterwalk are testament to the early wealth of the little port, as are the later houses around Bayard's Cove. At the mouth of the river lies the small church of St Petroc beside the castle of 1481, which looks across to its neighbor at Kingswear. At the other end of the town stands the imperial mass of the Royal Naval College, designed by Sir Aston Webb, and opened by Edward VII.

TOTNES Totnes is recognized as one of the most complete early towns in the country. The main street winds past 16th-and 17th-century merchants' houses, through the town walls at the East Gate, past the church, with the medieval Guildhall behind it, and eventually reaches the large motte-and-bailey castle. The remains of the shell keep, dating from the 14th century, are remarkable. The church of St Mary, with its unusually fine tower, was built by subscription in the mid 15th century.

WILLIAM
PRINCE OF ORANGE
AFTERWARDS
WILLIAM III
KING OF GREAT BRITAIN & IRELAND
LANDED NEAR THIS SPOT
5TH NOVEMBER 1688

Above: The remains of medieval farmhouses on Hounds Tor

Dartington Hall

DARTINGTON The extensive medieval house of John Holland, Duke of Exeter, half-brother of Richard II and stepson of the Black Prince, is set within glorious gardens ★ and includes his tiltyard. The Great Hall was built between 1388 and 1399. Holland's symbol of the wheatear surrounds the white hart of Richard II on the boss in the entrance porch. The imaginative revival of the buildings and the grounds in the 1920s and 1930s is due to the Americans Leonard and Dorothy Elmhirst, who financed the creation of **DARTINGTON COLLEGE**, a large, liberal school and college of the arts; **HIGH CROSS** was built in 1931-2 by William Lescaze in the International Modern style. The sharp geometric light-filled rooms house a fine contemporary collection of art and craft work.

SALCOMBE This is largely a late 19th- and early 20th-century resort with charming villas (some Arts and Crafts) set in subtropical gardens overlooking the water. One of these, at the far end of the town past Fort Charles, is **OVERBECKS**, an Edwardian house full of curiosities, in terraced grounds with a wide range of unusual plants.

BUCKFAST Buckfast Abbey is the site of perhaps the richest medieval Cistercian monastery in the West of England. In 1882 it was acquired by the Benedictine Order, which began to erect a temporary church (now the Chapter House) in the same year. The large church was mostly built by the monks themselves of grey limestone with Ham stone dressings and an interior of Bath stone, and was dedicated in August 1932. Many of the more spectacular furnishings are by Bernhard Witte of Aachen and date from the late 1920s.

DARTMOOR covers an area of over 200 square miles, extending between Okehampton, Tavistock, Ivybridge and Moretonhampstead. The central granite plateau is wild and remote, its small depressions filled with treacherous bogs and morasses. The tors – granite outcrops in contorted forms – dominate the skyline, and are sometimes surrounded by great

Buckfast Abbey's nave and exterior view

clusters of granite slabs and boulders of extraordinary shapes. The foothills are softer, characterized by deep ravines and gentle, sparsely wooded green valleys with charming villages such as **NORTH BOVEY** or **WIDECOMBE IN THE MOOR**.

MORETONHAMPSTEAD One of the main centers for touring Dartmoor, this was once a thriving wool town. Little survives from the early days apart from the church and the colonnaded almshouses of 1637. There are many prehistoric remains in

he area; cairns, hut circles and stone circles at Butterdon and
Mardon Downs and hill forts at Wooston, Cranbrook and
Prestonbury.

MERRIVALE The Rows are among the most accessible of the
early remains on the moor. Two rows of small stones, one 850
feet and the other 590 feet in length, lead to a large circle of
upright stones. Nearby there are cairns, hut circles and a

menhir (a single standing stone). Here also is the King's Tor
quarry, among the most important on the moor.

OKEHAMPTON The castle was begun by Baldwin de Brionne,
Sheriff of Devon after the Conquest. In about 1170 it passed
into the hands of the Courtenays, who held it until 1538. It lies
above the rushing waters of the West Okement on a natural
spur; the square Norman keep is a reminder of its original
defensive purpose. The later, early 14th-century building was
of a more ceremonial nature and incorporated the large Great
Hall and several lodgings.

*Above: Lydford Gorge
Above left:
Okehampton Castle*

LYDFORD The little village lies above the swiftly flowing
waters of the Lyd, which passes through a very dramatic
60-foot gorge viewed from narrow precipitous paths cut into
the cliffs.

TAVISTOCK At one end of the main street is a statue of Sir
Francis Drake ▲ *240*, the famous son of the town. **ENDSLEIGH
COTTAGE** (1810) was built by Sir Jeffry Wyattville in the most
picturesque of styles and enjoys exceptional views out across
the Tamar valley. The grounds are by Humphry Repton.

CASTLE DROGO ★ Perhaps the last castle to be built in
England, Castle Drogo was conceived on a grandiose scale by
Julius Drewe, who had made a fortune early in life from his
large chain of Home and Colonial grocery stores. His
architect was Sir Edwin Lutyens ▲ *416*, who was charged with
building a medieval-style castle with walls 6 feet thick. The
first schemes were grand and costly, the finished design more
economical but still monumental. Work started in 1911/12 and
finished in 1930, the year before Drewe's death. The plain
exterior is of granite, with huge mullioned windows and a
castelated parapet; the only relief is the large Drewe lion
carved above the entrance door, which even has its own
portcullis. The interior is notable for its cool, wonderfully
controlled spaces; the long vaulted corridors; and the wide,
dramatic staircase that leads down to the paneled Dining
Room. The ornamental grounds lie some way from the house.
Yew hedges surround the circular croquet lawn; beyond, along
a shrub-lined path, is a large rectangular rose and herbaceous
garden with corner pavilions of hornbeam.

*Above: Castle Drogo.
The Library has a
fine oak-coffered
ceiling, and a massive
billiard table in the
anteroom, from which
it is divided by a
granite arch.*

BUCKLAND ABBEY
(above and below) To a greater degree than in many other houses converted into homes after the Dissolution, the form of the original Abbey church is easily discernible. After Sir Francis Drake became rich from his voyages and from royal patronage, he purchased the property from Sir Richard Grenville and it is now largely a memorial to this great Devon seadog. His famous drum is kept here, together with many other mementos and portraits. Fire ravaged the mansion in 1938; but the nearby Tithe Barn, some 159 feet long, survives as a testimony to the wealth of the Cistercians who bred sheep on this part of Dartmoor from 1278.

Right: Portrait of Sir Francis Drake, 1591, after Gheeraerts, now at the National Maritime Museum
Below: the Drake Chamber at Buckland Abbey

PLYMOUTH An important fishing and trading port from early times, Plymouth was largely destroyed by German bombs in 1941, though small Elizabethan houses are still to be found in the winding streets around the former Fish Market. Nearby is a row of commemorative stones recording many of the perilous voyages that have started from here, including that of the *Mayflower* in September 1620. The hill behind is crowned by the protective walls of the Citadel. The present complex was begun in 1666 by Charles II, who perhaps also feared the Parliamentary leanings of the Plymouth citizens. With both Ionic pilasters and Corinthian columns, great carved trophies and statues in niches, it is one of the greatest baroque compositions of the South West. Inside the massive walls lie the Chapel of St Katherine and a range of messes, barrack blocks and other types of accommodation. THE HOE, famous as the place where Sir Francis Drake was playing bowls as the Spanish Armada approached, is still the favorite Plymouth promenade. The CITY MUSEUM AND ART GALLERY, at Drake Circus, opposite the recently founded University of Plymouth, has large and notable collections. Chief among these must be the Cottonian Collection of early drawings, prints and bronzes inherited and then amplified by the local 19th-century antiquary William Cotton. He also collected items belonging to local artists, such as Sir Joshua Reynolds, born at Plympton St Maurice. The work of later West Country artists is well represented and includes one of the greatest of the Newlyn School ▲ *245* works, *The Fish Sale on a Cornish Beach*, by Stanhope Forbes.

DEVONPORT William III established the Royal Naval Dockyard on the bank of the broad Hamoaze in 1691. During the next century the many naval engagements of the developing Empire saw Devonport's rapid expansion. Within the Yard is a number of fine early buildings such as the Roperies of 1763-72, and The Terrace of 1692, while outside are many latter naval residences, such as Hamoaze House (1795, built for the Duke

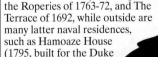

Richmond) and the Port Admiral's ouse of 1808-10. In the civilian part of e town Ker Street is terminated by the rious composition of a Greek Town Hall 821), a remarkable Egyptian-style stitution (1823) and a Doric column mmemorating the creation of the rough in 1824.

ALTRAM ★ is the finest surviving 18th-ntury house in the county, with much rk by Robert Adam (between 1768 and 82) for the Parker family. George Parker acquired a Tudor use in 1712; subsequent generations clothed this (still ident in the central core) with more fashionable and nvenient apartments and furnished the rooms. The Parkers re also noted patrons of the arts, particularly of Sir Joshua eynolds, and there are many pictures by him in the house. so represented is the work of his pupil James Northcote, other Devonian, together with Reni, Rubens, de Hooch and gelica Kauffman. The Saloon is the great room of the use, with its Venetian window, massive mirrors designed by dam and a carpet echoing the tripartite panels of the ceiling, signed by Thomas Whitty of Axminster in 1770. The red lvet-hung Morning Room, the pillared Drawing Room, the sidal-ended Dining Room, and the Library are other table ground-floor rooms, while on the first floor some of e rooms are decorated with 18th-century Chinese llpapers of the finest quality. The view from the grounds is longer as idyllic as it once was, but there are still interesting ildings to visit: an orangery, a converted chapel, a temple, a ck chapel, an amphitheater and three grottos.

Saltram House

Top: Theresa Robinson, Mrs Parker, and her son, later 1st Earl of Morley by Sir Joshua Reynolds (1723-92)

The Dining Room at Saltram House, with plasterwork by Joseph Rose and inset paintings by Antonio Zucchi and Francesco Zuccarelli

Adam vase and pedestal, Saltram House

Left: Cotehele House
Below center: Lanhydrock House

ANTONY Set within the extensive lawns and avenues of a landscape designed by Humphry Repton, this very early 18th-century house follows designs by James Gibbs, but the actual architect is unknown. Within the pinkish granite walls is a remarkable collection of famil and other portraits, modern pictures, fine furniture and tapestries, formed by members of the Pole and Carew familie

MOUNT EDGCUMBE The main house of the Egcumbes was built between 1547 and 1554 with four corner towers and a great central hall rising above the roof line. There is much to see in the ground the Earl's garden near the house; the formal French and Italian and then English gardens at the foot of the hill; and the temples, ruins and other features scattered throughout.

COTEHELE ★ This ancient estate was th home of the Edgcumbes from the 15th century. The present house became their secondary residenc after the construction of Mount Edgcumbe, and therefore slumbered until renovations in 1862 transformed the old service range into a dower house. The original state rooms survive in a remarkable way; filled with Flemish and English tapestries and curious and ancient furniture, they have not changed since Nicholas Condy recorded them *c.* 1840. Four four-poster beds have survived with a variety of elaborate, rare and early hangings, and chairs in the Punch room surviv with their early 18th-century covering of "Queen Anne's tatting". Beyond the delightful gardens is the Prospect Tower the Chapel in the Woods and the manorial Mill.

LANHYDROCK ★ Nestling under the protective lee of a hill, the ancient home of the Robarteses was destroyed by fire in 1881. A that survived the conflagration was the Gate House and the Long Gallery, with its outstanding 17th-century plasterwork ceiling depicting Old Testament scenes; both were built soon after S Richard Robartes purchased the property in 1620. The Victoria rebuilding is remarkable for the comprehensiveness of their well-planned state and service rooms. The ancient parish church lies beyond the formal gardens.

The long avenue leading to the house was originally laid out in the 1640s, and has fine views of **RESTORMEL CASTL** Now a ruined shell keep on top of a conical hill, the castle forms perfect circle, 110 feet in diameter, with domestic apartments within the curtain wall. It dates large from the 13th century.

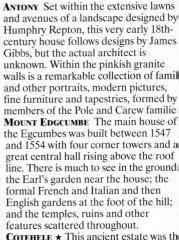

The Edgcumbe family coat-of-arms

ST MAWES
The trefoil-shaped castle at St Mawes (below) was built on the orders of Henry VIII between 1540 and 1543. It commands the eastern banks of the Carrick Roads and looks toward its larger sister fortress at Pendennis
▲ *244.*

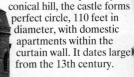

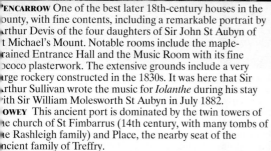

PENCARROW One of the best later 18th-century houses in the county, with fine contents, including a remarkable portrait by Arthur Devis of the four daughters of Sir John St Aubyn of St Michael's Mount. Notable rooms include the maple-grained Entrance Hall and the Music Room with its fine rococo plasterwork. The extensive grounds include a very large rockery constructed in the 1830s. It was here that Sir Arthur Sullivan wrote the music for *Iolanthe* during his stay with Sir William Molesworth St Aubyn in July 1882.

FOWEY This ancient port is dominated by the twin towers of the church of St Fimbarrus (14th century, with many tombs of the Rashleigh family) and Place, the nearby seat of the ancient family of Treffry.

THE ROSELAND PENINSULA A tranquil part of the county, with quiet sandy beaches, attractive villages such as VERYAN, with its entrances guarded by early 19th-century circular cottages to keep out the Devil, and the ancient fishing ports of MEVAGISSEY, GORRAN HAVEN and PORTLOE.

TRURO Cornwall's county town is set in a deep valley, with the three spires of the CATHEDRAL ● 86 at its center, rising imperiously above the clustered roofs of the shops and houses. The foundation stone of the cathedral was laid in 1880. The architect was John Loughborough Pearson, whose son Frank oversaw its completion in 1920. It is Early English in style, with spires covered with copper (one of Cornwall's principal minerals). The nave appears to be twisted, thanks to the retention of the ancient parish church of St Mary, but rises magnificently to a range of stone vaults. The Baptistery on the south side is unusually rich and complex, with a highly decorative mosaic floor. THE ROYAL CORNWALL MUSEUM in River Street houses the county's collection of archeology, with many items relating to the history of the area. They include silver and coins; Plymouth porcelain made from the locally mined china clay; a fine collection of pictures of the county and its inhabitants; and others by artists such as Stanhope Forbes and Patrick Heron, who made their homes here. It also houses the exceptionally fine Rashleigh collection of geological specimens. The gardens at TREWITHEN ★, created at the beginning of the 20th century by George Johnstone, are outstanding, with a wide range of flowering shrubs.

Above left: Mount Edgcumbe
Above: Trelissick Garden ★ is famed for its early shrubs, the fine Dell garden and its extensive herbaceous borders.

Truro Cathedral

THE LOST GARDENS OF HELIGAN surround the large 18th-century house that was once home to the Tremaynes. In recent years the extensive walled gardens have been authentically and painstakingly restored, and include such rarities as a pineapple pit. The rhododendron garden, the valley garden with its tree ferns and the Italian garden are among Heligan's most memorable features. The largest garden restoration scheme in Europe, it has been the subject of a number of books and a television series.

Mount Edgcumbe House and Park by W. du Busc

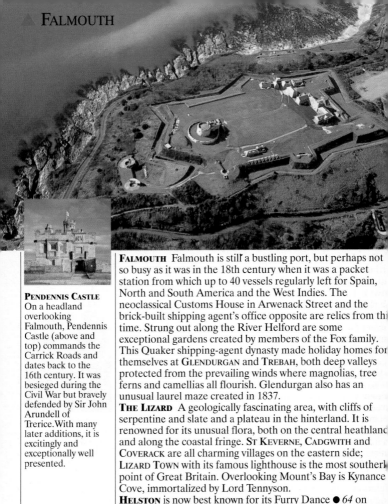

PENDENNIS CASTLE
On a headland overlooking Falmouth, Pendennis Castle (above and top) commands the Carrick Roads and dates back to the 16th century. It was besieged during the Civil War but bravely defended by Sir John Arundell of Trerice. With many later additions, it is excitingly and exceptionally well presented.

Minack Theatre

FALMOUTH Falmouth is still a bustling port, but perhaps not so busy as it was in the 18th century when it was a packet station from which up to 40 vessels regularly left for Spain, North and South America and the West Indies. The neoclassical Customs House in Arwenack Street and the brick-built shipping agent's office opposite are relics from this time. Strung out along the River Helford are some exceptional gardens created by members of the Fox family. This Quaker shipping-agent dynasty made holiday homes for themselves at GLENDURGAN and TREBAH, both deep valleys protected from the prevailing winds where magnolias, tree ferns and camellias all flourish. Glendurgan also has an unusual laurel maze created in 1837.

THE LIZARD A geologically fascinating area, with cliffs of serpentine and slate and a plateau in the hinterland. It is renowned for its unusual flora, both on the central heathland and along the coastal fringe. ST KEVERNE, CADGWITH and COVERACK are all charming villages on the eastern side; LIZARD TOWN with its famous lighthouse is the most southerly point of Great Britain. Overlooking Mount's Bay is Kynance Cove, immortalized by Lord Tennyson.

HELSTON is now best known for its Furry Dance ● *64* on May 8, its name taken from *fer*, the Cornish for "fair". The Penrose Estate nearby has extensive walks, some around the Loe Pool, the largest freshwater lake in the county.

PENZANCE was a prosperous town thanks to its mining, maritime and tourist industries, and its wealth is reflected in the elegant terraces and squares of Regency houses, the Egyptian House in Chapel Street and the many grand houses on its outskirts.

Trengwainton Garden

The **PENLEE HOUSE MUSEUM AND ART GALLERY**, set in lovely subtropical gardens, has recently been remodeled to accommodate a superb collection of Newlyn School pictures. There are also galleries devoted to the rich archeology of the area, together with its flora and fauna. The region's geology is best described at the **ROYAL GEOLOGICAL MUSEUM** in St John's Hall, one of the largest granite buildings in the world. **TRENGWAINTON GARDEN** lies in a sheltered valley to the west. In the unusual and extensive early 19th-century walled gardens,

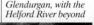

Glendurgan, with the Helford River beyond

with their raised beds, Sir Edward Bolitho planted a wide range of tender and exotic plants in the 1930s and later created an outstanding stream garden that has color throughout the year. The terrace at the top of the garden has a panoramic view back across Mount's Bay to Lizard Point. **NEWLYN** is the largest fishing port of the South West. Dozens of vessels still regularly leave its large sheltered harbor; the **PILCHARD MUSEUM** is well worth a visit. A bronze line at the entrance to the harbor marks the level of the sea as

recognized throughout the world. **NEWLYN ART GALLERY** has an adventurous contemporary art exhibition program.
LAND'S END This remote, largely level peninsula that rises northward to the Penwith Moors is windswept and mysterious; Neolithic, Bronze Age and Iron Age remains are scattered all around. At **LAND'S END** itself is a sizeable, largely modern tourist complex which includes restaurants, exhibitions (one concentrates on the many travelers who trek from here to John O'Groats) and a stimulating high-tech Lost Labyrinth visitor experience. At **ZENNOR** is the more peaceful **WAYSIDE MUSEUM**, displaying artifacts from the area, and the church of St Senar, with its famous pew carved with a mermaid. **PENDEEN** and **ST JUST** were two of the main mining centers of the far west, of which remains can be seen at **GEEVOR** and **LEVANT**. At **PORTHCURNO** is the fascinating **MUSEUM OF SUBMARINE TELEGRAPHY**. The cables that left Porthcurno beach in the late 19th century helped to form the British Empire and changed the face of the world. The open-air **MINACK THEATRE** (below) nearby has a regular series of week-long productions during the summer months.

NEWLYN SCHOOL
A group of artists working in Newlyn around 1880–1910, influenced by the Impressionists, became known as the Newlyn School; key members were Stanhope Forbes and Walter Langley. A good range of their work is on display at the Penlee Art Gallery, including Langley's *Among the Missing*, 1884 (above). More recent Newlyn School works are shown at the Newlyn Gallery.

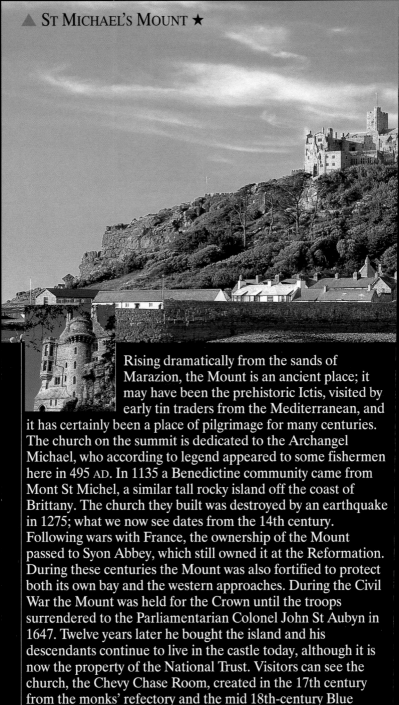

Rising dramatically from the sands of Marazion, the Mount is an ancient place; it may have been the prehistoric Ictis, visited by early tin traders from the Mediterranean, and it has certainly been a place of pilgrimage for many centuries. The church on the summit is dedicated to the Archangel Michael, who according to legend appeared to some fishermen here in 495 AD. In 1135 a Benedictine community came from Mont St Michel, a similar tall rocky island off the coast of Brittany. The church they built was destroyed by an earthquake in 1275; what we now see dates from the 14th century. Following wars with France, the ownership of the Mount passed to Syon Abbey, which still owned it at the Reformation. During these centuries the Mount was also fortified to protect both its own bay and the western approaches. During the Civil War the Mount was held for the Crown until the troops surrendered to the Parliamentarian Colonel John St Aubyn in 1647. Twelve years later he bought the island and his descendants continue to live in the castle today, although it is now the property of the National Trust. Visitors can see the church, the Chevy Chase Room, created in the 17th century from the monks' refectory and the mid 18th-century Blue Drawing Rooms made within the walls of the Lady Chapel. Piers St Aubyn, a cousin of the then owner, made major additions to the castle in the 1870s. The views from the terraces are magnificent.

CELTIC CROSS
Cornwall has many ancient granite crosses, which either marked pilgrimage routes or were used as meeting places by preachers.

CHAPEL INTERIOR
The 14th-century chapel has been visited by pilgrims for centuries. The view above shows the east end.

BLUE DRAWING ROOM
The large Blue Drawing Room was formed out of the Lady Chapel in the early 18th century and houses pictures by Gainsborough, Zoffany and John Opie.

Above: Chysauster Ancient Village, near Penzance, is a deserted Roman village with eight well-preserved houses. Right: Tresco Abbey Garden

SCILLY ISLES This archipelago lies some 28 miles off Land's End. Of the hundred or so islands, only five are inhabited; the largest is **ST MARY'S**. From here, boats leave regularly for the other islands, with their white sandy beaches, glorious sea views and flower fields protected from the boisterous winds by thick hedges. **TRESCO** with its **ABBEY GARDEN** ★ is one of the most popular destinations. Founded in the grounds of a former Benedictine Abbey by Augustus Smith, Lord Proprietor of the Isles in the mid-19th century, it is now famous for its subtropical grounds where exotic plants such as aloes, mimosa and palm trees line the terraced pathways. Recent introductions include a variety of sculpture and the Valhalla collection of ships' figureheads.

PENZANCE TO BUDE

A Cornish Engine: Taylor's shaft, East Pool mine

ST IVES White beaches and one of the most picturesque roofscapes in the county have long attracted artists to the cobbled streets of Porthminster and Porthmeor. Many of the fishermens' cottages, often reached by exterior staircases spread out from the harbor, have now been converted into craft galleries or restaurants. The **TATE ST IVES** ★ is housed in an impressive 1993 building with wide windows looking out over Porthmeor Beach. The fascinating collection includes works by Ben Nicholson, Barbara Hepworth, Naum Gabo and local artists of the St Ives School. Hepworth sculptures can also be seen in the **BARBARA HEPWORTH MUSEUM AND SCULPTURE GARDEN**.

REDRUTH AND CAMBORNE The towns, whose fortunes are intertwined with the tin and copper industries, represent Cornwall's industrial heartland. The last mine, South Crofty, still lingers on, but its future is very uncertain. The **CAMBORNE SCHOOL OF MINES** has an outstanding geological museum, some of whose specimens have been presented by its students (who come from all over the world). At **GWENNAP PIT** an amphitheater formed from fallen mine

Left: the Great Hall at Trerice showing the Jacobean plasterwork ceiling
Top: "People in a wind" by Kenneth Armitage, 1950
Above: Tate Gallery, St Ives

vorkings now seats over 1,000 people. It is a memorial to John Wesley, who visited the Pit 18 times between 1762 and 1789.

NEWQUAY A bustling, largely Victorian, resort spread out along he cliffs, with fine views along the coast in both directions; much used by wind-surfers. Two miles away, but seemingly in a different age, is **TRERICE**, an Elizabethan manor house with Dutch-inspired gables built by Sir John Arundell. Several of the rooms have elaborate plasterwork ceilings and overmantels, and contain fine furniture, pictures and clocks.

PADSTOW Above the town, and set in its own deer park, is **PRIDEAUX PLACE**, where the Prideaux family has lived since the 1530s. There is a fine 17th-century plasterwork ceiling with biblical scenes in the Great Chamber. Much renovation in the Gothick style took place about 1810, including a memorable staircase hall and library. The Reading Room is decorated with late 17th-century paneling.

TINTAGEL A popular, tourist-orientated village, dominated by the Arthurian myths encouraged by the poems of Lord Tennyson. The ancient **CASTLE** on the steep headland of Tintagel Island, has long been a defensive site; there is also an Iron Age enclosure, a Roman signal station and a Celtic monastery. There are Roman remains in the Norman church of St Merteriana, which is set in flower-strewn fields high above the village, and whose tower is visible for many miles around. In Fore Street **THE OLD POST OFFICE** is a 15th-century manor house in miniature that was used in the mid-19th century as a Letter Receiving Office for the area.

Tintagel, above, was traditionally the setting for King Arthur's Court.

Prideaux Place

Launceston Castle

BOSCASTLE One of the few harbors on this treacherous coast: a flourishing coastal trade took place here until the arrival of the railways in the 1890s. Above the clustered cottages of the port are the Forrabury Stitches, medieval field strips still farmed in the traditional, communal way. Some way up the Valency Valley is the church of St Julitta, which was restored by the young Thomas Hardy in 1871-2.

LAUNCESTON Dominated by the ruins of the motte-and-bailey Norman Castle, the town is the gateway to Cornwall on the northern route; any invader would have been intimidated by the strength of the King's defences on the high outcrop overlooking the River Tamar. Nearby, the carved granite church of St Mary Magdalene ★ is notable for the work to the south aisle undertaken by Sir Henry Trecarrel between 1511 and 1524.

BUDE TO BARNSTAPLE

BUDE A pleasant and traditional holiday resort which is divided by the Bude Canal. More ancient is the adjoining town of Stratton, on whose outskirts the Battle of Stamford Hill was fought in 1643, when the Royalist Sir Beville Grenville led his troops to victory. The house at STOWE built

Clovelly harbor

by his son John Grenville, Earl of Bath, and completed in 1680, stood above the cliffs near Kilkhampton. Akin to Belton House in Lincolnshire ▲ *359*, it was a two-storey brick house with a hipped roof crowned with a cupola, its elaborately decorated rooms and staircases were removed to other houses in the area (such as Prideaux Place ▲ *249*) when it was demolished in 1739.

CLOVELLY Best approached along the 3-mile Hobby Drive through hanging woods above the precipitous coast, the village is justly famed for its beauty. Much of its character dates from between the wars, so would not have been known to Charles Kingsley, whose father was the rector here, and who describes the village in *Westward Ho!* (1855).

WESTWARD HO! Took its name from Kingsley's novel, and is a small resort set behind the Pebble Ridge. Rudyard Kipling attended the United Services College here from 1878 until 1882 and described the place in *Stalky and Co* (1899).

BIDEFORD The main feature of the bustling port is the 24-arch medieval bridge over the River Torridge. Each arch is different, as the structure was paid for by a variety of donors

Early Christian memorial stones in the old cemetery beneath the lighthouse at Lundy

and guilds. In the 17th century there was an important North American trade in pottery, tobacco and Newfoundland fish. Some of these links are commemorated in the Church of St Mary, where a window engraved by Laurence Whistler commemorates one of Devon's great heroes, Sir Richard Grenville, whose family did much to expand the town.

GREAT TORRINGTON Sometimes known as the "English Jerusalem" – because of its position on a high escarpment, clustering around the castle and protected by a horseshoe bend in the River Torridge – the town is visited principally by those interested in its large glassworks. A couple of miles out of the town is **ROSEMOOR**, based on a fine shrub and tree garden established by Lady Anne Palmer, but now greatly supplemented by other gardens (notably a rose garden, magnificent in June). It is now owned by the Royal Horticultural Society.

BARNSTAPLE North Devon's main town and, like Bideford, made rich through its trade with North America in the 17th and early 18th centuries. The River Taw is crossed by an ancient 14-arch bridge leading into the heart of the town, which is dominated by the motte of the early castle.

ILFRACOMBE The wild and romantic scenery of the North Devon coast where it meets Exmoor greatly appealed to the Victorians, who flocked to this new resort either by narrow-gauge railway from Barnstaple or by paddle-steamer from the ports of the Bristol Channel.

LUNDY This 3-mile-long island has a remote and windswept character. There is a lighthouse at either end, and a church built in 1896 by the owner and aptly named incumbent, the Reverend H.G. Heaven, near the castle.

View from Penally Hill showing Meachard Island and Boscastle harbor at high tide.

Hartland Point, looking out toward Lundy Island

Above: Arlington Court is filled with the idiosyncratic collections of Miss Rosalie Chichester
Above right: the Morning Room

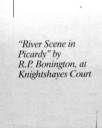

The Victorian neo-Gothic hall at Knightshayes Court

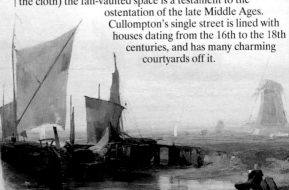

"River Scene in Picardy" by R.P. Bonington, at Knightshayes Court

PARRACOMBE St Petrock is an early medieval church, whose 16th-century pews were augmented in the 18th century by large box pews, a pulpit with sounding board, and a painting of the Commandments, the Lord's Prayer and Royal Arms.

ARLINGTON COURT This commodious Regency house has a plain Victorian exterior, relieved only by a single-storey Doric porch, and lavishness within. Along the south front are three intercommunicating reception rooms with delicate colored plaster ceilings divided by pairs of scagliola columns and housing William Blake's great but mysterious *Allegory*.

TIVERTON The handsome church of St Peter was enriched by John Greenway, a merchant whose sailing vessels are represented on the outside of the south porch and aisle. The interior of the porch has an elaborate vault, with an Assumption of the Virgin above the entrance door. **TIVERTON CASTLE**, built by Richard de Redvers in 1106, contains armor and items relating to Joan of Arc.

KNIGHTSHAYES COURT ★ In 1869 William Burges was commissioned to build a Gothic house for the Heathcoat-Amorys, whose lace- and net-making factory in Tiverton is visible from the main rooms. Built of local stone, the three-storey house has several extravagant and colorful interiors. A good collection of pictures includes Old Masters, and a charming watercolor of the works outing to Teignmouth in 1854. The outstanding garden lies in lightly wooded grounds to the east of the house. A wide range of tender and exotic shrubs grow here, as on the formal terraces nearer the house, which also feature a topiary fox hunt.

BICKLEIGH The castle, although now much altered, is still approached through a restored 15th-century gatehouse and charming gardens. In the 17th-century farmhouse wing is a remarkable carved overmantel.

CULLOMPTON The 100-foot tower of the church of St Andrew ★, built just before the Reformation, dominates the town. Justly famous is the Lane aisle of *c.* 1526, begun by John Lane, a cloth merchant. Heavily decorated both inside and out with symbols of his trade (ships, cloth shears, merchant's mark and teasels, which were used for brushing the cloth) the fan-vaulted space is a testament to the ostentation of the late Middle Ages. Cullompton's single street is lined with houses dating from the 16th to the 18th centuries, and has many charming courtyards off it.

SOUTH MIDLANDS

Lucy Worsley

1. HEREFORD 2. LUDLOW 3. LEDBURY 4. GLOUCESTER 5. WORCES

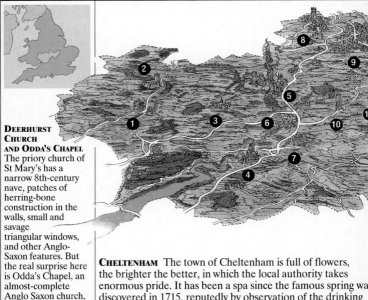

DEERHURST CHURCH AND ODDA'S CHAPEL

The priory church of St Mary's has a narrow 8th-century nave, patches of herring-bone construction in the walls, small and savage triangular windows, and other Anglo-Saxon features. But the real surprise here is Odda's Chapel, an almost-complete Anglo Saxon church, which was discovered during the chance repair of an ordinary-looking half-timbered house in 1885.

Above: the Pittville Pump Room, Cheltenham

Mosaic detail from Chedworth Roman Villa

CHELTENHAM The town of Cheltenham is full of flowers, the brighter the better, in which the local authority takes enormous pride. It has been a spa since the famous spring was discovered in 1715, reputedly by observation of the drinking habits of some pigeons. A visit from the Royal Family for five whole weeks in 1788 confirmed the reputation of the purgative powers of the waters, and Cheltenham has been in fashion ever since. At the heart of this activity is the domed Pittville Pump Room, set in a park. The town flourished particularly in Regency times, when neo-Grecian houses were laid out along carefully planned tree-lined avenues. Many of the elegant crescents and terraces of houses survive, with their caryatids and filigree iron verandas. The town is also home to the exclusive Cheltenham Ladies' College and an art gallery with a very good Arts and Crafts section.

ELKSTONE CHURCH Hidden away beneath the tall trees in the churchyard, Elkstone possesses an extraordinary 12th-century church. The now-blocked north door and narrow windows were designed for slender Normans. Visitors can creep up the spiral staircase leading to an unusual dovecote over the chancel, but if you find the stairs are too narrow, you can still see the blocked doves' entrances in the east wall outside.

CHEDWORTH ROMAN VILLA In this remote valley, it is possible to imagine the builders of the villa, with its baths, nymphaeum and hypocausts, seeing themselves as the last civilized outpost of a distant empire. The dining-room floor mosaic includes the figure of a Briton wearing the *birrus Britannicus*, the woolly cloak the Romans assumed that the British wore. The two courts of the villa are now topped by a 19th-century hunting lodge built on the spoil heap of the excavations, which were paid for by the Earl of Eldon. It houses a museum, with photographs of earnest Victorian visitors.

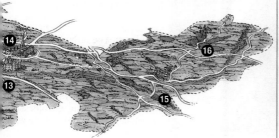

The massive squat tower of Tewkesbury Abbey dominates the town.

HAILES ABBEY (above) Vigorous excavation in the 1960s revealed the footings of the east range and chapterhouse of monastery, founded in 1246 by Richard, Earl of Cornwall.

Sudeley Castle shown in a Claude Lorrain painting and a contemporary photograph

TEWKESBURY ABBEY After the battle of Tewkesbury in 1471, the Yorkists were massacred by Lancastrians inside the Abbey, where they had taken refuge. The sanctuary door is plated with Yorkist armor. The most grotesque feature, in the ambulatory, is the 15th-century *memento mori* carving of a decaying corpse being eaten by giant worms. Inside the Abbey, 14 stout Norman pillars bear down on the nave.

BELAS KNAPP A steep climb up through the woods above Sudeley Castle leads to the long barrow of Belas Knapp, where over 30 skeletons have been found. It was first excavated in the 18th century and since 1930 it has been presented as a "restored" long barrow. Three burial chambers have external entrances, but the north end has a "false" entrance between two piers of earth.

WINCHCOMBE The way to Sudeley Castle passes through the little town of Winchcombe. Here a street called "Tobacco Row" is a last vestige of the English tobacco industry, which was crushed in order to give the colony of Virginia a monopoly. The town has a "wool" church and plenty of Tudor buildings.

SUDELEY CASTLE The overwhelming impression at Sudeley Castle is of a suave 1930s version of Elizabethan grandeur. The first buildings on the site were erected in the early 15th century, and an Elizabethan courtyard and apartments survive beneath later additions. The house is now surrounded by recently created gardens.

HAILES ABBEY The melancholy remains of the cloister in their peaceful country setting draw visitors here. Its most famous artifact was the Relic of the Holy Blood, a gift from the founder's son in 1270, which was an attraction for pilgrims. It even merited an oath from Chaucer: "By the blode of Crist that is in Hayles".

▲ GLOUCESTER

GLOUCESTER CATHEDRAL The nave (below), dominated by heavy Norman pillars, forms the first chapter of a textbook of architectural styles from different periods which make up the rest of the fabric. The cloister (bottom) contains 20 perfect carrels where the monks studied in silence outside their library. The cathedral also boasts the first example of fan-vaulting.

GLOUCESTER ★ Gloucester, surprisingly, has its own harbor master, and has always been an inland port. The cathedral rises up over a crossing-point of the Severn and looks down on a recently excavated 2-acre Roman forum. The two main streets, which cross near the cathedral, run on Roman lines. The museum contains the oldest-known backgammon set, along with watercolors by Turner.

Gloucester's CATHEDRAL has something in common with the wool churches of the county, although there is much here that hints at its previous use as the church of a Benedictine monastery dating from *c.* 679. The cathedral has several superb Renaissance tombs, including Thomas Machen's in the north aisle. He and his wife are shown with their four little sons and four little daughters, and their three tiny dead children. But the best known is the alabaster tomb of Edward II, whose body was brought here after his murder at Berkeley Castle in 1327. The Sharpness canal was opened in 1827 to make ship traffic less dependent on the Severn, and the area of warehouses around the DOCKS developed from the revived business of importing grain. Fourteen warehouses still stand, and now form a vibrant tourist and shopping center.

PRINKNASH ABBEY The site of the old house at Prinknash was described by Horace Walpole as "on a glorious but impracticable hill, in the midst of the little forest of beech, and commanding Elyseum". The hill now commands the sprawl of Gloucester, but the view is still staggering. Prinknash Abbey is an extraordinarily ugly yellow building built after designs by Goodhart-Rendel and Broadbent; the chapel, with its chunky colored glass, can be visited. The monastery houses about 25 Benedictine monks and has in its grounds their pottery where fascinatingly kitsch plates are made.

PAINSWICK Painswick is built of silvery-grey stone, which appears to best effect in the smart houses of its prosperous main street. This part of the countryside, especially the valley to the east and the village of Sheepscombe, was made the ideal of bucolic rural life in Laurie Lee's *Cider with Rosie*. ST MARY'S CHURCH ★ in the middle of the town is a wool church with nave and tower from the 1480s and some marvelous tombs. The churchyard contains 99 beautifully groomed yew trees but the famous "clipping" service that takes place each September has nothing to do with the manicuring of the yews; the word in fact means "encircling", and the custom is for children to link hands to encircle the whole church.

Benjamin Hyett, who built the mellow 18th-century Painswick House, changed the course of garden history in the 1740s

OWLPEN MANOR Owlpen (opposite, top left) is one of the most picturesque manor houses in England. Its three gables are all different but "illog-ically satisfactory", according to James Lees-Milne. The terraced garden, largely 19th-century in form, influenced Gertrude Jekyll and Vita Sackville-West and their idea of gardens as outdoor chambers. Indoors, the 16th-century painted cloths in the Great Chamber are the most interesting feature. These are a rare survival of the oilcloths which used to cover most domestic walls and show Joseph and his brothers in a forest of gargantuan trees.

when he created **PAINSWICK HOUSE ROCOCO GARDENS.** Instead of overwhelming visitors with a grand axial front garden, he used a combe behind the house to create a garden with some vistas but with many winding paths.

BERKELEY CASTLE ★ is built of a pinkish stone, "rose red and grey ... the colour of old brocade", according to Vita Sackville-West. The 14th-century castle is hidden under layers of later use and the famous cell where Edward II was murdered for incompetence and perversion (with a red-hot poker) is a melancholy little room. It is within the keep, erected on the site of a Norman motte, and probably incorporating early fabric erected soon after 1067 by Fitz Osborn, Earl of Hereford. There was some rebuilding work in the early 1900s.

FRAMPTON ON SEVERN This low, damp village by the ship canal has the largest village green in England. The shaggy meadow covers four acres and is surrounded by some pretty houses. Facing each other across the pond are the old manor house and its replacement: the timbered manor farmhouse, and the provincial baroque of Frampton Court.

WOODCHESTER PARK MANSION Sheltering below the heights of Minchinhampton Common is the shell of a Victorian mansion. The building was never completed, and now provides an intriguing skeleton of a house where work was abandoned in the late 1860s after 14 years of effort. It is now sometimes used for training courses in historic building techniques. The mansion is a mile's walk along the National Trust's valley and past its chain of five 18th-century lakes.

TETBURY CHURCH Work began on rebuilding the demolished medieval church of St Mary's in 1777 to a supremely elegant and soaring Gothic design.

TETBURY CHURCH (below) The high box pews are accessible only from the aisle or from the unusual passages that run around the outside of the church, so that (according to David Verey) entering a pew is like entering a box at the Opera House.

FRAMPTON COURT (below) The Court has an interesting Dutch-style ornamental canal in the garden, topped by a Gothick orangery, which is now a most unusual house.

Sezincote

Sezincote

CIRENCESTER Cirencester, or "Ziren" as it is sometimes known locally, was for a while the second most important town in the Roman province of Britain. The Icknield Way, the Fosse Way and Ermine Street all meet here at a junction of Roman roads. The town is now agricultural, architecturally rich because of the buildings paid for by fat wool profits.

CHURCH OF ST JOHN THE BAPTIST This is one of the largest of the churches built with the profits of the wool trade. The scale of the church is stupendous: the porch toward the market is three storeys high and the Perpendicular tower rises from stout battlements.

NORTHLEACH A silvery-stone town as picturesque as any in the Cotswolds, Northleach mercifully lacks tourists. The great wool church of St Peter and St Paul contains brasses showing the wool merchants who built it: the best known stands with one foot on a wool pack and the other on a ringletted sheep.

BARNSLEY HOUSE GARDENS ★ The village manor house has a tasteful new garden created by Rosemary Verey, with two 18th-century summerhouses.

STOW-ON-THE-WOLD Windy Stow-on-the-Wold used to be an important changing post for coach travelers, and formerly possessed no less than 27 inns. The enormous market place was used, of course, for selling sheep. The animals would be funneled into the square along the narrow alleys, or "tunes", around it. Many of them were of the famous and productive breed of "Cotswolds Lions".

SEZINCOTE ★ Sezincote is a remarkable house to find in this most English of landscapes: a Regency version of an Indian Moghul palace. Designed by Samuel Pepys Cockerell for his brother after a trip to India, its copper onion dome and "peacock tail" arches, typical of Rajasthan, contrast with a landscape park in the style of Sir Humphry Repton. Sir Charles Cockerell's own bedroom, in a separate wing, is built like a tent supported by wooden spears. It is not surprising that the Prince Regent visited Sezincote in 1806 when he was thinking of building the Pavilion at Brighton ▲ 188-9, although he chose another architect.

BOURTON-ON-THE-WATER This famous village has become interesting as a case study of the tourist industry in overdrive.

Barnsley House (below); the Laburnum Walk (right) and The Potager (bottom)

The picturesque village with a tame river running through it is better known now for its miniature model village, ice cream shops, enormous car parks and bank holiday traffic jams.

CHASTLETON When the National Trust opened Chastleton in 1997, it was heralded as a new approach in conservation: the work done to the house was supposed to go no further than repair, rather than restoration. This approach was carried through to keeping 1950s plastic light switches as well as the triumphant Jacobean textiles. Chastleton is an amazing marriage of exciting Jacobean architecture, including a long gallery with a barrel plaster vault, with an accumulation of the curiosities of everyday life. Outside are a Victorian topiary and the lawn where the game of croquet was invented and codified by owner Walter Whitmore Jones.

CHIPPING CAMPDEN The archetypal Cotswolds wool merchants' town, Chipping Camden is full of lavish stone early-Renaissance houses. The whole town was revitalized in 1902 for a short while by C. R. Ashbee's "Guild of Handicrafts", which moved out of London's East End in search of a rustic idyll. Ashbee himself restored the house of William Grevel, "flower of all wool merchants of England", which is the prettiest house in the main street with its tall bay window, built about 1380.

HIDCOTE MANOR GARDENS ★ After the Boer War, Major Lawrence Johnston retired to Hidcote to devote himself to gardening. His creation has been described as "a cottage garden on the most glorified scale".

SNOWSHILL MANOR Snowshill Manor is the remarkable creation of Charles Paget Wade, who lived alone for many years in the small cottage next door while using the manor house to entertain guests with his collections of curiosities. "I have not bought things because they were rare or valuable", he said, "but of interest as records of various vanished handicrafts." There is a room in the roof full of "boneshaker" bicycles, for example, and another containing 26 suits of Japanese samurai armor displayed on mannikins in a terrifying array.

STANWAY The ensemble of manor house, barns, church and gatehouse at Stanway makes it a jewel of a place. Its plan is an Elizabethan oddity, with a long, south-facing range and the hall at one side, so that the rooms look over the newly restored 1750s gardens behind with pyramid and cascade.

HIDCOTE MANOR GARDENS
Small enclosures crammed with plants lead one into another over 10 acres in a kind of "haphazard luxuriance", presided over by two little gazebos. Johnston's trips to China and South Africa brought back new plants to England.

Above: Snowshill Manor

Left: Stanway Gatehouse

259

The Cotswolds are not true hills, but uplands or "wolds", full of sheep enclosures or "cots". The character of the villages comes from the stone, Jurassic limestone originally formed in a warm and shallow sea

● *20-1*. Plentiful and easily worked, it was the obvious material for the increasingly prosperous sheep farmers and wool merchants to use for their churches and manors from the 14th century onward. Renaissance and baroque ideas arrived slowly, and with many intriguing and distinct local variations as Cotswolds craftsmen adapted them. The bare grassland slopes of the Cotswolds were cropped by thousands of sheep, but now that grazing is no longer economic, many are reverting to scrub, and habitats for orchids and butterflies are being lost. Villages like Broadway and Bourton-on-the-Water are admittedly beautiful, but the visitor can only marvel at the horrors that too many tourists can wreak on a place. Painswick, Northleach and Stanway are much more rewarding. The stone varies from soft, mellow shades in the north Cotswolds to more sober colors in the south.

BIBURY
This ravishingly pretty village (left) suffers from too many tourists, who are lured by its picturesque building, mill ponds, streams and little bridges. The main attraction is Arlington Row. Built in the late 14th century as farm buildings, these were converted to cottages in the 17th century.

Top: Snowshill
Above left: Vineyard Street, Winchcombe
Above: Painswick

DRY STONE WALLS
These are built without cement, the stones arranged carefully into resilient structures.

Right: Slad

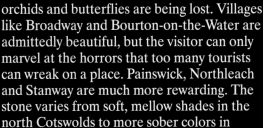

Above:
St Briavels Castle
Above right:
pulpit, St Mary and
All Saints' church,
Fotheringay,
Northamptonshire

ST BRIAVELS CASTLE
The massive gate-
house was built in the
1290s by skillful royal
masons, and acted
like a keep in that it
could be defended
from the back
entrance as well as
the front.

WESTBURY COURT
At Westbury Court
(below), two long
canals in the Dutch
style were made
between 1690 and
1715. A tall pavilion
reconstructed by the
National Trust
provides views over
the long lines of the
canals, and the rows
of yew pyramids and
holly balls reflected
in them.

FOREST OF DEAN TO ROSS-ON-WYE AND LEOMINSTER

FOREST OF DEAN The trees of the Forest of Dean are not all
ancient: 30 million acorns were planted in the 1800s. This was
after the centuries of depredations to the Royal Hunting
Forest (designated by the Normans in the early 11th century).
The Forest was important as an industrial area for mining coal
and minerals. The foresters have always had a kind of special
regional autonomy: they enacted forest law at the "Speech
House", now a pub, in the middle of the forest. Anyone born
within 100 miles of St Briavels still has rights, as a "free-miner",
to mine his own coal.

NEWLAND The giant church of Newland is sometimes called
"The Cathedral of the Forest". It dominates the village from
its huge square churchyard surrounded by almshouses and the
old grammar school. Inside are two important pieces of forest
history: the stone monument of the "Forester of Fee" shows
his 15th-century huntsman's outfit, and a brass in the south
aisle of unknown date shows a medieval miner with his pick,
holding a candlestick in his mouth.

CLEARWELL CAVES The free-miners used surface mines called
"scowle holes", but at Clearwell they burrowed deeper into a
natural cave system in search of iron and minerals used in
cosmetics. The long chambers are littered with debris and
mining equipment, often knocked together by the free-miners
from unlikely materials. In the furthest cave, an iron ladder
leads enticingly down to the deeper levels.

ST BRIAVELS CASTLE The "castle" is really a hunting lodge
used by King John, and his royal apartments have now been
converted into a youth hostel. There were mini-portcullises
defending even the entrances to the porters' lodges off the
entrance passage. In later times it was a debtor's prison, and
the debtors' scribbled complaints on the walls provide gloomy
decoration in some of the youth hostel bedrooms.

WESTBURY COURT GARDENS Down by the Severn lie some of
the most interesting 17th-century gardens in England. They
are rare not because of their design – which is common in
pictures of houses in the 1690s – but because they survive
in their original layouts.

Left and below left: Goodrich Castle

ROSS-ON-WYE Ross-on-Wye, upon its high hill, has something Italian about its situation, and this appealed to the 18th-century tourists who traveled up the Wye in steamers as a cheaper substitute for the Grand Tour. On the way, they admired the picturesque ruins of Goodrich and Monmouth castles ▲ 472, and visited natural features such as the rocky spire of Symonds Yat as their boats wound through the border country where the Wye now marks the division between England and Wales.

GOODRICH CASTLE The survival of so much fabric at Goodrich makes it seem like a "proper" castle, especially as you pass over the moat by the flimsy bridge from the monumental D-shaped barbican. The white Norman keep stands surrounded by later ranges of apartments and curtain wall in red sandstone.

A decorative carving on a pew in Much Marcle church

OFFA'S DYKE This massive earthwork runs, but not continuously, from the Welsh coast to the Severn at Sedbury. It was built in the 8th century by the Saxon King Offa of Mercia, over a 10-year period. It is a reminder of the turbulent character of this border area, and a particularly good section survives at Lyonshall, south of Moccas. There is now an Offa's Dyke long-distance footpath.

KILPECK CHURCH ★ It is astonishing that the carving at Kilpeck church has survived so well, with so little weathering, since Norman carvers made it. The corbels around the outside show a sequence of staggeringly concise and characterful animals, motifs, figures, and a rude sheila-na-gig. Around the door elongated men grapple with decorative spirals while over it birds' faces look down with the huge sad eyes of cartoon characters.

Church of Saints Mary and David, Kilpeck

HELLEN'S HOUSE, MUCH MARCLE This 17th-century brick manor house is a mellow fusion of earlier periods, although Jacobean plaster ceilings and fireplaces dominate inside.

ST MARY'S CHURCH AT KEMPLEY It is worth making a detour to remote St Mary's to see the Wheel of Life on the north wall of the nave, one of the many medieval wall-paintings here dating from the 13th century onward. Spreading across the tunnel vault is a picture of Christ seated uncomfortably on a rainbow, which was rescued from beneath Reformation whitewash in 1872.

Berrington Hall

MOCCAS COURT
Moccas has an expansive Capability Brown park bounded by another meander of the Wye. The strictly classical exterior in stark red brick by Robert Adam belies the opulent interiors, which include a circular Etruscan room. It was built in the 1770s for the Cornewall family.

LEDBURY The parish church in the little town of Ledbury is crammed with monuments, including those to the five little sons and five kneeling daughters carved on the Renaissance Skynner Tomb. The narrow cobbled street called Church Lane is lined with excellent Herefordshire timbered houses jutting out toward each other, but the best of them is the Market House with its timber columns and herring-bone walls.

EASTNOR CASTLE Begun in 1812, this is Sir Robert Smirke's wonderful 19th-century version of a 13th-century marcher baron's castle from about the time of Edward I, for the newly created first Earl Somers. The porte-cochere and bay windows sit between the four battlemented and machicolated towers.

HEREFORD Hereford lies in another bend of the River Wye; the restored early 14th-century tower of its red sandstone cathedral juts up over the low town. It was at its most important in the 13th century after Edward I conquered Wales, when it was in the powerful grip of the Mortimer family who controlled much of the border territory.

Hereford **CATHEDRAL**'s south transept is its oldest part, built from 1080 onward. The nave was added *c.* 1100, although the windows were enlarged 250 years later. The tower and part of the nave fell down on Easter Monday, 1786, and James Wyatt was appointed as architect for the restoration work; he tried, with varied success, to retain and unite all the surviving works of previous periods.

EASTNOR CASTLE
(above) The interiors have little of the medieval about them, but do contain a drawing room designed and furnished by Pugin, with a splendid Gothic chandelier that was shown at the Great Exhibition in 1851.

MAPPA MUNDI, the famous map of the world dated from 1289, was put up for sale by the cash-starved cathedral in the 1980s, and after a considerable panic, was returned to Hereford by benefactors. The map, now displayed in subdued light in its new building, shows Jerusalem at the center, and England at the extreme edge of the known world. Other parts are populated by absurd monsters and a man up among the fjords who appear to be skiing.

LEOMINSTER The agricultural town of Leominster is famous today for its antique trade, which finds an appropriate home

The complex staircase at Berrington Hall has hints of the baroque fantasies of Piranesi.

Above: plasterwork staircase, Croft Castle

among old coaching inns and picturesque black-and-white buildings. The 1633 town hall, now moved from its original position, is decorated with male and female busts. In an interesting parallel between the hierarchies of architecture and society, the frieze says that the columns below support the building as "noble gentry ... support the honour of a kingdom". Originally the Priory of St Peter and St Paul provided a focus for the town, and its swarthy red-brick church survives. Close by the west door is an interesting carving of a hairy "Green Man", a medieval fertility symbol, and outside stands a ducking stool, apparently still in use as late as 1809.

BERRINGTON HALL The fashionable architect Henry Holland was summoned to Herefordshire after Thomas Harley had made a fortune supplying uniforms and pay to the British Army in America. The site of his new Hall was chosen by Capability Brown, whose undulating park and lake survive.

CROFT CASTLE Croft Castle is a pleasant mixture of castle and country house. Fourteenth-century round corner towers flank a 18th-century front with mock-castle battlements and nostalgic Gothic Revival windows, hinting at the exuberant Georgian Gothic staircase inside. Outside, avenues traverse the huge park, one lined with 350-year-old Spanish chestnuts and another with silver birches, leading to Cock Gate. The Iron-Age fort of Croft Ambrey is a steep 40-minute walk away.

EVESHAM TO WORCESTER TO KIDDERMINSTER

VALE OF EVESHAM Evesham is the market town for the fruit-growing Vale of Evesham, which is snowed under with white apple blossom in the spring. The town stands on the bank of the River Avon, and its nub is the ruined Benedictine Abbey. The Norman gateway with its 15th-century timbered upper storey leads out into the town.

PERSHORE ABBEY ★ Pershore is a pocket-sized Georgian town. Entering from the southeast, you pass the six-arched medieval bridge over the Avon. Climbing the hill, you reach the long main street of little red-brick houses, mainly 18th century. Off the market place is the yellow stone Abbey, of which only the stump of the nave, the crossing, transepts and chancel survive. Its bulk seems out of scale with the town; originally the nave was nearly as long as those of Gloucester or Tewkesbury abbeys. The townsmen purchased the surviving section of the Abbey to use as their church at the time of the dissolution when the rest was destroyed.

BERRINGTON HALL
On a knoll stands the extremely sleek and simple classical house, begun in 1778. Indoors is an astonishingly lavish classical interior, full of ideas picked up in France by Henry Holland.

Bronze of Sir Edward Elgar, English School, 20th century

ELGAR'S BIRTHPLACE MUSEUM
The tiny red-brick cottage in the village of Lower Broadheath markets itself vigorously and has a hefty new visitor center. The cottage, although quite pretty, is more interesting for Elgar's letters in his spidery handwriting and his musical manuscripts, which lie scattered on his desk. A statue of the composer himself stands outside Worcester Cathedral, and the celebratory Three Choirs and Malvern Festivals still make this a musical part of the country.

Wichenford Court Dovecote

DOVECOTES often provide an architectural mini-history of an area's building styles; here, at Wichenford, it is the expected little black-and-white timbered tower, containing 57 nesting boxes.

Above: The park at Croome D'Abitot is special because many of its temples and ornaments survive, and are being gradually restored.

BESFORD CHURCH Besford, on the way to Croome Park, is a unusual tiny timber-framed church, constructed out of units almost 5 feet square, with diagonal beams for strength, and probably dating from the 14th century. Inside the stone lip o the rood loft is an interesting pre-Reformation survival.

CROOME D'ABITOT PARK AND CHURCH The current Croome Court was begun in 1751, and is a typical house of its time wi stern Palladian façade and park landscaped by Capability Brown. What is unusual in this case is that Brown seems to have had a hand in the design of the house as well. His patro was the 6th Earl of Coventry, whose friends, such as Sanderson Miller, also pitched in with ideas. Croome d'Abit church is itself an eye-catcher on a rolling hill, designed in a perfect early Gothic Revival style outside – possibly also by Capability Brown – and with an interior by Robert Adam, including the crisp and elegant font and pulpit with fanciful ogee curves.

MALVERN HILLS Great Malvern has been compared to an Indian hill station, and ha something of the same air of genteel retirement as it creeps up the sides of the

WORCESTER CATHEDRAL (below) Most of the interior is very consistently and harmoniously 13th- and 14th-century in character, while the exterior is largely Victorian.

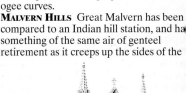

Malvern Hills. The best hotels are higher up, with astounding views over the Vale of Evesham. When Elgar lived in Malvern his house looked this way, and his works are often thought of as anthems to this stretch of English countryside. It is possible to walk along the length of the humpy spine of hills in a day, rising and falling to the three passes. Hollybush Pass is an ancient route used by packhorses travelling from Droitwich to South Wales. Queen Victoria added greatly to the town's reputation by coming to take the waters, which have a remarkably low mineral content as they filter quickly through the granite to over 60 springs. In the town, the remains of the priory form the nucleus for a splendid collection of 19th-century hotels and villas. There is also the Winter Garden concert hall, where George Bernard Shaw promoted the annual Malvern Festival.

WORCESTER There are too many cars in Worcester; but there are also interesting buildings, such as the splendid red-brick 1720s Guildhall decorated with busts of worthies, and the Royal Worcester factory, parts of which can be visited. The town is a center for the porcelain industry and has its own museum of porcelain.

The highlights of WORCESTER CATHEDRAL are the two royal tombs. Before the high altar lies the unpopular King John. He is positioned, as he himself specified, between the tombs of St Wulfstan and St Oswald. His effigy, with its neatly combed hair and beard, dates from the 1230s. To his right is Prince Arthur's Chantry, where Henry VIII's elder brother lies. The chantry is a confection of delicate vaulting and 88 tiny sculpted figures, many decapitated in the Reformation. Worcester was the first town to declare itself for King Charles in the Civil War, and the very last to surrender. It was after defeat at the Battle of Worcester in 1651 that Charles II had to flee and hide from Cromwell. He planned his final campaign in the COMMANDERY, which is a timber-framed house near the cathedral with a lofty open-roofed great hall and some stained glass. The building now contains a Civil War exhibition.

WICHENFORD COURT DOVECOTE Wichenford has a remote but attractive timbered dovecote surrounded by apple trees. The birds entered through doors in the lantern, and provided the fresh meat that was otherwise so scarce in the winter.

LOWER BROCKHAMPTON HOUSE Lower Brockhampton lies in a verdant valley, and survives because later owners typically chose the better views from the hillside above to build the 18th-century Brockhampton House.

KIDDERMINSTER The town of Kidderminster is historically a center of carpet-making, but today worth visiting only to board the Severn Valley Railway, which winds north up the magnificent Severn valley to the much more interesting Bridgnorth.

Spetchley Park, a dignified Regency house of Bath stone built for the Berkeley family, with a large garden and deer park

Worcester Cathedral

A fire began at 8pm on September 7, 1937 that was to ruin one of England's most luxurious houses. Coachloads came out from Birmingham to watch Witley Court burn. When his trustees purchased the house for him in 1837, William Ward, 1st Earl of Dudley, was one of the richest men in the world; visitors later remembered the family Christmas tree being hung with real jewels for the ladies to choose from. An earlier house was completely remodeled in the 18th century before the Earl of Dudley's confident Italian palace emerged in Bath stone cladding. He employed garden-designer Nesfield to lay out the grand parterres, but the best features are the stupendous fountains of Perseus and Flora. Perseus was played only twice a week, as the reservoir which powered it needed to be pumped full. The gigantic ruins of the house are a melancholy monument to the industrialist's immense extravagance.

THE CONSERVATORY
The skeleton remains of the vast conservatory (left) which was one of the 1st Earl of Dudley's additions.

SCULPTURE GARDEN
The extensive landscaped grounds of Witley Court have now been made into modern sculpture garden, including works by Dame Elisabeth Frink (1930-93).

PERSEUS AND ANDROMEDA FOUNTAIN
Perseus on Pegasus flies to the rescue of Andromeda in James Forsyth's fountain. The main jet was formerly 120 feet high.

The red-brick façade of Hanbury Hall

HARVINGTON HALL
John Wall, Harvington Hall's 17th-century owner and Catholic priest, was the last man to be executed for his faith in England, in 1679.

Harvington Hall

HARTLEBURY CASTLE Most of the house was rebuilt after near-demolition during the Civil War; but the old moated site of the castle was retained, and the interior of the Great Hall is more obviously 15th-century than its delicate 18th-century exterior. One of the hip-roofed wings contains a pretty fan-vaulted chapel. The castle has been the home of the bishops of Worcester for centuries, and the servants' quarters in the north wing contain the Worcestershire County Museum, which includes a collection of vacuum cleaners.

CHADDESLEY CORBETT Chaddesley Corbett is a typical Worcestershire village with early Georgian brick houses and a plethora of yeomen's timber-framed houses.

STOKE PRIOR The church contains unusual columns with carefully delineated leaves for capitals, but the main attraction here is the Avoncroft Museum of Buildings. It displays buildings relocated bodily from elsewhere, which include a 1940s pre-fab, a working windmill and the national collection of telephone booths.

HARVINGTON HALL Owned by the Catholic Church, Harvington Hall is a medieval house inside an irregular Elizabethan brick carapace and encircled by a moat. It is famous for its many and various priest-holes, secret passages, trapdoors, and a false stairway, used to hide away the priests sheltered by its Catholic owners from potential Protestant persecutors. The most elaborate hole is off the library, and involves going through the fireplace into a small room with a removable floor. Beneath the floor is a hiding place, with an escape chute to the moat below.

HANBURY HALL The Hall, completed in 1701 according to a date over the door, is the perfect substantial country home of a squire at the turn of the 18th century.

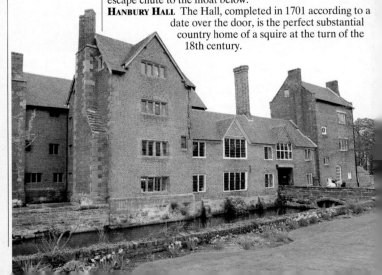

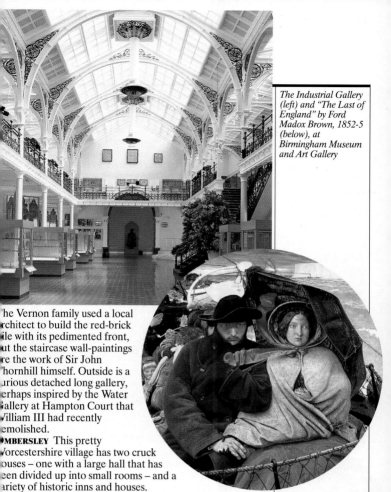

The Industrial Gallery (left) and "The Last of England" by Ford Madox Brown, 1852-5 (below), at Birmingham Museum and Art Gallery

he Vernon family used a local
rchitect to build the red-brick
ile with its pedimented front,
ut the staircase wall-paintings
re the work of Sir John
hornhill himself. Outside is a
urious detached long gallery,
erhaps inspired by the Water
allery at Hampton Court that
Villiam III had recently
emolished.

MBERSLEY This pretty
Vorcestershire village has two cruck
ouses – one with a large hall that has
een divided up into small rooms – and a
ariety of historic inns and houses.

IRMINGHAM This enormous industrial city has a surprisingly
brant center where landmarks include the ponderous but
rcheologically accurate and impressive classical temple of
irmingham Town Hall, and "The Rotunda", a cylindrical
.yscraper that dominates the city's skyline. St Philip's
athedral has stained-glass windows by Edward Burne-Jones.
he city now boasts an impressive **SYMPHONY HALL**, which
pened in 1991 with acoustics designed by Russell Johnson
hich are said to be among the best in the world. It is home
f the City of Birmingham Symphony Orchestra, conducted
y Sakari Oramo, and also provides a showcase for the world's
est international orchestras.

lodern art thrives at the **IKON GALLERY**, an interesting use
or the 19th-century school building that houses it. Regularly
nanging exhibitions of contemporary artists have given it its
novative reputation. The polite 18th-century **SOHO HOUSE**
 a surprising find in the middle of Birmingham. Its owner,
dustrialist Matthew Boulton, made his money in the
earby Jewellery Quarter where his factory – along with
any others – made buckles, clocks and silver plate from
e 1750s onward. As his friends were the engineers and
inkers of the later 18th century, it is not surprising
 find that his house had innovative central heating, and
at he designed his own eccentric furniture.

BIRMINGHAM MUSEUM AND ART GALLERY
Birmingham has England's largest provincial museum, and is a mecca for Pre-Raphaelite enthusiasts. Rossetti, Holman Hunt and Millais are well represented. There is a whole room of Edward Burne-Jones's overwr ought ladies, a good collection of watercolor landscapes, including those of David Cox, Birmingham's answer to Constable, and a continental collection that is especially strong on Italian painting from the 17th century.

BOURNVILLE This suburb, which gives its name to its very own line of chocolate, is a famous planned settlement by the Quaker Cadbury family, owners of the confectionery company and much land in Birmingham. The (8,000) houses of their workers were influenced by Arts and Crafts Utopian ideas, and timber-framed buildings were brought from elsewhere to create a bucolic atmosphere. Even today inhabitants have to keep their gardens tidy. The factory museum of Cadbury World gives more information about the family and their philanthropic traditions, as well as free samples.

Below: the Royal Shakespeare Theatre Bottom: Stratford's statue of Shakespeare

STRATFORD-UPON-AVON TO RUGBY

Stratford-upon-Avon is one of Britain's major tourist attractions because of the Shakespeare connection. He was born here, married a local woman, Anne Hathaway, and had three children with her, before he moved to London. Various memorials in the town pay tribute to him.

ROYAL SHAKESPEARE THEATRE ★ The cult of Shakespeare did not develop until the later 18th century, and there was probably no official theater at all in Stratford in his own time beyond inn courtyards. The theater which looms over the Avon and the hordes of tourists and theater-goers won a competition to replace the one burnt down in 1926 Its architect was Elisabeth Scott, making it the first important public building in the country to be designed by a woman. In a spare brick design with Art Deco echoes, it was thought locally to be very avant-garde in 1932. The burnt theater which it replaced was built in 1879; it exists remodeled as the Swan auditorium, a smaller theater-in-the-round at the back of the Main House ▲ 56. It offers the more intimate experience of round Elizabethan theaters such as the now-reconstructed Globe in London ▲ 57. More experimental plays are put on at a third theater called "The Other Place".

HOLY TRINITY No visit to Stratford is complete without walking along the river from the theaters toward the oldest part of town and the church, a spacious, mainly Perpendicular structure. Gerard

Johnson's alabaster bust of Shakespeare, dating from after his death in 1616, shows him pretentiously adopting the pose and Latin inscription of a scholar.

SHAKESPEARE BIRTHPLACE The fact that so little is really known about Shakespeare's life does not deter the Shakespeare Birthplace Trust, who valiantly make the most of the half-timbered building, heavily restored, in which Shakespeare's father lived and worked. He was perhaps a glover or wool-merchant, and his son

William could have been born here, but there is nothing to prove it. The Shakespeare Memorial Gardens mark the site of William's own house, New Place. It was demolished in 1759, reputedly because its owner could no longer bear the stream of pilgrims. In a previous effort to stem the tide, he'd also taken the step of cutting down a mulberry tree that Shakespeare was supposed to have planted.

ANNE HATHAWAY'S COTTAGE Owned by the Birthplace Trust, this cottage makes a more satisfying visit because of its pretty cottage garden. The thatched cottage contains 17th-century furniture, but its association with Shakespeare is far more important to visitors; Anne Hathaway married Shakespeare in 1582, when she was already pregnant with their first child, but there is no evidence that he kept in touch with her once he had moved to London.

CHARLECOTE PARK Charlecote was for many years considered to be the ultimate Elizabethan manor house, standing in meadows next to the River Avon in a park where Shakespeare was once caught poaching Sir Thomas Lucy's deer. Once you have passed through the magnificent and genuinely Elizabethan gatehouse, you enter George Hammond Lucy's Victorian recreation of Elizabethan times, with some rich furnishings from Beckford's Fonthill ▲ *208*.

CHARLECOTE PARK
G.H. Lucy greatly extended the house in the Elizabethan style and fitted out the lavish and ponderous interiors that survive today. Some of them contain incongruous but impressive Indian furniture.

273

Warwick Castle's Norman remains are now swamped by a substantial Victorian country house sandwiched between 14th-century towers, but its skyline is still a dramatic turreted mass, perched over the river with a working watermill below. Warwick Castle was a real pioneer of the heritage industry: the Earls of Warwick gave up treating their house as a home long before World War I and welcomed the visitors in. The 5th Earl of Warwick and his wife Daisy first staged a historical "pageant" in 1893, and the castle now contains a series of themed attractions. The waxworks in the Victorian suite, which tell the story of a "Royal Weekend Party" that included the 5th Earl and Daisy, are excellent and disconcertingly lifelike – especially as living people in costume mingle with them.

WAXWORKS
Daisy, Countess of Warwick, dressed by her maid.

GREAT HALL
The 14th-century Great Hall, later heavily remodeled, contains Oliver Cromwell's macabre death mask.

Right: Lord Leycester Hospital and its founder, the Earl of Leicester
Below: "The Disrobing of Christ" by El Greco, at Upton House

UPTON HOUSE

Upton is a pretty but minor 17th-century house extended in the 1920s by the 2nd Viscount Bearsted. He was the son of a "modern-day Dick Whittington", Marcus Samuel, 1st Viscount, who was born in London's East End but finished up as founder of Shell and the city's Lord Mayor. The gardens are beautiful.

ALCESTER is a pleasant, small market town, as it was in Roman times, and Roman finds are still frequently made in the surrounding fields.

LORD LEYCESTER HOSPITAL

Originally the guilds' hall, it was established by the Earl of Leicester as a home for old soldiers. Eight of the "Brethren" still live here, and can be spotted by their uniforms of black cloaks, silver chains, and medals with Leicester's bear.

COUGHTON COURT The Throckmortons still live at Coughton Court with its magnificent central gatehouse tower, built around 1530, which rises to four turrets on the fourth storey. There are stunning views over the hunting park.

RAGLEY HALL Ragley, designed in 1680, is an early and earthy forerunner of the Palladian piles which were to dominate the 18th century. Its 17th-century windows line an immensely long façade, to which a portico with stumpy columns was added in 1780. Many architects have been involved in alterations. Inside, the scale of Gibbs's Great Hall is overwhelming. The French furniture is magnificent, and the late Marquess of Hertford's contemporary tastes can be seen in Graham Rust's mural in the south Staircase Hall. The park and lake, designed by Capability Brown, are as popular as the house.

Packwood House gateway

PACKWOOD HOUSE Semi-rural Packwood House is a creation of the 1930s. A careful and beautiful collection of furniture and paintings put together by Graham Baron Ash enlivens this manor house. He also added a medieval hall. The famous garden is crammed with yews, supposed to represent the crowd gathered to listen to the Sermon on the Mount.

BADDESLEY CLINTON This is one of only two 14th-century moated manor houses surviving (the other is Ightham Moat ▲ 173). The moat that surrounds Baddesley Clinton was dug in the 13th century, and the cluster of buildings around the three-sided court has a venerable air. Two ranges date from the 15th century, while the third was added by the Elizabethan Henry Ferrers, whose descendants lived in the heavily Victorianized house until 1939.

COUGHTON COURT

(above) Visitors today look down over the gabled wings added slightly later, and the Georgian remodeling of the main block to either side. The house also contains some lovely Largillière portraits.

WARWICK The well-known fire of 1694, about which there is a video in the Warwickshire Museum, destroyed most of medieval Warwick. The result was a new neat Georgian town which would be attractive even without its castle. There are many splendid post-fire houses from the turn of the 18th century with hearty pilasters and hipped roofs.

LORD LEYCESTER HOSPITAL The medieval hospital consists of a well-preserved domestic interior, complete with great hall and courtyard with galleries like a coaching inn.

UPTON HOUSE The 1st Viscount Bearsted's son bought Upton House principally to display his pictures, and his changes to the house made it notoriously uncomfortable to live in, especially the now-recreated double-height picture room which was intended to be used as a drawing room. But it is admirable for displaying his astonishing picture collection, which includes works by Bosch, El Greco, Hogarth and Reynolds. Left: *Morning,* by William Hogarth.

KENILWORTH CASTLE Sir Walter Scott's stirring tale of the Elizabethan court was set here, so topographically accurately that he provided a plan for readers. Toward the end of the 14th century, after 250 years of royal warfare and sieges, John of Gaunt converted the almost-impregnable Kenilworth into a pleasure palace. The huge bulk of the tower glows pink, and once must have been wonderfully reflected in the lake, or "Mere", which surrounded it until the Civil War when the causeway dam was breached. Henry V was responsible for creating the moated garden known as the "Pleasance".

COVENTRY TO NORTHAMPTON AND CORBY

COVENTRY CATHEDRAL On November 14, 1940, an air-raid destroyed much of medieval Coventry. Since then, the city has been largely ruined by car plants and inhuman urban planning, but much was redeemed by Basil Spence's cathedral, built in 1962, with the ruins of the old church used as a forecourt. Benjamin Britten's *War Requiem* was first performed here. The cathedral contains Spence's sculptural Crown of Thorns, Graham Sutherland's superb tapestry of an enormous Christ with a minuscule man standing beneath him, and Epstein's sculpture of St Michael overcoming the Devil near the entrance steps.

MIDDLETON CHENEY CHURCH The medieval church was heavily restored in the 1860s, and visitors come here to see the famous stained glass by William Morris's company of decorators. The vicar in the 1860s was a friend of Burne-Jones, whose subjects here include the young men in the burning fiery furnace, in the north aisle. Other windows are by Philip Webb.

KINGS SUTTON CHURCH King's Sutton church is described by the great art historian Nicholas Pevsner as having "one of the finest, if not the finest, spire in this county of spires". Gaily crocketed and decorated, it dates from the 14th century, although it was rebuilt in the 19th. Outside, on the village green, the stocks still await miscreants.

Epstein's "St Michael vanquishes the Devil", near the main entrance of Coventry Cathedral

KENILWORTH CASTLE (below) Today, a good deal of 16th-century fabric survives, showing how Robert Dudley, Earl of Leicester, added the new lodgings, the more convenient gatehouse entrance, and the stables needed for a Tudor mansion and pleasure garden.

EARLS BARTON CHURCH
Unbuttressed and massive, this Saxon church
is latticed with decorative long and short
stones to make blind arcades and bizarre
stripes – possibly in imitation of the timber
towers that must have just preceded it.

Right: Fawsley Church

FAWSLEY COURT
The house at Fawsley
is now a luxurious
hotel. Many footpaths
traverse its rolling
18th-century park and
weed-choked lakes.
The parish house
stands alone on a
hilltop and contains
the interesting
alabaster tombs of the
Fawsley family.

WASHINGTON
John Washington left
his family home of
Sulgrave Manor for
Virginia in 1656. He
never returned and
became the great-
grandfather of the
first President of the
United States.

*Right: Queen
Eleanor's Cross at
Geddington
Above: The Great
Chambers, Canons
Ashby*

*Below: Stoke Park
Pavilions*

SULGRAVE MANOR Sulgrave
Manor is a pleasant 17th-
century wool-stapler's manor
house, with a wing added in the
early 18th century. Sir Reginald
Blomfield rather mistakenly
reconstructed a large part of
the central block in 1921.

EDGCOTE HOUSE Edgcote
House and church make a
pleasant prospect: the plain and
restrained 18th-century manor
house is flanked by gargantuan
stables and the church, which
contains beautiful alabaster figures reclining on chests –16th-
century members of the Chauncey family.

CANONS ASHBY Canons Ashby is unusual as a house of the
16th and 17th centuries which has escaped extensive later
alterations. Its tower looks down on to a famous baroque
garden with Italianate yews, recently restored. Inside, the
plasterwork of the Dryden family home is outstanding, and
some painted decoration survives on areas of paneling. The
small room with early 18th-century painted pilasters cut out of
card like stage scenery is unique.

NORTHAMPTON The town center boasts
some surprisingly good buildings,
including the sumptuous Sessions House
by Henry Bell (built shortly after
Northampton's terrible fire of 1674)
Godwin's fantastically Venetian town
hall, and a terraced house in Derngate
with an interior by Charles Rennie
Mackintosh. The town museum has an
enormous collection of shoes, as the
main industry here was once boot-
making, and a small collection of Italian
baroque paintings.

QUEEN ELEANOR'S CROSSES Outside
Northampton to the south is Delapré
Park, which still follows the boundary of the meadow or "pré"
that gave its name to the Cluniac nunnery of De-la-pré Abbey
now absorbed into a later country house. On its edge stands
an elaborate canopied 13th-century cross. Edward I's Queen
Eleanor died in Nottinghamshire in 1290, and
her forlorn husband set up crosses at each
place where the procession carrying her body
back to London stopped for the
night (the last
being Charing
Cross).

Cottesbrooke Hall

ALTHORP ★ The low and rambling house, whose external appearance owes much to the work of Henry Holland in the 1780s, consists of extra layers added to a house originally begun in 1573. It contains very fine 17th- and 18th-century English portraits, spectacular Van Dycks, Reynolds and Italian paintings. The stables are now a museum dedicated to the memory of Diana, Princess of Wales. Althorp was her childhood home.

HOLDENBY HOUSE Holdenby today is a only a tiny fragment of the prodigious mansion of two courts built by Sir Christopher Hatton, who won Elizabeth's favor by his excellent dancing and became her Lord Chancellor. Holdenby was one of a handful of the huge houses built to welcome the queen on her summer pilgrimages, and was staggeringly vast. The outline of the gardens can still be seen as earthworks, and the gateways into the lower court still stand although bereft of their walls.

Holdenby House

BRIXWORTH CHURCH Brixworth is a great barn of a church, not surprisingly as it was essentially an early Christian basilica, as befits the former seat of a bishop. Parts of its fabric date probably from as early as the 7th century. Pevsner claimed that, in size at least, "it surpasses all other Anglo-Saxon churches in England". The crushingly heavy arches of Roman bricks were once open and led to now-missing aisles.

COTTESBROOKE HALL Brixworth church stands firmly in the center of the great axial prospect from the front of Cottesbrooke Hall. The Hall, begun in 1702, is a smiling house in red brick with gay white pilasters and two curving wings stretched out toward outbuildings. Inside is an exceptional collection of art, largely featuring horses and hunting.

LAMPORT HALL Lamport Hall's main façade is like an encyclopedia of Palladian styles, the central block being by John Webb in the 1650s and the wings added 80 years later by Francis Smith of Warwick. Built by the Isham family (whose witty motto is "I sham not"), it contains excellent Royalist paintings, as well as the original fireplaces and other features found in Webb's own drawings.

KELMARSH HALL Now being restored by a trust, the bland red-brick façade of Kelmarsh Hall, built by James Gibbs in the early 18th century, hides exceptional stuccowork inside. The lodges, to James Gibbs's designs, date from the 1960s.

CASTLE ASHBY ★ is an Elizabethan monster, whose three-sided courtyard is persistently attributed to Inigo Jones. Its roofline is crowded with turrets, which bring up the twisting staircases in the corners of the building, and crowned with a homily in 2-foot high letters about the importance of home.

STOKE PARK PAVILIONS Inigo Jones's name appears in a history of Stoke Park, where he could well have designed the lodges that are all that survive of a 17th-century house built for Sir Francis Crane, owner of the famous Mortlake tapestry works.

GREAT BRINGTON VILLAGE
The church contains the outstanding fan-vaulted Spencer chapel with effigies, including that of John, Earl Spencer (above), and the extraordinary Sir Edward Spencer in the process of being resurrected out of his funerary urn.

279

Kirby Hall, west front and parterre

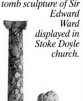

Above: Rushton Triangular Lodge
Above right: Rockingham Castle

KIRBY HALL
The grounds of Kirby Hall, an approximation of the 1680s parterre garden – made by the gardening Hattons – has been recreated by English Heritage with cut-work grass platts, conical yews, and box trees in tubs.

INSIDE BOUGHTON HOUSE ★
Boughton House has a superb collection of paintings, furniture, and textiles. It also contains an almost untouched suite of 17th-century apartments.

Rysbrack created the tomb sculpture of Sir Edward Ward displayed in Stoke Doyle church.

KETTERING AREA

RUSHTON HALL AND TRIANGULAR LODGE ★ Sir Thomas Tresham, sheepfarmer, recusant and builder, is one of Northamptonshire's famous characters. His Roman Catholicism put him into prison during the reign of Elizabeth I, but he amused himself there by sketching out the endless Christian symbols which obsessed him and still decorate his buildings. His house at Rushton is full of triangular symbols of the Trinity, and garden walks led to his warrener's lodge, built on a triangular plan and replete with Trinitarian symbols.

ROTHWELL MARKET HALL Sir Thomas Tresham's market house in Rothwell was never completed, but its elaborate cruciform plan is a hallmark of Tresham's, decorated with religious mottoes and heraldic devices.

LYVEDEN NEW BIELD The "new building" stands on the hill above the "old building", amid spectacular Elizabethan water-gardens that include canals, an orchard and high earth pyramids. The tall New Bield – whose top storey was never built – was an intriguing destination for a garden stroll or period of secluded study.

ROCKINGHAM CASTLE Rockingham Castle has now descended from its Norman motte – today a garden feature – and sprawls along a bluff with views of the Welland Valley spreading below. The royal castle, which King John visited at least 14 times, later became a hotch-potch of Tudor accommodation including a long gallery, updated by Salvin in the early 19th century. He heightened the medieval character of the castle with castellations and a tower. Rockingham has an interesting collection of 20th-century paintings.

BOUGHTON HOUSE ★ The "English Versailles", has the most arrogant of loggias, and Frenchified pavilions with Mansard roofs: the work of the 1st Duke of Montagu at the end of the 17th century. Not surprisingly, he had been the British ambassador to France.

DEENE PARK ★ The Brudenell family were Tresham's neighbors and rivals. Their house is much more conservative, with a medieval core, 17th-century wing and tower, and interesting portraits, some of Lord Cardigan, leader of the Charge of the Light Brigade.

KIRBY HALL The peaceful Kirby Hall echoes with the screams of peacocks. The house is nostalgic in plan, but has some of the earliest and most flamboyant Renaissance decoration, including giant pilasters around the inner courtyard.

HOME COUNTIES

Emily Cole

1. NEWBURY 2. ABINGDON 3. OXFORD 4. BANBURY 5. READING

St Albans

St Albans started life as a large and important center of Roman activity. Verulamium, as the city was known, was founded around AD 43 in the valley of the River Ver (now a pretty park). Although only fragments of original buildings are left standing, excavations have revealed – among other things – a mid-2nd-century theater and foundations of the basilica. Verulamium Museum contains many fascinating finds.

CATHEDRAL From the site of Verulamium you can walk up Abbey Mill Lane and ascend the hill where St Alban died a martyr in AD 209. Little remains of the Benedictine monastery founded in 793 except a big 14th-century gatehouse and, of course, the abbey church (cathedral since 1877). St Albans Cathedral was built from the late 11th century through to the 1400s and has a remarkably long body (the nave reaches almost 300 feet). The interior is impressive though gloomy, mainly because a series of fine screens cut off the vista from the west end to the beautiful early 14th-century Lady Chapel at the far east. Important surviving features are the numerous medieval wall paintings and the three chantry chapels. The shrine of St Alban, originally erected c. 1302-8, was found in 2,000 pieces in 1872 and reassembled. It is still overlooked by the rare surviving early 15th-century timber watching loft. St Albans is known for its market and range of attractive buildings. The CHURCH OF ST MICHAEL is a very interesting structure retaining Saxon nave and chancel walls and Norman aisles. It is famous for containing a monument to Sir Francis Bacon, who died in 1626. The CLOCK TOWER is an unusual survivor of 1403-12 and stands conspicuously at the center of the old market square. One of the most attractive roads in St Albans is Fishpool Street, which runs down to KINGSBURY MILL, of 16th-century origin and now a museum.

HEMEL HEMPSTEAD Hemel Hempstead is often thought of as a new town and, indeed, was designated as such in 1947. Nevertheless, the old town is unexpectedly attractive. The large Norman CHURCH OF ST MARY remains exceptionally complete, with a rib-vaulted chancel of c. 1150.

ASHRIDGE ESTATE This estate of over 4,000 acres that runs across a ridge of the Chiltern Hills on the borders of Herts and Buckinghamshire offers extensive walks through woodland, downland and commons, with a chance to view Sir Jeffry Wyatville's monument to the 3rd Duke of Bridgewater (erected 1832).

GORHAMBURY (above) At Gorhambury stand the remains of the courtyard house built 1563-8 by Sir Nicholas Bacon, Lord Keeper of the Great Seal under Elizabeth I. Of special note is the hall porch with early Renaissance detailing. To the east stands new Gorhambury House designed by Sir Robert Taylor and begun between 1777 and 1784.

St Albans Cathedral: a view from the southwest showing the mainly 11th-century crossing tower and south transept (below right) and the nave looking west (below). The flat ceiling dates from the 1400s.

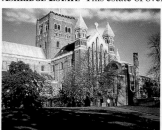

6. Henley-on-Thames
7. Buckingham
8. Windsor
9. Haslemere
10. Guildford
11. High Wycombe
12. St Albans
13. Bedford
14. Dorking
15. Hertford
16. Bishop's Stortford

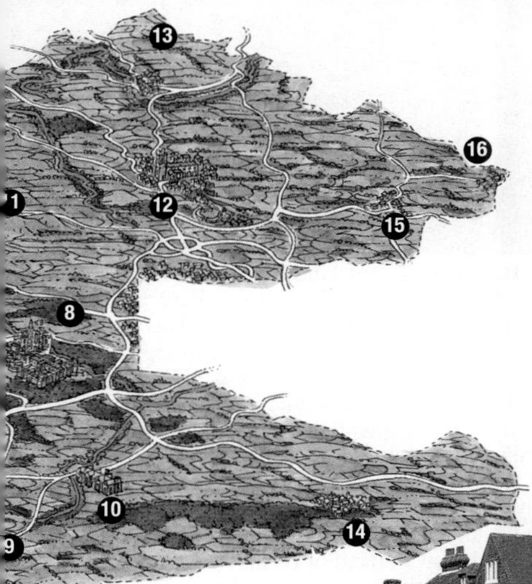

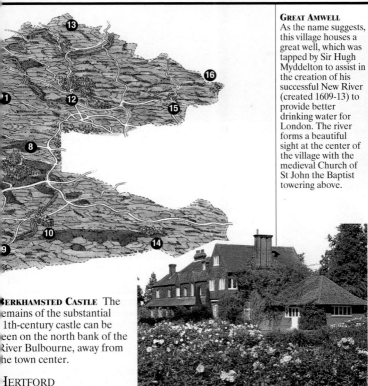

Great Amwell
As the name suggests, this village houses a great well, which was tapped by Sir Hugh Myddelton to assist in the creation of his successful New River (created 1609-13) to provide better drinking water for London. The river forms a beautiful sight at the center of the village with the medieval Church of St John the Baptist towering above.

erkhamsted Castle The emains of the substantial 1th-century castle can be een on the north bank of the River Bulbourne, away from he town center.

The Gardens of the Rose (above) These glorious gardens arranged around an attractive late-Victorian house known as Bone Hill, are run by The Royal National Rose Society and are only 2 miles south of St Albans at Chiswell Green. This is an important collection, with over 30,000 roses and companion plants including more than 100 varieties of clematis.

Hertford

Iertfordshire's county town remains a homely place with a nixture of historic and modern buildings. Not much survives f the once important castle, but what there is (parts of urtain walling and a 15th-century gatehouse, Gothicized luring the 1700s) lies set in tranquil parkland in the center of own by the river. Hertford is well known for its antique hops, riverside pubs, and busy shopping areas.

Bengeo At Bengeo, on higher ground immediately north of Iertford, is one of the best-preserved Norman churches in he county. St Leonard's has been little altered since the 100s and has a rare surviving chancel with apse.

Vare Ware has an imposing 14th- and 15th-century parish hurch (St Mary's), with five-stage west tower and transepts. Vorth a special look is the sumptuous late 14th-century font carved with figures of saints and angels.

Broxbourne, with its large, open green traversed by the New River, has a lively character and many charming spots, mostly centered around the extensive Lea Valley Regional Park.

Left: St Leonard's church, Bengeo, showing the large Norman apse with round-headed windows

Hatfield House (right) and the 15th-century Bishop's Palace (below), with projecting porch and knot garden

GEORGE BERNARD SHAW
Shaw lived in the Edwardian Shaw's Corner in Ayot St Lawrence from 1906 until his death in 1950. The house retains interesting personal relics and the summerhouse where he wrote.

ST PAUL'S WALDEN
All Saints' Church boasts a remarkable classical screen separating the chancel (remodeled in 1727) from the medieval nave. Edward Gilbert, the man responsible for this wonderful 18th-century work, lived at nearby The Bury.

Knebworth House: the battlemented skyline of mainly 19th-century provenance seen from the formal garden designed by Lutyens (right), and the Banqueting Hall (far right)

HATFIELD HOUSE ★ An outstanding Jacobean house built 1607-12 for Robert Cecil, 1st Earl of Salisbury, after he had exchanged the site with James I for nearby Theobalds. The house was probably designed by Robert Lyminge (also responsible for Blickling Hall, Norfolk ▲ *355*) and is set in an extensive great park with woodland, formal gardens, herb and scented garden, and a splendid maze laid out by the present Lady Salisbury. It features a stunning south front with loggia and clock tower attributed to Inigo Jones, a Great Hall with beautifully carved screen by John Bucke, magnificent staircase and Long Gallery (*c.* 160 feet). The house contains treasures such as the Rainbow Portrait of Elizabeth I, Hilliard's Ermine Portrait, rare tapestries, and paintings by Sir Joshua Reynolds. The surviving brick ranges of the great **BISHOP'S PALACE** built *c.* 1480-90, where Mary Tudor and Elizabeth I spent their childhoods, can be seen to the west of the house. The **CHURCH OF ST ETHELDREDA** contains the splendid monument to Robert Cecil (d. 1612), with sculpture by Maximilian Colt.

STEVENAGE

Although it looks perfectly commonplace today, Stevenage new town was famous in the 1940s and 1950s for having one of Europe's first completely pedestrian centers. In Old Stevenage is **ST NICHOLAS'S CHURCH**, with Norman tower and some 15th-century choir seats with misericords.

AYOT ST LAWRENCE The **CHURCH OF NEW ST LAURENCE** is an ambitious and unusual building of 1778-9 designed by Nicholas Revett (of *Antiquities of Athens* fame) in the Greek Revival style. Ayot St Lawrence was also home to George Bernard Shaw; his former house, Shaw's Corner, is situated in the southwest end of the village.

KNEBWORTH HOUSE Knebworth House, approached through a large and impressive park, has been home to the Lytton family since 1490. However, the battlemented, Gothic appearance of the house dates mainly from the 19th century.

Benington Lordship gardens (right and below), and a mock Norman gateway (far right)

The interior includes a Banqueting Hall with early 17th-century screen and paneling, a fine staircase and armory, and a sumptuous early Victorian State Drawing Room. The CHURCH OF ST MARY within the house's grounds contains the Lytton Chapel with excellent early 18th-century monuments.

ASHWELL This large and well-preserved village contains the beautiful 14th- and 15th-century CHURCH OF ST MARY with its splendid west tower (176 feet) and light and spacious interior. There is a detailed scratching of the south side of Old St Paul's Cathedral on the north wall.

HITCHIN An interesting town, its wealth during the late medieval period proudly demonstrated by the spacious CHURCH OF ST MARY. A visit is well rewarded by the series of excellent roofs, screens and monuments.

RAVENSBURGH CASTLE This vast, oval Iron-Age hill fort survives on the summit of Barton Hills beyond Hitchin, close to the Bedfordshire county boundary.

BISHOP'S STORTFORD

Bishop's Stortford is a busy town and presents a real architectural mix. One of the earliest buildings is THE BLACK LION on Bridge Street, a 16th-century inn with exposed timber-framing. ST MICHAEL'S is a good, late medieval town church with an airy interior, original roofs and a pulpit made locally in 1658.

MUCH HADHAM A short drive from Bishop's Stortford and one is in another world. This charming little village still has an unspoilt, typical Hertfordshire main street with several good cottages and large 18th-century houses. The mainly 14th-century CHURCH OF ST ANDREW has two uncharacteristically modern head-stops to its west door: a king and a queen; they are by the famous sculptor Henry Moore (1898-1986) who lived and worked at nearby Perry Green. His studios, workshops, and now a new gallery (Sheep Field Barn) are owned and maintained by THE HENRY MOORE FOUNDATION and are open for visits by appointment only. In this lovely, secluded part of the countryside Moore's sculptures can be seen at their best, dotted haphazardly round the garden and fields.

BENINGTON ★
The chief interest of this attractive village is Benington Lordship, a Queen Anne house reworked during the 19th century in the neo-Norman style. The hilltop gardens are open to the public and feature beautiful herbaceous borders, lakes, castle ruins, and verandah teas. The neighboring Church of St Peter retains an important medieval tomb chest with effigies.

Sculptures by Henry Moore can be seen at Perry Green, near Much Hadham, where the artist lived and worked

Opposite page (top row)
The 15th-century timber-framed courthouse at Lon
Crendon (left); Boarstall Tower, a 14th-century gatehous
with later alterations (center); the mid-17th-century re
brick front of Princes Risborough Manor House (righ

JORDANS
In Welders Lane, a Friends' Meeting House of 1688 survives. It is a modest structure of considerable historic interest, having been built by Isaac Penington immediately after the Toleration Act.

The picturesque 16th- or 17th-century cottage where John Milton lived can be visited at Chalfont St Giles. Top: a portrait of the poet, aged 10, on display in the cottage.

THE CHILTERNS

The beautiful Chiltern Hills, a long escarpment famous for its beechwoods and walks, provide a striking contrast to the built-up suburbs of London. Many peaceful villages nestle within this undulating landscape.

KING'S LANGLEY King's Langley owes its name to a royal palace that formerly stood to the west of the High Street, a site now occupied by school buildings. The medieval CHURCH OF ALL SAINTS contains a monument to Edmund of Langley (born here in 1341), fifth son of Edward III.

TRING The late 19th-century character of Tring is mainly attributable to the wealthy Rothschild family, who acquired Tring Park in 1873. The WALTER ROTHSCHILD ZOOLOGICAL MUSEUM (Akeman Street) opened to the public in 1892 to display the remarkable collections of Lionel Walter, 2nd Baron Rothschild (d. 1937), and was bequeathed to the British Museum in 1938. The museum is an extraordinary survival, over-brimming with all kinds of stuffed creatures.

CHALFONT ST GILES A large village with two noteworthy sights. First, there is the CHURCH OF ST GILES, retaining a cycle of wall paintings of *c.* 1330. Second is MILTON'S COTTAGE (21 Deanway) where John Milton fled to escape the 1665 plague and where he completed his epic *Paradise Lost*. The cottage and its garden are open to the public and there is a small museum.

STOKE POGES It is easy to be put off by the proximity of busy modern Slough, but Stoke Poges remains a characterful village with interesting connections. The handsome CHURCH OF ST GILES boasts fine stained glass and monuments. One of two lychgates leads to the old churchyard that inspired Thomas Gray to write his "Elegy in a Country Churchyard". The GRAY MONUMENT to the east was erected in 1799 to designs by James Wyatt and is adorned with quotations from the poem.

AYLESBURY

Aylesbury has expanded gradually since it replaced Buckingham as the county town in the 18th century, but experienced a period of very rapid growth in the 1960s culminating in the 1973 completion of the ring road. Thus, it now presents a rather mixed appearance with few major attractions. Worth a look is the BUCKINGHAMSHIRE COUNTY MUSEUM (Church Street), housed in well-restored buildings that include an 18th-century grammar school. It contains the magical Roald Dahl Children's Museum (Dahl lived and wrote in Bucks) and displays on the county's heritage.

HARTWELL At Hartwell is one of England's most perfect 18th-century churches in the Gothic style, ST MARY'S, built 1753-5 to designs by Henry Keene. This superb little building (now disused) sits on a mound near HARTWELL HOUSE, an important country house of the early 17th and 18th centuries remodeled as a hotel in 1986-9.

PRINCES RISBOROUGH Like Kings Langley, Princes Risborough takes its name from a royal manor, one which

xisted until 1628 when it was presented to the City of London y Charles I. The major interest of the town is its stately red-rick **MANOR HOUSE** built probably in *c.* 1630-50 and much eworked by the Rothschild family from 1886.

ONG CRENDON A large and attractive village, formerly nown for its needle-making, which retains a number of good nedieval buildings, many of cruck construction. The 15th-entury **COURT HOUSE** in the high street is particularly npressive and has a jettied upper floor over a stone base. The pper chamber was used as a manorial courtroom from the eign of Henry V until the 19th century.

ETHER WINCHENDON HOUSE This s a very interesting medieval and udor manor house remodeled etween 1798 and 1803 in the oothick style. The fine quality of the rieze and linenfold paneling in the rawing room suggest royal onnections, and indeed the early 6th-century owner, Sir John aunce, was one of Henry VIII's rivy Councillors.

OARSTALL At Boarstall there are two fascinating survivals: **OARSTALL TOWER** is an early 14th-century stone gatehouse ltered in the late 1500s or early 1600s, all that remains of a ortified medieval manor house. On a nearby lake surrounded y woodland is Boarstall's more peculiar sight, a **DUCK DECOY** f *c.* 1697 in complete working order.

WADDESDON MANOR Every county has its most prominent ountry house and this is Buckinghamshire's, a spectacular isplay of French Renaissance architecture which seems straight ut of Touraine. Waddesdon Manor was built as a show piece n 1877-89 by Baron Ferdinand de Rothschild (his architect vas the Belgian Hippolyte Destailleur) and contains one of he world's most significant collections of French decorative rt. There are paintings by English, Dutch and Flemish nasters and genuine 18th-century *boiseries* from Parisian *ôtels.* The 19th-century gardens are among Britain's best and oast a parterre, Rococo aviary of 1889, and 18th-century talian statues, recently restored.

CHILTERN OPEN AIR MUSEUM
(left and above)
This museum offers the visitor a unique chance to get to know the historic buildings of the region, not through photographs or drawings, but by exploring the re-erected structures themselves, many saved from demolition. These include a fully furnished 1940s prefab house, a tin chapel, a 19th-century toll house, and a blacksmith's forge.

The garden front of Waddesdon Manor with 18th-century Italian statues in the fountain

DODDERSHALL PARK, near Quainton (open by appointment only), forms three sides of a courtyard, with timber-framed ranges of *c.* 1520 to the east and north, and a brick addition of 1689 to the south. Of particular interest are the Tudor Hall and Great Chamber.

WING ALL SAINTS ★ is a well-known church and rightly so, for it retains a 9th-century crypt, nave, and a beautiful 10th-century polygonal apse. Such ambitious design indicates that the church probably housed the relics of an important saint.

HIGH WYCOMBE is a large, sprawling town built around the steep Wye Valley that has always been an important point on the main Oxford to London road (now bypassed by the M40). The most significant sights include the fine Palladian GUILDHALL of 1757 by Henry Keene and the spacious CHURCH OF ALL SAINTS. The church contains an excellent monument to Henry Petty, Earl of Shelburne (d. 1751) by Peter Scheemakers.

HUGHENDEN MANOR The private retreat of prime minister, statesman and writer Benjamin Disraeli, who lived here from 1848 until his death in 1881, has a dramatic red-brick exterior as remodeled in 1862-3 by E.B. Lamb. The Gothic-style interior contains Disraeli's study and mementos of his life; the attractive gardens have been recreated following the designs of his wife, Mary Anne.

Hughenden Manor: a portrait of Disraeli by Sir Francis Grant, 1852 (top), and the inner hall (above)

WEST WYCOMBE The focus of this pretty village is WEST WYCOMBE HOUSE and PARK. The spectacular Italianate appearance of the mansion is largely due to additions made between *c.* 1750 and 1764 by Sir Francis Dashwood MP, best known as creator of the infamous Hell-Fire Club, and features superb Palladian interiors. Its Park is an exquisite and perfectly preserved 18th-century landscape with lakes, temples and buildings, some designed by Nicholas Revett. On the nearby hill stand the DASHWOOD MAUSOLEUM and the medieval CHURCH, sumptuously remodeled in the mid-1700s. The church tower is finished with a golden ball, which contains seats for ten people. Halfway down the hill are the amazing WEST WYCOMBE CAVES made by Dashwood in 1750-2.

Cliveden: the south front looking out over the gardens from the 17th-century terrace (below) and a portrait of Nancy Astor (who lived in the house with her family) by John Singer Sargent, 1906.

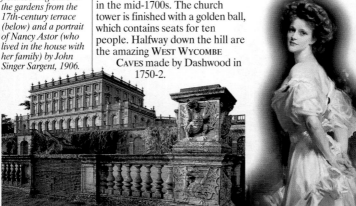

CLIVEDEN The estate comprises 375 acres of beautiful gardens and woodland set around an Italianate country house built in 1850-1 and designed by Charles Barry. Cliveden offers spectacular views along the Thames Valley and there is a parterre, rose garden and water garden with a Chinese pavilion made for the Paris Exhibition of 1867. The Octagon Temple of 1735, designed by Giacomo Leoni, was converted into a chapel during the 1800s and has a lovely Byzantine-style interior. Three rooms of the house (converted to a hotel in 1984-6) are open to the public.

CHENIES MANOR HOUSE is a handsome building of the 15th and 16th centuries, formerly owned by the Russells (later Dukes of Bedford). It has much to offer: Tudor tapestries and furniture, hiding places, a sunken garden and two mazes.

MARLOW Despite industrial growth around the edges of the town, Marlow retains a historic character, with the River Thames as its central focus. The impressive MARLOW SUSPENSION BRIDGE, built in 1829-31, provides an interesting contrast to the nearby CHURCH OF ALL SAINTS rebuilt in 1832-5 by C.F. Inwood. In Station Road is the excellent MARLOW PLACE of *c.* 1720, ascribed to Thomas Archer, and in West Street is ALBION HOUSE where Shelley lived and where his wife Mary worked on the story of Frankenstein.

ASCOTT This pretty house was originally a Jacobean farmhouse but was substantially remodeled for Leopold de Rothschild in 1873-88. Its interior and black-and-white appearance date from 1937-8. There are handsome gardens with an unusual topiary sundial.

IVINGHOE FORD END WATERMILL is the county's only working watermill to survive with its original machinery. The building was first recorded in the 1700s but has been restored, capturing the atmosphere of a late 19th-century corn mill.

West Wycombe House (above left); Temple of Venus (top) and a stunning neoclassical ceiling in the Tapestry Room (above).

ASCOTT
The house contains a marvelous collection of paintings, sculpture, furniture and ceramics (including Chinese porcelain). Below: Venus and cherubs in chariot; bottom left: *Interior* by Ludolph de Jongh; bottom right: cabinet.

MENTMORE TOWERS Mentmore's architect, Sir Joseph Paxton, is best known for his mid-19th-century Crystal Palace, but this remarkable Elizabethan Revival house (1850-5) has the same grandeur and magnitude; it was sold in 1978 and is no longer open to the public.

Top: Mentmore Towers, and the glass-roofed central hall (above right)
Above: the Chinese Room at Claydon House and a picture of Sir Edward Verney, 1868

Palladian Bridge, and Vanbrugh's Rotonda at Stowe (bottom)

BUCKINGHAM

Thanks to the removal of court and administrative business to Aylesbury, Buckingham has remained unspoilt and full of atmosphere. There are plenty of good buildings, many constructed after a major fire of 1725. Worth a special look are the TOWN HALL finished in 1784 and the very handsome OLD GAOL (Market Hill) built in 1748, now a museum. Fortunately one important medieval building escaped the fire, the BUCKINGHAM CHANTRY CHAPEL. This chapel was rebuilt in 1475, retaining a rich Norman doorway, and was rebuilt again in 1875 by Sir Giles Gilbert Scott.

STOWE LANDSCAPE GARDENS ★ are rightly famous throughout Europe, for it was here, in the 18th century, that the English art of landscape gardening was born. The gardens are remarkable for being so little altered and none of the original splendor or breathtaking beauty has been lost. The contoured landscape, covering an immense 325 acres, is dotted with buildings and temples by some of the greatest architects of the period. These include the TEMPLE OF BRITISH WORTHIES (1735) by William Kent, Gibbs's GOTHIC TEMPLE of 1741-2, the PALLADIAN BRIDGE (1719), and Vanbrugh's ROTONDA (c. 1719). The effect is intoxicating, so much so that it is easy to miss the garden's central focus, STOWE HOUSE, now a public school. The house does well in deserving such a position, especially the south front of 1770-4 by Robert Adam, and contains beautiful neoclassical interiors including the marble saloon of 1775-88.

MAIDS' MORETON ST EDMUND'S is an attractive church said to have been built in the mid-1400s by two maiden sisters. The wide, well-lit nave and chancel retain much of their original roofs, and there is an elaborate sedilia.

The south front of Stowe House, built in 1770-4 to designs by Robert Adam

CLAYDON HOUSE, Middle Claydon. This is the surviving part of an extraordinary mansion built *c.* 1757-69 by Ralph, 2nd Earl Verney, designed to rival Stowe. From the plain stone exterior you enter a Rococo wonderland, with three main reception rooms adorned with the most fantastic plasterwork in England. The main staircase is itself a major work of art. The upper rooms are no less lavish, and on display is the bedroom used by Florence Nightingale, a relation of the Verneys, who lived in the house on and off for 50 years.

WINSLOW A small but historic town, the Winslow Estate having been granted by King Offa to St Albans in 795. The Church of St Lawrence has good wall paintings of *c.* 1500 but the main sight is **WINSLOW HALL** (1700-4). This is the perfect example of a William and Mary house and has fine, virtually unaltered interiors. The design is convincingly attributed to Christopher Wren.

The dignified front of Winslow Hall, probably by Wren

STEWKLEY ST MICHAEL'S is the most complete Norman church in Buckinghamshire and was built probably in *c.* 1150-80. The vista from west to east, with zig-zag arches, is magnificent.

BLETCHLEY PARK Milton Keynes is, on the whole, to be avoided but this house offers something a little different. Bletchley Park, built in the 19th and early 20th centuries, was made famous during World War II as the government's intelligence center. It was here that Enigma and Colossus, the world's first large electronic valve computers, helped to crack Nazi codes.

CHICHELEY CHICHELEY HALL is a fine house built between 1719 and 1724. Its interiors demonstrate some excellent workmanship, including a screen possibly by Flitcroft, and there are pretty formal gardens. Previously the home of Admiral Lord Beatty, it contains a small naval museum, but is privately owned and occupied.

James Gibbs's Gothic Temple of 1741-2, a conspicuous and important part of Stowe's 18th-century landscaped gardens. It is built on a triangular plan.

OLNEY A delightful small town, once known for its lace-making, with some good Georgian architecture. Of special note is the COWPER AND NEWTON MUSEUM in Orchard Side (Market Place) where displays on the town's history are shown in the former house of poet William Cowper (1731-1800), alongside many personal relics. The 18th-century pulpit, used by Cowper's friend John Newton, is preserved at the 14th-century church, where he was curate.

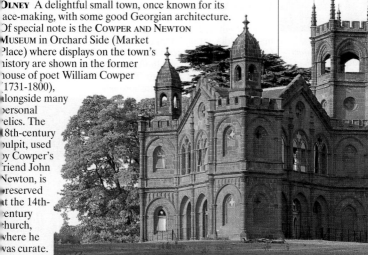

"Piazzetta San Marco" by Canaletto, 1358, at Woburn Abbey

*Center: Dunstable Priory, the west front
Above: the porch, All Saints, Chalgrave*

Elephant House at Whipsnade

DUNSTABLE

Dunstable is a modern town that retains one building of outstanding interest, the 12th-century **DUNSTABLE PRIORY**. This church represents the principal surviving part of an Augustinian priory founded in 1131 by Henry I. The west front is impressive, and inside is an excellent Norman font, probably recut during the 1800s.

LUTON Bedfordshire's largest town, once known for its straw-plait and hat making, is worth a visit only for its **CHURCH OF ST MARY**. Although now seen in a modern context, the church is of Norman origin. Note the font of *c.* 1330-40 with fine canopy, the Easter Sepulchre, and Hoo and Wenlock Chapels. Not far from the town is **LUTON HOO** (not open), a vast and magnificent country house begun in 1764 for the Earl of Bute, which features work by Robert Adam and Sir Robert Smirke; it was remodeled at the turn of the last century.

CHALGRAVE Chalgrave has a small unspoilt church, typical of the county, which was consecrated in 1219. Worth a closer look are the wall paintings of *c.* 1310 and the two 14th-century monuments of knights.

TOTTERNHOE At Totternhoe is another of Bedfordshire's delightful churches, **ST GILES'**, retaining an excellent late medieval nave roof with carved beams and bosses. There are remains of a castle at the end of a promontory site.

WHIPSNADE A steady stream of visitors have marveled at Whipsnade Wild Animal Park since it opened in 1931. The park is home to over 2,500 animals, many endangered, and there are 1930s buildings by Lubetkin and Tecton.

WOBURN ABBEY An understandably popular venue with plenty to offer any visitor. First there is the house, home of the dukes of Bedford for nearly 400 years, a magnificent, mainly 18th-century building that takes its name from a Cistercian abbey founded here in 1145. The interiors include the Grotto of *c.* 1630 and the Venetian Room containing 21 views of Venice by Canaletto. The fine art collection includes works by Claude, Cuyp, Gainsborough and Van Dyck. There are also

The sumptuous 18th-century State Bedroom at Woburn Abbey

Elizabeth I by Gower, detail of a painting at Woburn Abbey

gardens, an extensive deer park, and an unusually exciting safari park.

EATON BRAY The exterior of the Church of St Mary may not look like much, but inside are the exquisite 13th-century arcades and a font of *c.* 1235-40. Note the ironwork of the south door.

BEDFORD

Bedford was described in Daniel Defoe's *A Tour Through the Whole Island of Great Britain* as a "large, populous and thriving town, and a pleasant well-built place". The town has four medieval churches, the best of which is St Paul's, a 19th-century Shire Hall by Waterhouse, and a Town Hall of which the beautiful Harpur's School (1756) forms the left part. The River Ouse flows lazily through the town's center and is ideal for boating. Worth a visit is the **CECIL HIGGINS ART GALLERY** (Castle Close), former home of Bedford brewers, the Higgins family. Adjoining the 19th-century mansion is a modern gallery displaying a collection of watercolors, prints and ceramics. In the High Street is a statue of John Bunyan, author of *The Pilgrim's Progress*, who preached and was imprisoned here. The Swan Hotel, built in 1794, contains the re-erected staircase from Ampthill's Houghton House ▲ 294.

The Venetian Room at Woburn Abbey contains 21 views of Venice by Canaletto

Statue of John Bunyan in Bedford, by Sir J.E. Boehm, 1874

▲ BEDFORD

WREST PARK This 19th-century French château-style house, in its 18th-century park, was formerly home to the de Grey family, whose mausoleum is at nearby Flitton. The gardens cover over 90 acres and include a parterre and orangery.

FLITTON The entire east end of the 15th-century CHURCH OF ST JOHN THE BAPTIST is taken up by the de Grey Mausoleum, a remarkable series of rooms containing the 16th- to 19th-century monuments of the de Grey family. A more impressive statement of family pride is rarely to be seen.

AMPTHILL Ampthill is a typical Bedfordshire town with a market dating back to 1219 and some attractive buildings, particularly in Church Street and Woburn Street. The CHURCH OF ST ANDREW contains an unusual monument to Richard Nicoll (d. 1672) with the cannon ball that killed him embedded in the pediment. There are two major houses on the town's outskirts, AMPTHILL PARK of 1694 and HOUGHTON HOUSE. Houghton House is said to have been started c. 1615 and was then home to the Countess of Pembroke, sister of poet Sir Philip Sidney. Only the impressive remains can now be seen, for the house was dismantled in 1794. The Jacobean elevations are adorned with splendid frontispieces of c. 1635-45 which have been attributed (on no evidence) to Inigo Jones.

OLD WARDEN Old Warden has a church interesting for its interior over-brimming with woodwork, mainly Belgian, collected from 1841 by Lord Ongley. One mile away is WARDEN ABBEY, a small and odd-looking remnant of an early Tudor house built on the site of an abbey founded in 1135. For those who like a walk in picturesque surroundings there is the SWISS GARDEN (Biggleswade Road), laid out in the early 1800s.

Top: View of the gardens at Wrest Park, from the house, with the parterre in the foreground.
Above: Monuments in the De Grey Mausoleum at Flitton
Above right: Hinwick House, with projecting wing

Brasses depicting Isabel Conquest with her husband and son, Church of All Saints, Houghton Conquest

ELSTOW A Benedictine nunnery was founded at Elstow in *c.* 1075 and its beautiful 12th- and 13th-century nave survives in the **CHURCH OF ST MARY AND ST HELEN**, the

Moot Hall, Elstow, exterior (top) and interior, upper floor showing beamed roof (above)

pride of the village. Also of note are the so-called Chapter House near the building's west front and the detached 15th-century campanile. The remains of early 17th-century **HILLERSDON HALL** are nearby, as is the fine **MOOT HALL** of *c.* 1500 where John Bunyan and his adherents often met.

HINWICK This village has two memorable manor houses, Tudor **HINWICK HALL** with an early 18th-century east front, and the handsome classical **HINWICK HOUSE** of 1709-14.

BUSHMEAD Bushmead Priory is a rare surviving refectory range from an Augustinian priory founded in 1195. The building has a good timber roof and contains wall paintings and fragments of stained glass.

Below: Gold Bull in High Steet, Bedford
Below left: the refectory range at Bushmead Priory

HOUGHTON CONQUEST A village worth visiting for the excellent brasses of Isabel Conquest (d. 1493) and her husband and son contained in the 14th- and 15th-century **CHURCH OF ALL SAINTS**.

TURVEY Turvey's church, of Anglo-Danish origin, boasts some exquisite 13th-century ironwork to its south door, similar to that at Eaton Bray ▲ *293*. The high quality points to royal craftsmanship and it may have been produced by Thomas of Leighton, who was responsible for the railings surrounding Queen Eleanor's monument in Westminster Abbey.

BROMHAM Bromham has a good working watermill and art gallery, attractively sited by the River Ouse, and a bridge and causeway dating from the late 1200s. The Church of St Owen contains a fine brass to Thomas Wideville (d. 1435) and his two wives.

NORTHILL The much restored medieval **CHURCH OF ST MARY** has one outstanding feature: its rich stained-glass windows of 1664 by John Oliver.

WILLINGTON Henry VIII's Treasurer of the First Fruits and Tenths, Sir John Gostwick, was probably responsible for the **CHURCH OF ST LAWRENCE**. This is unusual in having been built all in one period, *c.* 1530-40. It contains the helmet worn by Gostwick at the Field of the Cloth of Gold.

FELMERSHAM
The Church of St Mary (above), one of the finest Early English buildings in all the Home Counties, is located in the quiet setting of Felmersham. St Mary's was built between *c.* 1220 and 1230/40 and has a noble west front, fine interior and screen.

EGHAM

Top: Aerial view of Royal Holloway College showing its rectangular plan enclosing two courtyards.
Above: the central hall at Taplow Court

Egham was the home of the Denham family, including 17th-century poet Sir John, whose father's monument (d. 1639) can be seen in the CHURCH OF ST JOHN THE BAPTIST. This shows a figure rising from the grave above a well-carved charnel house and is possibly by Maximilian Colt. Otherwise, there is little to see in this village on the Thames. Half a mile west, however, is ROYAL HOLLOWAY COLLEGE, the *magnum opus* of Victorian architect W.H. Crossland. The college, one of the country's first to be built especially for women, dates from 1879-87 and is in the French Renaissance style. The silhouette is impressive with its numerous tourelles and cupolas. The fine art gallery has a collection amassed mainly in 1881-3 including work by Landseer, Luke Fildes and Frank Holl. Crossland's lesser known HOLLOWAY SANATORIUM, opened in 1884, is the companion building to the college and has a good front in the Continental Gothic style. Both buildings take the name of their founder Thomas Holloway, a man who made his fortune selling the popular Holloway's Pills.

A detail of the vast and impressive Royal Holloway College, built in 1879-87 by W.H. Crossland.

RUNNYMEDE At Runnymede near Egham are the famous riverside meadows where in 1215 King John granted the Magna Carta (Great Charter) to the English people. The area, given to the National Trust in 1931, has pretty woodland and grassland, and there are memorial buildings including some by Lutyens. Here, too, is a memorial to John F. Kennedy. On a high escarpment above Runnymede is **COOPER'S HILL MEMORIAL**, built in 1953 by Sir Edward Maufe to commemorate the many members of the Allied air forces killed in 1939-45. The spot offers magnificent views of the surrounding countryside and the memorial itself demonstrates an imaginative use of space.

COOKHAM In 1891 the well-loved artist Stanley Spencer was born in this pretty village by the Thames, a place that inspired him throughout his life. The **STANLEY SPENCER GALLERY ★**, opened in 1962 in a converted chapel in the heart of Cookham, contains an important collection of his work including *The Last Supper* of 1920 and *Beatitudes of Love: Contemplation* of 1937.

BURGHCLERE At Burghclere, just over the Hampshire border near Newbury, can be seen the Sandham Memorial Chapel with interior walls completely covered by Spencer's remarkable murals depicting World War I.

TAPLOW Taplow Court is the much remodeled manor house of Taplow with an exterior largely due to work of 1855-60 by William Burn. The house boasts a rich hall at its center, built in the neo-Norman style and dating from the 1830s. Taplow Court became well known in the early 1900s as its owners, Lord and Lady Desborough, entertained an elite group known as "The Souls" here. The house is set high above the Thames and offers beautiful views and gardens. It is just across the county boundary from Cliveden ▲ 293. Southwest of Taplow Court, in the old churchyard, is a fascinating and important Anglo-Saxon **BURIAL MOUND** which was opened in 1883. The grave goods and finds can be seen in the British Museum ▲ 136-9.

The old **CHURCH** was demolished in 1828 and rebuilt on a new site (Boundary Road). It contains a brass to Nichole de Aumberdere of *c.* 1350, traditionally the earliest surviving brass of a civilian in England. The fine **MAIDENHEAD BRIDGE** is by architect Sir Robert Taylor and was built in 1772-7.

DORNEY A remote and charming area centered upon **DORNEY COURT**, a house of late medieval origin remodeled in *c.* 1900 in the style of *c.* 1500. The many-gabled brick exterior faces typical English parkland; inside there is a hall and parlor wing of *c.* 1470 and a good staircase.

BISHAM There are two buildings of particular interest in this delightful village by the River Thames – house and church. **BISHAM ABBEY**, now a country club, started life as a preceptory of the Templars, was an Augustinian priory after 1337, and was an abbey for only three years before being dissolved. Despite much that is medieval, what we see today is mainly the 16th-century work of the Hoby family. Note the fine chimneypiece and overmantel in the hall. The **CHURCH OF ALL SAINTS** has a Norman west tower but was over-restored in the 1800s. It contains the exquisite alabaster monument to Lady Margaret Hoby (d. 1605) which carries four swans, the family's supporters.

ASCOT
Ascot is known chiefly for its racecourse, which has been regularly attended by royalty since the 1700s when the first race was run. Most of the buildings seen today date from the 20th century, but the atmosphere remains historic.

"Pumpkin" by George Stubbs

Right. Aerial view of the castle

Angle tower and walling

Windsor, England's largest and most outstanding castle, was founded *c.* 1080 by William the Conqueror on a cliff-top site by the Thames Valley. What we see today is a fascinating mix of architecture from medieval times through to the 19th century. The castle contains the spectacular St George's Chapel, State Apartments and Semi-State Apartments (which house works by Holbein, Van Dyck, Rubens, Hogarth and Lawrence and a collection of historic furniture), the famous Queen Mary's Doll's House, and workplaces or residences of people such as the castle's Constable. Here, the wealth and glory of the country's monarchs is everywhere demonstrated with sumptuous interiors, carved work, and craftsmanship of the highest quality. Visitors can walk along the North Terrace built and loved by Elizabeth I and watch colorful ceremonies in the Quadrangle. A serious fire in 1992 did considerable damage, but all has now been comprehensively and beautifully restored, with new elements.

ST GEORGE'S CHAPEL
The chapel choir (right) is hung with banners of the Knights of the Garter; the east window is by Clayton and Bell.
Above: the stunning south front of St George's Chapel, begun in 1475.

QUEEN'S BALLROOM
Opposite, bottom left:
this detail of the ballroom shows Van Dyck's portrait of the sons of the Duke of Buckingham.
Opposite, bottom right: the opulent State Bedchamber.

Entrance tower / gate house

Above, left and right: the tranquil 35-acre Savill Garden contained in Windsor Great Park

Top: Basildon Park's impressive entrance front by John Carr (right), and the Octagonal Drawing Room (left)

Above: the Royal Mausoleum at Frogmore House

Saint Paul by Pompeo Batoni, from Basildon Park

WINDSOR AND ETON

WINDSOR Windsor Great Park offers acres of beautiful scenery on ancient, royal land connected to the castle by Charles II's 2-mile lime avenue known as the Long Walk. The SAVILL GARDEN, contained within the south part of the park, is of particular note. It has streams and ponds and offers a spectacular display of flowers including azaleas, camellias and primulas. There is also Virginia Water, an artificial lake created by the Duke of Cumberland of Culloden fame, the Valley Gardens, and columns from Roman buildings brought from Leptis Magna in 1817. HOME PARK, generally closed to the public, contains 18th-century Frogmore House and the 19th-century mausoleum of Prince Albert and Queen Victoria, open on one day a year. Windsor itself is a pleasant riverside town with several uncommonly good buildings, including the Town Hall completed by Wren in 1689-90.

ETON Eton College was founded in 1440 by Henry VI and is one of England's best-known public schools. The college buildings incorporate much important medieval work including Lupton's Range with a gatehouse of 1517-*c.* 1520. The chapel was built *c.* 1449-75 and has an impressive interior with some accomplished 15th-century wall paintings. Eton is still surrounded by pretty open fields.

READING A Cluniac abbey was founded at Reading in the year 1121 and the town was well loved by English monarchy. Today, despite the survival of fragments of the abbey (the Church of St Lawrence was originally the abbey's "chapel without the gates"), Reading is a modern university town centered around the rivers Kennet and Thames. The BLAKES

LOCK MUSEUM has displays on canals, mills, fishing and boat-building. The MUSEUM OF READING, contained in the 19th-century town hall, features the world's only full-size replica of the Bayeux Tapestry, painstakingly stitched by 35 Victorian ladies. It also has displays on the town's earlier origins, with Roman life depicted in the Silchester Gallery. Silchester ▲ *200* (in Hampshire) was an ancient capital of the Atrebates tribe, rebuilt after the Roman conquest and inhabited till the 6th century.

BASILDON PARK, Lower Basildon. This elegant Georgian mansion dates from 1776-83 and was built by John Carr for Sir Francis Sykes. The

interior retains fine plasterwork, a tall staircase and, in the center of the garden front toward the Thames, the unusual Octagonal Room probably by Victorian architect J.B. Papworth, which houses part of the fine collection of mainly Italian Baroque art assembled by Lord and Lady Iliffe. The house is set among pleasure gardens in an area rich in downland and woodland walks.

SWALLOWFIELD PARK An H-plan house rebuilt in 1689-91 by William Talman for the 2nd Earl of Clarendon, and substantially remodeled again in 1820. John Evelyn wrote that the gardens were "as elegant as 'tis possible to make a flat by art and industrie and no mean expense". Note especially the rich, re-erected doorway by Talman.

ENGLEFIELD HOUSE Only the gardens of this attractive house, mainly 19th-century but Elizabethan in origin, are open to the public. They feature woodland, rose and herbaceous borders, and are set in an extensive deer park. In the grounds stands Englefield's typical High Victorian church by Sir Giles Gilbert Scott, with good monuments.

Swallowfield Park's Drawing Room (above left) and the entrance front with porte-cochère added c. 1820 (above)

Lupton's Gatehouse at Eton College, facing the School Yard

NEWBURY

Newbury is a pleasant town on the River Kennet. Its good 16th- to 18th-century buildings reflect its former prosperity, having been the center of a booming cloth-making trade. This industry was established by John Smallwood (also known as Jack O'Newbury or John Winchcombe) who lived in the early 16th century and was responsible for the nave of the fine **CHURCH OF ST NICHOLAS** built in c. 1500-32. In Wharf Road is the fascinating timber-framed **CLOTH HALL** built in 1626-7, now a museum.

WELFORD PARK This good Queen Anne house is worth visiting for its lovely grounds, gardens and peaceful riverside walks. The house is open by prior arrangement only.

AVINGTON Avington's **CHURCH OF ST MARK AND ST LUKE** is a fine example of a small and unspoilt Norman country church which survives in a picturesque setting with a large cedar tree. Inside is a Norman font with well-carved figures.

COMBE At Combe, a remote hamlet south of Walbury Hill, is the remarkable **COMBE GIBBET**, a tall gallows on a Neolithic barrow. Its isolation and aspect is disturbing even today.

DONNINGTON CASTLE Donnington Castle was mainly destroyed during one of the longest sieges of the Civil War, but the earthworks and remains are unexpectedly impressive. The castle was originally licensed in 1386; of that time is the imposing twin-towered gatehouse.

WICKHAM The **CHURCH OF ST SWITHIN** displays two interesting architectural styles, genuine Anglo-Saxon and 19th-century neo-medieval. The chief early survival is the projecting south-west tower. Of the later period (1845-9 by Benjamin Ferrey) are the ornate interiors of nave and chancel. Note the completely out-of-context papier mâché elephants supporting the aisle roof. They were shown at the Paris Exhibition of 1862.

Combe Gibbet

RIVER AND ROWING MUSEU
In 1999 a museum dedicated to the a
and history of rowing and the riv
opened in Henley. It is housed in
building by David Chipperfiel

STOKE ROW
The little village of
Stoke Row contains
the obscure domed
Maharajah's Well
(above), presented in
1863 by the
Maharajah of
Benares. Exotic
features are the onion
dome and cast-iron
elephant.

*Below: Some of the
14th-century remains
at Greys Court
Right: The well-
preserved watermill at
Mapledurham*

Mapledurham House

Oxfordshire is a large and varied county moving from the flat,
fertile lands around the River Thames to the hilly Cotswolds
by the Gloucestershire boundary. Henley is a beautiful
example of the former, with a broad, straight stretch of the
Thames that constitutes the finest regatta course in the
country. Architecture from a range of periods is represented
with special sights including the attractive bridge rebuilt in
1786 by William Hayward and the Kenton Theatre of 1805.
The medieval church has a prominent tower supposedly built
by John Longland, Bishop of Lincoln in 1521-47.

ROTHERFIELD GREYS The main sight near this village is
GREYS COURT, a mansion built probably in the early 1500s
among the interesting ruins of a semi-fortified 14th-century
manor house. Greys Court was altered in the 17th to 19th
centuries and features some splendid Rococo plasterwork.
There is a well-house, a wheel-house with rare surviving
donkey wheel, and the so-called Cromwellian Stables. The
Bachelor's Hall takes its name from a Latin inscription
reading "Nothing is better than the celibate life". The village
CHURCH contains an excellent brass to Lord Robert de Grey
(d. 1387) and a superb Jacobean alabaster and marble
monument to the Knollys family.

STONOR PARK is a substantial house set in a remote valley at
the Oxfordshire edge of the Chiltern Hills. The building's
sash-windowed, Georgian appearance conceals some good
medieval work, for the house has belonged to the recusant
Stonor family since the 12th century. The simple detached
Roman Catholic chapel dates from the 1300s and was
remodelled internally between 1796 and 1800.

MAPLEDURHAM A well-preserved village near the Thames,
which contains the large Elizabethan **MAPLEDURHAM HOUSE**
begun in *c.* 1585 by Sir
Richard Blount, whose
monument can be seen in the
adjacent CHURCH. The house
has a pretty red-brick exterior
and fine Tudor and Jacobean
staircases and ceilings. It was
reworked in the late 18th-
century and of that date is
the private chapel. Nearby is
a lovely, fully restored
watermill.

FAWLEY A mile north of
Henley is **FAWLEY COURT**,
begun in 1684 for Colonel
William Freeman and
attributed to Christopher
Wren. Despite alterations of
the 18th and 19th centuries,
including work by James
Wyatt, the house retains its
late 17th-century plan and
some exquisite original
plasterwork. It also contains
a museum with a collection
of sabres and documents that
originally belonged to
Polish kings.

The red-brick façade of Milton Manor, with stone dressings.

Above: the well-preserved almshouses at Ewelme
Below: detail of the Jesse window at Dorchester Abbey

DORCHESTER was an early Christian center of England and a cathedral city from 634 to 707. Although nothing from that period survives, one important Norman building does, the huge late 12th-century **ABBEY CHURCH** ★. The church was remodeled in the later medieval period, the most impressive alterations being lavished upon the east end from the late 1200s to the early 1300s. The famed sculpture includes the carved "Jesse" window and the immense east window, of a fantasy and elaboration unparalleled in England. Also of note are the very well-preserved lead font of *c.* 1170, the medieval stained-glass and monuments.

EWELME This village was formerly home to the Chaucer family. Alice, Duchess of Suffolk, grand-daughter of Geoffrey Chaucer, lived here during the 1400s and the handsome group of church, school and almshouses that she built still survives. Alice's grisly *memento mori* can be seen in the church, as can 15th-century screens, a font, and a spectacular font cover.

ABINGDON grew up around the Augustinian abbey founded in 675, of which only fragments now remain. Most impressive is the late 15th-century gatehouse attached to the medieval Church of St Nicholas. The mainly 15th- and 16th-century **CHURCH OF ST HELEN** contains an exquisite painted ceiling of *c.* 1390 in the north aisle.

KINGSTON BAGPUIZE HOUSE This dignified, tall brick house was built *c.* 1720 and retains its original cantilevered staircase, paneled rooms, and some good pictures and furniture. The attractive gardens contain some fine trees and shrubs. The curious name of house and village derives from the de Bagpuize family who held the manor from 1086.

MILTON MANOR HOUSE An uncommonly good building of its period with a tall, plain 17th-century center and short matching wings added in 1776. The house has been attributed (on no evidence) to Inigo Jones. The large park has lakes and mature trees and there are also animals and shire horse cart rides.

SUTTON COURTENAY A large, pleasant village containing some above-average medieval domestic buildings. Most interesting is the **NORMAN HALL**, a rare surviving manor house of *c.* 1190–1200. There is also a **MANOR HOUSE** incorporating the 13th-century hall range amid 15th- and 17th-century additions.

WALLINGFORD A riverside town of ancient origins, with several good 18th-century buildings including the Church of St Peter (1760–9). At the north-east section of the town are the earthworks and fragmentary remains of the **CASTLE**.

ARDINGTON This village is worth a visit for **ARDINGTON HOUSE**, built in 1721 in the Vanbrughian style. The hall contains an imperial staircase and there is a good plasterwork ceiling to the dining room. Also of note is the **CHURCH**, of Norman origin but richly decorated during the 1800s.

STEVENTON
Steventon has an unusual, roughly paved causeway which runs from the medieval church to the Green. Fronting on to it by Mill Street are the timber-framed Priory Cottages, former monastic buildings which contain the medieval Great Hall of the original priory.

CHARNEY BASSETT
The Church of St Peter at Charney Bassett retains some Norman work, including the carved south doorway with 11th-century tympanum. The adjacent Manor House, remodeled in the 1800s, incorporates the beautiful late 13th-century solar wing of a hall-house.

WHITE HORSE Northeast of Uffington is the famous prehistoric hill figure which gives the Vale its name, a massive stylized horse cut into the chalk downs. It was probably made during the 1st century and is best seen when the sun is low in the sky.

VALE OF THE WHITE HORSE

UFFINGTON Uffington is a small village with chalk-built cottages and a fine cruciform CHURCH built in *c.* 1250. On nearby White Horse Hill is UFFINGTON CASTLE, a fort probably dating from the Iron Age. It is one of many camps built along the ancient Ridgeway.

WAYLAND'S SMITHY Just north of the Ridgeway is Wayland's

Portrait of Elizabeth of Bohemia, by Gerard Honthorst, at Ashdown House

Smithy, a Neolithic chambered tomb surrounded by a circle of beech trees. Its name probably derives from a Scandinavian myth in which Wayland the Smith has a white horse, although the nearby White Horse is later in date.

ASHDOWN HOUSE South of Ashbury is the Dutch-style Ashdown House, built in *c.* 1660 by the Earl of Craven and described by Pevsner as "the perfect doll's house". It was built for Elizabeth of Bohemia ("The Winter Queen"), sister of Charles I (though she never went there), and contains a few portraits from her collection.

KELMSCOTT The great 19th-century artist and designer William Morris made his country home at Kelmscott near the Gloucestershire border, and the MANOR HOUSE in which he lived from 1871 until 1896 remains an eminently picturesque and tranquil place. The house was built in *c.* 1570 and has a north wing added in the late 17th century. It contains a fascinating collection of works by Morris and his equally talented associates, such as Burne-Jones and William de Morgan, from tiles around fireplaces to carpets on the floor, as well Morris's own possessions.

KINGSTON LISLE was probably built originally in *c.* 1677 and is a fine Palladian house set in 140 acres of attractive parkland with three spring-fed lakes. The *pièce de résistance* of the house is its interior, dating mainly from *c.* 1825-30, with a remarkable series of vaulted rooms and an extraordinary flying staircase. In the village can be seen the BLOWING STONE, formerly on the Ridgeway, a perforated sarsen which produces a loud sound when blown. According to legend, Alfred the Great used the stone to muster his armies against the Danes.

BUSCOT PARK★
Buscot Park is a Georgian house of *c.* 1770 best known for containing the series of 1890 paintings by Burne-Jones called *Sleeping Beauty (Briar Rose)*. It also houses the Faringdon Collection of furniture and pictures, and has an early 20th-century water garden by Harold Peto (above). In the village is Buscot Old Parsonage, a Cotswold stone house of *c.* 1700 on the banks of the Thames.

WITNEY

Witney is an interesting town with a 17th-century BUTTER CROSS in its Market Place. It has long been known for its blanket-

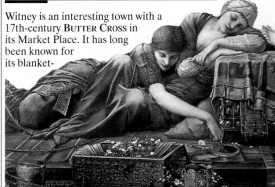

Detail from "Sleeping Beauty (Briar Rose)" by Edward Burne-Jones, 1890.

...aking trade and along the High Street can be seen the ...storic BLANKET HALL of 1721. The large and handsome ...hurch of St Mary, set back behind a long green, dates from ...e 13th to 15th centuries.

...URFORD One of Oxfordshire's most perfect villages. The ...one-built main street runs down to the River Windrush and ...lined with many good late medieval houses. The fine 12th- ...nd 15th-century church ★ was a point of debate in the late ...800s when William Morris protested at its restoration. The ...ector is reputed to have responded: "The church Sir is mine, ...nd if I choose to I shall stand on my head in it."

...ORTH LEIGH A hilltop village which has the remains of a ...rge Roman villa. The CHURCH OF ST MARY was originally ...uilt in *c.* 1000-50. Of note are the impressive mid-15th- ...entury Wilcote Chapel and the early 18th-century Perrot ...hapel built by Christopher Kempster.

...OGGES Immediately south of Witney is ...ogges, with its MANOR FARM MUSEUM, an ...-shaped house incorporating work of ...1250. The rooms have been furnished ...depict life in the 1800s.

...INSTER LOVELL On an enchanting spot ...the River Windrush stand the remains ...MINSTER LOVELL HALL, an important ...5th-century house built by William, Lord ...ovell. The CHURCH is another 15th- ...entury survivor and has a spacious ...terior containing a good effigy of a ...ovell knight.

...WINBROOK This small village was the ...ome of the Fettiplace family until the ...arly 19th century. In the CHURCH can be ...en the family's two splendid ...onuments. The earliest is of *c.* 1613 and ...e later dates from *c.* 1686, but both follow the same design ...ith near-identical reclining effigies arranged bunk-fashion ...gainst the wall. Nancy Mitford and her family are buried in ...e churchyard.

One of the striking 17th-century monuments to the Fettiplace family which adorn Swinbrook church.

...AMPTON Bampton is a well-known center of morris-dancing, ...hich still goes on along its village street. ...he important cruciform CHURCH, of ...orman origin, has a fine spire and ...ouble-tiered Easter Sepulchre.

GREAT COXWELL
The manor of Great Coxwell once belonged to Beaulieu Abbey in Hampshire ▲ *200*, which explains the magnificent Tithe Barn which survives here.

OXFORD

Christch Church Cathedral crossing tower (below), and interior with vaulting (below right)

ASHMOLEAN MUSEUM ★
The Greek Revival mid-19th-century masterpiece of C.R. Cockerell is famed as the country's first museum to be opened to the public (1688, in its original home, now the Science Museum). Its impressive collections range from Egyptian antiquities to 20th-century art.

It is not only its numerous collegiate buildings ▲ *308-11* which give Oxford its unique character. Many of the city's most important landmarks are University buildings, especially the domed **RADCLIFFE CAMERA**, built in 1737-49 to designs by James Gibbs, and the **SHELDONIAN THEATRE** (the University's ceremonial hall) of 1663-9, Wren's first work of architecture. **CHRIST CHURCH CATHEDRAL ★** doubles as a college chapel and is worth a special visit. It was begun in the late 1100s as a priory church and carries an exquisite vault of *c.* 1500. Also of note are St Frideswide's Shrine and watching loft, the monuments, and the other monastic remains. Christ Church is unique in having a **PICTURE GALLERY**, a wonderful 1960s building by Powell and Moya containing the college's fine collection of paintings and drawings by the Old Masters.

The impressive **DIVINITY SCHOOL** was begun in *c.* 1420 for the teaching of theology and contains a marvelous vault finished in 1483 by William Orchard. The neighboring **BODLEIAN LIBRARY**, opened in 1602, is one of the largest in the world. Note particularly the five-tiered and five-ordered entrance tower of 1613-24. Even the University's **BOTANIC GARDEN** boasts important architecture. Its three gateways were built in 1632-3 by Nicholas Stone for Charles I.

The large and imposing **UNIVERSITY MUSEUM** was built in the Gothic style by Benjamin Woodward and opened in 1860.

C.R. Cockerell's Ashmolean Museum of 1841-5

Collections are displayed in the glass-roofed Museum Court, and aim to assemble "all the materials explanatory of the organic beings placed upon the globe". The **PITT RIVERS MUSEUM** was added at the north-east in 1885-6 and houses wonders of anthropology including shrunken heads and painted masks.

"The Hunt in the Forest" by Paolo Uccello (1397-1475), Ashmolean Museum

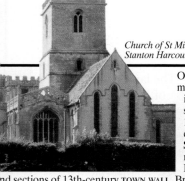

Church of St Michael, Stanton Harcourt

Oxford also offers many fine churches including the stately, mainly 14th- and 15th-century **CHURCH OF ST MARY**, the remains of a Norman **CASTLE**, and sections of 13th-century **TOWN WALL**. Bringing the city right up to date is the **MUSEUM OF MODERN ART** (MOMA) in Pembroke Street with enjoyable, constantly changing exhibitions and events. The lovely River Cherwell that runs through the city is a good means of exploration; punts may be hired at Magdalen Bridge.

BECKLEY The site of **BECKLEY PARK** is an ancient one and belonged to King Alfred in the 9th century. The handsome, unusually well-preserved brick house which stands today was built in c. 1540, probably by Lord Williams of Thame. It is situated by the historic remains of three rectangular moats.

STANTON HARCOURT This delightful village is focused upon an outstanding group of buildings consisting of manor house, church and parsonage. **STANTON HARCOURT MANOR HOUSE** represents the remains of a substantial medieval house, much of it demolished c. 1750. Particularly impressive are Pope's Tower of c. 1460-71, named after Alexander Pope who lodged here in 1717-18, and the spectacular Great Kitchen of the late 1300s. The Norman **CHURCH OF ST MICHAEL** was richly remodeled in the 13th century and has a fine chancel with rare screen. The Harcourt Chapel, added c. 1470, has been attributed to William Orchard and retains its original roof and stained glass. The stately **PARSONAGE**, next to the medieval fish ponds, is a little-altered house of c. 1675.

THAME A historic market town with several good 15th- to 17th-century buildings and inns. Note especially the **SPREAD EAGLE** of c. 1740, which was made famous by John Fothergill's *Innkeeper's Diary* (1931). The large **CHURCH OF ST MARY** is imposingly set beside the River Thame, a tributary of the Thames. To the west can be seen the interesting medieval **PREBENDAL HOUSE** with a fine chapel of c. 1250.

IFFLEY
At Iffley is one of the country's most beautiful Norman churches. St Mary's was built c. 1170-80 and is decorated with zig-zag and beakhead designs (below left and right, west front and detail).
Northwest of the church is the Old Parsonage, built mainly c. 1500 but of Norman origin. From here one has a fine prospect of both the nearby church and the distant skyline of Oxford.

RYCOTE CHAPEL
Rycote is worth visiting for its small and lovely Chapel of St Michael (above, left and right), founded in 1449, furnished in the 1600s and little altered since. The interior features a musicians' gallery and two beautiful early 17th-century roofed pews, the south one supposedly set up for Charles I's visit of 1625.

The Radcliffe Camera (left), built in the 1700s as a library

The larger and busier of England's two oldest University towns, Oxford still retains all its character and picturesqueness. The University has early origins, with Merton, University and Balliol colleges all founded during the 13th century. Nearly all the colleges are built around spacious green quadrangles and have a chapel and hall, but their design is by no means repetitive. Many of the country's finest architects have left their mark here, including Wren at Christ Church and Queens, Hawksmoor at All Soul's, Wyatt at Oriel and Butterfiel at Keble. Even the 1960s architecture of St Catherine's College by Danish architect Arne Jacobsen is outstanding. But it is the older colleges such as Magdalen, Christ Church and New College that make a trip to Oxford worthwhile. It is also these colleges which give Oxford its most distinctive characteristic: a remarkable skyline of spires, pinnacles and towers ▲ *310-11.*

TOM TOWER
On the right is Christ Church's magnificent Tom Tower, viewed from Tom Quad. The upper part was built by Wren in 1681-2. St Edmund's Hall is pictured above.

NORTH QUAD
All Soul's College
(above) was built
mainly in the early
18th century to the
designs of Nicholas
Hawksmoor.

Right: Merton
College, seen from
Christ Church
Meadow.

Far right: Balliol
College, much rebuilt
in the 19th century.

**THE BODLEIAN
LIBRARY** (left)
The masterly
frontispiece to the
Bodleian Library's
entrance tower,
located in the
School's Quadrangle
and built in 1613-24.

PECKWATER QUAD
Peckwater Quad,
Christ Church, was
built in 1705-14 and
designed by Henry
Aldrich.

▲ OXFORD COLLEGES ★

*Aerial view
Blenheim Pala*

WOODSTOCK

BLENHEIM PALACE ★
The largest and grande
baroque house in the
country, built in 1705-2
for the first Duke of
Marlborough. The palac
was paid for mainly by
Queen Anne and the nation, a prodigious thank-you gesture
for the Duke's long campaign against Louis XIV of France.
The house was designed by Sir John Vanbrugh with help from
Nicholas Hawksmoor, and is a truly majestic sight. The
interior is no less impressive with its beautiful Great Hall,
gilded State Apartments, 180-foot-long library, and chapel.
Among the palace's exceptional collections are the well-
known Marlborough Victories tapestries.

*Blenheim Palace,
Sir Winston Churchill's
Birth Room*

DITCHLEY PARK Ditchley Park, completed in 1722, is one of
James Gibbs's best and most significant buildings. The house
has a typical Palladian plan and features interiors by William
Kent and Henry Flitcroft. It is now used for conferences.
ROUSHAM Rousham House was built *c.* 1635 and much
remodeled by William Kent from 1738 to 1740. The
GARDEN ★, also designed by Kent, was one of the first to
abandon the principles of formal planning, and has been littl
altered since. It includes the seven-arched Praeneste, the
Temple of Echo or Townesend's Building, and Venus' Vale.

GREAT TEW
A beautiful little
village, created
mainly in the early
19th century. Great
Tew is the epitome of
the English
picturesque, with
thatched cottages
(above) and gardens
over-brimming with
delphiniums, holly-
hocks and lupins.

*Right: Chastleton
House grotesque
work, detail
Below right: The
"King's Men"
circle, Rollright
Stones
Below: Blenheim
Palace, Water
Terraces*

CHIPPING NORTON

An important market town made wealthy in the 1400s by its
thriving wool trade, which retains plenty of good buildings,
many refronted in the 1700s. The late 15th-century nave of th
CHURCH OF ST MARY is splendid, with its timber roof and
expanse of glazing.

CHASTLETON HOUSE, a magnificent building in golden
stone of the early 17th century, has well-preserved
interiors richly adorned with chimneypieces and
plasterwork, and includes a tunnel-vaulted Long
Gallery and first floor Great Chamber.

ROLLRIGHT STONES Close to Great Rollright i
this fascinating prehistoric site. The main stone
circle is known as the King's Men; set slightly
apart are the huge King Stone and a group
known as the Whispering Knights. Various folk
legends attach to the stones: one claims they were
king and his army petrified by a witch's spell.

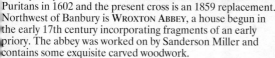

Broughton Castle exterior (far left) and the drawing room with its ornate 16th-century ceiling (left)

BANBURY The **BANBURY CROSS** from the well-known nursery rhyme "Ride a Cock Horse" was destroyed by Puritans in 1602 and the present cross is an 1859 replacement. Northwest of Banbury is **WROXTON ABBEY**, a house begun in the early 17th century incorporating fragments of an early priory. The abbey was worked on by Sanderson Miller and contains some exquisite carved woodwork.

BLOXHAM This lovely village is home to one of Oxfordshire's stateliest churches, **ST MARY'S ★**, built mainly in the 14th and 15th centuries. Its splendid spire is a prominent landmark and is probably by the same unknown masons who worked at Adderbury's equally good church. Note the corbel table and the elaborately painted 15th-century rood screen.

BROUGHTON CASTLE ★ is one of the county's most complete medieval houses, begun *c.* 1308 and still surrounded by its impressive moat. The castle was remodeled during the later 1500s, but the original hall and a 14th-century domestic chapel both survive. The house is usually attributed to John de Broughton, a knight of Edward I, whose effigy can be seen in the church.

DEDDINGTON An early market town built of golden stone with several good old houses. **LEADENPORCH HOUSE** on New Street, the main Oxford to Banbury Road, dates from *c.* 1315. At the southeast of Deddington are the substantial earthworks of the **CASTLE** where Piers Gaveston, unfortunate favorite of Edward II, lodged in 1312.

Top: St Mary's church spire, Bloxham
Above: Banbury Cross

Broughton Castle knot garden

Below: Claremont lake from across the ha-ha, Anon., c. 1740

Opposite page (top): the mainly Edwardian entrance front of Polesden Lacey

CLAREMONT LANDSCAPE GARDEN (above) This beautiful garden on the south edge of Esher was created in the 18th century and worked on by Vanbrugh, William Kent, Bridgeman, and Capability Brown. It has been well restored by the National Trust and includes a lake with an island, a turf amphitheater and a grotto.

The Gothic Tent of c. 1740, Painshill Park

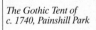
Box Hill, Surrey

WEYBRIDGE

This suburban town is named after the River Wey which joins the Thames here. Weybridge has been pressed upon by London since the 1930s but retains an open, leafy character. It is of mixed architectural merit but does have some historic features. For example, the Tudor walling in Thames Street formerly belonged to OATLANDS PALACE, an important royal residence rebuilt by Henry VIII from 1538.

CHATLEY HEATH Here can be seen the curious CHATLEY HEATH SEMAPHORE HOUSE, a five-storeyed tower built as part of an early 19th-century chain of semaphore stations. Messages could be sent between Whitehall and Portsmouth in less than a minute.

WISLEY At Wisley is the famed ROYAL HORTICULTURAL SOCIETY (RHS) GARDEN which extends to 240 acres. It is a wonderful place to explore and observe the countless varieties of plants. The spring flowering azaleas and rhododendrons are especially fine.

PAINSHILL PARK AND LANDSCAPE GARDEN ★ One of the county's finest landscape gardens, Painshill was laid out from the 1740s by the Hon. Charles Hamilton. A massive cast-iron water wheel pumps water out of the River Mole to feed the 14-acre lake, which has an island containing some interesting structures. There are also a crystal grotto, Gothic Tent or Umbrello, and huge cedar trees.

ESHER Esher is a pleasant if busy town with an interesting history. Bishop Waynflete of Winchester once lived in the 15th-century ESHER PLACE, of which only the fine gatehouse survives, gothicized by William Kent in c. 1730. In the CHURCH OF ST GEORGE is the handsome Newcastle Pew, built in 1725-6 and possibly by Vanbrugh.

CARSHALTON

Carshalton has a picturesque town center with a series of delightful bridges and ponds. CARSHALTON HOUSE in Pound Street, now a school for girls, is a Queen Anne mansion with good 18th-century interiors. The grounds were

laid out by Charles Bridgeman in the early 1700s. Of particular note is the Water Tower by Henry Joynes, a pupil of Vanbrugh, which pumped water from the river to supply the house. There is also LITTLE HOLLAND HOUSE at 40 Beeches Avenue, built and furnished for himself by the artist and craftsman Frank Dickinson from 1902 onward.

Left: the garden at Goddards by Gertrude Jekyll
Below: the Hon. Mrs Ronald Greville by Carolus-Duran, at Polesden Lacey

DORKING

Dorking, once known for its edible snails, is a good place from which to explore the surrounding countryside. LEITH HILL rises to the southwest of the town and reaches – with the help of an 18th-century Gothic tower – exactly 1000 feet. It is the highest point in the southeast of England and provides magnificent views all around, especially to the Weald at the south. One mile north of Dorking is BOX HILL, a beautiful area of woodland and downland which also offers fine views.

POLESDEN LACEY Polesden Lacey was once Sheridan's house, but was heavily remodeled in 1906. It is beautifully set amid unspoilt gardens and grounds, with views south toward the North Downs. The house contains the fine collections of the brewer William McEwan and his daughter the Hon. Mrs Ronald Greville, which are particularly notable for their Dutch and Early Italian paintings and majolica.

REIGATE HILL AND GATTON PARK North of the ancient town of Reigate is this area on the North Downs escarpment. It offers walks through lovely woodland, parkland and downland with breathtaking views all around.

ABINGER At Abinger Common is GODDARDS, an imposing house built by Sir Edwin Lutyens in 1898-1900 and reworked by him in 1909-10. It started life as a ladies' hostel and has a delightful garden laid out by Gertrude Jekyll.

CHALDON
Worth a detour is Chaldon's Church of St Peter and St Paul, which contains an important wall painting of *c.* 1200. The painting represents the Purgatorial Ladder; its devils and images of the Seven Deadly Sins are quite unnerving.

The summit of Leith Hill, the highest point in the southeast

Caryatid figure, detail of the Adam fireplace in the Drawing Room at Hatchlands

The two-storeyed entrance hall at Clandon Park

HATCHLANDS PARK (right) This impressive country house was built in 1756-7 for Admiral Boscawen, hero of the Battle of Lagos Bay. Hatchlands is set in a delightful park landscaped by Humphry Repton and its interiors feature work by Robert Adam. In the house can be seen the Cobbe Collection, the world's largest group of early keyboard instruments associated with figures such as Bach, Mozart, Chopin and Purcell.

LOSELEY HOUSE Just south of Guildford is the outstanding Loseley House, built for Sir William More in 1561-9. The setting is magnificent with rolling parkland, a walled garden, and a huge Cedar of Lebanon. Treasures include the so-called Nonsuch fittings in the Great Hall and an overmantel dated 1570, supposed to have been made from one of Elizabeth I's traveling cases.

The many-gabled north front of Loseley House, built in 1561-9 for Sir William More (below) and the Great Hall (above right)

GUILDFORD

Essayist and politician William Cobbett described Guildford as "the prettiest, and taken altogether the most agreeable and most happy looking town that I ever saw in my life". It is now the busy center of Surrey, but still has picturesque qualities and some excellent buildings. In the steep main street is the elegant Guildhall refronted in 1683, the Tudor Grammar School founded in 1509, and the adjoining red brick Abbot's Hospital built in 1619-22 by George Abbot, Archbishop of Canterbury.

GUILDFORD HOUSE MUSEUM at 115 High Street features a range of changing exhibitions, and is contained in a superb town house of 1660. To one side of the main street are the remains of the ancient castle, with an 11th-century motte and impressive 12th-century tower keep. In cobbled Castle

Arch is Guildford Museum, founded in 1898. The museum houses Surrey's largest collection of archeology, local history and needlework, with relics of local figures such as Gertrude Jekyll and Lewis Carroll. There is no historic cathedral at Guildford, the present building having been started in 1936 to designs by Sir Edward Maufe, but there is the fine, mainly Norman **CHURCH OF ST MARY**.

RIVER WEY AND GODALMING NAVIGATIONS AND DAPDUNE WHARF The River Wey opened to barge traffic in 1653 and offered a valuable new trade route between Guildford and London. In 1764, the Godalming Navigation opened and enabled barges to move a further 4 miles upriver. The whole

section of water is now maintained by the National Trust, and the pretty 20-mile towpath is open to walkers. Reliance, a restored Wey barge moored at the historic Dapdune Wharf in Guildford, contains an interesting display on the waterway's past. Exploration of the area, with its various locks and boat houses, can be done on foot, by canoe, rowing boat, or even by horsedrawn barge.

SHALFORD This small village is worth a visit for its lovely, 18th-century Shalford Mill on the banks of the River Tillingbourne.

CLANDON PARK ★ Clandon Park is a beautiful Palladian house rebuilt by Giacomo Leoni from 1713 to 1729 and little altered since. The plain brick exterior does nothing to prepare one for the stunning two-storeyed Marble Hall, which has fireplaces and overmantels by J.M. Rysbrack. Clandon Park contains Hannah Gubbay's collections of 18th-century furniture and ceramics and houses both the Ivo Forde Meissen collection of *Commedia dell'arte* figures and the Queen's Royal Surrey Regiment Museum. The 18th-century Maori Meeting House in the garden comes as quite a surprise.

CHARTERHOUSE Just north of Godalming, an ancient center of cloth-making, rises the impressive Gothic skyline of Charterhouse School, moved here in 1872 to buildings designed by P.C. Hardwick. Later additions are the Great Hall of 1885 by A.W. Blomfield and the detached chapel of 1922-7, built as a war memorial by Sir Giles Gilbert Scott.

Shalford Mill

The interior of the memorial chapel at Charterhouse

Charterhouse School, its Gothic skyline punctuated with spires

COMPTON This rural village is remarkable for two things: its ancient Church of St Nicholas and the Watts Gallery. The church was originally built in the 11th century but its most memorable work dates from the later 1100s. This period is represented mainly by the impressive two-storeyed sanctuary separated from the chancel by a late 12th-century guard rail, one of the country's earliest pieces of church woodwork. The Victorian painter and sculptor George Frederic Watts lived at Compton for much of his life. Over 350 of his works are displayed in the Gallery, built in 1903 near his county home, Limnerslease. Also open to the public is the CEMETERY CHAPEL designed by Watts' wife Mary. The circular interior is covered in ornate Celtic-style and Art Nouveau decoration.

Watts Chapel (detail), Compton

FARNHAM

Farnham is a fascinating town to visit, with fine buildings from a range of periods and pretty scenery. Most imposing is FARNHAM CASTLE which served as home to the Bishops of Winchester for over 800 years. Special sights are the Norman shell keep and the so-called Fox's Tower built by Bishop Waynflete in 1470-5. Farnham is well known for its high-quality Georgian architecture, which can be seen at its best in West Street and Castle Street. WILLMER HOUSE (38 West Street) of 1718 is especially handsome and has a noble, cut-brick façade. It now serves as the Museum of Farnham and has displays on various subjects including local history. Next door is the equally good SANDFORD HOUSE. In Bridge Square is the house where William Cobbett was born, now a pub bearing his name. A good way to explore the town is to follow the excellent Farnham Heritage Trail.

WAVERLEY ABBEY Two miles southeast of Farnham are the mainly 13th-century ruins of Waverley Abbey, England's first Cistercian monastery, founded in 1128.

DUNSFOLD
This village in the Weald close to Sussex boasts the unusually complete Church of St Mary and All Saints (above), built *c.* 1270, probably by royal masons. Inside, the later medieval bell turret is supported by a four-post cage and there are some good 13th-century pews.

HASLEMERE

This small town among wooded hills near the Sussex border became popular in the late 1800s. Many good Arts and Crafts houses are to be seen, including some by Voysey and E.J. May. Close by is HINDHEAD, described by William Cobbett as "the most villainous spot God ever made", probably because of its notorious highwaymen. It is an excellent place from which to view the surrounding landscape and has lovely walks among heath and woodland.

Right: a leafy, hillside view characteristic of the Winkworth Arboretum
Below: Farnham Castle showing the post-medieval alterations

WINKWORTH ARBORETUM ★ This arboretum was created in the early 20th century and is now home to over 1,000 different shrubs and trees, many rare. The spring show of azaleas and bluebells is spectacular. At nearby Hascombe is the CHURCH OF ST PETER of 1864, one of the most accomplished buildings erected by Henry Woodyer.

HAMBLEDON One of the best things in this picturesque Surrey village is OAKHURST COTTAGE, a small timber-framed house of the 16th century with a typical cottage garden.

EAST ANGLIA

Ian Collins

Waltham Abbey

Waltham Abbey gatehouse

Waltham Abbey started off as a church founded under Canute to house a black stone crucifix, unearthed in Somerset and famed for healing powers. It was the last of the 600 monasteries Henry VIII dissolved, but demolition spared part of the Norman nave. Reduced to a parish church, it was embellished in Victorian Gothic style by William Burges, with Burne-Jones stained glass. The romantic stave church of **St Andrew's at Greensted-juxta-Ongar** has Norman flint, Tudor brick and Victorian glass and Anglo-Saxon carpentry (the nave beams date to 850). **St Mary's Great Warley**, designed by Charles Harrison Townsend, is a temple to Art Nouveau: dove-crowned spire, silvery apse and banded, barrel-vaulted nave festooned with lilies. **St Margaret's Margaretting** has an intricate 15th-century timber belltower.

Hill Hall and **Copped Hall** – with Italian and Flemish gardens laid out from 1883 by Charles Eamer Kempe – were both gutted by fire. Hill Hall, with a monumental mural cycle from 1570, was a women's prison; currently it is not open to the public.

Kelvedon Hatch
A modest-looking bungalow at Kelvedon Hatch was built in 1952 with 40,000 tons of concrete. It hides a network of blast-protected underground rooms – a base for 600 "key personnel" in a nuclear war. The bungalow bunker is now Essex's oddest tourist attraction.

Ingatestone Hall is a red-brick, step-gabled mansion just south of Chelmsford with a gatehouse and clock tower begun in 1540 for Sir William Petre, minister under Henry VIII and Edward VI. Rewarded for organizing the Dissolution of the Monasteries, he now lies elaborately entombed in the Petre chapel of St Edmund's Church.

Hill Hall

Maldon This Blackwater port saw an epic battle in 991 with the Vikings (elderberries are still called "Danes' Blood" locally). The home of Maldon Sea Salt has two medieval churches: Gothic All Saints, with a triangular tower and window saluting

Ingatestone Hall

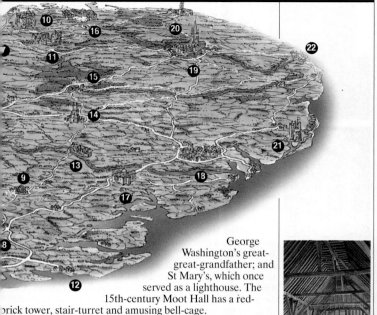

George Washington's great-great-grandfather; and St Mary's, which once served as a lighthouse. The 15th-century Moot Hall has a red-brick tower, stair-turret and amusing bell-cage.

ST CEDD'S CHAPEL, in the marshes behind Bradwell-on-Sea, was founded by the missionary around 654. It is the nave of a larger building and was used as a barn from the 17th century until 1920. Tudor Bradwell Lodge's neoclassical additions and decorations were commissioned in the 1780s.

LAYER MARNEY TOWER, the highest Tudor gatehouse in England, arose around 1520 as the entrance to a planned palace worthy of the 1st Lord Marney, Henry VIII's Keeper of the Privy Seal. His death in 1523, followed by that of his son in 1525, ended the male line and the building project. Both lords have terracotta tombs in the local church they endowed (not least with a fresco of St Christopher). The gatehouse is flanked by two octagonal towers, with eight tiers of large windows designed for display rather than defence. Topping the red and blue-glazed brick structure in place of battlements are scalloped-shaped terracotta gables with dolphins.

COPFORD CHURCH The Romanesque frescos were probably part of original 1140s building plans. The best shows Christ encircled by angels, apostles and a rainbow.

COGGESHALL Thomas Paycocke, the wealthiest cloth merchant in Tudor Coggeshall, built a fine timber-framed house in 1505 known as **PAYCOCKE'S**. It contains exquisite wood carving and linenfold paneling, plus a display of Coggeshall lace. Coggeshall Grange Barn is Europe's earliest timber-framed barn, dating from 1140; with nave and side aisles, this was where the monks stored their tithe-tax tenth of farm production. Two nearby 13th-century Cressing Temple Barns, each formed from over 500 oaks, were built for the Knights Templar and used by farmers until 1985.

Interior of Coggeshall monastic grange barn

Left: Layer Marney Tower
Above: Little Coggeshall, oblique view of grange barn

Top: St John's Abbey
Above: St Botolph's
Priory

COLCHESTER

Britain's oldest recorded town was once a Celtic trading port under Cunobelin. It became a Roman citadel, stormed by Boadicea but rebuilt with mighty, still-visible walls. A Norman castle, whose keep is now a museum housing a wealth of ancient Roman artifacts, covered the Temple of Claudius. Anglo-Saxon builders used Roman bricks in the tower of the well-preserved Holy Trinity church, now a museum of social history.

ST BOTOLPH'S PRIORY – founded around 1100 as the Augustinian order's first English base – has the remains of a Norman church wrecked in a Civil War siege. **ST JOHN'S ABBEY**, a late 11th-century Benedictine monastery, was reduced to its 15th-century flint-paneled gatehouse in the same conflict (a vault shows the track of a Cromwellian cannonball). **HOLLY TREES** is an early Georgian house hosting the town's military museum as well as a survey of domestic life; and the **MINORIES** is a late Georgian house turned art gallery, with a charming garden, linked to the Pissarro family. **BOURNE MILL** was built in 1591 as a fishing lodge – its stepped gables show the influence of Flemish weavers, whose half-timbered houses survive in the Dutch Quarter.

FINGRINGHOE CHURCH Overlooking the Colne Estuary, this 14th-century church has a square-topped tower striped with flint and limestone, and chequered flushwork and brickwork decorating a battlemented porch and parapet. Lawford, now merging into Manningtree, has a church with an elaborately carved 14th-century chancel and a tower in patchworked brick, flint, freestone, puddingstone and septaria.

ST OSYTH'S PRIORY was founded in 1118 where Saxon princess and sainted nun Osytha was beheaded by the Danes (she is said to have walked for 3 miles with her head under her arm). The 15th-century flint and stone flushwork gatehouse is an important survival of monastic architecture and regional style. After the Dissolution of the Monasteries the priory was turned into a country house by Lord D'Arcy (the noble family memorials can be seen in the village church) and remodeled in the 18th century. Outside the village the medieval St Claire's Hall lies amid farms which once supplied the priory with dairy produce.

COLNE VALLEY
The valley of the River Colne at Chappel is crossed by a 32-arch railway viaduct of 1847. Aping a Roman aqueduct, it celebrates the age of steam. The village station now hosts the East Anglian Railway Museum.

COLNE ESTUARY
The Colne estuary and creeks around Mersea Island have been prized for their oyster beds since the 19th century. The shellfish, a staple food turned delicacy, is celebrated each October in a banquet in Colchester Town Hall.

Bourne Mill,
Colchester

Below: The Old Lighthouse, Harwich

HARWICH

Harwich has been a key port for over a thousand years, and has links with seafarers Drake, Raleigh, Frobisher, Nelson and Christopher Jones, master of the *Mayflower* which carried the Pilgrim Fathers to America. Samuel Pepys ▲ *329* was its Member of Parliament when the town was the main base of the King's Navy. Note a treadwheel crane of 1667, a Napoleonic fort and the Low Lighthouse (now a maritime museum).

WALTON-ON-THE-NAZE and FRINTON are restrained resorts – the former with a pier dating from 1830, the latter with green sward and The Homestead, a model villa of 1905 by C.F. Voysey. Holland-on-Sea, Clacton-on-Sea (with its 1873 pier) and Jaywick have covered 5 miles of sandy coast in shacks, bungalows and seaside amusements. The glare and volume build up for the great blast of Southend-on-Sea, sprawling between Shoeburyness and Leigh, and boasting the world's longest pier, complete with electric railway.

DEDHAM VALE This stretch of the Stour Valley – now designated an Area of Outstanding Natural Beauty – is lovingly preserved much as John Constable ▲ *342* knew and painted it. Dedham, the village where the artist went to school, has timber-framed and Georgian houses and a 16th-century church with interesting commemorative pews. Castle House (now a museum) was home to the equestrian painter Sir Alfred Munnings.

HALSTEAD The white weatherboarded Townsford Mill straddles the River Colne. Originally a CORN-MILL, it was converted by Samuel Courtauld in the early 19th century for silk manufacture (the factory operated until 1982). The medieval church contains monuments to the Bourchier family of Stanstead Hall.

CASTLE HEDINGHAM (above) The de Vere family acquired this after the Norman Conquest and retain the remains of the baronial tower-keep which Aubrey de Vere built in 1140 and King John besieged in 1215. It has two 100-foot corner turrets, a banqueting hall and minstrels' gallery. The brick bridge over the moat may have been built to welcome Henry VII in 1498.

Top: House in Dedham
Above: River Stour

Above: Courtauld Mill, Halstead

Transfixed by a golden reflection in its mirror-like lake, this glorious house appears untouched by time. Looks, however, can deceive. The Benedictine abbey of Walden, dating from 1140, was suppressed by Henry VIII and the property handed to Lord Chancellor Sir Thomas Audley (who helped dispatch Sir Thomas More and queens Anne Boleyn and Catherine Howard). Remodeled as a great Jacobean "prodigy" house, Audley End was relaunched in 1614 by Lord Treasurer the 1st Earl of Suffolk to please a visiting king. Four years later the Earl was disgraced. Charles II later bought the hall as a base for Newmarket races. After decline and demolition, Sir John Griffin Griffin ordered a Georgian overhaul, with Capability Brown landscaping and neoclassical rooms by Robert Adam. From the 1820s the 3rd Lord Braybrooke added an opulent "Jacobean" suite, ousting some of the Adam parts. A wartime secret training center for the Polish section of the Special Operations Executive, Audley End passed to English Heritage, which recreated Adam features in the 1960s.

THE GREAT HALL

Although dating from the early 17th century, the "Jacobean" Great Hall was decorated and furnished by the third Lord Braybrooke more than 200 years later.

THE STATE BED

The State Bed, in the Howard Bedroom, was commissioned by Sir John Griffin Griffin to celebrate his elevation to the peerage in 1784 – and in anticipation of a royal visit.

PAINTINGS

Still Life by Dutch Old Master Pieter Claesz was recently returned to Audley End. A west view of the house is shown in the mid 18th-century naive painting.

One of five chimneyboards painted by Biagio Rebecca shows the antique Borghese vase.

325

▲ SAFFRON WALDEN

Shell House, Hatfield Forest

SAFFRON WALDEN is named after the saffron crocus that yielded a dye and a herb and brought the town medieval prosperity. A Norman castle keep survives in ruins. Around the Perpendicular church – the largest parish church in Essex, with a soaring 1831 spire – many timber-framed houses are beautifully preserved, with color washes and molded plasterwork pargeting. Bridge End Gardens contain a Georgian domed summerhouse and Victorian planting, but its lawn maze on the edge of the common may pre-date the Reformation. The Victorian museum of the Quaker banker and arts patron Francis Gibson reopened in 1987 as the Fry Art Gallery. It features artists of northwest Essex – especially mid-20th-century painters and craftspeople who clustered around Edward Bawden in the historic village of Great Bardfield.

Hatfield Forest

A GLASS WONDER
Stansted Airport, rising from the fields like a glass cathedral in the mid 1980s, is one of Sir Norman Foster's most successful buildings. Environmentalists remain unmoved.

Right: Thaxted

PATRICK BRONTË
Wethersfield Church, with copper-clad spire, names Patrick Branwell Brontë, father of the novelists, on its list of curates. He jilted a local farmer's daughter and moved to Yorkshire. Years later, when a widower with a young family, he wrote proposing marriage and received a stinging rejection.

FINCHINGFIELD is a picture-postcard village, with thatched and tiled cottages, church, green, pond and white post windmill. A 15th-century guildhall is now a museum. Here too is Spains Hall, an Elizabethan manor house, with a 300-year-old cedar of Lebanon in its garden. Of the pastoral Cistercian abbey site at Tilty, a lofty 13th-century "Chapel-outside-the-Gates" survives as the parish church. And a remnant of a medieval royal hunting ground at Hatfield Forest contains great pollarded hornbeams and oaks, and a lakeside SHELL HOUSE decorated in 1759.

THAXTED ("a place where thatch comes from") traded wool and cutlery and remains rife with medieval timbering. The 15th-century Guildhall's timbers were stripped of paneled plasterwork in 1910, creating a trend which has outraged East Anglian historian Norman Scarfe. Gustav Holst wrote *The Planets* in a cottage in Monk Street (now gone). "Daisy", Countess of Warwick ▲ 274, and mistress of Edward VII, who lived at Easton Lodge, hired Harold Peto to design Italianate and Japanese gardens and made Thaxted's 14th-century church (now with her memorial chapel) a Christian Socialist center. Her friend H.G. Wells moved here in 1912.

NEWMARKET The center of British horse-racing since the 17th century; the National Horse Racing Museum is housed in the former Regency Subscription Rooms. It sports a bronze figure of the most famous racehorse of all, Hyperion, and stands next to the Jockey Club Newmarket Heath, where James I hunted hares, became a pleasure ground under Charles II; George Stubbs painted several horses here. Rowley Mile Course is the world's longest and widest racecourse, and stables and stud farms stretch for miles.

Jockey Club, Newmarket

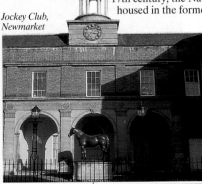

ANGLESEY ABBEY is the remains of a 12th-century Augustinian priory, converted into a private house by

the Cambridge carrier Thomas Hobson, after whom the saying "Hobson's Choice" is named. Its most striking features were created by Huttleston Broughton, later the 1st Lord Fairhaven, from 1926. He adorned the abbey with teeming art collections (jade, clocks, silver, Chinese lacquer, Chippendale desks, paintings by Claude and Etty, and views of Windsor) and surrounded it with spectacular gardens. Statuary includes Corinthian columns from Chesterfield House and female graces from Stowe. Finest are the four marble urns carved for Wanstead House by Delvaux and Scheemakers.

ELY

Looming over the city of Ely – and the level landscape for miles around – is a magnificent CATHEDRAL ★, dubbed "the Gothic wedding cake" or "the Ship of the Fens". The original abbey was founded by St Etheldreda in 673 but sacked by the Danes two centuries later. A new monastery became the last stronghold of Anglo-Saxon resistance to the Normans, as Hereward the Wake exploited the watery defences of the Isle of Ely. In 1081 Abbot Simeon began the transformation of a modest abbey into a Romanesque masterpiece. The process lasted for 268 years, until the arrival of the Black Death. Plague probably prevented the replacement of the nave and transepts' wooden roofing (the Victorians added the ceiling paintings). The wooden OCTAGON ▲ 74, Ely's finest feature, was a speedy and apparently gravity-defying successor to a

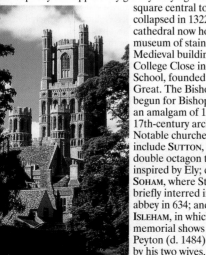

square central tower which collapsed in 1322. The cathedral now houses a museum of stained glass. Medieval buildings in the College Close include King's School, founded by Alfred the Great. The Bishop's Palace, begun for Bishop Alcock, is an amalgam of 15th- and 17th-century architecture. Notable churches hereabouts include SUTTON, with its double octagon tower clearly inspired by Ely; cruciform SOHAM, where St Felix was briefly interred in a doomed abbey in 634; and soaring ISLEHAM, in which a brass memorial shows Thomas Peyton (d. 1484) supported by his two wives.

Above: Anglesey Abbey and caryatid in the park (top)
Above left: "The Landing of Aeneas" by Claude, displayed at Anglesey Abbey

WHAT'S IN A NAME?
The name Ely derives from Eel Island. St Dunstan was said to have been so furious when local monks broke their vows of celibacy that he turned all the offenders into eels.

TAWDRY ST AUDREY?
St Etheldreda died of a throat tumor which she blamed on a youthful fondness for heavy jewelry. Her name was shortened to St Audrey and annual fairs were held across England in her honor. Cheap trinkets on offer, including "St Audrey's necklaces", gave us the word "tawdry".

Left: Ely Cathedral

▲ Huntingdon

*Right: Hinchinbrooke House
Below: Kimbolton Castle and
(below right) its Saloon*

THE MAZE AT HILTON
The Turf Maze at Hilton was cut in 1660 by William Sparrow; his stone memorial is now at the center. But a maze may have existed here in earlier times – possibly to thwart the devil, who was thought capable of traveling only in a straight line.

HUNTINGDON This country town, facing Georgian Godmanchester across the River Ouse, sleepily presided over England's third smallest county until Huntingdonshire was swept into Cambridgeshire in 1974. London overspill development has wrought much destruction – of 16 medieval churches, only two remain. It is famous for two of its Ministers of Parliament: Oliver Cromwell and John Major. Henry VIII gave the ruined Benedictine priory at Hinchin Brook, a mile or so west of Huntingdon, to Richard Cromwell, Oliver's great-grandfather, for help in closing fenland monasteries.

HINCHINGBROOKE HOUSE (now a school) emerged from the rubble. Oliver's uncle raised it to ever-greater Jacobean heights – prompting the king to pay many visits – until the expense ruined him. Richard Cromwell also acquired the important Benedictine Abbey at Ramsey, founded in 969. It stones were later used to refurbish some Cambridge colleges.

BUCKDEN is a village of brick and timber houses a short distance southwest of Huntingdon. Catherine of Aragon, discarded by Henry VIII, was sent to Buckden Towers – whose restored 15th-century gateway and massive Great Tower are now occupied by Roman Catholic Claritian missionaries. The ousted queen was then moved to **KIMBOLTON CASTLE** for two final years before she died and was buried at Peterborough Cathedral. The castle, a school since 1950, was remodeled by Sir John Vanbrugh and Alessandro Galilei in the early 18th century. Other delights are a 1690s Great Hall, Robert Adam gatehouse and Pellegrini panels in the chapel and on the staircase.

HOUGHTON WATERMILL, 3-4 miles east of Huntingdon, is a working, weatherboarded mill on a site where corn has been

OLIVER CROMWELL, the only commoner to head the British state, was born into local gentry in 1599. His birthplace is lost but the Grammar School he attended – once part of the 12th-century Hospital of St John – has a museum in his honor (admire the Lord Protector's felt hat, gaiters and death mask). As a rising force in Puritan politics, he rallied Parliamentary forces during the Civil War from the Falcon Inn. St Ives erected a Cromwell statue in 1901, spurred by his five years as a farmer in the town. Another museum is located in the house in Ely to which he moved following a family bequest; here you can play Roundheads and Cavaliers. Cromwell's head, paraded on a pike after the Restoration, eventually went to his old Cambridge college, Sidney Sussex. In the 1960s it was buried in the ante-chamber to the chapel.

ground for over a millennium. Its gallery exhibits the work of local artists.

HEMINGFORD GREY MANOR The manor house at Hemingford Grey (left), datin? from 1130, is said to be the oldest continuously inhabited house in England. Restored and opened to the public by the late Lucy Boston, it was the setting for her series of *Green Knowe* books. She laid out the garden with irises, roses and topiary.

Wimpole Hall

CAMBRIDGE

Formed at the head of navigation on the River Cam, and the junction of Roman roads from London to Lynn and Lincoln to Colchester, this thriving city of grand buildings and narrow streets contrives to be both a center and a backwater. It is a gorgeous blend of golden stone, green spaces, books, punts and bicycles. The FITZWILLIAM MUSEUM ★ *331*, designed by George Basevi in 1834 and aptly described as a scaled-down British Museum, is crowded with treasures, from ancient Greek pottery to French Impressionist paintings. In the bewitching house-museum of Kettle's Yard you can doze in an armchair, read the art books or admire the eclectic taste of donor Jim Ede (a key collector of 20th-century art; prominent are works by Henri Gaudier-Brzeska, Alfred Wallis and David Jones). You can punt along the river in the wake of Rupert Brooke, for tea under the apple trees in The Orchard. Cambridgeshire prairies hold England's most fertile soil and many overlooked historical sites. The Gog Magog Hills contain several Iron Age earthworks; DEVIL'S DYKE is the longest of several Saxon defensive ditches, stretching 7 miles from Reach to Wood Ditton.

MADINGLEY HALL Red-brick Madingley Hall, near the American Military Cemetery, is chiefly Tudor but its Gothick Gateway is a 15th-century relic from the Old Schools in Cambridge, moved in 1754. Now a college conference center, the Hall saw a final confrontation between Prince Albert and his wayward son, the future Edward VII, who lodged here when a student. Victoria's consort caught a chill from damp sheets and this, rather than Buckingham Palace's dodgy drains, may have killed him days later.

DUXFORD During the Battle of Britain, the celebrated fighter pilot Douglas Bader flew from Duxford. The site has been saved as the Imperial War Museum's airfield, with exhibits that include a B17 Flying Fortress, B52, Spitfire, Mustang, Vulcan, Victor and Concorde prototype. Duxford Chapel is a medieval remnant of the Hospital of St John.

WIMPOLE HALL This 18th-century house is the largest in Cambridgeshire, even after Elsie Bambridge used her father Rudyard Kipling's royalties to fell two wings. Its abiding glories are a James Gibbs library and chapel (the latter, 50 yards from the church of a lost village), with murals by Sir James Thornhill, the Bambridges' collection of conversation-pieces and narrative painting, and Sir John Soane's domed Yellow Drawing Room. The 3,000-acre park, with ruined Gothick tower, Chinese bridge and 2-mile Great Avenue, is by Charles Bridgeman, Capability Brown and Humphry Repton. Soane also designed Wimpole Home Farm, 1794, now home to rare animal breeds.

Above and above left: Yellow Drawing Room, Wimpole Hall

SAMUEL PEPYS (1633–1703), diarist, philanderer, scholar and civil servant, inherited his uncle's farmhouse in Brampton. He attended Huntingdon grammar school and Magdalene College. While a Cambridge student, he was once punished for being "scandalously overseene in drink". He bequeathed his books and manuscripts to Magdalene College, including the coded diaries that long remained undeciphered and unpublished.

Left: "The Crack Shot" by James Tissot, Wimpole Hall

▲ COLLEGES OF CAMBRIDGE ★

Left, from top:
Emmanuel College;
Mathematical Bridge;
Clare College

Supposedly founded by unruly students expelled from Oxford in 1209, Cambridge suspects it is an even older center of learning – indeed, the oldest in the land. Legend has St Amphibulus the Martyr as the first University Chancellor in AD 289. Monastic scholarship certainly spread from Ely ▲ *327* and the first college, Peterhouse, was built next to a St Peter's Church in 1284. Another 27 followed down the centuries – the latest, University, in 1965. Compact Cambridge nurtured the genius of Milton, Newton, Byron, Darwin and Keynes. Its academic prestige spreads ever wider, lately helping to spawn the surrounding high-tech industries of Silicon Fen. Grounds and courtyards, and sometimes libraries and chapels, are open to the public. If nothing else, see King's College Chapel, Trinity College's library and Great Court, the Palladian Senate House and the Fitzwilliam. The Backs by the river and the Botanic Gardens are calm oases even when Cambridge is teeming.

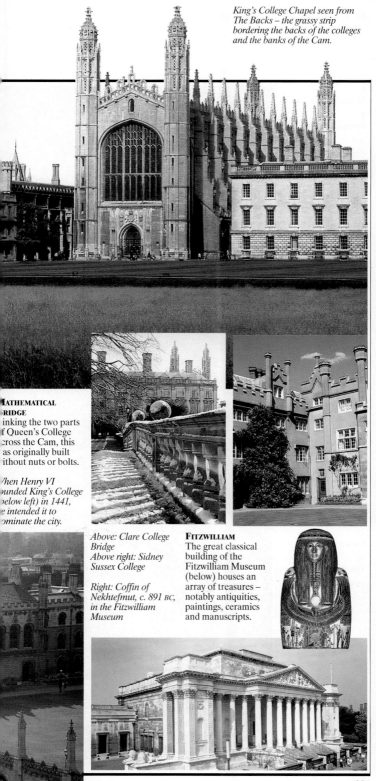

King's College Chapel seen from The Backs – the grassy strip bordering the backs of the colleges and the banks of the Cam.

MATHEMATICAL BRIDGE

Linking the two parts of Queen's College across the Cam, this was originally built without nuts or bolts.

When Henry VI founded King's College (below left) in 1441, he intended it to dominate the city.

Above: Clare College Bridge
Above right: Sidney Sussex College

Right: Coffin of Nekhtefmut, c. 891 BC, in the Fitzwilliam Museum

FITZWILLIAM

The great classical building of the Fitzwilliam Museum (below) houses an array of treasures – notably antiquities, paintings, ceramics and manuscripts.

▲ COLLEGES OF CAMBRIDGE

1
Magdalene College

2
Bridge of Sighs

3
St John's College

4
Trinity College

5
Gonville & Caius College

6
Old Schools

7
King's College Chapel

8
Clare College

9
King's College

10
Great St Mary's Church

11
St Catharine's College

12
Queens' College

13
Mathematical Bridge

14
Christ College

15
Corpus Christi

16
Peterhouse

17
Pembroke College

18
The Backs

19
Cam

Left and below left:
Impington Village
College

WICKEN FEN

Britain's oldest nature reserve is a unique fragment of the watery wilderness that once covered East Anglia. Complete with wooden windpump, it harbors rarities such as the eel-pout, fen violet and swallowtail butterfly.

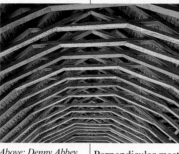

Above: Denny Abbey timber-beamed ceiling, and a reconstructed interior painted by Terry Ball (above right)

IMPINGTON VILLAGE COLLEGE, north of Cambridge, is a brilliant building designed in 1938 by Walter Gropius (with Maxwell Fry) after his rescue from Nazi Germany. Sadly, other commissions were not forthcoming and the Bauhaus giant moved on to America.

Interesting local churches include **WILLINGHAM**, with its 14th-century beacon tower, hammerbeam roof and lofty interior which hosted large-scale medieval ordinations (293 priests produced from one service); the Perpendicular masterpiece at Burwell, beside the site of King Stephen's Castle; and Ickleton, where an otherwise disastrous arson attack in 1979 uncovered 12th-century frescos.

DENNY ABBEY The stone-built remains of the 12th-century abbey resemble a farmhouse – fittingly so, in view of the now-adjoining Farmland Museum. Former residents include Knights Templar, Franciscan nuns and the Countess of Pembroke.

Denny
Abbey

Below: Peterborough Cathedral and its choir (below left)

⦙ETERBOROUGH

⦙terborough is a peculiar place. Once a separate soke (judicial ⦙trict), it is now a Midland outpost claimed by East Anglia; ⦙d it is also the only ancient city to become a New Town. ⦙mid a vast modern sprawl the old name of Gildenburgh ⦙Golden Borough") is still reflected in a stupendous ⦙THEDRAL ★. A monastery was founded here by King Paeda of ⦙ercia in 654. The present Norman building is one of only ⦙ree churches in Europe with an early ⦙inted wooden ceiling in its nave; the ⦙stern end, added in 1500, has superb ⦙n vaulting. It was elevated to a cathedral ⦙ the Dissolution of the Monasteries ⦙anks to the tomb of Catherine of ⦙agon in the north choir aisle. Mary ⦙ueen of Scots was interred in the south ⦙le for 25 years after her execution at ⦙theringay, until her son James I ⦙moved her remains to Westminster ⦙obey. A portrait of Old Scarlett, gravedigger for both ⦙eens, hangs on the west wall.

⦙THEDRAL SQUARE is graced by a 17th-century guildhall ⦙ote the arms of Charles II under the clock) which replaced a ⦙dor Butter Cross. The Priestgate Museum is rich in Roman ⦙lics and in bone models and straw marquetry work from a ⦙poleonic prisoner-of-war camp at Norman Cross. The jail site ⦙ now a field flanked by the A1, the old governor's house and ⦙ eagle-topped stone column saluting the 1,770 Frenchmen ⦙o died here between 1796 and 1816.

Above and center: Ramsey Abbey gatehouse and estate office

⦙MSEY ABBEY The important Benedictine abbey at Ramsey, ⦙unded in 969, was acquired by Richard Cromwell, Oliver's ⦙eat-grandfather. Its stones were used to refurbish Caius, ⦙ng's and Trinity colleges in Cambridge and to construct the ⦙lage church tower (a building now with William Morris ⦙ained glass). The Cromwells built a great house, destined in ⦙er years to become a school, on the plundered site. A richly ⦙rved 15th-century gateway survives as an historic ⦙onument. Nearby Bodsey House, dating from the 13th ⦙ntury, was the country seat of the last **ABBOT OF RAMSEY** ⦙til the Cromwells relieved him of its upkeep.

⦙TON HALL A mix of medieval, Gothic and classical styles, ⦙is has been home to the Proby family for 350 years. The ⦙rary is one of the finest in private hands, with more than ⦙,000 books – including Henry VIII's prayer book, inscribed ⦙ the Tudor king and two of his wives.

Elton Hall

Peckover House

LONGTHORPE TOWER Sites of interest around Peterborough include these remains of a fortified manor house (3 miles west of the city). Its great chamber contains the finest 14th-century domestic wall-paintings in northern Europe. Nearby STIBBINGTON HALL, noted for its elegant Jacobean façade.

THORPE HALL (now a Sue Ryder home) is a rare example of a stately home built during the Commonwealth. Its Dutch profile, richly carved staircases and ornate plaster ceilings reflect the taste of its Puritan founder, Oliver St John – a former ambassador to Holland and husband of Cromwell's beloved cousin, Elizabeth. There is also the slit-windowed stump of **THORNEY ABBEY**, which is in fact the nave of an otherwise demolished cathedral-sized building, founded in 657 and dissolved by Henry VIII. Its stones were carted off to build Cambridge's Corpus Christi College.

BARNACK Stone for Peterborough Cathedral and for many local churches and houses came from Barnack. The quarry was exhausted in the 18th century, but the site survives as a picnic spot dubbed "the Hills and Holes". Nearby Etton has a fine Early English church and Elizabethan manor house. Moated **WOODCROFT CASTLE** with a 13th-century tower, was a Royalist outpost besieged by the Roundheads in 1649.

Above: Arms of Charles II, Guildhall, Peterborough
Above right: mural depicting the Wheel of Five Senses at Longthorpe Tower
Right: Longthorpe Tower

BARNACK CHURCH
Barnack church is a beautiful blend of Saxon and Early Gothic – a pre-Conquest tower, with long and short stones, ascending to an octagonal belfry and spire of around 1200. Much interior interest, especially a late Saxon seated Christ in Majesty carving found under the floor in 1931.

A few miles north of Peterborough, off the A15, lies the village of **HELPSTON**. The surrounding fields, which "Peasant Poet" John Clare (1793-1864) saw as sacred Northamptonshire, are now annexed by Cambridgeshire. Where he raged against enclosure, we weep for lost hedges. A farm-boy at seven, Clare mourned lost loves in lyrical and heart-rending verse – penned, from 1841, in a Northampton asylum. He had felt exiled even in Northborough, 3 miles from his home village, where Lord Fitzwilliam offered him a cottage (Oliver Cromwell's widow and son-in-law are buried in the parish church – the latter, John Claypole, having presided over the remodeled 14th-century manor house). The poet's memorial and tomb at Helpston draw literary pilgrims. At the nearby nature reserve of Castor Hanglands, where Clare wandered, nightingales still sing.

WISBECH The market town and port of Wisbech has splendid Georgian buildings on either bank of the Nene at North and South Brink. Social reformer Octavia Hill was born at 7 South Brink (now a museum) in 1838. She also co-founded the National Trust, which now owns the early 18th-century **PECKOVER HOUSE** on North Brink, former home of Quaker banker Jonathan Peckover. This elegant townhouse has outstanding plaster and wood rococo decoration and a Victorian walled garden with orangery and fernery. Nearby there is a memorial to Thomas Clarkson by Sir George Gilbert Scott with a copy of Wedgwood's anti-slavery reliefs. Wisbech also has a good museum in a handsome Georgian circus.

MARCH CHURCH ★ has a unique dedication to ST WENDREDA, but is chiefly famous for one feature: its carved roof. A double hammerbeam structure built between 1470 and 1520 appears to be held aloft only by some 200 winged angels, saints and apostles ● 74.

Above left: the Dining Room at Peckover, and the gardens (above)

THORNHAM PARVA
Thornham Parva's tiny Romanesque thatched church contains an immense treasure – England's largest surviving medieval altarpiece. Made around 1336 for Thetford Priory, the retable was found in a woodpile in 1927.

Left: March church roof
Below: John Clare memorial, Helpston

FLAG FEN
At Flag Fen, a unique survival in England, peat has preserved some of the million timbers used to build a fortified island 3,000 years ago. Marks from Bronze Age axes are still visible.

Below: Euston Hall:
the lake and grounds;
"Mares and Foals" by
George Stubbs

St Mary's Churc
Bury St Edmun

BURY ST EDMUNDS Rebuilt in
traditional materials after a 1608 fire,
Bury has a thousand listed buildings.
A monastery founded here in 630 won
fame 250 years later when the body of
Edmund, East Anglia's martyred king,
arrived from Hoxne. In 1214 a band of
barons secretly met the Archbishop of
Canterbury amid pilgrimage crowds and
swore to make King John concede
Magna Carta rights. Of the abbey's great church only rubble
walls remain, set in the lovely abbey gardens. The Norman
Gate is now a belfry for the Cathedral Church of St James
– a Tudor church elevated in 1914. Nearby, 15th-
century **ST MARY'S CHURCH** has an angel roof
and the tomb of Mary, sister of Henry VIII
who completed the effort of earlier rioters to end
the abbey's power. The Regency Theatre
Royal, by William Wilkins, is both period
piece and working playhouse. The
Athenaeum assembly room of 1789 has
an Adam-style ballroom. Dickens put
the Angel Hotel in *The Pickwick Papers*.
The Manor House Museum has the
Gershom-Parkington collection of
clocks, watches and sundials. The 1861
Corn Exchange sports a Ceres statue and
a portrait of Queen Victoria, while
Robert Adam's Market Cross has comic
and tragic masks to denote a market hall
and theater. Moyse's Hall, a Norman
merchant's house turned jail, workhouse
and police station, is now a museum.

EUSTON HALL Set in a park
landscaped by John Evelyn, William
Kent and Capability Brown, Euston
Hall rose in the 1660s, was renovated along Italianate lines in
1902 and much reduced in 1951. The Hal
was built and the church remodeled by
Bennet, Earl of Arlington, Secretary of
State to Charles II,
whose only
daughter
married

THE TOWN OF CLARE
Clare, an interesting
small town with earth-
works from an Iron
Age hill fort and a
Norman motte, also
boasts the remains of
England's first Austin
Friars priory, founded
in 1248, again used by
the Augustinian
order. Beside the
churchyard the
Ancient House
Museum, once a
priest's house, is
pargeted with
luxuriant foliage and
dated 1473.

*Right: Augustus John
Hervey, Vice-Admiral
of the Blue, later
3rd Earl of Bristol,
by Thomas
Gainsborough,
Ickworth House*

*Ickworth
House*

Left: Melford Hall
Below left: Pompeiian Room, Ickworth

he 1st Duke of Grafton (the king's son by Lady Castlemaine). Dukes of Grafton have lived here ever since, surrounded by amily portraits by Van Dyck, Kneller and Lely.

CKWORTH HOUSE With its central rotunda and curving wings, ckworth House is unique and oddly unsettling. It was begun for Frederick, 4th Earl of Bristol and Bishop of Derry (who never returned from Italy to see it) by Francis Sandys in 1795 as a gallery for his Grand Tour acquisitions, most of which were later seized by the French. Frederick's grand-daughter, Lady Caroline Wharncliffe, designed the stucco panels within the portico; Casimiro and Donato Carabelli did the neoclassical figures and friezes around the outside of the rotunda. Major aintings (including a Velázquez) and grand furnishings hiefly reflect the late Regency taste of the 4th Earl's son and eir. His successor, the 3rd Marquess of Bristol, added ompeian Room frescos (actually copied from excavated urals in Rome's Villa Negroni acquired by the Earl Bishop).

ONG MELFORD A 3-mile long Georgian and Tudor main treet, now crammed with antique shops, gives way to a broad reen leading to the hilltop church.

HOLY TRINITY ★ is a Suffolk Perpendicular gem – with majestic alls of stone and flint flushwork and surviving 15th-century tained glass. **MELFORD HALL** looks much as it did when William Cordell moved here in 1578. Inside, admire the paneled anqueting hall, Regency library, and a display of watercolors by ormer guest Beatrix Potter. Moated red-brick Kentwell Hall, egun in the 1550s, has a brickwork maze in the form of a udor rose and regular "historical ecreations".

Left and above:
Kentwell Hall,
Long Melford

LAVENHAM ★
Lavenham is a timber town still flaunting 15th-century wool wealth. The Guildhall (above) has dominated the Market Place since 1529, when the Guild of Corpus Christi received its charter to regulate the wool trade (after weaving begun by Flemish migrants had actually peaked). The timbering of the Swan Inn and Wool Hall behind it is particularly fine. Little Hall is now home to the Suffolk Preservation Society, and a former Benedictine priory turned rectory contains Elizabethan wall-paintings. But the main showpiece is the huge church, with its 140-foot tower, superb carved screens and soaring artistry in knapped flint and dressed stone.

Kedington St Peter and St Paul – Barnardiston monument

Opposite page, top row (left to right): Blythburgh Holy Trinity; All Saints, Acton; Walpole Old Chapel near Halesworth

Suffolk was once known as "Silly Suffolk", from "selig" meaning "holy". The county landscape is still dominated by the towers of 500 medieval churches. Below Bungay lie the ancient villages of The Saints – six with the name of Elmham and four Ilketshalls. South Elmham St Cross has Suffolk's best-preserved Anglo-Saxon building. Everywhere flint is the main building block, often knapped and set with dressed stone in beautiful flushwork paneling. Twenty churches have thatched roofs and several (including Blythburgh, Mildenhall and Needham Market) have magnificent carved ceilings. Many churchyards, some with 17th-century tombstones, are now nature reserves. Suffolk churches are treasure-houses containing over 100 monumental brasses, 150 painted rood screens and forests of carved wood. Cromwell's commissioner William "Smasher" Dowsing, who came from Laxfield, destroyed thousands of "superstitious images and inscriptions" between 1649 and 1660. Much stained glass was lost – but Aldeburgh church is now brightened by John Piper's brilliant memorial window for Benjamin Britten ● *58* (who lies, with tenor Peter Pears, in the churchyard).

Covehithe: a church in a church

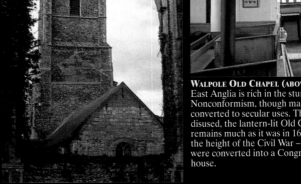

WALPOLE OLD CHAPEL (ABOVE)
East Anglia is rich in the sturdy halls of Nonconformism, though many have been converted to secular uses. Though now disused, the lantern-lit Old Chapel at Walpole remains much as it was in 1647 when – during the height of the Civil War – two cottages were converted into a Congregational meeting house.

HOLY TRINITY
At Blythburgh Holy
Trinity (above),
Suffolk Perpendicular
soars at its most
majestic to a ceiling
of winged angels.
Medieval carvings –
including the Seven
Deadly Sins and the
Seasons – adorn the
bench ends.

Elizabethan pulpit,
St Nicholas Church,
Denston

From the pulpits of St Nicholas, Denston
(left) and Kedington (right) preachers address
a congregation of carved animals.

Below: façade of Gainsborough's House, Sudbury, painted by Peter Jones, 1991
Bottom: Flatford Mill, Willy Lott's Cottage, early 17th century

THOMAS GAINSBOROUGH AND JOHN CONSTABLE
It is remarkable that two founding fathers of naturalistic English landscape painting ● 96-7 should have been born within 14 miles of one another, in the remote Stour Valley. Constable (1776-1837), aged 12 when Gainsborough (1727-88) died, literally followed in the older artist's footsteps as he absorbed and celebrated the East Anglian scene. But whereas there is a much-visited patch around Dedham called Constable Country, Gainsborough Country has reclaimed its anonymity. It is hidden in woods and fields and churches around Sudbury and Hadleigh, in cottages and country houses whose owners helped to make his name as a portrait painter, before the glory years in Bath and London. One of his best and earliest commissions, of the newlywed Mr and Mrs Andrews on their elevated estate outside Sudbury, is a tart tribute now in the National Gallery. While Gainsborough ended up feted in Pall Mall, Constable found his radical painting was most appreciated in France – he went on to influence, via the Barbizon School, Impressionism (which Philip Wilson Steer brought back to Suffolk in sun-drenched scenes of Walberswick in the 1880s). Both Gainsborough and Constable are buried in London, in Kew and Hampstead respectively.

SUDBURY This wool-turned-silk-weaving and market town, whose poverty shocked Daniel Defoe, has lately soaked up London overspill. Of three medieval churches, redundant St Peter's on Market Hill now hosts concerts; ancient St Gregory's was rebuilt in 1365 by Simon Sudbury who, when Archbishop of Canterbury, was beheaded in the 1381 Peasants' Revolt (his skull is preserved in the vestry – the teeth long since sold off as holy relics). Gainsborough Street contains the painter's birthplace, which has now been converted into a museum in his honor. The imposing red-brick façade was added by the painter's father, who also admired the mulberry tree in the walled garden. H.E. Kendall's Italianate Corn Exchange of 1841 has been brilliantly converted into a skylit library and information center. There are fine riverside and meadow walks.

NAYLAND Just outside this Stour-side village, Wissington (or Wiston) has a hall enlarged by Sir John Soane in 1791 for Samuel Beachcroft, Governor of the Bank of England (Soane

also did Tendring Hall at Stoke-by-Nayland, now demolished save for a gaunt doorway). It stands next to a small Norman church with 13th-century frescos, including a picture of St Francis preaching to the birds. Pastel-shaded Nayland – where Alston Court dates from 1480, with a hooded doorcase added in *c.* 1700 – is ranged around the church. Constable's 1809 painting of Christ blessing bread and wine still hangs over the altar. His only other religious work is now removed from Brantham church to Ipswich's Christchurch Mansion Museum. Nearby Stoke-by-Nayland is another finely

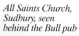

*All Saints Church,
Sudbury, seen
behind the Bull pub*

*Above: Hadleigh
Guildhall*

preserved village, with an arcaded Tudor porch to the church, 16th-century Guildhall and Maltings, oak-framed cottages and the popular Angel Hotel.

FLATFORD MILL (not open) is now a Field Study Centre but will be forever linked with John Constable who drew and painted it and whose father owned it. The National Trust has signposted several footpaths fringing the fields and following the banks of the Stour. Views extend to farmer Willy Lott's cottage, depicted in Constable's *The Hay Wain*. Bridge Cottage has also been opened as a Constable Museum, with tea-garden, shop, information center and boat hire – allowing visitors to meander in the wake of Constable family barges. In East Bergholt, the painter's birthplace has been replaced by a house called Constables, but his parents lie undisturbed in the churchyard. The church has a memorable bell-tower built like a dovecote.

HADLEIGH Hadleigh is one of Suffolk's most pleasing towns, where eclectic vernacular architectural styles spanning six centuries are lovingly preserved. The church's broach spire rises for 135 feet above a 14th-century tower. The grand red-brick Deanery Tower was built in 1495, more than half a century after the timber-framed **GUILDHALL**, with its two overhanging upper storeys. The latter building, little altered and still used for local functions, abuts the 1851 Town Hall and the 1813 Corn Exchange. Toppesfield Hall now houses the tourist information center.

HINTLESHAM HALL is a restored Elizabethan mansion, whose fine plasterwork ceilings can be viewed by guests at what is now a prized hotel and restaurant (opened under previous owner Robert Carrier in 1972). A Palladian façade added from 1725 is visible from a public footpath passing through the wooded park.

HAUGHLEY PARK (below) is a well-restored red-brick Jacobean hall set in wooded parkland. Its gabling was removed in 1824 and returned in the 1960s after fire gutted much of the interior. The village church stands beside Suffolk's biggest Norman motte and bailey castle.

*Top: Doorway of the
River House, Sudbury
Above: Haughley Park
grounds*

Haughley Park

*Left and below:
Helmingham Hall
gardens*

PIN MILL
On the Orwell estuary, this mill produced wooden pegs for boat-building and inspired Arthur Ransome to write *Swallows and Amazons*. Many artists have painted the sail-rife scene. The Butt and Oyster pub has been licensed since 1553.

HELMINGHAM HALL ★ is a moated mansion raised in the reign of Henry VIII, and made to look more castle-like by the Nash battlements added to its Georgian façade. The Hall has been home since 1485 to the Tollemache family, who founded Ipswich's Tolly Cobbold brewery in 1886 and whose monuments adorn the church. Only the exceptional 400-acre grounds are open. The drawbridge is still raised every night.

IPSWICH Although heavily redeveloped in recent decades, Ipswich retains the street pattern of a mighty Anglo-Saxon port. At one time the half-timbered town was among the seven richest in England – a period best illustrated in the 15th-century Ancient House, with molded ceilings and pargeted walls of around 1670. Thomas Wolsey, a butcher's son born in Silent Street in 1472, founded the Cardinal College of St Mary in 1528 when he was Henry VIII's Lord Chancellor. Work halted with his downfall, to leave only a modest gateway. Tudor Christchurch Mansion, on the site of a 12th-century priory, was almost demolished in the Victorian period before it was preserved as a marvelous museum and art gallery. The Unitarian Meeting House, built by the carpenter Joseph Clarke in 1699, has two huge ship-mast columns and a carved pulpit. Its façade reflects in the black glass of Norman Foster's 1975 Willis Faber insurance building.

WOODBRIDGE This medieval port turned marina on the Deben is best viewed from the river, or from the 108-foot church steeple. A restored 17th-century tide mill is driven from a pond filled twice daily; six-storey Buttrums Mill, dating from 1835, is also revived. This delightful town, with a museum in the 15th-century Moot Hall, still displays its Tudor and Georgian prosperity. The red-brick Shire Hall of 1570 is linked to Thomas Seckford, Elizabethan Master of the Court Rolls, whose ghost is said to haunt nearby Seckford Hall (now a hotel), wailing that his legacy to the poor was stolen by the rich. Poet Edward Fitzgerald, who translated *The Rubaiyat of Omar Khayyam* and is buried in Boulge churchyard, put Tennyson up at the Bull Hotel (then left him to pay the bill). Timber-framed and moated **OTLEY HALL** emerged in the reign of Henry VII and expanded under James I. It was once the home of explorer Bartholomew Gosnold (d. 1607), who discovered Cape Cod. Little Glemham Hall is an Elizabethan house with a severe Georgian façade added by the North family.

Above: the Linenfold Parlour at Otley Hall and the exterior (below)

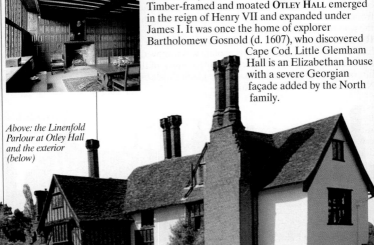

Butley Priory

BUTLEY PRIORY Begun in 1171, this became Suffolk's second-richest medieval convent after Bury. Its early 14th-century gatehouse, whose carved stone and flint flushwork has been described as "one of the noblest monuments of English monasticism", is reserved as a private house.

FELIXSTOWE is an Edwardian resort with elegant hanging gardens along the promenade and elaborate, no-longer-grand hotels and villas. To the south, alongside a sprawling container port, the Landguard Point nature reserve has rare coastal plants and a fort of 1718 built to guard the entrance to Harwich harbor.

SUTTON HOO A hillside above the Deben is contoured with burial mounds. One has yielded a treasure ship, almost certainly of Raedwald, king of the East Angles, who died in 625 and whose Wuffinga Dynasty set up their Great Hall in Rendlesham Forest. The astonishing Sutton Hoo treasure can be seen in the British Museum ▲ *138-9* and there is a new museum presenting the site.

Above and left: Landguard Fort in Felixstowe

ORFORD CASTLE Henry II's formidable fortress, by which he hoped to control the coast and to intimidate baron Hugh Bigod, is now reduced to defensive banks and ditches and a near-perfect central keep almost 100 feet high. There are commanding views from the top. The tower's 18 sides and three square turrets contain a labyrinth of rooms and passages constructed in 1165-7. The castle was captured by the French in 1217, during fighting after the death of King John.

ALDEBURGH ("Old Borough" in Old English) was a town of ancient importance, with the timber-framed Moot Hall at its heart. Now the Tudor museum backs onto the beach, as a swathe of land has been lost to the sea. Below the town, Britain's most northerly Napoleonic Martello tower survives, although a surrounding village

ORFORD NESS is Europe's largest vegetated shingle spit. A secret military site for 70 years from 1913, it is now a nature haven, particularly for rare plants, and birds – adjacent Havergate Island is an RSPB reserve. A ferry leads to a 5-mile walk.

Left: Orford Castle

was drowned. The birthplace of poet George Crabbe has many literary links: at Strafford House, on Crag Path, Darwinian disciple Edward Clodd drew Hardy, Meredith and Gissing to rationalist gatherings; Wilkie Collins set his novel *No Name* here; Laurens van der Post and Susan Hill wrote here. The Aldeburgh Festival, founded in 1948 by Lowestoft-born Benjamin Britten ● *59*, singer Peter Pears and Eric Crozier, and later converting Snape Maltings into a concert hall, draws arts enthusiasts each June.

THORPENESS North along the shingle beach from Aldeburgh, hiding Sizewell nuclear power station (sole blot on the Suffolk Heritage Coast), is this bizarre half-timbered holiday village begun in 1910 by estate owner Glencairn Stuart Ogilvie and architect W.G. Wilson. Looming over a

THE WILD MAN OF ORFORD
According to Ralph of Coggeshall, writing in 1207, a merman was caught in fishing nets in the 1160s. He remained mute, even when tortured and hung up by his feet, and showed no reverence in church. Finally freed, the Wild Man of Orford was last seen swimming out to sea.

Framlingham Castle

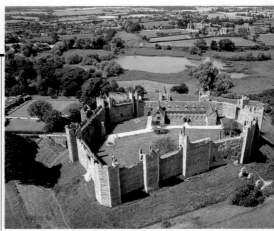

Leiston Abbey

*"House in
the Clouds",
Thorpeness*

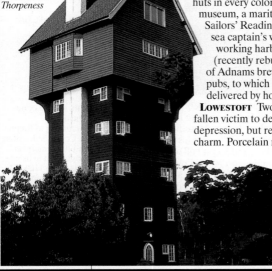

pleasure lake, the "House in the Clouds" is both dwelling and water tower.

DUNWICH Surrounded by sea and the important nature havens of Minsmere and Dunwich and Walberswick heaths – marsh, moor and forest attracting birds such as harriers, avocets and bitterns – is a village which in the early 13th century was England's sixth greatest town. Dunwich Museum charts a 750-year decline – the last of eight or more churches toppled over the cliff in 1904. Remaining ruins are the Norman apse of a lepers' hospital and the curtain wall and gateway of a friary dating from 1290. See, too, the nearby romantic ruins of LEISTON ABBEY, with its restored 1380s Lady Chapel and Tudor gate-turret.

WALBERSWICK On either side of the River Blyth, linked by an old railway bridge and a little summer ferry, are the artists' retreat of Walberswick and the town of Southwold. Like Covehithe to the north, Walberswick dismantled its noble church in the 17th century and set a humbler structure in the ruins. Southwold has greens built as fire-breaks after a 1659 inferno, and beach huts in every color. There is also a town museum, a maritime museum in the Sailors' Reading Room donated by a sea captain's widow in 1864, a working harbor, a lighthouse and (recently rebuilt) pier. The home of Adnams brewery is packed with pubs, to which the beer is still delivered by horse-drawn drays.

LOWESTOFT Two-pier Lowestoft has fallen victim to development and depression, but retains flashes of charm. Porcelain made here in the second half of the 18th century can be seen in the museum at Oulton Broad. The Maritime Museum is also worth visiting. Lowestoft became a seaside resort

thanks to railway speculator Samuel Morton Peto, who commissioned Somerleyton Hall (a spirited mock-Jacobean affair with Italian campanile) from John Thomas in the 1840s. He added a model village before going bust and selling to forebears of the current Lord Somerleyton.

FRAMLINGHAM CASTLE Built and rebuilt by the rebellious Bigod Earls of Norfolk in the 12th century, Framlingham's first castle was surrendered to Henry II in 1157, and the second was seized by John in 1216. Thirteen outer towers survive, linked by a curtain wall and topped with the fake chimneys by which the Howards disguised a clapped-out castle as a Tudor mansion. Mary Tudor waited here in 1553 until her succession was secure. From Wall Walk there are views over The Mere to Framlingham College, founded in 1865. **FRAMLINGHAM CHURCH ★** boasts the finest English renaissance tombs in the country, including that of the 2nd Duke of Norfolk, victor of Flodden (1513), and his helmet.

BECCLES This former wherry port with Georgian streets (Ballygate, Puddingmoor, Northgate) was linked by "score" alleys to the Waveney. Fires devastated the town in the 17th century, but Elizabethan Roos Hall, with its pedimented windows, red-brick bays and step-gables, survives, as does Leman House (conspicuous with its fine brick and flint façade and Tudor-style windows of 1631), a museum and former school. The church, with double-storey porch and detached Perpendicular tower, is where Nelson's parents wed.

BUNGAY Wrecked by fire in 1688, and with its Butter Cross erected the following year, Bungay bears many signs of Georgian prosperity. An abandoned castle of the Bigod barons was heavily quarried, and for a time a romantic lady novelist wrote in a folly between the two gate towers. But the town's literary star is Black Shuck, a ghostly dog which ran amok in the church one stormy Sunday in 1577 and was often sighted across East Anglia thereafter. This phantom inspired Conan Doyle's *The Hound of the Baskervilles*.

Houses overlooking the beach in Thorpeness (top)

Dunwich Heath (above)

OTTERS
The recent return of otters to many English rivers owes much to the breeding programme of the Otter Trust at Earsham, whose pens and pools can be visited.

SAXTEAD GREEN POST MILL (below) is a beautifully preserved white beacon of a windmill dating from 1796. A mill has turned on this site since at least 1309.

Norfolk's vast congregation of flint churches boasts more medieval survivors (650) than any other English county. South Walsham has two churches in one churchyard, and – if we count a ruin – Reepham has three. While 50 churches certainly contain Saxon fabric, most of the round towers so common hereabouts may also have pre-Norman origins. All but a handful of England's 180 or so round tower churches are in East Anglia; two-thirds are in Norfolk alone. More than 100 saints are recorded in glass, paint, wood and stone, and there are some

particularly fine painted rood screens (at Ludham, Loddon and Attleborough, for example) and angel-supported hammerbeam roofs (Knapton, Necton). While most parish churches offer interesting monuments in brass or marble, Stow Bardolph near Downham Market has a memorial that is now unique outside those in Westminster Abbey: a scarily-lifelike wax effigy of Sarah Hare, who died in 1744.

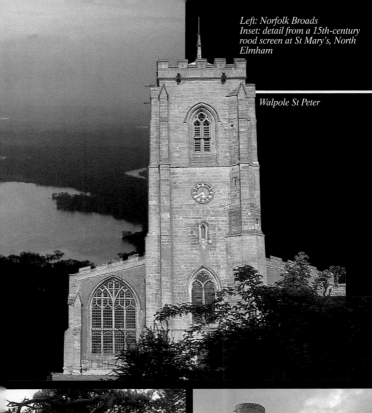

Walpole St Peter

Top: tower of Wymondham Abbey
Above: St Mary's, Shelton

Left: St Peter Mancroft

Top: St Margaret's, Hales
Above: St Peter Mancroft, with a sundial over the doorway

Right: Castle Rising
Below: West Walton
Church

CASTLE RISING
The ruins of the
imposing Norman
Castle Rising, which
once held Queen
Isabella (the "She-
Wolf of France"), are
surrounded by
immense earthworks.
Having helped to
murder her husband
Edward II in 1327,
Isabella was detained
here and elsewhere by
her son Edward III
for 27 years. She
wanted for nothing,
save power, freedom
and, ultimately,
sanity.

THE FENS Blurring the boundaries between land and water, and
between Norfolk, Cambridgeshire and Lincolnshire, these form
a geometric grid of fields and dykes resembling a Mondrian
painting. Drainage began in Roman times, but accelerated from
the 17th century under Dutch engineer Cornelius Vermuyden.
The tide of history was resisted by Fen Tigers – eelers and
wildfowlers – who sabotaged the first Denver Sluice. The New
Sluice was designed by Sir John Rennie, builder of London's
Old Waterloo Bridge. Both can be seen beside a fine windmill.
Although sinking fenland remains menaced by rising tides,
most is now under the plough. The old pattern of winter
flooding is preserved at the Welney Washes, which is now a
lake for migrant Bewick's and whooper swans.

KING'S LYNN ★ This unsung town holds streets of ancient
merchant houses, fine civic buildings and both Tuesday and
Saturday market places. Soon after the Norman Conquest the
Bishop of Norwich founded a priory, beside the River Ouse,
and the church of St Margaret (the latter, despite its leaning
pillars, remains firmly rooted in the community.) Bishop's
Lynn, renamed after the Dissolution of the Monasteries (and,
fittingly, a Royalist outpost during the Civil War) prospered as
a port, but eventually fell into decline. Many medieval,
Tudor and Georgian buildings survive because the town
became too poor to wreck them. Beside the docks, where
vessels from the Baltic and beyond have landed for a
millennium, are medieval warehouses and the 1683 CUSTOM
HOUSE by architect Henry Bell. Once a theater, where
Shakespeare probably acted, the early 15th-century St
George's Guildhall now hosts arts festivals. The slightly later
HALL OF THE TRINITY GUILD sports a checkerwork front of flint
and stone with an Elizabethan extension. This pattern is
echoed in the 1895 Town Hall.

Hall of the Trinity
Guild, King's Lynn

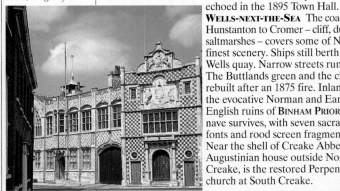

WELLS-NEXT-THE-SEA The coast from
Hunstanton to Cromer – cliff, dunes,
saltmarshes – covers some of Norfolk's
finest scenery. Ships still berth at
Wells quay. Narrow streets run to
The Buttlands green and the church,
rebuilt after an 1875 fire. Inland lie
the evocative Norman and Early
English ruins of BINHAM PRIORY. The
nave survives, with seven sacramental
fonts and rood screen fragments.
Near the shell of Creake Abbey, an
Augustinian house outside North
Creake, is the restored Perpendicular
church at South Creake.

*Left and below:
Cley-next-the-Sea*

WALSINGHAM The most remarkable religious architecture – and atmosphere – is found at Walsingham where, in 1061, the Virgin Mary told Richeldis de Fauvraches to build a replica of the Holy House at Nazareth. Pilgrims flocked from all over medieval Europe. Augustine guardians of the shrine built a church whose great east window can be seen in abbey gardens entered through a 15th-century gateway in the village street. Off the Friday Market, the Great and Little Cloisters and Pilgrims Hall of a ruined Franciscan Friary are still visible. As pilgrimages revived, a red-brick church arose in the 1930s on the shrine's original site. Patriots and pilgrims visit the seven parishes of the Burnhams, beyond the picturesque village green of Burnham Market, for Horatio Nelson (1758-1805), who gave eye, arm and ultimately life for his country, was born in Burnham Thorpe rectory. The White Ensign flutters from the tower of the restored church and oak from the flagship *Victory* has been carved into the lectern and crucifix. Nelson Hall and a time-warp local pub without a bar also pay tribute.

CROMER, like its neighbor and rival Sheringham, grew from fishing village to holiday resort thanks to the railways. It boasts hotel-crowned cliffs and crab pots, pier and cherished lifeboat (hail the memory of heroic coxswain Henry Blogg). The 160-foot church tower once served as a lighthouse. Lovely scenery can be enjoyed along the coast via the picture-postcard villages of Salthouse, CLEY and Blakeney, and through the Glaven Valley to painted and prettified Holt.

SHERINGHAM PARK ★ was laid out among wooded hills by the masterly East Anglian gardener-architect Humphry Repton (1752-1818). Born at Bury St Edmunds and buried at Aylsham, he executed over 220 landscape designs across England, around 30 of them in Norfolk and Suffolk. Sheringham, with its superb walks and viewing towers, dazzling rhododendron and azalea displays, is among his best.

*Above: Binham Priory;
Left: Felbrigg Hall's
"Old London Bridge"
by Samuel Scott, and
the Drawing Room*

FELBRIGG HALL ★ has another Repton park, with fine lake and woodland walks, this time adorning a celebrated 17th-century house remodelled by Palladian architect James Paine around 1750. Compare the south and west fronts if you want to see the revolution that took place in English architecture between the 1620s and the 1670s. The hall contains original 18th-century furniture, William Windham's Grand Tour paintings and a Gothic library. A parkland church once served a vanished village.

COASTAL PATHS
The 93-mile Peddars Way and Norfolk Coastal Path starts at Knettishall Heath near the Suffolk border and extends via Castle Acre, Brancaster and Blakeney, to Cromer.

Two of Britain's finest surviving Palladian houses, surrounded by deer-stocked parkland, and stuffed with stately treasures, are linked in name, style and location. Both appear slightly alien and austere at first glance, but closer attention brings immense rewards. Houghton was built in the 1730s for Sir Robert

Walpole, first and longest-serving British Prime Minister, using architects Colen Campbell and Thomas Ripley. The magnificent interior decorations and furnishings are the result of William Kent's first major commission. But by 1730 Kent had also provided Thomas Coke with rough plans for Holkham Hall and raised an 80-foot obelisk. The house, with much added inspiration from Lord Burlington and Grand Tour memories, was begun four years later but not completed until 1762. Holkham's classical calm belies the fervor of revolutionary agricultural ideas tested on the estate by another Thomas Coke ("Coke of Norfolk"), great nephew and heir of the founder.

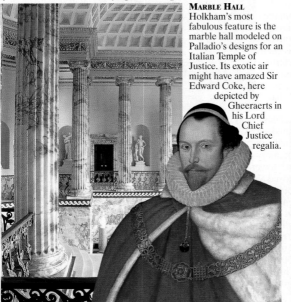

MARBLE HALL
Holkham's most fabulous feature is the marble hall modeled on Palladio's designs for an Italian Temple of Justice. Its exotic air might have amazed Sir Edward Coke, here depicted by Gheeraerts in his Lord Chief Justice regalia.

FURNITURE
Kent's designs for Houghton and Holkham included some of the finest achievements in English furniture. This sumptuous chair was created with no expense spared for Sir Robert Walpole – whose wild spending at Houghton included £1,200 on gold lace for the Green Velvet State Bed.

HOLKHAM

Left and opposite, we see how faithfully William Kent's brilliant design for Holkham was realized.

ART TREASURES

Both halls are still bursting with original treasures – like the Chinese export dinner service with Sir Robert's coat-of-arms at Houghton (left). But the Walpole collection of Old Master paintings went to Catherine the Great of Russia, and now graces St Petersburg's Hermitage Museum. Holkham's celebrated Leonardo Codex manuscript is now owned by Bill Gates.

INTERIORS

From the North Tribune at Holkham (above left) to the Saloon at Houghton (above), the two halls were conceived as a symphony – aiming at a harmony of architecture, art and furnishings. But it may have taken centuries for all the vivid notes to blend.

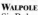

SOCIETY BEAUTY

John Singer Sargent's 1919 portrait of the late Marchioness of Cholmondeley shows a society beauty who was to prove a doughty custodian of Houghton. Born Sybil Sassoon, she lived to her nineties and was a much-loved figure in Norfolk.

WALPOLE

Sir Robert Walpole, pictured here by John Wootton, graduated from Norfolk squire to national leader. He wanted Houghton Hall to reflect his elevated status – commissioning a grand family house in which royalty, aristocracy and foreign dignitaries could also be entertained.

VAN DYCK

Van Dyck's equestrian portrait of the Duc d'Arenberg adds yet more nobility to the walls of Holkham.

▲ Great Yarmouth

Old Merchant's House, Great Yarmouth

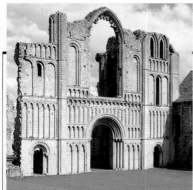

Castle Acre Priory (above) On a hilltop site on the pre-Roman Peddars Way, the fortified village of Castle Acre lies in the outer bailey of a long-gone Norman castle. The Cluniac priory once beckoned pilgrims with the arm of St Philip. It is now East Anglia's largest and loveliest monastic ruin. St Andrew's church has two treasures from 1400: a "wine-glass" pulpit and a rood screen portraying the Twelve Apostles.

Great Yarmouth gave us the bloater, kipper and fish finger. Now the neon-l town is more gaudy than great. Bombs and bulldozers have spared the birthplace of Anna Sewell; but of 200 medieval alleys called The Rows – hun with nets and thronged with children until the last war – little remains. Restored 17th-century merchants' houses at least hint at old glory days. The splendid South Quay, deemed by Defoe the loveliest in England, can be glimpsed around the Elizabethan House Museum (with its Conspiracy Room, where Charles I's trial was allegedly plotted). The Maritime Museum for East Anglia, in a forme shipwrecked sailors' refuge, is a joy. A Norfolk Nelson Museum will open in Easter 2001 on South Quay.

The moated 15th-century **Caister Castle** was built for Sir John Fastolf (model for Shakespeare's Falstaff), and alleged funded by ransom money paid for a French knight captured Agincourt. It was subsequently besieged, as the Paston mercantile family and the Duke of Norfolk fought for ownership. Now a motor museum, the castle is reputedly visited one midnight each year by a ghostly carriage pulled b four headless horses.

Burgh Castle is one of nine remaining Roman "Forts of th Saxon Shore" and among the earliest survivals of East Anglian flint architecture. Burgh Castle, or Gariannonum, was built in the late 3rd century and abandoned around AD 408. Now land-locked, it originally stood on a broad bay. Three sides of the fort's massive walls still loom large, together with bastions built to hold catapults. St Fursey founded a monastery here in the early 7th century.

Grimes Graves

Waxham Great Barn, a giant Tudor relic, dates fro the 1540s. It was built by the enterprising Woodhouse family who took stone from the nearby dissolved priories of Hickling, Ingham and Broomholm.

The Regency market town and aristocrati retreat of **Swaffham** was based on a Palladian market cross and a medieval legend. Lured to London by a dream, the Pedlar of Swaffham met a stranger who mocked his hopes of finding fortune – saying he himself had had a dream about a Swaffham pedlar who struck gold in his garden. Soon the ex pedlar had excavated wealth enough to build the north aisle of the grand Church of St Peter and St Paul (note, too, the double hammerbeam roof held aloft by 192 angels). He and his dog are portrayed on the prayer desk in the chancel.

Aylsham is a pleasing wool town of 18th-century houses where John of Gaunt held court. The great glory of the area the Jacobean **Blickling Hall** set in a Repton-linked estate formal gardens, park, lake, woods and farmland. The yew hedges alone, framing the symmetrical red-brick façade, are marvel. Designed for Lord Chief Justice Sir Henry Hobart, probably by Robert Lyminge (also associated with Felbrigg Hall ▲ *351* and Hatfield House ▲ *284*), the present hall succeeds a moated medieval manor. It boasts a long gallery

brary plus collections of furniture, pictures and tapestries. And it may be haunted by Anne Boleyn, whose family owned the earlier building until her execution by Henry VIII. Her heart is said to be buried in the nearby church at Salle.

VOLTERTON HALL Baron (Horatio) Walpole, brother of the Prime Minister, commissioned Thomas Ripley to build Wolterton Hall. In 1740, when it was still incomplete, he bought the moated Mannington Hall (dating from 1460) miles away. The current Lord Walpole still divides his time between both Norfolk seats. The Bulwer Long family have been based at Heydon for 600 years. Their Elizabethan hall borders an idyllic estate village: church, pub, post office, blacksmith's forge and houses gathered around a green.

The mounds and hollows of **GRIME'S GRAVES**, in a forest clearing, form Britain's largest group of neolithic flint mines. One of the 360 pits is open to the public: a ladder descending

Blickling Hall: exterior (top left), Great Hall and staircase (top right), and Sir Henry Hobart, by Daniel Mytens, c. 1624

to low tunnels where the flint was dug out with antlers before it was fashioned into tools and weapons for export. The name may have been coined by Anglo-Saxons who perceived "graves" (here meaning depressions) created by "Grime", a nickname for Woden, god of war and magic. This most powerful Saxon deity was later linked to Satan and to many eerie earthworks (such as Devil's Dyke and Devil's Ditch).

THE NORFOLK RURAL LIFE MUSEUM, at Gressenhall, is housed in a former workhouse dating from 1776. It also operates a working farm.

OXBURGH HALL ★ is a splendid moated manor built in 1482 for the Bedingfelds, who still live here. Henry VII visited and Mary Queen of Scots was detained here, working exquisite embroideries with Bess of Hardwick ▲ 382, wife of her custodian. The rooms progress from medieval to Victorian. The gardens contain a 1835 Roman Catholic chapel by Pugin, and a Victorian French parterre. Terracotta Bedingfeld tombs are in a chapel attached to the ruined parish church.

Oxburgh Hall: the King's Room (above), the late 17th-century staircase (above left) and exterior (below)

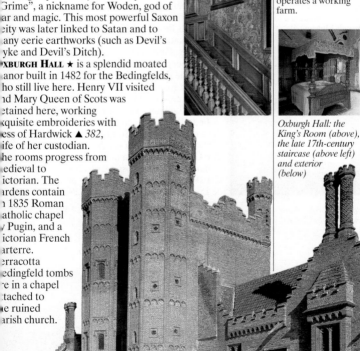

▲ Norwich

Norwich Cathedral

NORWICH

Norwich is a modern metropolis with a medieval heart, crowned by equally magnificent castle and cathedral. At night thanks to superb civic lighting, it becomes a gigantic theater set. Norwich is dotted with remnants of 14th-century walls and gates. It once boasted a different pre-Reformation church for every Sunday and a pub for each weekday. Most churches survive, although the majority are redundant and converted to other uses. The CHURCH OF ST JULIAN, where the medieval mystic wrote her *Revelations of Divine Love*, was rebuilt after bombing in 1942. ST ANDREWS HALL, the former nave of a Dominican friary completed in 1471, has been a public hall since the Reformation; adjoining Blackfriars Hall was the friary's chancel. Nonconformist Norfolk has bequeathed two gems in Colegate: the 17th-century Old Meeting House; and John Ivory's OCTAGON CHAPEL of 1754.

CASTLE Squat and square on its huge mound, the Norman castle keep decorated with blind arcades watches over the city Now a museum, its dungeons hold hideous death masks and its galleries ravishing early 19th-century local landscapes by Crome, Cotman and their Norwich School followers. There is an ancient market between the 15th-century Guildhall and majestic St Peter Mancroft Church. Ahead of and above the canvas-covered stalls lies the 1930s edifice of City Hall, with its campanile and guardian lions whose shadows rear up in the illuminated evenings. Pause in George Skipper's Art Nouveau Royal Arcade and peep into the amazing marble and mahogany interior he designed for Norwich Union. At every turn – along antique streets like Bridewell Alley (where there is a local museum in a 14th-century merchant's house), Tombland and cobbled Elm Hill – the cathedral's soaring spire provides a pointer. In its shadow lie NORWICH SCHOOL (founded 1553; star old boy, Horatio Nelson), the handsome houses of The Close and, hidden in Bishopgate, the remarkable Great Hospital of 1249.

CATHEDRAL Much of it was built by Bishop Herbert de Losinga between 1096 and 1119, and it boasts a wealth of wonders (marrying Norman and Gothic for richer and richer). Three details must not be missed: 400 colored bosses in England's largest cloisters; the Despenser Reredos, an altarpiece painted in 1380s Norwich; and 60 carved misericords relating witty and bawdy tales.

NORFOLK BROADS
The Broads ■ *28* cover 220 square miles of wetland northeast of Norwich. The terrain ranges from the vast lake at Hickling and the tidal Breydon Water, to dykes, water-meadows and impenetrable marshes. Rare flora and fauna include marsh orchids, swallowtail butterflies and the elusive bittern. One of the best vantage points for surveying these wetlands, whose history is set out in a Broads Museum at Stalham Staithe, is the tower at Ranworth church (note the finest Gothic rood screen in Norfolk).

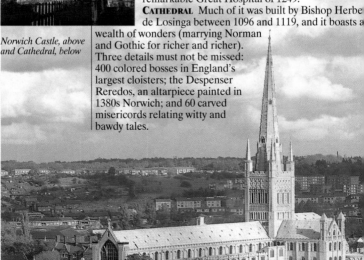

Norwich Castle, above and Cathedral, below

NORTH MIDLANDS
Neil Burton

▲ Stamford to Gainsborough

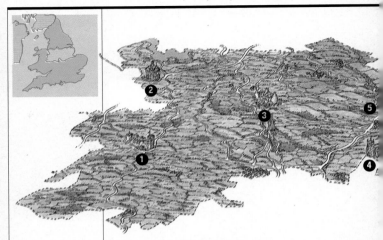

Stamford to Gainsborough

Below right:
Burghley House

Below: Statue of
Minerva, on
P.E. Monnot's tomb of
John, 5th Earl of
Exeter (d.1700) in
St Martin's Church,
Stamford

Stamford ★ A perfect small Georgian town that has been used for countless film locations, although the church steeples that punctuate the skyline serve as a reminder that Stamford has an older past, still visible in many places. **All Saints church** is the hub of the town and much more conspicuous than the 18th-century town hall in St Mary's Street. Most of the buildings are of the excellent local building stone, and a large proportion are still owned by the Cecil family from nearby Burghley House. Many of the 18th-century houses which line the streets have ornamental door and window surrounds copied directly out of the pattern books of the time.

Burghley House ★ Just beyond the boundary of the town, this is one of four great houses built by William Cecil, Secretary of State to Elizabeth I. Begun in the 1550s and finished by 1587, Burghley was meant for showing off, and the enormous stone palace with its fantastic silhouette of towers and chimneys is an unforgettable sight. The rooms inside were redecorated in the 1680s by the 5th Earl of Exeter and the ceilings of the state rooms covered with paintings by Antonio Verrio – most spectacularly in the Heaven Room. The Cecil family's huge collection of paintings covers the walls.

Grimsthorpe Hall is a magnificent muddle. The great north entrance front and the cavernous stone great hall behind it are the work of Sir John Vanbrugh, architect of Blenheim Palace and Castle Howard. Vanbrugh was employed to rebuild the whole house, but he died in 1715 and the Tudor house round its courtyard, wit

*elow left: Burghley House gate
dges and (bottom) the Great Hall
elow right: Lady Adelaide Talbot
° Lord Leighton, Belton House*

8. NOTTINGHAM **9.** GAINSBOROUGH **10.** MELTON MOWBRAY **11.** GRANTHAM **12.** LINCOLN **13.** STAMFORD **14.** BOSTON

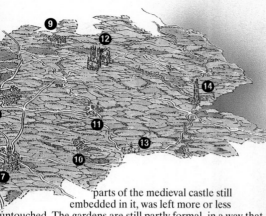

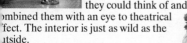

parts of the medieval castle still embedded in it, was left more or less untouched. The gardens are still partly formal, in a way that complements Vanbrugh's work.

GRANTHAM Grantham was clearly a highway town and takes much of its character from the fact that the Great North Road passed through the center of it. There are countless inns, notably THE ANGEL AND ROYAL HOTEL, with its 15th-century carved stone front where King Richard III signed the Duke of Buckingham's death warrant; the inn is still serving its original function 500 years later. The other conspicuous building and a monument to the medieval wealth accumulated from the wool trade is the CHURCH OF ST WULFRAM ★ with its staggeringly tall spire.

WOOLSTHORPE MANOR Seven miles south of the town is a limestone house of about 1620, where Isaac Newton was born in 1642 and where, in 1665, he discovered the principles of differential calculus.

HARLAXTON MANOR Westward of Grantham lies the wildest and most fanciful 1830s mansion in England. The architects – first Anthony Salvin then William Burn – copied parts of all the major Jacobean houses they could think of and combined them with an eye to theatrical effect. The interior is just as wild as the outside.

BELTON HOUSE ★ Built for Sir John Brownlow between 1685 and 1688, it still gives an excellent impression of a great late 17th-century mansion. The inside has some splendid plaster ceilings, wood carvings and much furniture and silver of the period, as well as Soho tapestries, a fine cross-section of 17th-century English portraiture, and remnants of a major collection of Old Masters. One room is entirely decorated with large bird paintings by Hondecoeter.

SIR ISAAC NEWTON (1642-1727) was a mathematician whose discoveries laid the foundations for much of the progress in science since his time. Besides inventing calculus, he solved some of the mysteries of light and, most importantly of all, evolved the theory of

gravity. Newton was born at Woolsthorpe Manor and educated at Grantham Grammar School and Trinity College, Cambridge. During the 1680s he formulated his three laws of motion and from them derived the theory of universal gravitation that was published in his book *Philosophiae Naturalis Principia Mathematica* (1687). Newton helped to resist the efforts of King James II to make Cambridge University Roman Catholic and was rewarded by being made Master of the Royal Mint in 1693 and later President of the Royal Society.

Belton House

359

BELVOIR CASTLE ★

The medieval castle has gone and there is nothing to be seen of the great classical house of the 1650s except a model in the ballroom. The present castle is a Gothic fantasy begun by the 5th Duchess of Rutland in 1801, destroyed by fire in 1816 and immediately rebuilt. The site, on a hill overlooking the flat Vale

of Belvoir, is superb, and the castle with its array of towers, turrets and battlements looks spectacular and romantic. Inside are the cold and cavernous great staircase and ballroom in a Gothic style copied from Lincoln Cathedral while the Elizabeth Saloon – named in honor of the 5th Duchess – is immensely opulent, with a gilded and painted ceiling, French gilt wall carvings and French furniture and carpet.

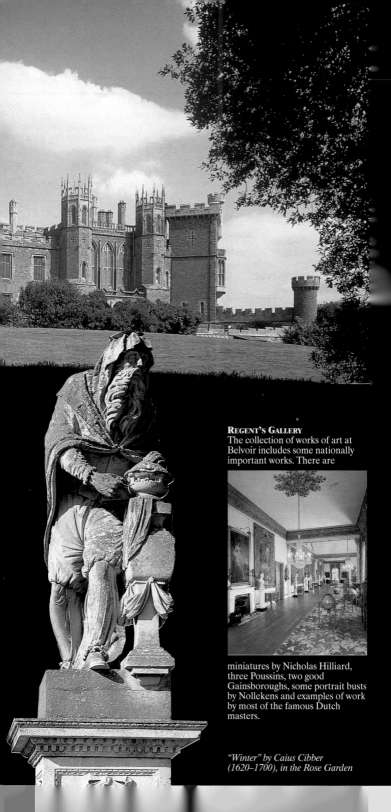

REGENT'S GALLERY

The collection of works of art at Belvoir includes some nationally important works. There are miniatures by Nicholas Hilliard, three Poussins, two good Gainsboroughs, some portrait busts by Nollekens and examples of work by most of the famous Dutch masters.

"Winter" by Caius Cibber (1620–1700), in the Rose Garden

TORKSEY
At Torksey the Roman Fosse Dyke joins the River Trent and links it to the River Witham. By this means the Romans were able to reach the Midlands. Torksey was once second only to Lincoln, with wharves all along the river bank, but has shrunk almost to nothing. Isolated on the edge of the Trent are the impressive remains of Sir Robert Jermyn's Elizabethan mansion Torksey Castle.

Right:
Tattershall Castle

BOSTON Boston is a remote and evocative town; it was once a wealthy seaport but the river silted up, and although ships still come in, the wealth seems to have evaporated. The town and the flat fenland for miles around are dominated by BOSTON STUMP ★, the immensely tall tower of the great medieval church of ST BOTOLPH which stands between the river and the broad market square. The Stump itself is 272 feet high – a monument to the daring medieval builders – and the church is one of the largest in the country. Around the market square are streets full of Georgian houses; one of the best is FYDELL HOUSE, a substantial town mansion built in 1726.

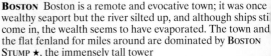

TATTERSHALL CASTLE
The great red-brick tower keep was built by Ralph Cromwell, Treasurer of England between 1430 and 1450, and contained the state rooms that he added to an earlier castle. Only the keep and a small gatehouse survive inside a water-filled moat. Cromwell also paid for the building of the magnificent CHURCH OF THE HOLY TRINITY, which stands next to the castle, as well as some almshouses and a college for priests.

GUNBY HALL The home of the Massingberd since the 18th century is a building of 1700, with wood-paneled interiors typical of that date and an attractive garden. Gunby has strong associations with the poet Alfred, Lord Tennyson.

LOUTH An utterly delightful small town, tucked away beyond the Lincolnshire Wolds. This range of low wooded hills provides welcome relief from the flat fields of sugar beet that are typical of east Lincolnshire. Louth is mainly Georgian in character, but the CHURCH OF ST JAMES ★ dates from the 15th century. Its tall slender spire was completed in 1515.

Gunby Hall (top) and the Oak or West Drawing Room (above)

LINCOLN Lincoln has perhaps the best site of any English cathedral town because the CATHEDRAL ★ itself, together with the castle, stands on the edge of a dramatic ridge, down which the cobbled streets of the medieval town run to meet the more modern part built on the banks of the river and extending to the railway station. The cathedral dominates the countryside for miles. It is quite simply one of the most stunning medieval buildings in England and is full of experiments in construction of every kind, in vaulting and ornament. The building is essentially of three periods: the west front is Norman; the transepts, choir and nave are Early English (13th century); and the towers are Perpendicular (14th century). The west front originally looked much more like a castle than a church but it was ornamented and extended by Bishop Alexander with a screen of sculpture. In 1185 much of the cathedral fell down; it was rebuilt by Bishop Hugo (usually known as Little St Hugh). Construction began in 1192 with the eastern

DODDINGTON HALL
Doddington (below left and right) is a late Tudor mansion which lies back from the main road behind its pretty brick gatehouse. The perfect balance of the main front suggests a good architect, and Doddington is probably the work of Robert Smythson, who also designed Hardwick Hall in Derbyshire ▲ *382-3*. Although the outside

ansepts and continued until the nave was roofed in 1233. In ɛ 1260s the Angel Choir was added at the east end of the ɪthedral: a brilliant early example of English High Gothic, ɪth exceptionally rich carved stonework, including the carved gures that give the choir its name.

round the cathedral is the ˙eensward of Minster Yard, fringed ɣ the Bishop's Palace and the large ɔuses of the cathedral canons. The ɑrd was once enclosed by a fortified ɑll, which can still be seen in many ɪaces. The main gate through the wall was the EXCHEQUER ˙ATE, opposite the west front of the cathedral. Beyond the ˙te lies LINCOLN CASTLE, still enclosed by its wall, and the old ɔwn. Here are several very early buildings, including THE ˙W'S HOUSE in Steep Hill, a rare survival of a domestic ɹilding of the 12th century. AUBOURN HALL stands at one end f the village next to the old church.

ˌRANT BROUGHTON CHURCH ★ is late medieval with exquisite ɔne carving. The chancel was rebuilt in the 1870s by George ɔdley, a leading Gothic revivalist, who refitted the rest of the ɪterior.

of the house has hardly changed since it was finished in 1600, most of the rooms inside were re-done in the 1760s for Sir John Hussey Delaval.

Aubourn Hall

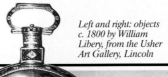

Left and right: objects c. 1800 by William Libery, from the Usher Art Gallery, Lincoln

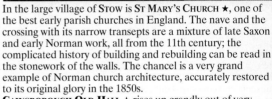

USHER ART GALLERY
Built in 1927 with money left by James Ward Usher, whose collection of watches, portrait miniatures, blue and white china and antique silver were the foundation of the present collection. There is a good collection of paintings by the watercolorist Peter de Wint, who was associated with the town (above right, *Lincoln from the South West*). For the poetic visitor, Tennyson's cloak and large-brimmed hat are also on display.

Chancel and crossing, St Mary's Church, Stow

St Mary's Church, Stow

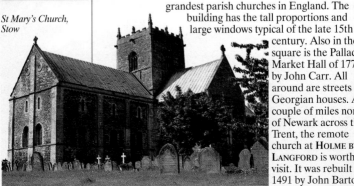

In the large village of STOW is ST MARY'S CHURCH ★, one of the best early parish churches in England. The nave and the crossing with its narrow transepts are a mixture of late Saxon and early Norman work, all from the 11th century; the complicated history of building and rebuilding can be read in the stonework of the walls. The chancel is a very grand example of Norman church architecture, accurately restored to its original glory in the 1850s.

GAINSBOROUGH OLD HALL ★ rises up grandly out of very ordinary urban surroundings, proclaiming itself a late medieval house of the first importance. Sir Thomas Burgh entertained King Richard III here in 1484, and Sir Thomas's enormous Great Hall with its elaborate timber roof survives, along with the great kitchen and other catering rooms. The kitchen is possibly the most complete medieval kitchen in England. Other parts of the mansion were rebuilt in the 1590s

NEWARK

Newark is a handsome town on the River Trent which became rich from the wool and coal shipped up the river. It was defended by a strong castle, but during the Civil War it was besieged by Parliamentary forces, who damaged the castle walls. The town was important as a staging place on the Great North Road and as a center of agriculture. Some of the great sheds built for malting still survive at its edge. At its heart is the broad and active market square with the splendid medieval CHURCH OF ST MARY MAGDALEN ★ – one of the grandest parish churches in England. The building has the tall proportions and large windows typical of the late 15th century. Also in the square is the Palladian Market Hall of 1774 by John Carr. All around are streets of Georgian houses. A couple of miles north of Newark across the Trent, the remote church at HOLME BY LANGFORD is worth a visit. It was rebuilt in 1491 by John Barton out of profits from the wool trade, and is a perfect and moving example of a Tudor church.

LAXTON A few miles north of Newark (south of Worksop) is the village of Laxton, remarkable as the only place left in the country that still uses the medieval open field system of cultivation, with all the land surrounding the village divided into long strips.

SOUTHWELL is a quiet little town, completely dominated by the superb **MINSTER CHURCH ★** – a cathedral since 1884, and one of the most glorious churches in England – which stands serenely in its grassy close. Begun in about 1108, the nave of the Minster with its small windows and blunt pyramid-roofed west towers conveys better than anywhere else the typical character of the larger 12th-century churches, as does the interior with its massive columns. The eastern parts of the Minster were rebuilt in the 13th century: first the chancel and then, after 1288, the octagonal chapter-house, with exquisite stone carving of international importance. Dotted round the edge of the Close are the ruins of the Bishop's Palace and a series of prebendal houses for senior clergy; many of these are medieval but with Georgian fronts. Charles I spent his last hours at liberty at the Saracen's Head.

Gainsborough Old Hall

NOTTINGHAM

In 1697 the traveler Celia Fiennes called Nottingham "The neatest town I have seen". For centuries Nottingham was famous for its lace-making, and large red-brick Victorian lace factories still dominate that part of the town known as the Lacemarket, but nowadays Nottingham is more famous as the home of Boots the Chemists. The ground is hilly, and the changing levels and unexpected views make it an exhilarating town to walk in. Its highest point is Castle Rock, now dominated by the long low outline of the Duke of Newcastle's 17th-century mansion, built on the site of the castle keep and burnt out in 1831 by rioters who resented the Duke's opposition to parliamentary reform. In 1878 the building was restored as the City Museum and Art Gallery. The rock beneath the castle is honeycombed with caves. The center of the town is still the market place, where the large stone Council House was built in the late 1920s. Behind it is High Pavement, which contains two excellent museums and the great medieval parish church. High Pavement Chapel has been converted into a lace museum; the old Shire Hall with its late Georgian front now houses the fascinating Museum of Law, where visitors can ponder the whole process from the court rooms to the cells and the gallows. **ST MARY'S CHURCH** is the second largest parish church in the county after Newark.

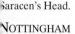

Above: St Mary Magdalene, Newark

Newstead Abbey

WOLLATON HALL East of
Nottingham center lies
Wollaton Hall (left), one of
the most spectacular
Elizabethan houses in
England, built for Sir Francis
Willoughby in the 1580s as a
display of the wealth gleaned
from his coal mines. The
house stands on a hill and has four great corner towers; its
tower room soars up in the middle. It is now a natural history
museum and its grounds, which include a great stable block
and a spectacular Camellia House, are a public park.

NEWSTEAD ABBEY The west front is all that survives of the
abbey church, but the cloister was turned into a large house by
the Byron family who acquired Newstead in 1540. By the time
the 6th Lord Byron (the poet) inherited in 1798, the house
was in a bad way; one of his friends called it "a heap of
rubbish". But Byron himself loved the place and his dog
Bosun is buried in the abbey ruins. In 1818 the house was sold
to the Wildman family, who restored it in early Gothic style.
The house is open to the public and contains many relics of
the poet, who is buried in Hacknall Church. Newstead is
surrounded by large and elaborate gardens; the huge lake was
used in the 1770s for miniature sea battles. Pretty mock 18th-
century forts still survive on the edge of the lake.

HOLME PIERREPOINT The mansion is now tucked away
behind a Water Sports center. It is a curious house –
part Tudor, part Jacobean and part
Victorian – the remains of a
much larger
building.

*Above right: Wollaton
Hall
Below: Holme
Pierrepont*

D.H. LAWRENCE (1885-1930) was born at Eastwood in Nottinghamshire, the son of a coal miner and a schoolteacher. His novel *Sons and Lovers* in 1913 followed his elopement with his university teacher's German wife Frieda. He produced *The Rainbow* in 1919 and *Women in Love* in 1921.

SHERWOOD FOREST has entered romantic legend as the greenwood with outlaws and splendid trees. Reality was sadly different. The soil was so poor it was not worth cultivating and was left to go wild as scrubby wood and heath, useful only for hunting. The Norman kings made Sherwood a royal forest. After the monasteries of Rufford, Newstead, Welbeck and Worksop were dissolved by Henry VIII, their lands reverted to the aristocracy. This part of Nottinghamshire became known as "The Dukeries" because of the large number of great ducal estates and mansion houses nearby, including Clumber Park, Welbeck Abbey and Thoresby Hall.

RUFFORD ABBEY The Savile family made a mansion out of the old abbey church in the 17th century. The family left in the 1950s and part of the house was demolished. English Heritage now cares for the abbey remains and the outbuildings and grounds have been made into a country park.

THORESBY HALL The great house at Thoresby, which was once the home of the Duke of Kingston, has been rebuilt three times. The present Victorian mansion has now been converted into a hotel.

CLUMBER PARK Another mansion of the Dukeries, this was built by the Duke of Newcastle in the 1760s. It was enlarged in the 19th century but pulled down in 1938 when the future of such great houses seemed bleaker than it does now. Fortunately the large and splendid park, with a serpentine lake, Victorian walled garden, glasshouses and apiary, is in the care of the National Trust.

WORKSOP is a little town that was once the center of a coal field and also part of the Dukeries. Both the coal and the private estates are much less in evidence now. Medieval Worksop clustered round **WORKSOP PRIORY**, a splendid late 12th-century church that stands on the eastern edge of the town. On the southern edge are the fragments of the Duke of Newcastle's great mansion of Worksop Manor. Across the road down a track is a hidden architectural gem: Worksop Manor Lodge – a tall mansion of about 1600 which is now, improbably, a pub.

MANSFIELD has a pleasant center which recalls its Georgian past, but the town became a focus for industry – especially coal and stockings – during the 19th century.

ROBIN HOOD
Robin of Sherwood (above) has become the best-known outlaw hero of the English Middle Ages. It is not certain whether he was an historical figure or whether the various ballads about him that appeared in the 14th and 15th centuries were romantic or political fiction. In either case, his portrayal as a generous outlaw, robbing the rich to give to the poor, has proved enduring. The democratic good fellowship of Robin Hood and his merry men (including Little John and Friar Tuck), as contrasted with the grasping and inhuman ways of the Sheriff of Nottingham, has been taken up countless times in books, films and dramas as a classic commentary on oppressive government.

Above left: Clumber Park Bridge
Left: Clumber Chapel

Worksop Manor stables

Staunton Harold Hall

Over the west door of Staunton Harold is an inscription which begins "In the yeare: 1653 when all things sacred were throughout ye nation Either demollisht or profaned Sir Richard Shirley Barronet Founded this Church whose singular praise it is to have done the best things in ye worst times, and hoped them in the most callamitous [sic]."

LEICESTER CITY MUSEUM AND ART GALLERY ★
The museum in New Walk has good British paintings from the 18th to 20th century. There is also a fine collection of German Expressionist art, and the remains of the famous Rutland dinosaur.

BELGRAVE HALL ★
North of Leicester town center is Belgrave Hall, a small country house built about 1710 for Anne and Edmund Cradock. There are handsome iron entrance gates and the rooms are furnished to illustrate life in a moderately well-to-do 18th-century family.

ASHBY DE LA ZOUCH A pleasant little town concentrated around the gently sloping Market Street. Hidden away at the top end of the street is **ST HELEN'S CHURCH**, a large 15th-century building with Victorian additions, which stands within the original enclosure of **THE CASTLE**, first built in the 12th century by the Earls of Leicester but turned into a very comfortable mansion by Edward IV's friend Lord Hastings in the 1470s. Many of his buildings survive, but they are roofless and ruined.

STAUNTON HAROLD The house and church at Staunton Harold stand next to each other by a lake within the park. The house has a handsome 18th-century exterior that conceals a complicated building dating back to the 15th century. The church is almost unique in being built during the Commonwealth. It is entirely Gothic in style; inside, all the original woodwork survives along with a sumptuous wrought-iron screen by the Derbyshire blacksmith Robert Bakewell, all under a handsome painted ceiling of the 1650s.

LEICESTER

Leicester is a thriving town with a large Asian population and two universities. It has been a trading center since Roman times, and in the 19th century it became the center of the stocking industry. The best preserved reminder of Roman Leicester is the **JEWRY WALL**, a stone and tile wall over 20 feet high which is now thought to have been part of a Roman public bath house. The Saxons incorporated the wall into the porch of the **CHURCH OF ST NICHOLAS** but it now stands by itself. The church also survives and its Anglo-Saxon nave is the oldest building in the town. **ST MARTIN'S CHURCH**, originally the medieval parish church, has been a cathedral since 1927. Immediately opposite the west front is the medieval **GUILDHALL** with its enormous Great Hall.
LEICESTER CASTLE is worth a visit for the **CHURCH OF ST MARY DE CASTRO** and the former **COURT HOUSE**, built within the Norman Great Hall. Just outside the Castle enclosure is the

EWARKE, with the NEWARKE HOUSES
USEUM formed from two early buildings.
AKHAM is now once again the county
wn of Rutland. It is an attractive place,
anding near the huge man-made lake
nown as Rutland Water, and possesses one nationally
mportant building. The main walls of OAKHAM CASTLE have
ow been reduced to grassy banks, but at its center survives
e best preserved early great hall of any English castle, dating
om about 1190. Both inside and out the form is very like that
 a church nave. This is most evident in the interior, with its
one arcades, although the walls covered with horseshoes tell
 different story. Since the late Middle Ages the Lord of the
anor of Oakham required every nobleman to forfeit a
orseshoe on his first visit to the town. To judge by the shoes,
me of the horses must have been larger than elephants. On
e edge of the castle enclosure are ALL SAINTS CHURCH,
hose tall spire dominates the town, and the OLD GRAMMAR
CHOOL building of 1584.

PPINGHAM Best known for its school; the original building of
584 still survives next to the church, while the 19th- and 20th-
entury school buildings are grouped together on the edge of
is little town very like the Oxford and Cambridge colleges.
YDDINGTON village, just south of Uppingham, contains the
EDE HOUSE, built in the 15th century as a palace for the
ishop of Lincoln and then converted into an almshouse, or
edehouse, for old men. STANFORD CHURCH, just across the
ounty boundary in Northamptonshire, is worth a detour to
e the outstanding stained glass and monuments inside.

Above: Lyddington Bede
Above left: the Great Hall, Oakham Castle

STANFORD HALL
This large and spacious William and Mary house is in an ample park next to the River Avon. The house was begun in 1697 and finished about 30 years later. The interior, with its paneled rooms, has changed little since the 1730s. Percy Pilcher, the first man in England to fly, was killed when his machine crashed at Stanford; a replica of his plane is in the stable block. Stanford also boasts a collection of Jacobite portrait and relics.

Stanford Hall ballroom (left) and library (above)

*Below and center:
Lichfield Cathedral
Below right: Hoar
Cross Church*

*Opposite pag
Sandon Orange
(left) and Chea
sedilia (righ*

SAMUEL JOHNSON
(1709-84), better
known as Dr Johnson,
is chiefly famous as
the compiler of the
first *English
Dictionary* and for the
forceful comments on
his contemporaries
faithfully recorded in
the *Life of Dr
Johnson*, written by
his friend and
admirer James
Boswell. Johnson was
born in Lichfield, the
son of a bookseller, in
whose stock he read
widely. After Oxford
he tried teaching,
married and in 1737
settled in London,
where he earned a
living by writing,
although he suffered
intermittently from
physical and mental
illness and from
poverty. His
Dictionary appeared
in 1755; in 1765 he
issued an edition of
Shakespeare; and in
1778 he embarked on
his *Lives of the
English Poets*.

ALTON TOWERS
Now best known as a
colossal leisure park,
at the center of Alton
Towers is the ruined
shell of the vast
Gothic mansion
house of the Talbots.
The garden has also
survived more or less
intact, with
ornamental trees and
garden buildings that
include an elaborate
glass conservatory.
There is also a lovely
pagoda fountain.

LICHFIELD

Lichfield has a long history and a medieval street pattern but
it is visually a Georgian town, which is appropriate for the
home of Dr Johnson. The red sandstone **CATHEDRAL OF
ST MARY AND ST CHAD** ★ with its three conspicuous spires ha
its origins in Bishop Hedda's church of 700, but nothing is le
of that, nor of the Norman cathedral. Most of the present
building belongs to the period 1220–80; the easternmost par
were added before 1350. The west front is richly carved,
although all the figures were replaced in the 19th century.
The cathedral, the smallest but perhaps the most graceful in
England, and its precinct are separated from the rest of the
town by two pools or meres.

TAMWORTH CASTLE, in the center of this much rebuilt town, i
remarkably well preserved. It still has a stone keep on top of
the tall castle mound, and several of the other castle building
including the Jacobean great hall, remain intact.

WALL is the curious modern name for the Roman settlement
of Letocetum, which was an important staging post on the
Roman military route to North Wales. The site has been
excavated and there is a good little museum.

HOLY ANGELS CHURCH ★, Hoar Cross is a fine church by
George Bodley, one of the leading Victorian church
architects. It was built between 1872 and 1876 to
commemorate Hugo Ingram of Hoar Cross Hall. The church
is all of stone, in the Decorated style. The interior with its
soaring chancel is furnished with extreme richness.

STAFFORD is an ancient town which has been a manufacturin
center since the late Middle Ages: first wool, then shoes, the
engineering. It is also an attractive place with good public
buildings, including the handsome Shire Hall of 1795 and
plenty of 17th- and 18th-century houses. The tiny church of
St Chad has superb Norman stonework.

SHUGBOROUGH is famous for its house, 18th-century park and fine collection of garden buildings. The house, which belonged to the Anson family, is a building of the 1690s enlarged in the 1750s with money from Admiral George Anson (who captured a Spanish Treasure Galleon) and again in the 1790s by Samuel Wyatt. He added the giant colonnade across the main front and cased the whole house in slate painted to look like stone. The interior decoration is mostly by his plasterer Joseph Rose. In the park are a host of garden buildings: the Chinese Pavilion dates from Admiral Anson's time, but the Tower of the Winds, the Doric Temple and Lantern of Demosthenes are all by the connoisseur architect James "Athenian" Stuart and are among the very first buildings in England in the Greek Revival style.

IZAAK WALTON'S COTTAGE is a small timber-framed and whitewashed cottage which was given to the town of Stafford by Izaak Walton, who died in 1683. Walton is best known as the author of *The Compleat Angler*, with its reflections on the pleasures of fishing; the cottage is devoted to his memory.

INGESTRE HALL is a brick Jacobean house which has suffered many alterations, especially in the 19th century. **ST MARY'S CHURCH**, which stands close to the Hall, is dated 1676 and is almost certainly by Sir Christopher Wren – it is very like a City church with elaborate plaster ceilings.

SANDON PARK is a large mid-Victorian mansion in the Jacobean style, designed by William Burn for the Earl of Harrowby, with a splendid Victorian conservatory. The village has lots of Arts and Crafts houses.

BARLASTON HALL is an exquisite Georgian villa of the 1750s, probably designed by Sir Robert Taylor and spectacularly sited on top of a steep rise.

Barlaston Hall

ST GILES CHURCH CHEADLE ★
This church with its very tall very thin spire, is the masterpiece of A.W. Pugin, prophet of the Gothic Revival in England. He wanted to make Cheadle "a perfect revival of an English parish church of the time of Edward I" and his client, Lord Shrewsbury, had the money to make this possible. Architecture and fittings are of the best and richest. Next to the church stands the School and Convent, also by Pugin.

Shugborough, painted by Nicholas Dall, c. 1768

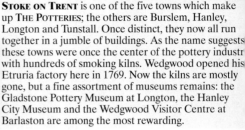

Gladstone Pottery Museum

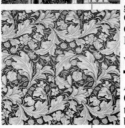

*Top: Wightwick Manor
Above: Leicester
wallpaper by J.H.
Dearle from Morris &
Co in the Morning
Room at Wightwick*

STOKE ON TRENT is one of the five towns which make up **THE POTTERIES**; the others are Burslem, Hanley, Longton and Tunstall. Once distinct, they now all run together in a jumble of buildings. As the name suggests these towns were once the center of the pottery industry with hundreds of smoking kilns. Wedgwood opened his Etruria factory here in 1769. Now the kilns are mostly gone, but a fine assortment of museums remains: the Gladstone Pottery Museum at Longton, the Hanley City Museum and the Wedgwood Visitor Centre at Barlaston are among the most rewarding.

WOLVERHAMPTON

After his defeat at the Battle of Worcester in 1651 King Charles I took refuge at **MOSELEY OLD HALL**. The small timber-framed manor house looks rather different now because it was encased in purple brick in the 1870s, but the interior has altered little and the rooms have been furnished in an appropriate manner.

WESTON PARK, together with its stables, the parish church and the impressive buildings of the Home Farm all stand together on the edge of the enormous park. The house was built for the Wilbrahams in 1671, probably to the designs of Lady Wilbraham herself; she also designed the stables and church. In the 18th century the Bridgeman family made many alterations. The furnishings are of a high standard, including a Gobelins Boucher tapestry room, and there are many superb paintings.

CHILLINGTON HALL has been with the Giffard family since the 12th century. The house is Georgian but its layout was dictated by an earlier house. The main front with its heavy portico is by Sir John Soane who carried out major alterations in the 1760s and made a saloon by putting a domed roof over what had been the great hall of the Tudor house. The park was landscaped by Capability Brown and is an excellent example of his informal landscaping.

WIGHTWICK MANOR ★ is a Victorian house with decorations by various artists of the Pre-Raphaelite movement. The house was built in the late 1880s for Mr Mander, a paint manufacturer, in a brick and timber style copying local examples. The interior decoration was done by Morris & Co. and fabrics and wallpapers designed by William Morris survive in almost every room; there is also stained glass by Kempe, tiles by de Morgan and much art metalwork. Against this background are paintings by Burne-Jones and his contemporaries and plenty of the Jacobean furniture, Persian rugs and the blue and white china that was popular with the "advanced" taste of the 1890s.

Ironbridge Gorge

IRONBRIDGE GORGE is a dramatic narrowing of the River Severn where it joins a valley called Coalbrookdale. In the 18th century it was a center of the British iron industry and the whole area is now a collection of museums devoted to industry, ceramics, decorative arts and living history, all bringing to life this crucial part of the Industrial Revolution. At the center of it all is the **IRON BRIDGE**, built in 1778; the first large bridge in the world to be built wholly of iron.

At **LILLESHALL ABBEY** are the extensive and evocative ruins of an abbey of Arroasian canons founded in 1148. The chancel is Norman, the crossing and nave Transitional.

BOSCOBEL HOUSE is small timber-framed house, famous as the refuge of King Charles I after the Battle of Worcester. For one day of his stay here the King hid in a nearby oak tree. Although the original "Royal Oak" has been carried away piecemeal by souvenir hunters, the house itself has been restored to tell the story. Just south of it lies **WHITELADIES**, the ruins of a small priory of Augustinian canonesses.

BUILDWAS ABBEY nestles within a loop of the River Severn, its cloisters between the church and the river. The monks were of the Cistercian order, whose buildings were austere and without much ornament, but beautifully placed. The massive nave walls and the crossing are well preserved.

Wenlock Priory

BENTHALL HALL is a late Tudor mansion built between 1580 and 1618 for the Benthall family. It has pleasant paneled rooms, several of which contain the rare Caughley porcelain made in the district in the late 18th century.

MUCH WENLOCK is a pleasant little town with a large and picturesque medieval dwelling house – the Prior's Lodge – dwarfed by the ruined remains of a Cluniac priory.

BRIDGNORTH has a spectacular site on a tall sandstone cliff above the River Severn. The broad high street is lined with Georgian houses; at its center stands the town hall of 1652.

MORVILLE HALL is a small Elizabethan house, so similar to Wilderhope and Shipton ▲ *374* that it must be by the same builder. The interior was made more comfortable in the 18th century.

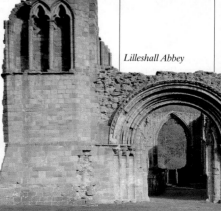

Lilleshall Abbey

Ludlow Castle

WILDERHOPE MANOR is a gray stone Tudor house hidden away in the Corvedale valley, miles from anywhere. Now a Youth Hostel, the interior is still of interest for its original wooden spiral staircase and plasterwork with the initials of the builders, Francis and Ellen Smallman.

SHIPTON HALL nearby is cousin to Wilderhope and dates from the 1580s. It has a pretty setting at the top of a rise, with the stables on one side and the parish church on the other. The house was "modernized" in the mid-18th century and given a handsome Georgian hall and staircase.

THE WHITE HOUSE at Aston Munslow is a small farmhouse that has evolved steadily since the 14th century. The farm outbuildings shelter an excellent collection of farm vehicles and implements from hay-wains to billhooks.

WHITTON COURT
This attractive house was enlarged in Tudor times and again in the 17th century. The interior has much good 17th-century paneling and a handsome Tudor screen in its great hall.

DUDMASTON HALL ★ (below left) was built about 1700, a substantial red-brick house which was modernized in the Regency period when a new main stair was inserted. The house contains both period furniture and good collections of Dutch flowerpieces and 20th-century art. There is also a dramatic garden, laid out in a steep dingle falling down to a large lake.

LUDLOW ★ is one of the most unspoilt towns in England, well known through A.E. Housman's *Shropshire Lad* and more recently distinguished for a number of excellent restaurants. The town's hilltop site makes the red sandstone tower of the **CHURCH OF ST LAURENCE** visible for miles. Near the church and the pretty market place are the impressive ruins of **LUDLOW CASTLE**, which was one of the strongest in the Welsh Marches and in the 15th century became the seat of the seat of the Lord President of Wales. The buildings of the town are an attractive mix of black-and-white timber-framed – including the famous Feathers Inn – and Georgian.

STOKESAY CASTLE is a romantic fortified manor house built just when the English were turning from castles to houses. Attached to a small 12th-century stone tower is a great hall built for Laurence de Ludlow, a cloth merchant who bought Stokesay in 1281. He also added a solar and a second tower, but since then the only addition has been the decorative little gatehouse built in 1590.

"Flamenco Dancers" by Sonia Delaunay, 1916, at Dudmaston

Stokesay Castle

Far left: Stokesay
Castle gatehouse
Left: Attingham Park

HODNETT HALL GARDENS

There are 60 acres of woodland shrubs and flowers at Hodnett, which have been carefully planted to give the garden a changing character from early spring to late autumn.

Left: The Hon. Henrietta Hill, Marchioness of Ailesbury, by Sir Thomas Lawrence, hanging in the drawing room at Attingham Park
Far left: Dining room, Attingham Park

The **LONG MYND** is a ridge which rises abruptly to the south west of Shrewsbury; open, wild and barren, with rocks and mountain pasture but with rich and fertile valleys folded away among the hills. Tucked into the western side of the Mynd is CHURCH STRETTON, very much a Victorian hillside resort, from where a lane leads to CARDING MILL VALLEY with its spectacular scenery and challenging walks. Across the Mynd toward the border with Wales is the little town of CLUN, rising steeply from the medieval bridge of the river and with a spectacular ruined CASTLE looking out over open country.

SHREWSBURY Like many of the best English towns, this stands on a hill, which gives it a memorable skyline of spires and towers. The center was built within a large loop of the river and a great deal of Tudor Shrewsbury still remains: an area of twisting streets known as "shuts", given picturesque names like Dogpole, Wyle Cop and Grope Lane. At the neck of the loop are the ruins of the castle with its Norman walls. Among the highlights of the town are the great CHURCH OF ST MARY ★, the circular Georgian CHURCH OF ST CHAD, the old buildings of Shrewsbury School (now the LIBRARY) and the brick and timber-framed ROWLEY'S HOUSE (now a museum), built at the end of the 1500s for the town's richest family.

ATTINGHAM PARK is an impressive house built for the 1st Lord Berwick in the 1780s and altered by the architect John Nash in 1805. The park was landscaped by Humphry Repton in the 1790s. The handsome main rooms, with excellent original neoclassical decoration by George Steuart, are arranged in two main apartments either side of the entrance hall. Beyond the hall is Nash's picture gallery with its iron and glass ceiling, and his main staircase with reeded wooden walls meant to look like drapery. Across the main road on the other side of Atcham village can be glimpsed a small Italianate villa by John Nash called CRONKHILL, which was built for the estate steward.

WALCOT

Beyond the southern end of the Mynd lies Walcot, a large redbrick house in splendid grounds with a large lake in front, which was built for Clive of India in the 1760s to designs by Sir William Chambers.

Clun Castle

Haughmond Abbey

PITCHFORD HALL
Built around 1570, Pitchford Hall is a fine example of a large Elizabethan timber-framed house with gables. In the grounds a huge lime tree bears an extraordinary and elaborate Tree House built in about 1750.

HAUGHMOND ABBEY was an abbey of Augustinian canons founded in about 1135. It lies with its east boundary against Haughmond Hill, and some of the walls have their lower parts cut out of the solid rock. The Abbey church has almost completely disappeared, but other parts of the monastery complex survive to a good height.

CONDOVER HALL is a large and handsome Elizabethan house, built of stone in the 1590s. The interior contains some good 18th-century decoration.

WROXETER is the fourth largest Roman city in Britain. Much of it has now been excavated and remains are impressive, especially those of the Bath House. Finds from the excavations are displayed in a museum.

AROUND CHESHIRE

CHESTER ★ has kept its medieval walls; the full circuit is nearly 2 miles in circumference, and within them are a splendid cathedral and lots of half-timbered houses. It is a city of colors, with red sandstone and black-and-white half timbering. In the center many houses have covered galleries for pedestrians at first-floor level, known as THE ROWS, which make Chester unique in England. The CATHEDRAL is red sandstone; although a whole series of Victorian

A folly in Hawkstone Park

Above and top: Chester Cathedral

Beeston Castle

restorations added spindly towers and pinnacles to the exterior, the inside is impressive, especially the choir of 1260–1320. The most remarkable thing about the nave is that the north side was built almost a hundred years after the south side. CHESTER CASTLE, founded by William the Conqueror, was almost entirely replaced in the 1790s by a group of handsome public buildings by the architect Thomas Harrison. These are major monuments of the Greek Revival style, especially the entrance gate, which recalls Berlin's Brandenburg Gate, and the Shire Hall with its semi-circular front.

MAIDEN CASTLE at Broxton is an Iron Age hill fort built on a promontory of land and defended by two massive earth ramparts, 7 feet high in places ● *68*.

ECKFORTON CASTLE has a splendid site challenging the medieval Beeston Castle ▲ *378*, but is wholly Victorian – a romantic fortress designed by Anthony Salvin and built by Lord Tollemache in the late 1840s as the centerpiece of his huge estate. Everything about the building is convincing: massive stonework, winding stairways, vaulted ceilings, huge stone chimneypieces. The wonder is that it was ever intended to be a comfortable gentleman's residence.

BEESTON CASTLE stands majestically on an isolated rocky crag which forms part of the defences. The inner parts of the castle, which was begun in the 1220s, are very ruined apart from the gatehouse, but seven towers of the outer walls still stand. Beeston was a royal castle until the Civil War.

NANTWICH was a salt town. Together with Middlewich and Northwich it grew rich from the salt industry which flourished in Roman times, but salt-making had ceased here by the 19th century. ST MARY'S CHURCH ★ is an impressive building with an unusual octagonal crossing tower and a very elaborate vaulted ceiling in the chancel. The church stands in the middle of the town, with pleasant streets radiating from the churchyard. An inscription carved on the outside of CHURCHE'S MANSION in Hospital Street reads "Rychard Churche and Margerye Churche his wife Mai IIII Thomas Clease made this worke, anno dni MCCCCLXXVII in the XVIII yeare of the reane of our noble queene elesabeth." The timber house that Mr Clease built for Richard Church in 1577 is an excellent example of a Tudor merchant's house, adorned with the elaborate timber patterns that were universally popular in the West Midlands at that time.

HAWKSTONE PARK
The Park belongs to Hawkstone House, an interesting Georgian building. It was made by Sir Richard Hill, mostly in the 1790s, and is a good example of late Georgian landscaping, making use of dramatic natural features and a genuine medieval ruined castle to produce something thrilling and romantic.

IRON-AGE FORT
Old Oswestry, on the edge of the town of the same name, is a magnificent Iron Age hill fort, nearly 40 acres in extent, with three huge earthen banks later enclosed by an enormous double rampart.

Little Moreton Hall

CHOLMONDELEY CASTLE
Cholmondeley is an early 19th-century house in the castle style by Robert Smirke, architect of the British Museum, built in a good position with a view over the lake and fine landscaping. There was an earlier house, of which the chapel still survives with a complete set of fittings from the Civil War period.

St Mary's Church, Acton

DORFOLD HALL is a Jacobean house built for Ralph Wilbraham in 1616, of smoky red brick with the patterns known as diaperwork. Although the builders made an effort to produce a symmetrical main front, the rest of the house looks a bit jumbled, and some of the interior rooms were redone in the late 18th century.

ACTON has a church that is the usual English mixtu of medieval work and thorough Victorian restoration, but it contains some outstanding monuments to the Mainwaring family and also som carved Norman stonework.

LITTLE MORETON HALL ★ is perhaps the best-know timber-framed building in England; the elaborate patterns of its walls appear on National Trust tea towels in thousands of homes. The higgledy-piggledy parts of the house are grouped round a courtyard. Across from the entrance is the great hall and the rooms either side, completed about 1480. Two bulging bay windows were added in 1559, as a carved inscription records. The rest of the house, including the front range with its long gallery crazily perched on top, were finished by 1580. Since then littl has been changed.

KNUTSFORD is an attractive town, with a Georgian parish church and a nicely winding main street, whose most conspicuous building – looking like a mad escapee from Gaudi's Barcelona – is the King's Coffee House of 1907.

TATTON PARK ★ has a calm, elegant stone exterior which yiel no clue to the fact that the western half was built in the 1790s by the architect Samuel Wyatt and the eastern half 20 years later by his nephew Lewis Wyatt. The Egerton family spent much money decorating and furnishing the interior, and the effect is still rich. Most of the furniture was made for the house by Gillows of Lancaster, the leading furniture makers of northern England. It contains an important collection of Old Masters, including Chardin's *La Gouvernante*, and three versions of B.W. Leader's *Manchester Ship Canal*.

NETHER ALDERLY MILL is a large watermill dating from the 15th century, with two overshot waterwheels. The Victorian machinery has been fully restored to working order and the mill is operated regularly.

CAPESTHORNE HALL has a very striking spiky silhouette, the product of two rebuildings in the last century. The handsome main rooms contain a varied collection of furniture.

GAWSWORTH HALL is a picturesque, rambling timber-framed house mostly built in the 15th century and originally twice as big as it is now. There is one long show front with a splendid three-story bay window.

ADLINGTON HALL comprises an attractive mixture of brick and timber buildings grouped round a quadrangle. They are all the work of various members of the Legh family who have been at Adlington since 1315. Most spectacular is the great hall, completed in 1505 but improved with larger windows in 1581. The hall has an elaborate hammerbeam roof, with a "ceilure" (decorative canopy) at the high end and a fine 17th-century organ by "Father" Smith. The grand stable block was added in 1749 as part of improvements, which included the 1757 south front with its ungainly portico.

LYME PARK is a very large, splendid stone building, partly 16th, partly 18th century, with some impressive rooms. The Tudor house of Sir Piers Legh is still standing, but is hardly visible because it was refaced in stone by the architect Giacomo Leoni in 1725 when he was called in to modernize it. He added the west side and refaced the courtyard walls to look like an Italian palace. The square tower was added in 1816 to house the servants. Some of the rooms are Tudor, some early Georgian, and there are important collections of portraits (many lent by the National Portrait Gallery) and English clocks. The garden has a conservatory and the deer park is enormous with a windswept tower called the Cage, also rebuilt by Leoni, to observe them from.

STYAL QUARRY BANK MILL was built in the wooded valley of the River Bollin in 1784 by Samuel Gregg. The river drove the massive wheel, and labor was supplied by pauper children, who lived in the apprentice house. The original building still survives, although the mill was enlarged several times. It has been restored to working order and is displayed to explain the growth of the textile industry.

DUNHAM MASSEY HALL ★ is a large, plain red-brick Georgian house of 1732, built on the site of a Tudor house for George Booth, 2nd Earl of Warrington. The house contains excellent collections of Georgian paintings, Stuart and early Georgian furniture, exceptional Huguenot silver and a famous carving of the *Crucifixion* by Grinling Gibbons. Most of the state rooms were renovated in the early 1900s under the direction of Percy Macquoid, a furniture expert who took care to provide appropriate decorations.

Lyme Park

TABLEY HOUSE
This Palladian mansion was designed by John Carr of York for the Leicester family (later Lords de Tabley) and built in 1761-7 to replace Tabley Old Hall, which stood on an island in the lake. It is a handsome red-brick building with fine rooms containing furniture by Gillow and Chippendale. The 17th-century chapel was rebuilt in 1927, but the college chapel interior was well restored.

Top left: Tatton Park
Top right: Dunham Massey
Above left and right: Lyme Park

▲ DERBYSHIRE

Below: Haddon Hall
Bottom: Peveril Castle

THE PEAK DISTRICT NATIONAL PARK
This area covers a large region that stretches from Ashbourne in the south to the craggy and remote High Peak District west of Sheffield. Characteristic of the area are the buildings and field walls made with gray limestone.

Buxton Crescent

DOWN THROUGH DERBYSHIRE

BUXTON has been a spa since Roman times and the Buxton water still provides a healthy income for the local council. In the 18th century the Duke of Devonshire, who owned most of the land, decided to turn Buxton into a fashionable center and paid for the building of the handsome BUXTON CRESCENT in 1780. Designed by the Yorkshire architect John Carr, it originally contained hotels and lodgings for those who had come to take the waters. The Crescent and the gardens that rise opposite form the center of this small town, which hosts a festival each summer. Poole's Cavern, outside the town, is a spectacular succession of natural caves.

PEVERIL CASTLE, begun by William Peveril, who was William the Conqueror's bailiff for the locality, was an immensely strong castle paid for with revenue from the local lead mines. Although ruined since the 17th century, it is still spectacular: the walls of the keep still survive at their original height, and the building dominates the village of Castleton below it.

BAKEWELL is a cheerful little town on the River Wye, whose church has a large collection of carved Saxon stone fragments

EYAM is famous as the village that nobly shut itself off from the rest of the world in 1666 when the plague had been brought here from London. There are some nice houses round the churchyard. Set back from the main street behind a formal garden is EYAM HALL, built in 1676.

HADDON HALL ★ is a gray stone house of the Middle Ages: a romantic jumble of battlemented walls, towers and chimneys, built round two small courtyards and standing on a wooded slope above the river. It was abandoned by the Manners family in 1700 but was carefully restored by the 9th Duke of Rutland in the 1910s and 1920s. The kitchens still have medieval bread cupboards and troughs for salting meat.

DOVEDALE is one of the most famous of the beautiful dales that make Derbyshire so popular with walkers.

MATLOCK is a curious town, being made up of a series of almost separate villages. One of these villages, Matlock Bath, became quite popular in the 18th and 19th centuries as a spa. The landscape, with its tall cliffs, is spectacular and from many parts of the town the Victorian folly of Riber Castle dominates the skyline.

CROMFORD Downriver from Matlock is Cromford, where Richard Arkwright started the first successful water-powered cotton-spinning mill in 1771. His mill still survives and is being restored. Arkwright also built a village for his workers, and other large mills along the valley. His partner Jedediah Strutt developed another important industrial center at **BELPER**, where the great sluices that channeled the water for the mills can still be seen. Strutt was also responsible for the **NORTH MILL** of 1804, which now contains a small museum.

DERBY

Derby is still a large and thriving town, although it is no longer the great center of railway building it once was, and many of its Georgian buildings have gone. ALL SAINTS CHURCH, now a cathedral, has a large 16th-century west tower, but the rest is a handsome Georgian structure by James Gibbs, containing Bess of Hardwick's tomb ▲ 382. Sloping

down from the cathedral is ST MARY'S GATE, which has fine houses and the massive COURT HOUSE (1660s) at the bottom, while the MUSEUM has a remarkable collection of paintings and drawings by Joseph Wright of Derby.

Dovedale

KEDLESTON HALL ★ The parkland here sweeps up from the lake to the long main front of the house built for Sir Nathaniel Curzon, 1st Lord Scarsdale, between 1759 and 1765. The first architect was Matthew Brettingham, and "Athenian" Stuart designed the great Marble Hall, but before the house was finished Robert Adam took over. He designed a completely new and highly original south front based on a Roman triumphal arch, and reorganized the interior, with a view to showing off Lord Scarsdale's important collection of pictures, many of which are set into the walls. Most of the rooms have Adam ceilings and many have furniture and metalwork by him

*Below left: The fireplace in the Marble Hall, Kedleston
Below right: Garden arbor, Melbourne Hall*

as well. The park was what he was first invited to design, and contains a variety of garden buildings, including a delightful Fishing Pavilion and Boat House (recently restored).

DALE ABBEY benefits from a delightful site below sandstone cliffs; but little remains of the medieval abbey founded here in about 1200 other than the footings of the walls and the great arch of the chancel east window.

REPTON SCHOOL dominates the small town of the same name and incorporates many of the buildings of the Priory, which was turned over to educational use in 1557 by Sir John Port; but long before that Repton was the capital of the Kingdom of South Mercia. A monastery was founded here in the 7th century. The parish church of ST WYSTAN probably incorporates some of the monastery church; the crypt at the east end, now partly underground, was built around AD 800.

A Robert Adam design for the wall of a book room at Kedleston, which was never executed.

MELBOURNE is a pleasant little town with a very fine Norman church. MELBOURNE HALL nearby is not a large house, but it has a handsome front of 1725 which looks down over the sloping formal garden ★, flanked by great yew hedges to a formal pond. Beyond the water is a small wrought-iron arbor or summer seat, made in the early 18th century by the famous smith Robert Bakewell.

BESS OF HARDWICK'S HOUSES

Hardwick Hall

Hardwick Hall ★ is a monument to a remarkable architect and a remarkable woman. The architect was Robert Smythson, the greatest English designer of his day, and the woman was Elizabeth, Countess of Shrewsbury – or Bess of Hardwick – four times married and great builder. Chatsworth ★ was originally built by Bess's second husband, Sir William Cavendish. It is now one of the very few great private houses in England where the splendor of the rooms and the extraordinarily rich collection of drawings, paintings, objects and furniture give at least a passing impression of the enormous wealth of the great ducal families.

Seadog table in the State Withdrawing Room at Hardwick Hall

HARDWICK HALL

The Old Hall still survives, in ruins, but after 1590 Bess set about building a brand new house a short distance away. The new house is very tall, and its buff stone walls are pierced by huge windows. Few Elizabethan houses look as crisp and modern. At the top of the house are the high state rooms, including the spectacular High Great Chamber and Long Gallery, and on the floor below the smaller and more comfortable family apartments. The Flemish tapestry above (c.16th century) hangs in the Green Velvet Room.

Elizabeth of Hardwick, att. Rowland Lockey, 1592, Hardwick Hall

CHATSWORTH (above) is a great classical house in enormous grounds. The first Chatsworth was Elizabethan, but each of its four sides was rebuilt in turn between 1687 and 1707 by the 1st Duke of Devonshire. Many of its rooms still retain their early Georgian character, with painted ceilings and carved decoration – most notably the State Apartments, which are of overpowering splendor. Chatsworth has exceptionally fine collections of paintings and furniture and a number of *trompe l'oeil* panels, of which the violin (left) is an example.

SUDBURY HALL ★ is a comfortable red-brick house whose rooms have some of the richest Charles II decoration in England. Building started in about 1662 and was finished by 1700. The exterior is an odd mixture of Jacobean features (mullioned windows and a two-storey porch) with the tall roof typical of the years after the Civil War. The rooms follow the familiar Jacobean arrangement of great hall, several parlors and first-floor long gallery, but the plasterwork by Bradbury and Pettifer and woodcarving by Edward Pearce (with an overmantel by Grinling Gibbons) are exceptional.

CHESTERFIELD has an enormous market place in the center of town. The **CHURCH OF ST MARY AND ALL SAINTS** is nationally famous because its lead and timber spire has warped into a comically twisted shape. The church beneath the spire is a large, handsome building.

Top: Sutton Scarsdale Hall
Center: Bolsover Castle
Above: Pillar Chamber and fireplace at Bolsover

SUTTON SCARSDALE is a dramatic ruin facing a slope that was once an open-cast coal mine. The remaining shell is mostly the house built in the 1720s for the Earl of Scarsdale. Shreds of decoration cling to the walls, but some rooms were exported to the Philadelphia Museum in the US.

BOLSOVER CASTLE lies on the same ridge as Hardwick, but overlooks an industrial landscape rather than a country estate. The fantastic house of the Cavendishes roughly follows the outline of the earlier castle, but the buildings date mostly from the 17th century and many are now ruined. The Little Keep is a pretend medieval castle; the architect was once again Robert Smythson. Built between 1612 and 1620, the keep is full of small rooms whose rich ornamentation compensates for the lack of furniture. The main living range stretching away from the Keep is roofless, yet has extraordinary decoration, and there is also a huge and handsome Riding School (the Cavendishes were mad about horses and dressage).

WINGFIELD MANOR at South Wingfield is the ruined mansion of Ralph, Lord Cromwell, Treasurer of England. It was built in 1440-55 round two courtyards. The buildings are of the highest quality. In the 1770s the house was abandoned but during the last century it was absorbed into a working farm.

Chesterfield Church of St Mary and All Saints

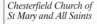

THE NORTH EAST
Jane Hatcher

1. Halifax   2. Ilkley   3. Huddersfield   4. Sheffield   5. Leeds   6. Fountains Abbey

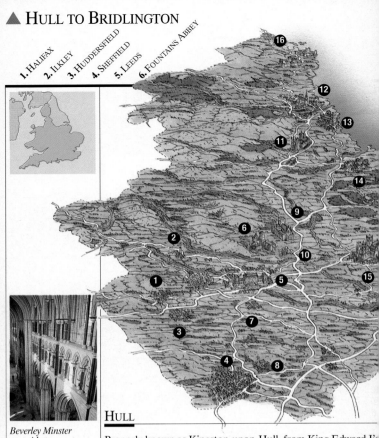

Hull

Beverley Minster east-side transept

MUSEUM OF SLAVERY Wilberforce House and adjacent Georgian houses now hold exhibitions on the history of slavery and the campaign for its abolishment. It is the only museum of its kind in Britain.

BEVERLEY MINSTER is a medieval gem, with double transepts and a twin-towered West front.

Properly known as Kingston-upon-Hull, from King Edward I's acquisition in 1293, Hull's maritime history is epitomized by the handsome Trinity House complex, still catering for young and old with a school and almshouse. **WILBERFORCE HOUSE,** a merchant's house of *c.* 1660, was the birthplace of anti-slavery campaigner William Wilberforce in 1759. **MAISTER HOUSE** of 1744-5, a Georgian merchant's residence, has a fine staircase with wrought-iron balustrade by Robert Bakewell. The finest Decorated church in the area is at **PATRINGTON**.

The **HUMBER BRIDGE,** spanning the wide river estuary, leads to Barton-on-Humber, where **ST PETER'S** incorporates an Anglo-Saxon church consisting of a fine tower with pilaster strip decoration, flanked by west and east annexes. **NORMANBY PARK** is a Regency house of 1825-30 by Sir Robert Smirke, an interesting exercise in the assemblage of cubes, with a restored Victorian garden.

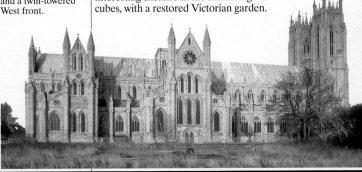

THORNTON ABBEY gatehouse is a tour de force of medieval pomp, having been enlarged to provide luxurious quarters for the abbot. Its licence to crenelate was granted in 1382, and the addition of an outer barbican made it even more ostentatious.

Above: Thornton Abbey, a fragment of the Decorated-Gothic Chapter House

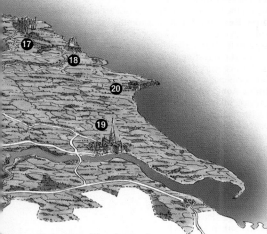

BURTON CONSTABLE HALL is mostly Elizabethan, in brick with stone dressings, with ogee-topped turrets and large mullioned-and-transomed windows. Inside, most rooms have been Georgianized – with some decoration in a Jacobean Revival style – but there is a magnificent Long Gallery.

BEVERLEY MINSTER ★ Internal details include delightful musicians still playing their instruments along the nave wall canopies, and in the choir the ogee-canopied Percy Tomb is a sumptuous example of Decorated intricacy. The choir stalls of 1520, a fine work by the Ripon School of Woodcarvers, have misericord seats carved with intriguing secular scenes. The north wall of the north transept, then leaning badly, was pushed back into verticality 1716-20 by a timber frame with a screw mechanism which could be tightened as it succeeded in its task. This ingenious contraption was devised by the York carpenter-architect William Thornton in conjunction with the more famous Nicholas Hawksmoor. The latter also designed the choir pavement, a dramatic geometric pattern in black and white marble. Another set of fascinating misericords can be found in **ST MARY'S CHURCH ★**, rebuilt by the guilds of Beverley – one of medieval England's most prosperous towns – after damage caused by the central tower's collapse in 1520.

SLEDMERE HOUSE represents generations of building by the Sykes family, including a 1751 reconstruction, 1780s additions, and a rehabilitation after a fire in 1911. The interior looks convincingly Georgian as the original plaster molds were used. There is a grand staircase, a recently regilded library, some fine portraits, including Romney's *Sir Christopher and Lady Sykes Stepping Out*, and an amazing Turkish bath room.

BURTON AGNES HALL (below) Built in 1601-10 by the great northern Elizabethan architect Robert Smythson, this building is entered through a gatehouse and by a yew avenue. The main front is meticulously symmetrical, even to the extent of having twin tower porches. A screens passage leads into a great hall, where a magnificent screen is carved with the Twelve Tribes of Israel, and the alabaster overmantel with the Parable of

the Wise and Foolish Virgins. An inventive staircase, supported on paired newel posts connected by round arches, rises past rooms hung with an excellent collection of Impressionist paintings (unusual if not unique in a English country house) to an elegant Long Gallery (above).

387

BRODSWORTH HALL (drawing room, right; South Hall, far right) was built 1861-3 as a house in which to entertain guests and display the white marble Italian sculptures collected by Charles Sabine Thellusson.

PAINE'S MANSION HOUSE (above) Doncaster has one exceptionally fine Georgian building, the Mansion House of 1748, designed by the architect James Paine as a place for the mayor to entertain on a lavish scale, and indeed for him to live in during his year of office. It is a handsome Palladian villa, surrounded by other lesser buildings, with a fine Venetian window flanked by pedimented windows lighting the first-floor banqueting room, which has exquisite Italianate plasterwork.

"A Convalescent" (c. 1876) by James Jacques Joseph Tissot, Mappin Art Gallery, Sheffield

DONCASTER The town's large parish church, dedicated to England's patron saint, St George, was rebuilt in 1854-8 by the great Victorian church architect Sir George Gilbert Scott. Another Victorian architect who had a hand in the design was Sir Edmund Beckett, later Lord Grimthorpe, a native of Doncaster who also designed clocks – most famously the one on the tower of the Houses of Parliament, in London.
MONK BRETTON PRIORY was founded in 1154 as a Cluniac house, an order rare in Yorkshire, but after a number of disputes it became Benedictine in the late 13th century. The most interesting parts of the coal-blackened ruins are the 15th-century gatehouse and the prior's quarters, which show evidence of frequent upgrading and embellishment.
ROCHE ABBEY (below right) near Rotherham is, by way of contrast, built of almost dazzlingly white magnesian limestone. A Cistercian monastery, founded in 1147, its water courses form a conspicuous part of the design of the claustral buildings. The transepts provide an interestingly early example of the Early English style of Gothic architecture. So spectacular is the site that the ruins were incorporated into Capability Brown's 18th-century landscaping scheme for the nearby country house of Sandbeck Park.

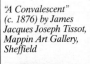

BRODSWORTH HALL is less Italianate than Italian, being designed by an architect from Lucca in Tuscany who never visited the site. The house was built from a £700,000 inheritance, legal disputes over which lasted for 60 years and were eventually resolved by the House of Lords – providing Charles Dickens with the idea for his novel *Bleak House*. The will in question was that of London banker Peter Thellusson, and the house was built by his great-grandson, Charles Sabine Thellusson. The house retains most of its original decorations, including the wall painting imitating marble, and wallpaper, as well as specially woven carpets and the Minton tiles which match them. Visitors can also marvel at the large number of water closets in the house, and glimpse Victorian "below stairs" life.

Sheffield

Sheffield is famous for cutlery, and there is still a Cutlers' Hall (the company was regulated from 1565 and by 1578 the city already had about 60 silver hallmarks). Silver plating was invented about 1750. Steel was made in small clay crucibles from about 1740. The factory age came late to Sheffield, and most of the historically important developments took place in

small workshops and forges. Sheffield's hills provided many good sites for the harnessing of water power, and this fascinating era has been preserved and presented to the public in a series of industrial museums within the Sheffield area. Set on a steep hill overlooking the city, PARK HILL FLATS is a vast concrete complex of flats housing about 3,500 people in "streets in the sky", designed 1956-61 by the then city architect J.L. Womersley. It has been such an outstandingly successful example of 20th-century public housing that it is now the country's largest Grade II* listed building.

To the south of the city is BEAUCHIEF ABBEY, originally a house of Premonstratensian canons. The west wall of the abbey church remains, incorporated interestingly if somewhat incongruously into a chapel of ease added c.1660. This is quite a period piece, still containing its original 17th-century furnishings, including box pews and squire's pew, and pulpit, reading desk and clerk's pew.

CONISBROUGH CASTLE, the inspiration for Sir Walter Scott's Rotherwood in *Ivanhoe*, has a superb late-12th century keep. A fine example of Norman military architecture, circular in plan, its battered base is ingeniously connected to six buttresses which project deeply and are also canted in plan. The extraordinarily thick walls contain staircases and passages for circulation, but could not easily be pierced for windows, so the interior must have been extremely dark when originally roofed. On the top floor is the private oratory with rib vaulting and richly carved bosses. The ground-floor chamber could be reached only from above, by a central eye in its stone vault, through which water could be drawn up from a well.

The dining room with sumptuous Rococo plasterwork in Nostell Priory

THE FRIENDS' SCHOOL (above) at Ackworth, a village south of Wakefield, began as a Foundling Hospital in 1758, but was bought in 1778 by John Fothergill, a medical doctor, who opened it as a Quaker school the following year. The large building is low-key Georgian in character, as befits the unostentatious philosophy of the Friends.

HEATH Only a mile south-east of Wakefield, which still retains waterfront warehouses, lies the attractive village of Heath, where a vast green common is surrounded by stone houses, mostly old, and a few of considerable grandeur. **HEATH HALL**, in core a Queen Anne house, was extended and given handsome Rococo interiors by the great John Carr of York, who was born at Horbury, on the other side of Wakefield, where he designed a handsome Georgian church.

Little remains of **PONTEFRACT CASTLE**, though it played a major role in medieval history, and it was here that Richard II died (or was murdered). It was besieged during the Civil War.

NOSTELL PRIORY ★ is of two architectural periods, only a generation apart in the early-to-mid 18th century. The Palladian house was begun in 1735 by the amateur architect Colonel James Moyser, with modifications by the young James Paine who created some sumptuous Rococo interiors for Sir Rowland Winn. His son and namesake succeeded in 1765 and brought in Robert Adam to extend the house and design rooms with superb plasterwork and thus to create one of his most unified classical design schemes. Otley-born cabinet-maker Thomas Chippendale furnished the house, providing everything from the magnificent desk in the library to the chopping block in the kitchen. Most of his work survives in the rooms for which it was designed. The priory has some noteworthy pictures.

Just within the grounds of Nostell Priory can be found **WRAGBY** parish church, an embattled Perpendicular building with a chancel dated by inscription to 1533. The church windows contain several hundred small panels of Swiss stained glass, forming one of the finest such collections to be found outside Switzerland, some dating from as early as 1514.

LEEDS This large city has a long history – there is an Anglo-Saxon cross in Chantrell's fine early-Victorian parish church in Kirkgate, which was one of the first designs to foretell a return to the Catholic tradition in an Anglican setting – and Briggate disguises a medieval town plan. Prosperity in the cloth markets of Leeds in the 17th century led to increased status, reflected in St. John's Church, New Briggate, externally Perpendicular Gothic Survival, internally magically Laudian. Expansion in the 18th century resulted in the handsome early-

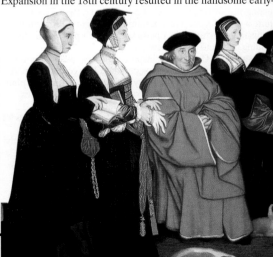

A late-16th-century copy of Holbein's celebrated lost conversation piece representing Sir Thomas More and his family, Nostell Priory

Georgian Holy Trinity Church, Boar Lane. More major industrial success in the 19th century was expressed by several important industrial monuments, including Joseph Bonomi's linen mill for Sir John Marshall, copied from the Temple of Edfu in the 1830s, and St Paul's House, Thomas Ambler's 1878 Hispano-Moorish warehouse for the ready-made clothing pioneer Sir John Barran. Public buildings of note are Cuthbert Brodrick's splendidly-towered Town Hall of 1853-8 and his elliptical Corn Exchange of 1861-3. Noteworthy also are the arcades, starting with Thornton's of 1878 – primly Victorian – to the County Arcade of 1898 by the theater architect Frank Matcham and exuberantly Art Nouveau. In this "Victorian Quarter" can be found the famous northern branch of Harvey Nichols, representative of the late-20th century revitalization which has seen Leeds become again a vibrant city and a shopping Mecca.

TEMPLE NEWSAM, 4 miles east of the center, houses a museum – of English decorative art, furniture and painting – which does great credit to the City of Leeds. Some pictures are from the historic collection of the Irwin family and some from the collections at Leeds City Art Gallery. The house, forming three sides of a large courtyard, is in brick, and mainly of the early 17th century, but one range is a century earlier and survives from the house where Henry, Lord Darnley, the second husband of Mary, Queen of Scots, was born in 1545. Later internal alterations have included an impressive Georgian remodeling of the long gallery by the architect Daniel Garrett in 1738-45, with magnificent Italianate plasterwork, and handsome fireplaces and door-cases in the style of William Kent. The original furniture is also displayed here.

A further collection of oriental art, fashion, 19th-century decorative art and modern craft and design is displayed at **LOTHERTON HALL** at Aberford, northeast of Leeds, a Victorian house with an Edwardian garden.

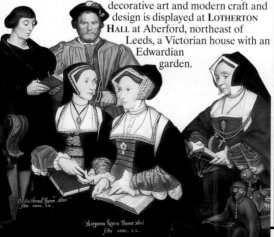

KIRKSTALL ABBEY

The Abbey, 3 miles west of the center of Leeds, was once a remote and typically Cistercian site in the valley of the River Aire. Founded in 1152, this was a large monastery, of which there are extensive remains, particularly of the church, including its massive crossing tower, and the vaulted chapter house. The public have access to the cloister, but the presentation of the ruins overall is disappointing, although the Abbey House Museum in the former gatehouse contains a lively folk museum.

Kirkstall Abbey

HENRY MOORE

The Leeds City Art Gallery pays tribute to Moore (1898–1986), who was born in Yorkshire and attended the Leeds School of Art. Its Henry Moore Collection, just inside the front entrance to the gallery, is inspiring.

BRAMHAM PARK, an early 18th-century country house illustrated in the second volume of Colen Campbell's *Vitruvius Britannicus*, was probably designed by its owner, Robert Benson, later first Lord Bingley, Lord Mayor and Member of Parliament for York, and a favorite of Queen Anne. A long, low house built of magnesian limestone, its interiors mainly date from after a major fire in 1828, but there are magnificent early 18th-century formal water gardens, also laid out by Lord Bingley, in a manner much influenced by French fashion, with ponds, cascades, a canal and beech hedges.

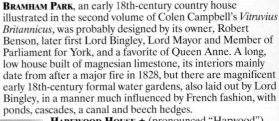

Huddersfield Railway Station of 1847, with an impressive portico worthy of a Roman temple.

HAREWOOD HOUSE ★ (pronounced "Harwood") provides an outstanding experience for visitors. Children can explore an adventure playground, all ages can take pleasure in fine gardens, country walks and a Capability Brown landscape, but above all adults can marvel at the splendors of the house. The construction of Edwin Lascelles' mansion in 1759 was financed from the proceeds of West Indian sugar plantations. It was built of beautiful honey-colored ashlar sandstone to a design by John Carr of York, with alterations by Sir Charles Barry, and has outstanding interiors by Robert Adam. Standing somewhat pugnaciously in the entrance hall, which is lined with Doric half-columns in a dark red imitation of porphyry, is Jacob Epstein's great marble statue of Adam – punning on the name of the architect-decorator – carved in 1939. Visitors are strongly advised to take up the option of following the tour of the house recorded by its expert owner, Lord Harewood. It is also well worth walking across the park to the redundant Church of All Saints, which contains six outstandingly good medieval alabaster recumbent effigies of medieval owners of manors in the parish. They provide detailed insight into costume and jewelry of their period.

Shibden Hall, Halifax, a late-medieval timber-framed house later partially encased in stone, which now houses a museum.

ART AT HAREWOOD
Harewood House is well worth a visit for its superb paintings alone, including works by El Greco, Gainsborough, Reynolds, Turner and Girtin. It also boasts a fine collection of Chippendale furniture.

Further splendors of West Yorkshire include Huddersfield Railway Station, Shibden Hall and **HALIFAX PIECE HALL**, the former Georgian cloth market of 1779, built on an enormous scale to provide individual rooms for the hundreds of merchants who traded in the lengths of woollen cloth produced in local cottages.

BRADFORD The industrial revolution came late to Bradford, which thus has many large and handsome Victorian buildings, notably the Gothic Revival

Harewood House

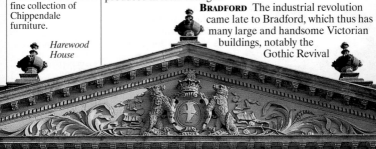

The Brontë Parsonage Museum (dining room, left), containing much of the furniture added when Charlotte became famous, and now a Brontë shrine.

WHITE WELLS
The whitewashed White Wells on the Ilkley moorside, still containing the spa bath, can be visited if the owner has hoisted a Union Jack to indicate it is open.

own Hall of 1873 and Venetian Gothic former Wool Exchange f 1864-7, both by local architects Lockwood and Mawson. ittle Germany is an area of erstwhile warehouses for expensive orsted cloth, much of which was always exported. The arehouses, like huge Italian palazzi, rise high above narrow one-setted streets. Lister's Manningham Mill of 1871-3 akes a huge presence felt on the skyline with its immense alianate mill chimney. At SALTAIRE, a model village built r Sir Titus Salt, whose fortune was made from alpaca, his rmer mill now houses an exciting art gallery dedicated the works of David Hockney ▲ *104*.

AST RIDDLESDEN HALL, a 17th-century yeoman-clothier's anor house with mullioned windows and oak paneling, is mplemented by solidly-constructed, and very Yorkshire, oak rniture, needlework and pewter of the period. At Haworth, a hilltop reached by a arrow stone-setted road, is the arish church of 1879 and, cross its graveyard, the older ARSONAGE of 1778 which, from 320, was the home of the Rev. atrick Brontë, his three ovelist daughters and drunken on Bramwell. Inspired by the ea's bleak moors, winter inds and damp mists, the sters produced their novels, sing masculine pseudonyms so at their writing would be ken seriously.

East Riddlesden Hall, the ruinous range of 1692

OMBALD'S MOOR, a wild open space at above 1300 feet, is ch in prehistoric remains, including rock-engravings. Among e fanciful shapes nature has carved from the rocks are the Cow and Calf".

KLEY, most famous for the song *On Ilkla Moor Bah Tat*, was fashionable 19th-century spa. Wealthy West Riding usinessmen liked to retire to Ilkley, and in 1906 one of them ommissioned a villa from the architect Sir Edwin Lutyens , *416*: "Heathcote", visible from Grove Road and King's oad, was the turning point when Lutyens changed from the rts and Crafts to a classical style, and formed a miniature rototype for his great buildings in New Delhi.

SPOFFORTH CASTLE (right) was one of the strongholds of the famous Percy family. Built very early in the 14th century, in attractive pinkish sandstone, it is partly hewn out of the rock from which the stone was quarried. Access to the upper floors and the roof was by a stair turret which has a charming spired top.

RIPON CATHEDRAL (below) Of particular interest inside are the choir stalls of 1489-94, carved in Ripon by William Brownfleet. The seats have canopies above, and misericords below carved with humorous scenes of medieval life and Bible stories, including Jonah leaving the whale, pigs dancing and making music. Some of the carvings are thought to have inspired Lewis Carroll – Charles Lutwidge Dodgson – with fanciful ideas for *Alice in Wonderland*, while his father was a canon of Ripon.

HARROGATE was once an important spa. Several of the wells can be seen, many with an elegant classical well-head. The town is now famous for floral displays, particularly splendid in spring when the large open **STRAYS** are edged with crocuses. Also of note are the **VALLEY GARDENS**, and **HARLOW CARR GARDENS**. Harrogate's spa heritage is represented by the Victorian and Edwardian **ROYAL PUMP ROOM**. An Art Nouveau flavor is evident in shops with colored and curving glass windows, and cast-iron canopies – most famously on **BETTY'S** tea shop.

RIPLEY CASTLE, a fortified manor house which has been owned by the Ingilby family for nearly 700 years, has a 15th-century gatehouse, a 16th-century pele tower with priest-hole and Georgian interiors. Ripley village is a charming exercise in 1820s Gothick town planning, inspired by places in Alsace-Lorraine. **ALLERTON PARK** is a mid 19th-century baronial castl with a fairytale skyline visible from the A1, from which can also be seen the classical Temple of Victory.

The attractive market town of **KNARESBOROUGH** has a ruined medieval **CASTLE** overlooking the deep gorge of the River Nidd, various rock-cut **SHRINES** and **MOTHER SHIPTON'S CAVE**, associated with uncanny predictions and a petrifying well.

STOCKELD PARK, designed by James Paine (1758-63), is an intriguing synthesis of Vanbrughian and Palladian architecture whose pedimented three-storey centerpiece is flanked by wing with broken pediments. Inside is an impressive staircase.

RIPON is a small cathedral city with a handsome square

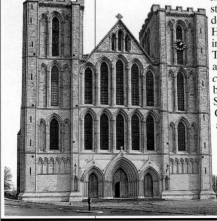

Market Place set around the oldest stone obelisk in the country, designed by the architect Nicholas Hawksmoor in 1702. It was repaired in 1781, hence the inscribed date. The town's patron saint is St Wilfric abbot of a monastery founded here *c*. 660, who built a church destroyed by the Vikings in 950 (although its Saxon crypt survives below Ripon Cathedral). After it was refounded as a collegiate church, a rebuilding program was begun in the late-12t century that has left us Norman transepts; its completion in the 1220s provides us with one of the country's finest Early English compositions, the west front almost classical in

Norton Conyers (left), and its walled garden (below)

its symmetry. The choir was altered early in the 14th century, the large east window having geometric tracery of *c*.1300, and the sedilia and piscina typically Decorated motifs. The nave was enlarged with fine Perpendicular arcades in the early-16th century, but this building phase was interrupted by the Reformation, hence the lop-sided and only partly-rebuilt central crossing arch. The church became a cathedral in 1836.

MARKENFIELD HALL is magical: a moated medieval manor house built in 1310 and little altered except for the addition of an Elizabethan gatehouse.

NEWBY HALL ★ The *pièce de résistance* is the Tapestry Room, with a set of breathtaking tapestries commissioned from the Gobelins factory by the house's young owner William Weddell, while on his Grand Tour in 1765-6. The tapestries around the doors, windows and fireplace, give an impressive effect of a room decorated with garlands of florists' blooms, as for a party; even the shadows are woven into them. They are to designs by Boucher and are unusual in that they have a dark grey, rather than pink background, and that the entrepreneur was an "emigré" Scot, Jacques Nielsen. Weddell's Grand Tour portrait by Pompeo Batoni hangs on the stairs. He also brought home an outstanding collection of Roman sculpture, for which he built a new gallery.

BOROUGHBRIDGE The **DEVIL'S ARROWS** alongside the minor Boroughbridge-Roecliffe road are three megaliths from a large late-Neolithic or early-Bronze Age monument.

ALDBOROUGH ROMAN TOWN, once Isurium Brigantum, was the main settlement of Roman Britain's largest Iron Age tribe, the Brigantes. An unusual example of a high-status Roman civilian settlement, it had a grid-plan of streets and a central forum, near which were shops and offices. Only a small area of its large site is exposed, including parts of the town's red-sandstone defensive wall, and two fine tesselated pavements from the same luxury town house. In the site museum there are some very high quality Roman artifacts and in the parish church, near the forum, can be seen a Roman carving of the god Mercury.

NORTON CONYERS (left) A charming house, medieval in origin but externally of 17th-century appearance with eye-catching Dutch gables and mullioned-and-transomed windows. Since 1624 it has been in the Graham family, who hosted various 17th-century royal visits. Charlotte Brontë came here in 1839 – it is thought she was given the idea for Mrs Rochester in *Jane Eyre* from the legend of a mad woman once confined to its attics. There is an enormous 18th-century walled garden which is still cultivated, and a very early example of a ha-ha.

Aldborough Roman Town, mosaic pavement

Newby Hall

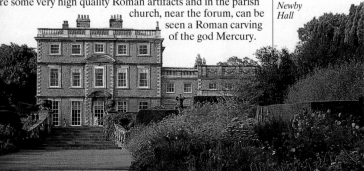

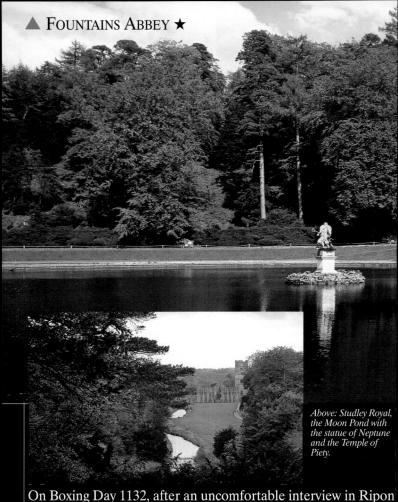

Above: Studley Royal, the Moon Pond with the statue of Neptune and the Temple of Piety.

On Boxing Day 1132, after an uncomfortable interview in Ripon with Archbishop Thurstan, 13 disaffected Benedictine monks of St Mary's Abbey in York headed toward the wild, secluded valley of Skelldale. Adopting the Cistercian Rule, they built FOUNTAINS ABBEY, which became that order's wealthiest monastery in Britain. The movingly beautiful ruins, epitomizing medieval monasticism, include the lay-brothers' 12th-century Transitional nave, the monks' Early English choir – extended by an Eastern transept, the Chapel of the Nine Altars, and (contrary to the Order's rules) Abbot Huby's impressive tower added *c.*1500. After the Dissolution, Stephen Proctor built from the stones the Jacobean FOUNTAINS HALL. In the aftermath of the 1720 South Sea Bubble, Chancellor of the Exchequer and Member of Parliament for Ripon John Aislabie retired to his local seat, and created at STUDLEY ROYAL a spectacular water garden, canalizing the River Skell and building temples. His son William was able to include in the landscape the real romantic "folly" of Fountains Abbey.

FOUNTAINS HALL
The mansion (above) built 1598-1611, partly from stones from the ruined abbey, to a design by Robert Smythson.

FOUNTAINS ABBEY
The church from the west (above), showing the lay-brothers' nave and Abbot Huby's tower.

Right, Fountains Abbey, east front

Above and right:
Middleham Castle

YORKSHIRE DALES A series of beautiful valleys running west to east, their rivers eventually becoming the River Ouse. Each dale is V-shaped, with relatively steep sides and little flat bottom land, so they are unsuitable for arable agriculture, but the meadows produce a crop of herb-rich hay. The field barns that so characterize the landscape in this area were built to house cattle and provide storage for the hay.

SKIPTON CASTLE, partly 13th-century with early-14th century round towers and later additions, was damaged in the Civil War, then restored by the formidable Lady Anne Clifford.

BOLTON ABBEY ★ was founded by Augustinian canons *c.* 1151. Their ruined choir has intersecting round arches creating pointed arches, typical of *c.*1170. The nave subsequently became the parish church, and only in 1983 was the west tower, still unfinished when the abbey was dissolved, transformed into what is now its porch.

BARDEN TOWER, the lodge of the Verdurer who controlled the ancient forest where wild boar were hunted, was remodeled as a large tower-house in the reign of Henry VII, and restored again by Lady Anne Clifford in 1658-9.

BOLTON CASTLE, on a site commanding much of Wensleydale, can be firmly dated because the original building contract of 1378, written in French, survives for what was clearly another phase of a part-completed structure. The builder was John Lewyn, a master-mason of national reputation, and the client Richard Scrope, Lord High Chancellor in 1379, when a licence was granted for the castle's crenelation. The ingenious plan gives it major importance in the history of military architecture. Four ranges of buildings which contained a large number of self-contained apartments, of varying size but each with its own fireplace and garderobe, as well as a communal chapel, great hall, kitchen and service rooms, surround and thus protect a central courtyard on to which the rooms could have large windows while still having almost unbreached walls to the outside for defence. Because it was comfortable and well-appointed as well as secure, Mary Queen of Scots was imprisoned here by Queen Elizabeth I in 1568.

The gatehouse of Skipton Castle, carved with the Clifford family's motto "Desormais"

MIDDLEHAM CASTLE has an exceptionally large Norman keep and added medieval curtain walls. This Neville stronghold became the home of Richard, Duke of Gloucester, later Richard III, through his wife Anne Neville.

JERVAULX ABBEY, one of North Yorkshire's many ruined Cistercian abbeys but privately owned, still retains something of the character of an 18th-century park, providing a habitat for a treasure-plot of wild flowers.

RICHMOND The market town of Swaledale, whose 18th-century prosperity from Swaledale wool and lead-mining is demonstrated by its Georgian **THEATRE ROYAL**. Seating fewer than 200 in an unforgettable atmosphere of intimacy with the stage – and one's neighbors – it is the best-preserved Georgian theater surviving. Most old theaters were altered in Victorian times, but this one simply closed and was used for other purposes; it was restored and reopened as a theater in 1963.

RICHMOND CASTLE, one of the country's first stone-built Norman castles, was begun *c.*1071 when William the Conqueror granted the "Honour" of Richmond to his kinsman Alan Rufus of Brittany. From the late 11th century date the curtain walls and the great hall – Scolland's Hall – named after one of the castle's stewards. In the mid-12th century a later earl, Conan, built the magnificent keep, still dominating the town which grew up around the castle on the steep hillside above the River Swale.

EASBY ABBEY was a Premonstratensian house, founded in 1155 by Roald, Constable of Richmond Castle, from which Easby is visible. The canons' impressive refectory has fine geometric windows. The abbey gatehouse stands roofless but otherwise complete, even to its stone vaulting. Easby's parish church, St Agatha's, was here before the abbey, which enclosed it within its precinct. This little church contains some surprises – the chancel has mid-13th century wall paintings, depicting on the North wall scenes from the Garden of Eden, and four of the Labours of the Months, with New Testament scenes on the South Wall; also a cast of a very fine Northumbrian cross shaft dating from *c.* 800.

MIDDLEHAM JEWEL
The Middleham Jewel was discovered near the Castle by a metal detector in 1985, and is now on display in the Yorkshire Museum in York. It is an exquisite example of the medieval goldsmith's art, minutely engraved with a Nativity scene on the back, and the Holy Trinity on the front, where there is a sapphire. A pendant, it probably contained religious relics and hung around the neck of a rich man, possibly King Richard III.

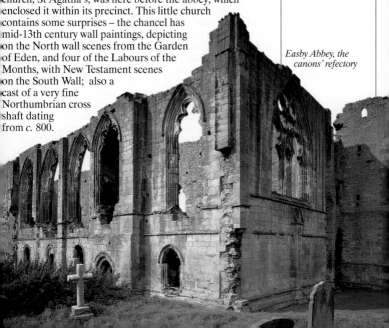

Easby Abbey, the canons' refectory

*Mount Grace Priory,
the small church*

RIEVAULX ABBEY
(right) was the first
Cistercian house in
Yorkshire, founded in
1131 directly from
Clairvaux. This
section is the Early
English choir.

MOUNT GRACE PRIORY is the most
complete English Carthusian
house. Unlike other religious
orders where monks lived
communally, here each monk lived
in isolation in his own two-storey
cell to which most of his meals
were brought, being passed to him
through a hatch designed to
prevent him seeing the servant.
Each cell had an ingeniously
contrived water supply and
drainage system. The cells are
arranged around a very extensive courtyard; but the church
and other communal areas are relatively compact, for
numbers in Carthusian monasteries were small. Although a
National Trust site, Mount Grace is administered by English
Heritage, who have very impressively recreated the interior of
one of the cells, and also have a good display on medieval
monasticism in the 17th-century entrance.

COXWOLD An attractive village, with interesting buildings
flanking the main street, which climbs up to its parish church

BYLAND ABBEY
(below) The ruins
include medieval
pavements in tiles of
various colors and an
amazing variety of
geometric patterns.

of St Michael – a splendid Perpendicular building
of *c.* 1430 with an unusual octagonal tower at its
western, uphill, end. At the southern side of the
church can be seen the tombstone of Laurence
Sterne, perpetual curate here in 1760-8. He was
buried in Bayswater, London, but the stone was
moved here in 1969 when that churchyard was
redeveloped. Inside the church, which has medieval
roof timbers, are Georgian furnishings largely
installed in Sterne's time. Of particular note is the
unusual U-shaped 18th-century altar rail, the space
in the chancel being made particularly narrow by
huge monuments.

NEWBURGH PRIORY became an Elizabethan country house
after the Augustinian canons' religious house was dissolved in
the 16th century; later alterations include chimneypieces,
paneling and Italian plasterwork. In the attic is said to be the
tomb containing Oliver Cromwell's headless body.

BYLAND ABBEY has one of the most memorable west fronts of
any monastic ruins, the semicircular half of its rose window
suspended from its flanking turret. The Cistercian monks
finally began Byland in 1177 after various aborted attempts at
settlement nearby. **GILLING CASTLE** contains the country's
finest Elizabethan Great Chamber, complete with heraldic

Pickering Castle

lass windows dated 1585, pendant rib ceiling, lozenge wall
aneling, and a painted frieze depicting the family trees of the
Yorkshire gentry, as well as the Fairfax family's musicians. In
rigin a 14th-century tower house, Gilling Castle also has
arly-Georgian wings with Rococo plasterwork by the Italian
Giuseppe Cortese.

HELMSLEY is an attractive market town of white stone
uildings with red pantile roofs, dominated by **HELMSLEY
CASTLE**, which is surrounded by two very impressive rock-cut
itches. As well as medieval structures there is an Elizabethan
ange with carved woodwork and fireplaces. The castle's living
ccommodation was eventually superseded by that of
DUNCOMBE PARK, a somewhat brooding Vanbrughian
omposition of c.1713 by Yorkshire gentleman-architect
William Wakefield. Much of the interior dates from rebuilding
fter a major fire of 1895, but the landscaped garden is largely
 survival of the early 18th century – the Stephen
witzer/Charles Bridgeman period. On one side there are a
erpentine bastion and a creepy yew walk, and on another a
arge lawn enticing the visitor to a curving terrace, flanked at
ach end by a temple, with splendid views down into the valley
f the River Rye, and of the estate's outstanding specimens of
rees. Accessed by a separate route, **RIEVAULX TERRACE** is also
art of the same designed landscape but of mid 18th-century
ate, and thus more romantic in concept, although also with
andsome temples at each end. A feature
f the vistas from both terraces is
RIEVAULX ABBEY, another of North
Yorkshire's many splendid monastic ruins.

NUNNINGTON HALL, a small stone country
ouse mainly of 17th-century date, has
ome early sash windows, dating from
687, and some exuberantly baroque gate
iers. The collection of miniature
nteriors is particularly popular with visitors. **SUTTON PARK** is a
id-18th century Georgian house in brick with surprisingly
orid plasterwork.

Sutton Park

PICKERING is a busy market town. Its parish church has late-
edieval wall paintings depicting a number of saints, many
nduring gruesome deaths. **PICKERING CASTLE** (opposite page)
 a fine example of a motte-and-bailey castle. **EBBERSTON
HALL** is a stately home in miniature, built in 1718 by Colen
Campbell and Palladian in character. Behind it is an
vergrown Italianate water garden of early date.
Close by are the **NORTH YORK MOORS**, an upland landscape
ith heather-covered moors and pretty villages.

*Above: Nunnington
Hall, the fine open-
well staircase*

SHANDY HALL
(above left)
Novelist Laurence
Sterne, author of
*The Life and Opinions
of Tristram Shandy,
Gentleman* (1759-67),
lived in this 15th-
century house in
Coxwold. Above left
is the study where
he wrote.

Whitby Abbey

WHITBY

A cliff-side town with a fishing harbor below and many fascinating corners to explore. The town's most famous sailor was Captain James Cook, who explored the Pacific Ocean in the 1760s and 1770s. Jewelry carved from local jet became very fashionable as mourning wear in Victorian times.

On the headland at Whitby is the 12th-century Church of St Mary, its interior still Georgian with galleries, box pews and a splendid three-decker pulpit of 1778.

WHITBY ABBEY ★ stands proudly on a cliff-top, where its Gothic ruins belie an earlier period of history; it was a community fo both monks and nuns, founded by St Hilda in AD 657. Here i 664 a Synod debated many contentious issues of the Early English Church and decided on the method of calculating the date of Easter which still pertains. This monastery was destroyed by a Danish invasion in 867.

SCARBOROUGH One of the country's earliest seaside resorts i the 17th century, it became famous as a spa. There are some elegant Regency villas and terraces, notably the curving CRESCENT; also the ROYAL HOTEL, which has a splendid staircase hall, and the former GRAND HOTEL, a vast Victorian concoction by Cuthbert Brodrick. Between two fine bays of sands projects a headland topped by SCARBOROUGH CASTLE, where only half of the handsome 12th-century keep survived the Civil War; the North Sea has taken a similar proportion o the site of a Roman Signal Station. In the graveyard of the parish church of St Mary, Anne Brontë is buried. The church of ST MARTIN ON THE HILL is a gem for Pre-Raphaelite devotees, with work by Bodley, Morris, Burne-Jones, Rossett and Brown. The Art Deco former Odeon cinema of 1936 by Harry Weedon became, 60 years later, the home of Alan Ayckbourn's plays, the STEPHEN JOSEPH THEATRE, founded in 1955 as a "theater-in-the-round" by the playwright's eponymous mentor, a son of the actress Hermione Gingold.

YORK

Eboracum to the Romans, who built a large military fortress and also a high-ranking civilian *colonia* here; Eoforwic to the Anglo-Saxons, and Jorvik to the Danes – hence its present name. York was the Second City of medieval England, and to this day the Lord Mayor of York gives precedence only to the Lord Mayor of London at national events. There are almost 2 miles of CITY WALLS surviving, with four gateways or "bars", and 18 churches remain of the 40 which served the medieval city in addition to its great Minster and numerous monastic houses. York has preserved many timber-framed houses and shops, such as the famous SHAMBLES Trade was regulated by craft guilds, the scale of the MERCHANT ADVENTURERS' HALL giving some idea of the

BENINGBROUGH HALL ★ is an elegant early 18th-century brick house with an exquisite marquetry staircase (below), and contains pictures from the National Portrait Gallery. Center: the Drawing Room at Beningbrough.

WHARRAM PERCY (below right)
Excavations over 41 seasons at Wharram Percy, a deserted medieval village, produced evidence of a Yorkshire Wolds community's 5,000-year stratified history.

importance. When the great Royalist city fell to the Parliamentarians after a lengthy siege in 1644, Charles I knew that his crown was lost. The **MANSION HOUSE**, where the Lord Mayor still lives during his year of office, was built in 1725 and Lord Burlington's **ASSEMBLY ROOMS** of 1730 provided a venue for elegant Georgian balls. Visitors can experience 18th-century elegance in **FAIRFAX HOUSE**, a handsome town house furnished with an outstanding collection of Georgian antiques, especially clocks. Nearby is the castle, **CLIFFORD'S TOWER**, a shell-keep set on a Norman motte. The **CASTLE MUSEUM**, with its famous recreated streets, occupies adjacent Georgian prison buildings. Not far away is the **JORVIK VIKING CENTRE**, recreating the sights and smells of 10th-century York. York offers a wide variety of museums and galleries, including Roman and natural history collections in the **YORKSHIRE MUSEUM** in the Museum Gardens next to the medieval ruins of **ST MARY'S ABBEY**, and the **YORK CITY ART GALLERY** which has a fine collection of ceramics as well as excellent pictures.

FOSTON OLD RECTORY was built by the Georgian divine and wit Sydney Smith while incumbent of Foston-le-Clay for twenty years from 1806, before he returned to London as a canon of St Paul's Cathedral.

Castle Howard (below), the Mausoleum by Hawksmoor (bottom left) and the hall (bottom right)

CASTLE HOWARD ★ was, amazingly, Sir John Vanbrugh's first attempt at architecture, and also the first English house to be crowned with a dome. Begun in 1699, it is a baroque master-piece, and has magnificent gardens with lakes and many landscape features, including a symmetrical Temple of the Four Winds, and a classical Mausoleum.

KIRKHAM PRIORY, on an idyllic site beside the River Derwent, has a very impressive late-13th century gatehouse with crocketed gablets and much carving.

The Rose Window

York Minster stands on the site of several earlier minsters – the word is an Old English contraction of the Latin *monasterium*. By cubic measurement, this is England's largest cathedral. Here, on Easter Day 627, King Edwin of Northumbria was baptized by St Paulinus, and the crypt has evidence of Roman and Norman buildings on the site. The mid-13th-century transepts were built by Archbishop Walter de Gray, and the north transept's tall lancets, the "Five Sisters", have original grisaille glass. The geometric windows of the chapter-house occupy the entire width of its eight sides: there is no central column, despite the large span, because the vault here, as in the rest of the Minster, is of wood, hence its susceptibility to major fires. The immense nave was begun in 1291, the Perpendicular Choir and Lady Chapel completed in 1405. The twin west towers, finished in 1472, were the last medieval addition.

STAINED GLASS
York Minster is a treasure-house of medieval stained glass. The Rose Window glass is of *c.* 1500, commemorating the marriage of Henry VII of Lancaster and Elizabeth of York, which ended the Wars of the Roses; it narrowly survived the fire in the south transept on July 9, 1984. The East Window, larger than a tennis court, glazed by John Thornton of Coventry 1405-8, shows the Creation and Fall of Man from Genesis and the Revelation of St John.

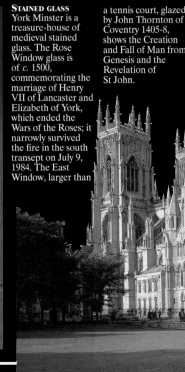

THE NAVE AND CHOIR
An unusual view of the huge nave (above left), without its normal seating, shows the Georgian pavement designed by William Kent and Lord Burlington. The choir stalls (above right) were put in after a fire in 1829 deliberately started by religious fanatic Jonathan Martin, brother of the painter John Martin.

EXTERIOR FROM THE SOUTHEAST (BELOW)
Outside the south door is a statue of Constantine the Great, who was proclaimed Roman Emperor in York in 306, and who made Christianity the official religion of the Roman world.

Detail of the Great East Window

Top: Barnard Castle and the River Tees

Above: Silver mechanical swan, 18th-century, Bowes Museum

BOWES MUSEUM
On the outskirts of Barnard Castle is this huge structure commissioned by John Bowes and his French wife Josephine in 1869 in the style of French château. Bowes Museum contains an outstanding collection of furniture and paintings.

GUISBOROUGH TO BERWICK-UPON-TWEED

MIDDLESBROUGH'S major feature is the Transporter Bridge, a marvel of steel engineering opened in 1911, to carry workers across the River Tees without obstructing busy shipping lanes below. **GISBOROUGH PRIORY**, founded for Augustinians by Robert de Brus early in the 12th century, was rebuilt after a fire of 1289. Nearby is an early dovecote, and in Guisborough [sic] parish church is a richly carved chest tomb from the priory. **ORMESBY HALL** was the Palladian ancestral home of the Pennyman family, its handsome stable block now the home of Cleveland police horses.

BISHOP AUCKLAND takes its name from the Bishop of Durham's palace, **AUCKLAND CASTLE**, where the Early English chapel, once the great hall, with shafts of Frosterley marble from Weardale, is the burial place of John Cosin, Bishop of Durham 1662-72, famous for his black oak church furniture. Nearby is an elaborate Deer House. **BARNARD CASTLE** grew up around an older castle built by Guy de Baliol.

BOWES CASTLE, a few miles to the south-west, is a ruined Norman keep of the time of Henry II, the only stone building on the site, the rest being earthworks. In the church is the dedication stone of a building in the Roman fort of Lavatrae within the boundary of which the church lies.

DURHAM

Durham perches spectacularly on a narrow promontory in a loop of the River Wear. **DURHAM CASTLE**, not only a motte-and-bailey fortress but also a palace for Durham's Prince Bishops, became the University of Durham in 1837, and is a residence for present-day students who eat in the magnificent great hall with

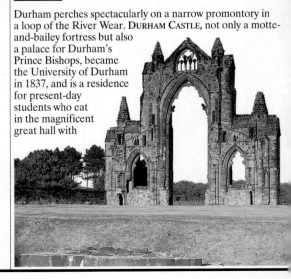

Gisborough Priory, the east wall of the choir. The large central window, originally with decorated tracery, frames a view of the Cleveland Hills.

HADRIAN'S WALL ▲

Durham Castle

creens passage and buttery, and food cooked in a medieval kitchen. An exquisite early-Romanesque vaulted chapel dates from c.1080, another splendid chapel from the 1540s, a Norman gallery has a richly-sculpted round-arched entrance, and Bishop Cosin's Black Oak Staircase is of the 1660s.

HADRIAN'S WALL, a World Heritage Site, 73 miles long, marking the northern edge of the Roman Empire, ran from Wallsend on the Tyne westward to Bowness on the Solway. Ordered to be built by the Emperor Hadrian in the 120s AD, the boundary consisted of a substantial stone wall with a ditch facing the "barbarians" and an earthwork called the *vallum* on the southern side. In addition to forts, spaced about a day's march apart, there was a milecastle every Roman mile, with two turrets between each. The turrets formed watch towers

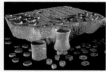

and the milecastles formed sheltered look-out positions with a gateway through the border; each fort, rectangular in design, provided accommodation for Roman troops and their supplies. A civilian settlement, or *vicus*, grew up near most forts, so not all archeological discoveries are of a military type.

CHESTERS This fort provides particularly well-preserved examples of gateways in its surrounding wall. In the center are remains of barrack blocks, the headquarters building, and next to it the commanding officer's house and his private bath-house with a well-preserved hypocaust heating system. Outside the fort can be seen extensive remains of the soldiers' bath-house, an elaborate complex of rooms for hot and cold, dry and steamy conditions, plus changing facilities. Chesters lies beside the North Tyne River, and the remains of a Roman bridge abutment can been seen here.

HOUSESTEADS Visitors to this fort pass first through its *vicus*, then its south gate. Nearby is a large-scale latrine. Other buildings excavated include the headquarters building, commanding officer's house, barrack blocks, granaries and a hospital. Slightly further west, and just south of Hadrian's Wall on the Stanegate, is Chesterholm or **VINDOLANDA**, which has in recent years produced some of the most exciting finds ever discovered on Hadrian's Wall. The wet ground conditions here have preserved organic material, including leather shoes and, best of all, thousands of small wooden tablets still containing traces of cursive ink writing, including private letters.

CORBRIDGE
Just south of Hadrian's Wall can be seen the remains of Corstopitum, the Roman town that was occupied longer than any other site in the area. It was established in the 80s AD and survived until the Romans withdrew from Britain early in the 5th century. Corbridge, strategically located

at the junction of two major Roman roads – Dere Street and the Stanegate – became an important supply depot, and the remains of extensive granaries can be seen. The site museum contains many fine Roman artifacts. Pictured above left are a bronze jug, gaming board and glass flask used to carry oil, from the site.

Hadrian's Wall, the world's most famous Roman frontier.

Perceptively epitomized by Sir Walter Scott "Half church of God, half castle 'gainst the Scot", Durham impresses unforgettably. Externally it is powerful, when viewed either from level ground to the north with full lengthwise elevation demonstrating the central tower's satisfying dominance, or from the River Wear below to the west front; internally it is awesome with its rhythm of stout piers and round arches. The country's first exercise in rib vaulting, Durham was begun in 1093 as a Benedictine Priory under a Prince Bishop. Here was the shrine of St Cuthbert. Also of note are the Transitional Galilee Chapel added to the west end containing the Venerable Bede's tomb, the delicate Neville Screen behind the High Altar, a fine Gothic work of 1380 despite the loss of 107 alabaster statues at the Reformation, and the contemporary tomb of Bishop Hatfield, surmounted by the Bishop's throne – the loftiest in Christendom.

NAVE ARCADE
The cylindrical columns are decorated with a lozenge pattern carved by using the same ingenious template of an 'X' on each stone. The composite piers of shafts have cushion capitals and there is a triforium gallery above. Among the tombs are the damaged alabaster effigies of John Lord Neville, died 1388, and his wife Matilda, on an elaborate tomb chest.

The Sanctuary door knocker

CATHEDRAL VIEWS
Durham Cathedral commands the view from across the River Wear. The twin west towers dwarf the Galilee Chapel added to the west end in the Transitional period between Norman and Gothic architecture. The tall central lantern tower dominates the composition externally, as well as admitting light into the crossing area of the cathedral. Inside, the round Norman arches and stout piers create an awe-inspiring rhythm.

Gibside Chapel, interior of the central dome

Hexham Abbey (right)

GIBSIDE CHAPEL
West of the Penshaw Monument, in an important landscape setting, once grand, then derelict, now being restored, is Gibside chapel, designed by James Paine and begun in 1760 as a mausoleum for the Bowes family, who owned the Gibside estate. A Greek cross in plan, it is an exquisite exercise in centralized design, with a tall, three-decker pulpit below the central dome.

NEWCASTLE UPON TYNE

Pons Aelius to the Romans, who bridged the Tyne here, Newcastle is a handsome yet vibrant city. Dominated by a fine 12th-century castle built for Henry II, it has two cathedrals: the medieval St Nicholas with its stone "crown", an open lantern supported by flying buttresses on its west tower, and the Roman Catholic St Mary designed by A.W.N. Pugin, with fine Victorian stained glass. Newcastle's architectural character is predominantly early 19th century. The elegant Grey Street has been described as the finest curved street in Europe; at the top is the Grey Monument, a huge Doric column surmounted by a statue of Earl Grey, the Prime Minister responsible for the Reform Act of 1832. Grey Street was part of a new town center development resulting from the successful interaction of three remarkable men: builder-cum-entrepreneur Richard Grainger, architect John Dobson and town clerk John Clayton. There are some medieval buildings, handsome Georgian churches, a good railway station also by Dobson, several fine bridges over the Tyne, and many museums including the Laing Art Gallery and the University Natural History Museum. The road south from Gateshead is now dominated by the impressive ANGEL OF THE NORTH, a huge late-20th-century sculpture in iron by Antony Gormley. It has joined the PENSHAW MONUMENT of 1844, a Doric temple, roofless like a miniature Parthenon, sited on an exposed hilltop where it was erected by public subscription to the 1st Lord Durham, a champion of Parliamentary Reform with Lord Grey, and later Governor of Canada.

SUNDERLAND Once a major shipbuilding and glass-manufacturing center, the city is now home to the National Glass Centre. Nearby is the Anglo-Saxon church at Monkwearmouth, a sister monastery to that at Jarrow, both founded by Benedict Biscop, in 674 and 681 respectively. At Jarrow, where the Venerable Bede wrote his famous *History of the English*

The "Angel of the North", Antony Gormley's impressive sculpture

Church and People and died in 735, there is the original dedication stone of 685.

SEATON DELAVAL Vanbrugh's mature masterpiece of 1718-19 for Admiral George Delaval, and more Palladian than his earlier works. The dominant central block is flanked by lower arcades and end pavilions which break forward to enclose on three sides a deep court, which faces the North Sea. The central block is very theatrical, heavily rusticated and turreted. The once-grand interior now gauntly bears the scars of a disastrous fire in 1822.

HEXHAM The Moot Hall in Hexham is a 15th-century fortified gatehouse. **HEXHAM ABBEY ★**, a medieval priory which became the parish church after the Dissolution, is mainly Early English in date, but has a fine Saxon crypt which survives from St Wilfrid's church of 675-80. The crypt was built of reused Roman stones, to which still adheres some Anglo-Saxon plaster.

AYDON CASTLE near Corbridge is a remarkably complete example of a Northumberland fortified house as evolved over several medieval centuries. Its great hall is displayed with replica furniture. Belsay Castle is a smaller medieval tower house, with a ruined Jacobean wing.

BELSAY HALL, CASTLE AND GARDENS Belsay Hall is an interesting essay in a very austere version of the Greek Doric order. The quarry from which came the stone to build the house became a quarry garden later in the 19th century. The central atrium (above) of Belsay Hall is exactly 100 feet square in plan. The principal rooms are sited around it.

WALLINGTON HALL is in core a late-17th-century courtyard house, which was much altered in the early 18th century, most notably by Daniel Garrett. The exterior is rather austere, but inside there is some delightful Rococo plasterwork created by Italian *stuccatori*. In the 19th century, after the house had been inherited by the intellectual Trevelyan family, the central court was roofed in to form a two-storeyed hall, around which historical scenes of Northumberland life were painted by William Bell Scott, with flowers added by amateur artists, including John Ruskin and Pauline, Lady Trevelyan.

KIRKHARLE, near the village of Cambo, was the birthplace of Lancelot "Capability" Brown in 1716.

WALLINGTON HALL KITCHEN GARDEN
The 18th-century kitchen garden, some distance from the house, was recreated as an enchanting flower garden in the 1930s. From it can be seen the owl house – the owl was the crest of the Fenwick family who lived at Wallington in the 17th century.

Wallington, the Central Hall (below) and the Portico House (bottom) overlooking the pond in the garden.

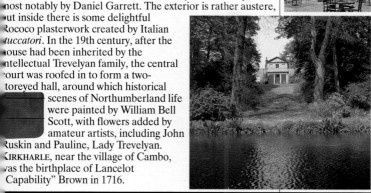

One of the largest inhabited castles in England, Alnwick has been the Percy family home since 1309, and is still the main residence of the Duke of Northumberland. Parts of the building are 14th century, although some of the medieval effects, including the distinctive stone figures lining its defensive walls, date from the 18th. An expensive restoration program begun in 1854 by the architect Anthony Salvin was partly a Victorian Gothicization, but also resulted in some good 19th-century classical interiors. It removed, however, most of the 18th-century creations of Robert Adam, of whom the 1st Duke of Northumberland was one of the most extravagant patrons. The present splendid interior is complemented by a sumptuous collection of paintings that includes works by Titian, Canaletto and Van Dyck. The castle has a dramatic outlook over the River Coquet and a Capability Brown landscape; the present Duchess plans to create a modern garden within the walls of the former kitchen garden.

The Library

Ebony veneer cabinet originally made for the apartment of Louis XIV at Versailles

The Keep, seen from the middle bailey

Dunstanburgh Castle's spectacular ruins include a large gatehouse with round towers.

Lord Armstrong sitting in the inglenook fireplace of the dining room at Cragside (right), painted by Henry Hetherington Emerson.

Cragside, Art Nouveau electric lamp

NORTHUMBERLAND NATIONAL PARK, stretching 40 miles north from Hadrian's Wall to the Cheviot Hills, contains some of the most spectacular, but surprisingly little visited, scenery in the country. There are many attractive towns and villages, including Warkworth, which has a complete Norman church and a medieval fortified bridge.

WARKWORTH CASTLE was a stronghold of the Percy family. Its Lion Tower, which formed the porch to the Great Hall, took its name from the Percy Lion carved on a boss of the ground-floor vault. The three-storey keep, ingeniously constructed on a Norman motte, is a superb example of military architecture: it takes the form of a square over which is superimposed a Greek cross; all the outer corners are chamfered, and from its center rises a taller turret. Built *c.*1400, it provided tower-house accommodation on a very grand scale.

CALLALY CASTLE began life as a typical Northumberland pele tower, but during the 1800s and 1900s was transformed into a classical mansion of complex form. It has plasterwork created by the Lafranchini, the same Italian *stuccatori* who worked on Wallington.

ALNWICK was walled in 1434 and the Hotspur Gate survives. A town of fine spaces, it crouches like a barbican to its castle. The Lion Bridge was designed in 1773 by Robert Adam, who also designed buildings for the Castle's extensive park, including a Gothick summer-house in the ruins of Hulne Priory, one of the earliest Carmelite houses in England, and the prominent Brizlee Tower, also a Gothick composition of 1781, for the picturesque-loving 1st Duke of Northumberland.

DUNSTANBURGH CASTLE, standing spectacularly above the North Sea on a promontory of dolerite rocks, can be reached only on foot; the path from Craster skirts the silted-up harbor where Henry VIII's fleet was found, after it had been lost for 3 weeks on a voyage from Scotland. Dunstanburgh was begun after the English loss at Bannockburn, and is thus a few years later than Edward I's great Welsh castles – it also has a large gatehouse with round towers. Alterations were made 1380-4 by John of Gaunt as Lieutenant of the Scottish Marches.

CRAGSIDE, the best northern example of Norman Shaw's "Old English" style, has beautifully decorated rooms containing Victorian paintings; the drawing room has a carved marble inglenook weighing 10 tons. The house, designed for engineering magnate Lord Armstrong, was technically very advanced: it was the first private house to be lit by hydro-electricity and the kitchen was powered by hydraulics, as were many other features of the estate.

BRINKBURN PRIORY, founded for Augustinian canons in 1135, has an idyllic site beside the River Coquet. The fine Early English church ruins were restored for use in 1858.

BAMBURGH CASTLE, set on a craggy promontory, dates from Norman times but was restored by Lord Armstrong in the late 19th century. It contains a notable collection of armor. The **FARNE ISLANDS** constitute one of Britain's most

LINDISFARNE CASTLE
Interior view of the castle. Lutyens designed most of the furniture and even such details as door catches.

important bird sanctuaries. These spectacular islands may be visited from Seahouses, but are closed during the breeding season (May to July). Puffins, eider ducks and four species of tern are found here; they are generally fearless of man and can sometimes be observed at close quarters (visitors are advised to wear hats!). A large colony of seals may also be seen. St Aidan found solitude on the Farnes, and St Cuthbert built himself a cell on Inner Farne, where he died in 687. That spot is marked by St Cuthbert's Church, a small chapel built in 1370 and restored in the 1840s when parts of Bishop Cosin's furnishings from Durham Cathedral were brought here. West of the church stands Prior Castell's Tower, erected about 1500, with a first-floor chapel. From here are spectacular views of the dolerite cliffs of the other islands, and across to Bamburgh.

HOLY ISLAND is accessible at low tide by means of a causeway. St Aidan came in 635, invited from Iona by the Bernician King Oswald to establish a monastery, and St Cuthbert was Prior, and later Bishop. He was buried here in 687 but destructive Danish raids caused the monks to begin their prolonged wanderings with his body, eventually to end at Durham. The island is thus one of the holiest sites of Northumbrian Christianity and still a place of pilgrimage.

Lindisfarne Priory (left) and Castle (below left)

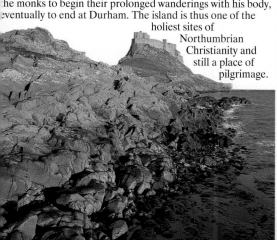

LOST GARDEN
Near Lindisfarne Castle there is a tiny walled garden laid out by Gertude Jekyll, whose design for it was lost for many years until a Durham professor of astronomy discovered it in a library in California.

Puffins on the Inner Farne Islands

LINDISFARNE PRIORY, re-established as a cell of Durham in 1093, is architecturally very similar to Durham Cathedral but on a smaller scale.

LINDISFARNE CASTLE ★, a 16th-century fort, was bought in 1902 by Edward Hudson, owner of *Country Life*, who commissioned Edwin Lutyens to convert the ruins into a small country house. Lutyens created a most attractive series of living spaces while successfully retaining the atmosphere of a castle.

▲ Berwick-upon-Tweed

Early 18th-century gravestone at Falstone (right), and c. 18th-century headstone in Hartburn churchyard (far right)

Portrait of Lutyens by his son Robert, 1959

Sir Edwin Lutyens (1869-1944), architect of Lindisfarne Castle, was at his best when blending old buildings with new, often with gardens designed by Gertrude Jekyll. Her knowledge of materials, and her network of friends and contacts, helped Lutyens to design numerous country houses, usually in an Arts and Crafts style. By 1906 he had moved into a version of the Classical style which was to reach its zenith at Viceregal Lodge in New Delhi. He designed the Cenotaph in London's Whitehall, originally as a temporary structure, but it was so successful that it was retained. He was knighted for his work with the Imperial War Graves Commission following World War I.

Ravensdowne Barracks, Berwick

Berwick-upon-Tweed is a border town which was finally declared English in 1483. Its situation demanded strong defences, and from medieval times Berwick was walled. During the reign of Queen Elizabeth I the walls were remodeled, with a series of bastions designed by Italian engineers, using Renaissance principles to take advantage of, and protect against, cannon fire. A series of wonderful views of the town, river and sea can be enjoyed by walking along the ramparts.

Ravensdowne Barracks (right), designed with advice from Vanbrugh and built 1717-25, was the first in Britain and housed 36 officers and 600 men. It is now the museum of the King's Own Scottish Borderers and the town museum, and contains many treasures collected by Sir William Burrell, a prosperous shipowner better known as the founder of the Burrell Collection in Glasgow. Burrell frequently used to drop into Berwick Town Hall and leave brown paper packages containing what are now priceless exhibits.

Cheviot Hills South of the Border are these hills, once a no man's land and war zone between Scotland and England, home of the "border reivers", feuding families who survived by raiding. The dangers of the area dictated the form of vernacular architecture found in these parts: the pele or bastle towers, miniature castles with a first-floor entry, few windows, and built in stone to resist attack by fire. High in the Cheviots is **Yeavering Bell**, an Iron Age settlement with surviving earthworks. Nearby was once the 7th-century palace of Edwin, King of Northumbria.

Chillingham Castle is a courtyard fortress, its licence to crenellate issued in 1344. One range was remodeled in the 17th century, and its gardens were laid out by Sir Jeffrey Wyatville in the 19th century. In the enclosed park is an ancient herd of wild white cattle.

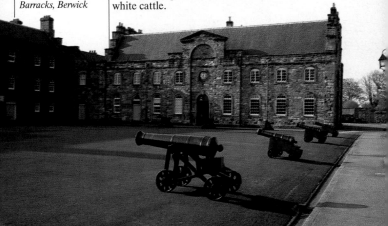

NORTH WEST
Frank Kelsall

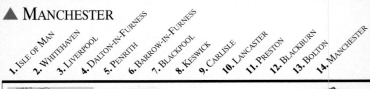

1. ISLE OF MAN
2. WHITEHAVEN
3. LIVERPOOL
4. DALTON-IN-FURNESS
5. PENRITH
6. BARROW-IN-FURNESS
7. BLACKPOOL
8. KESWICK
9. CARLISLE
10. LANCASTER
11. PRESTON
12. BLACKBURN
13. BOLTON
14. MANCHESTER

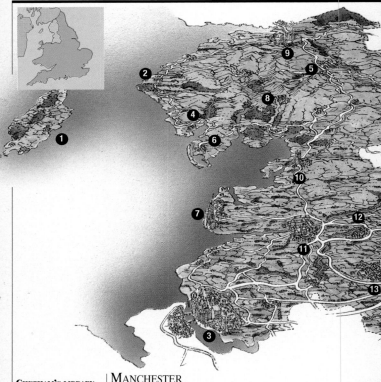

CHETHAM'S LIBRARY

The first floor contains the 17th-century bookcases and a reading room with a tympanum reminiscent of the woodwork of London's City churches ▲ *146-7*; the molded bases of the columns take the form, appropriately, of piles of books. This room also has one of the chained library chests that Chetham provided for several parishes near Manchester.

MANCHESTER

Although the only reminder of Roman Manchester is the reconstructed fort at Castlefield, there survives a fragment from the medieval city: a town church of size and quality, which became the new CATHEDRAL when Manchester was made a see in 1847. Essentially, it is a 15th-century collegiate church, established in 1421 by Thomas de la Warre. The chancel stalls of the early 16th century are among the best in England, with spiky canopies and cresting, and a set of misericords, carved with popular subjects such as men playing backgammon and dancing pigs.

Next to the cathedral is CHETHAM'S HOSPITAL. The buildings for the priests who served the collegiate church had a gatehouse (rebuilt 1816), a great hall and lodgings round a small quadrangle. After the Dissolution, they were sold in 1653 to trustees appointed by Humphrey Chetham to establish a school and a free public library.

The best city-center fragment of 18th-century Manchester is ST ANN'S CHURCH of 1709-12, at the head of the city's first square. Other buildings there include the ROYAL EXCHANGE, a grand, classical pile by Bradshaw, Gass and Hope (1914-21) with the Royal Exchange Theatre built inside a glass pod by Levitt Bernstein. The Barton Arcade to Deansgate has ornate iron and glass

One of a series of 12 murals by Ford Madox Brown, in Manchester's Town Hall

omes and tiers of balconies. Leading from the square to the athedral (and the Old Shambles, the last remains of timber-ramed Manchester, recently moved to this present site) is the ew street formed after the bomb explosion of 1997, marked y Marks and Spencer's newest and largest store (by the Building Design Partnership).

The principal 18th-century thoroughfares were Portland Street and Mosley Street, the latter with two fine, early 19th-century buildings – Thomas Harrison's PORTICO LIBRARY (1802-06), and Sir Charles Barry's CITY ART GALLERY. The gallery interiors house an especially good collection of Pre-Raphaelite and 20th-century British paintings. In Princess Street is Barry's Italianate Athenaeum of 1837, a trial run for the Reform Club in London, altered at the top after a fire. Art Gallery and ATHENAEUM are being joined with a new building to complete the block, designed by Michael Hopkins and Partners.

PRINCESS STREET has a fine collection of Italianate warehouses (Manchester's distinctive contribution to English building types, also seen in Charlotte Street).

KING STREET Commercial Manchester is most widely represented in King Street, a textbook of commercial architecture of the last 150 years. Here are Cockerell's Greco-Roman BANK OF ENGLAND (1845); Edward Salomons's Venetian Gothic REFORM CLUB (1870); Waterhouse's hard red-brick PRUDENTIAL ASSURANCE OFFICE (1881); Charles Heathcote's Edwardian aroque LLOYDS BANK (1912); and Lutyens' MIDLAND BANK 1929), with all the subtle proportions and detail of Lutyens at is best.

Of the same date is Harry Fairhurst's SHIP CANAL HOUSE, when finished the tallest building in Manchester; and Casson nd Conder's NATIONAL WESTMINSTER BANK (1966), clad in wedish granite, is a building whose merits now seem greater when contrasted with the overpowering Post-Modern resence of FRIENDS PROVIDENT HOUSE, set back behind King Street with Cockerell's Bank of England as its footstool.

The masterpiece of Manchester's 19th-century architecture is undoubtedly the TOWN HALL (below) by local-architect-made-good Alfred Waterhouse, completed in 1867. Waterhouse made his reputation in Manchester with the Assize Courts (bombed) and Strangeways prison, and the detailed design and completion of the Town Hall occupied him for nearly the rest of the century.

Manchester Cathedral

TOWN HALL
The Town Hall (below left) occupies a large triangular site, and the ingenious planning of this difficult plot is masterly. The principal front is on Albert Square, dominated by a tall tower and spire, and the main ceremonial rooms overlook the Square at first-floor level. The Great Hall fills the middle. From the low ground-floor vaulted entrance hall, the first-floor landing is reached by two monumental staircases, their subtle placement and composition smoothing the transition between the different axes of the entrance and the Great Hall. The building is beautifully decorated throughout, with details ranging from Puginian polychromy to Esthetic Movement sunflowers; what draws the eye most of all is the series of 12 murals in the Great Hall by Ford Madox Brown, representing the history of Manchester.

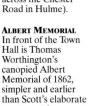

*View of Manchester
and Salford, 1734*

**THE CO-OPERATIVE
INSURANCE SOCIETY
TOWER** (1962)
dominates the north
of the city; designed
by G.S. Hay and Sir
John Burnet Tait and
Partners, it represents
one of the earliest
and best
introductions of the
modern American
skyscraper into an
English city.
Continuing love of
the new can been
seen in several
dramatic bridges
(by Whitby and Bird
across the Bridge-
water Canal,
Castlefield; by
Santiago Calatrava
across the Irwell at
Trinity Bridge; and by
Chris Wilkinson
across the Chester
Road in Hulme).

ALBERT MEMORIAL
In front of the Town
Hall is Thomas
Worthington's
canopied Albert
Memorial of 1862,
simpler and earlier
than Scott's elaborate
monument in
London ▲ *160*.

*Albert Memorial
(above and below)*

On the eastern fringe of the city center is ANCOATS, where
Schinkel sketched the eight-and nine-storey mills. Although
some have been rebuilt, the range fronting the Rochdale
Canal in Redmill Street is still awesome. The canal runs
through the southern heart of the city, and following a
towpath walk it is possible to emerge to view Watts'
Warehouse in Portland Street (now the Britannia Hotel) and
Lancaster and Bridgewater houses in Whitworth Street, the
high points at the beginning and end of Manchester textile
warehouse development in the 19th century.

The Rochdale Canal joins the Bridgewater Canal at
Castlefield. Warehouses with canal basins beneath them have
been converted into flats and offices, and the waterways are
crossed by new bridges. The most significant buildings now
form part of the MUSEUM OF SCIENCE AND INDUSTRY. The
former Liverpool Road Station (opened in 1830) is the oldest
surviving railway station in the world. It looks surprisingly
domestic. Behind, however, is a huge warehouse, along a
gentle curve of the railway track, brick with a robust timber-
framed structure within.

Urban regeneration is headed by Manchester's new concert
hall (1996), the BRIDGEWATER HALL by Renton Howard Wood
Levin, marked externally by fashionable *brise-soleils* and
internally by a spacious and cool entrance. It is set among new
office buildings. A short distance away is OXFORD ROAD
STATION (1960), an ingenious exercise in shell construction in
laminated timber, looking a bit like a miniature prototype of
the Sydney Opera House.

South of the center is the University, the older buildings by
Waterhouse between 1870 and 1900; the Manchester Museum
is part of the frontage to Oxford Road. Opposite is J.A.
Hansom's astonishing HOLY NAME OF JESUS (1869), stone on
the outside and terracotta within, the high and wide vault
supported on piers so slender that they appear to be built on
faith rather than calculation. Further south is the University's
WHITWORTH ART GALLERY of 1895 (J.W. Beaumont), housing
especially good English watercolors. In the same area is PLATT
HALL, a small country house designed (at least in part) in 1764
by Timothy Lightoler, which now houses a costume museum.
Further out is WYTHENSHAWE HALL, a 16th-century house now
standing in a park, and BAGULEY HALL, somewhat lost in the
huge housing estate laid out by Barry
Parker in 1931. The 14th-century
open hall lies between two wings
later in character, and boasts most
impressive timbering. Manchester's
major contribution to the classical
country house is HEATON HALL, to
the north of the city.
Set in more than
600 acres of
landscaped
grounds,
Heaton is a
major work
by James
Wyatt
(with
additions

Right: Cotton factory
Far right: L.S. Lowry's
"Coming from the Mill",
Salford Art Gallery

by Samuel and Lewis Wyatt) and the finest neoclassical house in the North West. The house is a 1772 rebuilding of an earlier villa. A long front faces south across the park, in fine sandstone with Coade stone details, with the typical Wyatt shallow-domed bow at the center. There are many good interiors, handsome chimney-pieces and plasterwork; the highlight is the circular first-floor cupola room, in the bow, with exquisite painted "Etruscan" decoration by Biagio Rebecca.

Several black-and-white timber-framed houses are within striking distance of Manchester. **BRAMALL HALL**, in Bramhall, is one of the best. Visitors can amuse themselves in an endeavor to sort out the original 15th- and 16th-century work from the 19th-century restoration and reproduction. **ORDSALL HALL**, in Salford, decorated inside and out with quatrefoil panels, retains a more obvious sense of antiquity, especially in the Great Hall. Both these houses are now local museums.

Above: Lark Hill Place, a reconstructed Victorian street in Salford Museum
Top: Platt Hall

SALFORD At Salford, urban church building can be traced from the Sacred Trinity, a nice Georgian box of 1752, through St Philip, a Commissioners' church of 1825 by Sir Robert Smirke and a near-exact copy of St Mary's in Wyndham Place, London, to the Roman Catholic Cathedral of 1855 by Weightman and Hadfield, with a splendid spire dominating the inner city. North of the center, at Pendlebury, is one of Bodley's finest churches, St Augustine's (1874), approached from the main road by a small gatehouse. The outside is brick and plainly detailed, the inside a lofty and majestic space with passage aisles through internal buttresses, and windows high in the walls, the whole derived from Albi. St Mark's Worsley (1846) is one of Sir George Gilbert Scott's best parish churches, with skilled workmanship and a lavish use of materials.

SALFORD MUSEUMS
Salford has two museums in historic buildings: a museum of mining in a villa designed by Charles Barry at Buile Hill, and the City Museum at the Crescent, one of the first public museums and libraries in England, overlooking Peel Park. A collection of paintings by Salford artist L.S. Lowry is shortly to be moved from here to a new Lowry Centre at Salford Quays, a dockland redevelopment at the eastern end of the Manchester Ship Canal.

Left: Wythenshawe Hall

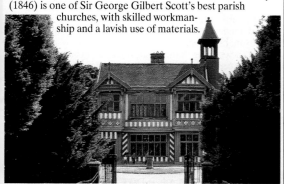

Above: the Whitworth Art Gallery
Left: Heaton Hall

421

▲ LIVERPOOL

ALBERT DOCK, opened 1845, is the best surviving example of an enclosed dock. The brick warehouses on monumental cast-iron arcades are built right to the quay edge, and have fireproof construction throughout. This is best seen inside the Maritime Museum housed in one of the warehouses. The Tate Gallery has its northern outpost here. The Dock Traffic Office (now Granada TV News) has giant Tuscan columns and pediment all in cast iron.

ANGLICAN CATHEDRAL (below) Built in a warm red sandstone, the Cathedral has a nave and chancel that appear short because of the dominance of the center: twin transepts flanking north and south portals, between them the tower, 330 feet high.

LIVERPOOL

The skyline of Liverpool is dominated by its two 20th-century cathedrals. Sir Giles Gilbert Scott's **ANGLICAN CATHEDRAL ★**, of 1903, is one of the last and most beautiful expressions of the Gothic Revival. While it took three generations to complete Scott's cathedral, the Roman Catholic Metropolitan Cathedral ● *90*, designed by Frederick Gibberd in 1959, took less than a decade from conception to completion. Built on the crypt of Lutyens's abandoned cathedral, designed in 1932, Gibberd's design puts the altar in the middle under the spiky lantern that crowns the 16 concrete trusses forming the structure; inside, these enclose a vast and airy space, and round their feet are the side chapels.

Next to the Anglican Cathedral is one of England's most dramatic cemeteries, formed in 1823 in a quarry. The entrance to the cemetery is guarded by a mortuary chapel, an exquisite miniature Greek temple designed by John Foster, who was also responsible for the finest monument in the cemetery, a small domed rotunda of 1836 commemorating William Huskisson, Liverpool M.P. and Minister, killed by a railway train at the opening of the Liverpool to Manchester Railway. In the city center the **BLUECOAT SCHOOL**, with its three ranges in an attractive provincial baroque (1716), now has shops, studios and meeting rooms, and an attractive garden. The best survivor of 18th-century Liverpool is the Town Hall in Dale Street, designed by John Wood of Bath in 1749, rebuilt after fire by James Wyatt at the end of the century. The arcaded and domed front looks down Castle Street. But what most impresses are the interiors, a suite of civic rooms, in *enfilade* right round the building, handsomely decorated and still with much original furniture.

Just to the north of Albert Dock Liverpool's "Three Sisters", commercial buildings facing the river,

The Royal Liver Building

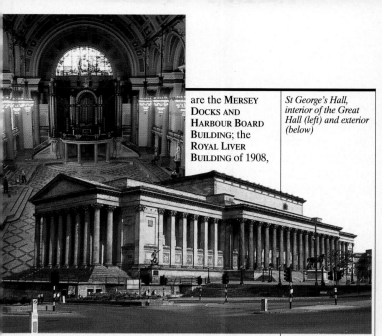

are the **MERSEY DOCKS AND HARBOUR BOARD BUILDING**; the **ROYAL LIVER BUILDING** of 1908,

St George's Hall, interior of the Great Hall (left) and exterior (below)

a pioneer American-influenced concrete-and-stone-clad skyscraper by W. Aubrey Thomas; and the **CUNARD BUILDING** of 1913 by Willink and Thicknesse. Next to these is the stone-clad ventilation tower to the Mersey Tunnel, by Herbert Rowse, with a nice relief sculpture of a begoggled motorcyclist by Tyson Smith.

The civic center of Liverpool must be **ST GEORGE'S HALL** (1839 onward) by Harvey Lonsdale Elmes, designed as a monumental Greek Temple raised on a podium. The east side, facing the station and St George's plateau, has a giant portico of 13 columns supporting an attic. The structure as well as the design is breathtaking: the main building is raised on great vaults of Piranesian splendor, and the hall is ceiled in hollow blocks to lighten the load. Elmes died young, and the principal interiors were designed by C.R. Cockerell. The great hall is a vast barrel-vaulted space, with five bays articulated by red granite columns, a richly plastered ceiling, much commemorative sculpture, enormous chandeliers and an immense floor of Minton tiles. At the north end, a more delicate small concert room has a gallery with an undulating front supported by draped ladies with their arms raised, and another wonderful chandelier. There are also two fine law courts – alas, no longer in use.

Away from the city center, up the hill and by the cathedrals, spreads Liverpool's once-fashionable residential district, now partly taken over by the university, which has colonized some of the Georgian houses and demolished many of them for new buildings; the contrast is seen most poignantly in Abercromby Square. Between the cathedrals is another Rowse building, the brown-brick **PHILHARMONIC HALL** of 1937; opposite is the **PHILHARMONIC HOTEL** of 1898, exotic within, and perhaps the finest pub interior in the North West with its plasterwork, beaten copper panels, ironwork and plaster caryatids.

ORIEL CHAMBERS
In Water Street stands Peter Ellis's Oriel Chambers (1864): a revolutionary iron-framed building with a clear proto-modern structural grid and an immense amount of glass. Nearby is Herbert Rowse's Barclays Bank, 1927, the epitome of French/American Beaux Arts classicism, popularized by Sir Charles Reilly's Liverpool School of Architecture (of which Rowse was a star pupil). Rowse also designed India Buildings, almost opposite, in similar fashion, with a shopping arcade running through the middle.

Liverpool Museum

Liverpool is worth visiting for its galleries alone. The Tate Gallery in the north and the collections of the various National Museums and Galleries on Merseyside provide a range of permanent and temporary exhibitions of enormous range. The visitor's pleasure is enhanced by the fact that all are housed in buildings of the greatest interest. The Tate and the Maritime Museum are in the converted warehouses at the Albert Dock and offer opportunities to see the fireproof structural engineering which makes the dock one of the principal monuments of 19th-century industrial and commercial architecture.

DEGAS
Woman Ironing, Walker Art Gallery

Below:
Dressing table by **THOMAS CHIPPENDALE**, rosewood and gilt, *c.* 1760. Lady Lever Art Gallery

THE CONSERVATION CENTRE
The most recent addition is the Conservation Centre in central Liverpool, converted out of the former Midland Railway's Goods Warehouse. The entrance hall is dominated by the statue of the Spirit of Liverpool removed for conservation from the top of the Walker Art Gallery, where a laser copied marble reproduction now stands.

THE LIVERPOOL MUSEUM AND THE WALKER ART GALLERY

The Liverpool Museum (Thomas Allom, 1860) and the Walker Art Gallery (Henry Vale, 1877) are both located in monumental classical buildings and both are due to expand in the near future, the Museum into the free classical and highly modeled and sculptured former Technical College (F.W. Mountford, 1902) and the Gallery into the former Sessions House (F & G Holme, 1884) at the top end of the gentle hill facing St George's Hall.

Top: **NICOLAS POUSSIN** *The Ashes of Phocion collected by his Widow*, Walker Art Gallery

Left: **JOSEPH WRIGHT OF DERBY** *Mr Fleetwood Hesketh*, Walker Art Gallery

Below: **ERCOLE DE'ROBERTI** *Pieta*, Walker Art Gallery

SUBURBAN MUSEUMS
Outposts of the museums are to be found in the suburbs of south Liverpool at Sudley House, an 1830s villa extended in the 1880s by the shipowner George Holt and still containing his collections, a monument to wealthy Victorian taste; and at Port Sunlight, across the Mersey on the Wirral, where the Lady Lever Gallery is the centerpiece of Lord Leverhulme's planned industrial settlement and again a monument to the eclectic tastes of a rich and discerning patron.

Bridge Cottage, Port Sunlight (below) and the Lady Lever Art Gallery (right)

FORMER BEATLE'S HOME
The building on the council estates that draws most visitors is probably the modest and unassuming No. 20 Forthlin Road, a 1950s house identical to its neighbors but famous as the home of Paul McCartney and now a shrine to Beatlemania. The house was recently acquired by the National Trust.

East of the city, CROXTETH HALL is a large country house, perhaps more rewarding for its estate buildings, especially a dairy (1861) by W.E. Nesfield, and a laundry by John Douglas. The farm has good buildings and the kitchen garden retains such curiosities as a heated wall and a mushroom house. Liverpool's other major house is SPEKE HALL, built for the Norris family round a small courtyard and surrounded by a moat crossed by a stone bridge. The exterior is characterized by much herring-bone framing and quatrefoil panels; the interiors have original molded timbers and fine plasterwork, especially in the Great Chamber, and elaborately carved chimneypieces.

PORT SUNLIGHT Across the Mersey is Port Sunlight, established in 1888, one of the largest of the industrial settlements set up by rich manufacturers. In the tradition of Saltaire and Bournville, Port Sunlight was the creation of Lord Leverhulme, and took its name from the soap that made his fortune. The estate falls into two halves: the southern section near the factory more picturesque and village-like, the northern section more formally planned around the LADY LEVER ART GALLERY ▲ *422-3* – a long, low, classical building of stone that contrasts with the brick, timber and plaster neo-vernacular of the housing round about. The Gallery, now part of the National Museums and Galleries on Merseyside, is a monument not only to Leverhulme's architectural patronage but also to his enthusiasms; it houses a wonderful collection of furniture (especially French 18th-century pieces) and 19th-century British painting and sculpture.

LANCASHIRE

North of the east–west conurbation of Liverpool and Manchester, Lancashire breaks into two clearly separated areas: the flat lands of the coast, and the hills of the west Pennines to the east. North of Manchester, the towns are heavily influenced by the remains of the cotton industry; the townscape of many is dominated by the multi-storey spinning mills and the lower weaving sheds, with their zig-zag north light roofs. These towns have clear identities, marked in many cases by town halls of remarkable pretension.

ROCHDALE The Town Hall (1866), by W.H. Crossland, is one of the high points of the secular Gothic Revival – gabled, traceried and with a tower finished by Waterhouse.
Further west, in **BOLTON**, the classical Town Hall (1866) by William Hill of Leeds has all the confidence of Leeds Town Hall. LE MANS CRESCENT, designed by local architects Bradshaw Gass and Hope in the 1930s, gives the center of

Speke Hall exterior (top) and Oak Drawing Room

Le Mans Crescent

Rochdale Town Hall (left and above left)

A COMPER CHURCH
Not far from Rochdale's Town Hall, in Toad Lane (where the origins of the Co-operative Movement are celebrated in a museum), is one of Ninian Comper's most remarkable churches, St Mary's, a rebuilding in 1909-11 of a 1740 church where classical Tuscan and Perpendicular Gothic are seamlessly blended and some of Comper's best woodwork is housed.

Bolton a metropolitan flavor. These buildings include an excellent local museum and gallery, which contains work by the Bolton-born American artist Thomas Moran. This strong architectural sense of civic pride is reinforced by one of the North's largest enclosed market halls, begun in 1853 and since extended to combine with a modern shopping center, and a large and lofty parish church rebuilt by Paley (1867). Suburban Bolton reveals the town's earlier origins.

HALL-I'-THE-WOOD A museum now best known as the place where Samuel Crompton invented the spinning mule, this is a fine black-and-white house of the 16th and 17th centuries with much decorative detail, repaired and reinstated when it was bought for the town of his birth by Lord Leverhulme, and done up by his Port Sunlight architects Jonathan Simpson and Grayson and Ould.

16th-century timbering at Hall-i'-the-Wood

Rufford Old Hall (left) and its Great Hall (below)

Turton Tower, near Darwen

Smithills Hall, Bolton

At **SMITHILLS HALL**, too, there is house with early origins (in this case 15th century), on a grander scale and with its open hall surviving, but with less appealing detail than at Hall-i'-the-Wood; and here there are 19th-century extensions by George Devey.

The earlier stages of the Lancashire cotton industry are best seen in the industrial museum at Helmshore, further north on the west Pennines, housed in old mill buildings with water-driven machinery. The attractive riverside site seems ages away from the "dark satanic mills" usually associated with industrialization. Not far away, in Rawtenstall, next to a mid-19th-century steam-driven mill, is an earlier handloom weaver's house with the typical range of top-floor windows to light the looms. The later phases of the industry can be seen at Wigan Pier, where the significance of the coal mines and the canals can be appreciated. At Trencherfield Mill, there is one of the largest working stationary steam engines.

ASTLEY HALL To the west, the signs of industry are less apparent. At Chorley, Astley Hall remains as a mid-17th-century great house: stone, old-fashioned in its asymmetrical composition and many of its details, especially the great areas of glazing reminiscent in quantity, if not in sophistication, of Hardwick Hall. Inside is a fine scrolly staircase, panel paintings of heroes as varied as Tamburlane, Elizabeth I and Christopher Columbus, and ceiling plasterwork of such barbaric character and so deeply undercut that the visitor fears to stand beneath.

RUFFORD OLD HALL ★ Further west still, as the land flattens out, is perhaps the finest of the medieval Lancashire black-and-white houses. Its 15th-century Great Hall is still open to the roof with wonderfully decorated hammerbeam trusses. Between the spere posts at the screens

Port Erin

passage end stands the only remaining movable screen, elaborately carved in as barbaric a fashion as the plasterwork at Astley Hall and so exotic that it reminded Sir Nikolaus Pevsner more of Indonesia than of Lancashire.

Further west still is SCARISBRICK HALL, equally richly carved and decorated, and one of A.W.N. Pugin's finest secular works: a part-remodeling of an earlier house for a client prepared to indulge some of Pugin's wildest ideas in planning and decoration, so that both spatial organization and detail are arresting. Moreover, Charles Scarisbrick, the patron, encouraged Pugin's antiquarian enthusiasms so that Pugin's fabric is interspersed with Flemish woodwork, including a 16th-century panel from Antwerp Cathedral. Scarisbrick Hall was then enlarged with a mini "Big Ben" clock tower by Pugin's son. Not far away, behind the coastal resort of Southport, is MEOLS HALL, 17th century in origin but now perhaps most remarkable for the works carried out in the 1960s by its then owner, Roger Hesketh. Hesketh maintained the 18th-century tradition of the gentleman-architect in an early 18th-century style, incorporating fragments rescued from demolished Lancashire houses and having in his home farm a Palladian cow-house, now listed, designed and built by himself.

Glass in the Falcon's Nest, Port Erin

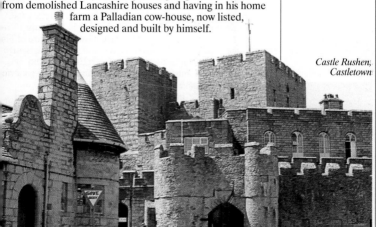

Castle Rushen, Castletown

ISLE OF MAN

The sovereign of the Isle of Man is the sovereign of England, but the island is practically independent and feels it. Green and hilly, it is attractive more for its isolation and open spaces than for its architecture, but there is a fine medieval castle at Castletown and attractive townscapes there and at Peel and Port St Mary. The island's capital, Douglas, has more the atmosphere of a Victorian seaside resort with terraces of hotels facing the sea, somewhat blemished by new building to accommodate offshore financial institutions. There are museums at Castletown and Douglas and an open-air folk museum at Port Erin. The Isle of Man's most spectacular monument is undoubtedly the water-wheel at Laxey, the largest of its kind in the world. The wheel is still turning, though now to no purpose as the lead mines it once drained no longer function; it is known as Lady Isabella, after the wife of the island governor in 1854 when it was commissioned.

Port Erin

Above: Colne parish church
Above right: Hoghton Tower

Samlesbury Hall exterior (bottom), and the Great Hall (below)

PRESTON

Preston stands in a loop of the River Ribble, its hilltop site marking its strategic position as the gateway to the further North West. The town has two buildings remarkable for their uncompromising architecture: ST WALBURGE'S CHURCH is the most impressive of a group of Roman Catholic churches, its spire dominating the south of the town. Built in the early 1850s by J.A. Hansom, it has all the structural adventure of his Holy Name Church at Manchester. Because of the height of the spire (the tallest non-cathedral spire in England) the church looks small; but inside, the steep hammerbeam roof on a wide aisleless church makes the internal space, lit entirely by patterned rather than pictorial windows, cavernous and forbidding.

In the town center is the HARRIS MUSEUM AND LIBRARY by local architect James Hibbert, a monumental classical building of the 1880s that would seem more at home in Germany than the north of England. It stands on a high podium, the front to the Market Place inscribed with the words "To Literature, Arts and Sciences" and the pediment filled to overflowing with sculpture. Above there is a square lantern, which lights a great central hall and staircase with sculpture by Thorwaldsen. The galleries contain work by the Preston artist Arthur Devis, including his self-portrait.

East of Preston the towns represent the northern outcrop of the Lancashire textile industry, stretching in a string from Blackburn to Colne. They can be bleak in the winter, but their buildings of sandstone and millstone grit, often now cleaned of industrial grime, can be attractive in the sun. The industrial urban landscape is very evident and in Darwen, with the India Mill chimney of almost 300 feet, is near overpowering. Most local museums have something on textiles (Blackburn's is especially noteworthy) but except perhaps for the

St Walburge's Church

430

GAWTHORPE HALL (left) At Padiham is Gawthorpe Hall, built in 1600 and perhaps the region's best example of that compact Elizabethan planning associated with the designs of Robert Smythson. Of its original interiors, the best is a splendid long gallery. Gawthorpe was restored and improved in 1850 by Sir Charles Barry and is now as much a monument to him as to its first builder, Lawrence Shuttleworth. Barry worked for the Kay-Shuttleworths, whose family collection of needlework, together with portraits from the National Portrait Gallery, makes Gawthorpe treasured for its contents as well as its architecture.

Weavers' Triangle, a restored complex by the Leeds and Liverpool Canal in Burnley Town center, and Queen Street Mill (a working mill still with steam-driven looms), the most visited places are those that predate the industrial past.

HOGHTON TOWER, between Preston and Blackburn, was built in stone in the later 16th century, its gatehouse and battlements giving it a somewhat military air. Carefully restored in the 19th century and well maintained in its hilltop setting and admirable gardens, it has an almost unreal quality to it; it has been regularly used for film locations.

SAMLESBURY HALL, a few miles to the north and the most northerly of the great black-and-white houses, presents another open hall, this time with arched-braced crucks, its former screen now turned into a minstrels' gallery at the wrong end.

TOWNELEY HALL in Burnley is now in a somewhat municipalized setting, housing an art gallery. Towneley has a complex architectural history, its medieval origins now somewhat overlaid by later alterations that include works by Sir Jeffry Wyatville, best known for his work at Windsor Castle ▲ 298-9 and Zoffany's "Townley's Conversation Piece". What is most striking at Towneley, however, is the refitting of the hall in the 1720s, enriched by beautiful plasterwork by the Italian *stuccatori* Vassali and Quadri, with medallions of Roman emperors.

ACCRINGTON In a small, Arts and Crafts house designed by Walter Brierley in 1909 for a local factory owner, is the HOWARTH ART GALLERY, noted above all for its outstanding collection of Tiffany glass sent from New York to the town of his birth by an expatriate who had connections with the firm. Accrington is also the home of the hard red-brick made by Nori ("iron" backward), whose inability to weather gracefully has left its mark across much of the North West.

Above: Gawthorpe Hall exterior and Drawing Room

Towneley Hall

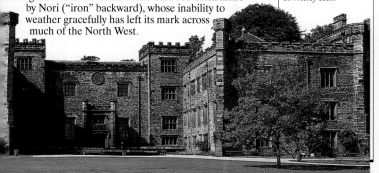

West of Preston, the flat land of the Fylde has a very different character. There is one major house, **LYTHAM HALL**, designed by John Carr and built in 1757-64. It is one of the first 18th-century houses to bring the principal reception rooms on to the ground floor, although the external order still creates a *piano nobile*; it has a major Fuseli.

BROWSHOLME HALL
(above and top)
Remote in wooded countryside, this Tudor hall is an attractive stone house first built in the 16th century but altered, especially by Wyattville in the 1820s; the exterior is notable for its robust frontispiece of three superimposed classical orders. The Parker family have lived here for centuries, and the furniture and pictures reinforce the feeling that this is an historic home rather than a public gallery.

Lytham Hall

BLACKPOOL TOWER is a landmark building which identifies its hometown more than any other in England. Opened in 1894, it was modeled on the Eiffel Tower, but whereas the Parisian prototype stands free, Blackpool Tower surmounts a seafront building housing the entertainments that made Blackpool a magnet for millions of holidaymakers. Within are two of Frank Matcham's best interiors, the Circus Arena, a Moorish fantasy, and the Ballroom, a Rococo extravaganza of plasterwork and decorative painting. Matcham produced a further fine interior for the Grand Theatre. The theme of rich interiors is maintained in the Winter Gardens, based on a theater of the 1870s but with many additions, each trying to outdo its predecessor in exotic ostentation, ending with the Galleon Bar, Baronial Hall and Spanish Hall of 1931, decorated in fibrous plaster by Andrew Mazzei, art director of the Gaumont Film Company.

North of the industrial areas in east Lancashire the landscape becomes pastoral, the hill farms nestling in sheltered spots and there are some picturesque villages, such as Downham and Slaidburn. Some of the small towns contain some of Lancashire's best early buildings: **WHALLEY** has the remains of a Cistercian abbey, of which the dormitory and the gatehouse are the best remaining parts, **CLITHEROE** has a castle, reputed to have the smallest stone keep in England; **RIBCHESTER** has Lancashire's best-known Roman remains, part of a fort established by Agricola in AD 79 and what is left of a 2nd-century bath-house. Much of this area was once the medieval park of the Forest of Bowland. Not far away, at **STONYHURST**, any domestic atmosphere that the 16th-century house of the Shireburnes once had is now lost beneath the activity of a major school. Like many Lancashire families, the owners of Stonyhurst maintained their Roman Catholic faith and in 179 the house was given to the Jesuits, whose English college in

the Low Countries had been forced to flee by the French Revolution. A Jesuit school Stonyhurst remains. The old house is approached by a long drive flanked by canals; to one side is the church added in the 1830s by J.J. Scoles, turreted *à la* King's College Chapel ▲ *332-3* and with an interior decorated in 1954 by Goodhart-Rendel.

LANCASTER

Lancashire's county town stands at the far north of the county. Its historic core centers upon the hilltop medieval castle and priory church. The CASTLE, now largely a prison, has an impressive 12th-century stone keep, still visible above the curtain walls, and an imposing early 15th-century battlemented gatehouse, called John of Gaunt's but in fact built by his son, Henry IV. The prison interiors, not easily visited, contain a good example of prison planning following John Howard's reforms, including a women's prison of 1818-21, designed by Joseph Gandy on the panopticon principle.

Other prison buildings were designed by Thomas Harrison, whose principal additions to the castle are accessible. These comprise the SHIRE HALL of 1796-8 – semi-circular, plaster-vaulted and timber-furnished in a beautiful Gothick style, decorated with hundreds of shields as a genealogical guide to Lancashire's history – and the CROWN COURT. The Grand Jury room retains its furniture made by Gillows workshops, where local craftsmen produced some of the best 18th- and 19th-century English furniture.

Next to the castle is the PRIORY, a handsome 15th-century church with a rebuilt west tower of 1753, entirely in keeping with the medieval church. The glory of the church is its set of 14th-century stalls, imported from an unknown source, with richly carved canopies and misericords.

As Lancaster prospered in the 18th century, the town spread down from the hill and along the Lune. The significance of Lancaster as the county town is seen not only in the Shire Hall but also in the JUDGE'S LODGING, a 17th-century house adapted for the visiting assize judges and now a museum containing an

CUSTOM HOUSE (left) The effect of Lancaster's growing coastal and international trade is evident in the warehouses facing the river: among them the Custom House in St George's Quay, now the Maritime Museum, an elegant Palladian building with an Ionic portico built by local architect (and furniture-designer) Richard Gillow in 1764.

Lancaster Castle

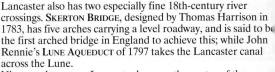

Lune Aqueduct

The Library in the Ruskin Centre

Ashton Memorial

outstanding collection of Gillow furniture, as well as in the former town hall, built in 1783, now the CITY MUSEUM.

Lancaster also has two especially fine 18th-century river crossings. SKERTON BRIDGE, designed by Thomas Harrison in 1783, has five arches carrying a level roadway, and is said to be the first arched bridge in England to achieve this; while John Rennie's LUNE AQUEDUCT of 1797 takes the Lancaster canal across the Lune.

Nineteenth-century Lancaster became the center of the linoleum industry. The leading lino maker was James Williamson, later Lord Ashton, and in Williamson Park stands the ASHTON MEMORIAL, occupying a site with magnificent views over Lancaster and Morecambe Bay. This monument to the Williamson family is an enormous Edwardian baroque confection designed by John Belcher. The architect was not local and the materials – white Portland stone and a green copper dome – seem alien as well; but the panache of the design, with the dome standing on a square base and lesser domes at the corners, can be appreciated in almost any context.

Lancaster became the seat of a new university in 1964. Like others of the time, the UNIVERSITY has a self-contained campus by architects Shepheard and Epstein to the south of the city, which is perhaps more noteworthy for its landscape architecture than for the individual buildings that made it up (although the chaplaincy with a clover-leaf plan and central spire is an inspiring effort of ecumenical planning). What will draw visitors, however, is the new RUSKIN CENTRE, designed by Richard MacCormac to house the books, manuscripts and drawings that belonged to John Ruskin. For those who associate Ruskin with Gothic, and especially Venetian Gothic, the building may not immediately call his name to mind; but its care for color, texture and decoration is entirely within the Ruskinian ideal.

North of Lancaster the scenery becomes wilder; even the motorways open up the vistas that appealed to the romantic sensibilities of the Lake poets.

LEIGHTON HALL The last major monument in Lancashire itself, this was the home of the Gillows from 1822, is still lived in by their descendants and is furnished with many of their best pieces. The house goes back to the 1760s, but it was prettily Gothicized by Richard Gillow when he bought it and then in a more scholarly way by Paley and Austin in the 1870s. Notable inside are the Hall, with its delightful cast-iron Gothic arcade, top-lit Billiard Room (Gillow was among the first to make billiard tables), and the altarpiece in the chapel; the Gillows, like many Lancashire families, held fast to their Catholic faith

John Ruskin, painted by William Gersham Collingwood, 1897

Crucifixion window in Kirby Lonsdale church

Leighton Hall

KENDAL

KIRBY LONSDALE Up the Lune Valley is Kirby Lonsdale, a town of attractive stone houses with a fine church. The view over the Lune was painted by Turner and described by Ruskin as one of the loveliest scenes in England. Nearby is Church Brow Cottage, a picturesque garden pavilion.

KENDAL Kirby Lonsdale guards the approaches to the Lake District from Yorkshire, while the southern key to the Lakes is Kendal, still attractive despite traffic and a shopping center. The most important attraction here is **ABBOT HALL** (1759), built by John Carr for Colonel Wilson so close to the town center and the church that it is a town house, but with its own grounds and outbuildings that give it a sense of space. The house is a late Palladian villa, with a central block and lower wings with Venetian windows. It now serves as an excellent museum and art gallery, with permanent collections downstairs and temporary exhibitions above; the outbuildings contain the Museum of Lakeland Life.

Close to Kendal are two major houses – Sizergh and Levens.

Below: Sizergh Castle exterior and (bottom), two of its paintings: Roger Strickland by Belle, c. 1697 (left) and Cecilia Strickland by Romney (right)

SIZERGH CASTLE is the typical accretive stone house of the North West. Its earliest surviving part is the mid-14th-century pele tower, while the whole is a mixture of additions given unity by the continuous ownership by the Strickland family (although it is now in the care of the National Trust), the

Cartmel Priory

exterior views enhanced by the wonderful garden setting. The interiors make Sizergh remarkable, above all, the great Inlaid Room, just recovered after a century in the Victoria & Albert Museum. The contents include Mary of Modena's personal portrait collection, and some very early Romneys.

LEVENS HALL ★, further west, is still in the hands of the Bagot family, whose continuous ownership goes back only three centuries. Levens, like Sizergh, is built round a pele tower and has many Elizabethan details comparable to those of its near neighbor. But it also has the improvements introduced after the sale of the estate in 1688, including a grand staircase, a room exquisitely lined with 17th-century Spanish leather, and

Levens Hall

perhaps the most famous topiary garden in England, laid out *c.* 1700 by Guillaume Beaumont, formerly gardener to James II. There are over 90 pieces of topiary, some over 30 feet high. The house has paintings by Rubens, Lely and Cuyp.

West of Levens in south Cumbria is Furness, once known as "Lancashire north of the sands".

CARTMEL At the center of Furness is Cartmel, an attractive small town, with its priory gatehouse surviving in the middle. Cartmel is dominated by its CHURCH ★, formerly an Augustinian priory which survived the Dissolution because it was also the parish church. But it has monastic size and architectural richness, the exterior distinctive in the way the square top stage of the central tower sits diagonally on the square of the crossing. Inside there is good joinery, 15th-century stalls with misericords, and an unusual screen of 1620 whose traceried panels may be Gothic Revival or survival. Best of all is the stone tomb of Sir John Harrington (died 1347); it is richly carved, with a base frieze of almsmen and mourners, and has a painted wooden ceiling.

Holker Hall

Lake Windermere

HOLKER HALL ★, near Cartmel is an old house Victorianized for the 7th Duke of Devonshire by Webster of Kendal in 1840 and by Paley and Austin of Lancaster in 1873, so presenting a textbook example of two stages of 19th-century domestic design. Still occupied by the Cavendish family, the house has very fine gardens. Works by Paxton were added to and amended by Thomas Mawson and again by the present owners. Medieval Furness was dominated by **FURNESS ABBEY**, established by the Savignacs in 1127 and Cistercian from 1147. The Abbey is now an impressive ruin in surroundings that still give some impression of the remoteness sought by the Cistercians. There is plenty of recognizable 12th-century detail (such as waterleaf capitals), especially in the transepts, and fine stone 15th-century sedilia in the choir. Most impressive of all are the remains of the 13th-century Chapter-house, entered from the cloister through beautifully moulded arches. Above the Abbey is the **ABBEY HOUSE HOTEL**, built by Lutyens for the managing director of the Barrow shipyard; not Lutyens at his best, but the best example of his domestic work in the region. Elsewhere in Furness there are monuments of very different character. Dalton Castle is a 14th-century tower in the middle of a charming little town. Its church (1882), with its big west tower, is one of Paley and Austin's finest, displaying their characteristic treatment of the chancel with differing arcades on north and south sides.

Above and below: Furness Abbey

CONISHEAD PRIORY, built 1821-36 by Philip Wyatt for Colonel Braddyll, is a folly of over-ambition which bankrupted its owner. A huge early Gothic Revival composition, it had neither the seriousness or quality of materials that marked later phases of the Revival. It has now found a new use as a Buddhist center: Wyatt's magnificent staircase frames a majestic statue of the Buddha. At Stott Park, discreetly set among the woodland, is **STOTT PARK BOBBIN MILL** (right), a working factory of 1835 whose products were an essential part of the textile revolution taking place 60 miles to the south in industrial Lancashire. Near Stott Park is **FINSTHWAITE**, perhaps Paley and Austin's most accomplished village church. Built in 1873, the small church is an exercise in 12th-century revival that is beautifully adapted to its site.

LAKE DISTRICT

Derwentwater

The Lake District is characterized by its small houses rather than by mansions. Some are visited as shrines to the famous, usually literary figures, who have lived there – William Wordsworth pre-eminent among them. Between 1777 and 1783, he attended the 16th-century grammar school at Hawkshead, which still stands. In Sawrey is Beatrix Potter's house, **HILL TOP**, and at Coniston is Brantwood, the house bought by John Ruskin ▲ *434* in 1871 and extended by him. It is a shrine to a prophet of 19th-century taste rather than a building of any great merit; but it has a fine site overlooking the lake.

GRASMERE, further north, has the greatest Wordsworth associations. **DOVE COTTAGE** is another piece of Lakeland vernacular architecture, where the poet lived from 1799 to 1808, a period meticulously covered in his sister Dorothy's journal. Here he lived simply, before moving to somewhat larger premises nearby at Rydal Mount, which remained his home until his death in 1850; his birthplace is in a fine Georgian town house at Cockermouth. All these three buildings now house Wordsworth memorabilia.

At some places it is possible to get a view of the traditional architecture of the Lake District less obstructed by the fame of those who have lived there. **TOWNEND** (near Windermere Troutbeck) is a yeoman farmer's house of 1626. The home of the Browne family until 1943, the house epitomizes both the remoteness of the Lake District in the 17th century and the domestic arrangements, house and furniture, which evolved to meet it.

William Wordsworth and the Drawing Room of his birthplace at Cockermouth

At **WINDERMERE** the buildings represent the increasing attractiveness of the Lake District to those who appreciated the landscape but whose money was often made elsewhere. In the middle of the lake, on Belle Isle, is one of the first buildings designed to take advantage of a picturesque site – the remarkable round house designed by John Plaw in 1774 for Thomas English, recently restored after fire damage. The house is now largely screened by trees, but can be glimpsed from boat trips on the lake.

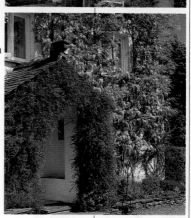

Hill Top, the 17th-century home of Beatrix Potter

STORRS HALL was remodeled by Joseph Gandy in 1808; projecting into the lake on a short causeway is Gandy's classical garden temple of 1804, commemorating admirals Nelson, Duncan, Howe and St Vincent.

More prominent still is **WRAY CASTLE**, a romantic silhouette of turrets on the west bank of the lake, designed in 1840 by the Liverpool architect Henry Horner for the Liverpool surgeon James Dawson. Windermere also attracted a remarkable group of Arts and Crafts houses: **BLACKWELL** (1900), by Baillie Scott for Sir Edward Holt, and **BROADLEYS** (now the Motor Boat Club) and **MOOR CRAG**, both 1898, by C.F. Voysey ● 89.

Rydal Mount, a 16th-century farmhouse with 18th-century additions, where Wordsworth lived from 1808-50

Further north, the Lake District centers on Keswick and Derwentwater. The latter, like Windermere, has a house on an island, in this case an 1840 villa. **KESWICK** itself has a fine early 19th-century town hall (now the Lake District National Park information center) and a church of 1838 by Anthony Salvin.

CASTLERIGG STONE CIRCLE Outside Keswick is this most immediately visible evidence of the prehistoric settlement of the Lake District, comprising 38 stones with a further 10 forming a unique rectangular enclosure within; current opinion dates it to perhaps 3000 BC, when the Lake District was the center of a trade in stone axes.

Castlerigg Stone Circle

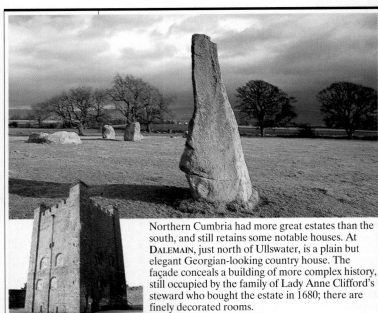

Northern Cumbria had more great estates than the south, and still retains some notable houses. At **DALEMAIN**, just north of Ullswater, is a plain but elegant Georgian-looking country house. The façade conceals a building of more complex history, still occupied by the family of Lady Anne Clifford's steward who bought the estate in 1680; there are finely decorated rooms.

LOWTHER CASTLE, outside Penrith, is now one of England's most impressive ruins, tended by grazing sheep. In 1806 Sir Robert Smirke built this huge house for the Earl of Lonsdale; it is classical in its composition but Gothic in its detailing, battlements and turrets. A century-and-a-half later this apparently unmanageable house was deliberately unroofed to avoid tax. Nearby, in Lowther Village, is one of the most interesting designs by the Adam brothers, a planned estate settlement of *c.* 1770 culminating in a crescent (originally intended to be a complete circus) of worker's houses, based on the ideas of fashionable Bath.

Top: the standing stones known as Long Meg & Her Daughter, Little Salkeld
Center: Appleby Castle
Above: Lowther Castle

Brough Castle

Further west is Appleby, straddling the route across the Pennines, with a fine main street, wide and gently curving, rising toward the castle. This has some good houses: **RED HOUSE** (1717), **WHITE HOUSE** (1756), and **LADY ANNE CLIFFORD'S HOSPITAL**, almshouses of 1651. **APPLEBY CASTLE** combines a medieval castle, a 12th-century

Below left: Brough Castle

Hutton-in-the-Forest

keep and curtain walls with a splendid 17th-century range in up-to-date country-house style, built in the 1680s for the Earl of Thanet, and housing Lady Anne Clifford's extraordinary family triptych. Her hand can also be seen in the Castle and even more so, beyond Appleby, in the wild Pennine countryside, at **BROUGH CASTLE**, a medieval construction on a Roman site, rebuilt after a Scottish invasion in 1174. It was restored by Lady Anne in medieval fashion so that now, as a ruin, the original and the restoration merge into a handsome whole that dominates the main road across the hills. Lady Anne's influence can be seen yet again at Brougham Castle, less dramatically sited just outside Penrith, where there is a fine 13th-century stone keep.

HUTTON-IN-THE-FOREST, between Penrith and Carlisle, is another house built round a medieval pele tower. The most impressive additions are those of the 17th century, first an old-fashioned long gallery of the 1640s on the first floor and originally built on an open arcade, and then, in exuberant late 17th-century fashion, a richly molded five-bay frontispiece, still with stone cross casement window.

Further north toward Carlisle is one of England's most improbable churches, at **WREAY ★**. Designed by Sara Losh as a memorial to her

THE IMAGE GARDEN
In the village of Reaghyll, south of Penrith, there is an unusual sculpture garden created in the early 19th century by a self-taught local man, Thomas Bland. Around 50 sculptures are arranged in "rooms", each with a specific theme – Shakespearean plays, Scottish poets, mythical characters, and so forth. It was created to commemorate the coronation of Queen Victoria and an event is held there every year on that date. It is not yet open to the public but the new owner intends to do so soon.

Right: Muncaster Castle exterior and interior

sister who died in 1835, the church is built in an eclectic neo-Norman/ Lombardic style which reflects Miss Losh's extensive travels and is decorated with wild carvings of plants and animals commissioned by her from a local carver; the woodwork is partly cut out of trees with the bark left on. The glass contains fragments from the Archbishop's Palace at Sens.

West of Carlisle, at Warwick Bridge, is Our Lady and St Wilfrid, a small Pugin church of 1841, Gothic in plan and detail, nicely decorated, and a key monument in the Puginian revolution that overtook church architecture in the 1840s.

West of the Lake District the Cumbrian coast is bleak and in many cases forlorn, as the industries that once made it thrive have gone. **MUNCASTER CASTLE**, passed by descent for nearly 800 years, has a medieval core, but the best of what is seen results from Anthony Salvin's rebuilding of 1862. His High Victorian interiors became even more opulent when the castle acquired the collections of the Ramsden family in the 1920s; at the same time the setting was changed with the creation of splendid gardens.

Further north, **WHITEHAVEN** is a town founded by the Lowther family and made prosperous from trade in coal and tobacco. It still has many good Georgian houses and an excellent Georgian church, **ST JAMES'S**, built in 1752 and designed by Sir William Lowther's steward, Carlisle Spedding. The galleries are supported on Tuscan columns with a full entablature, and themselves have Ionic columns supporting a ceiling with good stucco decoration.

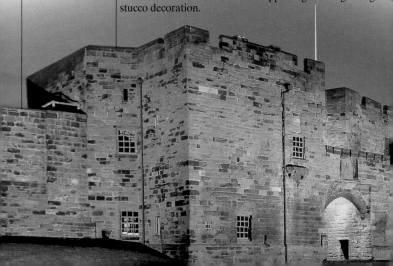

CARLISLE

Carlisle marks England's northwest frontier with Scotland and still has the atmosphere of a border city, even though most of the city walls have gone. Entering from the south, visitors pass through the citadel, originally built by Henry VIII's engineer

Stefan von Haschenberg and remodeled in 1810 by Sir Robert Smirke to provide the assize courts, housed in relatively low but massive towers, embattled and lit by ranges of Gothic windows. The military center of Carlisle is not here, however, but at the castle, where Mary Queen of Scots was imprisoned in 1568. It is based on a 12th-century keep and curtain wall, with wall walks and excellent views. It was much remodeled, as Carlisle's strategic position against the Scots meant that its facilities had to be constantly updated. There is a fine medieval gatehouse with portcullis; the keep contains carvings left by medieval prisoners. Buildings by both Henry VIII and Elizabeth testify to troubled Tudor times. There are 19th-century barracks; the Border Regiment Museum is in the former domestic quarters.

St James's Church, Whitehaven (above and left)

Within the city, shopping has been neatly fitted into the townscape, which centers around the Market Place at the junction of English and Scotch streets. Here is a Market Cross of 1682, a 17th-century Guildhall, and a rather humble 18th-century Town Hall.

Carlisle Castle cannons (left) and the outer gatehouse, keep and rampart wall (below)

Naworth Castle

NAWORTH CASTLE
The castle is a medieval house convincingly reinstated by Salvin after a fire in 1844, with fine decorative features, including a timber ceiling, imported from elsewhere. It has provided a setting for several films, including *Jane Eyre*.

Right and below left: Tullie House, staircase

Far right: Prior Salkeld's Screen in Carlisle Cathedral

The principal buildings are TULLIE HOUSE (1689), now the museum, with a fine staircase and classical details that recall those at Hutton-in-the-Forest ▲ *441*, and the cathedral.
CARLISLE CATHEDRAL, begun in 1102, is the smallest in England. Originally an Augustinian Priory, the church became the center of the diocese established by Henry I in 1133. Much of the 12th-century nave was destroyed by the invading Scottish army in 1645; what is left shows the Norman origins of the church. The chancel is Gothic, 13th and 14th century, spectacular for the carvings on the capitals of the arcades, representing the months of the year. Among the cathedral's most noteworthy features are the very fine east window; flowing tracery now filled with Hardman glass; some excellent joinery in the medieval stalls, richly canopied; Prior Salkeld's screen of *c.* 1541, a fine example of the Renaissance fashion for placing profile heads in medallions; and a pulpit originally from Antwerp. The cathedral is not visually dominant; in fact the city's highest building is the very fine chimney-stack to Dixon's Mill, 300 feet high, designed by Richard Tattersall in 1836, with William Fairbairn as engineer.

Carlisle Cathedral

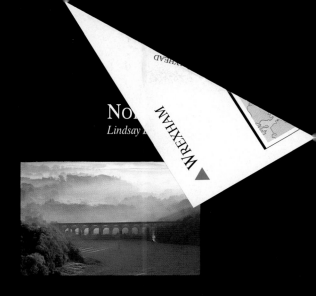

NO
Lindsay

WREXHAM

▲

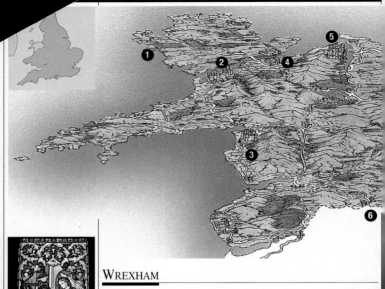

Stained glass window, Mold

ST GILES

The parish church of St Giles in Wrexham has the grandeur of a cathedral. Its ornate tower (1506) is extolled in a popular rhyme as one of the "Seven Wonders of Wales":
Pistyll Rhaeadr and Wrexham Steeple,/ Snowdon's mountain without its people,/ Overton yew trees, St Winefred's Wells/ Llangollen bridge and Gresford bells.
A replica of it was built in the 1920s at Yale, Connecticut.

WREXHAM

North Wales's largest town, equidistant from Offa's Dyke and the English border, developed from a market town into a substantial commercial center to meet the demands of a growing population dependent on the expanding coal and iron industries. The turn-of-the-century boom in house-building resulted in a proliferation of the locally produced Ruabon red brick.

YALE COLLEGE in Wrexham is said to be named after the Welsh word for hill (*iâl*). A replica of it was built in the 1920s at Yale, Connecticut, the University named after the Welsh benefactor, Elihu Yale, whose ancestors were members of a Denbighshire family and whose father emigrated to America in the 1640s. Elihu Yale's career included a period as Governor of the East India Company in Madras. The church interior is full of interest: a fine timber roof, enigmatic wall paintings, an impressive early 16th-century brass eagle lectern, and among the many monuments, a very theatrical one by Louis Roubiliac to Mary Myddelton (d. 1747) of Chirk Castle.

ALL SAINTS CHURCH, GRESFORD has at least two features in common with St Giles. They are both "wonders of Wales" (see left), and were built by Margaret Beaufort, the mother of Henry Vll.

MOLD (Yr Wyddgrug) is a market town based on a crossroads which rises to provide an elevated position for the town's most distinguished building, the parish church of St Mary's, another foundation of Margaret Beaufort. Mold is probably a corruption of the name of Norman de Montalt or de Mohaut, who established a stronghold here. On the hillside, as part of a civic complex of the 1970s, stands Theatr Clwyd, a highly innovative community arts center ● 56.

EWLOE is one of the least known of the castles in Wales. It is a Welsh castle, neither Norman nor medieval – the original was that of Edward I. Much of the fascination of Llywelyn ap Gruffudd's (d. 1282) stronghold, "built in the corner of the woods", is its unlikely defensive situation.

BASINGWERK ABBEY Originally of the Savigniac order, its remains were engulfed by industrial opportunism. It offers good views over the Dee estuary.

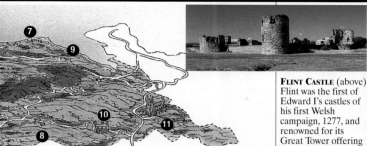

FLINT CASTLE (above) Flint was the first of Edward I's castles of his first Welsh campaign, 1277, and renowned for its Great Tower offering independent defence from the rest of the stronghold. Flint itself was designed as a bastide town.

St Winefride's Chapel and Holy Well

HOLYWELL owes its identity to a well whose curative properties were said to stem from the miraculous recovery of the 7th-century St Gwenfrewi (St Winefride) who, having escaped an attempted rape, was beheaded by her pursuer, Caradog, a chieftain, but brought back to life by her uncle, St Beuno. Above the shrine is a handsome chapel, which owes its existence to the patronage of Margaret Beaufort.

BASINGWERK ABBEY, originally Savigniac, had control over Saint Winefride's Well between the 13th and 15th centuries, but later became engulfed by industrial opportunism.

GREENFIELD VALLEY A walk through the Greenfield Valley, which is effectively interpreted through displays and signs, illustrates the economic history of this part of Wales. Agriculture, lead and copper smelting, and the making of brass and wire, were all dependent on hydraulic power, which according to Dr Johnson and Mrs Thrale's account of their Welsh journey of 1774 "turns 19 mills ... and [offers] an opportunity of seeing the cutting of a bar of iron at a stroke."

GRESFORD MONUMENTS
The interior of All Saints, Gresford is joyfully light, and rich in monuments. A recent acquisition is the depiction of the Gresford Disaster, an underground explosion in which over 250 died, and which is also commemorated in the local park. The Trevor Chapel is dedicated to the life of John Trevor of Trefalun, whose family seat, Trefalun Hall (1576), can be seen from the main road between Gresford and Rossett. Now divested of its gloomy 19th-century stucco, it is one of the first and most accomplished expressions of the Renaissance taste in Wales.

St Mary's Church, Mold

▲ ERDDIG ★

The Yorke family owned Erddig for more than 200 years until 1973, when Philip Yorke (the "Last Squire") gave it to the National Trust, who immediately undertook the task of repairing its advanced state of decay. Its remarkable state rooms still retain their 18th- and 19th-century furniture and fittings, including some beautiful Chinese wallpaper. Most rooms have no electric light. Kitchens, laundry, stables and sawmill, bakehouse, smithy and joiner's shop make up a fascinating range of outbuildings.

SCREEN GATES
The early-18th-century screen, strategically placed beyond the canal of the formal garden, is probably the work of the local Davies brothers, renowned for their exquisite craftsmanship as also seen at Chirk Castle ▲ *450.*

STATE BED
The early-18th-century State Bed, probably the most ornate piece of furniture in the house, suffered almost irreparable damage during the period of Erddig's neglect from the 1940s. It was expertly restored by the Victoria and Albert Museum in the 1970s.
Right (inset): detail showing the carved and gilt enrichments on the State Bed

SERVANT PORTRAITS
Erddig is fascinating for the glimpse it gives of life above and below stairs, and the series of "servant portraits" on display. Shown above is Thomas Rogers, a carpenter.

THE KITCHEN
The kitchen was built outside the main body of the house in the 1770s because of the owner Philip Yorke's fear of fire. An impressive room lit by a large Venetian window ● *83*, and full of fascinating culinary implements and utensils.

Above left:
Pont Cysyllte
Above center:
Rug Chapel
Above right:
Valle Crucis Abbey

LLANGOLLEN

Since 1947 this small market town, nestling below the slopes of the lovely vale of Llangollen, has been the scene of an international music festival held each year in July. Straddling the river Dee is another of the "Seven Wonders of Wales", a mid-14th-century bridge, popular with film-makers from all over the world.

PLAS NEWYDD Above the town, this house with its exuberant black-and-white decoration, was created by the "Ladies of Llangollen". Two friends of Irish extraction, Lady Eleanor Butler and the Honourable Sarah Ponsonby, came to Llangollen in 1780 and rented Pen-y-Maes, then no more than a rustic cottage. They transformed it into a *cottage orné* and renamed it Plas Newydd ("New Mansion"), a name given to several houses in Wales ▲ *452*. The Ladies were well enough known to receive visits from the foremost celebrities of the day, among them Sir Walter Scott, Richard Brinsley Sheridan and William Wordsworth (who referred to the house as a "low-roofed cot"). Known as "the two most celebrated virgins in Europe", they lived here for almost 50 years, until Eleanor died in 1829 at the age of 90 and Sarah two years later. During this time, they received the undying devotion of their servant Mary Caryll, who shares their three-sided memorial in the graveyard of the parish church. It is easy to understand what attracted them to Pen-y-Maes, perched above a wooded stream in front of the remains of the castle of Dinas Bran. The stream was given rustic bridges; gazebos and arches were created and a font from nearby Vale Crucis was given a suitably reverential setting.

VALLE CRUCIS (Glyn y Groes, "Vale of the Cross") takes its name from the 9th-century Pillar of Eliseg, a cross that once symbolized the royal house of Powys Fadog – although it has long since lost its significance.

CASTELL DINAS BRAN
Enough remains of Castell Dinas Bran ("Fortress of the Crow") to suggest its stature as a stronghold of the lords of Powys Fadog, who maximized the advantage of this originally Iron Age fort in order to repel Edward I's encroachment. One of the most prominently defensive sites in Wales, it commands tremendous views.

Chirk Castle

The riverside **RAILWAY STATION** at Llangollen is once again vibrant, thanks to the determination of voluntary enthusiasts who have opened the track as far as Carrog (a journey of 20 minutes). A few miles away, at Froncysyllte, Thomas Telford's Pont Cysyllte (1794-1805), carrying the Shropshire canal across the Dee at a vertiginous height, is still an awesome sight.

CHIRK CASTLE, built by Roger Mortimer, a staunch ally of Edward I, was meant to have been a stronghold, but only half of it was completed. Its evolution from medieval fortification to country house is a textbook study of the development of domestic architecture.

SNOWDON (YR WYDDFA)

The highest mountain in England and Wales, Snowdon (3,560 ft) was purchased by the National Trust in 1998. In the late 18th century, the cragginess of the whole Snowdonia range (Eryri) appealed to travelers whose journeys to the continent were made impossible by the Napoleonic Wars, and since then its popularity has never waned. After World War II it provided popular practice slopes for serious climbers who aspired to higher conquests elsewhere. For other visitors, the easiest of the ascents is the Llanberis Pass, which follows the track of the Snowdon Mountain Railway. This, the only rack railway in Britain, dates from 1896. Its base station is at Llanberis, near which the substantial Victoria Hotel testifies to the importance of the town as a tourist center in the 19th century.

DOLBADARN The tower of Dolbadarn, the castle of the Welsh princes painted by Richard Wilson and Turner, dominates the lakes of Padarn and Peris. Across the waters are the steep slopes of the Dinorwic Quarries, idle since 1969.

The National Museums and Galleries of Wales (NMGW) are responsible for the admirable **LLANBERIS SLATE MUSEUM**, staffed mainly by former quarry workers.

Snowdonia's other major slate "experience" is some distance away at **BLAENAU FFESTINIOG**, for most Welsh people a town suggesting not just slate, but rain. The Llechwedd ("slope") Slate Caverns date from the 1840s, and were opened to the public in 1972. Their success has been entirely due to the range and detail of their interpretation of a quarryman's life. The extensive underground tour offers some of the awesome fascination of Big Pit Mining Museum at Blaenavon, near Abergavenny.

Above left: Llanberis slate quarries
Above right: Valle Crucis Abbey

LLANGAR CHURCH (above, center) Reached by footpath across fields, the interior has remarkable wall paintings ranging over four centuries.

ROCK CLIMBING From Llanberis toward Capel Curig, the number of climbers on the rock faces of Llanberis Pass partly explains the importance of Pen-y-Gwryd Hotel. In the early 1950s it was the haunt of many of the world's finest climbers, among them Sir Edmund Hillary, Sir John Hunt and Sherpa Tensing, who conquered Everest in 1953, and who wrote their signatures on the ceiling of the public bar.

Llanberis, Snowdon railway

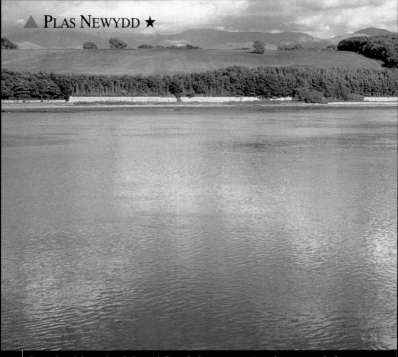

Plas Newydd ★

Overlooking the Menai Strait between Anglesey and the mainland is the Paget family's 18th- and 19th-century home, known as Plas Newydd. The best view can be enjoyed by sailing between Caernarfon and Beaumaris, passing under two of Wales's most famous bridges: Stephenson's Britannia and Telford's Suspension. The house, which itself boasts one of the best views in Wales (of the mountains of Snowdonia) owes much of its present appearance to James Wyatt, who enlarged it to a style and scale suitable for Lord Paget's new title, the Earl of Uxbridge. His son, who lost a leg at Waterloo while serving as

second-in-command to the Duke of Wellington, acquired the title of 1st Marquess of Anglesey and the elegance of his father's transformation of Plas Newydd proved admirably in keeping with his elevated status. With grounds laid out by Humphry Repton, Plas Newydd is probably Wales's most elegant 18th-century house, although its foundations are Tudor. It is now known principally for the vast mural in the Dining Room, painted by Rex Whistler in the 1930s – probably the largest canvas, and certainly the most romantic, in the British Isles. The house and gardens are open to the public.

SELF PORTRAIT
Rex Whistler interrupting his brushing in order to have his portrait painted – by himself: a characteristically whimsical joke. He can just be seen leaning on a broom halfway back (left).

MOTHER AND CHILD
Lady Caroline (Paget) Capel, eldest sister of the 1st Marquess, with infant asleep on her lap (right). By John Hoppner, 1794.

A ROOM WITH A VIEW
In 1937 Rex Whistler was commissioned by the 6th Marquess and Lady Anglesey to paint a mural for a dining room which they had created a year earlier from what had been a private theatre in the time of the 5th marquess, and a family chapel before that. Whistler's enchanting work is rich in pictorial allusions to the Paget family.

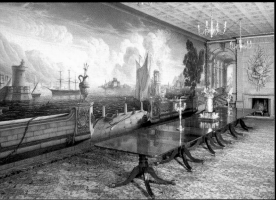

Opposite page: Plas Mawr, chamber over the parlor (left); kitchen (right)

BODRHYDDAN
The medieval core of the family house, Bodrhyddan (right) at Rhuddlan, has undergone many alterations and additions, most significantly in 1870 when W.E. Nesfield designed an elaborate west front. The original south entrance became the garden front, with parterres consistent with the 1696 date on the doorway. A pair of gate piers adds to the impression of 17th-century formality.

The gardens at Bodrhyddan Hall

THE STATUTE OF RHUDDLAN (1284) was a declaration of King Edward I's annexation of Wales, with its division into shires. The castle and hill were given to the Ministry of Works in 1944, and their care and supervision is now the responsibility of Cadw. (The donor, Admiral Rowley-Conwy, was appropriately a descendant of the castle's first constable).

Right and far right: Penrhyn Castle. The medieval origins of Penrhyn, refined in the 18th century, were swallowed up by Thomas Hopper's neo-Norman building.

RHYL

The building of **RHUDDLAN CASTLE** dates from Edward I's Welsh campaign of 1277. It was the first of the three concentric castles designed by the King's military engineer, Master James of St George (*c.* 1235-1308). Rhuddlan had the disadvantage of not being near tidal waters, a drawback overcome by the construction of a canal.

ST ASAPH'S CATHEDRAL hosts a music festival every September, the brain-child of the Welsh composer William Mathias (d. 1992). In the churchyard stands the Translators' Memorial to Bishop William Morgan and his collaborators in the Welsh translation of the Bible.

BODELWYDDAN CASTLE, a 19th-century building on much earlier foundations, now houses a part of the Victorian section of the National Portrait Gallery. The highly elaborate "Marble Church" nearby was built by a daughter of the house, in memory of her husband, Lord Willoughby de Broke.

CONWY (CONWAY)

Conwy is a 13th-century fortified town with 21 towers. Edward I's CASTLE took full advantage of a rock that controlled mountain and estuary. Access from the east was possible only by ferry until Thomas Telford's elegant suspension bridge was erected in 1825, a precursor of his other masterpiece that crosses the Strait to Anglesey. That bridge carried all the traffic until the present one was built in 1958. Like Caernarfon, Conwy is a two-warded castle and the disjointed shape of the Great Hall indicates how the fortress was built to obey the contours of the rock. Queen Eleanor's Chapel is one of the best preserved rooms in the castle.

ABBEY OF CONWY A hundred years before Edward completed his enterprise at Conwy, work had just finished on the church of this Cistercian abbey, founded by Llywelyn ap lorwerth as part of the Llys (court) of the Welsh princes, but transferred by Edward to a new site at Maenan in the Conwy Valley. The abbey was put to parochial use as the church of St Mary and All Saints. A fine rood screen and a late 15th-century font

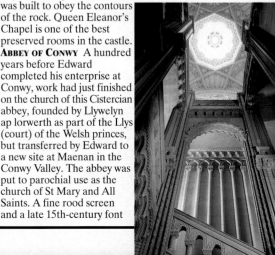

have avoided zealous 19th-century restoration. A bust celebrates the achievements of John Gibson, the distinguished Early Victorian classical sculptor and native of the town.

ABERCONWY HOUSE The town's oldest domestic building is on the corner of Castle Street and High Street; the timber jetties make a striking contrast with the rest of the stone house. Since 1990 the upper floors have been furnished to illustrate the use of the building, from its origins as a merchant's house to the period when it was a temperance hotel (1850-1910).

On the way to Llandudno, the Tudor house of GLODDAETH, now St David's College, has retained its principal feature: the 16th-century Great Hall, with its intricate painted plaster canopy at the dais end. The fireplace bears the motto of the Mostyn family: "Heb Dduw heb ddim; Duw a digon" ("Without God, nothing; with God, an abundance"). Prominent on the opposite hill is BODYSGALLEN, another Mostyn property, which was purchased by Richard Broyd as the first of his Historic House Hotels.

Although, like those at Powis Castle, BODNANT GARDENS ★ are of world distinction, they are much more recent, dating from the later part of the 19th century when Henry Pochin purchased the property.

PLAS MAWR, Conwy, (above left and right) is the display-case of Robert Wynn, an Elizabethan with all the right connections. Its refurbishment by Cadw in the mid-1990s highlights the social and architectural importance of Wynn's house, probably the best surviving example of its period in Britain.

"Burgomaster of Delft" by Jan Havicksz Steen from Penrhyn Castle, one of the finest picture collections in Wales

BANGOR

Bangor claims the beginnings of what is thought to be the oldest religious foundation in Britain: St Deiniol's Monastery, founded in the first half of the 6th century. The saint enclosed it with a wattled fence, the Welsh word for which was *bangor*. The present building dates from 1130, but was substantially altered between the 13th and 16th centuries and heavily restored by Sir George Gilbert Scott between 1868 and 1870. The University College of North Wales, a handsome building of the 1910s dominates the town. Bangor's 1,500-foot pier seems to stretch almost as far as Anglesey.

PENRHYN CASTLE was built as a gargantuan 19th-century display of wealth realized from the local slate, which roofed the ever-increasing towns and villages of the Industrial Revolution.

BEAUMARIS

It was at Beau Marreys, the Norman-French for "fine marsh", that Edward I chose to build a castle to guard the eastern extremity of the Menai Strait, whose western approach was already protected by the stern sentinel of Caernarfon. This coastal plain was the ideal terrain for the King's military surveyor, Master James of St George, to fulfil his ambition to design a genuinely concentric castle. Building began in 1295 and took almost another 50 years, by which time techniques of warfare had rendered the castle an anachronism.

Close to the castle is the COURT HOUSE, a plain rectangular building of 1614, although additions and improvements of the early 19th century indicate an increasing awareness of its dignity. The nearby prison, a suitably stern building of 1829, retains many of its original features, including a treadmill. The architect was J.A. Hansom (of "cab" fame) who was responsible for the fine Victorian terrace that characterizes Beaumaris as a fashionable resort. The PARISH CHURCH includes among its relics from the Priory of Llanfaes the

sarcophagus of King John's daughter Joan-Siwan, wife of Llywelyn Fawr (the Great).

PENMON East of Beaumaris the feeling of remoteness increases as one nears Penmon ("end of Mon"). It was here that Seiriol, a 6th-century saint, established his cell, later to become an Augustinian priory. Rebuilt in the 12th century, it is a remarkable survival; part of it now serves as a parish church.

The **ANGLESEY COLUMN** (Twr Marcwis) on the A5, not far from the Britannia Bridge, was built in 1816 to commemorate the first Marquess, second-in-command to the Duke of Wellington at Waterloo. His distinguished service on the battlefield cost him a limb, and gained him the nickname "Old One-Leg". A climb of over a hundred steps is rewarded by the most wonderful view of Snowdonia.

The elongated name of **LLANFAIRPWLL** (see left) was the fabrication of a 19th-century local tailor. The only attractive building is Telford's octagonal toll-house, less altered than others along the A5 as it crosses Anglesey in an almost straight line to Holyhead where there was a Roman fort, built to repel Irish marauders. Within its protective walls, Cybi, one

---

PENMON PRIORY (below) Few places in Wales impart such a sense of historical and spiritual continuity.

BEAUMARIS CASTLE (right) consists of an inner ward with four corner drum towers and one placed centrally on the west and east, an arrangement which dominated the octagonal outer ward, protected by 12 angle towers, and a northern and southern gatehouse. Both are out of alignment with their inner counterparts, not because of any lapse in the symmetrical design, but because of James's mastery of defensive tactics. The scale of the northern range, which mirrors that of the incomplete south range, indicates that Beaumaris was intended to accommodate royal apartments.

WHAT'S IN A NAME? The village with the longest name in Britain is Llanfairpwllgwyngyllgogerychwyrndrobwllllandysiliogogogoch, usually shortened to Llanfair PG or Llanfairpwll.

Caernarfon

of the most energetic of Christian missionaries, founded his monastery in the middle of the 6th century, and gave his name to the church which stands on the site. One of Anglesey's finest, it dates from the 14th century.

Although a packet service between Holyhead and Dublin existed in the 17th century, Holyhead grew considerably at the beginning of the 19th with the construction of a new harbor and with Telford's turnpike road (now the A5), the last toll road to be built in Britain. Holyhead Mountain is prominent because the rest of Anglesey is so flat, and it offers expansive views not only of Snowdonia, but also of the Irish coast and the Isle of Man. Particularly striking are the cliffs of **NORTH** and **SOUTH STACKS**, the latter with its lighthouse of 1809, connected to the mainland of Holy Island by a bridge. The area, a vast breeding ground for colonies of sea-birds, is a nature reserve under the surveillance of the Royal Society for the Protection of Birds.

CAERNARFON

Edward I's fortress was more than a forceful means to overcome the Welsh. It was a statement of regal power through which he could relate to the glories of Constantinople, whose polygonal towers with their banded masonry Caernarfon emulated.

It was at **CAERNARFON CASTLE** ★ that Prince Charles was invested as Prince of Wales in 1969, in a ceremony designed by Lord Snowdon but largely based on that planned in 1911 for his great-uncle, the uncrowned Edward VIII. This had been the idea of David Lloyd George, the constable of the castle and M.P. for Caernarfon, to whom there is a statue in the square (Y Maes). The Queen's Tower houses the museum of the Royal Welch Fusiliers.

GLYNLLIFON
(above) On the A499 Caernarfon to Pwilheli road stands the proudly imperial screen surmounted by a lion and eagles that proclaims the entrance to Glynllifon, the estate of a once powerful Welsh family. The red-brick home which Sir Thomas Wynn (the 1st Lord Newborough) built in 1757 went up in flames in 1836, and was replaced during the next 10 years by a vast neoclassical stucco mansion. The grounds, open to the public, are well worth exploring.

CAERNARFON CASTLE
(below) The Romans adapted the name of the River Seiont for their settlement of Segontium, which Agricola established in AD 78 as an auxiliary fort. Fully excavated in the 1920s, it is now well explained in the site museum.

Right: Portmeirion
Far right: Plas yn Rhiw

PORTMEIRION ★
(right and above left)
is Clough Williams-
Ellis's fantasy
Italianate village. It
was built in the 20th
century and much
embellished with
buildings rescued
from demolition from
all over the country.

TRE'R CEIRI ★
Of all the ancient
sites in northwest
Wales, the most
impressive is the hill
fort of Tre'r Ceiri
("settlement of the
ramparts"),
crowning one of the
peaks of Yr Eifl
("The Forks",
corrupted to "The
Rivals"), above
Llanaelhaearn.
Surrounded
by a formidable
protective rampart,
it consisted of 150
or more closely
packed stone huts
of varying shapes
and sizes, dating
from between 400
and 150 BC.

LLEYN

The most far-flung of the settlements of the Lleyn Peninsula,
Aberdaron was the last place on the pilgrims' way to the
Island of Bardsey. The pilgrims' prayers were offered at the
clas (a Celtic monastery), later the parish church of St Hywyn,
itself challenged by the sea to such an extent that it was
abandoned at the beginning of the 19th century. The design
for its replacement caused so much wrath that the earlier
building was restored. In 1967, the Anglo-Welsh poet R.S.
Thomas came as a vicar. Two miles across the Sound (Y Swnt)
lies "The Island of 20,000 Saints", the final resting place of
pilgrims and holy men who came to its 6th-century monastery.
The spiritual importance of the island was such that three
pilgrimages there were judged to equal one to Rome.
Very much part of the Pilgrims' Way was the *clas* at CLYNNOG
FAWR, the principal shrine of St Beuno. The importance of the
site resulted in major rebuilding between the 15th and 16th
centuries, making it one of the finest Perpendicular churches
in North Wales. Past the next village of Llithfaen, the road
northwest leads to the dead-end Nant Gwrtheyrn. Although
associated with the 5th-century Vortigern, traditionally hated
for his betrayal of his people, the place has a far more positive
ring for the thousands of students of Welsh who have
benefited from residential courses in the quarrymen's village
of **PORTH-Y-NANT**, rehabilitated by a local trust after decades
of disuse.
PLAS YN RHIW, the smallest of the National Trust country
houses in North Wales, is also one of the most charming –
partly because of the history of a widow and her three
daughters, the Keating family, who saved this old manor house
and garden in their wooded setting, rising above Cardigan
Bay, from oblivion just before World War II. The 13th-century
Welsh castle of CRICCIETH, eloquent on its high promontory
overlooking Tremadog Bay, rivals Harlech for its views.
Equally eloquent was a local boy, David Lloyd George, the
Liberal Prime Minister, to whom there is a comprehensive
museum at Llanystumdwy, where he was brought up from an
early age at Highgate House. He retired to Ty Newydd, which
is within walking distance and is now used for writers'

...esidential courses. His memorial on the nearest banks of the River Dwyfor was designed by Sir Clough Williams-Ellis.

...LANRWST

...he steeply humped bridge of 1636, so often fancifully ...ttributed to Inigo Jones, is one of the town's endearing and ...nduring features, matched by the perilously placed but aptly ...amed TU HWNT I'R BONT ("beyond the bridge"), once a court ...ouse. Also beyond the bridge stands GWYDIR CASTLE. This ...as the seat of the illustrious Wynn family. Although much ...utilated, first by fire and then by vandalism, this enigmatic ...ouse and its gardens are now being restored by its current ...wners. On the nearby thickly wooded hillside is GWYDIR ...CHAF CHAPEL. The ceiling, with its naively painted angels, ...e handsomely decorated gallery (1673) at the west end, and ...e Oxbridge inward-looking pews, display the family pride ...vident in the Gwydir Chapel (1633) in the south transept of ...e parish church of St Grwst. This handsome, well-lit ...xtension not only houses monuments to the family, but also ...eputedly the sarcophagus of Llewelyn Fawr (the Great) from ...earby Maenan Abbey, where it had been originally brought ...om Aberconwy after Edward I's victory.

...Y MAWR ("Great House") is not a misnomer in a community ...f much lowlier habitations. It is the birthplace of William ...Morgan (1545-1604), the translator of the Bible into ...Welsh (completed 1588) who was regarded ...s the savior of the language. Morgan's ...henomenal achievement as ...young man from such a ...emote area – gaining ...place at St John's ...College, Cambridge ...probably has ...uch to do with the ...atronage of the ...Vynns of Gwydir ...ho recognized the ...alent of one of their ...enants' sons.

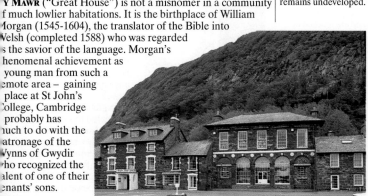

CASTELL Y BERE
(above) is probably
the most remote and
least known of the
castles of Wales. It
once had enormous
significance, since
Llywelyn ap
Iorwerth's stronghold
guarded the
mountainous route
between the estuaries
of the Dyfi and the
Mawddach. The
irregular plan of the
castle was dictated by
the natural rock
defences.

**PREHISTORIC
REMAINS**
On the A496 toward
Talsarnau stands
Y Lasynys, the
birthplace of one of
Wales's foremost
devotional writers,
Ellis Wynne
(1671–1734). The
burial chambers of
Carneddau Hengwm
lie south of Harlech,
and are reached by
a road offering
expansive views of
Tremadoc Bay.
The area is rich in
prehistoric remains,
and these two
Neolithic chambers
are among the most
interesting in Wales.

HARLECH

Harlech is renowned for the architecture of its castle, as well
as for its views of Snowdonia and the switchback outlines of
the Lleyn Peninsula. Its most significant military feature is the
innovative use of the gatehouse made by the King's engineer
Master James of St George (1235–1308), not only for defence
and storage but also for domestic accommodation of relative
comfort. This was feasible because of the depth of the rock-
cut ditch in front of it. On another two sides, nature provided
its own craggily precipitous protection, while allowing enough
level space on the rock itself for James to attempt a concentric
design. Harlech's defences proved inadequate when
confronted with Owain Glyndwr's attack of 1404 ● *41*, which
resulted in his establishing Harlech as a Welsh royal court.
COLEG HARLECH, a residential college, otherwise known as the
"College of the Second Chance" was founded in 1927 offering
opportunities to rural and industrial manual workers who
would otherwise have had little formal education. Theatr
Ardudwy, built in the 1970s but independent of the College,
offers a wide range of popular bilingual entertainment.

TYWYN

Tywyn is built on the site of a *clas*. Its lineage is indicated by
"Cadfan's Stone", which bears the earliest known written Welsh.
The town's railway museum is devoted to the history of the

narrow-gauge line of Tal-y-Llyn, which was
opened in 1865.
CRAIG YR ADERYN The valley is further
dominated by the dramatic
Craig yr Aderyn ("bird rock"),
the haunt of cormorants that
nest further inland here than
anywhere else in mainland
Britain.
LLANEGRYN CHURCH,
dedicated to saints Mary and
Egryn, is renowned for its
delicately wrought rood
screen. Prominent also are the
memorials to the owners of
the major estate in these
parts, PENIARTH ●

Harlech Castle

SOUTH WALES

Lindsay Evans

1. ST DAVID'S **2.** MILFORD HAVEN **3.** PEMBROKE **4.** GOWER PENINSULA **5.** FISHGUARD **6.** CARDIGAN **7.** KIDWELLY

ABERYSTWYTH

The west coast town of Aberystwyth owes its rapid development to the extension of the railway from Shrewsbury

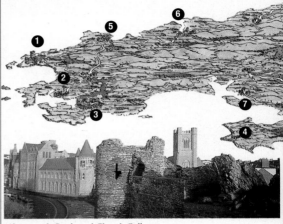

DEVIL'S BRIDGE

The town's handsome railway station is the terminus of the Vale of Rheidol Railway to Devil's Bridge (12 miles). "Devil's Bridge" is the adaptation of the Welsh name Pont Ar Fynach ("bridge across the river Mynach [monk]"). Both names relate to the legend of the devil who disguised himself as a monk in order to lure a girl across the

bridge. The present structure surmounts two older bridges: one medieval, the other 18th century. Nearby, the waterfall gushes down the gorge with a deafening roar.

Above: White Horse on a bar in Aberystwyth

University College, Aberystwyth

Aberystwyth Castle and Church College

in 1864. The history of the town dates back to the late 13th century with the construction of the Edwardian castle. Aberystwyth harbor, now relatively quiet, was built in order to export the lead of the Cardiganshire hills.

LAURA PLACE, with its fine houses and Assembly Rooms, illustrates the refinement of a fashionable seaside town of the 1820s. The High Victorian building at the southern end of the promenade started life as a hotel and then became the first UNIVERSITY COLLEGE OF WALES, opened in 1872, thanks to the support and subscriptions of a population anxious to have a national and non-sectarian university. Above the town, on Penglais, is the National Library of Wales, which has been built in stages since 1911. The Library is divided into three principal departments: Printed Books, Manuscripts and Records, and Prints, Maps and Drawings. Nearby is the Arts Centre, a development of the 1970s, incorporating expansive exhibition areas, a concert hall, and the THEATR Y WERIN (the People's Theatre). The town's Coliseum cinema (once a music-hall) now houses CEREDIGION MUSEUM, the museum of Cardiganshire life.

LLANBADARN In this village, a mile to the east of Aberystwyth, is the church of St Padarn, the 6th-century Celtic saint who founded his *clas*, or monastery here.

ABERAERON is a grid-patterned, planned town of commodious, clean-cut and confident houses, the result of the entrepreneurial talents of a local heiress. The outcome was the construction of a harbor, the development of a highly successful shipbuilding company, and one of the most pleasingly integrated towns in Wales. The harbor is now popular with yachtsmen.

LLANNERCHAERON is one of the small country houses that John Nash designed in west Wales in the 1790s. The property has a remarkable collection of estate buildings that have remained unaltered.

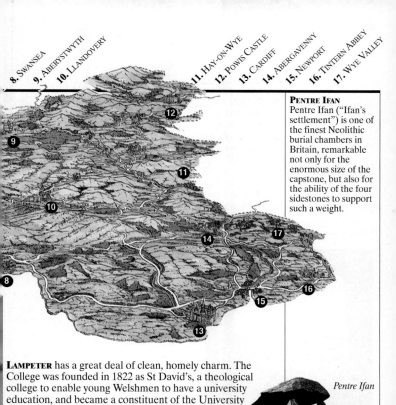

PENTRE IFAN
Pentre Ifan ("Ifan's settlement") is one of the finest Neolithic burial chambers in Britain, remarkable not only for the enormous size of the capstone, but also for the ability of the four sidestones to support such a weight.

Pentre Ifan

LAMPETER has a great deal of clean, homely charm. The College was founded in 1822 as St David's, a theological college to enable young Welshmen to have a university education, and became a constituent of the University of Wales in 1971.

CARDIGAN TO FISHGUARD

CILGERRAN The view of the castle enjoyed by 19th-century "tourists" as they came upstream from Cardigan (Aberteifi) is now seen only by coraclemen, but the castle's remains still convey its importance as a Norman stronghold. Painters such as Richard Wilson, Turner and de Wint have left us memorable views of the rock-perched stronghold high above the Teifi.

NEVERN In the churchyard of St Brynach, at Nevern (Nanhyfer), are a number of early Christian inscribed stones, and a majestic Celtic cross with intricately carved panels. One of the yews that form an avenue to the church is known as the "Bleeding Yew" because of the blood-red sap that drips from it. West of the church, cut into the rock, is the Pilgrim's Cross, probably a shrine on the route to St David's.

MYNYDD PRESELI, the highest ridge in Pembrokeshire, is the source of the "blue stones", reputedly transported from here along the Irish trade route to Stonehenge ▲ *212*. Preseli Mountain protects the ancient settlements of **TREFDRAETH** (Newport), Dinas and the Gwaun Valley.

Aberystwyth

St David's Cathedral

ST DAVID'S SHRINE
The shrine of
St David is in the
north side of the
presbytery. A casket
in a niche in the wall
behind the high altar
was reputed to hold
the bones of the
patron saint, but in
1996 tests revealed
the contents to belong
to the 13th century
rather than the 6th.

**ST DAVID'S
(TY DDEWI)** For
people visiting
St David's, the smallest city in Britain, it can be difficult
finding the cathedral dedicated to Wales's patron saint. Its
site, Glyn Rhosyn ("The Vale of the Rose") was vital for the
protection of this early Celtic foundation, from marauders as
well as from the elements. The cathedral, dating from the
1180s, underwent additions and alterations until well into the
20th century. None of them has distracted from its spirituality,
which gains much from the light flowing into the nave.
To the west of the cathedral is the **BISHOP'S PALACE** (late 12th-
15th centuries). Enough remains to give an idea of the

sumptuous formality of the building as well
as of its need for defence, exemplified by
first-floor principal rooms built over a
vaulted undercroft.
Signposts indicate the way to the chapel of
ST NON, St David's mother. Close by, the
holy well, with its 18th-century stone vault,
retained a reputation for healing powers
until after the Reformation.
Very prominent around the coast are the
islands whose names show their Norse
origins: Skokholm, Grassholm, and the
largest and best known of them, **SKOMER**, a
National Nature Reserve.

PEMBROKE

BISHOP'S PALACE
The scale and
magnificence of
St David's Bishop's
Palace (above) is due
to the flair and
originality of Henry de
Gower, who became
bishop in 1328.
Everything fell into a
sad decline when the
episcopal residence
was moved to
Carmarthen in 1536.

*Pembroke
Castle*

The town of Pembroke, a corruption of the Welsh *Penfro*
("Land's End") stands on a narrow rocky ridge above the river,
which provided a natural defence. Man-made protection took
the form of a town wall, parts of which still survive. In 1093,
Arnulph de Montgomery laid claim to the area, and a hundred
years later a new castle was built by William Marshall, who came
from a family remarkable for their castle-building ardor.
Forsaking the traditional rectangular shape, he introduced a
formidable cylindrical keep, with a domed roof, which still
dominates the town and its surroundings. In 1457, in one of
the towers, Margaret Beaufort, a 15-year-old girl already
three months a widow, gave birth to a son, Henry Tudor.
Twenty-eight years later he was to become King
Henry VII, the founder of the Tudor dynasty.
The origins of **PEMBROKE DOCK**, 2 miles north
of the tower, date back to

1814, when the Royal Naval Dockyard was established here. The original grid-iron layout of the town is intact, and a Martello tower (1849–57) still stands at either end of the dockyard.

MANORBIER has been described as "the pleasantest spot in Wales". The writer, who was justifiably proud of his birthplace, was Gerallt Gymro, Gerald of Wales ● *107*, whose *Itinerary through Wales* (1191) and *Description of Wales*, are both immensely important for their insights into and observation of early medieval Welsh life. The present castle at Manorbier was built after Gerald's death, and its effectiveness as a fortification was never put to the test, resulting in its relatively intact state today.

ST GOVAN'S CHAPEL must have sorely tested the endurance of early Christians as they tried to reach this simple cell at the bottom of a cliff, via the uneven steps whose total number, traditionally, differs between descent and ascent.

Although **STACKPOLE**, the great 18th-century house of the Cawdor family, was demolished in the early 1960s, the legacy of its enlightened landscaping can still be enjoyed. Stackpole Quay, once a limestone quarry, is much used for aquatic sports, and the area is an excellent center for exploring the coast and countryside.

TENBY The Welsh name for Tenby is Dinbych-y-Pysgod ("small fort of the fishes"), distinguishing it from its North Wales equivalent, plain Dinbych (Denbigh). The name is highly appropriate considering the sea-girt character of this ancient settlement. Its fortress dominates Castle Hill, which overlooks the two generous stretches of sand at North and South Beach, as well as the harbor from which boats go regularly to **CALDEY ISLAND** (Ynys Byr) and its Cistercian Abbey. Long stretches of the town wall still stand.

The parish **CHURCH OF ST MARY ★** has among its many memorials one to Robert Recorde (b. 1510), the inventor of the mathematical "equals" symbol. The town's early prosperity is conveyed by the Tudor Merchant's House, one of the first Welsh buildings acquired by the National Trust.

LAUGHARNE (Talacharn) is best remembered as the haunt of Dylan Thomas, whose village of Llareggub in *Under Milk Wood* was probably based on this sleepy estuary town. He lived with his wife Caitlin in the Boat House overlooking "the heron-priested shore". The rooms are now set out as a small museum of Thomasiana with audiovisual presentations of the poet's verse. On the cliff walk above is his writing shed, preserved as it was when he wrote there, with one window looking into trees and the other with a view down the estuary. The town has the remains of a 12th-century castle and the poet's simple grave is in the churchyard of St Martin's church.

CAREW CASTLE
The early 13th-century castle with 16th-century additions is situated on a tidal creek of the river. The eloquent ruins are maintained by the Pembroke Coast National Park. The early Christian monument, the Carew Cross, commemorates "Maredudd the King, son of Edwin" who was killed in 1035.

LAMPHEY
The Bishop's Palace at Lamphey (above) has an arcaded parapet similar to that at the palace at St David's. Beautifully landscaped to show off the handsome ruins, the spot manages to convey the serenity as well as the grandeur of episcopal life.

Oxwich Castle, general view from the west

GOWER PENINSULA

Gower Peninsula (Penrhyn Gwyr) stretches from Swansea between Swansea Bay and Carmarthen Bay, reaching its most western point at Worm's Head, one of the most remarkable promontories in Wales. Accessible for only two hours either side of low tide, it attracts walkers and naturalists; the less active can admire its primeval shape at the end of the broad grassy cliff-top walk from the tiny village of Rhosili. The glory of the area is the enormous sweeping beach that stretches northward in a generous arc. Untouched by modern development, it is reached only by paths, with one solitary white house standing between the sand and the Rhosili Downs, now the joy of hang-gliders. On the northern side of the beach near Llangennith are the remains of an Iron-Age hill fort occupying a site on Burry Holms, a tidal island like Worm's Head.

OXWICH On the south of the peninsula is another generous beach, overlooked by the "castle" of Oxwich. A fortified manor house rather than a purely defensive building, it owes much to the standing of its owner, Sir Rhys [or Rice] Mansel, whose name is closely associated with the early history of Glamorgan. His son, Sir Edward, added the east range, an ambitious project showing considerable Renaissance verve, but within 50 years of completion the property was leased and went into decline. Cadw, the Welsh Historic Monuments Society, undertook a program of repair and conservation in the 1980s. Between Rhosili and Oxwich, near Port Eynon, is PAVILAND CAVE, associated with the "Red Lady of Paviland" whose headless skeleton was discovered in 1823. (The "lady", stained with powdered red ocher, was later discovered to be a young man.)

Weobley Castle

ARTHUR'S STONE (below) On the minor road from Reynoldston over Cefu Bryn, this dolmen is much visited, not only as a renowned prehistoric monument, but because of the spectacular views from the site.

CAERPHILLY CASTLE (left and below) Gilbert de Clare, a powerful Marcher lord, built what was the largest non-royal castle in Britain at the end of the 13th century. It had a formidable structure and elaborate water defences.

Further east, near Parkmill, is PARC LE BREOS, otherwise known as PARC CWM, a Neolithic chambered cairn, 4th-3rd millennium BC, partially restored in the early 1960s. Another Neolithic chambered cairn stands off the minor road from Reynoldston over Cefn Bryn. It is much frequented, not only because of its gigantic dimensions but also because of the spectacular views from the site. North of Cefn Bryn, near Llanmadoc, is WEOBLEY, the only castle on the north coast of the peninsula, built on a site which has its own natural defences, with views across the Llwchwr estuary to the 19th-century development of Llanelli – a marked contrast to the agricultural calm of Llanmadoc. Dating from the late 13th century, it is a fortified manor house built round a small courtyard. The Gower Peninsula was designated an Area of Outstanding Natural Beauty in 1957, the first in Britain.

KIDWELLY CASTLE (above) The bow-shape was dictated by the naturally defended land above the river. It has an impressive twin-towered gatehouse which was a self-contained defensive unit. It dates from the early 14th century.

SWANSEA Most of the center of the town was rebuilt after merciless air bombardment in 1941, and it has since suffered from a great deal of civic indecision, with piecemeal development and improvements rather than a comprehensive planning strategy. The area around the mainline station has been woefully abandoned in favor of the Maritime Quarter. Some of the early 19th-century buildings near that enterprising development have been restored in recent years, notably the Old Guildhall in Somerset Place. In 1994 it became known as TŶ LLÊN, the National Literature Centre for Wales, with lecture rooms, a bookshop café, and an exhibition of Dylan Thomas's Swansea life. A close neighbor in the much-restored Cambrian Place is the handsome Greek Revival building designed in 1839 to house the Royal Institution of South Wales, now Swansea's official museum. The town's art gallery, the GLYNN VIVIAN, in Alexandra Road – one of the most dignified of its thoroughfares – has a comprehensive collection of the works of the two of the town's artists, Ceri Richards and the lesser-known Evan Walters, whose portrait of the "Cockle Woman" is memorable. Cockle women travel every week from Penclawdd in North Gower to their stalls in Swansea's covered market, which heaves with humorous exchange and banter, the true spirit of the town.

A cast-iron fountain canopy in Merthyr Tydfil c. 1890, in commemoration of Robert and Lucy Thomas, the pioneers of the South Wales steam coal trade.

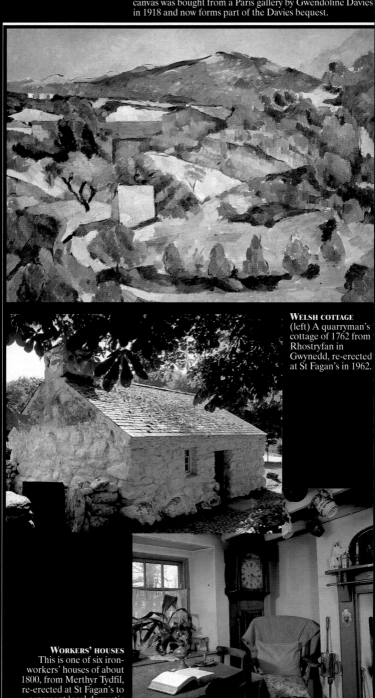

"MOUNTAINS AT L'ESTAQUE" (1878-80) Cézanne's oil on canvas was bought from a Paris gallery by Gwendoline Davies in 1918 and now forms part of the Davies bequest.

WELSH COTTAGE (left) A quarryman's cottage of 1762 from Rhostryfan in Gwynedd, re-erected at St Fagan's in 1962.

WORKERS' HOUSES This is one of six iron-workers' houses of about 1800, from Merthyr Tydfil, re-erected at St Fagan's to represent local domestic conditions.

MUSEUM OF WELSH LIFE In 1946 the 3rd Earl of Plymouth presented the Elizabethan house of St Fagan's Castle to the National Museum of Wales as a Folk Museum, the first of its kind in Britain. Now known as the Museum of Welsh Life, the range of re-erected buildings in the grounds is all-embracing, from man's earliest habitat to the sophistication of the castle itself.

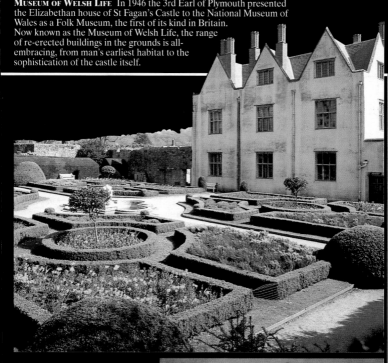

The National Museum of Wales opened in 1927 in one of the most distinguished buildings of Cardiff's splendid Edwardian baroque civic center, enclosed within Cathays Park. Its galleries display wide-ranging collections of silver, ceramics, fossils, dinosaur skeletons and shells, and it houses one of the finest collections of Impressionist paintings in the world, thanks to the bequest of local sisters Gwendoline and Margaret Davies ▲ *476*. For all its riches, it is little known outside Wales.

"LA PARISIENNE". Renoir's painting, exhibited at the First Impressionist Exhibition in 1874, was bought by Gwendoline Davies from the Grosvenor Gallery in 1913.

Ogmore Castle

From the Aesop Fable Wall at Castell Coch

The name "Cardiff" describes the town's origins: "the fort of the Taf". The castle is one of the most fascinating in Wales, showing its architectural development from the 6th century BC up until the 1900s. There were no significant changes after 1550 until the mid-18th century, when the property passed into the possession of the illustrious Scottish family, the Butes. The principal range was converted into a country house by the 1st Marquess in the 1770s, but a century later it was the 3rd Marquess who gave the castle its unmistakable outline and its highly ornate interiors, through which he was able to express his love of the Middle Ages and display his knowledge of religions and history. His architect and mentor in the great program that started in the early

Above: Cardiff Castle

Below: Coity Castle, a Norman castle, described in 1833 as "extensive and magnificent even in its ruins"

Bottom: the Drawing Room, Castell Coch

1870s was William Burges; between them they succeeded in spending the fortune which the 2nd Marquess had made by making Cardiff the coal metropolis of the world.

In the 1880s, the Marquess and Burges turned their sights to another Bute property, CASTELL COCH ("red castle" because of the color of its stone) on the wooded slopes of the Taf, 5 miles north of Cardiff. It was smaller, it was dramatically placed, and it had been neglected for four centuries. As at Cardiff, the decoration was based on genealogical, historical, religious and literary allusions.

PENARTH Similar in its growth from a small village, Penarth's docks were built after the completion at Cardiff. Its development was a result of the foresight of the Windsor family (the earls of Plymouth ▲ *468*), who clearly exercised considerable control over the town's expansion and the introduction of wide roads, wooded walks through parks, and an esplanade and pier with an Anglo-Indian-style pavilion.

South of Penarth is Lavernock Point, where in 1897 Marconi received the first-ever radio message, transmitted across the water from Flatholm.

ST FAGAN'S CASTLE has been turned into a folk museum, the first of its kind in Britain. By the 1990s the extent of land had increased to well over a hundred acres, allowing for a continuing program of acquisition of every type from all over Wales. This policy resulted in the Folk Museum being renamed the

Museum of Welsh Life ▲ *469*; it now exhibits agricultural buildings and rural homesteads, industrial cottages and a Miners' Welfare Hall. The castle has a fine collection of furniture, acquired by bequests and legacies since the 1940s, and the grounds include ponds, parterres and a rose garden.

LLANDAFF has retained its village atmosphere, although only a few miles away from the center of Cardiff. Its cathedral, dedicated to St Teilo, sits in a hollow, a situation similar to St David's and Bangor, and an indication of its early Celtic origin. The Green, with its preaching cross, conveys the atmosphere of a medieval settlement, although most of the houses are 19th century and later. Nearby is the twin-towered gatehouse that once led to the ruined Bishop's Castle.

The cathedral was much restored in the 19th century by John Prichard, whose other diocesan work is evident in Llandaff. The damage caused by a landmine in 1941 resulted in the replacement of the windows of the south aisle, and the installation of a flat roof for the nave. The most significant post-war addition was Sir Jacob Epstein's aluminium figure, *Christ, Majestas*.

OGMORE (OGWR) The castle, originally of earth and timber, was built by William de Londres and refortified in stone by his son, Maurice. Maurice is buried at **EWENNY PRIORY**, which he himself founded as a Benedictine community for a prior and 12 monks in 1141. The castle's principal attraction now is the long line of stepping stones to the opposite bank, and the path that leads to Merthyr Mawr, the estate village of thatched cottages. After the Dissolution, the nave at Ewenny continued as a parish church, and much of the rest of this strikingly simple early Norman building is still roofed and full of atmosphere.

ST DONAT'S CASTLE The 12th-century castle became, in the late 13th century, the property of the Stradling family, who retained it for over 400 years, transforming it from a fortified building into an impressive residence. In the 20th century it changed hands at least three times; one of the last private owners was William Randolph Hearst, the American newspaper tycoon and the inspiration for Orson Welles' film *Citizen Kane*. In the 1960s the castle became a school, known as St Donat's College, which was later changed to Atlantic College.

Above: Beaupre Castle
Left: Ewenny Priory

BEAUPRE
A trek through fields near St Hilary is an odd way to approach one of the Vale of Glamorgan's gems, Beaupre (above right). Plain and uninteresting from a distance, this courtyard house, often called "castle", has one of the finest Renaissance features in any Welsh house: a three-storey porch leading to the hall, each storey displaying a different architectural order.

Castell Coch

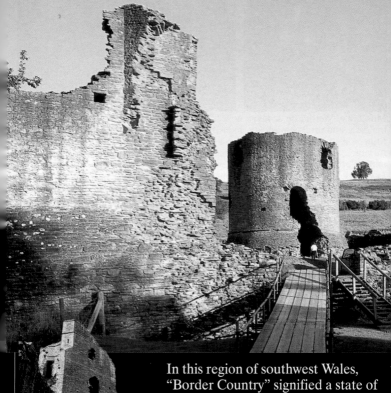

Grosmont Castle, inner face of south-western tower

In this region of southwest Wales, "Border Country" signified a state of mind, an indecisiveness of roots and allegiance. In Norman times, there was no such uncertainty. Here was frontier country: the line of demarcation was the river, and the choice was to conquer or to be conquered. Although Chepstow Castle ▲ *474-5* (1067) was of paramount importance in the enemy occupation of Wales, its builder, William Fitzosbern, Earl of Hereford, applied a similar strategy when establishing three separate wood-and-timber strongholds, which between them constituted a powerful unified defence system at assailable river crossings. These became known as "The Three Castles", or "The Gwent Trilateral". Nevertheless, each had its own identity: GROSMONT occupied a high position above the Monnow; SKENFRITH, a corruption of Ynysgynwr-aidd, was built on a stretch of water-edged land; while WHITE CASTLE took its name from the coloring of its walls, after being refortified in stone in the first decade of the 13th century by Hubert de Burgh (who similarly improved Grosmont and Skenfrith).

SKENFRITH

The distinctive feature of Skenfrith (below) is the formidable free-standing round keep. The walls of the castle rise to their original height in many places.

Below: Detail from a stone carving on a monument in the church at Skenfrith

WHITE CASTLE

Set in idyllic Monmouthshire countryside, near Llantolio Crossenny", the stern military aspect of White Castle was never put to the test.

Raglan Castle(top) and gateway (above)

MONMOUTHSHIRE

Monmouth has a building that is unique in Britain, and is the town's immediate badge of identity: the fortified Gatehouse protecting entry from across the Monnow. Little remains of the stone castle that replaced the original earthen stronghold, but the daunting appearance of Monnow Gate (1272) indicates that the castle would have been just as formidable. It was the birthplace in 1387 of "Harry of Monmouth" who became Henry V in 1413. A late 18th-century statue to Harry stands in the niche on the main front of the Shire Hall in the old market square – now Agincourt Square – as romantic a portrayal of a local hero as we could hope to see. Monmouth has more fine 18th-century houses than any other town in Wales, and commercial development has done little to demean its quiet dignity.

THE KYMIN The odd-sounding name is a corruption of the Welsh *Cae maen* ("field of stones"). A prominent hill above the town, it was so much appreciated by the gentlemen of the town that they formed a dining club which eventually necessitated the building of a banqueting room, The Round House. A few years after its completion in 1796, the same gentlemen, supported by local inhabitants, subscribed toward a Naval Temple, built nearby, to commemorate the victories of Nelson and other admirals. There is also an extensive collection of Nelson memorabilia in Monmouth Museum.

Chepstow Castle

CHEPSTOW (CASGWENT) The best way to appreciate the genius of William Fitzosbern's choice of ground is to approach Chepstow along the old Gloucester road, when its siting as the first Norman stronghold – and in stone – in Wales (1067) is immediately obvious. Chepstow sits on the narrowest point of a promontory on the Wye, with the protection of the river on one side and a deep ravine on the other. Subsequent additions were restricted to only two sides, accounting for elongated character of the castle.

Tintern Abbey

Parts of the town wall still stand, and the town gate resolutely challenged motorized traffic until the building of the first Severn Bridge. The main street hurtles down a steep hill toward the river. Half way is St Mary's church, which has retained its handsome Norman west door.

TINTERN ★ This great Cistercian abbey – the first in Wales – was founded in 1131 by Walter Fitz Richard, who had been granted the castle and lordship of Chepstow by Henry I. The building's extraordinary state of preservation sets it apart from most other monastic foundations in England and Wales. A great deal of the tracery remains unharmed, and that of the west window is especially exquisite. A visit to Tintern is not merely to come to a holy place, but also to wander round the ruins and beech woods that remain very much as Wordsworth described them.

RAGLAN CASTLE Enough remains of Raglan Castle to suggest its palatial concept. Had it not been a victim of the Civil War, it would have been more spectacular than either Powis or Chirk, two castles that succeeded in escaping from such irreparable damage. Everything about Raglan makes it different from other castles in Wales. It was begun as late as 1435 by William ap Thomas, with a five-storied hexagonal tower. His son, William Herbert, eventually the Earl of Pembroke, launched a rash scheme of embellishing the castle. The 3rd Earl continued the building tradition by creating terraces, formal gardens and a moat walk. Raglan was severely damaged during the Civil War and, after the Restoration, the family turned their sights toward Gloucestershire and the rebuilding of an inherited property: Badminton ▲ *223*.

LLANFIHANGEL COURT in the village of Llanfihangel Crucorney is a fascinating late 16th-century house whose original medieval hall plan is still evident.

ABERGAVENNY The importance of Abergavenny in the Middle Ages is reflected in the monuments in **ST MARY'S CHURCH ★**, established as a Benedictine priory in 1090; for it was here that the great families associated with the castle were buried. The result is a collection of tombs and effigies of exceptional importance, raising the church to rank with a major cathedral. Among the treasures is a 15th-century oak figure of Jesse ▲ *93*, an immensely commanding carving.

MUSEUM OF LOCAL HISTORY
A municipal park surrounds Abergavenny Castle above the Usk, and although only fragments remain, one of the towers was rebuilt in the early 19th century by the Neville family, owners of the property since the 12th century, for use as a hunting box. It now houses the Museum of Local History.

Llanfihangel Court: exterior and dining room (bottom)

TRETOWER COURT
(above) In recent years the sensitive development of the garden around this once prestigious house has recreated the horticultural tastes of Sir Roger Vaughan's time.

BRECON
(Aberhonddu) takes its name from a Welsh chieftain, Brychan; hence the county name of Brycheiniog, and the English corruption, Brecknock.

TRETOWER (Tretwr) derives its name from the Norman military settlement established at the end of the 11th century on the plain where the Rhiangoll flows into the Usk. The original timber was replaced by stone in the mid 12th century and the next generation introduced one of the most up-to-date innovations of military architecture: the cylindrical keep Within another generation, the family started to work on the Court, with a splendid Great Hall. The subsequent ambitious additions to the building were the work of Sir Roger Vaughan whose family had purchased the property in the 1420s. Insecurity caused by the Wars of the Roses ● *41* (as well as a wish to show off his status) accounted for Sir Roger's son Thomas's addition of a gatehouse and a wall-walk.

BRECKNOCK MUSEUM One of Brecon's most impressive badges of pride is T.H. Wyatt's Shire Hall (1842), since the 1970s home to the museum. The collection ranges from the county's earliest archeological remains to the first photographic images of town and country. Among the artifacts on display are those excavated at the Roman fort Y GAER, or "fort", a word normally followed by a geographical description – as in Caernarfon and Caerwent. Y Gaer, sometimes referred to as Brecon Gaer west of the town, was probably built within 20 years of the Roman conquest, and its site on the confluence of two rivers – the Usk and Yscir – was characteristic of the invaders' military tactics (as at Gobannium, later Abergavenny). Only part of the fort excavated by Mortimer Wheeler in 1926 is accessible. Bernard of Newmarch's castle was replaced in stone in the 13th century, and the remains of its Great Hall form part of the Castle Hotel. It was Newmarch who established the Church of St John the Evangelist, probably on the site of an earlier Celtic church. In 1923, after the disestablishment of the Welsh Church in 1920, this became the Cathedral of the Diocese of Swansea and Brecon.

The imaginative conversion of a 16th-century tithe barn in the

Tretower Castle

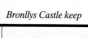
Bronllys Castle keep

1990s interprets the rich heritage of this relatively unknown early Christian place of worship.

BRONLLYS Like Tretower, Bronllys boasts a round keep. It is all that survives of the 13th-century stone reconstruction of a timber castle of the late 1080s, but the severe slope of the motte on which it stands gives some indication of its former defensive strength. It is an example of a first-floor entry stronghold, and the space beneath, reached by trap-door, would have been used for stores.

CRAIG-Y-NOS CASTLE ("rock of the night") is a romantic name for a romantic place. It was the diva, Adelina Patti, who transformed the property after 1885, by quadrupling its size with castelated additions and creating a private opera house where she could sing her favorite roles with her husband, Ernesto Nicolini. The 200-seat theater is used during the summer by a local operatic company. Her splendid Winter Garden now forms the framework of the Patti Pavilion in Swansea's Victoria Park. Below the "castle", used for antique fairs, the riverside grounds are part of the Craig-y-Nos Country Park.

HAY-ON-WYE (Y Gelli) In recent decades, Hay-on-Wye has become the largest center for second-hand bookshops in Britain, with its own self-styled "king", Richard Booth. The character of this idyllic market town was enhanced in the 1980s by the foundation of an annual Literary Festival held in late May. Hay stands at the head of what is known as "The Golden Valley", surrounded by glorious walking country. Nearby Clyro is associated with the Rev. Francis Kilvert, who was curate here from 1865 to 1872 and whose diaries evoke the feel of place and time so strongly that the area has become known as Kilvert Country. On a hillside a few miles away stands **MAESYRONNEN** ("field of the ash tree"). It epitomizes the spirit of religious dissent, whose independence could only be shown in remote farms and barns, as here. Founded in 1696, it is the oldest independent meeting house in Wales.

Hay-on-Wye clocktower (top) and one of the many bookshops for which the town is famous (above)

Below left: Clive of India (1725-74) by Nathaniel Dance. His son married the Herbert heiress of Powis. Below right: 1st Lord Herbert of Chirbury (1583-1648) by Isaac Oliver. Both are exhibited in Powis Castle. Bottom: Grand Staircase, Powis Castle, with walls painted by Gerard Lanscroon.

LLANDRINDOD WELLS The renown of Llandrindod Wells as a spa stems back to the 17th century, but most of the present buildings date to the late 19th. The gentility of a once-popular health resort is still evident, with a boating lake, an ornate Pump Room and a thickly wooded Rock Park, surprisingly unchanged; the shops in the main commercial street are still proud of their verandas. Four miles off the Llandrindod–Newtown road is the wonderfully secluded **CWM HIR** ("long valley"). The Abbey, never completed, was sacked in 1401 by Owain Glyndwr, who suspected its Cistercian monks of being spies of Henry IV. Traditionally, the body of Llywelyn ap Gruffudd ("The Last") was buried here after his death at Cilmeri, near Builth, in 1282.

LLANANNO CHURCH lies well below the road on the banks of the Ithon, just north of Llanbister. Its unprepossessing Victorian exterior houses an excellent early 16th-century screen. Christ occupies the central niche, with the Twelve Apostles on the right and 12 patriarchs and prophets on the left. The 19th-century restoration of the church spared the churchwarden's box pew of the late 17th century.

MONTGOMERY (Trefaldwyn) The parish church of St Nicholas has among its many splendid monuments an effigy of Owain Glyndwr's grandson, and the ornate canopied tomb of Richard Herbert and his wife, with their eight children.

The gardens at **POWIS CASTLE** ★, descending in terraces from the pink medieval castle, were the creation of a nephew of William III. Among the most memorable features are the enormous clipped yews contemporary with the terraces, forming a line of umbrellas over the niches below them. Balustrading, ornamental urns, statuary and wrought-iron gates all add to the fascination of the walk from the castle to the formal gardens at the base of the terraces.

GREGYNOG (below), north of Newtown was bought by Miss Gwendoline and Miss Margaret Davies after World War I, with the intention of making it a conference center and a focus for creative and artistic activity. Their bequest of Impressionists and Post-Impressionists is one of the major attractions of the National Museum of Wales, Cardiff, ▲ 468-9.

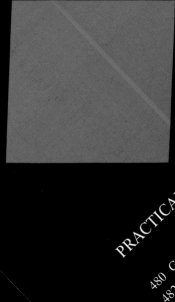

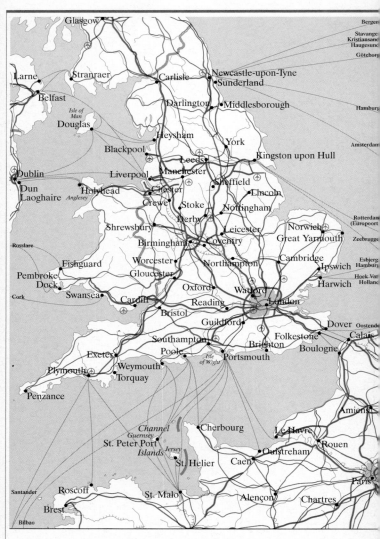

PASSPORTS AND VISAS

All overseas visitors to Britain need a valid passport. European Union (EU) citizens can also obtain entry with a registration card issued in their own country and they do not need a visa. Citizens of Australia, Canada, New Zealand, and the United States are also permitted to enter the country without a visa, but a passport with at least two months' validity is required. You must have proof of intention of return, such as a return ticket, as well as visible means of support during your stay, and the length of stay is restricted to six months.

WORKING RESTRICTIONS

EU citizens do not need a permit to work in Britain. Commonwealth citizens under the age of 27 are permitted to work for up to two years on a part-time basis as long as they have a Working Holiday Maker's Visa, issued abroad. Students from the United States can work in Britain for up to six months if they have a blue card, available through their home university.
Bunac
www.bunac.org
Tel. 020 7251 3472 is an organization that arranges exchange schemes for students from a variety of countries wishing to work abroad.

Note
The fares below quoted are for single, standard-class journeys.

EMBASSIES

→ IN THE UK

■ **American Embassy**
24 Grosvenor Square
London W1A 1AE
Tel. 020 7499 9000
www.usembassy.org.uk

■ **Australian High Commission**
www.australia.org.uk
Australia House, The
Strand, London WC2
Tel. 020 7379 4334

■ **Canadian High Commission**
www.canada.org.uk 1
Grosvenor Square
London W1K
Tel. 020 7258 6600

■ **New Zealand High Commission**
www.nzembassy.com
80 Haymarket,
London SW1
Tel. 020 7930 8422

→ IN THE US

■ **British Embassy**
3100 Massachusetts
Ave, Washington
D.C., 20008
(202) 588 7800
Apply online for a
visa:
*www.britainusa.com/
visas/*

■ **British Consulate
and Visit Britain**
Tel. 212 745 0200
(consulate)
Tel. 800 462 2748
(Visit BritainTourist
Authority)
www.britainusa.com
www.visitbritain.com

TRAVELING TO ENGLAND BY AIR

→ FROM THE US
Major airlines
operating from the
US to Britain include:

■ **Delta**
Tel. 1 800 241 4141
www.delta.com

■ **United**
Tel.1 800 241 6522
www.united.com

■ **American Airlines**
Tel.1 800 433 7300
www.aa.com

■ **British Airways**
Tel.1 800 247 9297
www.ba.com
They offer services
from all the main
American cities.

■ It is also worth
looking up the
following websites:
www.travelocity.com

www.orbitz.com
www.cheapflights.com

→ FROM EUROPE
A number of airlines
specialize in cheap,
"no frills" flights
between Britain and
many Europe.
Operators include:

■ **Easyjet**
Flies into London,
Bristol, Newcastle,
Nottingham and
Liverpool airports.
Tel. 0905 821 0905
www.easyjet.com

■ **Ryanair**
Flies into ten English
airports from many
European cities.
Tel. 0871 246 0000
www.ryanair.com

There are four major
international
airports around
London – Heathrow,
Gatwick, Stansted
and Luton – and a
smaller one, London
City Airport, which
serves Europe. Some
international
operators also fly
direct to Newcastle,
Birmingham, Leeds/
Bradford, Cardiff and
Manchester where
connections can be
made to one of the
many regional
airports.

→ HEATHROW
One of the largest
airports in the world,
15 miles west of
London, linked

to the city center:
■ **By underground**
Journey 45–55 mins;
£4

■ **By rail**
To Paddington
station via the
Heathrow Express,
operating at 17, 32,
47 and 02 mins past
the hour from
terminal 1, 2 and 3
(7 mins before from
terminal 4), from
5.10am– 11.40pm.
Paddington to
Heathrow: 10, 25,
40 and 55 mins past
the hour. Journey
15 mins; £14.50
*www.heathrow
express.com*

■ **By bus**
Coach service every
30 mins to Victoria
Station (5.40am–
9.35pm).
Journey 1 hr; £10
Tel. 020 7730 3499

→ GATWICK
28 miles south of
London, linked to
the center:
■ **By rail**
To Victoria station
via the Gatwick
Express
Tel. 0845 850 1530
*www.gatwickexpress.
com*
Every 15 mins from
5.50am–00.35am.
Victoria to Gatwick:
every 15 mins from
5am–11.45pm.
Journey 30 mins; £14

→ STANSTED
33½ miles northeast
of London, linked to
the center:
■ **By rail**
To London Liverpool
St Station. Every 15
mins from 5.30am–
11pm (00.30am at
week ends).
Journey 45 mins; £15
*www.stanstedexpress.
com*

→ LUTON
32 miles north of
London, linked to
the center:
■ **By rail**
Shuttle from airport
to Luton Airport
station, then train to
Kings Cross station.

Eight trains every
hour. Journey
45 mins; £11.20

→ LONDON CITY AIRPORT
Ten miles east of
London, linked to
the center:
■ **By underground
and DLR**
to London City
Airport station. £3

TRAVELING TO ENGLAND BY SEA
Several ports have
cross-Channel ferry
services. Dover to
Calais is the shortest
and most frequent
crossing, but there
are also good
services from
Folkestone to
Boulogne;
Portsmouth to
Cherbourg, Le Havre,
Caen and St Malo;
Plymouth to Roscoff
and Santander;
Harwich to Hamburg
and Hook of
Holland. Newcastle-
upon-Tyne to
Scandinavia.
For information:
■ **P&O**
Tel. 08705 980333
■ **Stena Line**
Tel. 08705 707070

TRAVELING TO ENGLAND BY RAIL
■ **Eurostar**
Passenger trains run
from Brussels and
Paris to London
Waterloo. Journey:
2 hrs 40 mins from
Paris; 2 hrs 20 mins
from Brussels.
Onward services are
available to
Manchester and
Birmingham, with
possible connections
to Wales.
Tel. 0870 5186 186
www.eurostar.com

■ **Eurotunnel**
shuttle trains take
cars, vans, coaches
and bikes from
Calais to Folkestone,
operating up to four
services per hour
throughout the day.
Journey 35 mins
(45 mins at night)
Tel. 08705 353535
www.eurotunnel.com

BY AIR

- **British Airways** Tel. 0870 850 9850
- **British Midlands** Tel. 0870 6070555
- **KLM UK** Tel. 08705 074074

are the main airlines with regular Shuttle services between national airports, but there are also several smaller companies. Unless you are traveling the length of the country, however, planes are only marginally quicker than trains if you include the time it takes to get to and from the airport.

BY RAIL

The British rail network is operated by 25 different companies, each covering particular regions and routes. However, you can buy a through ticket to your destination even if it requires travel on different networks.

> **National railway enquiries (times & fares)** Tel. 0845 7484950

There are nine termini in London, each serving different regions:

- **Paddington** (South West, West Country, South Wales & Oxfordshire)
- **Victoria** (South Coast, West Sussex & parts of Kent)
- **Waterloo** (Hampshire, Dorset & Surrey)
- **London Bridge** (Kent & East Sussex)
- **Liverpool Street** (Essex, Norfolk, Suffolk & Cambridgeshire)
- **Kings Cross** (North Midlands & North East)
- **Euston** (North West & North Wales)
- **St Pancras** (North Midlands)
- **Charing Cross** (South East)

Journey times from London by train (hours)	
Aberystwyth	5 ¼
Bath	1 ¼
Birmingham	1 ½
Brighton	¾
Bristol	1 ½
Cambridge	1
Cardiff	2
Carlisle	3 ½
Dover	1 ¼
Exeter	2
Liverpool	2 ½
Manchester	2 ½
Oxford	¾
Penzance	5
Stratford	2 ¼
Windermere	3 ¾
York	2

→ **RAIL PASSES**
Those planning to use the train frequently as a way of exploring Britain should buy a rail pass.
- **Britrail Pass** offers unlimited travel, without restrictions, throughout England, Wales and Scotland, and is available in a range of ticket validities.
- **Britrail Flexipass** is available for 4, 8 or 15 days of travel to be taken within a two-month period.
- **Consecutive Day Passes** are valid for 4, 8, 15, or 22 days (one month tickets also available), and give continuous travel over those periods.
Note: these passes cannot be bought in Britain; they can be purchased only through a Rail Europe office (or in some countries, a BritRail office), or through appointed sales agents.
- **The RailRover Pass** offers unlimited travel for 7 days or 14 days and can be bought in England.

> Train tickets can be booked at:
> *www.thetrainline.com*

BY BUS

Although bus services tend to be infrequent in the countryside, local buses run to regular timetables in most major cities, with many buses operating throughout the night. The cost of traveling around a city by bus can be reduced by purchasing a daily or weekly pass (available from newsagents), which have the added advantage that they can be used on all forms of public transport in that area.

BY COACH

For longer distances, traveling by coach is a reliable and cost-effective way of getting around the country.
- **Stagecoach** Tel. 01865 772250 *www.oxfordtube.com* is responsible for the Oxford Tube service (London to Oxford every 12-15 minutes; journey time from 90 mins; adult return fare £14) as well as operating a national service linking all the major cities in Britain.
- **National Express** Tel. 0870 5808080 is the largest national operator, with links to all the major towns and cities of England and Wales. Discounts are available to those aged 16-26, 60 and over, and to all students. The National Express Brit Xplorer Pass (available for 7, 14, or 28 days) is good value if you are planning to travel extensively around England and Wales. Tickets can be purchased from major international airports and large travel agents.

CAR HIRE

You can use a foreign-country-license within England for up to 12 months. To rent a car, you should be between 21 and 65 years of age. Car rental companies have offices at major aiports, main rail stations and most city centers. Car hire is expensive in the UK but some tour operators offer good fly-drive deals. In the more remote country areas, hiring a car is the only feasible way of getting around.The main companies are:
- **Avis** Tel. 08705 900500
- **British Car Rental** Tel. 020 8504 7676
- **Budget** Tel. 0870 1565656
- **Europcar** Tel. 0845 7222525
- **National Car Rental** Tel. 0870 4004579
- **Alamo** Tel. 08705 994000
You might consider joining one of the motoring organizations for 24-hour breakdown cover. The two largest in the UK are
- **AA** Tel. 0800 919595 and
- **RAC** Tel. 0800 550550
These organizations are able to offer additional services to their members, including help with route planning.

> For good places to eat within 5 mins of freeways, try *www.5minutesaway. co.uk*

Note
See p. 576 for a map of the London Underground

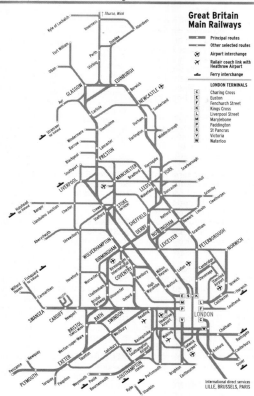

Great Britain Main Railways

▬▬▬	Principal routes
▭▭▭	Other selected routes
✈	Airport interchange
✈	Railair coach link with Heathrow Airport
⛴	Ferry interchange

LONDON TERMINALS

C	Charing Cross
E	Euston
F	Fenchurch Street
K	Kings Cross
L	Liverpool Street
M	Marylebone
P	Paddington
S	St Pancras
V	Victoria
W	Waterloo

International direct services
LILLE, BRUSSELS, PARIS

GETTING AROUND LONDON

→ BY SUBWAY

The quickest way to travel in London. Opened in 1863, the London subway (or Tube, or Underground) is the oldest in the world – and one of the most expensive (it will cost you a minimum of £3 for a single journey, unless you have a travelcard). The subway now covers areas as far as Watford or Epping.

■ **Network**
12 lines, as well as the Docklands Light Railway. There are six zones covering Greater London, charging different fares.

■ **Operating times**
Mon.–Sat. 5.30am– 12.30am, Sun. 7am– midnight (approx.)

→ BY BUS

Much cheaper than the subway, but less punctual.

■ **Lines**
Buses run from approx. 5am until 11.30pm. Bus maps are available from major subway stations. Check the front of the vehicle for its destination.

■ **Bus stops**
Compulsory bus stops are indicated by white-colored signs; request stops by red-colored signs (you must signal to the driver to stop).

■ **Fares**
For travel in central London you must buy a ticket before boarding (from yellow ticket machines by the bus stops). The fare per journey is £1.50. Travelcards again are much better value.

■ **Night buses**
From 11.30pm–6am for many routes (incl. the suburbs). Night buses are all indicated by the letter 'N' before the route number.

→ TICKETS

On the subway the further you travel, the more you pay. Travelcards are always better value.

■ **Oyster Card**
The Oyster card offers by far the best value for money and is valid for travel on the subway, suburban trains and buses. You can put a daily, weekly or monthly ticket on it, as well as top it up with money to pay as you go. Touch the card on the yellow card readers at stations and on buses. This card is issued at subway stations, some train stations many newsagents and outlets showing the Oyster logo.

London bus and underground information
Tel. 020 7222 1234

LONDON TAXIS

Black cabs can be hailed in the street when the yellow "for hire" sign is lit.

TIME

Greenwich Mean Time, the world's standard reference time since 1884, is eight hours ahead of Los Angeles, five hours ahead of New York, one hour behind Paris and ten hours behind Sydney.

CLIMATE

From November to February, the days are short (less than eight hours of daylight in December) and the weather is cold (under 50°F). April to September are the best months to visit, with July and August the busiest. Many attractions close between October and Easter, including most National Trust properties. Take an umbrella no matter when you visit: rain is possible at any time; the west coast is wetter than the east ● 20–21.

ACCOMMODATION

There is a list of recommended hotels on pages 517–38, all of which should be booked in advance. If you arrive in London without a hotel booking (not recommended), the accommodation offices at Victoria station, Heathrow and Gatwick will find a room for you. In other cities, ask for directions to the local tourist information center, as they will have lists of available accommodation; after hours, many display a notice in their windows listing local vacancies.There are several types of accommodation available:

■ **B & B's**
One of the most economic options is "bed and breakfast" in a private house. The quality varies; there are several guides to the best B & B's available in all good bookshops.
■ **Hotels**
These range from a room above a pub to grand country house hotels. The usual international chains are present.
■ **Short-term rental**
The National Trust rents out cottages, which tend to be very charming, in beautiful locations. Tel: 0870 4584411 for a brochure. www.nationaltrust.org.uk
The Landmark Trust rent more unusual buildings, such as castles, follies and medieval houses. *The Landmark Handbook* provides details. Tel: 01628 825925 www.landmarktrust.org.uk

TELEPHONE

■ **100** for a national operator
■ **155** for an international operator
■ **118 550, 118 118** or **118 000** for national directory enquiries
■ **118 505** for international directory enquiries
■ **00** to call overseas, followed by the country code, and then the required number (for some countries it is necessary to remove the first '0' of the telephone number)

→ **PUBLIC PHONES**
Public phone boxes take coins and phone cards, which can be purchased from newsagents and post offices. Credit cards are also accepted in a number of phone

COUNTRY CODES	
Australia	61
Belgium	32
Canada	1
France	33
Germany	49
Italy	39
Japan	81
Netherlands	31
New Zealand	64
Republic of Ireland	353
Spain	34
USA	1

boxes. The cheapest times to call are between 6pm and 8am Monday to Friday, and at weekends.

EMERGENCY SERVICES

Dial 999 for police, fire and ambulance services (calls are free and lines are manned 24 hours a day). An operator will ask which service you require and can provide first-aid advice in an emergency.

MEDICAL HELP

Accident victims should be taken to the nearest hospital with an Accident and Emergency department (check in a local telephone directory) or call 999 for an ambulance. Emergency medical treatment is available free at National Health Service (NHS) hospitals, but we strongly advise you to take out medical insurance to cover any other medical care which may be required. EU citizens, and those from countries with which Britain has reciprocal health arrangements, are entitled to free medical treatment under the NHS, but not all treatments may be covered so it it is still advisable to take out insurance. Local doctors (GPs)

will see visitors who fall ill in their area but you may be charged). Names and telephone numbers of local doctors can be found in the telephone directory for the relevant area or by calling NHS Direct on 0845 4647 who also provide free medical advice by telephone 24 hrs a day. www.nhsdirect.nhs.uk There are also walk-in medical centers at London Victoria and Waterloo stations.
■ **Non NHS services**
Several services provide doctors on 24-hour call, for a fee (up to £100 in the case of an evening house call): **Doctorcall** Tel. 020 7291 6666 can provide a doctor in London and the surrounding areas. **Doctors Direct** Tel. 020 7751 9701 serve central London only. Most chemists have a resident pharmacist who is trained to advise on medical problems and provide non-prescription medication for common ailments.

MONEY

Major credit cards used in Britain are Visa/Barclaycard, Access/Mastercard, AmEx and Diners Club. They are accepted at the majority of hotels, shops restaurants and petrol stations. Travelers' checks can be changed in

LOST CARDS
Mastercard
Call 0800 96 4767
Visa
Call 0800 89 1725
AmEx
Call collect
336-393-1111

banks, bureaux de change and hotel receptions. You can also use ATMs with the Cirrus/ Maestro or Plus symbols to withdraw cash, if you have the appropriate card. The pound sterling is divided into 100 pence. Coins are 1p, 2p, 5p, 10p, 20p, 50p, £1 and £2. Notes are £5, £10, £20 and £50.

VAT
A tax of 17½ percent is included in hotel and restaurant bills. If you come from outside the European Union, you may claim refunds of any Value Added Tax (VAT) on goods purchased. Ask for a form in

the shop where you make the purchase.

TIPPING
In restaurants, leave 10-15% if service has not already been included on the bill; some restaurants leave the total box empty on credit card slips so you can add a tip. Taxi drivers expect 10%. Porters in good hotels can be tipped £1, or 30p to 50p per piece of luggage. Barbers and hairdressers generally get 10 to 15% as a tip. Do not tip in pubs, cinemas or theaters.

POSTAGE
Post offices are usually open 9am–5.30pm Mon.–Fri.

and 9am–12.30pm on Sat. First class mail to a national address is generally delivered in one day and costs 32p for a standard-weight letter (under 100g), while second class mail takes slightly longer and costs 23p. Air-mail letters to European countries cost 44p, and to the Americas and Australasia the cost is 72p.

OPENING HOURS
Business hours are generally 9am–5.30pm Monday to Saturday, with late-night closing at 8pm one night a week. Most **shops** in central London are open until at least 7pm

during the week with late-night closing at 9pm. Many are also open on Sundays from noon to 6pm.

Banks are generally open 9am–5pm Mon.–Fri., with a number opening on Saturdays also. **Pubs** are generally open 11am–11pm daily (10.30pm on Sundays), but some are open until midnight, 1am or even later.

WELSH LANGUAGE

PRONUNCIATION
Welsh is a phonetic language; it sounds as it looks. Do your best with the ll and ch, for which there is no equivalent sound in English. Remember the following points:
■ Vowels are shorter and less drawled than in English
■ The stress is on the last syllable but one
■ ff = f ; f = v
■ c and g are hard, as in "anger"
■ dd = th, as in "then"
th = th, as in "thin"
■ w is a vowel = oo
■ y is a vowel = u, as in "hut" when alone or anywhere except the final syllable and = i, as in "hit", as a final syllable. *Mynydd* (mountain) is pronounced munith, with the th of "then", illustrating the two y sounds.

PLACE NAMES
These are often composites describing the location or history

of the place in question. The following glossary explains some of the commonly used terms:
abaty abbey
aber estuary
afon river
bach small
betws church, chapel
bryn hill
caer fort
capel chapel
carreg stone
castell / cas castle
clawdd dyke
clogwyn cliff
clun meadow
coed forest
cors bog
cwm valley
dan under
dinas city
dôl meadow
du black
fawr big
ffordd road
ffos ditch
gallt hill
glan shore
glyn glen
gwaun moor
gwyn white
heli salty
is below
llan parish
llech slate
llyn lake

maes field
mawr big
merthyr burial place of a saint
mynydd mountain
nant brook/stream, valley
newydd new
ogof cave
pant hollow
parc field
pen headland
penmaen promontory
pentre village
plas mansion
pont bridge
porth harbor
pwll pool
rhaeadr waterfall
rhos moor
rhyd ford
sarn causeway
tan under
traeth beach
traws across
tre town
trum ridge
twr tower
twyn knoll
ty, tai house, houses
y, yr 'r the
yn in
ynys island
ystwyth winding

So Plas Newydd means "new mansion"; Aberystwyth means

"winding estuary", Llantrisant means a "parish of three saints" and Porthmadog is a harbor town.

USEFUL PHRASES
How are you?
Sut mae?
Good morning
Bore da
Good afternoon
Prynhawn da
Good night
Nos da
How much? **Faint?**
Thank you **Diolch**
Open **Ar agor**
Hotel **Gwesty**
Bus **Bws**
Women **Merched**
Men **Dynion**

■ **Numbers**

1	un
2	dau
3	tri
4	pedwar
5	pump
6	chwech
7	saith
8	wyth
9	naw
10	deg
20	dau-ddeg
50	pum-deg
100	cant
200	dau gant
1000	mil

◆ CALENDAR OF EVENTS

JANUARY	WHAT	WHERE	WHAT ABOUT
MID	London international boat show	Earls Court, London	Over 600 exhibitors from around the world.
FEBRUARY			
BEG	Chinese New Year	Chinatown in London (Soho) and Manchester	Dragon parades.
MARCH			
MAR/APR	Ideal Home Exhibition	Earls Court, London	Consumer show featuring all that's new for homes and interiors.
END	Oxford vs. Cambridge Boat Race	River Thames, Hammersmith	University Rowing event held in Putney, London, since 1845.
END	International Antiques & Fine Arts Fair	Duke of York's, Chelsea, London	
APRIL			
WEEK 1	Chelsea Craft Fair	Chelsea, London	
END	British International Antiques Fair	Nat. Exhibition Centre, Birmingham	
VARIES	London Marathon		From Blackheath and Greenwich to the Mall, taking in Tooley St, Canary Wharf and back through Tower of London and Embankment.
MAY			
WKS 2-4	Brighton Festival	Brighton, Sussex	Country's biggest mixed arts festival.
MID	Festival of English Food and Wine	Leeds Castle, Kent	Celebration of England's gastronomic heritage.
MID-END	Chelsea Flower Show	Royal Hospital Chelsea, London	Plants and flowers of all seasons with displays of theme gardens. Tickets from Royal Horticultural Society.
MID-END	Hatfield Craft Fair	Hatfield House, Herts	Annual craft fair.
END	The Hay Festival	Hay-on-Wye, Wales	Book festival.
MAY/JUNE & SEP	Well Dressing Festivals	Various, Derbyshire	Originally a pagan form of water worship, and now the area's most recognized custom.
BANK HOL WEEKEND	International Beach Kite Festival	Weymouth Beach, Dorset	Hundreds of kite-fliers from Britain and overseas; displays, competitions etc.
WKS 2,3,4	Isle of Wight Walking Festival	all over island	Fun walks and serious challenges, themed walks etc.
END	Richmond Crafts Fair	Richmond, London	Summer craft fair, Queen Charlotte Hall.
MAY-JUN	Bath International Music Festival	Various (Bath), Somerset	All varieties of music represented.
MAY-AUG	Glyndebourne Opera Festival	Lewes, Sussex	World-famous opera festival.
JUNE			
WEEK 1	Derby Horse Race Meeting	Epsom Racecourse, Surrey	Contested for more than two centuries, the Derby is the most famous flat race in England.
WEEKS 2-3	Aldeburgh Festival	Aldeburgh/Snape Maltings Suffolk	Festival of classical music and opera.
AROUND THE 10TH	Trooping the Colour	Whitehall, London	Military parade to mark Queen's official birthday.
MID	Royal Ascot	Ascot, Berkshire	Social highlight of the horse-racing calendar.
MID	Wimbledon	Wimbledon, London	Lawn tennis championships held annually since 1884.
END JUNE	Alnwick Medieval Fair	Alnwick, Northumberland	Recreation of a fair dating from the Middle Ages with crafts, stage entertainment etc.
END JUNE/ BEG JULY	Glastonbury Festival	Glastonbury, Somerset	Rock festival.
JUN-JUL	City of London Festival	London	Music and the arts.
JULY			
BEG	International Musical Eisteddfod	Llangollen, N.Wales	International music and dance competition.
BEG	Henley Royal Regatta	Henley, Oxfordshire	International rowing event.
6TH	Barnes Fair	Barnes, London SW14	Annual fair held on Barnes Common.

JULY	WHAT	WHERE	WHAT ABOUT
MID	Haslemere (Dolmetsch) festival	Haslemere, Surrey	Early music.
MID	York Early Music Festival	York, Yorkshire	
MID	Cheltenham International Festival of Music	Cheltenham	
MID-END	Royal Tournament	Earls Court London	Display by the armed forces.
END	Womad	Rivermead, Reading Berkshire	Family-friendly rock festival.
END	Cambridge Folk Festival	Cambridge	UK's largest festival of folk music.
LAST WEEK	Whitstable Oyster Festival	Kent	Event including bands, stalls, dances, and tasting of oysters.
END JULY BEG AUG	Harrogate International Festival	Harrogate, Yorkshire	Music, theater, dance, comedy.
MID JUL-SEP	BBC Proms	Royal Albert Hall, London	Series of classical concerts. Founded by Sir Henry Wood in 1895.

AUGUST			
WEEK 1	Cowes Week	Cowes, Isle of Wight	Sailing regatta, over 900 boats – races, stalls, bands every night.
BEG	The Great British Beer Festival	Olympia, London	Biggest real-beer event in Britain.
BEG	Royal National Eisteddfod of Wales	Wales	Festival with cultural slant, dating back to 12th century; competitions in music, dance and the spoken word.
MID	Brecon Jazz	Various (Brecon) S.Wales	Major event in the British jazz calendar.
1-31	Dartington Summer School of Music	Near Totnes, South Devon	
1-31	Snape Proms	Aldeburgh	Music.
LAST WEEKEND	Notting Hill Carnival	Notting Hill, West London	West Indian street carnival.
BANK HOL	Reading Festival	Reading, Berkshire	Rock festival.
END	International Beatles Week	Liverpool, Merseyside	Various events celebrating the Beatles.
END	Ocean Festival	Newquay, Cornwall	Event attracting top British surfers.
AUG/SEP	Three Choirs Festival	Gloucester, Hereford and Worcester	

SEPTEMBER			
3RD WEEKEND	Great Autumn Flower Show	Harrogate, North Yorkshire	
1-30	North Wales International Music Festival (St Asaph)	North Wales	
SEP/OCT	Blackpool Illuminations	Blackpool Promenade, Lancashire	Illuminations covering a 6-mile stretch of Blackpool's promenade.

OCTOBER			
1-31	Norfolk and Norwich Festival	Norfolk	Music and the arts.
2ND WEEKEND	Goose Fair	Nottingham, Nottinghamshire	Traditional fair and fun fair.
WKS 2,3	Canterbury Festival	Canterbury, Kent	Music, drama and the arts.
WKS 2,3	Cheltenham Festival of Literature	Cheltenham (various), Gloucestershire	Longest-running literary festival in the world.
31ST	Hallowe'en	Countrywide	Games and costumes on the eve of All Saints Day.

NOVEMBER			
5TH	Guy Fawkes Day	England	Fireworks and bonfires to commemorate the arrest of Guy Fawkes in 1605 for attempting to blow up the Houses of Parliament.
2ND SAT	Lord Mayor's Procession	City of London	To mark the inauguration of the new mayor.

DECEMBER			
DEC 1-3	Richmond Crafts Fair	Richmond, London	Christmas fair, Queen Charlotte Hall
1ST THU	Lighting of Christmas Tree	Trafalgar Square, London	Mayor of Oslo turns on lights of tree donated each year by the people of Norway.

◆ THE BEST COUNTRY HOUSES

Selected by John Julius Norwich

NT after the name denotes
a National Trust property ◆ 496

BUCKINGHAMSHIRE
Claydon House (NT)
A Jacobean manor house remodeled in the 1750s with some of the most spectacular plasterwork in England. ▲ 291

CHESHIRE
Tatton Park (NT)
Handsome Wyatt mansion with fine pictures and a Japanese garden. ▲ 378

CLWYD
Erddig (NT)
One of the most fascinating houses in Britain; extraordinary evocation of backstairs life 100 years ago. ▲ 448-9

CORNWALL
Cotehele House (NT)
Medieval fortified granite manor house with wonderful tapestries. Time stands still. ▲ 242

Lanhydrock House (NT)
Gutted by fire in 1881 but still a show-stopper, with a breathtaking Long Gallery (which survived the flames) and kitchen quarters that are an education in themselves. ▲ 242

St Michael's Mount (NT)
No house in England boasts a more spectacular site, on a great crag projecting into the sea, by which it is cut off from the mainland for 20 hours a day. ▲ 246-7

DERBYSHIRE
Chatsworth
The grandest house in England, seat of Duke of Devonshire. Superb pictures, furniture, gardens, and park. ▲ 382-3

Haddon Hall
Perhaps the most romantic house in England, with the oldest kitchen in the country. Originally Norman, last altered in Elizabethan times. ▲ 380

Hardwick New Hall (NT) One of the great Elizabethan 'prodigy' houses, scarcely altered since its completion in 1597. ▲ 382

Kedleston Hall (NT)
Magnificent Palladian house with interior by Robert Adam. ▲ 381

DEVON
Powderham Castle
A fortified manor house of about 1400 with mostly 18th-century interior: lovely Music Room by James Wyatt and astonishing stucco work in the Great Staircase. ▲ 236

Saltram (NT)
Superb interiors by Robert Adam and outstanding collection of portraits by Sir Joshua Reynolds, a friend of the family. ▲ 241

Castle Drogo
Granite castle built for comfortable living, 1910-30, by England's foremost early 20th-century architect, Sir Edwin Lutyens. ▲ 239

GLOUCESTERSHIRE
Berkeley Castle
Superb medieval castle still inhabited

by the original Berkeley family. Edward II was murdered here in 1327. ▲ 257

GWYNEDD
Plas Newydd (NT)
Built by Wyatt in Gothic Revival style in a spectacular position overlooking the Menai Strait. Superb mural by Rex Whistler in the Dining Room. ▲ 450

HERTFORDSHIRE
Hatfield House
Begun in 1607 by Robert Cecil, chief minister to James I,

Kedleston Hall

and still occupied by his descendants. ▲ 284

KENT
Knole (NT)
One of the largest houses in England – the size of a village – and the most atmospheric. A world of its own. ▲ 172-3

Penshurst Place
Almost as big as its neighbor Knole, and, begun around 1340, well over a century older. Henry V and Edward IV both dined at the huge trestle tables in the Great Hall. ▲ 174

LINCOLNSHIRE
Belton (NT)
Perfect late 17th-century house with good carvings by Grinling Gibbons and others. ▲ 359

Belvoir Castle
Apotheosis of early 19th-century Gothic revival castle. ▲ 360-1

Burghley House
Tremendous creation of William Cecil, Secretary of State to Elizabeth I. Fine picture collection. ▲ 358

MIDDLESEX
Osterley Park (NT)
An Elizabethan house that has been virtually unaltered since it was remodeled by Robert Adam in 1761-80; all the furniture designed for it is still there. ▲ 168

Syon House
Originally a monastery founded by Henry V, now the Thamesside house of the Duke of Northumberland. Spectacular series of rooms by Robert Adam. ▲ 168

NORFOLK
Blickling Hall (NT)
Early 17th-century house with glorious plasterwork and magnificent gardens. ▲ 354-5

Holkham Hall
A Palladian palace designed by Thomas Coke, 1st Earl of Leicester and William Kent, who was responsible for the interiors and much of the furniture. ▲ 352-3

See also endpaper maps and contact details listed on pages *504-13*

Houghton Hall
Kent's Stone Hall is one of the great rooms of England. Superb pictures and plasterwork. ▲ *352-3*

Oxburgh Hall (NT)
Wonderful moated manor house begun in 1482. The King's Room, where Henry VII slept in 1487, had bed-hangings embroidered by Mary Queen of Scots. ▲ *355*

NORTHAMPTONSHIRE
Althorp
Late 18th-century mansion on earlier foundations, childhood home of Diana, Princess of Wales.
▲ *279*

Boughton House
Magnificent early 18th-century house on Tudor foundations with superb interiors and glorious furniture and pictures. ▲ *280*

Castle Ashby
Fine Elizabethan courtyard house with classical south front possibly by Inigo Jones. ▲ *279*

Deene Park
Originally Tudor, enlarged in later centuries. The Brudenells have lived here for twelve generations. ▲ *280*

NORTHUMBERLAND
Alnwick
Romantic border castle with an excellent art collection. ▲ *412-13*

OXFORDSHIRE
Blenheim Palace
Built 1705-25 by grateful government to designs of Vanbrugh as reward to 1st Duke of Marlborough for his success in wars with France.
▲ *312*

Broughton Castle
Not so much a castle as a fortified and moated manor house of about 1300, wonderfully little altered. ▲ *313*

POWYS
Powis Castle (NT)
A border stronghold with a glorious Tudor Long Gallery and the finest garden in Wales.
▲ *478*

SOMERSET
Montacute (NT)
One of the loveliest of Elizabethan houses. The upper floor is hung with superb Tudor and Jacobean portraits from the National Portrait Gallery.
▲ *231*

SUFFOLK
Ickworth (NT)
A vast rotunda with a wealth of pictures, furniture and works of art. ▲ *339*

SURREY
Clandon Park (NT)
The great marble Hall one of finest in England; wonderful furniture and plasterwork. ▲ *317*

Ham House (NT)
Begun 1610, with superb 17th-century furniture and pictures. ▲ *169*

SUSSEX
Petworth House (NT)
Late 17th-century house in French style. Don't miss the Grinling Gibbons' carvings or the glorious landscapes by J.M.W. Turner, who practically lived here in the 1830s.
▲ *192-3*

WILTSHIRE
Badminton
17th-century seat of Duke of Beaufort, where the game of badminton was invented. ▲ *223*

Dyrham Park (NT)
Perfect late 17th-century house, preserved virtually unchanged for nearly three centuries. ▲ *223*

Stourhead (NT)
Fine Palladian house completed 1724, with the finest landscape garden in England. ▲ *214-15*

Left: Blenheim Palace

Wilton House
Mid-16th-century house partially rebuilt in mid-17th, possibly by Inigo Jones. Six dazzling state rooms; the Double Cube is among the finest in England. ▲ *210-11*

YORKSHIRE (EAST RIDING)
Burton Constable
Fine Jacobean House, altered in mid-18th century but in the original style. ▲ *387*

YORKSHIRE (NORTH)
Beningbrough Hall (NT) Remarkable Baroque house with superb staircase hall and 18th-century portraits from the National Portrait Gallery. ▲ *403*

Castle Howard
The first work of Vanbrugh, featured in *Brideshead Revisited* television series. ▲ *403*

Newby Hall
17th/18th-century house with decoration by Robert Adam and superb gardens.
▲ *395*

Stourhead

YORKSHIRE (WEST RIDING)
Harewood House
Magnificent 18th-century house with Adam interiors; memorable collections of pictures, furniture and porcelain. ▲ *392*

Nostell Priory (NT)
Conventional Palladian exterior, but the interior is magnificent, decorated by Adam and with furniture by Chippendale, the house carpenter.
▲ *390*

Left: Petworth House

◆ THE MOST BEAUTIFUL GARDENS
Selected by Penelope Hobhouse

NT after the name denotes
a National Trust property ◆ 496

BUCKINGHAMSHIRE
Stowe Landscape Gardens
Vast 18th-century landscape worked over by Bridgeman, Kent, and Brown. Grass, trees, temples and vistas make Stowe unforgettable. ▲ 250

CAMBRIDGESHIRE
Anglesey Abbey (NT)
Gardens by Lord Fairhaven in the 1930s. Massive avenues, rose garden, hyacinth and dahlia garden. Fine sculpture set in hedged enclosures and alleys. ▲ 326-7

CORNWALL
Trewithen
18th-century house dominates vista through remarkable plantsman's garden. Woodland collection started by Col. Johnson in 1903; rhododendrons, magnolias from Asia brought in the 1920s. Formal walled garden. ▲ 243

CUMBRIA
Holker Hall
New formal gardens near house, superb woodland, tree collections, meadow. National collection of *Styracaceae*. ▲ 437

Levens Hall
Late 17th-century topiary garden, extended by Victorians. Beech alleys and view to superlative countryside. Box-edged beds of impeccable massed annuals set off monumental yew sculpture. ▲ 436

DERBYSHIRE
Chatsworth
400 years of garden development: 1700s cascade, canals, orangery, sculpture, "Capability" Brown landscape, Victorian glasshouses, Paxton rockery and a modern yew maze. ▲ 382-3

Melbourne Hall
Early 18th-century formal gardens, tunnels of yew, superb statuary by John van Nost. Robert Bakewell's exquisite wrought-iron 'Birdcage'. ▲ 381

DEVON
Dartington Hall
20th-century gardens (Beatrice Farrand and Percy Cane before 1939) designed around 14th-century tiltyard. Green terraces, fantastic steps, yew hedges and a Henry Moore sculpture, with interesting woodland planting. ▲ 238

Knightshayes Court (NT) Borders and terraces by 19th-century house with rare tender plants. Woodland garden since 1945 admirably maintained and imaginatively planted. ▲ 252

DORSET
Athelhampton
Compartmental garden designed by Inigo Thomas around medieval house in the 1890s. Further formal developments in last 50 years. ▲ 205

ESSEX
Beth Chatto Gardens
Garden and nursery. Ecological planting round pond, woodland. Gravel Garden.

GLOUCESTERSHIRE
Barnsley House
Designed by Rosemary and David Verey since 1951. Strong framework of alleys, laburnum and pleached lime walk, matching period of 17th-century house. Shrub roses, mixed borders and superb French-style potager. ▲ 258

Hidcote Manor (NT)
Designed as compartmental garden by Lawrence Johnson in early 20th century. Themed gardens, tapestry hedges, alleys, old roses, cottage-style planting. ▲ 259

GWYNEDD
Bodnant (NT)
Late 19th-century romantic woodland garden of conifers and rhododendrons. Formal terraces provide sheltered sites for tender plants. Lily Pool. ▲ 455

HERTFORDSHIRE
Hatfield House
Palace built in 1607, surrounded by formal gardens, imaginatively restored by Lady Salisbury. 16th-century knot garden by old Tudor Palace with authentic planting. Victorian maze. ▲ 284

KENT
Sissinghurst Castle (NT) Renowned 20th-century gardens designed and planted by Vita Sackville-West and Harold Nicolson. Yew hedges and pleached lime walks frame a white garden, 'hot' gardens, old roses, spring bulbs. ▲ 176

Sissinghurst

NORFOLK
Sheringham Park (NT) Finest Repton house and park (1812) for Abbot Upcher. In restoration. ▲ 351

OXFORDSHIRE
Buscot Park (NT)
Superb Harold Peto water-garden design feeds into 18th-century lake. Walled gardens border designs by Peter Coats and hop hornbeam tunnels by Tim Rees. ▲ 304

Hatfield maze

See also endpaper maps and contact details listed on pages 504-13

Rousham House

William Kent's finest design between 1737 and 1741: a virtuoso arrangement of buildings, follies, serpentine woodland rill and views to countryside. Walled gardens near the house predate Kent but have modern planting. ▲ 312

POWYS

Powis Castle (NT)
Formal 'hanging' terraces date to late 17th century. Decorated with clipped yews and fine lead urns. Spectacular border planting. ▲ 478

SCILLY, ISLES OF

Tresco Abbey
Begun by Augustus Smith in 1838. Windbreaks provide planting. Recently restored. Romantic landscape garden dates from 18th century designed by Copleston Warre Bampfylde. ▲ 231

STAFFORDSHIRE

Biddulph Grange (NT) Extraordinary Victorian gardens laid out from 1842. Recently restored. Themed Chinese and Egyptian gardens, conifer avenue, dahlia borders.

SURREY

Hampton Court Palace
Royal gardens from 16th century. 1691 maze, Fountain Garden and radiating lime tree avenues. William III's Privy Garden recently authentically restored. Vine

Great Dixter

Christopher Lloyd's famous garden around house restored by Lutyens in 1910. Fine topiary, mixed borders, 'hot' tropical bedding, wild flowers, naturalized bulbs. ▲ 176

Nymans Gardens (NT)

Historic collection of trees, shrubs, bulbs and flowers from 1885. Formal vistas and natural woodland planting. Topiary yew and box, geometric shapes and plump birds. ▲ 190

Sheffield Park (NT)

Brown and Repton park. Fine early 20th-century tree and shrub collection. Lake and woodland walks. ▲ 188

NATIONAL GARDENS SCHEME YELLOW BOOK is a useful listing of gardens throughout the UK belonging to this scheme. Tel. 020 8339 0931 www.ngs.org.uk

BED AND BREAKFAST FOR GARDEN LOVERS is available from BBGL, Handywater Farm, Sibford Gower, Banbury, Oxfordshire OX15 5AE www.bbgl.co.uk

WILTSHIRE

Iford Manor
Sir Harold Peto's early 20th-century garden. Italianate style on steep terraced slopes linked by steps. Pools, fountains, loggias, architectural fragments and evergreens. ▲ 216

Stourhead (NT)
Best-known English landscape garden begun in 1745. Valleys, lake, temples, grotto, hermitage. Victorian conifers and 20th-century rhododendrons. ▲ 214-15

YORKSHIRE, NORTH

Newby Hall
Outstanding, mainly 20th-century garden with beautiful plants, excellently and imaginatively looked after. Herbaceous borders, colored themes, seasonal gardens, tree and shrub collections. ▲ 395

Studley Royal (NT)
John Aislabie's masterpiece from 1720. Valley of River Skell opened out to make water garden, banqueting house, statues, octagonal tower, Temple of Piety and Temple of Fame. ▲ 396

semi-tropical conditions for exotic and rare tender plants. Primarily a plant collection held together by terraced structure. ▲ 248

SOMERSET

Hestercombe
Justly renowned for Edwardian Lutyens/Jekyll garden, on different levels. Lutyens for the stonework, Jekyll for the color planted in 1768. Jean Tijou gilded railings. ▲ 170

SUSSEX

Denmans
The modern designer John Brook's own garden. Walled gravel garden, architectural and foliage plants, dry stream bed with self-seeders, water garden, native planting.

*Above:
Sheffield Park*

Wakehurst Place (NT)
Original Loder tree and shrub collection, now part of the Royal Botanic Gardens of Kew. Rhododendrons, Himalayan plants, water garden, walled garden, a rock walk and winter garden.

◆ THE TOP 100 ENGLISH CHURCHES

Selected by Simon Jenkins

BERKSHIRE
Langley Marish
Private pew and sumptuous private library.

BUCKINGHAMSHIRE
Hillesden
Perpendicular clerestory, Dutch glass.

Wing
Saxon nave and crypt.

CHESHIRE
Nantwich
Octagonal tower, medieval stalls with canopies.

CORNWALL
Launceston
Exterior of carved granite decoration.

St Neot
Superb set of medieval windows.

CUMBRIA
Cartmel
Norman priory with fine Victorian glass.

Wreay
Victorian spinster's Lombardic labor of love.

DERBYSHIRE
Ashbourne
Cockayne and Boothby monuments adorn gateway to the Peak.

Melbourne
Vigorous Norman mini-cathedral of the Bishops of Carlisle.

DEVON
Crediton
Astonishing Buller memorial screen.

Cullompton
Virtuoso screen and fan vaulting in Lane aisle.

Ottery St Mary
Jumble of styles with vividly painted roof.

DORSET
Bournemouth, St Peter
Colorful 19th-century Gothic interior by Street.

Bournemouth, St Stephen
Pearson's quietly austere answer to St Peter's.

Christchurch
Norman core with dazzling Perpendicular chancel.

Milton Abbey
Nave and crossing of great abbey in valley setting.

Sherborne Abbey
Superb fan vaults of Ham stone.

Wimborne Minster
Loveable town church in mix of medieval styles.

ESSEX
Copford
Fine set of rare 12th-century wall paintings.

Thaxted
Adam & Eve window. Majestic Perpendicular spire.

Waltham Abbey
Saxon abbey revived by Burges; Burne-Jones windows.

GLOUCESTERSHIRE
Bristol, Lord Mayor's Chapel
Poyntz chapel; medieval glass.

Bristol, St Mary Redcliffe
Seafarers' foundation, with 'oriental' porch and vaulted nave.

Chipping Campden
Tall wool church with clothiers' tombs.

Cirencester
Cathedral of "woolgothic"; magnificent marketplace porch.

Deerhurst
Saxon church; 10th-century angel relief.

Fairford, St Mary
Unaltered medieval windows and woodwork.

Highnam
Colorful Anglo-Catholic memorial to patron's dead family.

Northleach
One of England's finest Gothic porches.

Tewkesbury
Massive Norman exterior encasing Despenser tombs.

Below: Fairford, St Mary

Above: Crediton, Devon. Above right: Barfreston, Kent

HAMPSHIRE
Romsey
Bold abbey survivor with Norman arcades.

Winchester, St Cross
Almshouse church with Norman features, rivalling the cathedral up the river.

HEREFORDSHIRE
Abbey Dore
Sublime location for early Gothic choir; 17th-century screen.

Kilpeck
Exotic Norman carvings in rich red stone.

Ledbury
Lofty chapter-house converted as baptistery.

Leominster
Superb decorated tracery; ancient ducking stool.

Shobdon
18th-century 'boudoir'; Gothic interior.

HUNTINGDONSHIRE
Barnack
Pink limestone church; Christ-in-Majesty carving.

Castor
Richly decorated Norman tower in Peterborough style.

KENT
Barfreston
Complete set of Romanesque decorations.

THE TOP 100 ENGLISH CHURCHES ◆

Selected by Simon Jenkins

See also endpaper maps

Top: Long Melford
Above: Hexham,
Northumberland

Stone (nr. Dartford)
Gothic carvings by
the masons who
worked on
Westminster.

LANCASHIRE
Liverpool, St Agnes
Pearson's Merseyside
masterpiece.

LINCOLNSHIRE
Boston
The 'Stump', the
highest tower in
England.

Brant Broughton
Perfect marriage
of 14th-century
interior and 19th-
century restoration;
rare 'defecating'
gargoyle.

Grantham
Finest of all Gothic
steeples.

Heckington
Exquisite exterior;
Gothic carvings.

Louth
Soaring
Perpendicular
steeple over fine
town church.

Stow
Pearson's free
restoration of fine
Norman church.

LONDON
**All Saints,
Margaret Street**
Butterfield's seminal
work of Victorian
revival.
**Christchurch,
Spitalfields**
Hawksmoor's
masterpiece
towering over
Spitalfields market.

**Holy Trinity,
Sloane Street**
London's best
gallery of Arts and
Crafts workmanship.

St Augustine, Kilburn
Dazzling work of
Anglo-French Gothic
by Pearson.

St-Mary-le-Strand
Gibbs's London
variant on a Roman
theme, sailing down
the Strand.

St Mary Woolnoth
Superb composition
of clustered columns
by Hawksmoor.

St Stephen Walbrook
Wren's finest City
church, a dome on
a square.

NORFOLK
**King's Lynn,
St Margaret**
Choir carvings;
Dutch brass of the
'peacock feast'.

**Norwich,
St Peter Mancroft**
Gigantic
Perpendicular town
church ablaze with
sunlight.

Salle
Lonely but mighty
Norfolk galleon in
the fields.

Walpole St Peter
Perfect East
Anglian church;
a study in light
on stone.

NORTHAMPTONSHIRE
Lowick
Fluttering octagonal
tower; superb
Gothic effigies.

Stanford
Every ecclesiastical
art on display in
small farmland
church.

Wellingborough
Comper's
masterpiece;
King's College
Chapel in industrial
suburb.

NORTHUMBERLAND
Hexham
Rare canons' night
staircase; 'Dance
of Death' painting.

NOTTINGHAMSHIRE
Clumber
Bodley's memorial
triumph; survivor of
old Clumber House.

Newark-on-Trent
Huge town church
with steeple to rival
Grantham.

OXFORDSHIRE
Bloxham
Finest work of
14th-century
Oxfordshire carvers;
Burne-Jones glass.

Burford
Wealthy merchants'
church of the upper
Thames valley, rich
in tombs.

Dorchester
Rare 'Tree of
Jesse' window
carvings.

SHROPSHIRE
Ludlow
Cathedral of the
Marches; Palmers
Guild chapel and
glass.

Shrewbury, St Mary
Newly restored
Gothic nave; superb
Continental glass.

SOMERSET
Bath Abbey
Angels' ladder
carving; stately fan
vault interior.

Crewkerne
Superb
Perpendicular
tracery; 'clean and
unclean' doors.

Dunster
Longest carved
screen; rare priory
garden.

Isle Abbotts
Gentlest of the
Somerset towers;
ideal Levels setting.

STAFFORDSHIRE
Cheadle
Pugin's Roman
Catholic masterpiece
of early Victorian
Gothic.

Hoar Cross
Bodley's museum
of Anglo-Catholic
design; superb choir
stall.

SUFFOLK
Framlingham
Mausoleum of 16th-
century Renaissance
tombs of the
Howard family.

Kedington
Rich furnishings;
dubbed 'Betjeman's
village Westminster
Abbey'.

Lavenham (below)
East Anglian tower;
rich merchants'
chapels.

WALES

Above: Bolton Abbey

Long Melford
Perpendicular gallery of clothiers' wealth; Clopton chantry with lily crucifix.

Mildenhall
Lacework east window; fluttering angels roof.

Southwold
Flint flushwork exterior; medieval choirstalls.

SUSSEX
Brighton, St Michael
Rival naves by Bodley and Burges; William Morris glass.

WARWICKSHIRE
Stratford-upon-Avon
Perpendicular chancel by river; Shakespeare's tomb.

Warwick, St Mary
Home of the mighty Beauchamps, with monuments to match.

WILTSHIRE
Devizes
Dark Norman chancel carvings.

Edington
Perfect work of mid-14th-century Gothic; colorful modern ceilings.

Malmesbury
Majestic half-ruin; Romanesque tableaux in porch.

WORCESTERSHIRE
Great Malvern
Rare medieval tiles and glass adorn strong Norman interior on hillside.

Great Witley
Gibbs interior next to gaunt ruined mansion; Georgian painted glass.

Pershore
Serene Early Gothic 'lancet' chancel.

YORKSHIRE, EAST RIDING OF
Beverley Minster
'Best' non-cathedral church in England; rich in building of all Gothic ages.

Beverley, St Mary
Rivals Minster; superb west front; minstrels carvings.

Patrington, St Patrick
Limestone jewel of early 14th-century Gothic, lost in Holderness.

YORKSHIRE, NORTH
Bolton Abbey
Immaculate setting in valley; botanical reredos.

Lastingham
Giant crypt capitals; wild moorland setting.

Selby
Abbey restored after fire; majestic east window.

Studley Royal
Explosion of Burges invention in Fountains Abbey landscape.

Whitby
Mariners' church; jumbled box pews.

ANGLESEY
Beaumaris
Handsome exterior, with fascinating interior fittings.

Llaneilian
Outstanding features from the 12th century onward.

BRECONSHIRE
Partrishow
Remote and rewarding, encompassing many centuries.

CAERNARFONSHIRE
Clynnog Fawr
Spacious and dignified Perpendicular on the site of 7th-century monastery.

DENBIGHSHIRE
St Marcella, Denbigh
Handsome monuments to Welsh notables.

Llanrhaeadr Dyffryn Clwyd
Glorious Jesse window; theatrical monument to county worthy.

FLINTSHIRE
Worthenbury
Completely 18th-century; boxed pews bearing arms of local gentry.

GLAMORGAN
Llantrithyd
Monuments of exceptional quality and interest.

St Mary's, Margam
12th-century abbey church, extravagant Mansel monuments.

MERIONETH
Llangar
Norman font, 17th- and 18th-century fittings. Cadw guardianship.

Rug Chapel
Private chapel, richly adorned in 17th century. Cadw guardianship.

MONMOUTHSHIRE
St Mary's Priory Church, Abergavenny
Distinguished monuments, particularly to the Herberts.

MONTGOMERYSHIRE
Llanidloes
Roof and nave rescued from Abbey Cwmhir after Dissolution.

Montgomery
Family monument, including the poet George Herbert and Lord Herbert of Chirbury.

PEMBROKESHIRE
St Mary's, Haverfordwest
Exuberant workmanship.

Nevern
Remarkable for Celtic associations.

St Mary's, Tenby
Rich in association, historically and decoratively, from Giraldus Cambrensis.

RADNORSHIRE
Diserth
Wonderfully untouched by the 19th century.

Presteign
Saxon origins, with a recently restored Flemish tapestry

WREXHAM
St Giles
Of cathedral quality, full of historic resonances.

All Saints, Gresford
Like Wrexham, a Margaret Beaufort foundation, and exquisite.

ANTIQUITIES

■ **Antiquarian Booksellers' Association**
Tel. 020 7439 3118
The senior trade body for dealers in antiquarian and rare books, manuscripts and allied materials.
www.aba.org.uk

■ **British Antique Dealers' Association**
Tel. 020 7589 4128
The leading trade association for antique dealers. Runs an annual Antiques Fair in Chelsea, London.
www.bada.org

ARCHITECTURAL HERITAGE

■ **CADW: Welsh Historic Monuments**
Tel: 029 2050 0200
Protects, conserves and promotes an appreciation of the built heritage of Wales.
www.cadw.wales.gov.uk

■ **Georgian Group**
Tel. 08717 52936
The Georgian Group campaigns against the maltreatment, neglect, and destruction of Georgian architecture, and promotes enjoyment of it. Regular program of study days and lectures open to the public.
www.georgiangroup.org.u

■ **Historic Houses Association**
Tel. 020 7259 5688
Exists to represent privately owned historic houses, gardens and parks, over 300 of which are open to the public.
www.hha.org.uk

■ **The Landmark Trust**
Tel. 01628 825920
Preservation charity working to rescue and then restore buildings of historic interest, including follies, mills, cottages and castles. Details available at www.landmarktrust.org.uk

■ **The National Monuments Record Centre**
Tel. 01793 414600
The public archive of English Heritage, containing over 12 million items of data on archeology, architecture, aerial photographs and maritime sites.
www.english-heritage.org.uk

■ **Royal Commission on the Ancient and Historical Monuments of Wales**
Tel. 01970 621200
Holds the leading national role in the management of the archeological, built and maritime heritage of Wales.
www.rcahmw.org.uk

■ **Royal Institute of British Architects**
Tel. 020 7580 5533
An organization representing 32,000 architects worldwide, whose wider aim is to bring architecture to the attention of a broad public. Open for exhibitions and talks. The RIBA's British Architectural Library is the largest and most comprehensive resource in the UK for information on all aspects of architecture.
www.architecture.com

THE ARTS

■ **British Academy**
Tel. 020 7969 5200
Society for the promotion of the humanities and social sciences. Details of lectures open to the public on www.britac.ac.uk

THE COUNTRYSIDE

■ **British Trust for Ornithology**
Tel. 01842 750050
Premier amateur bird research organization in Britain. Founded in 1932, it has over 20,000 members and other volunteers recording bird numbers and distribution.
www.bto.org

■ **Campaign to Protect Rural England (CPRE)**
Tel. 020 7981 2800
A national charity, which helps people to protect their local countryside. Information packs available.
www.cpre.org.uk

■ **Ramblers' Association**
Tel. 020 7339 8500
Campaigns to encourage walking, open up public footpaths, protect the countryside and secure the freedom to roam on open, uncultivated land. Its 417 groups organize walks.
www.ramblers.org.uk

■ **The Royal Forestry Society of England, Wales and Northern Ireland**
Tel. 01442 822028
Open to all those interested in trees. Its 21 divisions hold regular meetings.
www.rfs.org.uk

HORTICULTURE

■ **Brogdale Horticultural Trust**
Tel. 01795 535286
Home to the largest collection of fruit trees and plants in the world (2,300 different apple tree varieties). Daily tours held from March to November.
www.brogdale.org

■ **Garden History Society**
Tel. 020 7608 2409
Promotes the protection and conservation of historic gardens, parks, and designed landscapes, and advises on their restoration. Information leaflets available; regular workshops held.
www.gardenhistorysociety.org

■ **Royal Botanic Gardens Kew**
Tel. 020 8332 5000
Reflects the diversity of the world's flora through the 40,000 different types of plants on view in its giant glasshouses and extensive garden landscapes. Carries out research into plant sciences.
www.rbgkew.org.uk

■ **Royal Horticultural Society**
Tel. 020 7834 4333
The RHS brings gardening inspiration to over a quarter of a million members. Organizes the world famous Chelsea Flower Show; guardian of the RHS Garden in Wisley, Surrey. Holds regular lectures which are open to the public.
www.rhs.org.uk

SCIENCE

■ **Royal Geographical Society**
Tel. 020 7591 3000
A world center for geographers and geographical learning. Map Room open to public; library access by appointment.
www.rgs.org

■ **Royal Institution**
Tel. 020 7409 2992
Dedicated to promoting science through a variety of events including lectures, discussions and research. There is a small museum dedicated to those who have worked in the Royal Institution in the past.
www.ri.ac.uk

The National Trust plays an important part in the lives of millions of people: countryside in the Trust's care receives at least 50 million visits each year; around 13 million people visit properties for which a fee is charged; and over 500,000 school children benefit from the formal educational opportunities offered by the Trust at our properties.

As a charity independent of government, the Trust has depended on voluntary help and the financial contributions of members and many others since we were founded in 1895. Today, over 3.4 million people are members. Almost 40,000 volunteers give generously of their time each year to further our objectives.

The Trust's fundamental purposes are as relevant today as they were in the vision of the three founders – Octavia Hill, Canon Hardwicke Rawnsley and Sir Robert Hunter. They wanted to provide people with opportunities for recreation, both physical and mental, by preserving places of natural beauty or historic interest for ever. This ambitious aim is founded on a unique power vested in the Trust by Act of Parliament, to declare property inalienable. This means that it

cannot be sold, mortgaged or compulsorily purchased against the Trust's wishes without the consent of Parliament. This safeguard has encouraged tens of thousands of people to give and bequeath property (and chattels or furniture) as well as money for the purchase of land, in the knowledge that the Trust will look after them in perpetuity. Since the Trust's first acquisition, of a small area of cliffland above Barmouth, we have secured over 600,000 acres of countryside, as well as 700 miles of coastline, and over 300 historic houses and gardens. After the Country Houses Scheme of 1937 the Trust became a major safety net for houses under threat, and during the course of the subsequent half century it has saved many outstanding houses from sale and dispersal.

With this change of emphasis has come a widening of the Trust's cultural horizons. The recent acquisitions of three buildings – the house in Liverpool where John Lennon spent his childhood years, a courtyard of back-to-back houses in central Birmingham and The Homewood – a 1930's modernist house in Esher, Surrey – demonstrate our determination to maintain a contemporary interpretation of

the words "historic interest" that appear in the Trust's full title. **Most of the Trust's houses are surrounded by gardens**, the oldest of which dates from the 16th century. Many are of outstanding importance, making the Trust's collection of over 200 gardens the greatest in the world in charitable ownership. The Trust is now responsible for a remarkable diversity of properties, ranging in time from the largest prehistoric stone circle in Europe (Avebury, Wilts) to a 1950's council house (20 Forthlin Rd, Liverpool), in size from T. E. Lawrence's cottage retreat (Clouds Hill, Dorset) to one of the largest private houses in England (Knole, Kent). The nation's industrial heritage is represented by such important sites as Quarry Bank Mill (Cheshire), and the Trust looks after many wind- and watermills, religious buildings, dovecotes, villages, inns and public houses, buildings associated with famous people, and even a steam yacht (Gondola on Coniston Water). The range of landscapes includes large areas of the Lake District, spectacular coastline (such as Lundy Island, Devon), and The Lizard in Cornwall, and rare and valued habitats such as Wicken Fen (Cambs). The care of over 400 Sites of Special Scientific Interest and 31 National Nature

Reserves requires active management to maintain their scientific value and promote wildlife conservation.

Most of the countryside in the Trust's care is farmed – by nearly 2,000 farm tenants. Promoting the development of sustainable forms of agriculture is as important as the maintenance of hedges, dry-stone walls or hedge banks, dew-ponds, field barns or spinneys. Some of our cherished landscapes, especially in the uplands, are facing great economic pressure, and the Trust is trying to help farmers adapt, diversify and develop new forms of income such as farm-based tourism to enable them to continue to contribute to their rural community. Through promoting regional tourism and supporting farms and local jobs, the Trust's investment in rural areas makes a significant contribution to maintaining rural economies and sustaining the high quality environments that are their lifeblood.

THE NATIONAL TRUST
General queries: PO Box 39 Warrington WA5 7WD
Tel. 0870 458 4000 *www.nationaltrust. org.uk*

Adult membership costs £40.50 a year; family membership is £73.

English Heritage's role is to look after and champion the historic environment of England. We do this by providing services in three areas: improving understanding of the past by research and study; opening up our own properties across the country to be enjoyed today; and helping to protect the places, buildings and archaeological sites for their current owners and for future generations.

It is the historic buildings in our care which attract the most attention and are our most obvious public face. They range from major World Heritage Sites such as Stonehenge and Hadrian's Wall, through impressive castles, abbeys, and houses, to the smaller but still exquisite and evocative remains of prehistoric sites, Roman towns, and industrial buildings. Not only do we open most of these properties to the public, many free of charge, but we are also responsible for their care and conservation, so that they will continue to delight and educate our children. We take on new challenges too. Last year English Heritage took on the management of the spectacular Robert Adam designed Apsley House, the London home of the Duke of Wellington. This year we are delighted to have added Birdoswald Roman Fort in Cumbria to our sites spanning Hadrian's Wall.

England has around 365,000 listed buildings, 17,250 ancient monuments and 9,000 conservation areas, all protected by law from damaging change. We identify sites, buildings and landscapes of special national and local significance. This is called designation and it ensures that opportunities for change and development take informed account of the past.

We offer more than campaigns and advice. We give out over £30 million a year in grants to churches and cathedrals, buildings at risk from decay or neglect, archaeological investigations, and conservation areas, and we work with local authorities and other partners to set up regeneration schemes.

When English Heritage began in 1984, our income from visitors, membership, and site shops was in the region of £2 million a year. It is now around £30 million, all of which is reinvested into our work. In 1984 we had less than 100,000 members. Today we have more than 550,000, most of whom tell us that they join and remain members because they support our work. Our sites play host each year to over 500 special events, from battle re-enactments to historic plays.

What else do we do? We encourage curiosity by working with partners to increase public access to as much of the historic environment as possible. We fund the Civic Trust's Heritage Open Days which is England's biggest and most popular voluntary cultural event. The annual event includes free entry to attractions, local guided tours, town walks, plays and historical re-enactments, art festivals and children's activities.

We manage the Blue Plaques scheme. Blue plaques celebrate great figures of the past and the buildings that they inhabited. They open a window into another time by showing us where the great and the good have penned their masterpieces, developed new technologies, lived or died. Actors, authors, politicians, painters, scientists, sportsmen, campaigners and reformers – people from different countries, cultures and backgrounds – have all been commemorated in this way. The Blue Plaques scheme has been run by English Heritage since 1986, and continues to grow at a rate of around twenty plaques each year. In 2004, the scheme was extended across England on a region-by-region basis; there are already blue plaques in Merseyside, Birmingham, Southampton and Portsmouth. 2005 marked the 21st anniversary of the creation of English Heritage. We believe that during that period we have ensured that the historic environment of England is properly maintained and cared for. Looking forward, we are confident that, with the support of our members, visitors and the public at large, we can continue to ensure the best of the past informs our future.

Membership of English Heritage gives free entry to over 400 sites, an annual guidebook and a quarterly magazine – Heritage Today.

Adult membership costs £38 a year. Joint Adult membership costs £65. Up to 6 children accompanying members go free.

Members also receive half-price admission to historic sites in Scotland, Wales and the Isle of Man.

ENGLISH HERITAGE (Historic Buildings and Monuments Commission for England) General enquiries: PO Box 569 Swindon SN2 2YP Tel. 0870 333 1181 *www.english-heritage.org.uk*

◆ WALKING

By Robert Lloyd Parry

The English historian George Macaulay Trevelyan said in an essay in praise of walking that when he was feeling downhearted he consulted two doctors – his left foot and his right foot. Whatever your age, mood or fitness level, England and Wales offer some of the best rambles in Europe. Whether in the Docklands of London or the fenlands of East Anglia, almost everywhere you go you will see signs that direct you along a bridleway or footpath. Some of these are mere shortcuts, but many will lead you through landscapes of outstanding natural beauty.

Most of the walks recommended here form part of the network of long-distance routes that cross England and Wales. Expertly written guides to all these footpaths are available from most bookshops, and you are strongly advised to get hold of Ordnance Survey maps for the areas in which you are walking. The walks sketched here are at worst moderately strenuous. The more ambitious hiker is advised to seek counsel elsewhere.

■ **The Lake District**
Though it is becoming very difficult to find the kind of romantic solitude enjoyed by William Wordsworth, the Lake District still offers the walker the most dramatic scenery in England, and the peaks and fells around Buttermere give a fine taste of the area as a whole.
A 7-mile circular walk along The High Stile Ridge and back along the shore of Buttermere, affords some of the greatest views in Lakeland.
➜ Start at The Fish Inn in Buttermere. Just outside the village take the path marked 'Red Pike'. The steep ascent is rewarded by magnificent vistas from the top, whence one can see Buttermere,

Derwentwater, Ennerdale Water, Loweswater and Crummock Water. Continue along the undulating path along the ridge for roughly 2 miles, take care on the steep and difficult descent down, then return to Buttermere village through the lovely Burness Woods on the southern shore of the lake.

■ **Cumbria**
Alfred Wainwright, the godfather of Northern English hiking, wrote several detailed guides to rambles in the Lake District and these are worth consulting, but the jewel in his crown is the Coast to Coast walk, a beautiful 190-mile path that takes you across the North of England, through three national parks, from St Bee's Head in Cumbria to Robin Hood's Bay in North Yorkshire. Any stretch of this path will provide a satisfying day's hiking.
➜ Try walking from Kirby Stephen to Keld, a pleasant 11-mile hike into the heart of the Yorkshire Dales.

■ **North Yorkshire**
Walkers who made it to Robin Hood's Bay used to be entitled to a free pint in the Bay Hotel. Unscrupulous pedestrians have led the landlord to

withdraw this privilege, but the hotel makes a good starting point for an easy, well-signposted and bracing 7-mile walk along the cliffs toward Whitby, part of the 112-mile Cleveland Way.
➜ Climb up the steep High Street to the top of the village, and follow Mount Pleasant North Road which soon fades into a tree-lined footpath. Beyond a gate you find yourself high on the cliff above Ness Point. Simply follow the path as it gently meanders along the contours of the cliff through shady fields. After 6 miles you reach Saltwick Nab, a rocky promontory, at the bottom of which you can still see the remains of a 1914 shipwreck. Beyond are the ruins of Whitby Abbey, the town's charming harbor at the estuary of the river Esk and the best fish and chips in England.

■ **The Pennine Way** is the oldest and supposedly toughest of England's long-distance footpaths. It follows the Pennines, the backbone of England, up to Scotland. The 15½ mile stretch between Once Brewed and Bellingham makes for a long but fascinating day, starting off in the

shadow of Hadrian's Wall, then going through Wark Forest and the Northumberland National Park.

■ **Monmouthshire**
In the 8th century Offa, King of Mercia, built an earthwork frontier to divide his kingdom from the Welsh. The Offa's Dyke Path, a 168-mile ramble through the borders of England and Wales, follows this closely for about 60 miles. A long but easy-going walk between Tintern and Monmouth takes in the most impressive archeological remains, and has several delights of its own.
➜ Start off with a tour of the ineffably picturesque Tintern Abbey ▲ 474. You then have a choice of two alternative routes – one very easy path along the River Wye, another more undulating route closer to the Dyke – to Monmouth, a charming small town with plenty of hotels and eating places.

■ **The Thames Path** follows the river along the old towpath for 173 miles from its source near Cirencester to the Thames Barrier in London. Oxford makes a good base from which to sample day-long stretches of this route. Particularly recommended is the route south toward the village of Dorchester on Thames.

■ **Snowdonia**
Snowdonia has paths with views to match those of the Lake District. Snowdon is the highest peak in England and Wales and an ascent of this cold and craggy mountain is a tiring but very rewarding experience. There are several routes up the mountain, the most exciting of which – The Snowdon Horseshoe – is hard work and should really be attempted only by experienced hikers. A walk to the summit up The Pyg track, starting at Pen-y-Pass, is within

most people's capabilities.
From the top of the mountain, descend the south side along the Watkin Path which leaves you on the road to the charming village of Bedgellert.

■ **Kent**
For those of a spiritual and historical inclination The Pilgrims' Way, running 120 miles from Winchester Cathedral ▲ 198 to Canterbury Cathedral ▲ 182-3, holds many fascinations. This route, taken by pilgrims to venerate the memory of Saint Thomas à Becket, the Archbishop who was murdered in his Cathedral in Canterbury on December 29, 1170,

was established soon after the Saint's martyrdom. The exact route taken by the medieval pilgrims is often unclear and a detailed guidebook is essential. With this in hand, the approach to Canterbury from Chilham – the self-styled prettiest village in Kent – can still be an uplifting experience.

■ **Norfolk**
Peddar's Way is a very easy-going route following an old, straight Roman Road that meets up with the Norfolk Coast Path to form an undemanding 88½-mile long-distance path. The stretch from Holme-next-the-sea to Wells-next-the-sea

▲ 351 leads you through some pleasant coastal villages, offering good opportunities for swimming and birdwatching.

■ **Cornwall**
The longest long distance path in England and Wales snakes along the South West coast starting out in Minehead on the North of Exmoor and ending 594 miles later in Poole in Dorset. The section of the route from Porthleven to Lizard culminates in Lizard Point, the most southerly point in England. The clifftop views along the way are spectacular.

For details on the Ramblers' Association see page 495

For details on the Ramblers' Association see page 495

BIRDWATCHING

Birdwatching is one of the most popular leisure pursuits in England and Wales, and it is not hard to see why. The bird life of Britain is astonishingly diverse, considering its isolation from continental Europe. This is partly due to the wide variety of bird habitats to be found within small areas, including oak woods, heaths, farmland, lakes and marshes. But it is also because of the welcome the islands extend to migrant birds escaping the harsh climatic conditions of the great continents.
Perched out in the Atlantic, in the path of the warm Gulf Stream current, Britain experiences milder winters than the continental countries to the north and east. This makes it a natural

destination for winter visitors such as waders and wildfowl, whose continental breeding grounds freeze solid for months on end. The long coastlines and broad tidal estuaries provide safe, food-rich havens for these migrants, and about 40 percent of all the waders visiting north-west Europe spend the winter on British estuaries. Good places to visit include Cley marshland, the Ouse Washes and Minsmere reserve in eastern England, Slimbridge wildfowl reserve near Bristol in the west and Langstone Harbour in the south.
The mild, moist oceanic climate also ensures that there is plentiful food for summer visitors who migrate north to breed: birds such as

the swifts, swallows and nightjars that fly in every spring from Africa.
Some visitors are vagrants who overshoot their normal breeding grounds in France and turn up in southern England, causing great excitement among local birdwatchers. Such curiosities often turn up at Stodmarsh in Kent, which is also a wonderful site for marshland birds, while the New Forest in Hampshire is good for visitors such as nightjars and hobbies.
The most spectacular bird-watching, though, is to be found in spring on the rocky shores of the west and north. These rugged coasts provide cliff breeding sites for vast colonies of ocean birds

including guillemots, razorbills, gannets, puffins and fulmars. Almost 75 percent of the world gannet population breeds off British coasts, and 90 percent of the world's manx shearwaters. Some of the best sites are the Farne Islands and Bempton Cliffs in northeast England, and Skomer Island and the nearby coasts of southwest Wales.

◆ FISHING
By Tom Fort

It is striking how many foreign anglers one encounters on the rivers of Ireland, and how few on the rivers of England and Wales. Ireland markets its reputation for openness and the warmest of welcomes, whereas England and Wales tend to keep a little quiet about the treasured places.

Historically, the most celebrated fishing in England is that of the chalkstreams of Hampshire, Wiltshire, and Berkshire, where, according to the mythology, fat brown trout drift by beds of emerald weed in pellucid water, occasionally raising their well-bred snouts to suck in a passing mayfly. It has promoted the false notion that the cream of the sport is jealously preserved for a handful of privileged land-owners and their chums.

In fact, much of that chalkstream fishing isn't good, and prohibitively expensive. I can see little point in spending a small fortune pulling out fat, farm-fed stockies from the Test, when the further-flung parts of the land can provide some of the best river fishing for brown trout in Europe. That said, some very good chalkstream fishing in Hampshire can be supplied – at a price – by William Daniel at **Famous Fishing** (Tel. 01722 716210 www.famousfishing.co. uk). Much less pricey and just as good are the **Piddle and Frome** in Dorset, where Richard Slocock (Tel. 01305 848460) can arrange matters.

The further away you are from London, the more likely you are to be able to lay your hands on decent fishing at a sensible price. The most reliable and simple way to do so is to arrange to stay at one (or more) of the many good fishing hotels scattered around England and Wales.

Some of the best are to be found in southwest England. Staying at **Tarr Farm Inn** (Tel. 01643 851 507 www.tarrfarm.co. uk), in Exmoor National Park, you can wander the gorgeous Barle. The trout are small, but they are wild and numerous, and are by no means easy to deceive. The best-known anglers' hotel in Devon is probably the **Arundell Arms** (Tel. 01566 784 666 www.arundellarms.com) at Lifton. It arranges trout fishing on some lovely streams, and salmon and sea trout fishing when the season is right.

The **Half Moon**, (Tel. 01409 231376 www.halfmoonsheepw ash.co.uk) on the Torridge, specializes in sea trout and salmon; the **Rising Sun** (Tel. 01769 560447 www.risingsuninn.com) on the Taw, doesn't organize fishing anymore but will put you in touch with someone who does.

Another possibility is to explore the six or so Dartmoor streams owned by the Duchy of Cornwall, for which tickets are sold at a negligible price. **Brian Easterbrook** of Princetown (Tel. 01822 890488) is happy to advise.

There is also fine brown trout fishing in Wales, and for bigger fish. The **Gliffaes Country House Hotel** (Tel. 0800 146719) near Crickhowell has a lovely stretch of the Usk, where the dry fly fishing is properly challenging. And the Vyrnwy, near the English border, is much loved – **Howard Thresher** (Tel. 01363 774926) can supply tickets. Wales is famous for its sea trout which grow to a great size (12 to 15 pounders are caught each season), and demand specialized techniques. Access to a clutch of fisheries on rivers like the Towy, the Teifi, the Mawddach and many others can be organized through the excellent www. fishing-in-wales.com.

Heading north, there is – I am told, for I have not as yet had the opportunity to explore it for myself – some nice trout fishing in the Derbyshire streams, the Wye, the Dove, the Derwent, and the Manifold. **The Haddon Estate** (Tel. 01629 812855) controls some nice stretches. Cross the county border into Yorkshire, and you may find a cluster of notable rivers, among them the Wharfe, the Nidd and the Ure. **Bolton Abbey Estate** (Tel. 01756 710227) has 5 miles of the Wharfe. The **Buck Inn**, near Ripon Tel. 01677 422461) has fishing on the Ure.

My own heart, in a trout-fishing sense, belongs very much to northwest England. I caught my first little fish with a worm on a tiny stream in the Lake District, and for the young-at-heart who still relish a tramp across the fells, such fishing may still be had for nothing. Examine an Ordnance Survey map, and follow a ribbon of blue as far away from centers of population as you can get. Alternatively, there is decent free fly-fishing on several of the lakes – Ullswater, Coniston and Windermere among them. But I am primarily a river man, and a little way north is my river of rivers, the Eden. Sadly its once-great salmon fishing is a pale shadow, but the quality of the brown trout fishing remains amazingly high. At Appleby the **Tufton Arms** (Tel. 017683 51593 www.tufton armshotel.co.uk) can organize access to some of the best of it.

This a mere sample of what is on offer. I have not been able to touch on the magnificent coarse fishing to be found throughout the land; nor on the wealth of natural and artificial stillwaters (even in London itself) where trout may be caught; nor on the superb grayling fishing which can keep the flyfisher happy through the months of winter.

Fishing on the web
www.where-to-fish.com
www.fishing-in-wales.com

The sailing/watersports centers listed below offer approved sailing courses, as well as having dinghys/keelboats available for hire. Some offer residential courses and have on-site accommodation, while others may be able to arrange local accommodation for you. Many offer a range of watersport facilities, including windsurfing, canoeing, and courses in powerboating. Always telephone the center you wish to visit in advance, both to check the facilities available, and because it is necessary to pre-book in most cases.

LONDON

Royal Victoria Dock Watersports Centre
Tidal Basin Road
London E16 1AD
Tel. 020 7511 2326§

SOUTH EAST

Five Star Sailing Centre
Shore Rd, Warsash
Southampton
Hampshire SO31
Tel. 01489 885599
www.fivestarsailing.
co.uk

Neilson Active Holidays
Locksview,
Brighton Marina,
Brighton, East
Sussex BN2 5HA
Tel. 0870 9099 099
www.neilson.com

Southwater Watersports Centre
Cripplegate Lane,
Southwater
West Sussex RH13
Tel. 01403 734424
www.southwatersports.
co.uk

SOUTH WEST

Cool Cats Watersports
Sandbanks Hotel,
Sandbanks,
Poole, Dorset
BH13 7PS
Tel. 01202 701100
www.coolcatswater
sports.com

Shell Bay Watersports Centre
Ferry Rd, Studland
Dorset BH19 3BA
Tel. 01929 450399
www.shellbay.co.uk

THE WEST COUNTRY

Cornish Cruising
Falmouth Yacht
Marina, North
Parade, Falmouth
Cornwall TR11 2TD
Tel. 01326 211800
www.cornishcruising.
com

Southwest Lakes Ltd
Roadford
Watersports Centre,
Lower Goodacre,
Broadwoodwidger
Lifton, Devon PL16
Tel. 01409 211507
or
Upper Tamar Lake,
Kilkhampton,
Nr Bude
Cornwall EX23 9ST
Tel. 01288 321712
www.swlakestrust.
org.uk

Spinnakers Sailing Centre
The Harbour,
Exmouth
Devon EX8 1DX
Tel. 01395 222551
www.spinnakers.com

SOUTH MIDLANDS

Northamptonshire Watersports Centre
Pitsford Water,
Brixworth,
Northamptonshire
NN6 9DG
Tel. 01604 880248
www.northampton
watersports.com

HOME COUNTIES

Bray Lake Watersports
Monkey Island Lane,
Windsor Road,
Maidenhead,
Berkshire SL6 2EB
Tel. 01628 638860
www.braylake.com

Aqua Sports Co
Mercers Country
Park, Nutfield Marsh
Road, Merstham,
Nr Redhill
Surrey RH1 4EU
Tel. 01737 644288
www.aquasports.co.uk

EAST ANGLIA

Alton Watersports Centre
Holbrook Road,
Stutton,
Nr Ipswich,
Suffolk IP9 2RY
Tel. 01473 328408
www.altonwater.co.uk

Herbert Woods Boatyard
Herbert Woods,
Broads Haven,
Potter Heigham,
Norfolk NR29 5JD
Tel. 01692 670711
www.broads.co.uk

Sail Craft Sea School
Boatyard,
Main Rd,
Brancaster Staithe,
King's Lynn,
Norfolk PE31 8BP
Tel. 01485 210236
www.sailcraft.co.uk

NORTH MIDLANDS

Sutton-in-Ashfield Sailing Club
c/o 3 Ruby Gardens,
Kirkby-in-Ahsfield,
Notts NG17 7QH
Tel. 01623 599605
www.suttoninashfield
sailingclub.co.uk

NORTH EAST

Hawkhirst Adventure Camp
Hawkhirst, Kielder
Water, Nr Hexham,
Northumberland
NE48 1QZ
Tel. 01434 250217
www.members.aol.
com/hawkhirst

NORTH WEST

Derwent Water Marina
Portinscale,
Keswick,
Cumbria CA12 5RF
Tel. 017687 72912
www.derwentwater
marina.co.uk

The YMCA National Centre Lakeside
Newby Bridge,
Ulverston,
Cumbria LA12 8BD
Tel. 08707 273927
www.lakesideymca.
co.uk

WALES

Bala Adventure and Watersports Centre
Bala Lake Foreshore,
Pensarn Road,
Bala,
Gwynedd LL23 7SR
Tel. 01678 521059
www.balaadventure
andwatersportscentre.
co.uk

Pembrokeshire Activity Centre
Cleddau River Centre,
Cleddau Reach,
Pembroke Dock,
Pembrokeshire
SA72 6UJ
Tel. 01646 622013
www.pembrokeshire-
watersports.com

West Wales Wind-surfing & Sailing
Dale,
Nr Haverfordwest,
Pembrokeshire
SA62 3RB
Tel. 01646 636642
www.surfdale.co.uk

ROYAL YACHTING ASSOCIATION

RYA House,
Ensign Way,
Hamble,
Southampton,
Hants SO31 4YA
Tel. 0845 345 0400
Information on sailing centers in England and Wales is available on their website at
www.rya.org.uk

◆ GOLF

Green fees vary a lot according to the season and the course; call the club beforehand for price information

The most famous golf clubs in England and Wales – Wentworth, Royal Lytham St Annes, Sunningdale, Royal Berkshire, Sandwich, St Mellions, The Belfry and Royal Porthcawl in Wales – are exclusively members-only. All of the courses listed below welcome visitors, although there may be some restrictions: prior arrangement must be made to play; you may only be allowed to play on weekdays; a very few require a handicap certificate from visiting players. For exact details, and out of courtesy, telephone any club you plan to visit in advance.

LONDON

■ **Hendon Golf Club**
Tel. 020 8346 6023
Parkland course; 18 holes; designed by H.S.Colt.

■ **Riverside**
Tel. 020 8310 7975
Pay-and-play course; 9 holes. Prices on application.

SOUTH EAST

■ **E. Sussex National**
Uckfield, East Sussex
Tel. 01825 880088
American style layout; 2 x 18 holes.

■ **Freshwater Bay**
Isle of Wight
Tel. 01983 752955
Downland course overlooking the bay; 18 holes.

SOUTH WEST

■ **Bulbury**
Nr Poole, Dorset
Tel. 01929 459574
Parkland course in ancient woodlands; 18 holes.

■ **Oake Manor**
Taunton, Somerset
Tel. 01823 461993
Parkland course with water; 18 holes.

■ **Wrag Barn Golf and Country Club**
Highworth, Wilts
Tel. 01793 861327
Scenic parkland course; 18 holes.

THE WEST COUNTRY

■ **Perranporth**
Cornwall
Tel. 01872 57370
Links course with magnificent sea views; 18 holes.

■ **Royal North Devon**
Bideford, Devon
Tel. 01237 473824
Founded 1864. Links course; 18 holes; 9 hole pitch and putt.

■ **St Enodoc**
Wadebridge, Cornwall
Tel. 01208 863216
Links course set between sand dunes and views of the sea; two 18 holes.

SOUTH MIDLANDS

■ **Abbey Hotel Golf and Country Club**
Redditch, Worcs
Tel. 01527 406600
Modern parkland course; 18 holes.

■ **Kettering**
Northants
Tel. 01536 511104
Parkland course; 18 holes; designed by Tom Morris.

■ **Ross-on-Wye**
Hereford
Tel. 01989 720267
18-hole course set in pleasant woodland.

EAST ANGLIA

■ **Felixstowe Ferry**
Felixstowe, Suffolk
Tel. 01394 286834
Founded 1880. Championship links course; 18 holes.

■ **Hunstanton**
Old Hunstanton, Norfolk
Tel. 01485 532811
Founded 1891. Links course; 18 holes.

■ **Regiment Way**
Chelmsford, Essex
Tel. 01245 361100
Pay-and-play parkland course; 9/18 holes.

HOME COUNTIES

■ **Dunstable Downs**
Dunstable, Beds
Tel. 01582 604472
Downland course; 18 holes.

■ **Stoke Poges**
Park Road, Stoke Poges, Bucks
Tel. 01753 717171
Parkland course; 18 holes; designed by H.S.Colt.

■ **Moor Park**
Rickmansworth, Herts
Tel. 01923 773146
Parkland course with gardens by 'Capability' Brown; clubhouse Grade 1 Listed Building; Two 18 holes.

NORTH MIDLANDS

■ **Llanymynech**
Oswestry, Shropshire
Tel. 01691 830542
On Welsh border – 4th hole tee in Wales, green in England; 18 holes; Offa's Dyke part of its boundary.

■ **The Tytherington**
Macclesfield, Cheshire
Tel. 01625 506000
Modern parkland course; 18 holes; home of the WPGA European Tour.

■ **Uttoxeter**
Uttoxeter, Staffs
Tel. 01889 566552
Parkland course; views over Dove valley; 18 holes.

NORTH EAST

■ **Alwoodley**
Leeds, W Yorks
Tel. 0113 268 1680
Beautiful heathland course; 18 holes.

■ **Goswyck Golf Club**
Berwick-upon-Tweed, Northumberland
Tel. 01289 387256
Links course; 18 holes; designed by James Braid/ F. Pennick.

■ **Hallowes**
Sheffield, S Yorks
Tel. 01246 413734
Founded 1892; 18 holes; undulating moorland course.

■ **Seaton Carew**
Hartlepool
Tel. 01429 266249
Championship links course; 18 holes.

NORTH WEST

■ **Keswick**
Keswick, Cumbria
Tel. 017687 79324
Parkland/moorland course in the heart of the Lake District; 18 holes.

■ **Ulverston**
The Clubhouse, Ulverston, Cumbria
Tel. 01229 582824
Parkland course with stunning views of the Lake District mountains; 18 holes. £30–35 (summer), £15–20 (winter).

■ **Wallasey**
Merseyside
Tel. 0151 691 1024
Seaside links course; 18 holes.

WALES

■ **Ashburnum**
Burry Port, Carmarthenshire
Tel. 01554 833846
Championship links course; 18 holes.

■ **Royal St David's**
Harlech
Tel. 01766 780203
Founded 1894. Championship links course; 18 holes.

English Golf Union
Tel. 01526 354500
For a complete list of golf courses in England see *www. englishgolfunion.org.*

The Welsh Golfing Union
Catsash, Newport, South Wales NP18
Tel. 01633 430830
www.welshgolf.org.uk

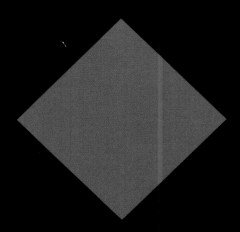

USEFUL ADDRESSES

*Most gardens and parks are open 10am–6pm, **most houses** 1–5.30pm, April 1 to October 31. But check beforehand. Hudson's Historic House and Gardens gives detailed opening times and admission prices.*

LONDON
MUSEUMS, HOUSES AND GARDENS

2 Willow Road, NW3
Tel: 020 7435 6166 (NT)

Albert Memorial, SW7
Tel. 020 7495 0916 (EH)

Apsley House, W1
Tel. 020 7499 5676

Banqueting House, SW1
Tel. 0870 751 5178

Buckingham Palace, SW1A
Tel. 020 7766 7300

Burgh House, NW3
Tel. 020 7431 0144
Free

Chelsea Physic Garden, SW3
Tel. 020 7352 5646

Chiswick House, W4
Tel. 020 8995 0508 (EH)

Eltham Palace, SE9
Tel. 020 8294 2548 (EH)

Fenton House, NW3
Tel. 020 7435 3471 (NT)

Ham House, Richmond
Tel. 020 8940 1950 (NT)

Hampton Court Palace, Surrey
Tel. 0870 752 7777

Kensington Palace and Orangery, W8
Tel. 0870 751 5170

Kenwood, NW3
Tel. 020 8348 1286 (EH)
Free but charge for parking

Kew Gardens, Richmond, Surrey
Tel. 020 8332 5655

Lambeth Palace, SE1
Tel. 020 7898 1200

Linley Sambourne House, W8
Tel. 020 7602 3316

Mansion House, EC4
Tel. 020 7626 2500
Open to groups only

Marble Hill House, TW1
Tel. 020 8892 5115 (EH)

Monument, EC3
Tel. 020 7626 2717

Osterley Park & House, TW7
Tel. 020 8232 5050 (NT)

Ranger's House, SE10
Tel. 020 8853 0035 (EH)

Royal Courts of Justice, WC2
Tel. 020 7947 6000

Royal Mews (Buckingham Palace), SW1
Tel. 020 7766 7300

Spencer House, SW1
Tel. 020 7499 8620

Strawberry Hill, TW1
Tel. 020 8240 4224

Sutton House, E9
Tel. 020 8986 2264 (NT)

Syon Park, TW8
Tel. 020 8560 0882

Wesley's Chapel, EC1
Tel. 020 7253 2262

MUSEUMS AND GALLERIES

Bank of England Museum, EC2
Tel. 020 7601 5491 *Free*

Bankside Gallery, SE1
Tel. 020 7928 7521

Barbican Art Gallery, EC2
Tel. 020 7638 4141

Bethnal Green Museum of Childhood, E2
Tel. 020 8983 5200
Free

British Museum, WC1
Tel. 020 7323 8000
Free

Cabinet War Rooms, SW1
Tel. 020 7930 6961

Carlyle's House, SW3
Tel. 020 7352 7087

Charles Dickens Museum, WC1
Tel. 020 7405 2127

Clink Prison Museum, SE1
Tel. 020 7403 0900

Courtauld Gallery, Somerset House, WC2
Tel. 020 7845 4600

Crystal Palace Museum, SE19
Tel. 020 8676 0700

Cuming Museum, SE17
Tel. 020 7525 2163
Free

Cutty Sark, SE10
Tel. 020 8858 3445

Design Museum, SE1
Tel. 020 7403 6933

Dr Johnson's House, EC4
Tel. 020 7353 3745

Dulwich Picture Gallery, SE21
Tel. 020 8693 5254

Fan Museum, SE10
Tel. 020 8305 1441

Faraday Museum, Royal Institution, W1
Tel. 020 7409 2992
Closed for renovation until 2008

Florence Nightingale Museum, SE1
Tel. 020 7620 0374

Foundling Museum, WC1
Tel. 020 7841 3600

Freud Museum, NW3
Tel. 020 7435 2002

Geffrye Museum, E2
Tel. 020 7739 9893 *Free*

Geological Museum,
See Natural History Museum

Guards' Museum, SW1
Tel. 020 7414 3428

Guildhall, EC2
Tel. 020 7606 3030

Gunnersbury Park Museum, W3
Tel. 020 8992 1612
Free

Hampton Court Palace, Surrey
Tel. 0870 751 5175

Hayward Gallery, SE1
Tel. 020 7921 0813

HMS Belfast, SE1
Tel. 020 7940 6300

Hogarth's House, W4
Tel. 020 8994 6757
Free

Horniman Museum and Gardens, SE23
Tel. 020 8699 1872
Free

Imperial War Museum, SE1
Tel. 020 7416 5000

ICA – Institute of Contemporary Arts, SW1
Tel. 020 7930 3647

Jewel Tower, SW1
Tel. 020 7222 2219 (EH)

Keats House, NW3
Tel. 020 7435 2062

Kew Bridge Steam Museum, TW8
Tel. 020 8568 4757

Leighton House, W14
Tel. 020 7602 3316

London's Transport Museum, WC2
Tel. 020 7379 6344

Lord's Tour & MCC Museum, NW8
Tel. 020 7432 1033

Madame Tussaud's, NW1
Tel. 0870 400 3000

Museum of Garden History, SE1
Tel. 020 7401 8865
Free

Museum of London, EC2
Tel. 0870 444 3852

Musical Museum, TW8
Relocating in 2007.
For info, write to 399 High St, Brentford TW8 0DU

National Army Museum, SW3
Tel. 020 7730 0717
Free

National Gallery, WC2
Tel. 020 7747 2885
Free

National Maritime Museum, SE10
Tel. 020 8858 4422

National Portrait Gallery, WC2
Tel. 020 7306 0055
Free (except major exhibitions)

Natural History Museum, SW7
Tel. 020 7942 5000

Orleans House Gallery, Twickenham
Tel. 020 8831 6000

Percival David Foundation of Chinese Art, WC1
Tel. 020 7387 3909
Free

Petrie Museum of Egyptian Archaeology UCL, WC1
Tel. 020 7679 2884
Free

PM Gallery and House, W5
Tel. 020 8567 1227

Queen's House, Greenwich, SE10
Tel. 020 8312 6565 *Free*

Royal Academy of Arts, W1
Tel. 020 7300 8000

Royal Observatory Greenwich, SE10
Tel. 020 8312 6565
Free

St John's Gate (Museum of the Order of St John), EC1
Tel. 020 7324 4070

Science Museum, SW7
Tel. 020 7942 4454
Free

Shakespeare's Globe, SE1
Tel. 020 7902 1500

Sherlock Holmes Museum, NW1
Tel. 020 7935 8866

(EH) = English Heritage property
(NT) = National Trust property

Sir John Soane's
Museum, WC2
Tel. 020 7405 2107
Free

Tate Britain SW1
Tate Modern, SE1
Tel. 020 7887 8000
*Free (except major
exhibitions)*

Theatre Museum, WC2
Tel. 020 7943 4700

Tower of London, EC3
Tel. 0870 7566060

Victoria & Albert
Museum, SW7
Tel. 020 7942 2000
Free

Wallace Collection, W1
Tel. 020 7563 9500
Free

Wellcome Trust,
NW1
Tel. 020 7611 8888
Free

Whitechapel Art
Gallery, E1
Tel. 020 7522 7888

William Morris
Gallery, E17
Tel. 020 8527 3782
Free

○ SOUTH EAST

HOUSES AND GARDENS

Appuldurcombe House,
Wroxall, nr Ventnor,
Isle of Wight
Tel. 01983 852484 (EH)

Arundel Castle,
Arundel, W. Sussex
Tel. 01903 882173

Basing House,
Basingstoke, Hants
Tel. 01256 467294

Bateman's, Etchingham,
E. Sussex
Tel. 01435 882302 (NT)

Old Bayham Abbey,
Lamberhurst, Sussex
Tel. 01892 890381 (EH)

Beaulieu (with National
Motor Museum,
Brockenhurst, Hants
Tel. 01590 612345

Bodiam Castle,
nr Robertsbridge,
E. Sussex
Tel. 01580 830436 (NT)

Boughton Monchelsea
Place, nr Maidstone,
Kent
Tel. 01622 743120
Pre-booked guided
tours only, for groups

Breamore House &
Countryside Museum,
Fordingbridge, Hants
Tel. 01725 512468

Broadlands, Romsey,
Hants
Tel. 01794 505010

Carisbrooke Castle,
Newport,
Isle of Wight
Tel. 01983 522107 (EH)

Charleston, Lewes,
E. Sussex
Tel. 01323 811265

Chartwell, Westerham,
Kent
Tel. 01732 866368 (NT)

Chiddingstone Castle,
Edenbridge, Kent
Tel. 01892 870347

Cobham Hall, Cobham,
Kent
Tel. 01474 823371

Deal Castle, Deal, Kent
Tel. 01304 372762 (EH)

Denmans Garden,
nr Chichester, Sussex
Tel. 01243 542808

Dover Castle, Kent
Tel. 01304 211067 (EH)

Down House,
Downe, Kent
Tel. 01689 859119 (EH)

Finchcocks,
Goudhurst, Kent
Tel. 01580 211702

Gad's Hill Place,
Higham-by-Rochester,
Kent
Tel. 01474 822366

Godinton House,
Ashford, Kent
Tel. 01233 620773

Goodwood House,
Chichester, W. Sussex
Tel. 01243 755040

Great Dixter House
& Gardens, Northiam,
E. Sussex
Tel. 01797 252878

Groombridge Place
Gardens,
Tunbridge Wells, Kent
Tel. 01892 861444

Hall Place, Bexley, Kent
Tel. 01322 526574
Free

Hammerwood Park,
East Grinstead,
W. Sussex
Tel. 01342 850594

Herstmonceux Castle,
Hailsham, E. Sussex
Tel. 01323 833816

Hever Castle,
Edenbridge, Kent
Tel. 01732 865224

Highclere Castle &
Gardens, Newbury,
Berks
Tel. 01635 253210

Hinton Ampner
Garden, Hants
Tel. 01962 771305 (NT)

Ightham Mote,
Sevenoaks, Kent
Tel. 01732 810378 (NT)

Knole, Sevenoaks, Kent
Tel. 01732 462100 (NT)

Leeds Castle,
Maidstone, Kent
Tel. 01622 765400
Open all year

Lullingstone Castle,
Eynsford, Kent
Tel. 01322 862114

Lullingstone Roman
Villa, Eynsford, Kent
Tel. 01322 863467 (EH)

Mottisfont Abbey,
nr Romsey, Hants
Tel. 01794 341220 (NT)

Netley Abbey,
Southampton, Hants
Tel. 01424 775705 (EH)
Free

Nymans Gardens,
nr Haywards Heath,
W. Sussex
Tel. 01444 400321 (NT)

Old Soar Manor,
Borough Green, Kent
Tel. 01732 810378 (NT)
Free

Osborne House, East
Cowes, Isle of Wight
Tel. 01983 200022 (EH)

Parham House &
Gardens,
nr Pulborough,
W. Sussex
Tel. 01903 744888

Penshurst Place &
Gardens, nr Tonbridge,
Kent
Tel. 01892 870307

Petworth House
& Park, Petworth,
W. Sussex
Tel. 01798 343929 (NT)

Pevensey Castle,
Pevensey, E. Sussex
Tel. 01323 762604 (EH)

Portchester Castle,
Portsmouth, Hants
Tel. 023 9237 8291 (EH)

Quebec House,
Westerham, Kent
Tel. 01732 866368 (NT)

Richborough Roman
Fort, Sandwich, Kent
Tel. 01304 612013 (EH)

Rochester Castle,
Medway, Kent
Tel. 01634 402276
(EH/local council)

Royal Pavilion,
Brighton, E. Sussex
Tel. 01273 290900

Sandham Memorial
Chapel, nr Newbury,
Hants
Tel. 01635 278394 (NT)

Scotney Castle Garden,
Tunbridge Wells,
Kent
Tel. 01892 891081 (NT)

Sheffield Park Garden,
nr Uckfield, E. Sussex
Tel. 01825 790231 (NT)

Sissinghurst Castle
Gardens,
nr Cranbrook, Kent
Tel. 01580 710701 (NT)

Squerryes Court
& Gardens,
Westerham, Kent
Tel. 01959 562345

Standen,
E. Grinstead, W. Sussex
Tel. 01342 323029 (NT)

Stratfield Saye House,
Basingstoke, Hants
Tel. 01256 882882

Titchfield Abbey,
Southampton, Hants
Tel. 01329 842133 (EH)
Free

Upnor Castle,
Upnor, Kent
Tel. 01634 718742 (EH)

Uppark,
Petersfield, W. Sussex
Tel. 01730 825857 (NT)

The Vyne,
Basingstoke, Hants
Tel. 01256 881337 (NT)

Wakehurst Place,
Ardingly, Sussex
Tel. 01444 894000 (NT)

Walmer Castle &
Gardens, Deal,
Kent
Tel. 01304 364288 (EH)

MUSEUMS AND GALLERIES

Airborne Forces
Museum, Aldershot,
Hants
Tel. 01252 349619

Aldershot Military
Museum, Hants
Tel. 01252 314598

Allen Gallery, Alton,
Hants
Tel. 01420 82802

Anne of Cleves House,
Lewes, E. Sussex
Tel. 01273 474610

Brading Roman Villa,
Isle of Wight
Tel. 01983 406223

Brighton Museum
& Art Gallery,
]\E. Sussex
Tel. 01273 290900
Free

Canterbury Royal
Museum & Art Gallery,
Kent
Tel. 01227 452747 *Free*

Curtis Museum,
Alton, Hants
Tel. 01420 82802

Dickens House Museum,
Broadstairs, Kent
Tel. 01843 861232

Fort Brockhurst,
Gosport, Hants
Tel. 023 9258 1059

Fort Nelson –
The Royal Armouries
Museum of Artillery,
Fareham, Hants
Tel. 01329 233734
Free

Jane Austen's House,
Chawton, Alton, Hants
Tel. 01420 83262

Maidstone Museum
& Art Gallery, Kent
Tel. 01622 602838
Free

Museum of
Archaeology,
Southampton, Hants
Tel. 023 8063 5904
Free

New Forest Museum,
Lyndhurst, Hants
Tel. 023 8028 3914

Southampton City Art
Gallery, Hants
Tel. 023 8083 2277
Free

Southampton
Maritime Museum,
Hants
Tel. 023 8022 3941
Free

Tudor House Museum,
Southampton, Hants
Tel. 023 8063 4906

Quex House & Garden,
Powell-Cotton Museum,
Birchington, Kent
Tel. 01843 842168

SOUTH WEST
HOUSES
AND GARDENS

Athelhampton,
Dorchester, Dorset
Tel. 01305 848363

Barrington Court,
nr Ilminster, Somerset
Tel. 01460 242614 (NT)

Bowood House &
Gardens, Calne, Wilts
Tel. 01249 812102

Brownsea Island,
Poole Harbour, Dorset
Tel. 01202 707744 (NT)

Chettle House,
Blandford Forum,
Dorset
Tel. 01258 830898

Claverton Manor,
Bath, Somerset
Tel. 01225 460503 (NT)

Cleeve Abbey,
nr Washford, Somerset
Tel. 01984 640377 (EH)

Clevedon Court,
Clevedon, Somerset
Tel. 01275 872257 (NT)

Corfe Castle,
Wareham, Dorset
Tel. 01929 481234 (NT)

Corsham Court,
Corsham, Wilts
Tel. 01249 701610

Dunster Castle,
nr Minehead, Somerset
Tel. 01643 823004 (NT)

Dyrham Park,
nr Chippenham,
Wilts
Tel. 01179 372501 (NT)

Farleigh Hungerford
Castle, Bath, Somerset
Tel. 01225 754026 (EH)

Fiddleford Manor,
Newton, Dorset
Tel. 0117 975 0700 (EH)
Free

Forde Abbey,
nr Chard, Somerset
Tel. 01460 220231

Great Chalfield Manor,
nr Melksham, Wilts
Tel. 01225 782239 (NT)

Hardy's Cottage,
nr Dorchester, Dorset
Tel. 01305 262366 (NT)

Hestercombe Gardens,
Taunton, Somerset
Tel. 01823 413923

Horton Court,
nr Chipping Sodbury,
Bristol
Tel. 01179 372501 (NT)

Iford Manor,
Bradford-on-Avon,
Wilts
Tel. 01225 863146

Kingston Lacy,
Wimborne Minster,
Dorset
Tel. 01202 883 402 (NT)

Lacock Abbey & Fox
Talbot Museum,
Chippenham, Wilts
Tel. 01249 730227 (NT)

Little Clarendon,
Salisbury, Wilts
Tel. 01985 843600 (NT)

Longleat House,
Warminster, Wilts
Tel. 01985 844400

Lulworth Castle,
Wareham, Dorset
Tel. 01929 400352
(discounted entry fee
for EH members)

Lydiard House,
Swindon, Wilts
Tel. 01793 770401

Lytes Cary Manor,
nr Charlton Mackrell,
Somerset
Tel. 01458 224471 (NT)

Mapperton House &
Gardens, Beaminster,
Dorset
Tel. 01308 862645

Mompesson House,
Salisbury, Wilts
Tel. 01722 335659 (NT)

Montacute House,
Montacute, Somerset
Tel. 01935 823289 (NT)

Old Wardour Castle,
Salisbury, Wilts
Tel. 01747 870487 (EH)

Philipps House & Dinton
Park, Salisbury, Wilts
Tel. 01722 716663 (NT)

Prior Park Landscape
Garden, Bath
Tel. 01225 833422 (NT)

Sandford Orcas
Manor House,
Sherborne, Dorset
Tel. 01963 220206

Sherborne Castle,
Sherborne, Dorset
Tel. 01935 812072

Sherborne Old Castle,
Sherborne, Dorset
Tel. 01935 812730 (EH)

Stourhead,
Warminster, Dorset
Tel. 01747 841152 (NT)

Tintinhull Garden,
Yeovil, Somerset
Tel. 01935 822545 (NT)

Westwood Manor,
Bradford-on-Avon,
Wilts
Tel. 01225 863374 (NT)

Wilton House,
nr Salisbury, Wilts
Tel. 01722 746720

Wolfeton House,
nr Dorchester, Dorset
Tel. 01305 263500

MUSEUMS
AND GALLERIES

Building of Bath
Museum – Countess of
Huntingdon's Chapel,
Bath, Somerset
Tel. 01225 333895

Bristol City Museum
& Art Gallery, Bristol
Tel. 0117 922 3571
Free

Coleridge Cottage,
Nether Stowey,
nr Bridgwater,
Somerset
Tel. 01278 732662 (NT)

Dorset County
Museum, Dorchester,
Dorset
Tel. 01305 262735

Fleet Air Arm Museum,
Yeovilton, Somerset
Tel. 01935 840565

Holburne Museum of
Art, Bath, Somerset
Tel. 01225 466669

Philpot Museum,
Lyme Regis, Dorset
Tel. 01297 443370

Roman Baths Museum,
Bath, Somerset
Tel. 01225 477773

Russell-Cotes Art
Gallery & Museum,
Bournemouth, Dorset
Tel. 01202 451800
Free

Salisbury & South
Wiltshire Museum,
Salisbury
Tel. 01722 332151

Swindon Museum
& Art Gallery, Wilts
Tel. 01793 466556
Free

Wiltshire Heritage
Museum, Devizes,
Wilts
Tel. 01380 727369

WEST COUNTRY
HOUSES
AND GARDENS

A La Ronde,
Exmouth, Devon
Tel. 01395 265514 (NT)

Antony House,
Plymouth, Cornwall
Tel. 01752 812191 (NT)

Arlington Court,
nr Barnstaple, Devon
Tel. 01271 850296 (NT)

Berry Pomeroy Castle,
Totnes, Devon
Tel. 01803 866618 (EH)

Bickleigh Castle,
nr Tiverton, Devon
Tel. 01884 855363

Bicton College Garden
& Arboretum,
Budleigh Salterton,
Devon
Tel. 01395 562400

Buckland Abbey,
Yelverton, Devon
Tel. 01822 853607 (NT)

Castle Drogo, Exeter,
Devon
Tel. 01647 433306 (NT)

Coleton Fishacre House
& Garden, Kingswear,
Devon
Tel. 01803 752466 (NT)

Chysauster Ancient
Village, Penzance,

Cornwall
Tel. 07831 757934

Compton Castle,
Paignton, Devon
Tel. 01803 875740 (NT)

Cotehele, Saltash,
Cornwall
Tel. 01579 351346 (NT)

Dartington Hall
Gardens, nr Totnes,
Devon
Tel. 01803 862367
By donation

Dartmouth Castle,
Devon
Tel. 01803 833588 (EH)

Endsleigh House &
Gardens, Tavistock,
Devon
Tel. 01822 870248

Killerton House
and Garden,
Exeter, Devon
Tel. 01392 881345 (NT)

Knightshayes Court,
Tiverton, Devon
Tel. 01884 254665 (NT)

Lanhydrock House,
Bodmin, Cornwall
Tel. 01208 265950 (NT)

Launceston Castle,
Launceston, Cornwall
Tel. 01566 772365 (EH)

Lost Gardens of
Heligan, St Austell,
Cornwall
Tel. 01726 845100

Mount Edgcumbe
House & Country Park,
Torpoint, Cornwall
Tel. 01752 822236

Okehampton Castle,
Okehampton, Devon
Tel. 01837 52844 (EH)

Oldway Mansion,
Paignton, Devon
Tel. 01803 207933
Free

Overbecks Museum
& Garden, Salcombe,
South Devon
Tel. 01548 842893 (NT)

Pencarrow,
Bodmin, Cornwall
Tel. 01208 841369

Pendennis Castle,
Falmouth, Cornwall
Tel. 01326 316594 (EH)

Powderham Castle,
Exeter, Devon
Tel. 01626 890243

Prideaux Place,
Padstow, Cornwall
Tel. 01841 532411

Rosemoor RHS Garden,
Grt Torrington,
Devon
Tel. 01805 624067

St Mawes Castle,
St Mawes, Cornwall
Tel. 01326 270526 (EH)

St Michael's Mount,
nr Penzance, Cornwall
Tel. 01736 710507 (NT)

Saltram House,
Plymouth, Devon
Tel. 01752 333500 (NT)

Shute Barton,
nr Axminster, Devon
Tel. 01297 34692 (NT)

Tintagel Castle,
Tintagel, Cornwall
Tel. 01840 770328 (EH)

Totnes Castle,
Devon
Tel. 01803 864406 (EH)

Trelissick Garden,
nr Truro, Cornwall
Tel. 01872 862090 (NT)

Trengwainton Garden,
Penzance, Cornwall
Tel. 01736 363148 (NT)

Trerice, Newquay,
Cornwall
Tel. 01637 875404 (NT)

Tresco Abbey Gardens,
Isles of Scilly
Tel. 01720 424105

Trewithen, Truro,
Cornwall
Tel. 01726 883647

Ugbrooke Park,
Chudleigh, Devon
Tel. 01626 852179

MUSEUMS AND GALLERIES

Allhallows Museum,
Honiton, Devon
Tel. 01404 44966

Barbara Hepworth
Museum & Sculpture
Garden, St Ives,
Cornwall
Tel. 01736 796226

Newlyn Art Gallery,
Penzance, Cornwall
Tel. 01736 363715

Penlee House Gallery
& Museum, Penzance,
Cornwall
Tel. 01736 363625

Plymouth City
Museum & Art Gallery,
Devon
Tel. 01752 304774
Free

Porthcurno Telegraph
Museum, Cornwall
Tel. 01736 810966

Royal Cornwall
Museum, Truro
Tel. 01872 272205

Tate Gallery, St Ives,
Cornwall
Tel. 01736 796226

Wayside Folk Museum,
Zennor, St Ives,
Cornwall
Tel. 01736 796945

SOUTH MIDLANDS
HOUSES AND GARDENS

Althorp, Northampton
Tel. 01604 770107

Baddesley Clinton,
Solihull, Warwickshire
Tel. 01564 783294 (NT)

Barnsley House,
nr Cirencester, Glos
Tel. 01285 740561

Belas Knap Long
Barrow, Cheltenham,
Glos (EH) Free

Berkeley Castle,
Dursley, Glos
Tel. 01453 810332

Berrington Hall,
nr Leominster,
Herefordshire
Tel. 01568 615721 (NT)

Boughton House,
Kettering, Northants
Tel. 01536 515731

Canons Ashby House,
Daventry, Northants
Tel. 01327 861900 (NT)

Charlecote Park,
Warwick
Tel. 01789 470277 (NT)

Chastleton House,
Moreton-in-Marsh,
Glos
Tel. 01608 674355 (NT)

Chavenage House,
nr Tetbury, Glos
Tel. 01666 502329

Chedworth Roman
Villa, Cheltenham, Glos
Tel. 01242 890256 (NT)

Cottesbrooke Hall &
Gardens, Northampton
Tel. 01604 505808

Coughton Court, nr
Alcester, Warwickshire
Tel. 01789 400777 (NT)

Croft Castle,
nr Leominster,
Herefordshire
Tel. 01568 780246 (NT)

Croome Park,
Severn Stroke, Worcs
Tel. 01905 371006 (NT)

Deene Park, Corby,
Northants
Tel. 01780 450278

Eastnor Castle, nr
Ledbury, Herefordshire
Tel. 01531 633160

Frampton Court, Glos
Tel. 01452 740267 (EH)

Goodrich Castle, Ross-
on-Wye, Herefordshire
Tel. 01600 890538 (EH)

Hailes Abbey,
Cheltenham, Glos
Tel. 01242 602398
(EH/NT)

Hanbury Hall,
Droitwich, Worcs
Tel. 01527 821214 (NT)

Hartlebury Castle,
nr Kidderminster, Glos
Tel. 01299 250416

Harvington Hall,
Kidderminster, Worcs
Tel. 01562 777846

Hellens, Ledbury,
Herefordshire
Tel. 01531 660504

Hidcote Manor
Garden, nr Chipping
Campden, Glos
Tel. 01386 438333 (NT)

Holdenby House &
Gardens, Northants
Tel. 01604 770074

Kelmarsh Hall,
Northampton
Tel. 01604 686543

Kenilworth Castle,
Warwickshire
Tel. 01926 852078 (EH)

Kirby Hall,
Corby, Northants
Tel. 01536 203230 (EH)

Lamport Hall &
Gardens, Northampton
Tel. 01604 686272

Lord Leycester
Hospital, Warwick
Tel. 01926 491422

Lower Brockhampton,
House Bringsty, Worcs
Tel. 01885 488099 (NT)

Lyveden New Bield,
nr Oundle,
Peterborough
Tel. 01832 205358 (NT)

Moccas Court,
Moccas, Herefordshire
Tel. 01981 500019

Odda's Chapel,
Deerhurst, Gloucester
(EH) Free

Owlpen Manor,
nr Uley, Glos
Tel. 01453 860261

Packwood House,
Solihull, Warwickshire
Tel. 01564 783294 (NT)

Painswick Rococo
Gdns, Painswick, Glos
Tel. 01452 813204

Ragley Hall, Alcester,
Warks
Tel. 01789 762090

◆ DIRECTORY

When an English Heritage or National Trust property is mentioned without a phone number, it means that the property consists of ruins or that only the exterior is visible.

Rockingham Castle, Market Harborough, Leics Tel. 01536 770240

Rushton Triangular Lodge, Kettering, Northants Tel. 01536 710761 (EH)

St Briavel's Castle, nr Monmouth, Glos (EH) *Free*

Sezincote, Moreton-in-Marsh, Glos Tel. 01386 700444

Snowshill Manor, nr Broadway, Glos Tel. 01386 852410 (NT)

Spetchley Park, Worcester Tel. 01905 345213

Stoke Park Pavilions, Towcester, Northants Tel. 01604 862172

Stanway Water Garden, Cheltenham Tel. 01386 584469

Sudeley Castle, nr Cheltenham, Glos Tel. 01242 602308

Sulgrave Manor, Banbury, Oxon Tel. 01295 760205

Upton House, Banbury, Oxon Tel. 01295 670266 (NT)

Warwick Castle, Warwickshire Tel. 0870 4422000

Westbury Court Garden, Westbury-on-Severn, Glos Tel. 01452 760461 (NT)

Wichenford Dovecote, Wichenford, Worcs Tel. 01527 821214 (NT)

Witley Court, Great Witley, Worcester Tel. 01299 896636 (EH)

Woodchester Mansion, Stroud, Glos Tel. 01453 861541

Woodchester Park, Stroud, Glos Tel. 01452 814213 (NT)

MUSEUMS AND GALLERIES

Anne Hathaway's Cottage, Stratford-upon-Avon, Warks Tel. 01789 292100

Avoncroft Museum of Historic Buildings, Bromsgrove, Worcs Tel. 01527 831363

Birmingham Museum & Art Gallery, West Midlands Tel. 0121 303 2834 *Free*

Cadbury World, Bournville, Birmingham Tel. 0121 451 4180

Commandery, Worcester Tel. 01905 361821

City Museum & Art Gallery, Gloucester Tel. 01452 396131 *Free*

Elgar's Birthplace Museum, Lower Broadheath, Worcs Tel. 01905 333224

Ikon Gallery, Birmingham, W. Midlands Tel. 0121 248 0708 *Free*

Museum of Worcester Porcelain, Worcs Tel. 01905 746000

Northampton Museum & Art Gallery Tel. 01604 837277 *Free*

Shakespeare's Centre Stratford-upon-Avon, Warks Tel. 01789 204016

Soho House, Birmingham, W. Midlands Tel. 0121 554 9122

Warwickshire Museum, Warwick Tel. 01926 412500/501 *Free*

HOME COUNTIES

HOUSES AND GARDENS

Ascott, nr Leighton Buzzard, Bucks Tel. 01296 688242 (NT)

Basildon Park, Reading, Berks Tel. 0118 984 3040 (NT)

Benington Lordship Gardens, Stevenage, Herts Tel. 01438 869668

Berkhamsted Castle, St Albans, Herts Tel. 01223 582700 (EH) *Free*

Blenheim Palace, Woodstock, Oxon, Tel. 01993 811091

Boarstall Duck Decoy, Aylesbury, Bucks Tel. 01844 237488 (NT)

Broughton Castle, Banbury, Oxon Tel. 01295 276070

Buscot Park, Faringdon, Oxon Tel. 01367 240786 (NT)

Bushmead Priory, Bedford Tel. 01799 522842 (EH) *Free*

Carshalton House, Carshalton, Surrey Tel. 020 8770 4781

Chastleton House, Moreton-in-Marsh, Oxon Tel. 01608 674355 (NT)

Chenies Manor House, Rickmansworth, Herts Tel. 01494 762888

Chicheley Hall, Newport Pagnell, Bucks Tel. 01234 391252

Clandon Park, Guildford, Surrey Tel. 01483 222482 (NT)

Claremont Landscape Garden, Esher, Surrey Tel. 01372 467806 (NT)

Claydon House, nr Buckingham Tel. 01296 730349 (NT)

Cliveden, Maidenhead, Berks Tel. 01494 755562 (NT)

Ditchley Park, Enstone, Oxon Tel. 01608 677346

Donnington Castle, Newbury, Berks (EH)

Dorney Court, Windsor, Berks Tel. 01628 604638

Englefield House, Reading, Berks Tel. 01189 302221

Farnham Castle, Bishops Palace, Surrey Tel. 01252 721194

Farnham Castle Keep, Surrey Tel. 01252 713393 (EH)

Fawley Court, Henley-on-Thames, Oxon Tel. 01491 574917

Ford End Watermill, Ivinghoe, Buck Tel. 01582 600391

Gardens of the Rose, St Albans, Herts Tel. 01727 850461

Goddards, Dorking, Surrey Tel. 01628 825920

Greys Court, Henley-on-Thames, Oxon Tel. 01491 628529 (NT)

Hatchlands Park, Guildford, Surrey Tel. 01483 222482 (NT)

Hatfield House & Gardens, Herts Tel. 01707 287010

Houghton House, Bedford (EH)

Hughenden Manor, High Wycombe, Bucks Tel. 01494 755573 (NT)

Kelmscott Manor, nr Lechlade, Glos Tel. 01367 252486

Kingston Bagpuize House, Abingdon, Oxon Tel. 01865 820259

Knebworth, nr Stevenage, Herts Tel. 01438 812661

Little Holland House, Carshalton, Surrey Tel. 020 8770 4781 *Free*

Loseley Park, Guildford, Surrey Tel. 01483 405120

Mapledurham Trust, Reading, Berks Tel. 01189 723350

Milton Manor House, Abingdon, Oxon Tel. 01235 862321

Minster Lovell Hall & Dovecote, Witney, Oxon (EH)

Moot Hall, Elstow, Bedford Tel. 01234 266889

Nether Winchendon House, Aylesbury, Bucks Tel. 01844 290101

Old Gorhambury House, St Albans, Herts (EH)

Painshill Park & Landscape Garden, Cobham, Surrey Tel. 01932 868113

Polesden Lacey, nr Dorking, Surrey Tel. 01372 452048 (NT)

Rousham House, Bicester, Oxon Tel. 01869 347110

Royal Horticultural Society Garden, Wisley, Surrey Tel. 01483 224234

Sandham Memorial Chapel, nr Newbury, Hants Tel. 01635 278394 (NT)

Stonor, Henley-on-Thames, Oxon Tel. 01491 638587

(EH) = English Heritage property
(NT) = National Trust property

**Stowe Gardens,
Buckingham**
Tel. 01280 822850 (NT)

**Stowe House,
Buckingham**
Tel. 01280 818282

**Swiss Garden,
Old Warden, Beds**
Tel. 01767 627666

**Taplow Court, nr
Maidenhead, Berks**
Tel. 01628 591209
Free

**Waddesdon Manor,
nr Aylesbury, Bucks**
Tel. 01296 653211 (NT)

**Welford Park,
Newbury, Berks**
Tel. 01488 608203

**West Wycombe Park,
Bucks** (NT)
Tel. 01494 513569
(April-Oct only)

Windsor Castle, Berks
Tel. 01753 831118 or
020 7766 730

**Winkworth Arboretum,
Godalming, Surrey**
Tel. 01483 208477 (NT)

Woburn Abbey, Beds
Tel. 01525 290666

**Wrest Park Gardens,
Rycot, Oxon**
Tel. 01525 860152 (EH)

MUSEUMS
AND GALLERIES

**Abingdon Museum,
Oxon**
Tel. 01235 523703
Free

**Ashmolean Museum,
Oxford**
Tel. 01865 278000
Free

**Buckinghamshire
County Museum and
Roald Dahl Museum,
Aylesbury**
Tel. 01296 331441
Free (County Museum)

**Cecil Higgins Art
Gallery, Bedford**
Tel. 01234 211222
Free

**Open Air Museum,
Chalfont St Giles, Bucks**
Tel. 01494 871117

**Cogges Manor Farm
Museum, Witney,
Oxon**
Tel. 01993 772602

**Cowper & Newton
Museum, Olney, Bucks**
Tel. 01234 711516

**The Egham Museum,
Surrey**
Tel. 01784 434483
Free

**Guildford House
Gallery, Surrey**
Tel. 01483 444740
Free

**Guildford Museum,
Surrey**
Tel. 01483 444751
Free

**The Henry Moore
Foundation,
Much Hadham, Herts**
Tel. 01279 843333

**John Milton's Cottage,
Chalfont St Giles, Bucks**
Tel. 01494 872313

**Museum of Farnham,
Surrey**
Tel. 01252 715094
Free

**Museum of Modern
Art, Oxford**
Tel. 01865 722733

**Museum of Reading,
Berks**
Tel. 0118 939 9800
Free

**Old Gaol Museum,
Buckingham**
Tel. 01280 823020

**Oxford University
Museum of Natural
History, Oxford**
Tel. 01865 272950

**The Pitt Rivers
Museum, Oxford**
Tel. 01865 270927
Free

**Riverside Museum,
Blake's Lock, Reading**
Tel. 0118 939 9800
Free

**Shaw's Corner,
Ayot St Lawrence,
nr Welwyn, Herts**
Tel. 01438 820307 (NT)

**Stanley Spencer
Gallery, Cookham
on Thames, Berks**
Tel. 01628 471885

**Verulamium Museum,
St Albans, Herts**
Tel. 01727 751810

**The Walter Rothschild
Zoological Museum,
Tring, Herts**
Tel. 020 7942 6171

**The Watts Gallery,
Guildford, Surrey**
Tel. 01483 810235
Free

EAST ANGLIA
HOUSES
AND GARDENS

**Anglesey Abbey &
Garden, Cambridge**
Tel. 01223 810080

**Audley End House
and Gardens, Saffron
Walden, Essex**
Tel. 01799 522842 (EH)

**Beth Chatto Gardens,
Colchester, Essex**
Tel. 01206 822007

**Binham Priory,
Binham-on-Wells,
Norfolk**
Tel. 01328 830362 (EH)
Free

**Blickling Hall, Garden &
Park, Norwich, Norfolk**
Tel. 01263 738030 (NT)

**Bourne Mill,
Colchester, Essex**
Tel. 01206 572422 (NT)

**Burgh Castle, Great
Yarmouth, Norfolk**
Tel. 01223 582700 (EH)
Free

**Castle Acre Priory,
nr Swaffham, Norfolk**
Tel. 01760 755394 (EH)

**Castle Rising Castle,
King's Lynn, Norfolk**
Tel. 01553 631330
(free for EH members)

**Coggeshall Grange
Barn, Colchester,
Essex**
Tel. 01376 562226 (NT)

**Copped Hall, Epping,
Essex**
Tel. 020 7267 1679

**Custom House,
King's Lynn, Norfolk**
Tel. 01553 763044
Free

**Denny Abbey &
Farmland Museum,
Cambridge**
Tel. 01223 860489
(EH/Farmland Museum)

**Euston Hall,
Thetford, Norfolk**
Tel. 01842 766366

**Elton Hall,
Peterborough, Cambs**
Tel. 01832 280468

**Felbrigg Hall, Garden
& Park, Norwich**
Tel. 01263 837444 (NT)

**Framlingham Castle,
Suffolk**
Tel. 01728 724189 (EH)

**Grime's Graves,
Thetford, Norfolk**
Tel. 01842 810656 (EH)

**Hadleigh Guildhall,
Hadleigh, Suffolk**
Tel. 01473 827752
Garden free

**Haughley Park,
Stowmarket, Suffolk**
Tel. 01359 240701

**Hedingham Castle,
nr Halstead, Essex**
Tel. 01787 460261

**Helmingham Hall
Gardens, Stowmarket,
Suffolk**
Tel. 01473 890363

**Hinchingbrooke House,
Huntingdon, Cambs**
Tel. 01480 375678

**Holkham Hall,
Wells-next-the-Sea,
Norfolk**
Tel. 01328 710227

**Houghton Hall, nr
King's Lynn, Norfolk**
Tel. 01485 528569

**Ickworth House, Park
and Gardens, Bury
St Edmunds, Suffolk**
Tel. 01284 735270 (NT)

Ingatestone Hall, Essex
Tel. 01277 353010

**Kentwell Hall, Long
Melford, Suffolk**
Tel. 01787 310207

**Kimbolton Castle,
Kimbolton,
nr Huntingdon, Cambs**
Tel. 01480 860505

**Landguard Fort,
Felixstowe, Suffolk**
Tel. 01394 277767 (EH)

**Layer Marney Tower,
nr Colchester, Essex**
Tel. 01206 330784

Leiston Abbey, Suffolk
Tel. 01223 582700 (EH)
Free

**Little Hall,
Lavenham, Suffolk**
Tel. 01787 247179

**Longthorpe Tower,
Cambs**
Tel. 01223 582700 (EH)

**Melford Hall,
Sudbury, Suffolk**
Tel. 01787 37922 (NT)

**Orford Castle,
nr Woodbridge,
Suffolk**
Tel. 01394 450472 (EH)

**Otley Hall, Ipswich,
Suffolk**
Tel. 01473 890264

**Oxburgh Hall, Garden
& Estate, King's Lynn,
Norfolk**
Tel. 01366 328258 (NT)

**Peckover House &
Garden, Wisbech,
Cambs**
Tel. 01945 583463 (NT)

**Ramsey Abbey
Gatehouse, Ramsey,
Cambs**
Tel. 01480 301494 (NT)
Free

**St George's Guildhall,
King's Lynn, Norfolk**
Tel. 01553 764864 (NT)

◆ DIRECTORY

Most gardens and parks are open 10am–6pm, *most houses* 1–5.30pm, April 1 to October 31. But check beforehand. Hudson's Historic Houses and Gardens gives detailed opening times and admission prices.

St John's Abbey Gate, Colchester, Essex (EH)

Saxtead Green Post Mill, Woodbridge, Suffolk
Tel. 01728 685789 (EH)

Sheringham Park, Upper Sheringham, Norfolk
Tel. 01263 820550 (NT)

Thorpe Hall, Peterborough, Cambs
Tel. 01733 330060
Gardens only open to public; free

Wimpole Hall, Royston, Cambs
Tel. 01223 206000 (NT)

Wolterton Park, Norwich, Norfolk
Tel. 01263 584175

MUSEUMS AND GALLERIES

Aldeburgh Museum, Moot Hall, Aldeburgh, Suffolk
Tel. 01728 454666

Clare Ancient House Museum, Clare, Suffolk
Tel. 01787 277662

Christchurch Mansion, Ipswich, Suffolk
Tel. 01473 433554
Free

Dunwich Museum, Saxmundham, Suffolk
Tel. 01728 648796
Free

East Anglian Railway Museum, Chappel, nr Colchester, Essex
Tel. 01206 242524

Elizabethan House Museum, Great Yarmouth, Norfolk
Tel. 01493 855746

Firstsite at the Minories Art Gallery, Colchester, Essex
Tel. 01206 577067

Fitzwilliam Museum, Cambridge
Tel. 01223 332900
Free

Flatford (Bridge Cottage), Colchester, Essex
Tel. 01206 298260 (NT)

Fry Public Art Gallery, Saffron Walden, Essex
Tel. 01799 513779

Gainsborough's House, Sudbury, Suffolk
Tel. 01787 372958

Great Yarmouth Row of Houses, Great Yarmouth, Norfolk
Tel. 01493 857900 (EH)

Gressenhall Farm and Workhouse, Gressenhall, nr Dereham
Tel. 01362 860563

Imperial War Museum, Duxford, Cambridge
Tel. 01223 835000

Kelvedon Hatch Nuclear Bunker, nr Brentwood, Essex
Tel. 01277 364883

Kettle's Yard, Cambridge
Tel. 01223 352124

Lowestoft and East Suffolk Maritime Museum, Suffolk
Tel. 01502 561963

Lowestoft Museum, Suffolk
Tel. 01502 511457
Free

Moyses Hall Museum, Bury St Edmunds, Suffolk
Tel. 01284 706183

Museum of the Broads, Stalham, Norwich, Norfolk
Tel. 01692 581681

National Horseracing Museum, Newmarket, Suffolk
Tel. 01638 667333

Norwich Castle & Art Gallery, Norfolk
Tel. 01603 493625

Oliver Cromwell's House, Ely, Cambs
Tel. 01353 662062

Stained Glass Museum, Ely Cathedral, Cambs
Tel. 01353 660347

Thaxted Guildhall, Dunmow, Essex
Tel. 01371 831281

Tine and Tide Museum of Great Yarmouth Life, Great Yarmouth, Norfolk
Tel. 01493 743 930

NORTH MIDLANDS

HOUSES AND GARDENS

Adlington Hall, Macclesfield, Cheshire
Tel. 01625 820875

Ashby-de-la-Zouch Castle, Leics
Tel. 01530 413343 (EH)

Aston Hall, Birmingham, W. Midlands
Tel. 0121 327 0062
Free

Attingham Park, Shrewsbury, Shrops
Tel. 01743 708162 (NT)

Aubourn Hall, Lincoln
Tel. 01522 788270

Beeston Castle, Tarporley, Cheshire
Tel. 01829 260464 (EH)

Belgrave Hall & Gardens, Leicester
Tel. 0116 266 6590 *Free*

Belton House, Grantham, Lincs
Tel. 01476 566116 (NT)

Benthall Hall, Broseley, Shrops
Tel. 01952 882159 (NT)

Biddulph Grange Garden, Stoke-on-Trent, Staffs
Tel. 01782 517999 (NT)

Boscobel House & the Royal Oak, Bishop's Wood, Shrops
Tel. 01902 850244 (EH)

Bolsover Castle, Bolsover, Derbs
Tel. 01246 822844 (EH)

Buildwas Abbey, Telford, Shrops
Tel. 01952 433274 (EH)

Burghley House, Stamford, Lincs
Tel. 01780 752451

Capesthorne Hall, Macclesfield, Cheshire
Tel. 01625 861221

Chatsworth House, Bakewell, Derbs
Tel. 01246 582204

Chillington Hall, Wolverhampton, Staffs
Tel. 01902 850236

Cholmondeley Castle Garden, Malpas, Cheshire
Tel. 01829 720383

Clumber Park, Worksop, Notts
Tel. 01909 476592 (NT)
Free for pedestrians

Clun Castle, Ludlow, Shrops (EH)

Doddington Hall, Lincoln
Tel. 01522 694308

Dorfold Hall, nr Nantwich, Cheshire
Tel. 01270 625245

Dudmaston, nr Bridgnorth, Shrops
Tel. 01746 780866 (NT)

Dunham Massey, Altrincham, Cheshire
Tel. 0161 941 1025 (NT)

Eyam Hall, Hope Valley, Derbs
Tel. 01433 631976

Fydell House, Boston, Lancs
Tel. 01205 351520 *Free*

Gainsborough Old Hall, Lincs
Tel. 01427 612669 (EH)

Gawsworth Hall, nr Macclesfield, Cheshire
Tel. 01260 223456

Grimsthorpe Castle, Bourne, Lincs
Tel. 01778 591205

Guildhall, Leicester
Tel. 0116 2532569
Free

Gunby Hall, nr Spilsby, Lincs
Tel. 01909 486411 (NT)

Haddon Hall, Bakewell, Derbs
Tel. 01629 812855

Hardwick Hall, Chesterfield, Derbs
Tel. 01246 850430 (NT)

Hardwick Old Hall, Chesterfield, Derbs
Tel. 01246 850431 (EH)

Harlaxton Manor, Grantham, Lincs
Tel. 01476 403000
(open one day a year only)

Haughmond Abbey, Shrewsbury, Shrops
Tel. 01743 709661 (EH)

Hawkstone Hall & Gardens, Shrewsbury, Shrops
Tel. 01630 685242

Hodnet Hall Gardens, Market Drayton, Shrops
Tel. 01630 685786

Holme Pierrepont Hall, nr Nottingham, Notts
Tel. 0115 933 2371

Ingestre Hall, Stafford, Staffs
Tel. 01889 270225

Kedleston Hall, Derby
Tel. 01332 842191 (NT)

Lilleshall Abbey, Oakengates, Shrops
(EH) *Free*

Lincoln Castle, Lincs
Tel. 01522 511068

Little Moreton Hall, Congleton, Cheshire
Tel. 01260 272018 (NT)

Ludlow Castle, Shrops
Tel. 01584 873355

Lyddington Bede House, Rutland
Tel. 01572 822438 (EH)

Lyme Park, Disley,
nr Stockport,
Cheshire
Tel. 01663 762023 (NT)

Melbourne Hall,
Derbs
Tel. 01332 862502

Morville Hall, nr
Bridgnorth, Shrops
Tel. 01746 780838 (NT)

Moseley Old Hall,
Wolverhampton,
Staffs
Tel. 01902 782808 (NT)

Newstead Abbey,
Ravenshead, Notts
Tel. 01623 455900

Oakham Castle,
Rutland
Tel. 01572 758440
Free

Peveril Castle,
Hope Valley, Derbs
Tel. 01433 620613 (EH)

Rufford Abbey,
nr Ollerton, Notts
Tel. 01623 822944
*Free but car park
charge*

Sandon Hall, Staffs
Tel. 01889 508004

Shipton Hall, Much
Wenlock, Shrops
Tel. 01746 785225

Shugborough,
nr Stafford, Staffs
Tel. 01889 881388 (NT)

Stanford Hall,
Lutterworth, Leics
Tel. 01788 860250

Staunton Harold
Church, Ashby-de-la-
Zouch, Leics (NT)
Tel. 01332 863822
(Calke Abbey)

Stokesay Castle,
nr Craven Arms,
Shrops
Tel. 01588 672544 (EH)

Sudbury Hall,
nr Ashbourne, Derbs
Tel. 01283 585337 (NT)

Sutton Scarsdale Hall,
Chesterfield, Derbs
Tel. 0870 333 1181 (EH)
Free

Tabley House,
Knutsford, Cheshire
Tel. 01565 750151

Tamworth Castle,
Staffs
Tel. 01827 709626

Tattershall Castle,
Lincoln
Tel. 01526 342543 (NT)

Tatton Park,
Knutsford, Cheshire
Tel. 01625 534400 (NT)

Walcot Hall, nr
Bishop's Castle, Shrops
Tel. 01588 680570

Wenlock Priory,
Much Wenlock,
Shrops
Tel. 01952 727466 (EH)

Weston Park,
nr Shifnal, Shrops
Tel. 01952 852100

Wightwick Manor,
Wolverhampton
Tel. 01902 761400 (NT)

Wilderhope Manor,
Much Wenlock, Shrops
Tel. 01694 771363 (NT)

Wingfield Manor,
South Wingfield,
Derbs
Tel. 01246 857436 or
01246 856456 (EH)

Woolsthorpe Manor,
Grantham, Lincs
Tel. 01476 860338 (NT)

MUSEUMS
AND GALLERIES

The Collection,
Lincoln
Tel. 01522 527980

Derby Museum
& Art Gallery, Derbs
Tel. 01332 716659
Free

Galleries of Justice
(Museum of Law),
Nottingham
Tel. 0115 952 0555

Izaak Walton's Cottage,
Stafford, Staffs
Tel. 01785 760278

Jewry Wall Museum
& Site, Leicester
Tel. 0116 225 4971
Free

Knaresborough Castle,
N. Yorks
Tel. 01423 556188

Leicester City Museum
and Art Gallery (New
Walk Museum and Art
Gallery), Leicester
Tel. 0116 255 4900
Free

Natural History
Museum, Wollaton
Hall, Nottingham
Tel. 0115 915 3900
Free weekdays

Newarke Houses
Museum, Leicester
Tel. 0116 225 4980

Nottingham Castle
Museum & Art Gallery
Tel. 0115 915 3700

Potteries Museum
and Art Gallery,
Hanley,
Stoke-on-Trent, Staffs
Tel. 01782 232323
Free

Rutland County
Museum, Leics
Tel. 01572 758440
Free

Shrewsbury Museum
& Art Gallery,
Shrewsbury, Shrops
Tel. 01743 361196
Free

Sir Richard Arkwright's
Cromford Mills, Derbs
Tel. 01629 824297
Free

The Wedgwood Story,
Stoke-on-Trent, Staffs
Tel. 01782 204218

NORTH EAST
HOUSES
AND GARDENS

Alnwick Castle,
Northumberland
Tel. 01665 510777

Auckland Castle,
Durham
Tel. 01388 601627

Bamburgh Castle,
Northumberland
Tel. 01668 214515

Barnard Castle,
Durham
Tel. 01833 638212 (EH)

Belsay Hall, Castle &
Gardens, nr Ponteland,
Northumberland
Tel. 01661 881636 (EH)

Beningbrough Hall
& Gardens, York
Tel. 01904 470666 (NT)

Bolton Castle,
Leyburn, N. Yorks
Tel. 01969 623981

Bramham Park,
Wetherby, W. Yorks
Tel. 01937 846000

Brinkburn Priory,
Morpeth,
Northumberland
Tel. 01665 570628 (EH)

Brodsworth Hall &
Gardens, nr Doncaster,
Yorks
Tel. 01302 722598 (EH)

Burton Agnes Hall,
Driffield, E. Yorks
Tel. 01262 490324

Burton Constable Hall,
Skirlaugh, E.Yorks
Tel. 01964 562400

Byland Abbey,
Helmsley, N.Yorks
Tel. 01347 868614 (EH)

Castle Howard,
York
Tel. 01653 648333

Chillingham Castle
& Gardens, nr Alnwick,
Northumberland
Tel. 01668 215359

Clifford's Tower,
Tower Street, York
Tel. 01904 646940 (EH)

Conisbrough Castle,
S. Yorks
Tel. 01709 863329 (EH)

Cragside, Morpeth,
Northumberland
Tel. 01669 620150 (NT)

Duncombe Park, York
Tel. 01439 770213

Dunstanburgh Castle,
Alnwick,
Northumberland
Tel. 01665 576231
(NT/EH)

Durham Castle,
Durham
Tel. 0191 334 3800

Easby Abbey,
nr Richmond, N.Yorks
Tel. 01748 822493 (EH)

East Riddlesden Hall,
Keighley, W. Yorks
Tel. 01535 607075 (NT)

Fairfax House, York
Tel. 01904 655543

Fountains Abbey &
Studley Royal Garden,
Ripon, N. Yorks
Tel. 01765 608888 (NT)

Gibside,
Burnopfield,
Newcastle upon Tyne
Tel. 01207 541820 (NT)

Gisborough Priory,
Redcar & Cleveland
Tel. 01287 633801 (EH)

Harewood House,
nr Leeds, W. Yorks
Tel. 0113 218 1010

Helmsley Castle,
N. Yorks
Tel. 01439 770442 (EH)

Kirkham Priory,
Whitewell-on-the-Hill,
Yorks
Tel. 01653 618768 (EH)

Lindisfarne Castle,
Holy Island,
Northumberland
Tel. 01289 389244 (NT)

Lindisfarne Priory,
Holy Island
Tel. 01289 389200 (EH)

Lotherton Hall,
Aberford, W. Yorks
Tel. 0113 281 3259

Markenfield Hall,
Ripon, Yorks
Tel. 01765 603411

Merchant Adventurers'
Hall, York
Tel. 01904 654818

Middleham Castle,
Leyburn, Yorks
Tel. 01969 623899 (EH)

Monk Bretton Priory,
Barnsley, S. Yorks (EH)
Free

Mount Grace Priory,
Staddlebridge,
N. Yorks
Tel. 01609 883494
(NT/EH)

Newburgh Priory,
Coxwold, Yorks
Tel. 01347 868435

Newby Hall & Gardens,
Ripon, N. Yorks
Tel. 01423 322583

Normanby Hall
Country Park,
Scunthorpe,
Humberside
Tel. 01724 720588

Norton Conyers,
nr Ripon, N. Yorks
Tel. 01765 640333

Nostell Priory,
Wakefield, W. Yorks
Tel. 01924 863892 (NT)

Nunnington Hall,
York
Tel. 01439 748283 (NT)

Pickering Castle,
Pickering, N. Yorks
Tel. 01751 474989 (EH)

Richmond Castle,
N. Yorks
Tel. 01748 822493 (EH)

Rievaulx Abbey,
nr Helmsley,
N. Yorks
Tel. 01439 798340 (EH)

Rievaulx Terrace and
Temples, Helmsley,
N. Yorks
Tel. 01439 748283 (NT)

Ripley Castle,
Harrogate, N. Yorks
Tel. 01423 770152

Roche Abbey,
Rotherham, S. Yorks
Tel. 01709 812739 (EH)

Scarborough Castle,
N. Yorks
Tel. 01723 372451 (EH)

Seaton Delaval Hall,
Whitley Bay,
Northumberland
Tel. 0191 237 1493

Shandy Hall,
Coxwold
Tel. 01347 868465

Skipton Castle,
N.Yorks
Tel. 01756 792442

Sledmere House,
Driffield, E.Yorks
Tel. 01377 236637

Spofforth Castle,
Harrogate, N. Yorks
Tel. 01904 601901 (EH)
Free

Stockeld Park,
Wetherby, Yorks
Tel. 01937 586101

Sutton Park, York
Tel. 01347 810249

Temple Newsam
House, Leeds, W. Yorks
Tel. 0113 264 7321

Thornton Abbey &
Gatehouse, Scunthorpe,
Humberside
Tel. 01904 601901 (EH)
Free

Wallington, Morpeth,
Northumberland
Tel. 01670 773600 (NT)

Warkworth Castle
& Hermitage,
nr Morpeth,
Northumberland
Tel. 01665 711423 (EH)

Whitby Abbey, N. Yorks
Tel. 01947 603568 (EH)

**MUSEUMS
AND GALLERIES**

1853 Gallery (housed
in former mill), Saltaire,
Shipley, W.Yorks
Tel. 01274 531163
Free

Aldborough Roman
Town & Museum,
Boroughbridge,
N. Yorks
Tel. 01423 322768 (EH)

Berwick Barracks,
Berwick-upon-Tweed,
Northumberland
Tel. 01289 304493 (EH)

Bowes Museum,
Barnard Castle,
Durham
Tel. 01833 690606

Bronte Parsonage
Museum, Keighley,
W. Yorks
Tel. 01535 642323

Calderdale Museum,
Piece Hall, Halifax,
W. Yorks
Tel. 01422 358300

Craft Centre & Design
Gallery, City Art
Gallery, Leeds, W. Yorks
Tel. 0113 247 8241
Free

Graves Art Gallery,
Sheffield, S. Yorks
Tel. 0114 278 2600
Free

Kelham Island
Industrial Museum,
Sheffield, S. Yorks
Tel. 0114 272 2106

Kirkstall Abbey,
Leeds, W. Yorks
Tel. 0113 2305492

Laing Art Gallery,
Newcastle upon Tyne

Tel. 0191 232 7734
Free

National Glass Centre,
Sunderland, Tyne &
Wear
Tel. 0191 515 5555
Free

Shibden Hall,
Halifax, W. Yorks
Tel. 01422 352246

Weston Park Museum
Sheffield, S. Yorks
Tel. 0114 278 2600

Wilberforce House,
Hull, Yorks
Tel. 01482 613902
Free

York Castle Museum,
N. Yorks
Tel. 01904 687687

York City Art Gallery,
N. Yorks
Tel. 01904 697968

Yorkshire Museum and
Gardens, York
Tel. 01904 687687

NORTH WEST
**HOUSES
AND GARDENS**

Appleby Castle,
Cumbria
Tel. 01768 353344

Ashton Memorial,
Lancaster
Tel. 01524 33318

Bramall Hall, Stockport,
Manchester
Tel. 0161 485 3708

Brough Castle,
Brough, Cumbria (EH)

Carlisle Castle, Cumbria
Tel. 01228 591922 (EH)

Cartmel Priory
Gatehouse, Grange-
over-Sands, Cumbria
Tel. 01539 536874 (NT)

Croxteth Hall & Country
Park, Liverpool
Tel. 0151 233 6910

Dalemain Historic
House and Gardens,
Penrith, Cumbria
Tel. 01768 486450

Furness Abbey, Barrow-
in-Furness, Cumbria
Tel. 01229 823420 (EH)

Gawthorpe Hall,
nr Burnley, Lancs
Tel. 01282 770353 (NT)

Hall i'th'Wood
Museum, Bolton, Lancs
Tel. 01204 332370

Heaton Hall,
Prestwich, Manchester
Tel. 0161 773 1231
Free

Hill Top,
Ambleside, Cumbria
Tel. 01539 436269 (NT)

Hoghton Tower,
Preston, Lancs
Tel. 01254 852986

Holker Hall,
Grange-over-Sands,
Cumbria
Tel. 01539 558328

Hutton-in-the-Forest,
Penrith, Cumbria
Tel. 01768 484449

Leighton Hall,
Carnforth, Lancs
Tel. 01524 734474

Levens Hall,
Kendal, Cumbria
Tel. 01539 560321

Lytham Hall, Lancs
Tel. 01253 736652

Meols Hall, Southport,
Merseyside
Tel. 01704 228326

Muncaster Castle,
Gardens & Owl Centre,
Ravenglass, Cumbria
Tel. 01229 717614

Naworth Castle,
Brampton, Cumbria
Tel. 01697 73229

Rufford Old Hall,
nr Ormskirk, Lancs
Tel. 01704 821254 (NT)

Rydal Mount &
Gardens, Cumbria
Tel. 01539 433002

Samlesbury Hall,
Preston, Lancs
Tel. 01254 812010

Sizergh Castle &
Garden, nr Kendal,
Cumbria
Tel. 01539 560070 (NT)

Speke Hall,
Liverpool
Tel. 0151 427 7231 (NT)

Townend,
Windermere,
Cumbria
Tel. 01539 432628 (NT)

Turton Tower,
Bolton, Lancs
Tel. 01204 852203

Wythenshawe Hall,
Manchester
Tel. 0161 998 5083
Free

**MUSEUMS
AND GALLERIES**

Abbot Hall Art Gallery,
Kendal, Cumbria
Tel. 01539 722464

Astley Hall Museum &
Art Gallery, Chorley,
Lancs
Tel. 01257 515555

(EH) = English Heritage property
(NT) = National Trust property

Blackburn Museum & Art Gallery, Lancs
Tel. 01254 667130
Free

Bolton Museum, Art Gallery & Aquarium, Lancs
Tel. 01204 332211
Free

City Art Galleries, Manchester
Tel. 0161 235 8888

Dove Cottage & Wordsworth Museum, Grasmere, Cumbria
Tel. 01539 435544

Gallery of Costume (Platt Hall), Rusholme, Manchester
Tel. 0161 224 5217
Free

Harris Museum & Art Gallery, Preston, Lancs
Tel. 01772 258248
Free

Haworth Art Gallery, Accrington, Lancs
Tel. 01254 233782
Free

Helmshore Mills Textile Museum, Rossendale, Lancs
Tel. 01706 226459

Lady Lever Art Gallery, Port Sunlight Village, Wirral
Tel. 0151 478 4136

Lancaster City Museum, Lancs
Tel. 01524 64637
Free

Lancaster Maritime Museum, Lancs
Tel. 01524 382264

Liverpool Museum
Tel. 0151 478 4399

The Lowry, Salford, Manchester
Tel. 0870 1112000
Free

Manchester Museum
Tel. 0161 275 2634
Free

Merseyside Maritime Museum, Liverpool
Tel. 0151 478 4499

Museum of Science and Industry, Manchester
Tel. 0161 832 2244
Free (except exhibitions)

Ordsall Hall Museum, Salford, Manchester
Tel. 0161 872 0251
Free

Ribchester Roman Museum, nr Preston, Lancs
Tel. 01254 878261

The Ruskin Library, Lancaster
Tel. 01524 593587
Free

Salford Museum & Art Gallery, Manchester
Tel. 0161 736 2649
Free

Smithills Hall Museum, Bolton, Lancs
Tel. 01204 332377

Stott Park Bobbin Mill, Ulverston, Cumbria
Tel. 01539 531087 (EH)

Tate Gallery, Liverpool
Tel. 0151 702 7400
Free (except exhibitions)

Towneley Hall Art Gallery & Museums, Burnley, Lancs
Tel. 01282 424213
Free

Tullie House Museum & Art Gallery, Carlisle, Cumbria
Tel. 01228 534781

Walker Art Gallery, Liverpool
Tel. 0151 478 4199

Whitworth Art Gallery, Manchester
Tel. 0161 275 7450
Free

Wordsworth House, Cockermouth, Cumbria
Tel. 01900 824805 (NT)

SOUTH WALES
HOUSES AND GARDENS

Caerphilly Castle
Tel. 029 2088 3143

Cardiff Castle
Tel. 029 2087 8100

Carew Castle & Tidal Mill, Tenby, Pembs
Tel. 01646 651782

Castell Coch, Tongwynlais, Cardiff
Tel. 029 2081 0101

Chepstow Castle, Gwent
Tel. 01291 624065

Cilgerran Castle, Cardigan, Dyfed
Tel. 01239 621339 (NT)

Kidwelly Castle, W. Glamorgan
Tel. 01554 890104

Laugharne Castle, Carmarthenshire
Tel. 01994 427906

Oxwich Castle, Swansea
Tel. 01792 390359

Pembroke Castle
Tel. 01646 681510

Raglan Castle, Monmouthshire
Tel. 01291 690228

St Davids Bishop's Palace, Pembs
Tel. 01437 720517

Tintern Abbey, Monmouthshire
Tel. 01291 689251

Weobley Castle, Llanrhidian, Swansea
Tel. 01792 390012

MUSEUMS AND GALLERIES

Ceredigion Museum & Coliseum Gallery, Aberystwyth, Cardiganshire
Tel. 01970 633088
Free

Glynn Vivian Art Gallery, Swansea
Tel. 01792 516900
Free

The Nelson Museum, Monmouth
Tel. 01600 710630

Museum of Welsh Life, St Fagans, Cardiff
Tel. 029 2057 3500
Free

The National Museum & Gallery, Cardiff
Tel. 029 2039 7951
Free

Swansea Museum
Tel. 01792 653763
Free

Tudor Merchant's House, Tenby, Pembs
Tel. 01834 842279 (NT)

NORTH WALES
HOUSES AND GARDENS

Aberconwy House, Conwy
Tel. 01492 592246 (NT)

Beaumaris Castle, Anglesey
Tel. 01248 810361

Bodelwyddan Castle, Denbighshire
Tel. 01745 584060

Bodnant Garden, Colwyn Bay, Conwy
Tel. 01492 650460 (NT)

Bodrhyddan, Rhuddlan, Denbighshire
Tel. 01745 590414

Caernarfon Castle, Gwynedd
Tel. 01286 677617

Chirk Castle & Gardens Wrexham
Tel. 01691 777701 (NT)

Conwy Castle, Conwy
Tel. 01492 592358

Criccieth Castle, Gwynedd
Tel. 01766 522227

Dolwyddelan Castle, Ffestiniog, Gwynedd
Tel. 01690 750366

Erddig, nr Wrexham
Tel. 01978 355314 (NT)

Gwydir Castle, Llanrwst, Gwynedd
Tel. 01492 641687

Harlech Castle, Gwynedd
Tel. 01766 780552

Judge's Lodging, Presteigne, Powys
Tel. 01544 260650

Penrhyn Castle, Bangor, Gwynedd
Tel. 01248 353084 (NT)

Plas yn Rhiw, Pwllheli, Gwynedd
Tel. 01758 780219 (NT)

Plas Mawr, Conwy
Tel. 01492 580167

Plas Newydd, Anglesey
Tel. 01248 714795 (NT)

Portmeirion, Gwynedd
Tel. 01766 770000

Powis Castle & Garden, nr Welshpool, Powys
Tel. 01938 551929 (NT)

Rhuddlan Castle, Denbighshire
Tel. 01745 590777

Tretower Court & Castle, Crickhowell, Powys
Tel. 01874 730279

Valle Crucis Abbey, Llangollen, Clwyd
Tel. 01978 860326

White Castle, Llantilio, Crosseny, Abergavenny
Tel. 01600 780380

MUSEUMS AND GALLERIES

Beaumaris Gaol & Courthouse, Anglesey
Tel. 01248 810921

Brecknock Museum, Brecon, Powys
Tel. 01874 624121

Welsh Slate Museum, Llanberis, Gwynedd
Tel. 01286 870630
Free

◆ HOTELS AND RESTAURANTS

For the **restaurants**, the following
price bands have been used, according to
the price of a two-course meal (without wine):
■ = up to £15; ■ = £15–£20
■ = £20–£30; ⊞ = £30 and over

LONDON
GASTRONOMIC TREATS

LE GAVROCHE
43 Upper Brook St, W1
Tel. 020 7408 0881
www.le-gavroche.co.uk
Closed Sat lunch; Sun
*The baton passed from
founding father Albert
Roux to son Michel
some years back now,
and there was no
diminution in
standards, food or
service in this
unashamedly luxurious
restaurant. Michel's
cooking moves from
classic to contemporary
dishes with confidence,
ease, panache and
individuality. Silvano
Giraldin, the peerless
manager, who has
been with the
restaurant since it
opened its doors,
keeps the service the
finest in the country.
The wine list is an
oenologist's dream and
the set price lunch
(three courses and half
a bottle of wine for
£40) is one of the best
bargains in town.*
⊞

GORDON RAMSAY
68-69 Royal Hospital Rd,
SW3 Tel. 020 735 4441
www.gordonramsay.com
*Deservedly won its
third Michelin stars in
2000. The restaurant is
classically French in
almost every respect,
aside from the name
above the door. It is
small and elegant –
restaurants aiming for
triple stardom tend to
be. The service has
considerable charm,
and the food immense
elegance, poise and
brilliance. The
attention to detail is
prodigious, the effects
often close to sublime.
Altogether a pretty
senior experience.
Set meals available.*
⊞

ORRERY
55 Marylebone High St,
W1 Tel. 020 7616 8000
www.orrery.co.uk
*Sir Terence Conran
(for this is one of his
restaurants) has
created a deliciously
suave dining room out
of what is, essentially,
a long thin room. The
service is among the
most accomplished in
London, and the wine
list among the most
highly priced. But the
real glory of Orrery is
the food that comes
out of Chris Calvin's
kitchen – potent,
wonderfully crafted,
deeply considered, and
powerfully structured.
This is some of the
finest cooking in
London. The team here
are also responsible for
supervising the food
and service at the
Almeida (see p. 516),
Sir Terence's latest
bright young brasserie.*
■

THE SQUARE
6-10 Bruton St, W1
Tel. 020 7495 7100
www.squarerestaurant.
com
Closed Sat lunch; Sun
*Quite possibly the most
civilized restaurant in
London, The Square
breathes calm and
confidence. The rooms
stand full square in the
canons of modern
good taste, providing
an immaculate setting
for Philip Howard's
clever, graceful and
immensely tasteful
(quite literally)
cooking. It's only
afterward you realize
just how good the food
was and how enjoy-
able the experience.
Set lunches available.*
⊞

HOT YOUNG CHEFS

CLUB GASCON
57 West Smithfield, EC1
Tel. 020 7796 0600
Closed Sat lunch; Sun
*Instant hit with
virtually all critics since
it opened in 1998. Chef
Pascal Aussignac brings
flair and an innovative
sleight of hand to
the grand food of
southwest France –
foie gras, duck and
cassoulet – generally
lightening their impact
for the modern
stomach. Clean, clear
decor (though usually
cluttered with happy
eaters). Service pretty
French (read into that
what you like).*
■

LINDSAY HOUSE
21 Romilly St, W1
Tel. 020 7439 0450
www.lindsayhouse.co.uk
Closed Sat lunch; Sun
*An 18th-century town
house in the heart of
Soho that retains that
distinctive rakish feel
to it. This is largely due
to the chef and
proprietor Richard
Corrigan, who is larger
than life in every sense
of the word. His
cooking has an entirely
idiosyncratic brio and
style, muscular and
robust in flavor, but
with the lightest and
most delicate of
touches. Some of the
most distinctive and
innovative food in
the country.*
⊞

PETRUS
Berkeley Hotel,
Wilton Place, SW1
Tel. 020 7235 1200
www.gordonramsay.com
Closed Sat lunch; Sun
*Pétrus moved to the
Berkeley in November
2003. It is still an
elegant place serving
elegant food. Serious
too. Chef Marcus
Wareing is a protégé
of Gordon Ramsay so,
not surprisingly, his
cooking is also modern
French, characterized
by immense care and
restraint. That is not to
say it lacks flavor or
flair. Quite the
contrary. But it is
the kind of food that
sneaks up on you
rather than bangs you
over the head. Service
and wine list in
keeping with style of
the whole.*
■

PIED À TERRE
34 Charlotte St, W1
Tel. 020 7916 0786
www.pied-a-terre.co.uk
Closed for lunch Mon &
Sat; all day åSun
*This small, slightly
stark gastro-boutique
is now on its third chef.
Australian Shane
Osborne follows
Richard Neat and
Tom Atkin. His style
of food is generically
similar, involving the
careful balancing of
a number of strongly
characterized
ingredients. He does
not push the flavors
quite so hard as his
predecessors, but his
slightly more relaxed
approach pays high
dividends in subtlety
and substance. David
Moore, who has
survived the passing of
chefs, holds the front
of house together with
style and good humor.*
⊞

TOP ETHNIC RESTAURANTS

THE CINNAMON CLUB
The Old Westminster
Library, 30 Great Smith St
W1 Tel. 020 7222 2555
www.cinnamonclub.com
Closed Sat lunch; Sun
*Smooth as a pukka
sahib. Situated in the
old Westminster
Library it has kept on
the old paneling, some
of the books and the
air of studious calm.
New wave Indian
cookery, but none the
worse, or even, all the
better for that.
Delicate use of spices,
controlled exuberance
in the sauce
department, allied to
distinctly Western
traditions of plate
artistry (expertise
supplied by Eric Chavot
of The Capital).
Rumored to be moving
toward further Indian/
European fusion.*
■

HAKKASAN
8 Hanway Place, W1
Tel. 020 7927 7000
*The sexiest restaurant
in London, at the end
of a worryingly mean-
street alley. Brilliant
design, brilliant*

For **hotels**, the price bands are for a double room with en-suite bathroom for one night:
⊡ = up to £40; ⊡ = £40–£80; ⊞ = £80–120,
⊞ = over £112
For advice on finding a hotel, see also page 484

lighting, brilliant vibe. Service becomes part of the elaborate mise en scene. The brain child of Alan Yau, the man behind Wagamama, Hakkasan is at the other end of the scale of restaurant eating. The dim sum at lunch are quite possibly the best in London. The à la carte Chinese and Western-influenced (Chinese New Wave?) food is not far behind. Big cocktail list. There is also a deafeningly patronized bar. Hot spot – must book.
⊡

LOCANDA LOCATELLI
8 Seymour St, W1
Tel. 020 7935 9088
www.locandalocatelli.com
Closed Sun
Giorgio Locatelli was the king of the kitchen when Zafferano was the finest Italian restaurant in London. Now he has his own place, tacked onto the side of the Churchill Hotel. Senior retro-chic design by über-designer David Collins, reassuringly smooth service, classy Italian wine list, and Giorgio's stunning, French-influenced, indubitably Italian food. Flavor in all the right places. Rightly hailed by the critics. No wonder it is one of the most difficult London restaurants to get into.
⊞

MORO
34-36 Exmouth Market, EC1 Tel. 020 7833 8336
www.moro.co.uk
Closed Sat lunch; Sun
Sam and Sam Clarke (husband and wife) are largely responsible for giving a fashionable lick to the food of North Africa and Spain. Open-plan kitchen, modish, laid-back decor, long bar for tapas, plus formidable range of sherries. The food has a terrific, tastebud-tingling

appeal based on super-lative basic ingredients and a deft feel for how to combine them to bring the best out of them. Best bread in London.
⊡

ROYAL CHINA
24-26 Baker St, W1
Tel. 020 7847 4688
www.royalchinagroup.co.uk
It's surprising there aren't more top-class Chinese restaurants, given their overall numbers. The black mirrored and gold Royal China is consistently one of the best, particularly for dim sum. Big menu of Cantonese and Szechuan dishes produced with unusual delicacy and balanced flavors. Sister branches at 13 Queensway, W2 (Tel. 020 7221 2535), 68 Queen's Grove, NW8 (Tel. 020 7586 4280), 30 West Ferry Circus, E14 (Tel. 020 7719 0888).
⊡

TAMARIND
20 Queen St, W1
Tel. 020 7629 3561
www.tamarindrestaurant.com
Closed Sat lunch
Among the first Indian to move expectations up market in terms of food, decor, service and price. It would have to be in moneyed Mayfair, and why should top-class Indian food cost any less than French or Italian food of the same quality? North Indian cooking of Alfred Prasad balances fire with flavor and serious, sophisticated delicacy. Formal service and an intelligent wine list makes a good case for interesting food/wine matches.
⊡

ZAIKA
1 Kensington High St, W8 Tel. 020 7795 6533
www.zaika-restaurant.co.uk

Closed Sat lunch
Produces some of the most interesting food in London of whatever nationality. Happens to be Indian, but not of the slavishly authentic variety. Each dish is an object lesson in technical intelligence allied to superb taste. Spicing in particular is a joy, pointed but never excessive, fresh but not frenzied. The design of the place sympathetically matches classic Indian details with contem-porary metropolitan restaurant design. Lunch a mega-bargain (£10 for two courses, £12 for three courses).
⊡

CLASSIC INTERIORS

BELVEDERE
Holland Park (off Abbotsbury Rd), W8
Tel. 020 7602 1238
www.whitestarline.org.uk
Closed Sun eve
Yet another London landmark brought back to life by Marco Pierre White. Neo-classical splendor in bosky Holland Park Gardens; like a glorious summerhouse complete with vaulting ceiling and large scale picture windows to let the light flood in.The food follows MPW's tried and tested formula of the grand classics of French bourgeois cooking done with panache, plus a few dishes with a more contemporary feel. All the other bits and bobs – napkins, glass, tableware – are heavy gravity; wine list also has a certain weight to it (and its pricing), and the service is usually pretty crisp.
⊡

THE CRITERION
Piccadilly Circus, W1
Tel. 020 7930 0488
Closed Sun
Another outpost of Marco Pierre White's empire. He has rightly

been praised for creating this mighty monument to the Victorian fascination for the more imaginary exoticism of the Ottoman Empire. It is a Victorian vision of a Turkish seraglio, all mosaic, gilt and marble, built on the scale of a small railway station. The food is another level of clever reworkings of French bourgeois/brasserie classics, with an occasional wild card dish thrown in.
⊡

THE RITZ
150 Piccadilly, W1
Tel. 020 7493 8181
www.theritzlondon.com
The masterpiece of Cesar Ritz and Auguste Escoffier. The dining room has lost none of the beauty of its 19th-century homage to 18th-century design ideals. The ceiling is still lofty, the tall windows flood the place with light, the pinks and blues and golds of the wall and ceiling decorations are as fresh as ever (thanks to recent renovation). The kitchen has never quite aspired to these heights, but the food has a distinctive classical heft and a substantial elegance – like the service.
⊞

RULES
35 Maiden Lane, WC2
Tel. 020 7836 5314
www.rules.co.uk
It claims to be the oldest restaurant in London, and at first sight Rules seems to be caught in a time warp, all Edwardian illustrations, discrete dining areas, cigar smoke and clubby camraderie. On closer inspection it turns out to be a clever disguise for a model, modern watering hole, with serious cooking from Dick Sawyer using best British ingredients

For the **restaurants**, the following price bands have been used, according to the price of a two-course meal (without wine):
■ = up to £15; ■ = £15–£20
■ = £20–£30; ⊞ = £30 and over

(Aberdeen Angus beef, game in season etc). A short, intelligent, well priced wine list (and fixed priced lunch) and crisp service.
■

AL WAHA
75 Westbourne Grove, W2 Tel. 020 7229 0806
www.waha-uk.com
Al Waha might not get too many marks for original decor, although it's smart and comfortable, but it will always score highly for the excellence of its food. Classic Lebanese stuff. Modest lunchers can make do with a selection of top grade mezze. More serious eaters may like to explore the more exotic sections of the menu devoted to grills. The service is always ready to help and explain. A glass or two of stylish, hefty Lebanese wines ease any rights of passage.
■

ANDREW EDMUNDS
46 Lexington St, W1
Tel. 020 7437 5708
Much loved restaurant in miniature, an ebullient offspring of the print gallery next door. Modern European again, with vim and vigor. Short menu which changes daily. Terrific wine list. Popular and packed like a cheerful, egalitarian club.

GEALE'S
2 Farmer St, W8
Tel. 020 7727 7969
Classic fish and chippie all done up with loving care and back to serving hunks of fab fresh fish and chips as they should be, all golden and chunky. Eat in or take away. And a proper wine list as well as heavy-duty tea if you have a mind.
■

INCOGNICO
117 Shaftesbury Ave, Cambridge Circus, WC2
Tel. 020 7836 8866
www.incognico.com
The old master, Nico Ladenis, is actually resident in the South of France, but his spirit lives on in Shaftesbury Avenue, albeit in a rather cheaper form than the more famous eponymous restaurant of his heyday. The menu, which he supervises, is studded with French classics, produced with the famous attention to depth of flavors, supercharged sauces and all the rest. The dining room is smart and friendly. The staff are smart and friendly and the set price lunch is one of the bargains of the decade.
■

POPESEYE
108 Blythe Rd, W14
Tel. 020 7610 4578
Open evenings only; closed Sun eve
Basic stuff. Just top-class steaks grilled with absolute precision and served with utter simplicity and great quality chips. There's a bit more to it than that, such as a short but brilliant wine list with wines of a vintage, pedigree and reasonable price you won't find elsewhere. Also at 277 Upper Richmond Rd, SW15 (Tel. 020 8788 7733).
■

ST JOHN
26 St John St, EC1
Tel. 020 7251 0848
www.stjohnrestaurant.com
Closed Sat lunch; Sun
Chef's favorite, critics favorite, offal lovers' favorite. Fergus Henderson has turned this highly individual, stark, canteen-like space into a place of pilgrimage for anyone seriously interested in the contemporary eating. The food is plain but perfect

(mostly). The restaurant's motto 'Nose to Tail Eating' is slightly exaggerated, but it may be the only place in the country to have squirrel on the menu occasionally. The point is that it is very good squirrel, very well cooked.
■

ALMEIDA
30 Almeida St, N1
Tel. 020 7354 4777
www.conran-restaurants.co.uk
A pretty stylish place this is. Brasserie in the modern style, all calm creams and beiges. The service and food are supervised by the team at Orrery (see page 514), and the emphasis is on bistro staples. There's even a trolley laden with pates, terrines and rillettes etc, all produced with considerable eclat and authenticity. The service is brisk and the bill sometimes defies the value for money edict but it usually depends on how much you drink. Quiet at lunch, bustling at night.
■

BANK ALDWYCH
1 Kingsway, WC2
Tel. 020 7379 9797
www.bankrestaurants.com
Big, bustling, glass, stainless steel, mirrors and murals brasserie in the modern style. Food generally a very reliable mix of standard and well-worked new dishes. Service crisp. Price: medium to expensive (depending how much you drink). Good value fixed price lunch. Much liked by men and women in suits.
■

THE EAGLE
159 Farringdon Rd, EC1
Tel. 020 7837 1353
The first of the gastro-pubs, and in many

ways still the best. Smart but laid-back young professional customers seem to think so because they pack in in big numbers lunchtime and evening. Basic Mediterranean fare, with emphasis on Spain and Portugal. Lots of grills, mountainous salads and the finest steak sandwich in town. A few well-chosen wines and beers.
■

KENSINGTON PLACE
201-209 Kensington Church St, W8
Tel. 020 7727 3184
www.egami.co.uk
The original London brasserie all of 15 years old and still in classic form in spite of having changed hands – thanks to old hands staying on to greet the many regulars, and to the inspirational menu direction and cooking of wily Rowley Leigh. He is a stickler for great ingredients and sensible, terrific-tasting European cooking. Good wine list. Very good value set price lunch.
■

MIRABELLE
56 Curzon St, W1
Tel; 020 7499 4636
Another Marco Pierre White makeover, this time giving an elegant modern gloss to an upmarket old timer in Mayfair. High-quality tablecloths, napkins, glasses, cutlery and so forth, help to create the gravity of old-style class. The food is MPW's usual and dependable clever retro-classics over which he has waved a renovating wand. Remarkable wine list. And value-for-money fixed-price lunch.
■

NOURA
16 Hobart Place, SW1
Tel. 020 7235 9444

For **hotels**, the price bands are for a double room
with en-suite bathroom for one night:
▣ = up to £40; ▣ = £40–£80; ▣ = £80–120,
▦ = over £120
For advice on finding a hotel, see also page 484

www.noura.co.uk
Here's a novelty – a
Lebanese brasserie.
And it works very well.
Big, open space, as
sleek and chic as any
around. Burly waiters
look like enforcers,
but are crisp and
professional about
their business. Some
of the best bread in
London, hot and puffy
from the oven appears
regularly throughout
a meal. Hot and cold
mezze are very reliable
and help keep the
costs down, but
kebabs, fish and other
grills are also premier
division stuff. Lebanese
wines priced higher
than elsewhere, but
are very drinkable.
▣

CLASSIC HOTELS

CAPITAL HOTEL
22-24 Basil St, SW3
Tel. 020 7589 5171
www.capitalhotel.co.uk
Small but perfectly
formed privately
owned hotel situated
just behind Harrods.
Essence of stylish
good taste through-
out, with efficient,
knowledgeable and
friendly staff. The
hotel restaurant has
just come into highly
rated hands of Eric
Chavot, whose previous
form suggests tasty
and tasteful modern
French cooking.
▣/▦

**GORDON RAMSAY
AT CLARIDGE'S**
Brook St, Mayfair, W1
Tel. 020 7629 8860
www.gordonramsay.com
The suave old charmer
tends to get forgotten
in assessments of
London's hotel glory.
Recently awakened
from a deep, but
sumptuous, sleep by
the arrival of Gordon
Ramsay, or rather his
team, who have turned
the dining room,
revitalizing the kitchen
and the profile of the
hotel at the same time.
The menu is packed
with Ramsay dishes,

delivered with crisp
style, if not quite the
attention to detail as
the Master's own
kitchen; but then they
are feeding many more
mouths. So many more,
indeed, that you may
have to book as much
as two months ahead
if you want the highly
desirable fixed price
lunch.
▣/▦

THE HALKIN
5 Halkin St, SW1
Tel. 020 7333 1234
www.halkin.co.uk
Closed for lunch
Sat & Sun
Bijou boutique in quiet
Belgravia. Slickly
dressed staff; cool
dude lines of interior;
modern comforts out
of the top drawer; and
Nahm, where David
Thompson, Aussie
megastar, turns out the
best Thai food in
London, or quite
possibly anywhere else
for that matter. Dishes
are amazingly labor
intensive, not that you
would know in the
calm of the rather
cosmopolitanly neutral
dining room; but the
results are revelatory –
clean, precise, multi-
dimensional. Not for
cheap eats.
▦/▦

THE METROPOLITAN
19 Old Park Lane,
W1
Tel. 020 7447 1047
www.metropolitan.co.uk
All the surfaces are
smooth, minimalist,
glossy, curved and
immaculate. So are the
staff. Fashion-driven
hotel that draws
perma-tanned A-list
celebs and inter-
national high flyers.
The restaurant is called
Nobu and is the
London end of New
York original; kind of
East meets West and
the rest of the world
in innovative, highly
praised fish-based
menu. Wine list made
to match.
▦/▦

ST MARTINS
45 St Martins Lane, WC2
Tel. 020 7300 5500
www.morganshotelgroup.
com
An instant hit. Much
talked about Ian
Shrager/Philippe Starck
laying down a new
benchmark for London
hotel design. Soothing
white bedrooms which
change color according
to lighting and mood.
Smoothly friendly staff.
The restaurant, Asia de
Cuba, has raised an
eyebrow or two for its
innovative approach to
constructing a meal.
▦/▦

LONDON FRINGES

RESTAURANTS

REDMONDS
170 Upper Richmond Rd
West, SW14
Tel. 020 8878 1922
www.redmonds.org.uk
Closed Mon-Sat lunch;
Sun eve
Classic neighborhood
restaurant. Husband
and wife team,
Redmond and Pippa
Hayward, are one of
the ultra-reliable teams
in the business. She
runs the front of house
with a light and lively
hand. He cooks food
that may not be
exactly cutting edge,
but which invariably
you want to eat. Its
heart is in Europe, with
a leaning toward the
Med, but it is lit up by
occasional flashes of
the Middle and further
East. Excellent cheese
board firmly located in
Britain and Ireland.
▣

RIVA
169 Church Rd, Barnes
Tel. 020 8748 0434
Closed Sat lunch
Andrea Riva is one
of the finest
restaurateurs in the
country. He rarely, if
ever, misses a lunch or
dinner. He is the
presiding spirit, genial,
urbane, charming and
energetic in an

understated fashion.
The restaurant is small
and personal, and the
long-serving chef,
Francesco Zanchetta,
produces highly
flavored dishes
drawing on the ingre-
dients and techniques
of Northern Italy.
Model wine list.
▣

LA TROMPETTE
5-7 Devonshire Rd, W4
Tel. 020 8747 1836
www.latrompette.co.uk
Classy, sharp, smooth
and well run, slightly
formal, though relaxed
atmosphere. The food
– by owner/chef Olivier
Couillaud – is very well
produced, slightly to
gutsy side of the
middle-of-the-road,
Eurocentric; and very
pleasing it is too.
Model wine list at
ungrasping prices.
Altogether worth
visiting Chiswick for.
Or even living there.
▣

WHITE HORSE
14 Worple Way,
Richmond, Surrey
Tel. 020 8940 2418
www.fullers.co.uk
Tucked away in a little
lane a short walk from
Richmond Station, the
White Horse is a model
for a pub that serves
intelligent, precisely
cooked food in the
modern European vein.
Drinkers will feel just
as at home as eaters,
particularly if they like
Fuller's beers or any-
thing from the short
but discerning wine
list. The interior is
pleasingly unmucked-
about-with and
handsome, and the
prices reasonable.
▣

SOUTH EAST
(KENT, SUSSEX, ISLE OF WIGHT)

RESTAURANTS

36 ON THE QUAY
47 South Street,
Emsworth, Hants
Tel. 01243 375592

For the **restaurants**, the following price bands have been used, according to the price of a two-course meal (without wine):
🔳 = up to £15; 🔳 = £15–£20
🔳 = £20–£30; ⊞ = £30 and over

www.thirtysixonthequay.co.uk
Closed Sat-Mon lunch; Sun eve
Time your visit for fair weather and enjoy drinks in the courtyard garden overlooking Chichester harbor. Winter guests can be warmed by the cozy Mediterranean interior, and settle in while meals are prepared to order by chef/proprietor Ramon Farthing. The wait – to which the menu alerts the impatient – is well worth it (the place has a Michelin star after all), for dishes that are complicated and ambitious, and which usually hit the mark. Service is relaxed, but so will you be.
🔳

CIRCA
145 High St,
Lewes, East Sussex
Tel. 01273 471777
www.circacirca.com
Modern-looking Circa might not attract much attention in London, Leeds or Manchester but in the curlicued, streets of tasteful red brick Lewes it makes something of a statement. The cooking is characterized by knockabout, knockout flavors. It is difficult to ascribe the dishes to this tradition or that. There's a bit of everywhere interpreted in terms of British eating habits. Many of the ingredients and cooking techniques are Oriental, but the dishes are constructed along the unmistakable meat-with-sauce-and-two-veg lines that we know and love.
🔳

DEW POND
Old Burghclere, Hants
Tel. 01635 278408
www.dewpond.co.uk
Open evenings only;
Closed Sun & Mon eve
Elegantly respectable and cozy restaurant on the Hampshire/

Berkshire borders that's been in business for ten years, which says something for its ability to satisfy local demand. The cooking is firmly in the French camp, leavened with a lightness of touch and a deftness with flavors. The wine list favors the same country, and the service has charm. The quality and the price are in tandem – highish in both cases.
🔳

DOVE
Plum Pudding Lane,
Dargate, Kent
Tel. 01227 751360
Closed Mon lunch;
Tue & Sun eve
More restaurant than pub, but so it should be with cooking of some finesse. Bare tables, bare floorboards and photos of the Dove in years gone by establish a suitably informal note, and Nigel Morris's cooking has the same no-nonsense approach. It's essence is English. That's not to say that it's without subtley and sophistication, but flavor comes first. So it should. Keep an eye out for bargains on the wine list.
🔳

ONE PASTON PLACE
Brighton, East Sussex
Tel. 01273 606933
www.onepastonplace.co.uk
Closed Sun & Mon
What with the sea practically splashing in the front door, you'd expect fish to take pride of place on the menu. Actually, Paston Place is something of a rarity in the UK – a seaside restaurant that treats seafood seriously. Expect plenty of flavors on an up-to-the-minute menu, including some unusual pairings – scallops with a ragout of pig's trotters and lentils, for example – and clever use of

seasonal foods in a bright and breezy setting. Save room for pudding.
🔳

GRIFFIN INN
Fletching, East Sussex
Tel. 01825 722890
www.thegriffininn.co.uk
To step out of the glare of a hot Sussex day (or the gray damp of a winter day, come to that) into the cool, civilized crepuscular interior of the Griffin is to experience something close to nirvana. Brilliant beer, beautifully kept. Intelligent mostly Francofile cooking. Good wine list. Large garden at back with superb views over Downs. Deservedly popular.
🔳

PREZZO
21 Palmerston St,
Romsey, Hants
Tel. 01794 517353
www.prezzoplc.co.uk
One of a chain of restaurants where design and food are of equal importance. Where possible, outlets are located in beautifully restored, impressive buildings or buildings of local interest. This stunning premises was formerly an old manor house. As the name would suggest, the food on offer is Italian in style, with dishes ranging from a selection of pasta and pizza to fresh roast chicken, grills and homemade burgers.
🔳 / 🔳

READ'S
Macknade Manor,
Canterbury Rd,
Faversham, Kent
Tel. 01795 535344
www.reads.com
Closed Sun & Mon
After 24 years at Painter's Forstal, Faversham, the Pitchfords up and offed a few hundred yards away to a

restaurant with (very comfortable) rooms. The cooking retains the same high quality (and its Michelin star), rooted in France and based on immaculately sourced, usually local, ingredients. It's unshowy stuff, but it delivers true flavors with real finesse. Let's hope they stay another 24 years at the new gaff.
🔳/🔳

SAWYARDS
Manleys Hill,
Storrington, West Sussex
Tel. 01903 742331
www.sawyards.com
Closed Mon; Tue lunch;
Sun eve
Classic French cuisine served in a fine English brick-and-stone building dating from 1730. Three beautifully decorated dining areas, two of which feature wooden pillars and beams and one of which boasts an brick inglenook fireplace. The daily changing menu prides itself on the quality of the ingredients used, many of which are locally sourced. Dishes include starters such as terrine of roast chicken, foie gras and wild mushrooms, and main courses such as brill with lemongrass sauce and ratatouille millefeuille with eggplant sauce. Good wine list.
🔳

SIMPLY POUSSIN
The Courtyard,
Brookley Rd,
Brockenhurst, Hants
Tel. 01590 623063
www.simplypoussin.co.uk
Closed Sun & Mon
A Grail for the mycophage, or mushroom lover as we'd better call them. Actually there is a great deal more to Le Poussin than just mushrooms. Chef & proprietor Alex Aitken has a keen nose for all manner of top-notch local ingredients, many

For **hotels**, the price bands are for a double room
with en-suite bathroom for one night:
▣ = up to £40; ▣ = £40–£80; ▣ = £80–120,
▦ = over £120
For advice on finding a hotel, see also page 484

of them organic, which
he transforms with
a deft and highly
individual hand. A
good deal of thought
goes into the mighty
wine list too, ringing
the changes on the
house wine front.
Atmosphere is cozy
and intimate in a quiet
dining room with only
the occasional visual
reference to the
eponymous bird.
▣

TERRE A TERRE
71 East Street, Brighton,
East Sussex
Tel. 01273 729051
www.terreaterre.co.uk
Closed Mon; Tue &
Wed lunch
Vegetable heaven.
Indeed, one of the
few categorically
vegetarian restaurants
in Britain where the
dedicated carnivore
can eat and not be
profoundly
disappointed. That's
because the dishes
serve up flavor and
texture to an unusual
degree. The world is
plundered for
ingredients and
cooking techniques,
and the results piled
high in the plate with
colorful bravura. This is
excellent eating by any
standards; and the
crowds flocking to the
easy, breezy dining
room bear witness.
▣

THREE LIONS
Stuckton Road,
Stuckton, Hants
Tel. 01425 652489
www.thethreelions
restaurant.co.uk
Good things tend to
happen when a
talented chef with a
talented wife like Mike
and Jayne Womersley
take over old pubs.
Things get done
properly, sauces made
well, meat and veg
cooked with precision.
Don't be fooled by the
laid-back blackboard
menu – cooking here is
serious and assured,
with unfussy, intensely

flavored dishes
drawing on quality
local ingredients
(mushrooms, game,
fish). Potent puddings,
too. Pricier than pub
lunches, but furlongs
ahead in terms of
quality, and the wine
list has some absolute
bargains. There are
bedrooms too.
▣ / ▣

**WEST HOUSE
RESTAURANT**
28 High St,
Biddenden, Kent
Tel. 01580 291341
Closed Mon; Sat lunch;
Sun eve
Graham Garrett's
menu uses local
produce to create his
modern British/modern
European fare with a
distinctly seasonal
flavor. Typical dishes
include salmon with
honey-mustard
dressing, plum tomato,
goat's cheese tart with
caramelized onions
and noisettes of lamb
with apricot and
almond stuffing.
▣

**WHITSTABLE OYSTER
FISHERY CO**
Royal Native Oyster
Stores, The Horsebridge,
Whitstable, Kent
Tel. 01227 276856
www.oysterfishery.co.uk
Closed Mon
Something of a
character. This
converted boathouse
has had a Royal
Charter to serve oysters
since 1862 and
continues to dish up
simple, untampered-
with seafood to this
day, and top-dog
oysters, natch. Quirky
anti-decor – walls are
bare and floorboards
scrubbed. Similar
sensible reluctance to
mess around with the
flavor of the fish
pulled fresh from the
sea just along the
shingle beach outside
the window. Choice is
limited by seasons and
availability. Veg can be
dodgy and the wine
list is perfunctory, but

the fish is fresh and
usually faultless, and
that's the whole reason
to come here.
▣

CHEWTON GLEN
Christchurch Road,
New Milton, Hants
Tel. 01425 275341
www.chewtonglen.com
Chewton Glen, hard by
a corner of the New
Forest, has just grown
over the years in
resources and stature.
Now it represents the
acme of country house
luxury, what with
health clubs, golf
courses and the like.
There's food for the
faddist, although the
fully committed eat at
the Marryat restaurant.
Fish takes top billing
on this menu, though
there's enough for the
traditionalist to get his
or her teeth into.
Vegetarian options are
given proper
consideration, and
scaled-down dishes are
on offer for those with
an eye on the waistline
and the health club.
The wine list has an
encyclopedic quality,
with good-value
choices at all levels.
Service on a par with
the luxurious
surroundings.
▣ / ▦

EASTWELL MANOR
Eastwell Park,
Boughton Lees, Kent
Tel. 01233 213000
www.eastwellmanor.co.uk
Grand Victorian manor
house complete with
battlements. The
restaurant is both
grand and imposing,
service reassuringly
grand, and dishes
traditionally domed.
The French food (and
grand wine list) follows
in the same pretty
grand vein – few
surprises, but plenty of
simple yet effective
dishes, with luxuries a
regular feature. A bit
of gueridon work –
carving at the table –
adds to the theater.

Fixed price lunch and
dinner menus offer
good value.
▣ / ▦

GEORGE HOTEL
Quay Street,
Yarmouth, Isle of Wight
Tel. 01983 760331
www.thegeorge.co.uk
Handsome is as
handsome does, and
the George Hotel is
handsome, inside as
well as out. Built in the
late 17th century as a
home for the islands
governor (who would
probably have
welcomed the 21st-
century creature
comforts now on
understated display),
it is now arguably the
best eaterie on the isle.
The restaurant is smart
and formal, with a
generous sprinkling
of luxury ingredients
on a serious menu.
The cooking is pretty
classical and French in
its foundations, but
there's a good deal of
chef Kevin Mangoelles'
own vision on view
too, with a confident
handling of powerful
flavors. There is a
cheaper and less
formal brasserie,
with spot-on family-
oriented grub. Service
at both is friendly and
patient.
▣ / ▦

GRAVETYE MANOR
Vowels Lane, East
Grinstead, West Sussex
Tel. 01342 810567
www.gravetyemanor.co.uk
Gravetye Manor is a
stunning Elizabethan
mansion house set in
beautiful surrounds,
and now under the
ownership of Andrew
Russell and Mark
Raffan. The Michelin
starred, oak-paneled
restaurant offers
traditional English/
French fare using fresh
local produce. There
are two menus on
offer; a daily three-
course table d'hôte
menu and a seasonal
three-course menu.
▣ / ▣

◆ HOTELS AND RESTAURANTS

For the **restaurants**, the following price bands have been used, according to the price of a two-course meal (without wine):
■ = up to £15; ■ = £15–£20
■ = £20–£30; ⊞ = £30 and over

HOTEL DU VIN & BISTRO
14 Southgate St, Winchester, Hants
Tel. 01962 841414
www.hotelduvin.com
There's more than a touch of genteel elegance about this converted town house, and quite right too; Winchester is that kind of place. But it avoids pomposity in its hoteliering and cooking, with an ambitious menu long on Mediterranean influences rendered in a cheerful bistro style. Both clientele and staff are smart but relaxed. It's worth loosening the wallet restraints for the wine, which is a majestic selection, as you might expect if you knew that one of the co-proprietors, Gerard Basset, is an award-winning sommelier. Outposts in Henley-on-Thames, Tunbridge Wells, Brighton, Bristol and Birmingham.
■ / ■

QUEEN'S ROOM
Amberley Castle, Amberley, West Sussex
Tel. 01798 831992
www.amberleycastle.co.uk
Past the strolling peacocks and the working portcullis is an authentic medieval castle and a luxury hotel and restaurant strewn with suits of armor for the real historical experience. Menus dip a toe into the modern but those seeking a bit of Olde English indulgence will be satisfied with dishes such as pike in water souchy sauce. Dinner is a grand six-course affair with appropriately stiff service; lunch a speedier – and cheaper option.
■ / ⊞

SANDGATE HOTEL
Wellington Terrace, The Esplanade, Sandgate, Kent
Tel. 01303 220444
www.sandgatehotel.com
The Sandgate hotel is situated opposite a pebble beach with magnificent sea views. New owner and chef Stephen Piddock offers a menu of seasonal international cuisine. Menu includes dishes such as crab and asparagus lasagne with saffron butter sauce, noisettes of Romney marsh lamb with minted pea puree and garlic and thyme jus and corn-fed chicken with parma ham and spinach risotto.
■ / ■

SOUTH WEST
(DORSET, WILTSHIRE, SOMERSET)
RESTAURANTS

GEORGE AND DRAGON
High Street, Rowde, Wilts
Tel. 01380 723053
Closed Sun eve; Mon lunch
Gastropub as it should be, with the perfect combination of high-quality cooking and down-to-earth atmosphere. Olde worlde beams and very much of-this-world contemporary fish and seafood dishes chalked up unpretentiously on a blackboard. Beer and wines are excellent and prices don't wander too high. A classic of its kind, and classy with it.
■

THE PRIORY HOUSE RESTAURANT
1 High St, Stoke sub Hamdon, Somerset
Tel: 01935 822826
www.prioryhouse.co.uk
S sub H is a pretty, straggly kind of village not far from Yeovil, and the Priory House occupies the corner between the v of two streets. The restaurant, now under the ownership of husband and wife team Peter and Sonia Brooks, is pretty, well lit,

unpretentious and comfortable.
■

QUARTIER VERT
85 Whiteladies Rd, Bristol
Tel. 0117 973 4482
www.quartiervert.co.uk
Closed Sun eve in winter
Very jolly place, with a great shaft of Mediterranean sunlight, both deliberately evoked and metaphorical, lighting it up. Part tapas bar, part more serious (but still pretty informal) restaurant. Spanish influences are pronounced, but most of the Med gets a look in, the quality of flavors helped by very careful sourcing of ingredients, many of them organic. Very popular, with distinctly studentish overtones. Fair prices and good wines.
■

HOTELS

BISHOPSTROW HOUSE
Warminster, Wilts
Tel. 01985 212312
www.bishopstrowhouse.co.uk
The epitome of what metropolitan man and woman want from a civilized weekend out of town. Rose garlanded and garden girt, complete with gin-clear river for fishing. Other, more contemporary mod cons, too, such as indoor pool, gym, spa & tennis courts to ease away the tensions of modern living or fight the flab put on with easeful food in the dining room. Emphasis on comfort all round, in fact; but how many people actually read the books in the library?
⊞ / ⊞

CASTLE HOTEL
Castle Green, Taunton, Somerset
Tel: 01823 272671
www.the-castle-hotel.com
Restaurant closed

Sun eve
Creeper-clad creation of several generations of the Chapman family. The present pater familias, Kit, has propelled The Castle to the top of the hotel tree, partly by continual discrete upgrading of interior, and partly by championing champion British chefs – Chris Oakes, Gary Rhodes, Phil Vickery all got a start here. Now is the turn of Richard Guest to fly the flag for imaginatively modernised British cooking. Clearly his is another star turn, and has been rewarded by Michelin recognition.
■ / ■

CHARLTON HOUSE HOTEL
Charlton Rd, Shepton Mallet, Somerset
Tel. 01749 342008
www.charltonhouse.com
Oh, to be in England – and places don't come much more English than Charlton House, owned by the founders of Mulberry. Fabrics, furnishings, fixtures and fittings, all breathe the air of Mulberry's England (and if that's not enough, the factory shop is a stroll away). The Mulberry restaurant, though, has a more to-the-minute European feel, unstuffy and willing to use a variety of flavors and a healthy dollop of imagination. Vegetarian dishes show care, as does the wine list. Staff are chatty and helpful. There is a wonderful spa, too, should you feel the need to detress.
■ / ⊞

HOMEWOOD PARK
Hinton Charterhouse, Somerset
Tel. 01225 723731
www.homewoodpark.com
Tranquility, quiet, peace, comfort,

For **hotels**, the price bands are for a double room
with en-suite bathroom for one night:
▣ = up to £40; ▣= £40–£80; ▣ = £80–120,
▦ = over £120
For advice on finding a hotel, see also page 484

assurance – if that's
what you're looking
for then settle right
back and enjoy the
treat here. There's
nothing (except,
possibly, the bill) to
disturb or ruffle the
soul. Just work up
enough of an appetite
to enjoy some bold
and assured Michelin-
starred cooking.
Modern British dishes
presented with French
technical precision.
Staff are of a similar
Anglo-French mix, and
the service is highly
professional.
▣ / ▦

HOWARD HOUSE
Teffont Evias,
nr Salisbury, Wilts
Tel. 01722 716392
Restaurant closed
Mon lunch; Fri
www.howardshousehotel.
co.uk
A model of tranquil
civility, from the
creeper-clad exterior
through the orderly
garden, the soothing
fountain to the cool
elegance of the
interior. The cooking,
likewise, concentrates
on the essentials,
getting the ingredients
to speak up for
themselves with
apparent simplicity
(restraint of this kind is
only achieved by a
great deal of hard
work). Hold back for
the puddings and
travel widely through
the wine list.
▣ / ▦

**LITTLE BARWICK
HOUSE**
Barwick, Somerset
Tel. 01935 423902
www.littlebarwickhouse.
co.uk
Restaurant closed
Mon; Tue lunch; Sun eve
If you've survived in
business for 20 years,
you're obviously doing
something right.
Little Barwick House
is a small, warm,
comfortable, family-
run hotel. Tim and
Emma Ford are turning
out classy dishes in

keeping with our
gastro-curious times in
the high-toned, high-
ceilinged dining room.
Service is charming and
welcoming. Wine
list of exemplary
intelligence.
▣ / ▦

LUCKNAM PARK
Colerne, Wiltshire
Tel. 01225 742777
www.lucknampark.co.uk
Restaurant closed Mon-
Sat for lunch
Another monument to
the magnificence of
our country house
heritage. The
handsome Palladian
mansion in 500 acres
now caters for a
largely corporate
crowd, but gastro-
travelers can bypass
the conference suites
and head straight for
the chandeliered
restaurant, formerly
the ballroom, for some
finely judged food. No
real surprises on this
menu (unless you
count the occasional
Eastern spicing), but
plenty of gourmet
goodies to please the
palate. On the pricey
side.
▦ / ▦

MANOR HOUSE
Castle Comb,
Chippenham, Wilts
Tel. 01249 782206
www.exclusivehotels.co.uk
Grand – that's the
word that springs to
mind as you enter the
266-acre estate, with
its 18-hole champion-
ship golf course and
the manor house with
700 years of history.
Grand goes for the
food too, but it's well
considered grand, with
some complex and
interesting
combinations. Bills
tend to be on a grand
scale, too. Lunch
menus offer a cheaper
way for commoners to
indulge. Service is
charming if a touch
formal. Well-stocked
wine list for those with
a well-stocked wallet.
▦ / ▦

**OLIVE TREE AT THE
QUEENSBURY HOTEL**
Russell Street, Bath
Tel. 01225 447928
www.thequeensbury.co.uk
Restaurant closed
Mon lunch
Regency meets Tuscan
in this modernized
Bath town house
hotel, a popular
combination judging
by the local following
– it is so busy that
hotel residents need to
make reservations in
advance. Menus
change frequently,
sophisticated
Mediterranean dishes
are central and old
favorites, such as
Provençale fish soup,
never stay away for
long. Light and stylish
basement setting;
service is just as bright.
▣ / ▦

STOCK HILL HOUSE
Stock Hill,
Gillingham, Dorset
Tel. 01747 823626
www.stockhillhouse.co.uk
Lush, that's the word.
There's plenty of lush
about Stock Hill House
– and luxury, and
attention to detail.
The Hausers have been
here for 15 years, and
they know what
they're about. Lush
might not be the word
you would
immediately apply to
Austrian cooking, but
under Peter Hauser's
knowing hand, and
with a bit of help from
the rest of Europe
now, Austrian cooking
takes on an altogether
more sophisticated
gloss. Dumplings and
native bread pop up in
various guises and the
country also features
strongly on the wine
list. The kitchen
garden of this large
Victorian house is put
to good use.
Atmosphere is calm,
service unruffled.
▦ / ▦

SUMMER LODGE
Summer Lane,
Evershot, Dorset
Tel. 01935 83424

www.summerlodgehotel.
com
An idyllic setting, this
hotel, former dower
house of the Earls of
Ilchester, offers a
down-to-earth family-
run service with some
high-class cooking.
Chef Stephen Titman
prepares and cooks
every dish to order,
with quiet, unshowy
confidence. Despite
the sophistication of
the food the
atmosphere remains
homely; staff are
friendly and efficient.
Worth a visit just for
the afternoon tea.
▣ / ▦

WOOLLEY GRANGE
Woolley Green, nr
Bradford-upon-Avon,
Wilts
Tel. 01225 864705
www.woolleygrange.com
A rarity in Britain – a
hotel that goes out of
its way to make
children particularly
welcome and to cater
to their needs, such as
recognizing that they
may eat at different
times from their
parents. Caters to the
needs of grown-ups
too pretty well by way
of creature comforts,
and produces pretty
grown-up food in
the modern European
mold. Luxurious
and fun.
▣ / ▦

22 MILL STREET
22 Mill St,
Chagford, Devon
Tel. 01647 432244
Closed Sun; Mon &
Tue lunch
Why tiny Chagford
should be blessed with
two exceptionally fine
restaurants is
something of a
mystery, although they
could scarcely be more
different. 22 Mill
Street has the cozy,
intimate charm of a
small-scale enterprise –

For the **restaurants**, the following
price bands have been used, according to
the price of a two-course meal (without wine)
■ = up to £15; ■ = £15–£20
■ = £20–£30; ⊞ = £30 and over

the restaurant only seats thirty – but the food is of a quality that ensures those tables are fully booked. The menu poetry is austere and understated when compared to the assurance and brilliance of Duncan Walker's Eurocentric cooking. Wine list has been chosen with care and is unintimidating.
■

MICHAEL CAINES
Royal Clarence Hotel
Cathedral Yard,
Exeter, Devon
Tel: 01392 319955
www.royalclarencehotel.co.uk
Michael Caines has made his reputation as the chef who brought multi-stardom to Gidleigh Park. While not neglecting Gidleigh, he is now taking his inconsiderable gifts to a wider audience in a simpler and cheaper form at the Royal Clarence. While the Royal Clarence has the quiet majesty of years from the outside, it looks pretty bright, spry and on the ball inside, and no part looks brighter, spryer and more on the ball than the Caines wing of it. The cooking carries an unquestionable French pedigree - sophisticated, assured, but not full throttle haute cuisine – with the kitchen is well tuned in to local ingredients.
⊞ / ⊞

SEAFOOD RESTAURANT AND HOTEL
Riverside,
Padstow, Cornwall
Tel. 01841 532700
www.rickstein.com
Fish-lovers are said to book their holidays around a reservation at Rick Stein's phenomenally busy Seafood Restaurant

and Hotel. Helped by television exposure, no doubt, but the cooking here is top class. Ignore the token meat and veggie options and stick to the fish. Simple dishes highlight the quality of the local catch, but trademark inventive touches, such as Stein's goat fish curry, also hit the spot. High standards in service and the restaurant itself is modern and relaxing. Indulgent prices and you must book weeks in advance, at least.
⊞ / ■

HOTELS

ARUNDELL ARMS
Lifton, Devon
Tel. 01566 784666
www.arundellarms.com
A man may fish and eat well. And a woman, too. The Arundell Arms, a former coaching inn, is the fishing hotel par excellence, where everything is organized to favor the sportsman, including the cheer necessary at the end of a hard day on the water. In fact there's no need to be a fisherman to enjoy the place or the food. Provenance is important, with suppliers listed on a daily-changing menu, in which fish plays a central role in the five courses on offer. Cooking shows restraint in leaving good quality ingredients to speak for themselves. Staff are smilingly attentive. House wines start at £10.
■ / ■

BARTON CROSS HOTEL
Huxham, Stoke Canon,
nr Exeter, Devon
Tel. 01392 841245
All beams and thatch and charming gardens in this delightful hotel assembled out of several 17th-century cottages. Emphasis on comfort rather than

luxury. First-floor gallery and open fire in dining room. Cooking true to local ingredients, with emphasis on fish.
■ / ■

GIDLEIGH PARK
Chagford, Devon
Tel. 01647 432367
www.gidleigh.com
This stately pleasure dome is tucked away at the end of one of the windiest roads in the West Country. All 14 rooms have either a forest or river view. Subside into calm, cossetting luxury or take a turn around the magnificent garden before tucking into Michael Caine's two-Michelin-starred food. Highly personalized cooking with a distinct French accent. It's worth exploring proprietor Paul Henderson's legendary wine cellar too, although there is a generous selection of half-bottles. Service is faultless. Price includes breakfast and dinner.
⊞ / ⊞

HORN OF PLENTY
Gulworthy, Devon
Tel: 01822 832528
www.thehornofplenty.co.uk
Closed Sun & Mon lunch
Once a resting place for gastronomic pilgrims under Sonia Stephenson, the Horn of Plenty is once again playing to full houses under new owners. Some come for the views over the Tamar Valley. Some come for the creature comforts of the rooms. And some come for Peter Gorton's food, which livens up top notch local ingredients with trans-continental ideas with a sure, balanced and intelligent hand. Perhaps more a restaurant with rooms than a pukka hotel, but it is imbued with hospitality in the true sense of the word, and has a proper respect

for the word 'comfort'.
■ / ■

HOTEL TRESANTON
27 Lower Castle Road,
St Mawes, Cornwall
Tel. 01326 270055
www.tresanton.com
Transformed by Olga Polizzi, daughter of Lord Forte, this 26-room sea-view hotel has played host to a number of celebrity visitors. Design is key here and the place oozes charm. The nautical-themed restaurant looks out to the estuary and much of the menu devotes itself to local seafood. Service is unobtrusive but efficiently pampering.
■ / ⊞

THE ISLAND HOTEL
Tresco,
Isles of Scilly
Tel. 01720 422883
www.tresco.co.uk
Getting away from crowds (not many people); traffic (no cars – you get to the hotel by tractor); the 21st-century (as close to as you'll find in these sceptered isles). The hotel is the acme of modern comfort, with exceptional gardens and sea views. Food long on fish and shellfish cooked with élan, but there's intelligence brought to bear on non-marine produce as well.
■ / ⊞

LEWTRENCHARD MANOR
Lewdown,
Devon
Tel. 01566 783256
www.lewtrenchard.co.uk
Restaurant closed Mon lunch
Peace and quiet here, in a majestic hotel set in an Elizabethan manor house on the cusp of Dartmoor; the welcome is warmer than the moors, and a good deal more relaxed than the acres of paneling and carved oak might lead you to

For **hotels**, the price bands are for a double room
with en-suite bathroom for one night:
▯ = up to £40; ▣ = £40–£80; ▤ = £80–120,
▥ = over £120
For advice on finding a hotel, see also page 484

expect. The dining room preserves much of the Elizabethan passion for the ornate, but the food has a simplicity and robustness, with the flavors and local ingredients handled with exemplary sureness. The wine list wanders further afield, lingering on South Africa, and the house wines start at a very reasonable £10.
▥ / ▥

ST PETROC'S HOTEL & BISTRO
4 New St,
Padstow, Cornwall
Tel. 01841 532700
www.rickstein.com
The cadet branch of the Stein empire, St Petroc's is cheaper, laid-back, and you can sleep off your meal afterward in one of the charming, light, bright rooms. The dining-room offers informal bistro-style service and food. Fish is still the star attraction, woven into flavorsome French and Italian dishes with skill. Stylish setting and far easier to get a table here than at its more famous neighbor. It still isn't that easy in season.
▣ / ▤

WELL HOUSE
St Keyne, Cornwall
Tel. 01579 342001
www.wellhouse.co.uk
The valley was home to the curative waters of St Keyne's well and the personal touch at this friendly hotel can have a rejuvenating effect. Regional produce is fully exploited on the menu, but attention is paid to new trends and Italian dishes make an appearance. The set price menu changes daily – in recent years, the chef has changed almost as frequently, but standards remain high.
▣ / ▤

> ## SOUTH MIDLANDS
> ### (GLOS, HEREFORDSHIRE, WORCS, WARKS)

RESTAURANTS

BIRMINGHAM
Until recently the only gastronomic side of Birmingham celebrated was the numerous balti houses (of which Royal Naim, 417-19 Stratford Rd, Sparkhill – tel. 0121 766 7849 has a very sound reputation). Recently, however, Birmingham has become a site for successful chains, such as Le Petit Blanc (9 Brindley Place – tel. 0121 633 7333, www.lepetitblanc.com).

LE CHAMPIGNON SAUVAGE
24-26 Suffolk Rd,
Cheltenham, Glos
Tel. 01242 573449
www.lechampignon sauvage.co.uk
Closed Sun & Mon
A classic French restaurant de famille in this most English of towns with chefs, David Everitt-Mathias and his wife, of impeccable British pedigree. The stylish but low-key decor makes use of paintings from the local art college, to sit alonside equally creative cooking which is strong on sauces and meats. Mr E-M is a dab hand at devising cleverly balanced combinations which actually bring out the natural flavors of his ingredients. Desserts, too, are ambitious and striking. Set price menus and house wines provide excellent value for those eating on a budget. Service is a delight. Not surprisingly the restaurant recently gained a second Michelin star.
▣

CALLANDS
13-14 Meer St,
Stratford-upon-Avon,
Warks
Tel. 01789 269304
Odd that the home of Shakespeare should be almost devoid of adequate eating places. This more-than-adequate restaurant offers a menu of international, Mediterranean and modern British fare.
▥

CHURCHILL ARMS
Paxford, Glos
Tel. 01386 594000
www.churchillarms.com
Closed Sun eve in winter
Weekend visitors from London have turned this once-quiet watering hole into a local landmark. Part of Sonia Kidney/Leo Brooke-Little's Marsh Goose family (which also includes the Hare and Hounds at Foss Cross), it has become a classic gastropub which offers a more informal set-up. The menu changes twice daily, allowing for a great range of dishes and any number of cutting-edge capers. Proper ales properly cared for. No bookings, which can be nightmarish at weekends.
▯

THE LOUGH POOL INN
Sellack, Ross-on-Wye,
Herefordshire
Tel. 01989 730236
Closed Mon (winter);
Sun eve (winter)
A harmonious jumble of red tiled, whitewash- and-black-timber buildings in this unspoiled riverine just outside Ross on Wye. The dining room is agreeably unpreten-tious, with solid tables and comfortable chairs. The menu changes daily and features a highly tempting range of dishes based on proprietor Stephen Bull's intelligent and distinctive feel for various European

traditions, using high quality ingredients, local where possible. The beer is exemplary, there's a challenging range of ciders and perry (like cider but made with pears) and the wine list short but intelligently selective.
▯

LOVE'S RESTAURANT
15 Dormer Place,
Royal Leamington Spa,
Warcks
Tel. 01926 315522
Closed Sun & Mon
Stephen Love, chef and proprietor of Love's, is a chef with pedigree. He is an award winner. In 1997 he won the Roux Brothers Scholarship. That means, among other things, that he can do the basic things properly – make a sauce, reduce a stock, be precise about meat, treat vegetables with consideration and create toothsome pastry. In 2004 he won the title of National Chef of the Year, with a menu of lobster ravioli with langoustines and a celery broth, breast of pigeon with braised lentils and a pumpkin puree, and white chocolate mousse with banana and whisky ice cream.The cooking in this slightly somber basement restaurant is better, sounder and more satisfying than most London restaurants, if less flashy and fashionable. It is completely and unregenerately French, but there is nothing wrong with that.
▣

RESTAURANT BOSQUET
97A Warwick Rd,
Kenilworth, Warks
Tel. 01926 852463
www.restaurantbosquet. co.uk
Closed Sun & Mon
Another corner of this sceptred isle that is forever French, with a real Frenchman at the helm. Comfortable

For the **restaurants**, the following price bands have been used, according to the price of a two-course meal (without wine)
■ = up to £15; ■ = £15–£20
■ = £20–£30; ⊞ = £30 and over

dining room, and food with heft and hitting power. Classic stuff, with its roots firmly in Bernard Lignier's native southwest – long on flavor and richness and with a cavalier attitude to portion control. Changing dishes with the seasons and not fashion, local ingredients are well used, and duck is always in evidence somewhere on the menu. The wine list is exclusively French. Service is in the capable hands of Jane Lignier.
■

ROADE HOUSE
16 High Street, Roade, Northants
Tel. 01604 863372
www.roadehousehotel.co.uk
Closed Sun; Mon & Sat lunch
All nicely titivated, and now with room upstairs, the Roade House continues along its well-established, comfortable, sensible path. The menu provides a comforting mix of the classic and the not so classic. Dishes tend to gain in complexity as the meal progresses, with strong, well-defined flavors predominating. Game in season is particulary good, as are the desserts all year round. The wine list focuses on France, with a bit of help from other parts of the globe, and errs on the affordable side.
■

SIMPSONS
101-103 Warwick Rd, Kenilworth, Warwickshire
Tel. 01926 864567
www.simplysimpsons.com
Closed Sun & Mon
Simpsons is modern in mood, what with cream walls, tiled floor, and tall mirrors in bleached oak frames, but the effect is on the warm side of cool, and

curious bits of fake box topiary shaped like cork screws give the dining rooms a bosky appeal. The menu is modern, too, specifically modern French, with the odd Italian touch. The food is conceived within sensible boundaries and is immaculately cooked. The service is charming, energetic and efficient. All these are rare qualities, even in Kenilworth.
■

HOTELS

LOWER SLAUGHTER MANOR
Lower Slaughter, Glos
Tel. 01451 820456
www.lowerslaughter.co.uk
A bit of a picture postcard affair – 17th-century house, honey-gold Cotswold stone, village trim and neat, tasteful luxury in fixtures and fittings – that kind of thing. Dinner on the lavish side, in keeping with the clientele and its Michelin-starred status. Service and cooking – both Anglo-French – are spot-on, and the grandish dining room is a notable setting for pretty formal eating. The wine list is in keeping with the overall gravitas of the place, but worth a leaf through. Expect to come out considerably poorer but much happier.
⊞ / ⊞

LYGON ARMS
Broadway, Worcs
Tel. 01386 852255
www.lygonarms.com
Restaurant closed Mon-Sat lunch; brasserie open daily for lunch and dinner
Salman Rushdie hid out at this former coaching inn during the first few days of the fatwa against him. It's easy to see why. The Lygon Arms offers impeccable levels of luxury and indulgence, combined with a

seductive remoteness from the outside world. The Elizabethan banqueting hall that serves as a restaurant is decorated with heraldic shields and medieval armor, and there's also a minstrel's gallery. The menu is long, and not short on luxury. Some dishes verge toward the overcrowded, such is the energetic use of flavors and ingredients, but the overall quality is high. Head chef Martin Blunos won a Michelin star in January 2005.
⊞ / ⊞

THE TALBOT INN
Knightwick, Worcestershire
Tel. 01886 821235
www.the-talbot.co.uk
The realm of sisters Wiz and Annie Clift, on the banks of the River Teme. A true, traditional inn, relaxed, hospitable, kindly, old fashioned and unfashionably comfortable. The Clift sisters are gently passionate about local produce and many of the vegetables they grow in their organic garden. What cannot be eaten in times of glut, is pickled. They pick up the game from local shoots. They list their cheese, eggs, game, rabbit, meat, preserves and soft fruit suppliers. The cooking is rooted in an cosmopolitan English sensibility. It is without pretension. It is homely in the best sense of the word.
■ / ⊞

HOME COUNTIES
(BEDS, HERTS, BUCKS, OXON, BERKS, SURREY)

RESTAURANTS

BEETLE & WEDGE
Ferry Lane, Moulsford, Oxon
Tel. 01491 651381

www.beetleandwedge.co.uk
Idyllic setting beside the riverside in the former home of Jerome K. Jerome, and perfect for lazy summer evenings al fresco. Food is heartily and unfussily cooked, with no stinting on the butter or the booze, and portions are generous. Strong on organic ingredients too, on a menu that changes daily. The neighboring boat house offers a less formal menu, concentrating on fish and grilled meats, but the same high standards of preparation and service, which is unfailingly warm. A beetle and wedge, incidentally, is a boatbuilder's hammer and chisel, linked by a chain.
■

LA CHOUETTE
Westlington Green, Dinton, Bucks
Tel. 01296 747422
Closed Sat lunch; Sun
Very idiosyncratic; utterly disarming. Chef and proprietor Frederic Desmette juggles cooking and service single-handed at this thatched restaurant, producing dishes with a distinctive Belgian penchant for earth flavors – pheasant with chicory, for example, or salmon cooked in wheat beer. Good wine and Belgian beer (of course) are available. The £11 three-course lunch is a steal.

FAT DUCK
1 High St, Bray, Berks
Tel. 01628 580333
www.fatduck.co.uk
Closed Sun eve; Mon
Pyrotechnics on the plate. Chef and proprietor Heston Blumenthal is simply one of the two or three most inventive chefs in the country,

For **hotels**, the price bands are for a double room
with en-suite bathroom for one night:
▣ = up to £40; ▣ = £40–£80; ▣ = £80–120,
▣ = over £120
For advice on finding a hotel, see also page 484

constantly pushing at the borders of technique and flavor combinations, which on the menu seem bizarre (cod and cockscombs) but which are perfectly realized on the plate. Staff too are committed and charming, and the wine list is as dynamic as the food (there's a fabulous list of sherries). The Fat Duck received the culinary world's most prestigious accolade, a third Michelin star, in January 2004.
▣

THE GOOSE
Britwell Salome, Oxon
Tel. 01491 612304
Closed Sun eve
Every village should have one – a pleasing pub serving proper food. The menu at The Goose changes daily and relies heavily on local, often organic, ingredients. Service also comes with the local touch – friendly and obliging. Drink in the front, eat in the back where Michael North, formerly chef to Prince Charles at Highgrove, turns out high-quality, potent grub, without too much fuss but plenty of panache. The wine list is short but well priced and good beer.
▣

THE LEMON TREE
268 Woodstock Rd, Oxford
Tel. 01865 311936
www.thelemontreeoxford. co.uk
This very pleasant restaurant is smart without being overly formal. The walled garden and patio is the perfect setting for indulging in a relaxed lunch. The food is excellent but reasonably priced. Main courses include dishes such as free-range roast chicken breast with romesco sauce, poached smoked haddock with minted pea puree and slow cooked leg of lamb in red wine and rosemary sauce. Irresistable desserts.
▣

THE NETTLEBED
The White Hart Hotel, Nettlebed, Oxon
Tel. 01491 641245
www.whitehartnettlebed. com
The 30-seater Nettlebed restaurant is housed inside the White Hart Hotel. There is a smart fine dining room, very nattily decked out, serving fine food, and a bar which serves up rather cheaper and more robust fare. The cooking is supervized by Nick Seckington. The set menu changes daily depending on the season and market availability, while the seven-course tasting menu provides a top-notch gourmet feast.
▣

THE OLD PARSONAGE
1 Banbury Rd, Oxford
Tel. 01865 310210
www.oldparsonage-hotel.co.uk
An old haunt of Oscar Wilde, believe it or not. The luxury level will have come on a bit since he strutted his stuff as a student, and the food too. Nothing fancy, but plenty of modish elements sorted into appealing dishes at reasonable prices, as you might expect from a place owned by Jeremy Mogford, founder of the extremely successful Browns chain (now owned by Bass).
▣

L'ORTOLAN
The Old Vicarage, Church Lane, Shinfield, Berks
Tel. 0118 988 3783
www.lortolan.com
Closed Sun & Mon
L'Ortolan has had a bit of a makeover since John Burton-Race decamped for the metropolitan pastures. It is now in the hands of yet another graduate of Le Manoir aux Quat' Saisons academy of culinary arts, Alan Murchison. The atmosphere is notably more relaxed than formerly, but the cooking has the hallmarks of Raymond Blanc's love of complexity, balance and well defined flavors. The set price lunch is a particular bargain.
▣

LE PETIT BLANC
71-72 Walton St, Oxford
Tel. 01865 510999
www.lepetitblanc.co.uk
Brasserie offshoot of Mr Blanc's rather posher Le Manoir (see next page) and doing pretty well in this student-populated corner of Oxford. Tables are small and crowded together, but the atmosphere is buzzy and warm, and service is efficient. Food sticks to French favorites, and vegetarians are given more than a nod on the reasonably-priced menu (as are children – there is a menu just for them). Modern decor is courtesy of Terence Conran. Other outposts in Tunbridge Wells, Manchester, Cheltenham and Birmingham.
▣

SIR CHARLES NAPIER
Sprigg's Alley, Nr Chinnor, Oxon
Tel. 01494 483011
www.sircharlesnapier. co.uk
Closed Sun & Mon
Not the easiest place in the world to find, but worth the effort. Visit in summer to eat on the terrace amid the vines and wisteria, or venture inside to the eccentric pub-cum-dining room where wilfully mismatched furniture rubs shoulders with a collection of modern sculptures. The hand-written menus are full of interpretations of the latest ideas in modern British cooking. Exemplary cheeseboard. Wine list is excellent, as are the beers. Informal staff are charming and efficient.
▣

STRAWBERRY TREE
Radwell Rd, Milton Ernest, Beds
Tel. 01234 823633
Closed Sun-Tue
All thatch and pastel walls, the Strawberry Tree has something of the air of the tea-room it once was – ornaments and knick-knacks adorn the cottage interior. But this family-run restaurant (brothers Jason and Andrew Bona in the kitchen; parents John and Wendy Bona out front) offers food that is up-to-date and keeps an intelligent finger on the pulse of new trends. Ingredients are home-grown where possible, and local where not.
▣

WATERSIDE INN
Ferry Road, Bray, Berks
Tel. 01628 620691
www.waterside-inn.co.uk
Closed Mon & Tue
One of the rare three-Michelin-starred restaurants in Britain, with all the trimmings in the service and decor line that implies; and in the haute nature of the food. French through and through, of course. Alain Roux and head chef Russell Holborn turn out dishes of stunning precision – classic simplicity, not innovation, is the point here. Not quite immune to fashion,

For the **restaurants**, the following price bands have been used, according to the price of a two-course meal (without wine):
▪ = up to £15; ▪ = £15–£20
▪ = £20–£30; ▪ = £30 and over

but its dedication to the culinary arts is unchanging. The large wine list is predictably French and pricey. Service is pretty much perfect.
▪

HOTELS

CLIVEDEN
Taplow, Berks
Tel. 01628 668561
www.clivedenhouse.co.uk
The grandest of grand houses designed by Sir Charles Barry, architect of the Houses of Parliament, in the Victorian neo-classical style. This 39-room hotel was the former home of the Astor family and rendezvous for John Profumo and one Christine Keeler. Grandeur persists even if all the attention from tail-coated staff seems a little out-dated. Prices race upward through the menu at the restaurant, Waldo's. Daniel Galmiche took over as executive head chef in January 2005.
▪ / ▪

FEATHERS HOTEL
Market St,
Woodstock, Oxon
Tel. 01993 812291
www.feathers.co.uk
Inn cozied up to the entrance to Blenheim Palace, a hotch-potch of little rooms in which to seek refuge in comfortable sofas and good drinks. Food is consistently interesting and innovative, and portions are extremely generous, thanks to clever use of accompaniments. Wine list is excellent, although service is sometimes on the distracted side. Feathers are courtesy of the African Grey parrot at reception.
▪ / ▪

LE MANOIR AUX QUAT' SAISONS
Church Rd,
Great Milton, Oxon
Tel. 01844 278881
www.manoir.com

Landmark watering hole which just goes on getting more luxurious and other worldly by the year. Rooms are designer wombs in which to retreat from the stress of the world. Fifteenth-century manor house, with a bright and airy conservatory and more sedate dining room. Food from the kitchen of Raymond Blanc is intricate and exudes technical expertise, although straightforward dishes also shine. An open-minded menu has plenty of options for vegetarians, for offal devotees, and even children. Service is as formal and attentive, and is included in the – admittedly hefty – prices. Only two wines by the glass are on offer on what is a mammoth, French-leaning list, but this is a place to treat yourself. Not surprisingly has two Michelin stars.
▪ / ▪

THE VINEYARD AT STOCKCROSS
Stockcross,
Berks
Tel. 01635 528770
www.the-vineyard.co.uk
Delightfully OTT building with bizarrely OTT decor (and that's just the garden – the pond spews flames). The interior is thankfully more restrained and allows guests to concentrate on the food. John Cambell, formerly of Lords of the Manor, has taken over the reins from Billy Reid, so expect flavors pushed to the extreme, unusual combinations, and considerable complexity, handled with disciplined skill. The wine list is a masterpiece.
▪ / ▪

EAST ANGLIA
(ESSEX, CAMBS, SUFFOLK, NORFOLK)

RESTAURANTS

ADLARD'S
79 Upper St Giles,
Norwich, Norfolk
Tel. 01603 633522
www.adlards.co.uk
Closed Sun & Mon
For years David Adlard was a standard-bearer for serious eaters in East Anglia. Currently chef Tom Kerridge focuses on top-class dishes, using luxury ingredients to point up the qualities of a particular dish. It may sound fancy, but the end result is disarmingly simple, long on flavor, and balanced. The wine list is good value.
▪

LIGHTHOUSE
77 High St,
Aldeburgh, Suffolk
Tel. 01728 453377
www.lighthouserestaurant
.co.uk
A beacon of decent, basic cooking and reasonable pricing. Ham, egg and chips is on the lunch menu at this shop-turned-bistro, but when the ham is from Peasenhall, the eggs are free range and freshly laid and the chips are hand-crafted and on the chunky side, you know that this is a proper gastronomic experience. For dinner, stick to seafood, locally caught and judiciously prepared. Service is notably friendly and house wines peak at £11. ▪

MIDSUMMER HOUSE
Midsummer Common,
Cambridge
Tel. 01223 369299
www.midsummerhouse.
co.uk
Closed Sun & Mon
Leave the hurly burly of the dreaming spires behind. Stroll across the common to Midsommer House on

the banks of the River Cam, complete with bosky views from the conservatory dining room. Inventive French cooking with secure technique and taste, handling complex flavor and textures with aplomb.
▪

SCUTCHERS BISTRO
Westgate St,
Long Melford, Suffolk
Tel. 07000 728824
www.scutchers.com
Closed Sun & Mon
Deep in rural Suffolk, Scutcher's raises the vanguard of cheerful Med-evoking colors, with Designers Guild cerulean blue and buttercup yellow, and the odd splash of tart's toenail vermilion by way of light relief. There is a similar individuality about the food, which puts imprint on some of the staples of the modern menu. Ingredients are sourced with discrimination and cooked with appropriate care. The wine list is almost alarmingly reasonably priced. ▪

STRATTONS
4 Ash Close,
Swaffham, Norfolk
Tel. 01760 723845
www.strattonshotel.com
Opened Mon-Sat eves only
This Queen Anne villa may be stuffed to the dado rail with gew-gaws and knick-knacks in the manner of the Victorians, but it's a pleasantly relaxed place in the modern style. The handwritten menu is to the point, offering light, fresh starters, followed by meat, fish or a vegetarian option (just one of each), all cooked with assurance. Likewise, the wine list has handwritten notes on recommendations, and is spot-on. Most produce is bought locally and organic.
▪

For **hotels**, the price bands are for a double room with en-suite bathroom for one night:
▣ = up to £40; ▣ = £40–£80; ▣ = £80–120,
▣ = over £120
For advice on finding a hotel, see also page 484

LE TALBOOTH
Gun Hill, Dedham, Essex
Tel. 01206 323150
www.milsomhotels.com
Long-time servant of fine dining in Essex. Timbered restaurant, formerly a master weaver's cottage, looking over the river, and offering the opportunity of al fresco feeding, weather permitting. Despite the olde worlde beams, cooking is a cunning mix of magpie modern British and more traditional roasts and vegetables. Exemplary wine list.
▣

WELLS FINE DINING COMPANY
The Buttlands, Wells-next-the-sea, Norfolk
Tel. 01328 710209
www.thecrownhotelwells.co.uk
This former coaching inn offers a choice of relaxed meals in the bar area or more formal dining in the restaurant. Top quality ingredients are used to create a range of dishes featuring modern British cuisine and Pacific Rim-influenced fare. Good wine list.
▣

HOTELS
THE CROWN
90 High St, Southwold, Suffolk
Tel. 01502 722275
www.adnams.co.uk
Standard-bearer for Adnams the award-winning brewers, and showcase for Adnams the award-winning wine merchants, this former coaching inn has brilliant beers and a startling range of wines chosen to complement the menu (daily changing in the bar). The light, airy dining room lends itself to relaxed informality, although the cooking carries a serious clout. Seafood is great, and influences

cosmopolitan, all presented with precision. Staff are young, charming and efficient. Comfortable, cozy rooms.
▣ / ▣

MORSTON HALL
Morston, Norfolk
Tel. 01263 741041
www.morstonhall.com
Closed Mon-Sat lunch
Unpretentious country house hotel on the coast, in characteristic flint and brick. Predictably strong on fresh fish dishes. Chef and proprietor Galton Blackiston admirably resists the temptation to fuss with the flavor of the day's catch, and the menu (four courses, no choice) keeps it simple and well balanced.
▣ / ▣

NORTH MIDLANDS
(LINCS, NOTTS, LEICS, RUTLAND, STAFFS, SHROPS, CHESHIRE, DERBS)

RESTAURANTS
DARLEYS
Darley Abbey Mill, Darley Abbey, Derby
Tel. 01332 364987
www.darleys.com
Closed Sun eve
The old mill as we would have it be, smart and smiling. The dining room overlooks the river Derwent (tables are engineered to make the best of the view). The cooking is in the modern mode, but confidently handled, with a mix of the traditional and a touch of the Mediterranean. Service is hard-working and friendly.
▣

EPWORTH TAP
9-11 Market Place, Epworth, N. Lincs
Tel. 01427 873333
Closed Sun-Tue
Early gastro-pub. Longstanding local

with consistently good food and sense of familiar well-being. Loving attention to detail, local ingredients, generous approach to portion control. Outstanding wine list with some remarkable bargains.
▣

HARRY'S PLACE
17 High St, Great Gonerby, Lincs
Tel. 01476 561780
Closed Sun & Mon
Harry's Place only seats ten, but Harry Hallam's cooking has a virtuoso touch. The menu is short – two dishes per course – but then Harry cooks everything himself. He assiduously sources the finest ingredients, and then handles them with skill. The wine list is brief and to the point.
▣

HART'S
1 Standard Court, Park Row, Nottingham, Notts
Tel. 0115 911 0666
www.hartsnottingham.co.uk
Bright, modern interior (which shows no trace of its former incarnation as a hospital reception wing), with well-lit tables and a spirited atmosphere, Hart's is attracting a lot of attention in Nottingham. Food is similarly upbeat and contemporary across the range of mostly light dishes, with a fair choice for vegetarians. The brasserie sibling of proprietor Tim Hart's rather grander Hambleton Hall. Staff know what they're doing and do it well. Intelligently put together wine list.
▣

HIBISCUS
17 Corve St, Ludlow, Shropshire
Tel. 01584 872 325
www.hibiscusrestaurant.co.uk

Closed Sun & Mon; Tue lunch
Hibiscus is a relative newcomer in that gastro theme-park. The small dining room and little bar are girt with old oak paneling. The service, which is marshalled by the radiant Mme Bosi, wife of the chef, Henri Bosi, is friendly and charming. The cooking is in classic French tradition, beautifully balanced, with rigorous attention to detail and elegant saucing. There is a natural consideration for the dovetailing of ingredients, and an inherent understanding of the pleasure principles when it comes to eating. It isn't showy cooking. It's well-bred in the best sense of the word.
▣

MERCHANT HOUSE
Lower Corve St, Ludlow, Salop
Tel. 01584 875438
www.merchanthouse.co.uk
Closed Sun & Mon; Tue-Thu lunch
Festooned with Michelin stars, awards, and other guff, and rightly so. This is one of the most individual and accomplished restaurants in the country. Shaun Hill knows exactly what he is up to in the kitchen, and has an infallible feel for what goes best with what. He doesn't go in for frills, just for thrills – of which there are a lot. He works solo in the kitchen while wife Anja handles the small dining room with charm.
▣

MR UNDERHILL'S
Dinham Weir, Ludlow, Salop
Tel. 01584 874431
www.mr-underhills.co.uk
Opened evenings only. Closed Mon-Tue eve

◆ HOTELS AND RESTAURANTS

For the **restaurants**, the following price bands have been used, according to the price of a two-course meal (without wine):
■ = up to £15; ■ = £15–£20; ■ = £20–£30; ■ = £30 and over

Quite why Ludlow should assume the mantle of the culinary capital of the county is something of a mystery. This is another gem overlooking the River Teme beneath the walls of Ludlow Castle. A no-choice set dinner menu takes account of previously announced special requests, and results in a balanced meal focused on fresh ingredients handled with care, imagination and great technical skill by Chris Bradley. The wine list is sensibly priced, with some excellent bottles. A few delightful rooms if you need to sleep over after dinner.
■

OLD VICARAGE
Ridgeway Moor,
Ridgeway, Derbs
Tel. 0114 247 5814
www.theoldvicarage.co.uk
Closed Sun & Mon;
Sat lunch
Menus change about every six weeks at this serene country house, but prices remain fixed for three and four courses at lunch and dinner. Chef and proprietor Tessa Bramley has a magpie curiosity when it comes to cooking, and you'll find dishes reflecting an eclectic culinary sensitivity, with elements from any-where from England to the Far East, all handled with exemplary understanding of what they can contribute to a dish. It isn't a striving after originality or innovation, simply the reflection of her personality. The wine list is compact but covers most bases.
■

WIG & MITRE
30 Steep Hill,
Lincoln, Lincs
Tel. 01522 535190
www.wigandmitre.com
Another early entrant

into the gastro-pub stakes. Menus change with the days and the seasons here, making the best of what local suppliers have to offer. No rules and a distinct lack of pretension means you can eat all day if you want to. The format encourages local regulars rather than one-off gourmet sensation seekers. Traditional dishes win out, although modern dishes get a look in. The fish is especially fine. Service is brisk and smiling.
■

WINTERINGHAM FIELDS
Winteringham, Lincs
Tel. 01724 733096
www.winteringhamfields.com
Closed Sun & Mon
A model of inspired industry. Husband and wife team, Germain and Annie Schwab, surrounded by a myriad of Victorian knick-knacks, have, little by little over the years built this 16th-century farmhouse turned restaurant-with-rooms into one of the outstanding hostelries in the country. Germain Schwab's two Michelin-star food undeniably takes center stage. Influences of Schwab's native Switzerland may peek in here and there, but for the most part it is highly sophisticated cooking of a highly individual nature. All-round top drawer operation.
■

HOTELS

ARKLE
The Chester Grosvenor
Hotel, Eastgate,
Chester, Cheshire
Tel. 01244 324024
www.chestergrosvenor.com
Restaurant closed
Sun & Mon
Luxury it is – in the reception area, in the

rooms, in the glass-topped dining room. Heavy duty silverware, crisp napery, the light gleaming on handblown glasses, the soft fall of the waiter's foot on plush carpet, the plate stacked with luxury ingredients – there's money to be spent here all right. And why not? The cooking is smooth, sophisticated and refined, in the classical French mode, with Italian touches here and there.
■/■

CALLOW HALL
Mappleton Rd,
Ashbourne, Derbs
Tel. 01335 300900
www.callowhall.co.uk
Restaurant closed Mon-Sat lunch; Sun eve
Family-run. Various members of the Spencers staffing kitchen, front of house, meeting and greeting. This brings a personal touch to this substantial Victorian pile, decorated very much in the Arts and Crafts tradition. The attention to detail shown by staff and the kitchen is equally diligent. The food is of the sensible Euro-centered school. Dinner is from a set-price menu, with a few choices at each of the five courses. Meat and game are strong points, and all dishes are generous in size.
■/■

FISCHER'S BASLOW HALL
Calver Rd, Baslow,
Derbs
Tel. 01246 583259
www.fischers-baslowhall.co.uk
Restaurant closed Mon lunch; Sun eve (except for residents)
Another family-run manor house hotel, Edwardian this time, all mullioned windows and civilized comfort. Max Fischer's cooking

is civilized and comfortable too, but with the extra zip of real élan. He's not afraid of the luxury ingredient, but he also has the intelligence and real skill to know when to leave things as they are, sometimes pointed up by herbs from the garden. Terrific cheeses. Cheaper Café Max also delivers the goods.
■/■

HAMBLETON HALL
Hambleton, Rutland
Tel. 01572 756991
www.hambletonhall.com
The epitome of civilized luxury. Like a Bentley, looking out over Rutland Water, Hambleton Hall purrs along with friendly, confident ease, with plenty of power in reserve, particularly in the kitchen. Aaron Patterson's cooking runs with the seasons, using top notch local raw materials as the starting point for often explosively inventive and intricate dishes. Prices reflect the quality and workmanship. The lengthy wine list is inviting, though a shorter list offers a few specially chosen recommendations.
■ /■

OVERTON GRANGE
Hereford Road,
Ludlow, Salop
Tel. 01584 873500
www.overtongrangehotel.com
Yet another of Ludlow's glories, actually just outside, on a slightly grander scale than the others, what with the oak-paneled dining room and the refined French cooking of Wayne Vickerage. It is classical in basis, but lightened and leavened for the modern taste, long on sauces, and rather shorter on veg. Service is friendly and the wine list global.

For **hotels**, the price bands are for a double room with en-suite bathroom for one night:
▣ = up to £40; ▣ = £40–£80, ▣ = £80–120, ▦ = over £120
For advice on finding a hotel, see also page 484

Rooms of the very comfortable country house hotel variety.
▣ / ▣

NORTH EAST
(YORKS, DURHAM, NORTHUMBERLAND)
RESTAURANTS

3 YORK PLACE
3 York Place, Leeds
Tel: 0113 245 9922
www.no3yorkplace.co.uk
Closed Sun; Sat lunch
Some of the finest dining in Leeds is to be had at this relaxed, friendly restaurant, which has an extremely eclectic clientele. Head chef Martel Smith and restaurant manager Denis Lefrancq offer a stunning menu of modern British food with a French twist. Either order à la carte or try the dégustation menu, which is made up of seven of the establishment's signature dishes.
▣

ANGEL INN
Hetton, N. Yorks
Tel. 01756 730263
www.angelhetton.co.uk
Four hundred year-old sister (or brother?) to General Tarleton (see Hotels), at the top of a steep hill in the middle of the Yorkshire dales. Lots of small, comfortable, beam-laden rooms. Choice between laid-back pub grub at the bar, or a more formal dining experience in the restaurant. Cooking in the mainstream of modern European, and done with real edge to it. The restaurant is also strong on game and old-fashioned English desserts (queen of puddings, sticky toffee pudding). Brilliant beers; even better wine list, with lots by the glass, including some very serious stuff. Very popular.
▣

ARMSTRONGS
102 Dodworth Rd, Barnsley, S. Yorks
Tel. 01226 240113
www.armstrongsrestaurant.com
Pared-down restaurant – they have shown the red card to lunches, vegetarian menus and special deals, and now offer only a set three-course dinner from Tue to Sat – and indeed pretty much everything else here has been stripped to its essentials, from the rather sparse decor to the simple cooking. The essentials, though, are very good; ingredients are strong and dishes creative but uncrowded. European influences are evident, and desserts are imaginative.
▣

BISTRO 21
Ayley Heads House, Aykley Heads, Durham
Tel. 0191 3844354
Closed Sun & Mon
Terry Laybourne stretches out a long arm from his Newcastle base. The setting is clean, uncluttered wood and white decor. Good value cooking of real substance.
▣

BOX TREE
35-37 Church St, Ilkley, W. Yorks
Tel. 01943 608484
www.theboxtree.co.uk
Closed Sun eve; Mon and for lunch Tue-Sat
Others come and go, but the Box Tree, like the Mississippi in the song, just rolls on. North country opulence of decor makes a fitting setting for proprietor/chef Simon Gueller's cooking. Every detail gleams brightly down to the petits fours, breads and coffee. Blockbuster wine list – 800 bottles. Luckily, sommeliers are steeped in knowledge and sensible with it.
▣

BRASSERIE FORTY FOUR
44 The Calls, Leeds, W. Yorks
Tel. 0113 234 3232
www.brasserie44.com
Closed Sun; Sat lunch
Bright and breezy brasserie in modishly converted 19th-century grain store right on the river Aire waterfront. Model modish food bestrides the world from pizzas to pastilla without losing sight of our own native traditions, particularly in the pudding line. Wine is similarly targeted for those not looking to spend a fortune. Chef Jeff Baker also looks after the sister restaurant, the smarter Pool Court.
▣

MAGPIE CAFE
14 Pier Rd, Whitby, N. Yorks
Tel. 01947 602058
www.magpiecafe.co.uk
Classic site for classic food. Three floors of a former merchant's house are home to the Magpie Cafe and rarely is there a free space on any of them. Fish and chips is the unpretentious fare on offer here, and with the fish market situated on the harbor directly opposite, there's no doubting the freshness of the raw materials. Generous portions and shorn of elaboration – fish and chips is what you get, save the occasional dab of lemon butter. Brilliant stuff.
▢

MCCOY'S BISTRO
The Cleveland Tontine, Staddlebridge, N. Yorks
Tel. 01609 882671
www.mccoysatthetontine.co.uk
Idiosyncratic basement creation of the McCoy family, all potted palms, dotty furnishings and accordion, and the self-assured house cat by the fire. Food is unaffectedly rustic and cheerfully contemporary by turns. Service is warm and the whole enterprise has a highly individual vitality.
▣

MELTON'S
7 Scarcroft Rd, York
Tel. 01904 634341
www.meltonsrestaurant.co.uk
Closed Sun; Mon lunch
Long-term gastronomic standard bearer in an historic city not much noted for its wealth of worthy watering holes. The husband and wife team provide a pleasingly relaxed base. Michael Hjort's cooking allies a sound mastery of classic techniques with superb primary ingredients. The results are splendidly in the great Franco/British tradition, with the emphasis firmly on the French. Very good-value early-evening menu.
▣

POOL COURT AT 42
44 The Calls, Leeds, W. Yorks
Tel. 0113 244 4242
www.poolcourt.com
Closed Sun; Sat lunch
The senior partner to Brasserie Forty Four. Sophisticated dining room chooses neutral tones for decor and saves the color for the Michelin-starred food. Plenty of luxuries amid the modern French and British dishes available, which are handled with confidence and founded on good, often regional (e.g. Whitby cod), ingredients. Service is sedate compared with the buzzy brasserie next door. A recipe comes with the bill to inspire the dedicated home cook.
▣

For the **restaurants**, the following price bands have been used, according to the price of a two-course meal (without wine):
🔲 = up to £15; 🔲 = £15–£20
🔲 = £20–£30; 🔲 = £30 and over

ROSE & CROWN
Romaldkirk, Co Durham
Tel. 01833 650213
www.rose-and-crown.co.uk
Fine, upstanding 17th-century inn with a fine, upstanding 17th-century feel (oak paneling, sconces and the like), and old-fashioned warmth of welcome. Eurocratic cooking isn't fancy, more straight from the heart as well as straight from the surrounding countryside. Delivers punchy flavors in unfussy style. Good bar snack for those not up for the proper dining room experience.
🔲

THE STAR INN
Harome, nr Helmsley,
N. Yorks
Tel. 01439 770397
www.thestaratharome.co.uk
Closed Mon
Pluperfect gastro-pub. Real fires. Real beams. Real beer. Real food. Easy-going warmth and friendliness disguise hard-working professionalism. Eat in the pub part, eat in the restaurant – it's all the same. Food mainstream British modified by European influences. Strong on local ingredients used imaginatively. Terrific wine line. A star all round, in fact.
🔲

THORPE GRANGE MANOR
Thorpe Lane,
Almondbury,
Huddersfield, W. Yorks
Tel. 01484 425115
www.thorpegrangemanor.co.uk
Closed Sun & Mon;
Sat lunch
Eighteenth-century manor house; five-year-old kitchen. But the team has found its feet quickly. A plethora of options here, from the carte to a series of special menus, and of styles – come at Sun lunchtime for roast beef or weekdays for food with a Franglo feel. Bread is good whatever the day. An army of staff.
🔲

THYME
32-34 Sandygate Rd,
Crosspool, Sheffield
Tel: 0114 266 6096
www.thymeforfood.co.uk
May look a bit like a successful dental practice outside and in, but the food is more gutsy than dainty. It's straight down the line, sensible, well-crafted, single flavors to the fore, pleasure on the line, satisfaction guaranteed, and at what can only be described as very fair prices. The wine list, particular, is packed with goodies at prices that make you wonder what other restaurants are charging for. The service is cheerful and attentive.
🔲

YORKE ARMS
Ramsgill,
Nr Pately Bridge,
N. Yorks
Tel. 01423 755243
www.yorke-arms.co.uk
Very much a friendly country atmosphere at this old beams-and-flagstones shooting lodge. Chef/proprietor Frances Atkins has put her culinary roots deep down into local traditions, notably with the local game and cheeses that appear on the menu, but she also handles newer trends with skill. Service is warm and wines good value.
🔲

HOTELS
DEVONSHIRE ARMS
Bolton Abbey,
N. Yorks Tel. 01756 710441
www.devonshirehotels.co.uk
Brasserie open daily (lunch and dinner);
Burlington Room open Tue-Sat for dinner and for Sun lunch
Country house hotel in an old coaching inn, owned by the Duke and Duchess of Devonshire, who have also kitted the place out with suitably swish furniture and art. Fortunately, prices at the Burlington are pitched at those of us less nobly born (the brasserie offers yet cheaper, lighter options). A fixed-price five-course dinner takes in global culinary styles, but with the emphasis on indulgence rather than exotica.
🔲 / 🔲

GENERAL TARLETON
Boroughbridge Rd,
Ferrensby, N. Yorks
Tel. 01423 340284
www.generaltarleton.co.uk
Partner to master restaurateur-cum-hotelier Dennis Watkin's Angel Inn at Hetton (see previous page), and similarly offering well-priced, well-executed food in European mainstream, made merrier by a Yorkshire approach to portions. Informal atmosphere. You're in no danger of forgetting where you are as the kitchen produces some ding-dong regional specialties. Service is unhurried, so settle in for a while. Old buildings, thoroughly modern bedrooms.
🔲 / 🔲

THE GRANGE HOTEL
1 Clifton,
York
Tel. 01904 644744
www.grangehotel.co.uk
An oasis of substantial comfort in the heart of the city. Brasserie, seafood bar and restaurant proper. Ubiquitous Eurostyle cooking, but carried through with proper conviction. Big wine list.
🔲 / 🔲

HAZLEWOOD CASTLE
Paradise Lane,
Hazlewood, Tadcaster,
N. Yorks
Tel. 01937 535353
www.hazlewood-castle.co.uk
A bit of Yorkshire grandeur. A real castle too, with Great Hall, State Drawing Room and all that. Bedrooms knee-deep in creature comforts. The restaurant menus are entitled Elementary, Indulgence and Extravaganza. Dishes try hard to impress, and many do. When the chefs stop to draw breath, simpler dishes work well. Popular with locals.
🔲 / 🔲

HORTON GRANGE
Seaton Burn,
Tyne & Wear
Tel. 01661 860686
www.horton-grange.co.uk
Closed Sun eve
Guests at this nine-room hotel might be surprised to find themselves looking out over a Japanese garden. The modern conservatory restaurant works very well, on both decor and food in the modern British idiom. Four-course dinners come complete with menu poetry which lists every ingredient on the plate, but balance and portions are well judged. As is the wine list, with plenty of decent tipples available by the glass.
🔲 / 🔲

**NORTH WEST
(CUMBRIA, LANCS,**
RESTAURANTS

60 HOPE STREET
61 Hope St, Liverpool
Tel. 0151 707 6060
www.60hopestreet.com
Closed Sun
Very much a modern (but not in-your-face modern) restaurant housed inside a handsome neo-classical Victorian bulding.

For **hotels**, the price bands are for a double room
with en-suite bathroom for one night:
▣ = up to £40; ▣ = £40–£80; ▣ = £80–120,
▦ = over £120
For advice on finding a hotel, see also page 484

Some fine cooking in the modern British idiom, with a sure handling of flavors and precise, inspired cooking. The front of house has a distinctive Scouser flair.
▣

BECHER'S BROOK
29a Hope St,
Liverpool
Tel. 01517 070 005
The appearance of this Georgian house in the city center is simple and functional rather than racy, but the food shows a considerable fleetness of foot in the contemporary mold of gastro-eclecticism, with a good range of countries represented on the plate at the same time.
▣

JUNIPER
21 The Downs,
Altrincham,
Greater Manchester
Tel. 0161 929 4008
www.juniper-restaurant.
co.uk
Closed Sat lunch;
Sun & Mon;
Michelin star flourishing in wealthy Altringham. Slick Italianate interior. Slick contemporary French cooking from chef Paul Kitching. Fish outstanding. Smart takes on traditional northern passion for offal. Painterly presentation – sauces come as rather Fauvist splashes of flavor. Service is unflappable. The food, like the wine, isn't cheap.
▣

TAI PAN
81-97 Upper Brook St,
Manchester
Tel. 0161 273 2798
Closed Sun & Mon
Another sign of the vigor of Chinese community in Manchester. Bright, breezy, big site above a Chinese supermarket. Too many standard formula, all-purpose fare, but dim sum

begins to push the envelope a bit, and the a la carte contains some genuine surprises that shows the kitchen on top of its game. Enterprising wine list. Perhaps not ready to challenge the legendary Yang Sing – the service isn't in the same class as the kitchen – but getting there maybe.
▣

MOSS NOOK
Ringway Rd,
Manchester
Tel. 0161 437 4778
Closed Sun & Mon;
Sat lunch
A bit of a time warp. It must have been like this in smart restaurants around the turn of the century, all drapes and red plush, but the cooking is of a quality right out of the classical mold – loads of luxury ingredients, beautifully cooked and artfully presented.
▦

NUTTERS
Edenfield Rd, Norden,
Rochdale
Tel. 01706 650167
Closed Mon
Pub-turned-restaurant, playground of TV chef Andrew Nutter, up on the moors. The food is impressive, with influences and presentation unremittingly fashionable, much given to towering constructions at present. This works rather well, thanks to the quality ingredients and a confidence in matching flavors. Service is decidedly more sober than the cooking.
▣

PAUL HEATHCOTE'S
104-106 Higher Rd,
Longridge, Lancs
Tel. 01772 784969
www.heathcotes.co.uk
Closed Mon
Paul Heathcote was a trailblazer for the renaissance of high-

quality cooking in the Northwest. Superb local ingredients and an unerring understanding for the textures and flavors of British cooking are transformed by high imagination and impeccable classical techniques into some of the most satisfying cooking in the country. Huge flavors derive from immense sophistication of the food. Service is unhurried and charmingly formal. A place for proper eating.
▦

PUNCH BOWL INN
Crosthwaite, Cumbria
Tel. 015395 68237
www.punchbowl.fsnet.
co.uk
Closed Mon; Sun eve
Stephen Docherty, chef/proprietor of the Punch Bowl (and the Spread Eagle, Sawley, Lancs. Tel. 01200 441202) is a properly trained chef (ex-head chef at Le Gavroche), so when he and his head chef Anthony Denis-Payne turn their attention to pub food you can be sure it will be a cut above the average. Several cuts, as it turns out. The place is utterly unpretentious. The food is without-frills-modern, and packs a formidable flavor punch. Wine and beer are predictably fine. Three charming rooms.
▣

SIMPLY HEATHCOTES
Jacksons Row,
Deansgate, Manchester
Tel. 0161 835 3536
www.heathcotes.co.uk
The lighter side of Paul Heathcote. A bright, modern brasserie, big on atmosphere and style. Food reflects the liveliness of the place, showing vigor and invention. There are plenty of fashionable Med-inspired dishes, but the regional

influences that are so evident at Paul Heathcote's restaurant in Longridge pop up here too. Young, breezy service suits the ambience.
▣

YANG SING
34 Princess St,
Manchester, Lancs
Tel. 0161 236 2200
www.yang-sing.com
Manchester landmark. Long acknowledged as the best Chinese restaurant outside London (and maybe inside it, too). After fire gutted the Princess Street premises in 1997, the restaurant operated out of a temporary home until late 1999. Standards have remained high despite the upheavals. Staff steer the uninitiated through the Cantonese menu, which offers more than the usual anglicized Chinese dishes. Vegetarians and children have menus of their own. Wine, though, sticks to mostly French bottles.
▣

HOTELS

BAY HORSE HOTEL
Canal Foot,
Ulverston, Cumbria
Tel. 01229 583972
www.thebayhorsehotel.
co.uk
Closed Sat & Mon lunch
Traditional inn, simply decorated, but home to exceptionally well executed modern British cooking. Lunches are generally informal, with dinner a smarter affair. Menus change weekly and make the very best of the ingredients available. Desserts in particular make splendid use of the seasons and traditional English recipes. Views over the Leven estuary add to the calming atmosphere, and real ales increase the feeling of well-being.
▣ / ▣

For the **restaurants**, the following price bands have been used, according to the price of a two-course meal (without wine):
◪ = up to £15; ◪ = £15–£20
◪ = £20–£30; ⊞ = £30 and over

HOLBECK GHYLL
Holbeck Lane,
Windermere
Tel. 015394 32375
www.holbeckghyll.com
The Victorians liked to do themselves in style, even when they were just out hunting. Holbeck Ghyll was built for the pleasure of the Lord Lonsdale of 1888, and a good many of the trappings still survive, including some of the finest views in the Lake District. His lordship probably wouldn't recognise the food, although he might approve of it. Unmistakable French basis, interpreted with an individuality and creativity a light touch and a sure palate. Strong on fish and very strong on puddings. Senior service wine list.
⊞ / ⊞

NORTHCOTE MANOR
Northcote Rd,
Langho, Lancs
Tel. 01254 240555
www.northcotemanor.com
It looks a bit high Edwardian, but once inside it's luxurious but totally unstuffy. Nigel Haworth's fine Michelin-starred cooking has its roots firmly in local traditions – black pudding, Eccles cake and Lancashire cheese ice cream all pop up here and there – blended seamlessly with modern European influences. Service is affable, obliging and capable, and the wine list broad.
◪ / ◪

SHARROW BAY
Ullswater,
Cumbria
Tel. 017684 86301
www.sharrowbay.co.uk
Now that Francis Coulson and Brian Sack, the two great founders have died, can this grand original among country hotels maintain the standards that made it the benchmark for 55 years? The answer seems to be yes. The new management is the old team without the guiding spirits, and so has been steeped in the traditions of Sharrow Bay for decades. Civilized comfort, enveloping hospitality, cooking that takes no cognisance of modern dietary practice, it is all balm to the soul and body.
⊞ / ⊞

UNDERSCAR MANOR
Applethwaite,
Cumbria
Tel. 017687 75000
Perched on a hillside, looking over Derwent Water, this Italianate manor house hotel is currently in the process of building 25 luxury appartments. It has a longstanding commitment to its food. Chef Robert Thornton has been here for a decade, and is an expert trend-surfer. Ingredients are always of top quality. Potent puddings. Wine list is geared to those of all budgets.
⊞ / ⊞

WHITE MOSS HOUSE
Rydal Water,
Grasmere, Cumbria
Tel. 01539 435295
www.whitemoss.com
Closed for lunch and Sun eve
Family-run country hotel, in property once owned by Wordsworth, with views over Rydal Water. Similarly, the food relies on what is found locally, with organic and wild produce a specialty. The five-course set menu (at one sitting for dinner, 8pm sharp) is not exactly cutting edge but consistently hitting the mark on taste and timing. The wine list is exemplary.
◪ / ◪

WALES
RESTAURANTS

CARLTON HOUSE
Dolycoed Rd, Llanwrtyd Wells, Powys
Tel. 01591 610248
www.carltonrestaurant. co.uk
Closed Sun; lunch by prior arrangement only
A restaurant with rooms rather than a true hotel, but with better food and nicer rooms than a good many pricier joints. Mary Ann Gilchrist has a fine nose for a (largely organic) ingredient and a restless culinary intelligence which embraces a good many culinary cultures. Fish is remarkably good, but then so are most things on the menu. Husband Alan dispenses wit, good humor and wisdom on the wine front.
◪

THE CROWN AT WHITEBROOK
Whitebrook,
Monmouthshire
Tel. 01600 860254
www.crownatwhitebrook. com
Closed Mon
The Crown thinks it is an auberge, but it is more like an inn which opts for challenging French cookery and pulls it off. Good use is made of local strengths such as Welsh lamb, but the French bias adds a classic touch to more rustic dishes. Wine is excellent value, and shares the same Gallic tendencies. Service is erratic but kindly.
◪

LE GALLOIS
6-10 Romilly Crescent, Canton, Cardiff
Tel. 029 2034 1264
www.legallois-ycymro.com
Closed Sun & Mon
Le Gallois sticks out in Romilly Crescent. Its long, flat glass frontage is something of a contrast to the cheerfully incidental , haphazard, domestic nature of most of the buildings in the street The cooking is distinctly French in technique, as you might expect from a chef who had spent his culinary formative years in the kitchens of a Hilton hotel but it is by no means a spiritless gallop through the traditional favorites. There is something of the pan-European approach favored by so many contemporary chefs, but there is something character-istically British about the actual structure of the dishes.
◪

MAES-Y-NEUADD
Talsarnau, Gwynedd
Tel. 01766 780200
www.neuadd.com
Comfy manor house on the edge of the Snowdonia National Park. Genteel interior foaming with lace and chintz. Cooking pretty up-to-date. Menu changes daily, culminating in the good value five-course dinner. Ingredients are sourced locally, so lamb is obviously a specialty, as are the cheeses. Vegetables travel a minimum distance from kitchen garden to plate and are prepared with consideration. Lunch is less elaborate and plenty cheaper.
◪

OLD RECTORY
Llanrwst Rd,
Llansanffraid Glan Conwy, Conwy
Tel. 01492 580611
www.oldrectorycountry house.co.uk
Closed Sun & Mon
From Snowdonia to Conwy Castle, that's the spectacular view you get from this charming, rather handsome house. Friendly staff will take note of food preferences when you book; the bilingual

For **hotels**, the price bands are for a double room
with en-suite bathroom for one night:
▣ = up to £40; ▣= £40–£80; ▣ = £80–120,
▦ = over £120
For advice on finding a hotel, see also page 484

menu is no-choice and
dinner is taken at just
the one sitting. Once
again impeccable local
ingredients are the key
to chef and proprietor
Wendy Vaughan's
restrained cooking.
▣

THREE MAIN STREET
3 Main St,
Fishguard, Pembs
Tel. 01348 874275
Lovely, refined
Georgian town house
hotel, which is light
and unstuffy inside.
A certain confidence
has descended on the
cooking here after a
decade of turning out
well-crafted dishes.
Organic ingredients
have been added
where possible.
Seafood and
vegetables are
particular strengths.
Lighter options are
available during the
day when the house
opens as a coffee shop;
booking is advised for
lunch.
▣

THE WALNUT TREE INN
Llandewi Skirrid,
Abergavenny,
Monthmouthshire
Tel. 01873 852797
www.thewalnuttreeinn.
com
Closed Mon; Sun eve
After 35 years Franco &
Anne Taruschio moved
on. Their place has
been taken by
Francesco Mattioli.
Aside from being able
to book a table and
pay by credit card, the
cheerful, unpretentious
style of the Walnut
Tree remains the same.
The happy eaters are
still managed with a
no-nonsense good
humor, and the
cooking remains
largely Italian of the
highest quality. There
are very few British
chefs who can do this
kind, any kind, of
Italian cooking
properly with
understanding and
respect for its essential
restraint, but Stephen

Terry seems to be one
of them.
▣

WYNNSTAY
Maengwyn St,
Machynllneth,
Powys Tel. 01654
702941
www.wynnstay-hotel.com
Gareth Johns, formerly
of the Red Lion Inn at
Llanfihangel-Nant-
Melan, is a champion
of all things Welsh and
culinary, although he
does draw on methods
and techniques from
beyond the borders of
the Principality to get
top notch local
ingredients showing
their best. The results
are very appealing,
hearty and subtle at
the same time. The
carefully modernized
18th-century coaching
inn, too, manages to
mix traditional style
with the contemporary
comforts with some
panache.
▣

YE OLDE BULLS HEAD
Castle St, Beaumaris,
Isle of Anglesey
Tel. 01248 810329
www.bullsheadinn.co.uk
Seventeenth-century
inn which has been
brought into line with
modern thinking with
the addition of a
conservatory brasserie
to complement the
existing restaurant. A
long-standing reliance
on local produce has
resulted in supplies of
top-class ingredients,
particularly meat and
fish, both of which are
handled well by the
kitchen, which is not
afraid to go for not-so-
traditional track. Brisk,
unfussy service.
▣

YNYSHIR HALL
Eglwysfach, Powys
Tel. 01654 781209
www.ynyshir-hall.co.uk
A place to potter.
This secluded white
Georgian mansion
offers an escape to a
more tranquil and
leisurely pace of life.

But the interior and
the pan-European
cooking have a certain
bravura and color
about them, both
carried off with a
certain panache.
▣

HOTELS

FAIRYHILL
Reynoldston,
Swansea
Tel. 01792 390139
www.fairyhill.net
Comfortable and
hospitable country
house hotel in one of
those lost corners of
Britain. Welcome as
charming as the rooms.
Ye olde log fires cede
to stainless steel in the
up-to-date dining
room, where modern
Welsh cooking offers
some surprise and
some more predictable
(and no less
accomplished for that)
dishes – Welsh lamb a
notable example. Wine
list is commendable,
with some bargains
and a good selection
of house wines.
▣ / ▦

LAKE COUNTRY HOUSE
Llangammarch Wells,
Powys
Tel. 01591 620202
www.lakecountryhouse.
co.uk
It's got the lot –
50 acres, a river,
handsome house,
soothing rooms, with
old-fashioned comfort
and decent grub. You
don't eat here looking
for racy informality.
The food is serious –
not without flair, but
uncontentious. The
wine list is a mighty
tome, with some
interesting choices,
although house wines
start at below £10.
▣ / ▦

LLANGOED HALL
Llyswen, Powys
Tel. 01874 754525
www.llangoedhall.com
Set in the sylvan Wye
Valley, draped with
Laura Ashley fabrics
(the owner is Sir
Bernard Ashley) and

s   ...ques,
th ...use is a dream
of rural tranquillity
designed in the high
Edwardian style by
Clough Williams Ellis.
Michelin-style food
(classical French with
the leavening breath
of lighter saucing and
shorter cooking),
Michelin-starred, and
with Michelin star-
styled prices. Pretty
damn comfortable, if
you can afford it.
▦ / ▦

PLAS BODEGROES
Nefyn Road, Pwllheli,
Gwynedd
Tel. 01758 612363
www.bodegroes.co.uk
Closed Mon; Tue-Sat
lunch; Sun eve
Grade II listed
Georgian manor house
hotel, but the interior
is modern and
unstuffy, with warm,
professional service.
Although Chris Chown
is a staunch advocate
of Welsh produce, he
doesn't let that inhibit
his considerable
culinary imagination
in putting together
traditional and not
so traditional dishes.
Puddings excel,
particularly pastry
dishes. Quality wine
list with about 20
house wines. Elegant,
comfortable bedrooms.
▦ / ▦

**ST DAVID'S HOTEL
& SPA**
Havana St,
Cardiff Bay, Cardiff
Tel. 029 2045 4045
www.thestdavidshotel.
com
The waterfront setting
continues inside this
liner-like hotel
(proprietor: Sir Rocco
Forte), with five-star
luxury, "deck"
balconies, blue wave
decor and lighthouse
cruet sets. The kitchen
at the Tides Bar and
Grill, overseen by
executive chef Stephen
Carter, uses the finest
fresh ingredients from
local suppliers.
▣ / ▣

"What two ideas are more inseparable than beer and Britannia?" proclaimed the 18th-century wit, bon viveur and vicar, Sidney Smith. Sadly, this may no longer be the case. Industrial brewing, consolidation within the industry, the switch to lager and, even worse, wine have all taken their toll on England's traditional tipple.

However, even if well-brewed, well-kept beers are not quite so universally available as they once were, there are still plenty left, with an encouraging number of new, small-scale breweries springing up, bringing their life-enhancing properties to otherwise parched parts of the country.

While the number of traditional, independent breweries has dropped, you will find many who have not just survived but thrived, tapping into local loyalties and brewing beers to reflect local tastes. Beer is one of the few expressions of regional identity left. London is blessed with two notable survivors, Young's of Wandsworth and Fuller, Smith and Turner of Chiswick. If you're in Suffolk, keep an eye open for pubs with Adnams and Greene King signs; in Lincolnshire for Bateman; Yorkshire for Black Sheep and Taylors; Wales for Brains; Oxfordshire for Brakspear and Hook Norton; Hampshire for Gales; Sussex for Harveys and 1648; Manchester for Joseph Holt; Cumbria for Jennings; Nottingham for Mallards; Staffordshire for Marston's; Dorset for Palmers (Britain's only thatched brewery); Kent for Shepherd Neame; Lancashire for Thwaites; and Wiltshire for Wadworths. You will also find some of these brewers' beers popping up as guest beers other pubs too.

The second positive development has been the creation of micro-breweries supplying local outlets. There are too many to mention, but among those worth keeping an eye open for are Uley beers around Stroud in Gloucestershire; Archers around Swindon in Berkshire; Beowulf around Birmingham; Blackawton around Totnes; Coniston in the Lake District; Exmoor around Wivelscombe in Somerset; Mordue around Tyne and Wear; Pitfield in London; St Peter's in Suffolk; Six Bells around Bishop's Castle in Shropshire; Woodforde's around Norwich in Norfolk; and York suitably around York.

Scan the shelves behind the bar for bottles such as Worthington's White Shield, St Peter's Golden Ale, Marston's Pedigree, Timothy Taylor's Landlord and Black Sheep Ale.

PUBS

You will find some pubs listed in the restaurant section because they blissfully combine fine food and fine beer. Below is a short list of pubs which are worth visiting for their historic or cultural associations as well as their good beer.

LONDON

GEORGE
off 77 Borough High St, London SE1
Tel. 020 7407 2056

DOVE
19 Upper Mall, London W6
Tel. 020 8748 5405

LAMB
94 Lamb's Conduit St, London WC1
Tel. 020 7405 0713

SOUTH EAST

MILBURY'S
Beauworth, Hants
Tel. 01962 771248

SOUTH WEST

HAUNCH OF VENISON
1 Minster St, Salisbury, Wilts
Tel. 01722 322024

OLD GREEN TREE
Green St, Bath
Tel. 01225 448 259

WEST COUNTRY

BLUE ANCHOR
50 Coinagehall St, Helston, Cornwall
Tel. 01326 562821

KING'S ARMS
South Zeal, Devon
Tel. 01837 840300

SOUTH MIDLANDS

HOWARD ARMS
Ilmington, Warwicks
Tel. 01608 682226

THREE KINGS INN
Hanley Castle, Worcs
Tel. 01684 592686

WEST END
9 Bull St, Stratford-upon-Avon
Tel. 01789 268832

HOME COUNTIES

BELL INN
Aldworth, Berks
Tel. 01635 578272

FALKLAND ARMS
Great Tew, Oxfordshire
Tel. 01608 683653

HOBGOBLIN
2 Broad St, Reading, Berks
Tel. 0118 950 8119

ROYAL STANDARD OF ENGLAND
Forty Green, Bucks
Tel. 01494 673382

EAST ANGLIA

ANGEL
Market Place, Lavenham, Suffolk
Tel. 01787 247388

NORTH MIDLANDS

ALBION
Park St, Chester
Tel. 01244 340345

GREEN MAN
Stamford, Lincs
Tel. 01780 753598

OLDE TRIP TO JERUSALEM
1 Brewhouse Yard, Castle Road, Nottingham,
Tel. 0115 947 3171

PRINCESS VICTORIA
Matlock Bath, Derbyshire
Tel. 01629 57462

NORTH EAST

BLUE BELL
Fossgate, York
Tel. 01904 654904

OLDE BLACK BOY
Hull, Yorkshire
Tel. 01482 326516

NORTH WEST

PHILHARMONIC DINING ROOMS
36 Hope Street, Liverpool
Tel. 0151 7072837

WALES

GOAT MAJOR
33 High St, Cardiff
Tel. 029 2033 7161

SLOOP
Porthgain
Tel. 01348 831449

The telephone numbers given below are those of the box offices.

MUSIC

MAIN ORCHESTRAS AND ENSEMBLES

LONDON

LONDON SYMPHONY ORCHESTRA
BBC Symphony Orchestra, Barbican Centre
Tel. 020 7638 8891
www.lso.co.uk

LONDON PHILHARMONIC ORCHESTRA
Philharmonia Orchestra, Orchestra of the Age of Enlightenment, and London Sinfonietta all at the Royal Festival Hall, South Bank Centre,
Tel. 020 7840 4200
www.lpo.co.uk

ROYAL PHILHARMONIC ORCHESTRA
Tel. 020 7608 8800
www.rpo.co.uk

ENGLISH CHAMBER ORCHESTRA
Tel. 020 8840 6565
www.englishchamber orchestra.co.uk/

ACADEMY OF ST MARTIN IN THE FIELDS
Tel. 020 7702 1377
www.asmf.org

LONDON MOZART PLAYERS
Tel. 020 8686 1996
www.lmp.org

CITY OF LONDON SINFONIA
Tel. 020 7621 2800
www.cityoflondon sinfonia.co.uk

HANOVER BAND
Tel. 01273 206978
thehanoverband.com

ACADEMY OF ANCIENT MUSIC
Tel. 01223 301509
www.aam.co.uk

KING'S CONSORT
Tel. 020 8995 9994
www.tkcworld.com

NASH ENSEMBLE
Tel. 020 8203 3025
Recitals and small ensembles at the

Wigmore Hall
Tel. 020 7935 2141
www.wigmore-hall.org.uk
And **Queen Elizabeth Hall** and **Purcell Room**
Tel. 08703 800 400

ALDEBURGH, SUFFOLK

SNAPE MALTINGS CONCERT HALL
Tel. 01728 687100

BIRMINGHAM

CITY OF BIRMINGHAM SYMPHONY ORCHESTRA
Tel. 0121 616 6500
www.cbso.co.uk

BOURNEMOUTH

BOURNEMOUTH SYMPHONY ORCHESTRA
Tel. 01202 670611
www.bsolive.com

BRISTOL

NATIONAL YOUTH ORCHESTRA OF GREAT BRITAIN
Tel. 0117 960 0477

CARDIFF

BBC NATIONAL ORCHESTRA OF WALES
Cardiff,
Tel. 0800 052 1812

LIVERPOOL

ROYAL LIVERPOOL PHILHARMONIC
Tel. 0151 709 3789
www.liverpoolphil.com

MANCHESTER

HALLÉ ORCHESTRA,
Manchester
Tel. 0161 237 7000

BBC PHILHARMONIC ORCHESTRA
Manchester
Tel. 0161 244 4001

NEWCASTLE UP. TYNE

NORTHERN SINFONIA OF ENGLAND
Newcastle upon Tyne
Tel. 0191 443 4661
www.thesagegates head.org.

OPERA AND BALLET

LONDON

ROYAL OPERA
(international repertory in original languages) and
ROYAL BALLET
Covent Garden,

Tel. 020 7304 4000
www.royalopera.org

ENGLISH NATIONAL OPERA (modern productions in English)
London Coliseum
Tel. 020 7836 0111
eno.org

ENGLISH NATIONAL BALLET
Tel. 020 7581 1245
www.ballet.org.uk

RAMBERT DANCE COMPANY
Tel. 020 8630 0600
www.rambert.org.uk

Also periodical opera seasons at:
SADLERS WELLS
Tel. 020 7863 8000, and in summer at the Almeida Theatre
Tel. 020 7359 4404
www.sadlerswells.com

BIRMINGHAM

BIRMINGHAM ROYAL BALLET
Tel. 0121 245 3500
www.brb.org.uk

CARDIFF

WELSH NATIONAL OPERA
Cardiff (and touring company),
Tel. 029 2063 5000
www.wno.org.uk

GLYNDEBOURNE

GLYNDEBOURNE FESTIVAL OPERA
Lewes, Sussex, also touring company;
01273 815000; box office 01273 813813
www.glyndebourne.com

LEEDS

OPERA NORTH LEEDS
(and touring company)
Tel. 0113 243 9999
www.operanorth.co.uk

NORTHERN BALLET
Leeds based,
Tel. 0113 274 5355

OXFORD

GARSINGTON OPERA,
Garsington Manor Oxford,
Tel. 01865 368201
www.garsingtonopera.org

CHOIRS AND CHORAL SOCIETIES

Apart from the choirs attached to the BBC or major symphony orchestras, there are a large number of amateur and semi-professional choirs like the Bach Choir, the Goldsmith's Choral Union, or the choral societies of northern England and Wales. Some of the finest British choral music can be heard in cathedrals and abbeys across the country (particularly at evensong) and in college chapels at Oxford, Cambridge and other universities (of which the choir of King's College, Cambridge is perhaps best known).

THEATER

LONDON WEST END

ALBERY THEATRE
Tel. 0870 060 6621
www.theambassadors.com/albery/

APOLLO THEATRE
Tel. 020 7834 6423

CRITERION THEATRE
Tel. 020 7839 8811

DONMAR WAREHOUSE
Tel. 0870 0606624
www.donmarware house.com

DUKE OF YORK THEATRE
Tel. 0870 060 6623
www.theambassadors.com/dukeofyorks/

GARRICK THEATRE
Tel. 020 7520 5690

GIELGUD THEATRE
Tel. 0870 8901105

LYRIC THEATRE
Tel. 028 9038 1081
www.lyrictheatre.co.uk

NEW AMBASSADORS THEATRE
Tel. 0870 060 6627
www.theambassadors.com

QUEEN'S THEATRE
Tel. 0870 950 0930

VAUDEVILLE THEATRE
Tel. 0870 890 0511

◆ THEATER

WYNDHAM'S THEATRE
Tel. 0870 950 0925

THROUGHOUT LONDON

**ALMEIDA,
ISLINGTON, N1**
Tel. 020 7359 4404
www.almeida.co.uk

**BARBICAN THEATRE
AND PIT, EC2**
Winter home to
the RSC, in summer
taken over by the
London International
Theatre Festival
Tel. 020 7638 8891
www.barbicantheatre.
co.uk

**LYRIC
HAMMERSMITH, W6**
Tel. 0870 050 0511
www.lyric.co.uk

OLD VIC, SE1
Tel. 020 7928 7616
www.oldvictheatre.com

**ROYAL COURT THEATRE,
SW1**
Tel. 020 7565 5000
www.royalcourttheatre
.com

**ROYAL NATIONAL
THEATRE, SE1**
Includes The Olivier,
The Lyttleton and
The Cottesloe
Tel. 020 7452 3000
www.nationaltheatre.
org.uk

**SHAKESPEARE'S GLOBE,
SE1**
Tel. 020 7401 9919
www.shakespeares-
globe.org

YOUNG VIC, SE1
Tel. 020 7928 6363
www.youngvic.org

PICK OF THE FRINGE

**BATTERSEA ARTS
CENTRE (BAC), SW11**
Tel. 020 7223 2223
www.bac.org.uk

THE BUSH, W12
Quality new writing,
Tel. 020 7610 4224

THE GATE, W2
Tel. 020 7229 0706

**THE KING'S HEAD,
ISLINGTON, N1**
London's original
pub theater
Tel. 020 7226 1916

BATH
THEATRE ROYAL
Tel. 01225 448844
www.theatreroyal.org.
uk

BIRMINGHAM
**BIRMINGHAM
REPERTORY THEATRE**
Tel. 0121 236 4455
www.birmingham-
rep.co.uk

BOLTON
THE OCTAGON
Tel. 01204 520661
www.octagonbolton.
co.uk

BRISTOL
**BRISTOL OLD VIC & NEW
VIC STUDIO THEATRE**
Tel. 0117 987 7877

CARDIFF
NEW THEATRE
Tel. 02920 878889
www.newtheatre
cardiff.co.uk

SHERMAN THEATRE
Tel. 029 2064 6900
www.shermantheatre.
co.uk

CHESTER
GATEWAY THEATRE
Tel. 01244 340392
www.gateway-
theatre.org

CHICHESTER
**CHICHESTER FESTIVAL
THEATRE** (from late
spring to early fall)
Tel. 01243 781312
www.cft.org.uk

COLCHESTER
MERCURY THEATRE
Tel. 01206 573948
www.mercurytheatre.
co.uk

COVENTRY
BELGRADE THEATRE
Tel. 024 7655 3055
www.belgrade.co.uk

EXETER
NORTHCOTT THEATRE
Tel. 01392 493493
www.northcott-
theatre.co.ukl

GUILDFORD, SURREY
YVONNE ARNAUD
Tel. 01483 440000
www.yvonne-
arnaud.co.uk

HORNCHURCH, ESSEX
QUEEN'S THEATRE
Tel. 01708 443333
www.queens-
theatre.co.uk

HULL
HULL TRUCK
Tel. 01482 323638
www.hulltruck.co.uk

KESWICK, CUMBRIA
THEATRE BY THE LAKE
Tel. 017687 74411
www.theatrebythelake
.com

LEEDS
**WEST YORKSHIRE
PLAYHOUSE**
Tel. 0113 213 7700
www.wyplayhouse.
com

LEICESTER
LEICESTER HAYMARKET
Tel. 0116 253 0021
www.lhtheatre.co.uk

LIVERPOOL
LIVERPOOL EVERYMAN
Tel. 0151 709 4776
www.everymanplay
house.com

MANCHESTER
CONTACT THEATRE
Tel. 0161 274 0600
www.contact-
theatre.org

LIBRARY THEATRE
Tel. 0161 236 7110

ROYAL EXCHANGE
Tel. 0161 833 9833

MILFORD HAVEN
TORCH THEATRE
Tel. 01646 695267
www.torchtheatre.org

MOLD, FLINTSHIRE
CLWYD THEATR CYMRU
Tel. 0845 330 3565
www.clwyd-theatr-
cymru.co.uk

UNDER LYME
NEW VIC
Tel. 01782 717962
www.newvictheatre.
org.uk

NEWCASTLE UP. TYNE
NORTHERN STAGE
Tel. 0191 230 5151
www.northernstage.co
.uk

THEATRE ROYAL
Tel. 0870 905 5060
www.theatreroyal.co.uk

NORTHAMPTON
**ROYAL DERNGATE
THEATRE**
Tel. 01604 6324811

NORWICH
THEATRE ROYAL
Tel. 01603 630000

OXFORD
OXFORD PLAYHOUSE
Tel. 01865 305305
www.oxfordplayhouse
.com

PLYMOUTH
THEATRE ROYAL
Tel. 01752 267222

RICHMOND,
NORTH YORKSHIRE
**GEORGIAN THEATRE
ROYAL**
Tel. 01748 825252
www.georgiantheatre
royal.co.uk

SCARBOROUGH
**STEPHEN JOSEPH
THEATRE**
plays old and new
by Alan Ayckbourne
plus new writing by
visiting playwrights
Tel. 01723 370541
www.alanayckbourn.
net

SHEFFIELD
SHEFFIELD CRUCIBLE
Tel. 0114 249 6000
www.sheffieldtheatres
.co.uk

STRATFORD-UPON-
AVON
**ROYAL SHAKESPEARE &
SWAN THEATRES**
Tel. 01789 403403
www..rsc.org.uk

SWANSEA
**SWANSEA GRAND
THEATRE**
Tel. 01792 475715

YORK
THEATRE ROYAL
Tel. 01904 623568
www.theatre-royal-
york.co.uk

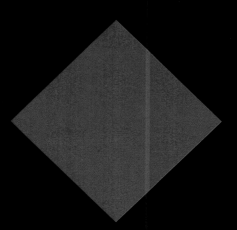

APPENDICES

ESSENTIAL READING
◆ *The English Heritage Visitors' Handbook* (annual)
◆ *The National Trust Handbook* (annual)
◆ *National Gardens Scheme Yellow Book*
◆ BORROW, GEORGE, *Wild Wales*, Gomer Press, 1995
◆ JENKINS, SIMON *England's Thousand Best Churches*, Allen Lane, The Penguin Press, 1999

ARCHITECTURE
◆ AMERY, COLIN, *Period Houses and their Details*, Architectural Press, 1978
◆ ASLET, CLIVE *Last Country Houses*, Yale, 1982
◆ BEARD, GEOFFREY, *The National Trust Book of English House Interiors*, Viking in association with the National Trust, 1990
◆ BURTON, NEIL, *Life in the Georgian City*, Viking, 1990
◆ CLIFTON-TAYLOR, A., *English Parish Churches as Works of Art*, Batsford, 1974
◆ CLIFTON-TAYLOR, A. and SIMMONS, JACK (ed.) *The Pattern of English Building*, Faber and Faber, 1987
◆ COOK, O., *The English Country House*, London 1974
◆ COOPER, NICHOLAS, *Houses of the Gentry, 1480-1680*, Yale, 1999
◆ CORNFORTH, JOHN, *London Interiors*, Aurum, 2000
◆ CORNFORTH, JOHN, *The Inspiration of the Past Country House Taste in the 20th Century*, Viking, 1985
◆ EVANS, LINDSAY *The Castles of Wales*, Constable, 1998
◆ GIROUARD, MARK, *Robert Smythson and the Architecture of the Elizabethan Era*, Barnes n.d., 1960
◆ GIROUARD, MARK, *Life in the English Country House*, Penguin, 1980
◆ HARRIS, JOHN, *The Architect and the British Country House 1620-1920*, The A.I.A. Press, Washington DC 1985
◆ HATCHER, JANE, *Richmondshire Architecture*, 1990
◆ HUSSEY, CHRISTOPHER, *English Country Houses* (3 volumes), Antique Collectors Club

◆ Jackson-Stops, GERVASE, (ed.), *The Treasure Houses of Britain, Five Hundred Years of Private Patronage and Art Collecting*, Yale, 1985
◆ JACKSON-STOPS, GERVASE and PIPKIN, JAMES, *English Country House Grand Tour*, Weidenfeld and Nicolson, 1985
◆ MASSINGBERD, HUGH and SYKES, CHRISTOPHER, *Great Houses of England and Wales*, Laurence King, 1994
◆ MCNEIL, TOM, *English Heritage: Castles*, Batsford, 1992
◆ MUNSON, JEREMY, *English Manor Houses*, Aurum
◆ NORWICH, J.J., *The Architecture of Southern England*, Macmillan, 1985
◆ PEVSNER, NIKOLAUS, *County by County* guides, Penguin, 1954 onward
◆ REPTON, HUMPHREY AND DAVIDS, STEPHEN, *Landscape Gardening and the Gardens of Georgian England*, Yale, 1999
◆ ROBINSON, J.M., *The Architecture of Northern England*, Macmillan, 1986
◆ ROBINSON, J.M., *The Latest Country Houses*, Bodley Head, 1984
◆ RUSSELL, J., *London*, Thames & Hudson, 1996
◆ SAUMEREZ-SMITH, CHARLES, *The Building of Castle Howard*, Pimlico, 1997
◆ SAUMAREZ SMITH, CHARLES, *18th Century Decoration*, Weidenfeld & Nicolson, 1993
◆ SEEBOHM, CAROLINE and SYKES, CHRISTOPHER SIMON, *English Country*, Clarkson Potter, N.Y. 1987
◆ SMITH, EDWIN and ARCHER, LUCY, *Architecture in Britain and Ireland: 600-1500*, Harvill Press, 1999
◆ SPENCER, CHARLES, *Althorp*, Viking, 1999
◆ SUMMERSON, J., *Georgian London*, Barrie & Jenkins, 1988
◆ SUMMERSON, J., *Architecture in Britain: 1530-1830*, Yale, 1953 (9th edition 1993)
◆ WEBB, G., *Architecture in Britain: The Middle Ages*, London, 1956

◆ WILLES, MARGARET (intro.), EINSIEDEL, ANDREAS VON and MACKENZIE, NADIA (photographs), *Historic Interiors*, National Trust, 1999
◆ WORSLEY, GILES, *Classical Architecture in Britain*, Yale, 1995

ART
◆ AMERY, COLIN, *A Celebration of art and architecture: the National Gallery Sainsbury Wing*, National Gallery, 1991
◆ *The Cambridge Guide to the Arts in Britain*, Cambridge, 1989
◆ COLLINS, IAN, *A Broad Canvas: Art in East Anglia since 1880*, Black Dog Books, 1999
◆ HARRIS, JOHN, *The Artist and the Country House, Sotheby Park, Bernet*, 1996
◆ HARDYMENT, CHRISTINA, *Literary Trails: Writers in their Landscape*, National Trust
◆ JANSON, H.E., *History of Art*, Thames & Hudson, 1997
◆ SPALDING, FRANCIS, *British Art since 1900*, Thames & Hudson, 1987
◆ VAUGHAN, WILLIAM, *British Painting: The Golden Age*, London, 1999
◆ WATERFIELD, GILES, *Art Treasures of England*, Merrell Publishers, 1998
◆ WATERHOUSE, ELLIS, *Painting in Britain 1530-1790*, Yale, 1993

HISTORY
◆ ARNOLD, C.J., *An Archaeology of the early Anglo-Saxon Kingdoms*, Routledge, an imprint of Taylor and Francis, 1997
◆ BLAIR, P.H., *Roman Britain and Early England 55 BC-AD 871*, W.W. Norton, 1966
◆ CHIPPINDALE, CHRISTOPHER, *Stonehenge Complete*, Thames & Hudson, 1994
◆ COLLEY, LINDA, *Britons, forging the nation 1707-1837*, Vintage, 1996
◆ FRASER, ANTONIA, *The Gunpowder Plot*, Weidenfeld & Nicolson, 1996
◆ FRASER, ANTONIA, *King Charles II*, Weidenfeld & Nicolson, 1979
◆ GILBERT, MARTIN, *The Dent Atlas of British History*, Dent, 1993
◆ HARDYMENT, CHRISTINA, *Behind the Scenes: Domestic Arrangements in Historic Houses*, National Trust, 1997
◆ HIBBERT, CHRISTOPHER, *The English, A Social History 1066-1945*, HarperCollins, 1987
◆ HIBBERT, C. and WEINREB, B., *The London Encyclopaedia*, Macmillan, 1983
◆ HOBSBAWM, E.J., *Industry and Empire: from 1750 to the present day*, Penguin, 1999
◆ JOHNSON, PAUL, *The Offshore Islands and History of the English People*, Phoenix, 1972, 1998
◆ LATHAM, ROBERT (ed.), *Shorter Pepys*, Bell & Hymen Ltd, 1985
◆ MORGAN, KENNETH O., (ed), *The Oxford Illustrated History of Britain*, Oxford, 1997
◆ MORITZ, CARL, *Journeys of a German in England*, Eland, 1999
◆ PORTER, ROY, *London and Social History*, Penguin, 1994
◆ PAXMAN, JEREMY, *The English*, 1999
◆ STRONG, ROY, *The Story of Britain: A People's History*, Hutchinson in association with Julia Macrae, 1996
◆ TINNISWOOD, ADRIAN, *The Polite Tourist: A History of Country House Visiting*, National Trust
◆ WOODCOCK, THOMAS and ROBINSON, JOHN MARTIN, *Heraldry in National Trust Houses*, The National Trust, 2000

NATURAL HISTORY
◆ ANGEL, HEATHER *The Natural History of Britain and Ireland*, London 1981
◆ CHINERY, MICHAEL, *Insects of Britain and Northern Europe*, 1993
◆ CORNISH, JOE et al., *National Trust Coast*, 1998
◆ *The Country Life Book of the Natural History of the British Isles*
◆ ELPHICK, JONATHAN, *A Guidebook to British Birds*, BBC/RSPB, 1997
◆ HOBHOUSE, PENELOPE, *Garden Design*, 1996
◆ READER'S DIGEST *Nature Lovers' Library Field Guides to Birds, Flowers, Butterflies*

Knopf Guides:
Front cover: View of Cheapside, 1823, drawn by W. Duryer and on stone by T. M. Barnes (litho) Museum of London, UK /Bridgeman Art Library
Everyman Guides
Front cover: Warwick Castle © Warwick Castle. Back cover: Chatsworth House © Chatsworth House Trust.
14 Coal miners © HG
14/15 Liverpool docks © HG
16/17 Epsom Derby © HG
17 Paper seller © HG
18 Sheep farmer © HG; Welsh woman © HG
20/21 Geological photos © Photoair
35 The Armada by Nicholas Hilliard, 1588, © Society of Apothecaries, London/BAL.
36 The Wicker Man, engraving, © MEPL. Stonehenge, print, 1695, © MEPL. Bronze Age gold bracelet, © R.Sheridan/Ancient Art & Architecture Collection. Mercury bronze, © R.Sheridan/ Ancient Art & Architecture Collection.
37 Stonehenge, plate 19 from 'The History of the Nations', aquatint, 19th century © Private Collection/The Stapleton Collection/ BAL. Claudius coin, © Ancient Art & Architecture Collection. First Invasion of Ireland, 1169, St Albans's Chronicle, late 15th century,© Lambeth Palace Library, London/ BAL. Anglo-Saxon Warriors, plate 14 from 'The History of Nations', aquatint, 19th century, © Private Collection/The Stapleton Collection/ BAL. The Round Table and The Holy Grail Roman de Tristan, late 15th century © Musee Conde, France/ Giraudon/BAL.
38 Portrait of William the Conqueror, English

School, 16th century, © Philip Mould, Historical Portraits Ltd, London/BAL. William killing Harold at the Battle of Hastings, 14th century, Decrees of Kings of Anglo-Saxon and Norman England, © British Library, London/BAL. Richard I, CHS pub. Colnaghi, aquatint, 1811, © MEPL. Thomas a Becket, from Butler's Lives of Saints, © MEPL.
39 Norman Conquest, Bayeux Tapestry, detail, © MEPL. Kings of England, from The Kings of England from Brutus to Henry III © British Library, London/BAL. King John of England, from Dresses and Decorations of the Middle Ages, Henry Shaw, © MEPL. King Edward I, from Dress and Habits of the People of England, Joseph Strutt, 1842, © MEPL.
40 100 Years War, from Chroniquers de l'Histoire de France, Ronjat, manuscript, © Bibliotheque Nationale/MEPL. Knight of the Garter, from Dresses and Decorations of the Middle Ages, Henry Shaw, 1858, © MEPL. The Great Plague of London, from Cassell's History of England, © MEPL. Chaucer at the Court of King Edward III by Ford Madox Brown, 1845-51, © Art Gallery of New South Wales, Australia/BAL
41 Caxton Printing Office by Daniel Maclise © Knebworth House, Hertfordshire/ BAL. Owen Glendower, engraving by Forrest, © MEPL. King Henry VI from A Book of Hours, English, 15th century, © Fitzwilliam Museum, University of Cambridge/BAL.
42 Portrait of Henry VIII by Hans the Younger Holbein, © Belvoir Castle,

Leicestershire/ BAL. The Armada, © Society of Apothecaries, London/BAL.
43 Sir Francis Drake by Isaac Oliver, © Victoria & Albert Museum, London/BAL. Queen Elizabeth I by John Bettes, © Explorer Archives/MEPL. Shakespeare and his Friends by John Faed, © Private Collection/BAL. Portrait of Shakespeare, title page from Mr William Shakespeare's Comedies, Histories and Tragedies, 1623, © British Library, London/BAL. Globe Theatre, engraving, detail, 1616, © British Library, London/BAL.
44 Execution of Charles I at Whitehall by Gonzales Coques, © Musee de Picardie, France/Giraudon/BAL. Oliver Cromwell by Christian Richter, (after official portrait by Samuel Cooper, 1708), enamel on vellum, © Wallace Collection, London/BAL. Death Warrant for Charles I, © MEPL. Great Fire of London, 1666 by Lieve Verschuier, © Museum of Fine Arts, Hungary/ BAL.
45 London Coffee House, engraving, © MEPL. Great Plague, engraving by Franklin in Ainsworth's 'Old St Paul's', 1847, © MEPL. William III & Mary II, R de Hooghe, © MEPL. Queen Anne by Edmund Lilly, © Blenheim Palace, Oxfordshire/BAL.
46 Sir Robert Walpole, John Woolton, © MEPL. Title page of the English Dictionary by Samuel Johnson, pub.1755, © Private Collection/BAL. South Sea Bubble pamphlet, © MEPL. Portrait of King George III by Anonymous, copy of painting by William Robinson, 1831, © The Crown Estate/BAL. Master Isaac Newton by Robert Hannah, 1905, oil on canvas, © The Royal Institution, London/BAL. Sir Isaac Newton's telescope at Woolsthorpe Manor, © NT/Tessa Musgrave.
47 The Duke of Wellington at Waterloo by Robert Alexander Hillingford, oil on canvas, © Private

Collection/Christie's Images/BAL. 'A Wellington Boot' satire, © Paul Pry/MEPL. Power loom weaving by Thomas Allom, 1834, engraving, © Private Collection/BAL. Regent's Park: Sussex Place, Thomas Shepherd, engraving by W.R.Smith, © MEPL. John Nash, statue in Regent St, London, © MEPL.
48 Queen Victoria by Sir Francis Grant, 1843, © The Crown Estate/BAL. Penny Post Poster, © Bruce Castle Museum Collection/ MEPL. Victoria Cross, Player's cigarette cards, © MEPL. H.R.H. Prince Albert by John Lucas, © The Crown Estate/BAL. Penny Red and Tuppenny Blue stamps, originals, © MEPL. Stephenson's 'North Star' Steam Engine, 1837, © Private Collection/BAL.
49 Passenger trains of the Liverpool-Manchester railway, © MEPL. The Adventures of Sherlock Holmes, cover, Newnes 6d Copyright Novels, © The Coupland Collection/MEPL. Portrait of Benjamin Disraeli by Henry Jr Weigall, 1880, © Philip Mould/Historical Portraits Ltd, London/ BAL. Discovery of Jack the Ripper victim, F. Fizzi in Famous Crimes, © MEPL. Jack the Ripper victim, Clair Guyot in Le Petit Parisien, 1890, © MEPL.
50 Queen Elizabeth II and Duke of Edinburgh, © Camera Press London/Rota. Whitehall Palace & St James's Park by Hendrick Danckerts (attr. to), © Ackermann and Johnson Ltd, London/BAL. Trooping of the Colour, © Camera Press London/ Stewart Mark.
51 State Opening of Parliament, © Camera Press London/Rota. Garter Ceremony, © Camera Press London/ Stewart Mark/Rota. Tower of London, © Camera Press London/ Stewart Mark. Crown Jewels, © Camera Press London. Royals Open Welsh Assembly, © Camera Press London/ Stewart Mark. George IV in

◆ PICTURE CREDITS

Coronation Robes by E.Scrivenor, engraving, © Guildhall Library, Corporation of London/BAL.
52 Lily Langtry, *Celebrities of the Stage*, © MEPL. WWI ration books, © MEPL. General Strike, 1926, © MEPL. Neville Chamberlain, © HG. WWI Trenches, © MEPL.
53 Morris Minor, in *Good Housekeeping*, © MEPL. Winston Churchill, © HG. The Blitz, © HG. WWII evacuees, © Bruce Castle Museum Collection/MEPL.
54 Clement Attlee by Baron, 1950, © HG. The Beatles, © HG. Miners' strike, © Steve Eason/HG. Margaret Thatcher, 1986, © HG.
55 *The Beggar's Opera, Scene III*, Act XI by William Hogarth, 1729, oil on canvas, © Yale Center for British Art, Paul Mellon Collection, USA/BAL.
56 Shaftesbury Avenue theatres, © Camera Press/Geoff Howard. Judi Dench, © Camera Press/GM. Harold Pinter and Tom Stoppard, © Camera Press/Richard Watts. *The White Devil*, RSC, 1996, © Shakespeare Centre Library, Stratford-upon-Avon.
57 *Jack and the Beanstalk*, at Drury Lane, c.1911, from The Play Pictorial no.102, © MEPL. Sir Henry Irving as Mathias in *The Bells*, © MEPL. Dame Alice Ellen Terry, photograph by Barraud, © MEPL. Oscar Wilde, prob. in *Daily Graphic*, 1890, © MEPL. Noel Coward, © Ida Kar/ MEPL. *Punch and Judy performance*, unnamed artist in 'Chatterbox', © MEPL. The Globe Theatre, © Camera Press/Theodore Wood. Fiona Shaw as Miss Jean Brodie, © Camera Press/Nigel Norrington.
58 Simon Rattle, ©Camera Press/Jon Blau. The Last Night of the Proms, © HG.
59 Sir Edward Elgar, portrait photograph, © Haags Gemeentemuseum, Netherlands/BAL. Benjamin Britten, © Auerbach FRPS, London. George

Frederick Handel, 1738, terracotta, © Fitzwilliam Museum, University of Cambridge/BAL. Huddersfield Town Hall, Choral Society, © Selwyn Green, Bradford. Black Dyke Band, © Huddersfield Town Hall.
60 *The Beggar's Opera, Scene III, Act XI* by William Hogarth, 1729, oil on canvas, © Yale Center for British Art, Paul Mellon Collection, USA/BAL. Covent Garden theatre showing Handel's organ, c.1808, © Museum of London. John Tomlinson as Gawain, 1991, © Clive Barda/Performing Arts Library, London.
61 Margot Fonteyn in *Firebird*, 1856, © HG. Henry Purcell, courtesy of the National Portrait Gallery, London. Joan Cross and Peter Pears in *Peter Grimes*, 1945, © Hulton Deutsch Collection, London. *John Bull at the Italian Opera* by Thomas Rowlandson, 1811, engraving, © Private Collection/BAL. Glyndebourne Opera House, © Mike Hoban. The Royal Opera House, Covent Garden, © Peter Mackertitch.
62 Manchester United football club, © Camera Press. Andre Agassi at Wimbledon, © Camera Press. Roger Bannister, © HG. Wimbledon, aerial view, © Camera Press/John Evans. Willie Carson at Ascot, © Fiona Hanson/PA News, London.
63 Daniel Herbert and Phillipe Bernat-Salles at Rugby World Cup, Cardiff, 1999, ©PA News, London. WIllie Carson at Epsom, © Dennis Oulds/HG. Matthew Pinsent and Steven Redgrave, Atlanta, Georgia, © Rebecca Naden/PA News, London. Ranjitsingh, © The Hulton-Deutsch Collection, London. David Gower, Cornhill Test, © Rex Features, London. Millennium Stadium © Huw Evans Picture Agency, Cardiff. Lord's Cricket Ground, © Edifice/Lewis. W.G. Grace, c.1880, © MEPL.

64 Guy Fawkes Night bonfire, © Rex Features, London. State Opening of Parliament, © PA News, London. Padstow Hobby Horse; Maypole; 'King William' play, Cornwall, © HG.
65 Coracle races, © Brian Robson/Rex Features, London. Beating the Bounds; pancake racing, © Rex Features, London.
66 Cheeses (main picture) & individual cheeses, © Christina Jansen.
91 *Peace - Burial at Sea* by J.M.W.Turner, © Tate Gallery, 2000.
92/93 *The Ambassadors* by Hans Holbein the Younger, 1533, oil on panel, © National Gallery, London/BAL. *Young Man against a Rose Tree* by Nicholas Hilliard, miniature, © Victoria & Albert Museum, London/BAL. Jesse tree courtesy of the Vicar and Churchwardens of St Mary's Church, Abergavenny.
94/95 *Mary Countess Howe* by Thomas Gainsborough, c. 1760, © EH. *The Roman Pontiff, Puis VII*, engraved by Samuel Freeman, pub. by A.Fullarton & Co. (engraving) by Sir Thomas Lawrence, (after), © Private Collection/BAL. *Portrait of Captain Coram* by William Hogarth, 1740, © Coram Foundation, London/BAL. *The painter's wife, Margaret Lindsay*, by Allan Ramsay, 1754-55, © National Gallery of Scotland, Edinburgh/BAL.
96/97 *Golding Constable's Flower Garden* by John Constable, 1815, © Ipswich Borough Council Museums and Galleries, Suffolk/BAL. *Old Walton Bridge over the Thames* by Giovanni Antonio Canaletto, 1754, oil on canvas, © Dulwich Picture Gallery, London/BAL. *The Harvest Wagon* by Thomas Gainsborough, c.1767, © The Barber Institute of Fine Arts, University of Birmingham/BAL. *Brignall Banks on the*

Greta by John Sell Cotman, pencil and w/c, Leeds Galleries and Galleries (City Art Gallery)/BAL.
98/99 *The Ancient of Days* by William Blake, © British Museum, London/BAL. *Cheetah and Stag with two Indians* by George Stubbs, c.1765, © Manchester City Art Galleries/BAL. *Lady Macbeth Seizing the Daggers* by Henry Fuseli, oil on canvas, © Tate Gallery, 2000.
100/101 *Work* by Ford Madox Brown, 1863, oil on canvas, © Birmingham Museums and Art Gallery/BAL. *The Railway Station* by William Powell Frith, 1862, oil on canvas, © Royal Holloway and Bedford New College, Surrey/BAL. *Isabella and the Pot of Basil* by William Holman Hunt, 1867, © Laing Art Gallery, Tyne and Wear/BAL. *Mother and Child (Cherries)* by Frederic Leighton, c.1865, oil on canvas, © Blackburn Museum and Art Gallery, Lancashire/BAL.
102/103 *The Juvenile Head (Self Portrait)* by Walter Richard Sickert, 1907, Southampton City Art Gallery, Hampshire/BAL, © Estate of Walter Richard Sickert, 2000. All rights reserved, DACS. *Figure Study II* by Francis Bacon, Kirklees Metropolitan Council, Huddersfield, Yorkshire/BAL, © Estate of Francis Bacon/ARS, NY and DACS, London 2000. *King and Queen* by Henry Moore, 1952-3, bronze sculpture, Yorkshire Sculpture Park/BAL, © Henry Moore Foundation. *Mother Marie Poussepin* by Gwen John, c.1915-20, The Barber Institute of Fine Arts, University of Birmingham/BAL, © Estate of Gwen John, 2000. All rights reserved, DACS. *The Resurrection of the Soldiers* by Stanley Spencer, 1928-29, mural, detail, Sandham Memorial Chapel, Hampshire/BAL, © Estate of Stanley Spencer, 2000. All rights reserved, DACS.

PICTURE CREDITS ◆

104 *Mr and Mrs Clark and Percy* by David Hockney, 1970-71, acrylic on canvas, © Tate Gallery, 2000/Tradhart. *Mah's Head (Self Portrait)* by Lucian Freud, 1963, © Lucian Freud/Whitworth Art Gallery, Manchester/BAL.
105 Charles Dickens, 1864, © HG. Kingsway tram subway, postcard, c.1905, ©MEPL.
106 Ancient Britons, © MEPL. Saint Bede the Venerable, woodcut, © MEPL.
107 William Shakespeare, by M.Droeshout, Frontispiece to First Folio, engraving, 1623, ©MEPL
108 Daniel Defoe, © MEPL. York, © MEPL.
109 *The Thames* by Thomas H.Shepherd, © MEPL. James Boswell by Evans, engraving, © MEPL. Tobias Smollett by Freeman, engraving, © MEPL.
110 Thomas Macauley by George Richmond, engraving, © MEPL. Henry James by Jeffrey Morgan, illustration, © MEPL.
111 Grasmere Lake and Village, Westmorland, by C. Mottram, after G.Pickering, engraving, © MEPL. William Wordsworth, c. 1820, © MEPL.
112 Beatrix Potter, 1889, © HG. Edward Morgan Forster, original illustration by Jeffrey Morgan, © Jeffrey Morgan/MEPL, courtesy of the Victoria &Albert Museum, reproduced by kind permission of Frederick Warne & Co.
113 Charles Dickens by J.Brown, engraving, © MEPL.
114 St.Ives, Cornwall, 1930, postcard, © MEPL.
115 Blaenau Ffestiniog, Wales, 1961, © Roger Mayne/MEPL. Dylan Thomas, 1946, from *A Nest of Singing Birds*, © HG.
116 Electric tram, Clapham Common, 1904, postcard, © MEPL. The Last Horse Tram in London, 1913, © Hulton Deutsch Collection Ltd. Alan Bennett, © HG.
118/9 Derwentwater © AH

120 Nymans © NT, West Wycombe Park © NT, Cottesbroke Hall and Gardens © Cottesbroke Hall, Dartmoor © AH, Winkworth © NT, Stonehenge © EH, Welshpool © AH, Isle of Wight © NY, Long Mynd © AH,
123 The City of London, © AH.
124 Map, Sylvie Rabbe. Main map, Atelier Duplantier (F.Lieval/M.Lagarde). Nelson's Column, © Nick Swallow. *Whistlejacket* by George Stubbs, 1762, oil on canvas, © National Gallery, London/BAL. St Martin-in-the-Fields, © AH.
125 Eros statue, © Nick Swallow. John Dryden plaque, © AH. London Coliseum, © Nick Swallow.
126 St Paul's church, Covent Garden, © Edifice/Lewis. *Tondo Taddei* by Buonarotti Michelangelo, stone sculptured panel, Royal Academy of Arts, London/BAL. Chinatown, Soho, © Nick Swallow.
127 Burlington Arcade, © Nick Swallow. Cenotaph, Whitehall; 10 Downing St, © AH.
128 Figure of Christ in Westminster Abbey, © EH. Interior of the House of Commons by Joseph Nash, 1858, oil on canvas, © Houses of Parliament, Westminster, London/BAL. The Palace of Westminster, © AH.
129 Westminster Abbey; Westminster Cathedral, © Nick Swallow. Big Ben, © Camera Press/Richard Gillard.
130/131 *The Saltonstall Family* by David de Granges, c.1636-7, oil on canvas; *Miss Cicely Alexander: Harmony in Grey and Green* by James Whistler, 1872-4, oil on canvas; *The Lady of Shallot* by John William Waterhouse, c. 1888, oil on canvas; *Peace-Burial at Sea* by J.M.W.Turner, 1842, oil on canvas, © Tate Gallery, 2000.
132 Banqueting Hall, Whitehall, © Crown Copyright, 1996. St James's Palace, © Nick

Swallow. The Victoria Monument, Buckingham Palace, © AH.
133 Spencer House: Great Hall; exterior, © Spencer House/Mark Fiennes. Cleopatra's Needle, © Emily Lane. Trooping the Colour, © Camera Press/Richard Gillard.
134 Easter Island Statue; The Portland Vase, © The British Museum, London. The British Library, © Irene Rhoden.
135 St Pancras Station hotel; exterior, © Peter Ashley; staircase, © AH. Portrait of Dickens by Samuel Laurence; Drawing Room at Dickens House, © Dickens House Museum.
136/137 The British Museum, exterior, © AH. Selene's Horse; The Great Disk; The Snettisham Great Torc; The Warren Cup; Rameses II, © The British Museum, London.
138/139 Egyptian coffin; Dying Lion Relief; Roman coins; The Rosetta Stone; Study of Adam by Buonarroti Michelangelo; Sutton Hoo Buckle; Bronze head of Hadrian; Human-headed bull and attendant genie, © The British Museum, London.
140 Sir John Soane's Museum: exterior; interior, © Martin Charles. Fleet Street, © Edifice/Lewis. Twinings Tea shop, © Nick Swallow. 'Ye Olde Cheshire Cheese' sign, © Edifice/Lewis.
141 Somerset House; Middle Temple Hall; Temple Gateway, © AH. Royal Courts of Justice: exterior, © Emily Lane; interior, © AH.
142 The Tower of London, © AH. The Crown Jewels, © Camera Press/John D.Drysdale. *St Paul's Cathedral* by Canaletto, 1754, oil on canvas, © Yale Center for British Art, Paul Mellon Collection, USA/BAL.
143 Lord Mayor's Coach, © Museum of London. Mansion House, Egyptian Hall, © AH. Sir Christopher Wren by Sir Godfrey

Kneller, engraved by E.Scriven, © MEPL. Old Bailey statue; Charterhouse Square gateway, © Nick Swallow.
144 College of Arms, © College of Arms. Bank of England, Great Hall, from Ackermann's 'Microcosm of London', 1809, by T.Rowlandson & A.C.Pugin, © Guildhall Library, Corporation of London/BAL. Stock Exchange; Royal Exchange, © Nick Swallow. The Bank of England, © AH.
145 The Monument, © AH. St Bartholomew, © Nick Swallow.
146 Temple church, © Nick Swallow. St Vedast spire, © AH. St Stephen, Walbrook, © Nick Swallow.
147 St Bride's spire; St Mary Woolnoth, © AH. All Hallows, © Nick Swallow
148 The Whitechapel Art Gallery, © AH. Geffrye Museum: interior; © Chris Ridley/Geffrye Museum; exterior, © Geffrye Museum. The Woodpecker, tapestry designed by William Morris, woven at Morris and Co., Merton Abbey, 1885, © William Morris Gallery, London E17. Christchurch, Spitalfields, © Emily Lane.
149 St Katharine's Dock, © Nick Swallow. Sutton House, Great Chamber, © NT/Geoffrey Frosh.
150 /151 Westminster Bridge, © Misha Aniket. Vauxhall Bridge, detail, © AH. Looking east from Waterloo Bridge, c.1830, © MEPL. Tower Bridge, © EH. *Old London Bridge* by Claude de Jongh, 1630, © EH/Jonathan Bailey. The Albert Bridge, © Camera Press/Richard Gillard. Millennium Bridge, © Norman Foster Associates.
152 Design Museum, © Jefferson Smith. Southwark Cathedral, detail; the London Eye; the Globe Theatre, © Nick Swallow.
153 *The Triumph of David* by Nicolas Poussin,c.1631-33. By Permission of the Trustees, Dulwich Picture Gallery. Horniman Museum;

541

PICTURE CREDITS ◆

191 Henry Frederick, Prince of Wales, attr. to Robert Peake, *c.* 1611, at Parham; The Great Hall, Parham, first printed in *The Antique Collector*, 1987, © Parham Park Ltd. Arundel Castle, © Arundel Castle. Walnut armchair, English, c.1685, at Parham, © Parham Park Ltd./Derek Gardiner and Michael Helmsley, Walter Gardiner Photography, Worthing.
192 Page from 15th century version of Chaucer's *Canterbury Tales*, at Petworth, © NT/Mark Fiennes. The Doric Temple, Petworth, © NT/Rupert Truman. *Mrs Robinson* by William Owen, at Petworth, © NT/John Hammond. Petworth through iron gates, © NT/J.Whitaker. *Thomas Wentworth, 1st Earl of Strafford* by Anthony Van Dyck, at Petworth, © NT/Roy Fox. *Lady Ann Carr, Countess of Bedford* by Van Dyck, at Petworth, © NT/A.C.Cooper.
193 *Jacob and Laban* by Claude, at Petworth, © Lord Egremont/NT/John Hammond. *Bucks Fighting at Sunset* by J.M.W.Turner, at Petworth, © NT/Trustees of Tate Gallery. North Gallery, Petworth, © NT/Andreas von Einsiedel. Limewood carved panel by Gibbons, at Petworth, © NT/Nicolas Sapieha. Bust of William III, at Petworth, © NT/AH. *Dewy Morning at Petworth* by J.M.W.Turner, at Petworth, © NT/Trustees of Tate Gallery.
194 Uppark, © NT/Matthew Antrobus. *Seapiece-Morning* by Joseph Vernet, at Uppark, © NT/John Hammond. Uppark, interior, © NT/Nadia MacKenzie. Chichester Cathedral, nave, © AH. Goodwood, exterior, © Goodwood Photo Library. Goodwood, interior, © Goodwood Photo Library/Tim Imrie Tait.
195 Lord Nelson by Sir William Beechey, oil on canvas, 18th century, © Cider House Galleries

Ltd., Surrey/ BAL. Freshwater, Isle of Wight, © NT/Joe Cornish. Quarr Abbey, interiors, © Don French.
196 Yarmouth Castle, © Skyscan Balloon Photography/EH. Appuldurcombe House, © EH. St Nicholas Chapel, Carisbrooke Castle, © EH. Osborne House, © EH.
197 Mottisfont Abbey, © NT/B.K.S.Surveys Ltd. Medieval Merchant's House, © EH. Titchfield Abbey, © EH. *In the Park (St James's Park)* by Malcolm Drummond, oil on canvas, 1912, © Southampton City Art Gallery, Hampshire/ BAL. *Perseus and the Sea Nymphs* by Sir Edward Burne-Jones, gouache, c.1876, © Southampton City Art Gallery, Hampshire/ BAL.
198 Winchester School: exterior; stained-glass window, © Emily Lane. Chawton © Chawton. Strathfieldsaye House, from *Old England*, © MEPL.
199 The Vyne, © NT/Vera Hunter. Casket in the Ante Room, The Vyne, © NT/James Mortimer. *Mamillius in Charge of a Lady of the Court* by Henry Fuseli, from the *Winters Tale*, c.1785-86, © NT/Christopher Hurst.
200 Palace House: interior; exterior, © National Motor Museum, Beaulieu. Breamore, © Breamore House. *Ablutions and Moving Kitbags*, by Stanley Spencer, 1939, at Sandham Memorial Chapel, © Estate of Stanley Spencer, 2000. All rights reserved, DACS/NT. *The Boy with the Bat*, c.1760, at Breamore, © Breamore House.
201 The Pantheon at Stourhead, © NT/Nick Meers.
202 Map, © Sylvie Rabbe. Main map, © Atelier Duplantier (F.Lieval/M.Lagarde). Wimborne Minster: south east view; stained-glass window; nave, © Woodmansterne Ltd, Watford.
203 Painted ceiling of the Saloon at Kingston Lacy, © NT/James

Mortimer. Kingston Lacy, south front, © NT/Rupert Truman. *Cardinal Camillo Massimi* by Diego Velasquez, at Kingston Lacy, © NT/Roy Fox. Fiddleford Manor, © EH.
204 Brownsea Island, © NT/B.K.S. Surveys Ltd. Durdle Door, © Nick Swallow. Brownsea Castle, © NT/Joe Cornish. Lulworth Castle: exterior; interior, © EH. Corfe Castle, © NT/Matthew Antrobus.
205 Dorchester, © Emily Lane. Maiden Castle, © Skyscan Balloon Photography/ EH. Great Hall, Athelhampton House, © Athelhampton House.
206 Mapperton, © Patrick Cooke. Parnham House, © Parnham House. Wolfeton House: Great Stairs, © Wolfeton House; exterior, © Michael J.Allen Photography, Dorset.
207 Forde Abbey: interior; exterior, © Forde Abbey. *Elizabeth I in Procession*, British School, at Sherborne Castle, © Sherborne Castle Estates. Sherborne Castle, detail, © Emily Lane.
208 Mompesson House, © NT/Susan Witney. Chapter House, Salisbury Cathedral, © Steve Day for Salisbury Cathedral. Malmesbury House, © Malmesbury House. Salisbury Cathedral, spire, © Steve Day. Sundial, Malmesbury House, © Malmesbury House.
209 Tisbury Barn, © The Lanes, London. Fonthill Abbey, © AH. Salisbury Cathedral, exterior, © Nick Swallow. Old Wardour Castle, © Skyscan Balloon Photography/EH.
210/211 Wilton House: Double Cube Room, © Wilton House Trust/Ian Jackson Photography, 1996; exterior, © Wilton House Trust/Ian Jackson Photography, 1998; Single Cube Room, © Wilton House Trust/Ian Jackson Photography, 1996; Palladian Bridge, © Wilton House Trust/Ian Jackson Photography, 1998; *Philip, 4th Earl*

and His Family by Sir Anthony van Dyck, in Double Cube Room, © Wilton House Trust.
212 Stonehenge, © EH. Avebury Stone Circle (main picture), © EH.
213 Longleat House, reproduced by permission of the Marquess of Bath, Longleat House, Warminster, Wiltshire, Great Britain. Windmill Hill, © AH. West Kennet Long Barrow, © EH. Avebury Stone Circle, © EH. Silbury Hill, © EH.
214/215 Stourhead: balustraded villa, © NT/Nick Meers; Cheere statue of Neptune, © NT/Nick Meers; the Pantheon, © NT/Nick Meers. *Flight into Egypt* by C. Maratta, at Stourhead, © NT/John Hammond. *Lady Hoare (Frances Acland)* by Francis Cotes, at Stourhead, © NT/John Hammond. The Temple of Apollo, © NT/Nick Meers.
216 Great Chalfield Manor, © NT. The Courts, Holt, © NT/George Wright. Westwood Manor, © NT/Neil Campbell-Sharp.
217 Farleigh Hungerford Castle, Lady Tower, © EH. The White Horse, Westbury, © AH. Farleigh Hungerford Castle, general view, © EH
218 Corsham Court, © Unichrome of Bath. Bowood House: exterior; the Orangery, © The Bowood Estate. William Henry Fox Talbot, photograph, at Lacock Abbey, © NT/Nick Carter. Lacock Abbey, exterior, © NT.
219 Corsham Court, interior, © Unichrome of Bath. Malmesbury Abbey: detail; door, © Emily Lane.
220 Assembly Rooms, Bath: Tea Room, © NT/John Bethell; Ballroom, © NT/Andreas von Einsiedel. Roman Baths, © Richard Tapscott. Baths with abbey church in background, © Simon McBride.
221 Royal Crescent, Bath. © AH. Landsdowne Tower, © Emily Lane.
222 *Henrietta Laura Pulteney* by Angelica

Kaufmann, oil on canvas, © Holburne Museum of Art, Bath. Prior Park, © Edifice/Darley. *Main Facade of the Holburne Museum* by Ray Williams, oil, © Holburne Museum of Art, Bath. Dyrham Park, © NT/Rupert Truman.
223 Dyrham Park: Diogenes Room, © NT/Andreas von Einsiedel; State Bed in the Queen Anne Room, © NT/Andreas von Einsiedel. *Peasant Woman and Boy* by Bartolomé Esteban Murillo, © NT/John Hammond. Claverton Manor, American Museum, © Claverton Manor.
224 Bristol Cathedral, © AH. Lord Mayors Chapel of St Mark on the Green, © Nick Swallow. Clifton Suspension Bridge, © Nick Swallow.
225 Wills Tower, © Nick Swallow. Nash cottages, Blaise Hamlet, © Nick Swallow.
226 Congresbury church: detail; exterior; © Nick Swallow. All Saints Church, Wraxall: stained-glass window; exterior, © Nick Swallow.
227 Stone circles, Stanton Drew, © Nick Swallow. Cottages, Stanton Drew, © Nick Swallow. Clevedon Court, © NT/John Blake.
228 Wells Cathedral: nave, © AH; astronomical clock, © Wells Cathedral Library and Archives; Vicars' Close, © Emily Lane.
229 Stone work at Wells, © Emily Lane. Wells Cathedral, exterior, © AH.
230 Glastonbury Abbey, © Glastonbury Abbey Church. Tower at Glastonbury, © NT/William R.Davis. Montacute, © NT/Nick Meers.
231 Lytes Cary Manor, © NT/Nick Meers. Barrington Court, © NT/Neil Campbell-Sharp. Elizabeth Knollys, Lady Layton, attr. to George Gower, 1577, at Montacute, © NT/Derrick E.Witty. *Colonel Edward Phelips*, attr. to Jacob Huysams, 1663, at

Montacute, © NT/Derrick E.Witty.
232 Tintinhull House Garden, © NT/Neil Campbell-Sharp. Tintinhull House Garden, © NT/Nick Meers. Cleeve Abbey, © EH. Exmoor National Park, © Emily Lane. Dunster Castle: exterior, © NT/ Magnus Rew; interior, © NT/ Bill Batten.
233 Oldway Mansion, Paignton, © Christina Jansen.
234 Map, © Sylvie Rabbe. Main map and Scilly Isles, © Atelier Duplantier (F.Lieval/M.Lagarde). Ottery St Mary, © Emily Lane. Exeter Cathedral, monument, © Emily Lane.
235 Exeter Cathedral: exterior, © Pitkin Unichrome; corbels, © Penwell Ltd. A la Ronde, Exmouth, © Emily Lane.
236 Powderham Castle: grand staircase; libraries, © Woodmansterne Ltd., Watford. Killerton, © NT/John Blake. Gentleman's frock coat and lady's bodice and skirt, at Killerton, © NT/Andreas von Einsiedel.
237 Berry Pomeroy Castle, © EH. Dartmouth Castle, © EH. Totnes Castle, © EH. Compton Castle, © NT/John Blake.William of Orange statue, Brixham, © Christina Jansen.
238 Hound Tor medieval village, © EH. Dartington Hall, © Christina Jansen. Buckfast Abbey: nave; exterior, © Christina Jansen.
239 Okehampton Castle, © EH. Lydford Gorge, © NT. Castle Drogo: exterior, © NT/Chris Gascoigne; library, © NT/James Mortimer.
240 Buckland Abbey: exterior; Drake Chamber, © NT/George Wright. Portrait of Sir Francis Drake by Marcus Gheeraerts (style of), oil on panel, 1591, © National Maritime Museum/BAL.
241 *Theresa Robinson, Mrs Parker, and Her Son, later Lord Morley* by Sir Joshua Reynolds, at Saltram, © NT. Saltram House: dining

room, © NT/Andreas von Einsiedel; exterior, © NT/Rupert Truman; Adam vase, © NT/Andreas von Einsiedel.
242 Cotehele House, © NT/Andreas von Einsiedel. Lanhydrock House, © NT/Rupert Truman. Edgcumbe coat of arms, © Mount Edgcumbe House and Country Park. St Mawes Castle, © EH.
243 Mount Edgcumbe House, © Mount Edgcumbe House and Country Park. Trelissick Garden, © NT/Stephen Robson. Truro Cathedral, © Edifice/Samer. *Mount Edgcumbe House and Country Park, Stonehouse and Plymouth* by W. du Busc, watercolor, c.1680, © Plymouth City Art Gallery.
244 Falmouth, © Crown Copyright/National Monuments Records Centre, Swindon. Pendennis Castle, © EH. Minack Theatre, © Minack Theatre.
245 Trengwainton Garden, © NT/Andrew Besley. Glendurgan Garden, © NT/Jerry Harpur. *Among the Missing* by Walter Langley, watercolor, 1884, © Penlee House, Gallery and Museum, Penzance.
246/247 St Michael's Mount: main picture, © NT/Oliver Benn; inset, © NT; chapel interior, © NT/John Bethell; Celtic cross, © NT; Blue Drawing Room, © NT/John Bethell.
248 Chysauster Ancient Village, © EH. Tresco Abbey Garden, © Tresco Abbey Gardens. Cornish Engines, Taylor's shaft, © NT/Andy Williams.
249 Great Hall, Trerice, © NT/Andreas von Einsiedel. *People in a Wind* by Kenneth Armitage, 1950, © Tate Gallery, St Ives. Tate Gallery, St Ives. The Medieval Castle AD1230 by Ivan Lapper, reconstruction drawing, © EH/Jeremy Richards. Tintagel Castle, © EH. Prideaux Place, © Prideaux Place.
250 Launceston Castle, © Skyscan Balloon Photography/EH. Clovelly Harbour, ©

Cornish Picture Library/Paul Watts.
251 Memorial stones at Lundy, © NT/Joe Cornish. View from Penally Hill, © Cornish Picture Library/Paul Watts. Hartland Point, © Cornish Picture Library/Paul Watts.
252 Arlington Court: portico entrance, © NT/Matthew Antrobus; morning room, © NT/Andreas von Einsiedel. Neo-Gothic Hall, Knightshayes Court, © NT/AH. *River Scene in Picardy* by R.P. Bonington, at Knightshayes Court, © NT/John Hammond.
253 Barnsley House Garden, The Laburnum Walk, © Barnsley House.
254 Map, © Sylvie Rabbe. Main map, Atelier Duplantier (F.Lieval/M.Lagarde). Imperial Gardens, Cheltenham, © Cheltenham Tourism Photographic Library. Chedworth Roman Villa, mosaic detail, © NT/Ian Shaw.
255 Tewkesbury Abbey, © Emily Lane. Hailes Abbey, © EH. Sudeley Castle: Claude Lorrain painting; view from Tithe Barn, © Sudeley Castle.
256 Gloucester Cathedral: nave; cloisters, © AH.
257 Chavenage House, Glos., © Chavenage House. Berkeley Castle: Great Hall; exterior; coat of arms, © Berkeley Castle. Tetbury Church, nave, © AH.
258 Sezincote, © Sezincote House. Sezincote, with gardens, © Sezincote House. Barnsley House: exterior; The Laburnum Walk; The Potager, © Barnsley House.
259 Chastleton House, © Edifice/Darley. Hidcote Manor, and Gardens, © NT/Andrew Lawson. The Gatehouse at Stanway, © Lord Neidpath. Snowshill Manor, © NT/Andreas von Einsiedel.
260/261 Arlington Row, Glos., © Edifice/Lewis. Snowshill; Vineyard St, Winchcombe; Painswick; Slad, © Steve Dovey/ Gloucestershire County Council. Fairford

Church, Glos., © Geoff Heyworth. **262** St Briavel's Castle, © EH. St Mary and All Saints church, © Peter Ashley. Westbury Court Garden, © NT/Stephen Robson.

263 Goodrich Castle: aerial view, © Skyscan Balloon Photography/EH; the Keep, © EH. Much Marcle church, detail, © Emily Lane. Church of Saints Mary and David, doorway, © AH.

264 Berrington Hall, © NT/John Blake. Moccas Court, © Emily Lane. Eastnor Castle, © Eastnor Castle.

265 Berrington Hall, staircase, © NT/Nadia MacKenzie. Croft Castle, staircase, © NT/J.Whitaker. Bust of Sir Edward Elgar, bronze, by English School, 20th century, © Private Collection/Philips, The International Fine Art Auctioneers/BAL.

266 Croome Landscape Park, © NT/Vera Collingwood. Wichenford Court, Dovecote, © NT/Dennis Davis. Worcester Cathedral, © Worcester Cathedral.

267 Brockhampton House, © NT/Nick Meers. Spetchley Park Garden, © Spetchley Park. Worcester Cathedral, interior, © Worcester Cathedral.

268/269 Witley Court: south front; Orangery wall; Poseidon fountain; south front detail; domed pavilion, © EH.

270 Hanbury Hall, © NT/Alasdair Ogilvie. Harvington Hall, © Ivanhoe Photography, Stourbridge.

271 The Industrial Gallery, Birmingham Museum & Art Gallery, © Birmingham Museums & Art Gallery. *The Last of England* by Ford Madox Brown, oil on panel, 1852-55, © Birmingham Museums & Art Gallery.

272 Royal Shakespeare Theatre, © Simon McBride. Shakespeare's statue, © Camera Press/Jon Blau.

273 Charlecote Park: exterior, © NT/Oliver Benn; Great Hall, © NT/Andreas von Einsiedel; Great Hall, detail, © NT/Derrick E. Witty.

274/275 Warwick Castle: aerial view; jousting at Warwick; east front with tower; bedroom; waxworks; Great Hall, © Warwick Castle, Warwick, England.

276 *El Espolio* by El Greco, panel, at Upton House, © NT/Upton House (Bearstead Collection)/AH. Lord Leycester Hospital, © Lord Leycester Hospital. Packwood House, iron gates, © NT/Richard Surman. Coughton Court, © NT/A.F. Kersting.

277 *Morning* by William Hogarth, at Upton House, © NT/John Hammond. *St Michael and the Devil*, at Coventry Cathedral, © Coventry Cathedral. Kenilworth Castle, © EH.

278 Earls Barton church, © All Saints, Earls Barton. Fawsley Court, © Emily Lane. Great Chamber, Canons Abbey, © NT/Andrew Haslam. Eleanor's Cross, Peter Ashley. Stoke Park Pavilions, © Stoke Park Pavilions.

279 Cottesbrooke Hall, © Cottesbrooke Hall, Northampton. Holdenby House, © Peter Marshall/Holdenby House. John, Earl Spencer effigy, Great Brington, © Emily Lane.

280 Kirby Hall, © EH/Nigel Corrie. Rushton Triangular Lodge, © EH. Rockingham Castle, © Skyscan Balloon Photography. Sir Edward Word, sculpture, Stoke Doyle church, © Emily Lane.

281 West Wycombe Park, balustrade, © NT/Vera Collingwood.

282 Map, © Sylvie Rabbe. Gorhambury, St Albans, © Edifice/Sayer. Main map, © Atelier Duplantier (F.Lieval/M.Lagarde). St Albans Abbey: interior; exterior, © St Albans Abbey.

283 The Gardens of the Rose, © Carl Wallace/Royal National Rose Society. St Leonard's church, © Malcolm Hill.

284 Bishop's Palace and Knot Garden, © Edifice/Sayer. Hatfield House, aerial view, ©

AH. George Bernard Shaw, © Karsh/Camera Press. Knebworth House: exterior; Banqueting Hall, © Knebworth House.

285 Benington Lordship: gardens (small picture), © Benington Lordship; gardens (large picture); mock Norman gateway, © Peter Ashley. Henry Moore sculptures at Perry Green, © Edifice/Darley.

286 Portrait of John Milton, old print from painting by Cornelius Janssen, © Woodmansterne Ltd., Watford. Milton's Cottage (both pictures), © Edifice/Sayer.

287 Long Crendon Courthouse, © NT/John Blake. Boarstall Tower, © NT/John Parry. Princes Risborough Manor, © NT/William R.Davis. Chiltern Open Air Museum: interior, © Steve Norris/Chiltern Open Air Museum; exterior, © Chiltern Open Air Museum. Waddesdon Manor, © Edifice/Sayer.

288 Hughenden Manor: The Right Hon.B. Disraeli MP by Sir Francis Grant P.R.A., 1852, © NT/John Hammond; Inner hall, © NT/John Bethell. Cliveden: exterior © NT/Oliver Benn; Nancy Astor by John Singer Sargent, 1906, © NT/John Hammond.

289 West Wycombe Park: exterior, © NT/Vera Collingwood; Temple of Venus, © NT/Alasdair Ogilvie; ceiling in the Tapestry Room, detail, © NT/John Bethell. Ascott: bronze fountain group, © NT/Vera Collingwood; *Interior* by Ludolph de Jongh, © HBR Thames & Chilterns/NT/John Hammond; writing desk in the common room, © NT/Angelo Hornak.

290 Mentmore Towers: exterior; central hall, © Mentmore. Claydon House: Chinese Room, © NT/Andreas von Einsiedel; *Sir Edmund Hope Verney - 3rd Baronet*, artist unknown, 1868, © NT/John Hammond. Stowe Landscape Gardens: Palladian

Bridge, © NT/Rupert Truman; Vanbrugh's Rotunda, © NT/Jerry Harpur.

291 Stowe House; Winslow Hall, © Edifice/Darley. Gothic Temple, Stowe, © AH.

292 *Piazzetta San Marco* by Canaletto, 1358, at Woburn Abbey, © Woburn Abbey. Dunstable Priory; All Saints, Chalgrave, © Peter Ashley. Elephant House, Whipsnade Zoo, © Edifice/Darley.

293 Woburn Abbey: State Bedroom; *Portrait of Elizabeth I* by Gower, detail; Venetian Room, © Woburn Abbey. Statue of John Bunyan, © Edifice/Sayer.

294 Wrest Park House and Gardens, © EH. Monuments at De Grey Mausoleum, Flitton, © EH. Hinwick House, © Peter Ashley. Brasses at Houghton Conquest church, © All Saints, Houghton Conquest.

295 Elstow Moot Hall; exterior; interior, © Elstow Moot Hall Museum. Gold Bull, High St, Bedford, © Emily Lane. Bushmead Priory, © EH. Church of St Mary, Felmersham, © Edifice/Cole.

296 Royal Holloway College; aerial view; interior, © Royal Holloway College; exterior, © Emily Lane.

297 Dorney Court, © Dorney Court. *Self Portrait (Adelaide Road)* by Stanley Spencer, 1939, Ex-Edward James Foundation, Sussex/BAL, © Estate of Stanley Spencer, 2000. All rights reserved, DACS. *Pumpkin* by George Stubbs, at Ascott, © Lord Rothschild/NT/John Hammond.

298/299 Windsor Castle: exterior (small), © Edifice/Sayer; Garter Throne Room, © The Royal Collection © 1999, HM Queen Elizabeth II/John Freeman; St George's Chapel, exterior, © AH; exterior (large), © Edifice/Sayer; aerial view, The Royal Collection © 1999, HM Queen Elizabeth II/Chorley & Handford; St George's Chapel (interior), The Royal Collection © 1999, HM

PICTURE CREDITS ◆

335 Peterborough Cathedral; exterior; the choir and crossing, © AH. Ramsey Abbey: gatehouse; estate office, © Peter Ashley. Elton Hall, © Peter Ashley.
336 Longthorpe Tower, © EH. Peckover House, © NT/Stephen Robson. Arms of Charles II, Guildhall, © Peter Ashley. Mural, Longthorpe Tower, © EH.
337 Peckover House; the Dining Room, © NT; gardens, © Peter Ashley. March church, ceiling, © Peter Ashley. John Clare Memorial, Helpston, © Peter Ashley.
338 Euston Hall: exterior; *Mares and Foals* by George Stubbs, © Euston Estate, Norfolk. Ickworth House: exterior, © NT/Rupert Truman. *Augustus John Hervey*, Vice-Admiral of the Blue by Thomas Gainsborough, © NT/John Hammond.
339 Melford Hall, © NT/Martin Charles. The Guildhall, Lavenham, © Emily Lane. Pompeian Room, Ickworth, © NT/Andreas von Einsiedel. Kentwell Hall: exterior; interior, © Kentwell Hall.
340 Barnardiston monument, Kedington, © Emily Lane. Covehithe, © Emily Lane. Walpole Old Chapel, © Peter Ashley.
341 Blythburgh Holy Trinity, exterior; All Saints, Acton; Walpole Old Chapel, © Peter Ashley. Blythburgh Holy Trinity, interior; St Nicholas, pulpit and animal carving, © Peter Ashley. Kedinton, carved animal, © Emily Lane.
342 Gainsborough's House: facade 1991 by Peter Jarvis, pencil, pen and ink and watercolor on board, © Gainsborough's House, Sudbury. Willy Lott's Cottage, © NT/Colin R.Chalmers.
343 The Bull and All Saints church, © Peter Ashley. Hadleigh Guildhall, © Hadleigh Guildhall. River House, doorway, © Peter Ashley. Haughley Park: grounds; exterior, © Haughley Park.

344 Helmingham Hall Gardens, © Helmingham Estate. Otley Hall: exterior; the Linenfold Parlour, © Otley Hall.
345 Butley Priory, © Butley Priory. Landguard Fort: inner entrance; Guardroom, © Peter Ashley. Orford Castle, © Skyscan Balloon Photography/EH.
346 Framlingham Castle, © Skyscan Balloon Photography/EH. Leiston Abbey; House in the Clouds, © Peter Ashley.
347 Beach at Thorpeness, © Peter Ashley. Dunwich Heath, © NT/John Miller. Saxtead Green Mill, © Peter Ashley.
348 Norfolk Broads, © AH. St Mary's, rood screen; St Peter's Mancroft, © Peter Ashley.
349 Walpole St Peter; © Peter Ashley. Wymondham Abbey, © Emily Lane. St Margaret's, Hales; St Mary's, Shelton; St.Peter's Mancroft, © Peter Ashley.
350 West Walton church, © Emily Lane. Castle Rising Castle, © EH. Guildhall, Kings Lynn, © Peter Ashley.
351 Cley-next-the-Sea: windmill; cottages, © Peter Ashley. Cley-next-the-Sea, aerial view, © AH. Binham Priory, © EH. Felbrigg Hall: *Old London Bridge* by Samuel Scott, 18th century, © NT/John Hammond; Drawing Room, © NT/Nadia MacKenzie.
352 The Coke Coat-of-Arms, © Holkham Estate. Holkham Hall: aerial view; Marble Hall; *Sir Edward Coke* by Gheeraerts, © Holkham Estate. Chair at Houghton Hall, © Jarrold Publishing, Norfolk.
353 Holkham Hall, The North Tribune, © Holkham Estate. Houghton Hall: The Saloon; Chinese plate; *Marchioness of Cholmondeley* by John Singer Sargent, 1919; *Sir Robert Walpole* by John Wooton, © Jarrold Publishing, Norfolk/Neil Jinkerson. *The Duc d'Arenberg* by Van Dyck, at Holkham, © Holkham Estate.

354 Castle Acre Priory, © EH. Old Merchant's House, Gt Yarmouth, © EH. Grimes Graves, © Skyscan Balloon Photography/EH.
355 Blickling Hall: exterior, © AH; the Great Hall, © NT/Nadia MacKenzie. Sir Henry Hobart, 1st Baronet by Daniel Mytens, c. 1624, © NT/John Hammond. Oxburgh Hall: King's Room, © NT/Bill Batten; West Staircase Hall, © NT/Mark Fiennes; exterior view, © NT/Matthew Antrobus.
356 Norwich Cathedral, nave, © AH. Norwich Castle, © Emily Lane. Norwich Cathedral, exterior, © AH.
357 *'Jason', His Groom and Sir Harry Harpur* by Sawrey Gilpin, at Calke Abbey, © NT/Christopher Hurst.
358 Map, © Sylvie Rabbe. Main map, © Atelier Duplantier (F.Lieval/M.Lagarde). Statue of Minerva, © Emily Lane. Burghley House, © English Life Publications Ltd.
359 Burghley House: exterior, © Peter Ashley; the Great Hall, © English Life Publications Ltd. *Sir Isaac Newton* by Sir James Thornhill, 1710, Trinity College, Cambridge, © BAL. *Lady Adelaide Talbot, Countess Brownlow*, by Lord Leighton from Belton, © NT/John Hammond. Lapis Lazuli cabinet, Belton House, © NT/Mark Fiennes.
360 Belvoir Castle: exterior; lake view, © Belvoir Castle; flower garden, © Arthur Pickett.
361 Belvoir Castle: Caius Cibber statue © Belvoir Castle; Regents Gallery, © Arthur Pickett.
362 Gunby Hall: exterior, © NT; Oak or West Drawing Room, © NT. Tattershall Castle, © NT.
363 Lincoln Cathedral, © AH. Lincoln Cathedral, detail, © Emily Lane.
364 Various objects by William Libery, © The Usher Gallery, *Lincoln*. *Lincoln from The South West* by Peter de Wint, © The Usher Gallery. Stow Church: chancel;

crossing; exterior, © Murray King.
365 Gainsborough Old Hall, © EH. St.Mary Magdalene, © Peter Ashley.
366 Newstead Abbey, © Emily Lane. Wollaton Hall, © AH. Holme Pierrepont Hall, © Emily Lane.
367 Robin Hood, bronze, © Camera Press. Clumber Park Bridge, © NT. Clumber Chapel, © NT. Worksop Manor Stables, © Emily Lane.
368 Staunton Harold: exterior, © NT/Brian Lawrence; east end; Chancel, © NT/John Bethell.
369 Oakham Castle, Great Hall, © Leicestershire Musuems, Arts and Records Service. Lyddington Bede House, © EH. Stanford Hall: ballroom; library; *The Quintet* by F. Torond, © Arthur Pickett.
370 *Portrait of Dr Johnson*, Anonymous, © Private Collection/BAL. Lichfield Cathedral: interior; exterior, © Emily Lane. Hoar Cross Church, © Emily Lane. *The West Front of Shugborough* by Nicholas Dall, c. 1768, © NT.
371 Sandon Orangery, © Emily Lane. Cheadle sedilia, © Emily Lane. Barlaston Hall, © Edifice/Darley.
372 Wightwick Manor, © NT/Rupert Truman. Leicester Wallpaper by J.H. Dearle, at Wightwick Manor © NT/Andreas von Einsiedel. Gladstone Pottery Museum, Stoke on Trent, © Gladstone Pottery Museum. *View of the Iron Bridge* by William Williams, 1780, © Ironbridge Gorge Museum, Telford/BAL.
373 Buildwas Abbey, © EH. Boscobel House, © EH. Wenlock Priory, © EH. Lilleshall Abbey, © EH.
374 Ludlow Castle, © G.B.Thomas, FRPS. Dudmaston Hall, © NT/Michael Caldwell. *Flamenco Dancers* by Sonia Delauney, 1916, at Dudmaston, © NT/Jonathan Gibson. Stokesay Castle, © EH.
375 Stokesay Castle gatehouse, © EH. Attingham Park, dining room, © NT/Oliver Benn.

Attingham Park: exterior, © NT/ Mike Williams. *Henrietta Maria Hill, Marchioness of Ailesbury,* by Sir Thomas Lawrence, © NT/John Hammond. Clun Castle, © EH.
376 Haughmond Abbey, © EH. Eastgate St, Chester, © Christine Hinze/MEPL.
377 Hawkstone Park, © Hawkstone Park. Chester Cathedral: exterior; © Judges of Hastings; interior, ©Unichrome (Bath) Ltd. Beeston Castle, © EH.
378 Little Moreton Hall, © NT/Rupert Truman. St Mary's Church, © St Mary's Church.
379 Lyme Park, exterior, © NT/ Nick Meers. Tatton Park, detail, © NT/Mark Fiennes. Lyme Park, entrance hall, © NT/Andreas von Einsiedel. Lyme Park, courtyard, © NT/ Nick Meers. Dunham Massey, Great Hall, © NT/Mike Williams.
380 Haddon Hall, © Haddon Hall. Peveril Castle, © Skyscan Balloon Photography/ EH. Buxton Crescent, © High Peak Borough Council.
381 Dovedale, © NT/Joe Cornish. Kedleston Hall, fireplace, © NT/Nadia MacKenzie. Melbourne Hall, © Derbyshire Countryside Ltd. Design for One Wall of a Book Room by Robert Adam, 1768, pen, ink and watercolor, at Kedleston, © NT/John Hammond.
382 Hardwick Hall: exterior, © EH; Flemish tapestry, detail, late 16th century, © NT/ John Hammond; State Withdrawing Room, © NT; *Elizabeth of Hardwick* by Rowland Lockey (attr. to), 1592(?), © NT/Hawkley Studios.
383 Chatsworth, aerial view, © AH. Chatsworth House: exterior; violin, © Chatsworth House Trust. Sudbury Hall, © NT/Andrew Butler. Sutton Scarsdale Hall, © EH. Bolsover Castle, © EH. Chesterfield Cathedral, © Edifice/Darley.

384 Sudbury Hall, © NT. Sulton Scarsdale Hall, © EH. Bolsover Castle: exterior; Pillar Chamber, © EH. Chesterfield Cathedral, © Edifice.
385 Dunstanburgh Castle, © NT/Lee Frost.
386 Map, © Sylvie Rabbe. Main map, Atelier Duplantier (F.Lieval/M.Lagarde). Beverley Minster: detail, © Emily Lane; exterior, © AH.
387 Thornton Abbey, © EH. Burton Agnes Hall: Long Gallery; exterior, © Burton Agnes Hall.
388 Paine's Mansion House, © Emily Lane. Roche Abbey, © EH. *A Convalescent* by James Jacques Joseph Tissot, *c.*1876, © Sheffield Galleries and Museums Trust/BAL.
389 Brodsworth Hall, Drawing Room, © EH. *A Corner of the Artist's Room, Paris* by Gwen John, *c.* 1907-09, © Sheffield Galleries and Museums Trust/ BAL, © Estate of Gwen John, 2000. All rights reserved, DACS. Brodsworth Hall, © EH. Conisbrough Castle, © EH.
390 The Friend's School, Ackworth, © The Friend's School. Nostell Priory: Dining Room, © NT/Mark Fiennes; *The Family of St Thomas More* by a follower of Holbein, © Lord St Oswald/NT.
391 Temple Newsam House: exterior; the Gothick Room; the Long Gallery, © Leach Studio Ltd, W.Yorkshire. Kirkstall Abbey, © Edifice/Hart-Davis.
392 Railway Station, Huddersfield, © John Morrison. Shibden Hall, © John Morrison. Harewood House, © Emily Lane.
393 Bronte Parsonage Museum: Portrait of Charlotte Bronte by J.H.Thompson; dining room, © The Bronte Society. White Wells, © Bradford Economic Development Unit (EDU). East Riddlesden Hall, © NT/Matthew Antrobus.
394 Spofforth Castle, © EH. Ripon Cathedral, © John Morrison.
395 Norton Conyers: house; garden, © Norton Conyers House.

Aldborough Roman Town, mosaic pavement, © EH. Newby Hall, © John Morrison.
396/397 Temple of Piety at Studley Royal, Fountains Abbey, © NT. Fountains Abbey: 'Surprise' view; west front, © NT/Matthew Antrobus. Fountains Hall, © NT/Mike Williams. Fountains Abbey, east front, © NT/Matthew Antrobus.
398 Middleham Castle: exterior, © EH; aerial view, © Skyscan Balloon Photography/EH. Skipton Castle, © Skipton Castle.
399 Bolton Abbey, © AH. Bolton Priory: exterior detail, © John Morrison. Jervaulx Abbey, © John Morrison. Easby Abbey, © EH.
400 Byland Abbey, © EH/Andrew Tryner. Mount Grace Priory, © EH. Rievaulx Abbey, © EH. Pickering Castle, © EH.
401 Sterne's study, © The Laurence Sterne Trust. Nunnington Hall, the Great Staircase, © NT/J.Whitaker. Sutton Park, © Sutton Park.
402 Whitby Abbey, © Sandy Boyle/Whitby Parish. St Mary's church, north side, © Sandy Boyle/Whitby Parish.
403 Beningbrough Hall: the Great Staircase, © NT/Andreas von Einsiedel; the Drawing Room, © NT. Wharram Percy Medieval Village, © EH. Castle Howard: aerial view; the Mausoleum; the Hall, © AH.
404 /405 York Minster: Rose Window, © Dean and Chapter of York/Jim Kershaw; East Window, and nave, © AH/Chapter Clerk, York Minster; the Choir, © Dean and Chapter of York/Newbury Smith Photographers; East Window, detail, © Dean and Chapter of York; exterior, © AH.
406 Barnard Castle, © EH. Silver Mechanical Swan, at the Bowes Museum, © Eddie Ryle-Hodges, Co.Durham. Gisborough Priory, © EH.
407 Durham Castle, © AH. Corbridge Roman Site: bronze jug;

gaming board; glass flask, © EH; aerial view, © EH. Hadrian's Wall, © NT/Mike Williams.
408/409 Durham Cathedral: floodlit view; nave arcade; exterior; interior detail, © AH.
410 Gibside Chapel, interior, © NT/Nick Meers. Hexham Abbey, © Hexham Abbey. 'Angel of the North', Gateshead, © Eddie Ryle-Hodges, Co.Durham.
411 The Pillar Hall, Belsay Hall, © EH. Wallington: Central Hall, © NT/Andreas von Einsiedel; the Portico House, © NT/Matthew Antrobus.
412/413 Alnwick Castle: Constable's Tower, © Edifice/Lewis; library, © English Life; keep from middle bailey, © Edifice/Lewis; exterior (main), © Edifice/Lewis.
414 Dunstanburgh Castle, © NT/Lee Frost. 1st Lord Armstrong of Cragside by Henry Hetherington Emmerson, at Cragside, © NT/Derrick E.Witty. Lamp, at Cragside, © NT/Andreas von Einsiedel.
415 Lindisfarne Castle, interior, © NT/Andreas von Einsiedel. Lindisfarne Priory, © Skyscan Balloon Photography/EH. Lindisfarne Castle, exterior, © NT/Joe Cornish. Puffins, Farne Island, © NT/Joe Cornish.
416 *Sir Edward Lutyens* by Robert Lutyens, by courtesy of the National Portrait Gallery, London. Gravestone at Falstone; Headstone at Hartburn churchyard, © Eddie Ryle-Hodges, Co.Durham. Ravensdowne Barracks: gate entrance; barracks square, © EH.
417 St George's Gate, Liverpool, © Emily Lane.
418 Map, © Sylvie Rabbe. Main map, © Atelier Duplantier (F. Lieval/M. Lagarde). Chetham's Library, Manchester, © Chetham's Library.
419 *Bradshaw's Defence of Manchester AD 1642* by Ford Madox Brown, mural,

at Manchester's Town Hall, © Manchester Central Library, Local Studies Unit. Manchester Cathedral, © Edifice/Cole. Manchester Town Hall, © Marketing Manchester.

420 The South West Prospect of Manchester and Salford by Robert Whitworth, engraving, 1734, reproduced by permission of Chetham's Library. Albert Hall Memorial, Manchester, © Marketing Manchester. Albert Hall Memorial, (angled view), © British Tourist Authority.

421 Cotton mills, Manchester, by Austin, in Baines' The Cotton Manufacture, engraving, © MEPL. Coming from the Mill by L.S.Lowry, 1930, © City of Salford Museums and Art Gallery. Platt Hall, © Manchester City Art Galleries. Lark Hill Place, at Salford Museum, © City of Salford Museums and Art Gallery. Wythenshawe Hall, © Manchester City Art Galleries. Heaton Hall, © Edifice/Cole. Gulbenkian Room, Whitworth Art Gallery, © Whitworth Art Gallery/University of Manchester.

422 Vase, made at Herculaneuin Pottery, Liverpool, c.1815, © National Museums & Galleries on Merseyside. Woman Ironing by Edgar Degas, c.1885, © Walker Art Gallery, Merseyside/Board of Trustees: National Museums and Galleries on Merseyside/BAL. Dressing table by Thomas Chippendale, rosewood and gilt, c.1760, © Lady Lever Art Gallery, Merseyside/National Museums and Galleries on Merseyside/BAL.

423 The Ashes of Phocion collected by his Widow by Nicolas Poussin, 1648; Portrait of Fleetwood Hesketh by Joseph Wright of Derby, 1769, oil on canvas; Pieta by Ercole de Roberti, c. 1490-96, oil and tempera on panel, © Walker Art Gallery, Merseyside/Board of Trustees: National Museums and Galleries on Merseyside/BAL.

424 Albert Dock, © Emily Lane. Anglican Cathedral, © Emily Lane. Royal Liver Building, © Edifice/Sayer.

425 St George's Hall: interior; exterior, © Emily Lane. Liverpool Museum, © Emily Lane.

426 Bridge Cottage, Port Sunlight, © Emily Lane. Lady Lever Art Gallery, interior, © Courtesy of the Board of Trustees of the National Museums & Galleries on Merseyside. Speke Hall: exterior, © NT/Rupert Truman; interior, © NT/Geoffrey Frosh.

427 Rochdale Town Hall, exterior, © David Brearley Photography, Sale/Rochdale Metropolitan Borough Council. Le Mans Crescent, Bolton, © Bolton Metro. Rochdale Town Hall, interior, © Rochdale Metropolitan Borough Council. Hall-i'-the-Wood, © Edifice/Cole.

428 Rufford Old Hall: exterior, © NT/Mike Williams; the Great Hall, © NT/Mike Williams. Turton Tower, © John Morrison. Smithills Hall, © Edifice/Cole.

429 Port Erin, © Emily Lane. Glass in the Falcon's Nest, Port Erin, © Emily Lane. Castle Rushen, © Emily Lane. Port Erin, view from Falcon's Nest, © Emily Lane.

430 Colne parish church, © Heritage Cards & Souvenirs Ltd. Hoghton Tower, © Hoghton Tower Preservation Trust. Salmesbury Hall: The Great Hall; exterior view, © Salmesbury Hall. St Walburge's church, © John Birtles.

431 Gawthorpe Hall: Barry's Staircase, © NT/John Bethell; exterior, © NT/Mike Williams; Drawing Room, © NT/Mike Williams. Towneley Hall, © Towneley Hall.

432 Brownsholme Hall: exterior; interior, © Brownsholme Hall. Lytham Hall, by permission of the Heritage Trust for the North West.

433 Custom House, St George's Quay, © Lancaster City Museums. Lancaster Castle, © Edifice/Darley.

434 Ruskin Library, University of Lancaster, © Edifice/Darley. Lune Aqueduct, © Jon Sparks ARPS. Ashton Memorial, © Williamson Park. Portrait of John Ruskin by William Gersham Collingwood, oil on canvas, 1897, © Ruskin Museum, Coniston, Cumbria/BAL.

435 Crucifixion window, Kirby Lonsdale church, © Kirby Lonsdale church. Leighton Hall, © Leighton Hall. Sizergh Castle: Roger Strickland by Belle, c. 1697, © NT/John Hammond; the Pele Tower, © NT/Alasdair Ogilvie. Cecilia Strickland nee Towneley by George Rombey, © NT/John Hammond.

436 Cartmel Priory, © Emily Lane. Levens Hall, © Levens Heritage/Levens Hall. Holker Hall: exterior; gardens, © Holker Hall.

437 Lake Windermere, © NT/Robert Thrift. Furness Abbey: exterior; interior, © EH. Stott Park Bobbin Mill, © EH.

438 Derwentwater, © AH. Wordsworth House: William Wordsworth by an unknown artist, © NT/John Hammond; Drawing Room, © NT/Richard Surman.

439 Home of Beatrix Potter, © Edifice/Weideger. Rydal Mount, © Rydal Mount and Gardens. Castlerigg Stone Circle, © EH.

440 Long Meg and Her Daughters, Little Salkeld, © John Morrison. Appleby Castle, © Appleby Castle. Lowther Castle, © Edifice/Darley. Brough Castle, © EH/Jonathan Bailey.

441 Brough Castle, aerial view, © Skyscan Balloon Photography/EH. Hutton-in-the-Forest, © C. Pemberton-Piggott.

442 Muncaster Castle: exterior; interior, © Muncaster Castle. Carlisle Castle, © EH.

443 St James's Church, Whitehaven, interior, © Malcolm Best. Carlisle Castle, cannons, © EH. St James's Church, exterior, © St James's Church, Whitehaven.

444 Naworth Castle, © Emily Lane. Old Tullie House: Victorian Foyer; Jacobean staircase, © Tullie House Museum & Art Gallery. Carlisle Cathedral: Salkeld Screen; exterior view, © Tony Wiseman ABIPP. Reproduced by kind permission of the Dean and Chapter of Carlisle Cathedral.

445 Chirk Aqueduct, © AH.

446 Map, © Sylvie Rabbe. Stained Glass Window, Mold, © Emily Lane. Main map, © Atelier Duplantier (F.Lieval/M.Lagarde).

447 Basingwerk Abbey, © CADW. Flint Castle, © CADW. St Winifred's Chapel and Holy Well, © CADW. Mold, © Emily Lane.

448 Erddig: bureau bookcase, © NT/Andreas von Einsiedel; State Bedroom, © NT/Andreas von Einsiedel; State Bed, © NT/Andreas von Einsiedel. Thomas Rogers, Carpenter, unknown artist, 19th century, © NT.

449 Erddig: across the canal, © NT/Rupert Truman; wrought iron gates, © NT/Rupert Truman; kitchen, © NT/Andreas von Einsiedel.

450 Pont Cysyllte, © Emily Lane. Rug Chapel, © CADW. Valle Crucis Abbey, east end, © CADW. Chirk Castle, © AH.

451 Llanberis quarries, © Emily Lane. Llangar Church, © CADW. Valle Crucis Abbey, general view, © CADW. Llanberis Snowdon railway, © Emily Lane.

452 The Menai straits, © NT/Martin Trelawny. Plas Newydd, © NT/Nick Meers.

453 Plas Newydd: mural by Rex Whistler, detail, © NT/John Hammond; mural in Rex Whistler room, 1936-37, © NT/John Bethell; Lady Caroline Capel by John

◆ PICTURE CREDITS

◆ INDEX

*Page numbers in **bold** refer to the Practical information section*

◆ INDEX

*Page numbers in **bold** refer to the Practical information section*

◆ INDEX

*Page numbers in **bold** refer to the Practical information section*

◆ INDEX

*Page numbers in **bold** refer to the Practical information section*

MAPS

Key

Areas of Outstanding Natural Beauty

National parks, the Broads and the New Forest Heritage Area

★ The main houses, gardens and churches mentioned in the guide

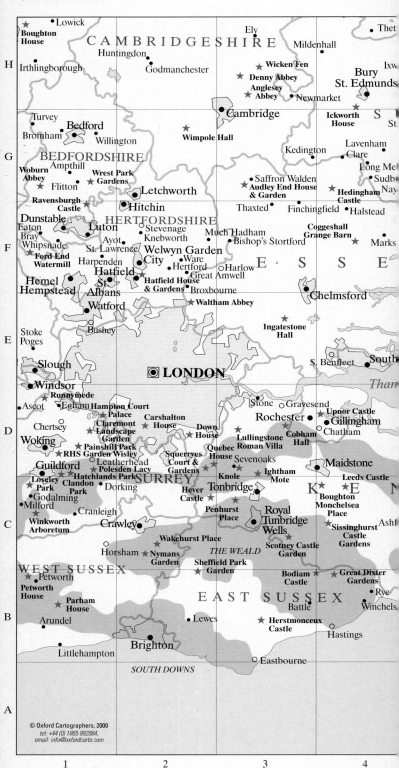

◆ **SOUTH EAST**

© Oxford Cartographers, 2000
tel: +44 (0) 1865 882884,
email: info@oxfordcarto.com

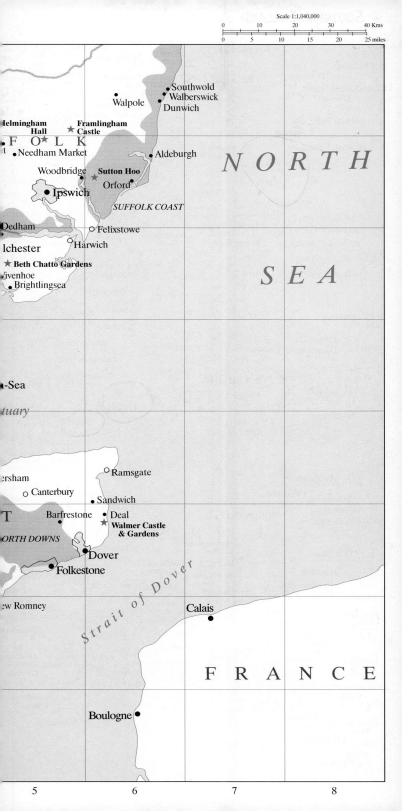

Scale 1:1,040,000

| 0 | 10 | 20 | 30 | 40 Kms |

| 0 | 5 | 10 | 15 | 20 | 25 miles |

Southwold
Walberswick
Walpole
Dunwich

Helmingham Hall   **Framlingham Castle** ★

F O★L K
t •Needham Market   •Aldeburgh   *N O R T H*

Woodbridge   **Sutton Hoo** ★
•Ipswich   Orford•
                    SUFFOLK COAST

Dedham   ○Felixstowe   *S E A*

Ilchester   ○Harwich

★ **Beth Chatto Gardens**
Vivenhoe
•Brightlingsea

a-Sea

tuary

ersham   ○Ramsgate
    ○Canterbury
                •Sandwich
T   Barfreston •Deal
NORTH DOWNS   ★ **Walmer Castle & Gardens**
                    •Dover
    •Folkestone   *Strait of Dover*

ew Romney   Calais
                                    •

                    Boulogne•   *F R A N C E*

5   6   7   8

SOUTHERN ENGLAND

Rhayader
Penybont
Llandrindod Wells
Disserth
Builth Wells
Knighton
Presteigne
Croft Castle
Woofferton
Shobdon
Berrington Hall
Leominster
Hartlebury Castle
Stourport-on-Severn
Witley Court
Lower Brockhampton House
Great Malvern
Worcester

H

WORCESTE
Spe
P.

Llanwrtyd Wells
Moccas Court
Llyswen
Bromlys
Brecon
Abbey Dore
Kilpeck
Hereford
Ledbury
Eastnor Castle
Croome Park
Tewkesbury
Odda's Chapel
Cheltenhar
Highnam
Per

G

BRECON BEACONS
Tretower Court & Castle
NATIONAL PARK
Partrishow
Llanfihangel
Crucorney
Abergavenny
Grosmont Castle
Skenfrith Castle
Monmouth
Goodrich Castle
Ross-on-Wye
Westbury Court Garden

White Castle
Raglan
Newland
St. Briavel's
DEAN NAT. FOREST PARK
Frampton Court
Glo
Elk
P.
Pain
Roco
Gard

F

Merthyr Tydfil
Ebbw Vale
Offa's Dyke
Tintern Abbey
Berkeley Castle
Owlpen Manor
Chave

Rhondda
Maesteg
Pontypridd
Abercarn
Pontypool
Usk
Cwmbran
Chepstow
Horton Court
Tetbur
Malme

E

BRIDGEND
Caerphilly
Llantrisant
Castell Coch
Newport
NEWPORT
CARDIFF
Portishead
Clevedon Court
Dodington Hall
Dyrham Park
Castle Co
Chippenh

Bridgend
Ogmore
Llandaff
Cardiff
Llantrithyd
THE VALE OF GLAMORGAN
Penarth
Barry
Wraxall
Bristol
Corsham
Great Cha
Manor
Bradford-on-Avon
Bath
Trowb

St. Donats
Weston-super-Mare
Yatton
Congresbury
Stanton Drew
Iford Manor
Farleigh Hungerford Castle
Westwood Manor
Westbury
Br

D

Bristol Channel
Banwell
Cheddar
Mendip Hills
Wells
Croscombe
Warminster
Longle
Hous

Minehead
Burnham-on-Sea
Dunster
Cleeve Abbey

EXMOOR NATIONAL PARK
Bridgwater
Glastonbury
Stourhead
Philipps F
& Dinton
Tisbu

C

S O M E R S E T
Dulverton
Hestercombe Garden
Taunton
Lytes Cary Manor
Sandford Orcas Manor Hoise
Purse Caundel Manor
Shaftes
Fiddlefo
Manor

Bampton
Barrington Court
Ilminster
Tintinhull Garden
Montacute House
Yeovil
Sherborne

B

Tiverton
Knightshayes Court
Uffculme
Cullompton
Chard
Crewkerne
Forde Abbey
Beaminster
Cerne Abbas
Mapperton
Blandford Forun
Milton Al

Bickleigh Castle
Killerton House & Garden
D E V O N
Honiton
Axminster
Shute Barton
Parnham House
Wolfeton House
Hardy's Cottage
Atthelham
House & Gardens

Exeter
Ottery St. Mary
Bridport
Lyme Regis
Seaton
Maiden Castle
Dorchester
Warel

Powderham Castle
Topsham
Sidmouth
Bicton College Garden & Arboretum
Lulworth Castle

Chudleigh
Budleigh Salterton

A

Ugbrooke Park
Exmouth
Dawlish
Weymouth

Newton Abbot
Teignmouth

Torquay
Easton

1   2   3   4

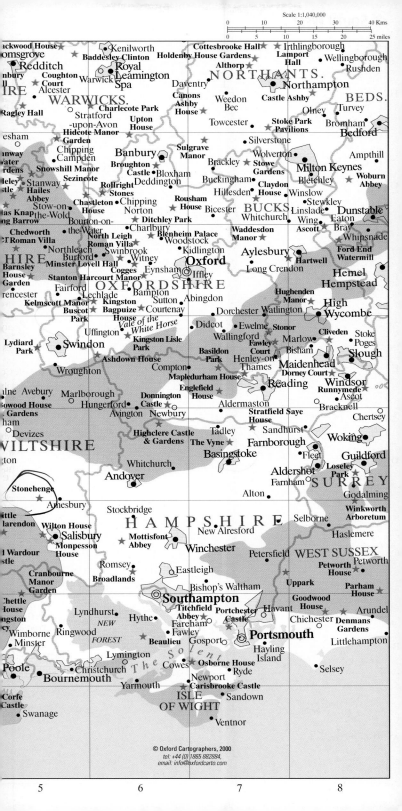

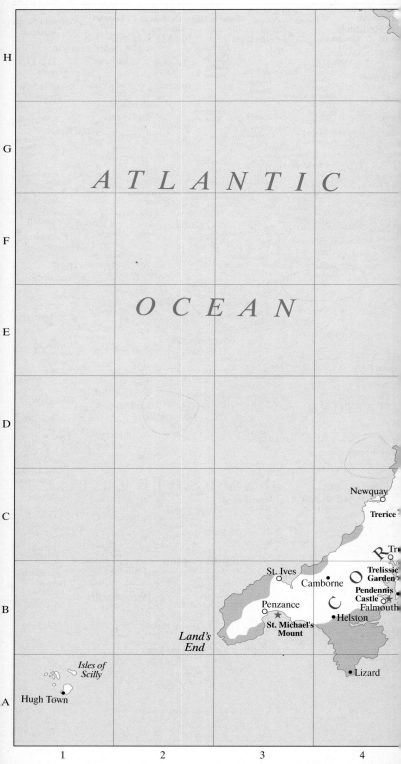

ATLANTIC

OCEAN

H

G

F

E

D

C

Newquay

Trerice

R Tr

B St. Ives

Trelissic Garden

Camborne

Pendennis Castle

Falmouth

Penzance

St. Michael's Mount

Helston

Land's End

A *Isles of Scilly*

Lizard

Hugh Town

1 2 3 4

Scale 1:1,040,000

| 0 | 10 | 20 | 30 | 40 Kms |
| 0 | 5 | 10 | 15 | 20 | 25 miles |

nbroke • Tenby
• Manorbier

Llanelli
Weobley Castle ★
SWANSEA
• Swansea ◉
Gower Peninsula
The Mumbles
Oxwich Castle

• Neath
Maesteg Rhondda
Port Talbot
• Margam
Bridgend •
Porthcawl •
BRIDGEND
• Llantrisant
• Ogmore
THE VALE OF
Llantrithyd
GLAMORGAN
St. Donats ★

Bristol   Channel

Lundy I.

Ilfracombe
○
Lynton • • Lynmouth
• Combe Martin
• Parracombe
★ Arlington
Court
Minehead
○
Dunster ★
Cleeve Abbey
EXMOOR
NATIONAL PARK

• Barnstaple

Westward Ho! •
• Clovelly
○ Bideford
Dulverton
Bampton •
Knightshayes Court

• Great Torrington

Tiverton
○
Bickleigh Castle ★
Cullompton
Killerton House & Garden ★
○ Crediton

Bude •

D E V O N
• Okehampton
Exeter ◉
Topsham ○

Tintagel •

Launceston
○

Castle Drogo ★
Moretonhampstead •
Lydford Castle ★ & Saxon Town

Powderham Castle ★
Chudleigh •
Ugbrooke ★ Exmouth
Park
Teignmouth •

rideaux Place
★ Pencarrow
St. Neot •
Bodmin ○
Lanhydrock ★
• Lostwithiel
St. Austell
○
• Fowey

Tavistock •
• Merrivale
Newton Abbot ○
DARTMOOR
NATIONAL PARK

Cotehele ★
• Yelverton
Buckland Abbey ★

Torquay •
Berry Pomeroy Castle ★
• Paignton
Dartingham ★
Hall Gardens
Totnes •
Brixham •

C O R N W A L L
Devonport
Antony ★
Plympton •
Saltram House ★
Plymouth
• Dartmouth

Mount Edgcumbe
House &
Country Park

Trewithen

awes

English   Channel

© Oxford Cartographers, 2000
tel: +44 (0) 1865 882884,
email: info@oxfordcarto.com

5   6   7   8

Ulverston
Grange-over-Sands
Kirkby Lonsdale
Conishead
Dalton in Furness
Hoker Hall
Leighton Hall
YORKSHIRE DALES NATIONAL PARK
Barrow-in-Furness
Furness Abbey
Carnforth
Morecambe
Settle
N O
H
Morecambe Bay
Lancaster
FOREST OF BOWLAND
Stocks Res.
Long Preston
Bo Ab
Skipton
Browsholm Hall
Eas Riddle Hal
G
L A N C A S H I R E
Clitheroe
Keighley
Haworth
Brontë Parsonage Museum
Blackpool
Samlesbury Hall
Burnley
Halifax
Lytham St. Annes
Kirkham
Preston
Blackburn
Accrington
Towneley Hall
Sowerby Bridge
Hoghton Tower
Helmshore
F
Meols Hall
Rufford Old Hall
Astley Hall
Chorley
Southport
Ormskirk
Formby
Liverpool
Leigh
Manchester
Bay
Kirkby
Ordsall Hall Museum
Salford
Stockport
Bramall Hall
Hoylake
Liverpool
Dunham Massey
E
Prestatyn
Birkenhead
Tatton Park
Adlington Hall
Lyme P.
Rhyl
Greenfield Valley & Basingwerk Abbey
Mersey
Port Sunlight
Wilmslow
Knutsford
Tabley House
Bodrhyddan
Neston
Macclesfield
DE
Rhuddlan
Flint
C H E S H I R E
Northwich
Capesthorne Hall
Bux
FLINT-SHIRE
Ewloe
Gawsworth Hall
PEAK
Denbigh
Hawarden
Chester
Beeston Castle
Little Moreton Hall
NAT
D
Llanrhaeadr
Peckforton Castle
Crewe
Biddulph Gran
Ruthin
Gresford
Dorfold Hall
DENBIGHSHIRE
Valle Crucis Abbey
Wrexham
Nantwich
Stoke-on-Tre
Erddig
Cholmondeley
Newcastle-under-Lyme
WREXHAM
Worthenbury
Longton
Llangar
Llangollen
Whitchurch
Chea
Rug
Corwen
Market Drayton
Stone
Uttoxet
Chirk Castle
Ellesmere
Sandon C
C
STAFFORD
Oswestry
Stafford
Hoar C Ch
P
Llanfyllin
SHR
Haughmond Abbey
Newport
Shugborough Estate
Lilleshall Abbey
O
Welshpool
Shrewsbury
Wellington
Oakengates
Weston Park
Boscobel House
W
Attingham Park
Telford
Shifnal
Chillington Hall
B
Powis Castle & Garden
Buildwas Abbey
Wolverhampton
Walsall
Montgomery
Much Wenlock
Wightwick Manor
E
Long Mynd
Church Stretton
W. Bromwich
Gregynod
Bridgnorth
Dudley
S
Newtown
Wilderhope Manor
Birmingham
Bishop's Castle
Dudmaston Hall
Stourbridge
A
SHROPSHIRE HILLS
Stokesay Castle
Kidderminster
Harvington Hall
Y
Ludlow
Hartlebury Castle
Bromsg
Knighton
Woofferton
Stourport-on-Severn
Chaddesley Corbett
Reddi

1   2   3   4

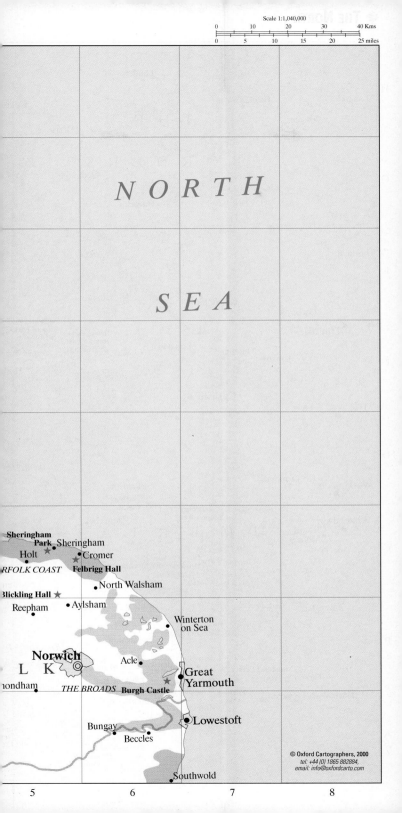

Scale 1:1,040,000

| 0 | 10 | 20 | 30 | 40 Kms |
| 0 | 5 | 10 | 15 | 20 | 25 miles |

N O R T H

S E A

Sheringham
Park Sheringham
Holt ● ★ ● Cromer
RFOLK COAST **Felbrigg Hall**

Blickling Hall ★
Reepham ● ● North Walsham
● ● Aylsham

Winterton
on Sea ●

Norwich
L K ◎ Acle ●

⊙ondham ● *THE BROADS* **Burgh Castle**
★ **Great**
Yarmouth

Bungay ● ◇ ● **Lowestoft**
Beccles ●

Southwold ●

© Oxford Cartographers, 2000
tel: +44 (0) 1865 882884,
email: info@oxfordcarto.com

5   6   7   8

H — Lanark
Biggar
Peebles
Lauder
Galashiels
T H E
Colds
Kelso

G — B O R D E R S
Selkirk
Jedburgh
Hawick
THE CH
81
THE CHS

F — Moffat
Thornhill
KIELDER
FOREST
PARK
NORTHUMBERLAND
NATIONAL
Langholm
Lockerbie

E — Dumfries
Gretna
Longtown
Housteads Roman Fort & Museum
Chesters Roman Fort & Museum
NORT
Annan
Brampton
★ **Hadrian's Wall**
Haltwhistle
Hexh

D — Carlisle
•Wreay
Solway Firth
NORTH PI

C — Workington
Cockermouth
○ Penrith
★ **Lowther Castle**
Whitehaven
Keswick ○ ★ **Castlerigg Stone Circle**
Cleator Moor
C U M B R I A
Appleby
•St. Bees
LAKE DISTRICT
Shap
Brough
Grasmere ★ **Dove Cottage & Wordsworth Museum**
Kirkby Stephen
Ambleside
NATIONAL PARK
Windermere

B — Ravenglass ★ **Muncaster Castle**
Kendal
Lake Windermere
○ **Abbot Hall Art**
Sedbergh
★ **Sizergh Castle**
★ **Levens Hall**
YORKSHIRE DA
Ulverston Cartmel
Kirkby Lonsdale
NATIONAL PA
Conishead Priory
Grange-over-Sands
Dalton in Furness •
★ **Hoker Hall & Gardens**
Leighton Hall

A — Barrow-in-Furness ★ **Furness Abbey**
Morecambe
Carnforth
Settle
Lancaster
Morecambe
Bay
FOREST OF BOWLAND
Long Pre
★ **Browsholm Hall**

1   2   3   4

© Oxford Cartographers, 2000
tel: +44 (0) 1865 882884,
email: info@oxfordcarto.com

·wick-upon-Tweed

**Lindisfarne Castle
& Priory**
★ *Holy I.*

●Bamburgh

N O R T H

·oler
★ **Chillingham Castle**

★ **Dunstanburgh Castle**

Alnwick●

★ **Warkworth Castle**

S E A

★ **Cragside**
Rothbury

Morpeth●

·ington

Seaton Delaval
★ **Hall**

**Newcastle-
upon-Tyne**

○Tynemouth

·don Castle

·rbridge

◎ **Sunderland**

·onsett

Durham

Hartlepool

D U R H A M

Bishop○
Auckland

○Redcar

Stockton-on-Tees

·arnard
·Castle

Middlesbrough

Darlington●

Guisborough●

Whitby○

·wes

Richmond●
★ **Easby Abbey**

Mount Grace
★ **Priory**

NORTH YORK MOORS

NATIONAL PARK

★ **Bolton Castle**

Northallerton●

Rievaulx Terrace
★ **& Temples**

●Lastingham

Scarborough

·iddleham
★ **Castle**

N   O   R   T

Thirsk●

★ **Helmsley**
★ **Duncombe Park**

●Pickering

Norton Conyers
★

Coxwold●

★ **Byland**
Abbey

★ **Nunnington Hall**

O   R

K

Ripon○

S

H

★
Newburgh
Priory

I   R   E

Fountains Abbey
& Studley Royal
★ **Estate**

Newby
★ **Hall**

★ **Sutton**
Park

●Malton

Castle Howard

Markenfield Hall
★
Ripley Castle★

Aldborough
Roman Town

★ **Kirkham**
Priory

★ **Sledmere**
House

·Boroughbridge

★

Knaresborough●

Beningbrough
Hall

★ **Bolton Abbey**

Stamford Bridge●

EAST RIDING

·ipton

Harrogate

●Hkley

Stockeld
★ **Park**

●Wetherby

◎ **York**

OF YORKSHIRE

5   6   7   8

H

Carmel H

• Malahide

ISLE
OF
MAN

• Ramsey

Holyhea

Dublin

Peel •

Holy I.

• Dun Laoghaire

Valley (Dyff

• Bray

Douglas •

G

Port Erin •

• Castletown

Isle of Man

Wicklow

F

I R I S H

Per

Plas-yn-Rhiw ★

• Arklow

Aberd.

E

S E A

Cara

D

B

C

Cardi •

**Cilgerran
Castle** ★

Fishguard •

Nevern •

B

*PEMBROKESHIRE
COAST N.P.*

*MYNYDD
PRESCELLY
536*

PEMBROKESHIR

Channel

• St. David's

• Haverfordwest

Pen

A

Milford Haven ○

**Carew Castle
& Tidal Mill** ★

Pembroke Dock •

• Pembroke

Tenb

• Manorbier

© Oxford Cartographers, 2000
*tel: +44 (0) 1865 882884,
email: info@oxfordcarto.com*

1   2   3   4

◆ LONDON UNDERGROUND

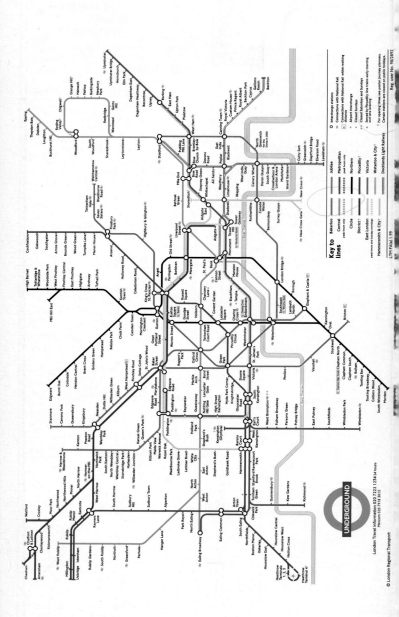

THE EDITORS' CHOICE ★

HAREWOOD HOUSE ▲ 392

YORK MINSTER ▲ 404-5

RUFFORD OLD HALL ▲ 42

BURGHLEY ▲ 358

LINCOLN CATHEDRAL ▲ 363

STUDLEY ROYAL ▲ 396-7

The places marked on the map are the editors' choice of the best churches, gardens and country houses. You'll find a full list with short descriptions of each on pages 488–93. Throughout the chapters of the book, you will also find stars beside the places we think deserve a detour on your visit.